MELODY • LYRICS • CHORDS | FOR ALL "C" INSTRUMENTS

THE ULTIMATE ROCK POP FAKE BOOK

THE ULTIMATE ROCK POP FAKE BOOK

FEATURING OVER 500 SONGS!

ISBN 978-1-4234-5339-0

HAL•LEONARD®
CORPORATION
7777 W. BLUEMOUND RD. P.O. BOX 13819 MILWAUKEE, WI 53213

Visit Hal Leonard Online at
www.halleonard.com

AFTERNOON DELIGHT

Words and Music by
BILL DANOFF

Moderately slow Country, in 2
F Gm7
Gon-na find my ba-by, gon-na hold her tight, gon-na grab some af - ter-noon de-light. My
F Gm7
mot-to's al-ways been "When it's right, it's right," why wait un-til the mid-dle of a cold, dark night
C7 Gm7
when ev-'ry-thing's a lit-tle clear-er in the light of day. And we know the
C7 F
night is al-ways gon-na be here an - y - way?
(1.,3.) Think-ing of you's work-ing up my
(2.) out this morn-ing feel-ing
Gm7
ap - pe - tite, look-ing for-ward to a lit-tle af-ter-noon de-light. Rub-bing
so po - lite, I al-ways thought a fish could not be caught who did - n't bite. But you
F Gm7
sticks and stones to-geth-er make the sparks ig - nite and the thought of rub-bing you is get-ting
got some bait a-wait-ing and I think I might like nib-bl-ing a lit-tle af-ter-
F C A7 Dm
so ex-cit-ing. noon de-light. Sky rock-ets in flight, af-ter-noon de-light,
Gm7 Am B♭ C7 F Gm7 Am B♭ C7 F
af - ter-noon de-light, af - ter-noon de-light.
1 2, 3 To Coda Gm7
Start-ed Be wait-ing for me, ba-by, when I
C7 Gm7 C7 D.S. al Coda
come a - round. We can make a lot of lov-ing 'fore the sun goes down.
CODA
Gm Am B♭ C F N.C.
Af - af-ter-noon de-light, af -
F
af-ter-noon de-light.

AGAINST THE WIND

Words and Music by
BOB SEGER

Medium Rock beat

G Bm
It seems like yes - ter - day, but it was long a - go.
And the years rolled slow - ly past. And I found my - self a - lone,
Instrumental

C G D
Ja - ney was love - ly. She was the queen of my nights, there in the dark - ness with the ra -
sur - round - ed by stran - gers I thought were my friends. I found my - self fur - ther and fur -

C G
- di - o play - in' low, and the se - crets that we shared,
- ther from my home, and I guess I lost my way.

Bm C G
the moun - tains that we moved, caught like a wild - fire out of con - trol till there was
There were oh so man - y roads. I was liv - in' to run and run - nin' to live. Nev - er

C D
noth - in' left to burn and noth - in' left to prove. And I re -
wor - ried a - bout pay - in', or e - ven how much I owed. Mov - in'
End instrumental Well, those

Em D G Em C
mem - ber what she said to me, how she swore that it nev - er would end.
eight miles a min - ute for months at a time, break - in' all of the rules that would bend,
drift - er's days are past me now. I've got so much more to think a - bout:

G Em D C
I re - mem - ber how she held me oh so tight, Wish I did - n't know now what I did - n't know
I be - gan to find my - self search - in', search - in' for shel - ter a - gain and a -
dead - lines and com - mit - ments, what to leave in, what to leave

D G Bm C G
then. A - gainst the wind, we were run - nin' a - gainst the wind. We were
gain. A - gainst the wind, lit - tle some - thin' a - gainst the wind. I
out. A - gainst the wind, I'm still run - nin' a - gainst the wind. I'm

C Bm Am C G
young and strong. We were run - nin' a - gainst the wind.
found my - self seek - in' shel - ter a - gainst the wind.
old - er now, but still run - nin' a - gainst the wind.

To Coda 1. 2. D.C. al Coda

CODA

C Bm D
Well, I'm old - er now, and still run - nin' a - gainst the

C G
wind, a - gainst the wind. A - gainst the

Repeat and Fade

AIN'T NO WOMAN (LIKE THE ONE I'VE GOT)

Words and Music by DENNIS LAMBERT
and BRIAN POTTER

Moderately
Fmaj7 Em7 Dm7 Fmaj7 Em7 Dm7
Ain't no wom - an like the one I've got.
Ain't no wom - an like the one I've got.
Fmaj7 Em7 Dm7 Dm7/G
Ain't no wom - an like the one I've got.
Ev - 'ry day the
Dm7 Am7 Dm7
sun comes up a - round her. She can make the birds sing har - mo - ny.
up when it's down I'm go - in', put a lit - tle mu - sic in my day.
Am7 Dm7 Am7
Ev - 'ry drop of rain is glad it found her. Heav - en must have
Would - n't be sur - prised if my love keeps grow - in' big - ger ev - 'ry
Dm7 G Fmaj7 Em7
made her just for me. When she smiles so warm and ten -
min - ute that she stays a - way. I would kiss the ground she walks
Dm7 Ab/Bb G/A F/G
- der, it's a sight for sore eyes to see.
on 'cause it's my word she'll o - bey.
Fmaj7 Em7 Dm7
Ain't no wom - an like the one I've got
Oh no they don't come bet - ter. to
Well, I kiss the ground she walks on.
Fmaj7 Em7 Dm7
make her hap - py does - n't take a lot.
She don't ask for things, no dia - mond rings.
She's a real good friend, right to the end.
Fmaj7 Em7 Dm7
So to - geth - er like a hand in glove.
Like pag - es in a let - ter.
I'm a lone - ly man when she's gone.
Fmaj7 Em7 Dm7
1 Dm7/G
2 Dm7/G
D.S. and Fade
Ain't no wom - an like the one I love.
She can build me

ALL ALONE AM I

English Lyric by ARTHUR ALTMAN
Original Lyric by JEAN IOANNIDIS
Music by M. HADJIDAKIS

Slowly, with feeling

F Dm G C Dm E7
All a - lone am I, ev - er since your good - bye, all a - lone with just the beat of my heart. Peo - ple

F Dm G C Dm G7 C
all a - round, but I don't hear a sound, just the lone - ly beat - ing of my heart.

G7
No use in hold - ing oth - er hands, for I'd be hold - ing on - ly emp - ti - ness.
No oth - er voice can say the words my heart must hear to ev - er sing a - gain.

Am E7
No use in kiss - ing oth - er lips, for I'd be think - ing just of your ca - ress.
The words you used to whis - per low, no oth - er love can ev - er bring a - gain.
All a -

F Dm G C Dm E7
lone am I, ev - er since your good - bye, all a - lone with just the beat of my heart. Peo - ple

F Dm G C
all a - round, but I don't hear a sound, just the

1. Dm G7 C
lone - ly beat-ing of my heart. All a -

2. Dm G7 C
lone - ly beat-ing of my heart.

ALL MY LOVING

Words and Music by JOHN LENNON
and PAUL McCARTNEY

Fab groove
Gm C7 F Dm B♭ Gm
Close your eyes and I'll kiss you, to - mor - row I'll miss you; re - mem - ber I'll al - ways be
tend that I'm kiss - ing the lips I am miss - ing and hope that my dreams will come
E♭ Gm C7 F Dm
true.
true.
And then while I'm a - way, I'll write home ev - 'ry day, and I'll
B♭ C7 F 1 N.C. 2 Dm
send all my lov - ing to you. I'll pre - All my lov - ing
D♭+ F Dm D♭+ F
I will send to you. All my lov - ing, dar - ling, I'll be true.

ALL I WANNA DO

Words and Music by KEVIN GILBERT,
DAVID BAERWALD, SHERYL CROW,
WYN COOPER and BILL BOTTRELL

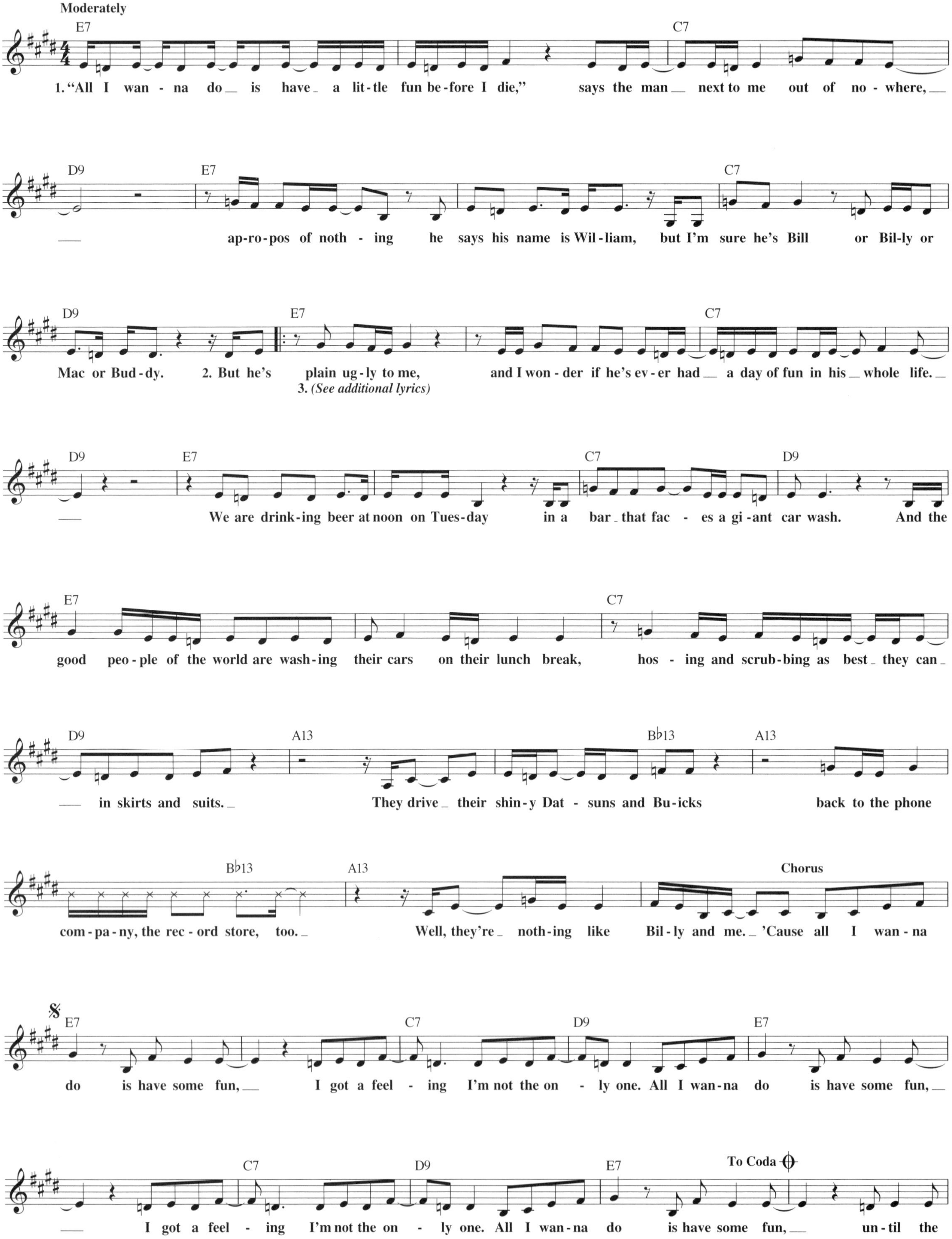

Moderately

E7 C7
1. "All I wan - na do _ is have _ a lit - tle fun be - fore I die," says the man _ next to me out of no - where, _

D9 E7 C7
_ ap - ro - pos of noth - ing he says his name is Wil - liam, but I'm sure he's Bill or Bil - ly or

D9 E7 C7
Mac or Bud - dy. 2. But he's plain ug - ly to me, and I won - der if he's ev - er had _ a day of fun in his _ whole life. _
3. *(See additional lyrics)*

D9 E7 C7 D9
_ We are drink - ing beer at noon on Tues - day in a bar _ that fac - es a gi - ant car wash. And the

E7 C7
good peo - ple of the world are wash - ing their cars on their lunch break, hos - ing and scrub - bing as best _ they can _

D9 A13 B♭13 A13
_ in skirts and suits. _ They drive _ their shin - y Dat - suns and Bu - icks back to the phone

B♭13 A13 Chorus
com - pa - ny, the rec - ord store, too. _ Well, they're _ noth - ing like Bil - ly and me. _ 'Cause all I wan - na

𝄋 E7 C7 D9 E7
do is have some fun, _ I got a feel - ing I'm not the on - ly one. All I wan - na do is have some fun, _

C7 D9 E7 To Coda
_ I got a feel - ing I'm not the on - ly one. All I wan - na do is have some fun, _ un - til the

C7 B7 E7 C7 D9
sun comes up o - ver San - ta Mon - i - ca Bou - le - vard.
B7 E7 C7 D9 E7
San - ta Mon - i - ca Bou - le - vard.
(Instrumental)
C7 D9 A13 B♭13
Oth - er - wise the bar is ours,
A13 B♭13 A13
and the day and the night and the car wash, too.
The match - es and the Buds and the
B♭13 A13
D.S. al Coda
clean and dirt - y cars, the sun and the moon. But all I wan - na
CODA
I've got a feel -
C7 D9 E7
- ing the par - ty has just be - gun. All I wan - na do is have some fun, I won't tell
C7 D9 E7 C7
you that you're the on - ly one. All I wan - na do is have some fun, un - til the sun comes up o - ver
D9 E7 C7 D9
San - ta Mon - i - ca Bou - le - vard, un - til the sun comes up o - ver San - ta Mon - i - ca Bou - le - vard.
E7 1, 2 C7 D9 3 C7 B7♯9 E
(Vocal 1st time only)

Additional Lyrics

3. I like a good beer buzz early in the morning,
And Billy likes to peel the labels from his bottles of Bud
And shred them on the bar.
Then he lights every match in an oversized pack,
Letting each one burn down to his thick fingers
Before blowing and cursing them out.
And he's watching the Buds as they spin on the floor.
A happy couple enters the bar dancing dangerously close to one another.
The bartender looks up from his want ads.
Chorus

ALL NIGHT LONG (ALL NIGHT)

Words and Music by
LIONEL RICHIE

Moderate Caribbean feel
A♭
G♭
B♭m
A♭
Well, my friends, the time has come raise the roof and have some fun.
Peo - ple danc - ing all in the street, see the rhy - thm all in their feet.

G♭
B♭m
A♭
Throw a - way the work to be done. Let the mu - sic play on (play on, play on.)
Life is good, wild and sweet. Let the mu - sic play on (play on, play on.)

G♭
B♭m
A♭
Ev - 'ry - bod - y sing, ev - 'ry - bod - y dance, lose your - self in wild ro - mance. We're going to
Feel it in your heart and feel it in your soul, let the mu - sic take con - trol. We're going to

G♭
B♭m
par - ti' ka - ra - mu, fi - es - ta, for - ev - er. Come on and
par - ti' lim - ing, fi - es - ta, for - ev - er. Come on and

Play 1st time only
A♭
G♭
B♭m
sing a - long: We're going to par - ty, ka - ra - mu, fi - es - ta, for - ev - er. Come on and

A♭
G♭
sing a - long:
sing my song:
All night long, (all night) all night, all night

A♭
G♭
long, (all night) all night, all night long, all night, all night
1
A♭
2
A♭
long, Oh. (all night) long, (all night) Yeah!

N.C.
G♭
Once you get start - ed you can't sit down.

N.C.
G♭
Come join the fun, it's a mer - ry - go - round.

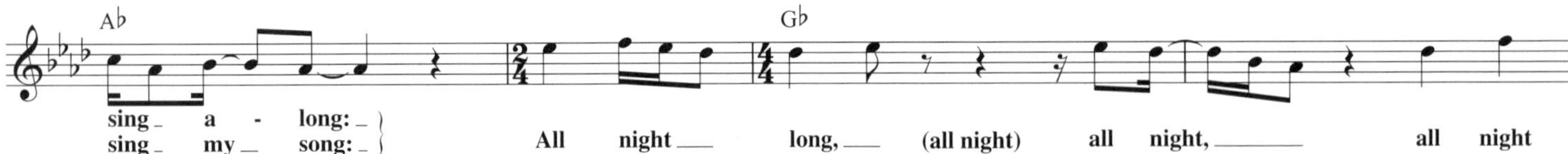

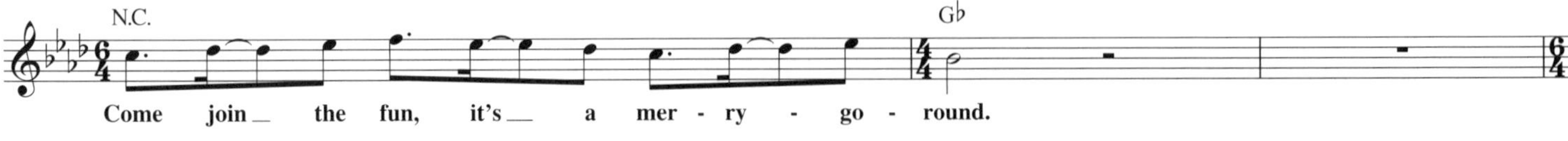

N.C.
Gb
Ev - 'ry - one's danc - ing their trou - bles a - way.
N.C.
Gbmaj7 Fm7 Gbmaj7 Fm7
N.C.
Come join our par - ty, see how we play! (Instrumental)
Gbmaj7 Fm7 Gbmaj7 Fm7
N.C.
Tom bo li de say de moi ya
Yeah, Jam - bo Jum - bo way to par - ti' o we goin' Oh, jam - ba - li.
Tom bo li de say de moi ya Yeah, Jam - bo Jum - bo.
Gbmaj7 Fm7 Gbmaj7 Fm7 Gb/Ab
Oh
Gbmaj7
Fm7
Ab
yes. We're gon - na have a par - ty all night
Gb
Ab
long, (all night) all night, all night long, (all night) all night,
Gb
all night long, all night, all night
Ab
Gb
long. (all night) (all night) Ev - 'ry - one you meet, they're
Ab
Gb
jam - ming in the street, all night long. (all night) (all night) (Instrumental)
Ab
Repeat and Fade
(all night) (all night)

AMANDA

Words and Music by
TOM SCHOLZ

Slowly

G C/G G Em Bm
Babe, to-mor-row's so far a - way. There's some-thin' I just have to say. I don't

C G/B Am G Dsus D
think I could hide what I'm feel-in' in-side an-oth-er day know-in' I love you.

G C/G G Em
And I, I'm get-tin' too close a - gain. I don't wan-na see it

Bm C G/B Am G
end. If I tell you to-night, will you turn out the light and walk a-way know-in' I love

D C/D G/D D Em Am7
you? I'm gon-na take you by sur-prise and make you re-al-ize, A-

D Em Am7 D
man - da. I'm gon-na tell you right a-way; I can't wait an-oth-er day, A-man - da. I'm gon-na

Em Am7 D Csus2
say it like a man and make you un-der-stand, A - man - da. I love you.

G C/G G Em Bm
And I feel like to-day's the day. I'm look-in' for the words to say. Do you

C G/B Am G D D7sus
wan-na be free? Are you read-y for me to feel this way? I don't wan-na lose ya.

G C/G G Em Bm
So, it may be too soon, I know. The feel - in' takes so long to grow. If I
C G/B Am G D C/D
tell you to - day will you turn me a - way and let me go? I don't wan - na lose you. (Instrumental)
G/D D Bm Em Am7 D
Em Am7 D Em Am7
(End instrumental) I'm gon - na take you by sur - prise and make you re - al - ize, A -
D Em Am7 D
man - da. I'm gon - na tell you right a - way; I can't wait an - oth - er day, A - man - da. I'm gon - na
Em Am7 D E
say it like a man and make you un - der - stand, A - man - da. Oh, girl. Instrumental
Bm7 E Bm7 E
(End instrumental) You and I, I
Bm7 E Bm7
know that we can't wait. And I swear, I swear it's not a lie, girl. To - mor - row may be too late.
C D G D/F# Em Em/D C C/B Am Am/G
You, you and I, girl, we can share a life to - geth - er. It's now or nev - er, and to - mor - row may be too
D C/D G/D D G C/G
late. Oh. And feel - in' the way I
G Em Bm Am Am/G D
do. I don't wan - na wait my whole life through to say I'm in love with you.

AMERICA
from the Motion Picture THE JAZZ SINGER

© 1980 STONEBRIDGE MUSIC
Words and Music by
NEIL DIAMOND
Moderately
Far, we've been trav - el - ing far, with - out a home but not with - out a star.
(Instrumental)
Free, on - ly want to be free. We hud - dle close, hang on to a dream.
On the boats and on the planes, they're com - ing to A - mer - i - ca.
Nev - er look - ing back a - gain, they're com - ing to A - mer - i - ca.
Home, don't it seem so far - a - way?
Oh, we're trav - el - ing light to - day, in the eye of the storm, in the eye of the storm.
Home to a new and a shin - y place. Make our bed, and we'll say our grace.
Free - dom's light burn - ing warm, free - dom's light burn - ing warm.
(Instrumental)

F/E F
Ev - 'ry - where a - round the world, they're com - ing to A - mer - i - ca.
Ev - 'ry time that flag's un - furled, they're com - ing to A - mer - i - ca.
G/F♯ G
Got a dream to take them there. They're com - ing to A - mer - i - ca.
Got a dream they've come to share. They're com - ing to A - mer - i - ca.
A
F♯m7
They're com - ing to A - mer - i - ca. They're com - ing to A - mer - i - ca,
D
Bm7
They're com - ing to A - mer - i - ca. They're com - ing to A - mer - i - ca to - day,
(Instrumental) to - day, to - day,
to - day, to - day,
A7sus
My coun - try 'tis of thee, (to - day,) sweet land of lib - er - ty, (to - day,)
of thee I sing, (to - day,) of thee I sing to - day.
Repeat and Fade
To - day, to - day.

ALL THE YOUNG DUDES

Words and Music by
DAVID BOWIE

Slowly
D D/C♯ Bm D/A
Well, Bil - ly rapped all night a - bout his su - i - cide, how he'd kick it in the head when he was twen-ty - five.
F♯m A D D/C♯
Speed jive, don't wan - na stay a - live when you're twen - ty five. And Wen - dy's steal - in' clothes from Marks and Sparks and
Bm D/A F♯m A
Fred - die's got spots from rip - pin' off the stars from his face. Funk - y lit - tle boat race. The
Em7 F♯7 Bm Bm/A G D
tel - e - vi - sion man is cra - zy, say - in' we're ju - ve - nile de - lin - quent wrecks. Oh, man, I need T V when I got
A A7 D D/C♯ Bm D/A
T - Rex. Oh, broth - er, you guessed, I'm a dude, man. (All the young dudes car - ry the news.
Lead vocal ad lib.
Am G F C/E C G C A D D/C♯ Bm D/A Am G
Boo - ga - loo dudes car - ry the news. All the young dudes car - ry the news. Boo - ga - loo dudes
F C/E C G C A D D/C♯
car - ry the news.) Lu - cy look - in' sweet 'cause he dress - es like a queen, but he can
Bm D/A F♯m A Asus A
kick like a mule, it's a real mean team. But we can love, oh yes, we can love. And my broth -
D D/C♯ Bm D/A
- er's back at home with his Bea - tles and his Stones. We nev - er got it off on that rev - o - lu - tion stuff.
F♯m A Em7
What a drag, too man - y snags. Now I drunk a lot of wine 'n' I'm feel - in' fine, got to
F♯7 Bm Bm/A G D A Asus A
race some cat to bed. Oh, is there con - crete all a - round, or is it in my head? Yeah! I'm a dude, Dad.
D D/C♯ Bm D/A Am G F C/E C G C A
(All the young dudes car - ry the news. Boo - ga - loo dudes car - ry the news.
Lead vocal ad lib.
Repeat and Fade
D D/C♯ Bm D/A Am G F C/E C G C A
All the young dudes car - ry the news. Boo - ga - loo dudes car - ry the news.)

ALL THROUGH THE NIGHT

Words and Music by
JULES SHEAR

Medium Rock
G D G Em7
All through the night, I'll be a - wake, and I'll be with you.
All through the night, this pre - cious time when time is new. Oh,
Bm C Am7
All through the night to - day know-in' that we feel the same with-out say - in':
G Em C Am7 D6
We have no past, we won't reach back. Keep with me for - ward all through the night.
G Em C Am7 D6
And once we start the me - ter clicks, and it goes run - ning all through the night.
To Coda
G Em Bm6 Bm G D
Un - til it ends, there is no end. All through the night
G D
stray cat is cry - ing, so stray cat sings back. All through the night they have for - got - ten what
G Em7 Bm
by day they lack. Oh, un - der those white street lamps there is a lit - tle chance
D.S. al Coda
C(add 9) Am7
they may see.
CODA
G D G Em7
Oh, the
Bm C(add 9) Am7
sleep in your eyes is e - nough. Let me be there, let me stay there a while.
G Em C Am7 D6
We have no past, we don't reach back.
Un - til it ends, there is no end.
Keep with me for - ward all through the night.
G Em C Am7 D6
And once we start the me - ter clicks, and it goes run - ning all through the night.
G Em Bm6 G Em C
Un - til it ends, there is no end.
Am7 D6 G Em C
1 Repeat ad lib.
Am7 D6
2
Am7 D6 G

AMERICAN WOMAN

Written by BURTON CUMMINGS, RANDY BACHMAN, GARY PETERSON and JIM KALE

Moderately slow
G
A - mer - i - can wom - an, gon - na mess your mind.
A - mer - i - can wom - an, she gon - na mess your mind.
A - mer - i - can wom - an, gon - na mess your mind.
G
A - mer - i - can wom - an, gon - na mess your mind. I say A, I say M, I say E,
I say R, say I, use C, say A, N.
A - mer - i - can wom - an, gon - na mess your mind.
A - mer - i - can wom - an, gon - na mess your mind.
A - mer - i - can wom - an, gon - na mess your mind.
G G7 Gdim Cm/G G(♯9)
E
(Instrumental)
(End instrumental)
A - mer - i - can wom -
E
an, stay a - way from me, A - mer - i - can wom - an, ma - ma let me be.
(2.,3.)(See additional lyrics)
Don't come hang - in' a - round my door, I don't wan - na see your face no more,
I got more im - por - tant things to do than spend my time grow - in' old with you. Now

1
woman, I said stay a - way. A - mer - i - can wom - an, lis - ten what I
say. (Instrumental) (End instrumental) A - mer - i - can wom -
2
- an, lis - ten what I say. (Guitar solo) A - mer - i - can wom -
3
- an, ma - ma let me be.
E
Go, got - ta get a - way, got - ta get a -
way, now go go go, I'm gon - na leave you, wom - an, gon - na leave you wom - an. Bye
bye, bye bye, bye bye, bye bye. You're
E
no good for me. I'm no good for you. Gon - na look you right in the eye,
tell you what I'm gon - na do. You know I'm gon - na
E
leave. You know I'm gon - na
Repeat and Fade
go. You know I'm gon - na leave. I know I'm gon - na go, wom - an. I'm gon - na...
(ad lib. vocal)

Additional Lyrics

2. American woman, get away from me
American woman, mama let me be
Don't wanna see your shadow no more
Colored lights can hypnotize
Sparkle someone else's eyes
Now woman, I said get away
American woman, listen what I say.

3. American woman, said get away
American woman, listen what I say
Don't come hangin' around my door
Don't wanna see your face no more
I don't need your war machines
I don't need your ghetto scenes
Colored lights can hypnotize
Sparkle someone else's eyes
Now woman, get away from me
American woman, mama let me be.

ANGEL BABY

Words and Music by
ROSE HAMLIN

Moderately slow

C Am Dm7 G7 C Am Dm7 G7
It's just __ like heav-en __ be-in' here _ with you, you're like __ an an-gel __ too good _ to be true, __

C Am Dm7 G C Am Dm7 G7
but af - ter all __ I love you, __ I do, an - gel ba-by, __ my an - gel ba-by. __

C Am Dm7 G7 C Am Dm7 G7
When you __ are near me __ my heart _ skips a beat, __ I can hard-ly stand on __ my __ own two feet, __

C Am Dm7 G7 C Am Dm7 G7 C Am
be-cause I love you, _ I love you _ I do, an - gel ba-by, __ my an-gel ba-by. __ Ooh, __ I love you, _

Dm7 G7 C Am Dm7 G7 C Am Dm7 G7
ooh, __ I do, no one could love you __ like __ I do. Ooh __ ooh __

C Am Dm7 G7 C Am Dm7 G7
ooh __ ooh. __ Please nev - er leave me __ blue __ and a - lone, __

C Am Dm7 G7 C Am Dm7 G
if you __ ev-er go __ I'm sure you'll _ come back home, __ be-cause _ I love you __ I love you __ I do,

C Am Dm7 G7 C Am Dm7 G7
an - gel ba-by, __ my an-gel ba-by. __ It's just __ like heav-en __ be-in' __ with you dear, __

C Am Dm7 G7 C Am Dm7 G
I could nev-er stay __ a-way without you near, __ be-cause _ I love you, __ I love you, __ I do,

C Am Dm7 G7 C Am7 Dm7 G7 C Am
an - gel ba-by, __ my an-gel ba-by. __ Ooh, __ I love you, _ ooh, __ I do, no one could love you _

Repeat and Fade

Dm7 G7 C Em7/B Am Dm7 G7 C Em7/B Am Dm7 G7
like __ I do. Ooh __ ooh __ ooh __ ooh. __

AMERICAN PIE

Words and Music by
DON McCLEAN

Freely
G D/F♯ Em7 Am C Em D
A long long time a-go I can still re-mem-ber how that mu-sic used to make me smile. __
G D/F♯ Em7 Am C
And I knew if I had my chance that I could make those peo-ple dance and

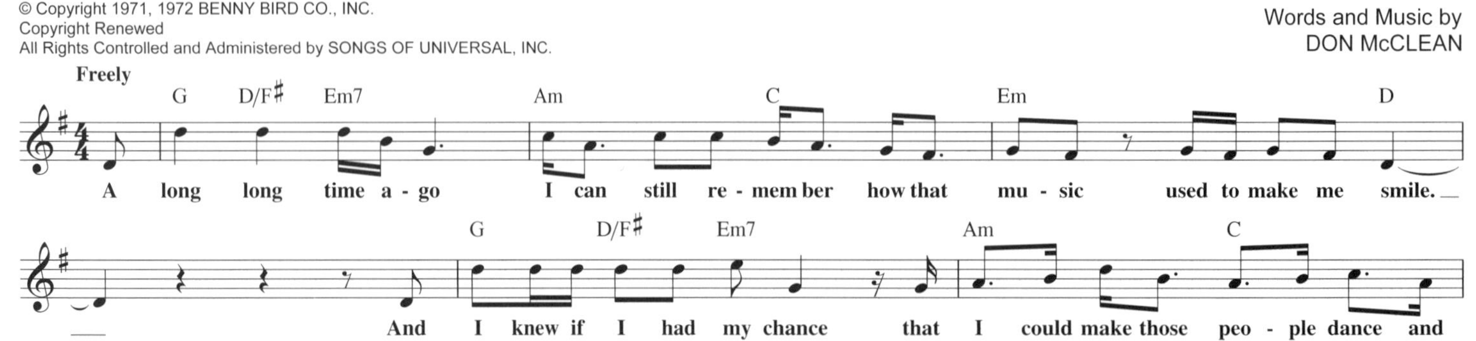

Em C D Em Am Em Am
may-be they'd be hap-py for a while. But Feb-ru-ar-y made me shiv-er with ev-'ry pa-per I'd de-liv er.
C C/B Am C D G D/F♯ Em
Bad news on the door-step, I could-n't take one more step. I can't re-mem-ber if I cried when I
Am7 D G D/F♯ Em C D7 G C/G
read a-bout his wid-owed bride. Some-thing touched me deep in-side the day the mu-sic died.
Moderately
G G C G D G C
So bye-bye, Miss A-mer-i-can Pie drove my Chev-y to the lev-ee but the
To Coda
G D G C G D Em
lev-ee was dry. Them good ol' boys were drink-in' whis-key and rye sing-in' this-'ll be the day that I
A7 Em D7 G
die, this-'ll be the day that I die. Did you write the
Am C Am Em
book of love and do you have faith in God a-bove? If the Bi-ble tells
D G D Em Am7
you so now do you be-lieve in rock and roll, can mu-sic save your
C Em A7 D
mor-tal soul and can you teach me how to dance real slow? Well, I
Em D Em D
know that you're in love with him 'cause I saw you danc-in' in the gym, you
C G A7 C D7
both kicked off your shoes. Man I dig those rhy-thm and blues. I was a
G D Em Am C
lone-ly teen-age bronc-in' buck with a pink car-na-tion and a pick-up truck. But
G D Em C D7
I knew I was out of luck the day the mu-sic died.
D.S. al Coda
G C G D7
I start-ed sing-in'
CODA
C D7 G
this-'ll be the day that I die.

ANNIE'S SONG

Words and Music by
JOHN DENVER

Moderately
Dsus G A Bm G D D/C♯ D/B
You fill up my sens - es like a night in a for - est, like the
D/A G F♯m Em G A7
moun - tains in spring - time, like a walk in the rain. Like a
G A Bm G D D/C♯ D/B
storm in the des - ert, like a sleep - y blue o - cean. You
D/A G F♯m Em A7 D Dsus D Dsus
fill up my sens - es, come fill me a - gain. Come let me
G A Bm G D D/C♯ D/B
love you, let me give my life to you. Let me
sens - es like a night in a for - est. Like the
D/A G F♯m Em G A7
drown in your laugh - ter, let me die in your arms.
moun - tains in spring - time, like a walk in the rain.
G A Bm G D
Let me lay down be - side you, let me al - ways be with you.
Like a storm in the des - ert, like a sleep - y blue o - cean.
D/C♯ D/B D/A G F♯m Em A7
Come let me love you, come love me a -
You fill up my sens - es, come fill me a -
1 D Dsus D Dsus
gain. You fill up my
2 D Dsus D
gain.

ANTICIPATION

Words and Music by
CARLY SIMON

Moderately
D G D
We can nev - er know a - bout the days to come,
you, how eas - y it feels to be with you. And
- row we might not be to - geth - er. I'm no
G Em7 Asus A D
but we think a - bout them an - y - way. And I won - der
how right your arms feel a - round me. But I, I re -
proph - et, and I don't know na - ture's ways. So I'll try and
G D G To Coda
if I'm real - ly with you now, or just chas - ing af - ter some
hearsed those words just late last night, when I was think - ing a - bout how
see in - to your eyes right now, and stay right here, 'cause
Em7 A D D7sus D G
fin - er day.
right to - night might be.
An - ti - ci - pa - tion,
Dmaj7 Em7 A
an - ti - ci - pa - tion is mak - ing me late, is
Em7 A
keep - ing me wait - ing. And I tell to - mor -
1 2 D.C. al Coda
CODA
Em7 A D Dmaj7 G6 D
these are the good old days. These are the good old days. And
G Em7 A D G6 D
stay right here, 'cause these are the good old days. These are the good old days.
Dmaj7 G6 D Dmaj7 G6 D
These are the good old days; these are the good old days.
Dmaj7 G6 D
These are the good old days.
(Instrumental)

AT MY FRONT DOOR

Words and Music by JOHN C. MOORE
and EWART G. ABNER, JR.

With a beat

G6
G7
Cra - zy lit - tle ma - ma come knock - ing, knock - ing at my front door, door, door.

C7
G6
D7
Cra - zy lit - tle ma - ma come knock - ing, knock - ing at my front door. Cra -

C7
G
- zy lit - tle ma - ma come knock, knock, knock - ing just like she did it be - fore I

G6
G7
C7
woke up this morn - ing with a feel - ing of des - pair, I tel - e - phoned my ba - by but she was - n't there. Heard

G
3
some - one knock - ing, and much to my sur - prise. There stood my ba - by, look - ing in my eyes.

D7
C7
G6
Cra - zy lit - tle ma - ma come Knock, knock, knock - ing just like she did it be - fore. If you

G7
got a lit - tle ma - ma and ya want to get a - long, teach your lit - tle ma - ma right from wrong.

C7
G6
Tell her that you love her like you did be - fore, she'll come knock, knock, knock - ing at your door.

D7
C7
G6
1
2
Cra - zy lit - tle ma - ma come knock, knock, knock - ing just like she did it be - fore.

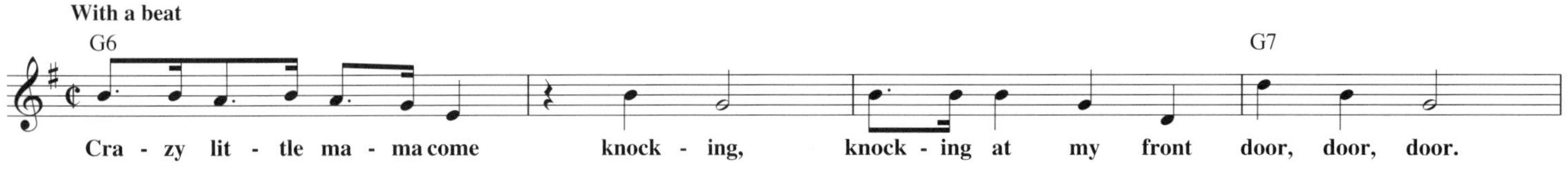

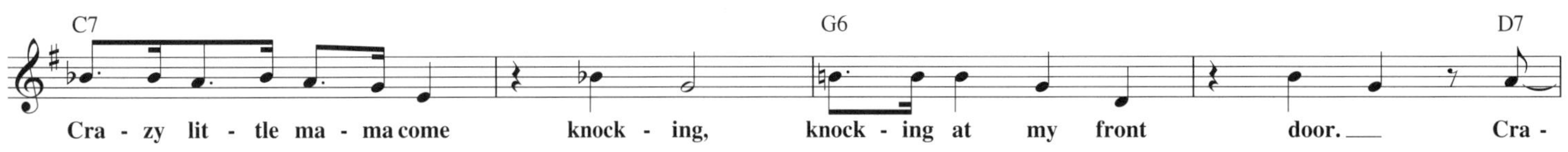

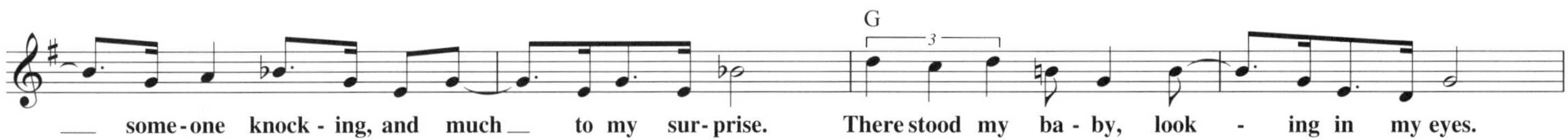

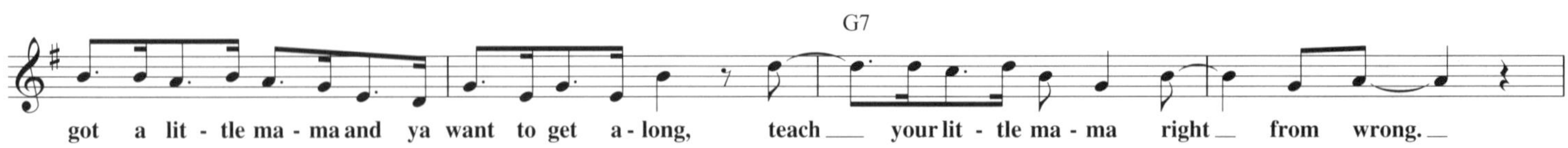

AXEL F

Theme from the Paramount Motion Picture BEVERLY HILLS COP

By HAROLD FALTERMEYER

BABY COME BACK

Words and Music by JOHN C. CROWLEY
and PETER BECKETT

Moderately slow
A♭/B♭
Gm7
Spend - in' all my nights, all my mon - ey go - in' out on the town.
All day long wear - in' a mask of false bra - va - do,

A♭/B♭
Gm7
Do - in' an - y - thing just to get you off of my mind But when the
try'n' to keep up a smile that hides a tear. But as the

A♭/B♭
Gm7
morn - ing comes, I'm right back where I start - ed a - gain. And
sun goes down, I get that emp - ty feel - ing a - gain.

A♭/B♭
B♭/C
C
try'n' to for - get you is just a waste of time.
How I wish to God that you were here.
Ba - by come back,

A♭maj7
Gm7
Cm
an - y kind of fool could see there was

Fm7
Gm7
Cm
some - thing in ev - 'ry - thing a - bout you. Ba - by come back,

A♭maj7
Gm7
Cm
you can blame it all on me. I was

To Coda
1
Fm7
Gm7
Cm
D♭maj7
wrong and I just can't live with - out you.

A♭/B♭
Gm7
2
Cm
D♭maj7
B♭sus
B♭
(Instrumental)
you.

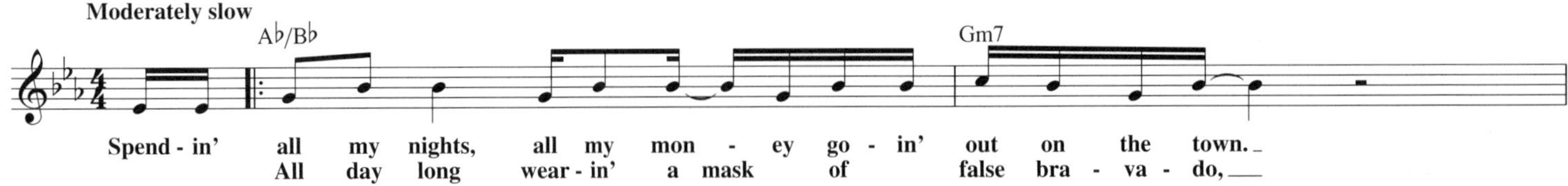

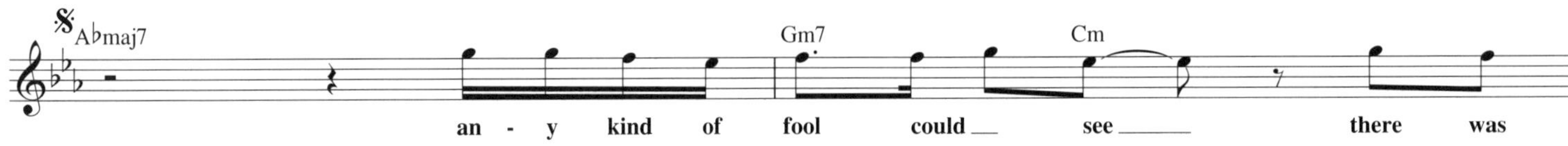

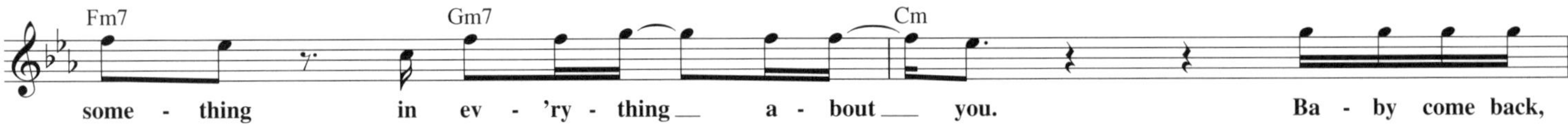

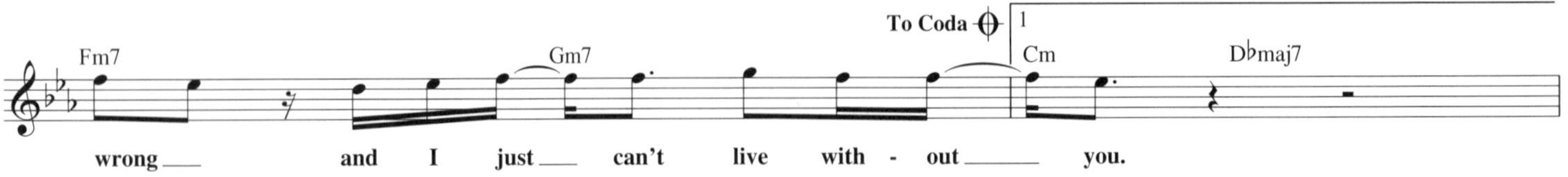

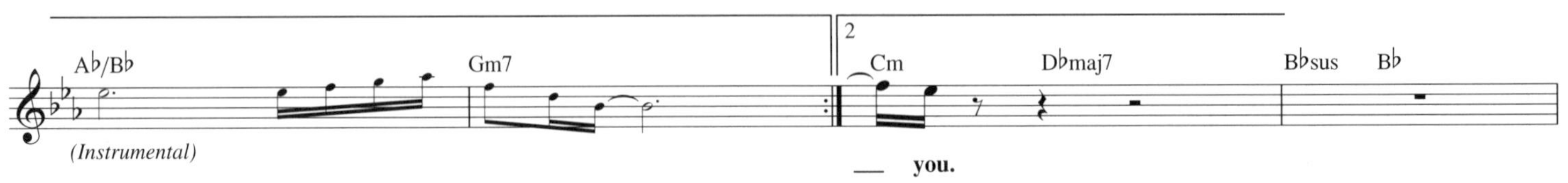

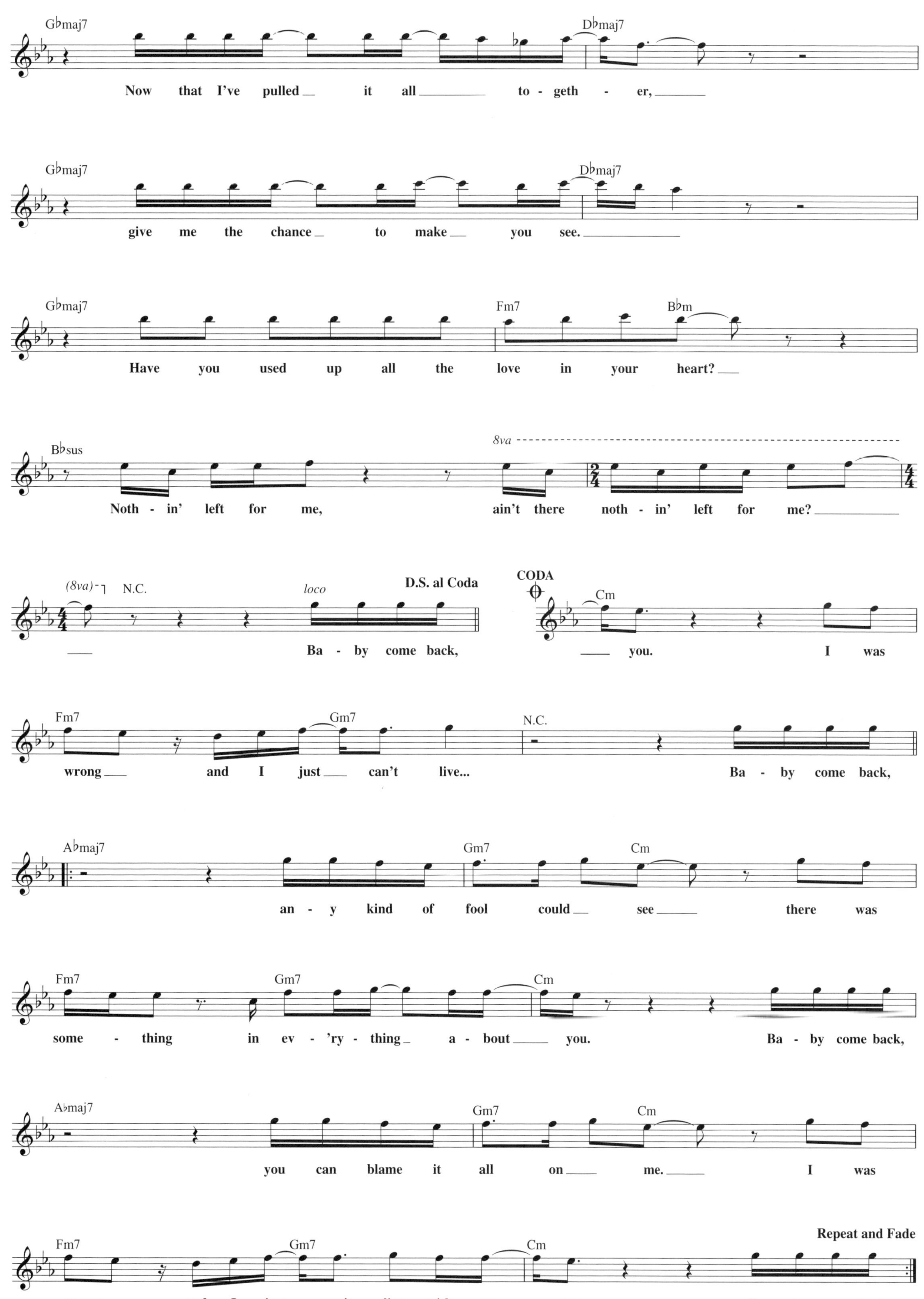
G♭maj7
D♭maj7
Now that I've pulled it all to - geth - er,
G♭maj7
D♭maj7
give me the chance to make you see.
G♭maj7
Fm7
B♭m
Have you used up all the love in your heart?
B♭sus
8va
Noth - in' left for me, ain't there noth - in' left for me?
(8va)
N.C.
loco
D.S. al Coda
Ba - by come back,
CODA
Cm
you. I was
Fm7
Gm7
N.C.
wrong and I just can't live...
Ba - by come back,
A♭maj7
Gm7
Cm
an - y kind of fool could see there was
Fm7
Gm7
Cm
some - thing in ev - 'ry - thing a - bout you.
Ba - by come back,
A♭maj7
Gm7
Cm
you can blame it all on me. I was
Fm7
Gm7
Cm
Repeat and Fade
wrong and I just can't live with - out you.
Ba - by come back,

BABY DON'T GET HOOKED ON ME

Words and Music by
MAC DAVIS

Slowly
A
D/A
A
Girl, you're get - tin' that look in your eyes; and it's start - ing to wor - ry me.
Girl, you're a hot - blood - ed wom - an, child, and it's warm where you're touch - ing me.

D/A
A
D/A
I ain't read - y for no fam - i - ly ties; no - bod - y's gon - na
But I can tell by your trem - bl - in' smile; you're see - ing way too

A
D/A
C♯m
C♯m7
F♯m
hur - ry me. Just keep it friend - ly girl 'cause I don't want to leave.
much in me. Girl, don't let your life get tan - gled up with mine.

Bm7
E7
A
Don't start cling - in' to me girl; 'cause I can't breathe.
'Cause I'll just leave you I can't take no cling - in' vine.
Ba - by, ba - by don't get

Bm
E7
A
hooked on me. Ba - by, ba - by don't get hooked on me.

Bm7
E7
'Cause I'll just use you then I'll set you free. Ba - by, ba - by don't get

D/A
1.
D
C♯m
Bm
A
hooked on me.
(Instrumental)

D/A
D/A
2.
D.C. and Fade
D
C♯m
Bm

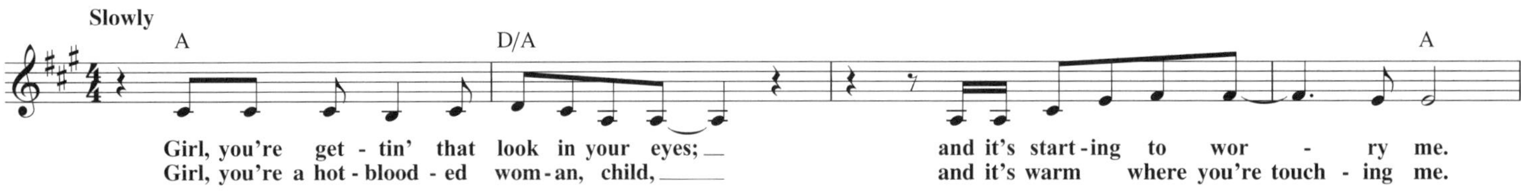

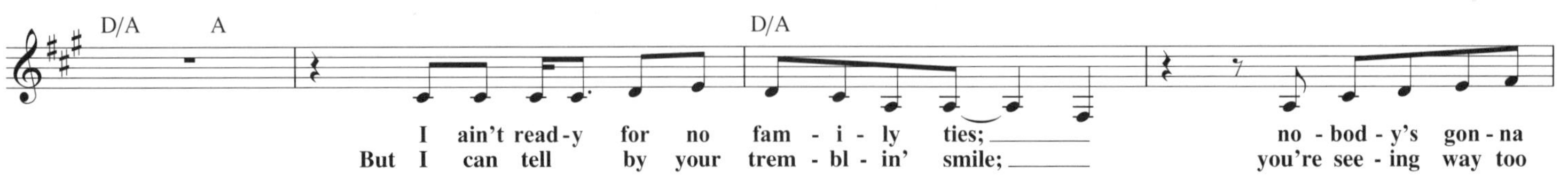

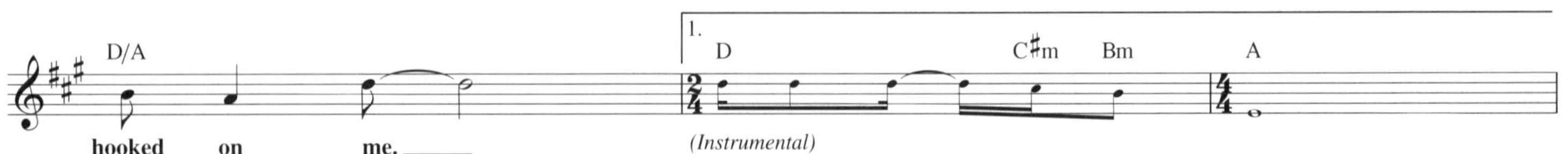

BABY, I'M-A WANT YOU

Words and Music by
DAVID GATES

Slowly, with feeling
A♭ B♭m7/A♭ A♭maj7 D♭ D♭/C B♭m7 D♭/E♭ Cm E♭/D♭ F7/A B♭m G♭maj7/A♭
Ba - by, I'm - a want you. Ba - by, I'm - a need you. You're the on - ly one I care e - nough to hurt a - bout.
lov - in' an' af - fec - tion. Giv - in' me di - rec - tion, like a guid - ing light to help me through my dark - est hour.
May - be I'm - a cra - zy; but I just can't live with - out your
Late - ly I'm - a pray - in', that you'll al - ways be a - stay - in' be - side me.
Used to be my life was just e - mo - tions pass - ing by;
To Coda
feel - ing all the while and nev - er real - ly know - ing why.
D.S. al Coda (take 3rd ending)
CODA
then you came a - long and made me laugh and made me cry; you taught me why.
Ba - by, I'm - a want you. Ba - by, I'm - a need you.
Oh, it took so long to find you, ba - by. Ba - by, I'm - a want you. Ba - by, I'm - a need you.
Repeat and Fade

BABY, IT'S YOU

Words and Music by MACK DAVID,
BURT BACHARACH and BARNEY WILLIAMS

Moderately slow

Ab Eb
It's not the way you smile that touched my heart.
You should hear what they say a - bout you.

Ab Eb
It's not the way you kiss that tears me a - part.
They say you've nev - er, nev - er, nev - er been true.

Cm Fm
Man - y, man - y nights roll by. I sit a - lone at home and cry o - ver
Does - n't mat - ter what they say. I know I'm gon - na love you an - y old way, what can I

1.
Eb Cm Ab Bb7
you. What can I do? I can't help my - self,

Eb Cm Eb Cm
'cause, ba - by, it's you. Ba - by, it's you.

2.
Eb Cm Ab Bb7
do when it's true. I don't want no - bod - y,

Eb Cm Eb
'cause, ba - by, it's you. Ba - by, it's you.

BAND ON THE RUN

Words and Music by
PAUL and LINDA McCARTNEY

Moderately bright
C Fmaj7
1. Well, the rain ex - plod - ed with a might - y crash as we fell in - to the sun,
2. un - der - tak - er drew a heav - y sigh see - ing no one else had come,
3. (See additional lyrics)
C Fmaj7 Em
and the first one said to the sec-ond one there, "I hope you're hav-ing fun."
and a bell was ring-ing in the vil - lage square for the rab - bits on the run.

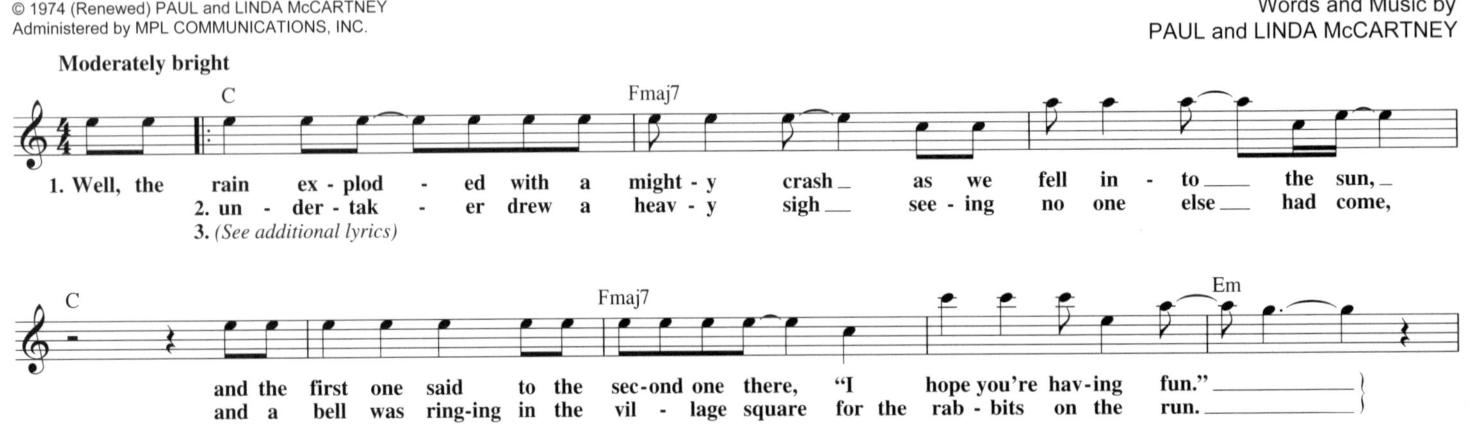

G C Em C Am
Band on the run, band on the run; and the
F C Fmaj7 N.C.
jail - er man and sail - or Sam were search - ing ev - 'ry - one. For the
C
band on the run, band on the run, band on the run,
1, 2 3
band on the run. 2. Well, the 3. Well, the band on the run.

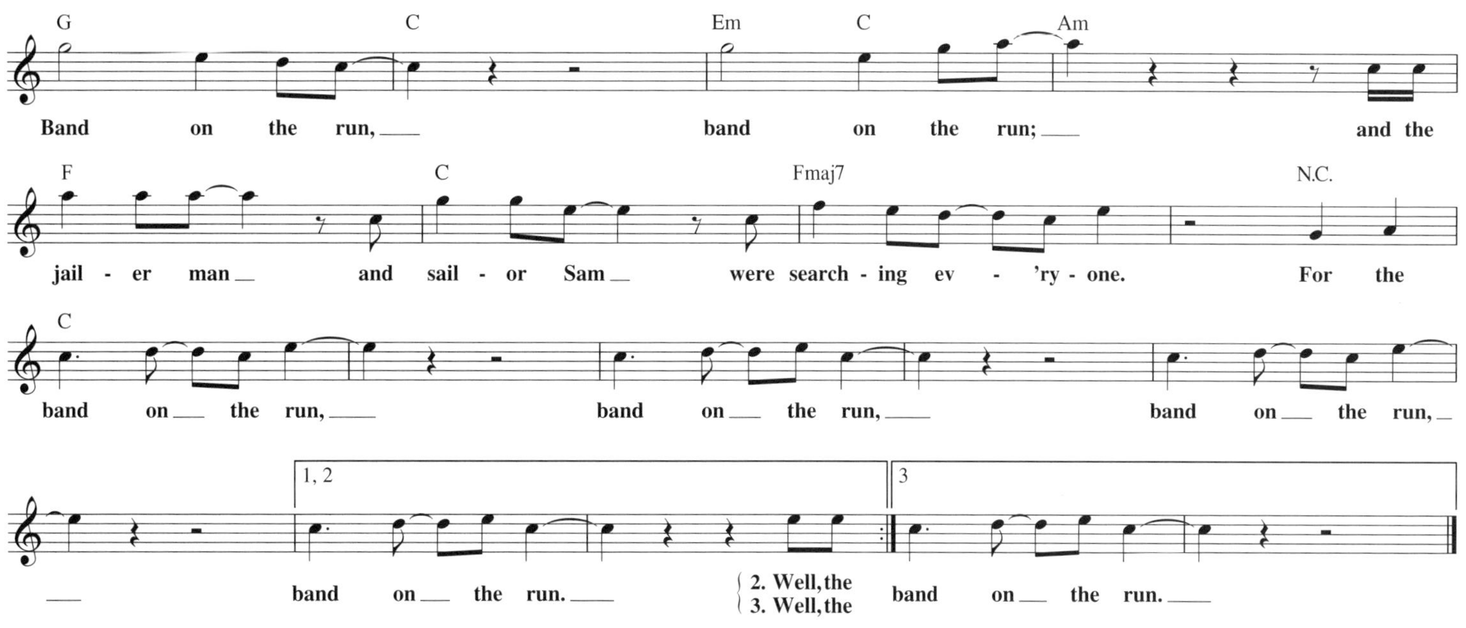

Additional Lyrics

3. Well, the night was falling as the desert world began to settle down.
In the town they're searching for us ev'rywhere but we never will be found.
Band on the run; band on the run;
And the country judge who held a grudge will search forevermore.
For the band on the run, band on the run,
Band on the run, band on the run.

BE MY BABY

Words and Music by PHIL SPECTOR, ELLIE GREENWICH and JEFF BARRY

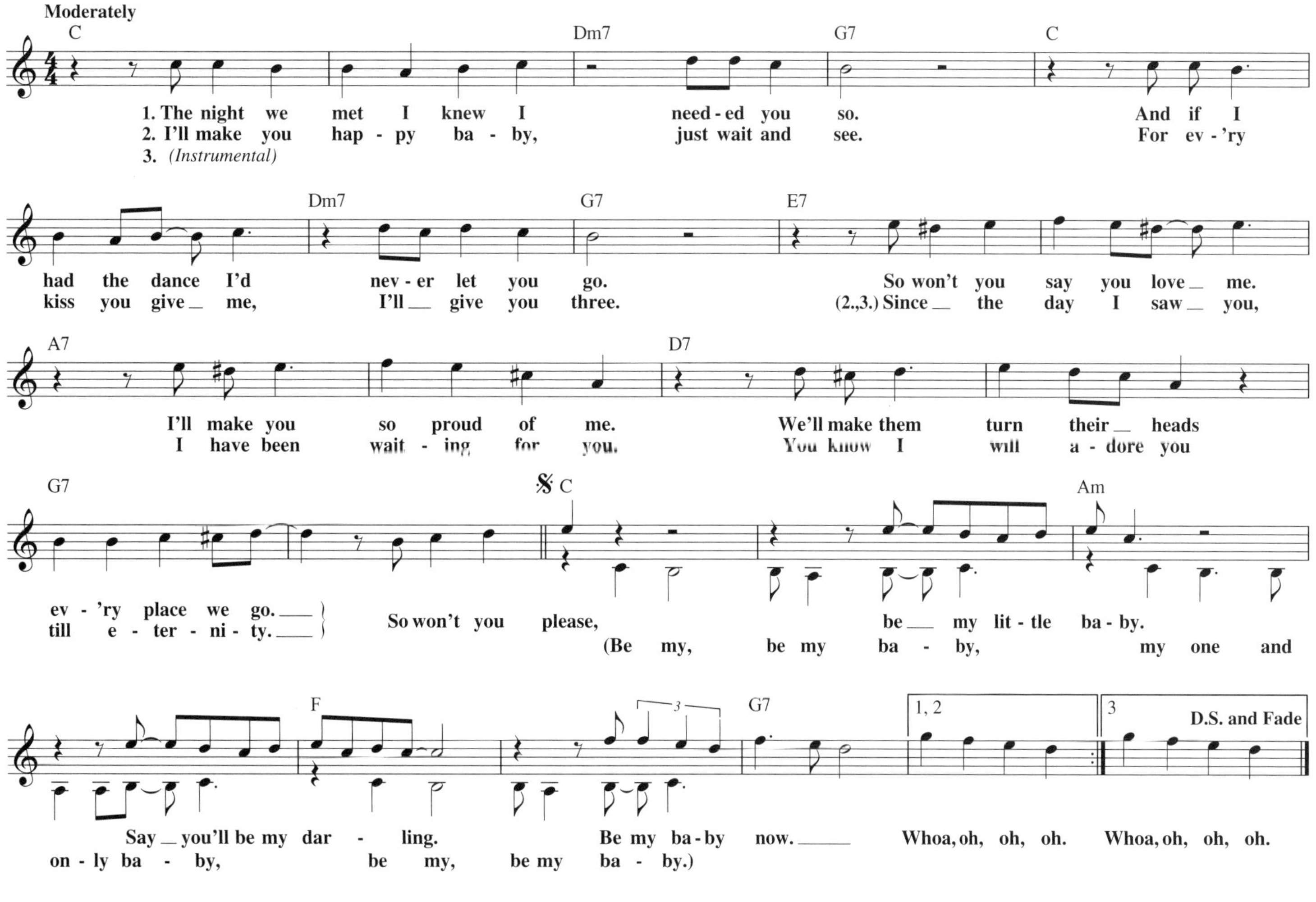

Moderately

C Dm7 G7 C
1. The night we met I knew I need - ed you so. And if I
2. I'll make you hap - py ba - by, just wait and see. For ev - 'ry
3. *(Instrumental)*

Dm7 G7 E7
had the dance I'd nev - er let you go. So won't you say you love me.
kiss you give me, I'll give you three. (2.,3.) Since the day I saw you,

A7 D7
I'll make you so proud of me. We'll make them turn their heads
I have been wait - ing for you. You know I will a - dore you

G7 𝄋 C Am
ev - 'ry place we go. / till e - ter - ni - ty. So won't you please, be my lit - tle ba - by.
(Be my, be my ba - by, my one and

F G7 1, 2 3 D.S. and Fade
Say you'll be my dar - ling. Be my ba - by now. Whoa, oh, oh, oh. Whoa, oh, oh, oh.
on - ly ba - by, be my, be my ba - by.)

BAD DAY

Words and Music by
DANIEL POWTER

Moderate groove
E♭5 A♭sus2 B♭sus
Where is the mo - ment we need - ed the most?
E♭5 A♭sus2 B♭sus
You kick up the leaves and the mag - ic is lost.
Cm Gm/B♭ B♭ A♭ E♭/G
They tell me your blue skies fade to grey. They tell me your pas - sion's gone a - way
Fm7 B♭
and I don't need no car - ryin' on.
E♭ A♭ B♭ A♭
You stand in the line just to hit a new low.
E♭ A♭ B♭
You're fak - in' the smile with the cof - fee to go.
Cm Gm/B♭ B♭ A♭ E♭/G
They tell me your life's been way off line. You've fall - en to piec - es ev - 'ry time
Fm7 B♭ N.C.
and I don't need no car - ryin' on be - cause you had a bad
E♭ A♭ Fm7 B♭
day. You're tak - in' one down. You sing a sad song just to turn it a - round. You say you don't
E♭ A♭ Fm7 B♭
know. You tell me don't lie. You work at a smile and you go for a ride. You had a bad
To Coda
Cm Gm/B♭ A♭ E♭/G
day. The cam - 'ra don't lie. You're com - in' back down and you real - ly don't mind. You had a bad
Fm7 B♭ E♭5 A♭sus2 B♭sus A♭ E♭5 A♭sus2 B♭sus B♭
day. You had a bad day. (Instrumental)

Cm Gm/B♭ A♭ E♭/G
Well, you need a blue sky hol - i - day. The point is they laugh at what you say
Fm7 B♭sus B♭ D.S. al Coda
and I don't need no car - ryin' on. You had a bad
CODA
Fm7 E♭/G
day. Oh, on a hol - i - day.
G♭ C♭
Some - times the sys - tem goes on the blink and the whole thing, it turns out wrong. You
G♭ C♭
might not make it back and you know that you could be well. Oh, that's strong and I'm not wrong,
B♭sus B♭ E♭5 A♭sus2
yeah. So where is the pas - sion when you need it the most?
B♭sus E♭5 A♭sus2
Oh, you and I. You kick up the leaves and the mag - ic is lost
B♭ N.C. E♭ A♭
'cause you had a bad day. You're tak - in' one down. You sing a sad
Fm7 B♭ E♭ A♭
song just to turn it a - round. You say you don't know. You tell me don't lie. You work at a smile
Fm7 D♭ Cm Cm(maj7)/B
and you go for a ride. You had a bad day. You've seen what you like. And how does it feel
Cm7/B♭ Cm6/A F9 A♭ B♭sus
one more time? You had a bad day. You had a bad
E♭ A♭ Fm7 B♭ E♭ A♭ Fm7 B♭
Repeat and Fade
day. (Vocal ad lib.) (Vocal ad lib. continues)

BAD MEDICINE

Words and Music by JON BON JOVI, RICHIE SAMBORA and DESMOND CHILD

Moderate Rock
Your love is like bad med - i cine, bad med - i - cine is what I need, whoa.
Shake it up just like bad med - i - cine. There ain't no doc - tor that can cure my dis - ease.
(Instrumental) (End instrumental) Bad med - i - cine. I
ain't got a fe - ver, got a per - ma - nent dis - ease and it - 'll take more than a doc - tor to pre -
don't need no nee - dle to be giv - ing me a thrill and I don't need no an - es - the - sia or a
scribe a rem - e - dy. I got lots of mon - ey but it is - n't what I need; gon - na
nurse to bring a pill. I got a dir - ty down ad - dic - tion that does - n't leave a track; I got a
take more than a shot to get this poi - son out of me. And I got all the symp - toms, count 'em
jones for your af - fec - tion like a mon - key on my back. There ain't no par - a - med - ic gon - na
1, 2, 3. First you need,
save this heart at - tack. When you need,
(that's what you get for fall - ing in love.) Then you
bleed, (you get a lit - tle but it's nev - er e - nough.) On your knees, (that's what you get for
fall - ing in love.) Now this boy's ad - dict - ed 'cause your kiss is the drug, whoa.
Your love is like bad med - i - cine, bad med - i - cine is

G5 F♯5 E5 G5 E5 A5 G5 F♯5 E5
what I need, whoa. Shake it up just like bad med - i - cine.
A5 G5 F♯5 E5 Gmaj7 A
There ain't no doc - tor that can cure my dis - ease.
So let's play doc - tor, ba - by, cure my dis - ease.
Bad, bad -
1 E(N.C.) 2 E5
med - i - cine. (Instrumental) I med - i - cine, is what I want.
Gmaj7 A E(N.C.)
Bad, bad med - i - cine. Oh it's what I need. I
need a res - pi - ra - tor 'cause I'm run - ning out of breath. You're an all night gen - er - a - tor wrapped in
B5
stock - ings and a dress. When you find your med - i - cine you take what you can get. 'Cause if there's
E N.C. E5
some - thing bet - ter ba - by, well, they have - n't found it yet, whoa. Your love is like
A5 G5 F♯5 E5 A5 G5 F♯5 E5
bad med - i - cine, bad med - i - cine, is what I need, whoa.
G5 E5 A5 G5 F♯5 E5 A5
Shake it up just like bad med - i - cine.
There ain't no doc - tor that can
Your love's the po - tion that can
1 G5 F♯5 E5 2 G5 F♯5 E5 Gmaj7 A
cure my dis - ease. cure my dis - ease. Bad, bad
E (N.C.) Gmaj7 A E5
med - i - cine, is what I want. Bad, bad med - i - cine. (Instrumental)
Gmaj7 A N.C. G5 F♯5 E5
Bad, bad med - i - cine.

...BABY ONE MORE TIME

Words and Music by
MAX MARTIN

Moderately

Cm G7/B G7 E♭ Fm G Cm
Oh, ba - by, ba - by, how was I sup - posed to know that some - thing was - n't right here?
Oh, ba - by, ba - by, the rea - son I breathe is you. Boy, you've got me blind - ed.

G7/B G7 E♭ Fm G Cm
Oh, ba - by, ba - by, I should - n't have let you go. And now you're out of sight, yeah.
Oh, pret - ty ba - by, there's noth - ing that I would - n't do. It's not the way I planned it.

G7/B G7 E♭ Fm G Cm
Show me how you want it to be. Tell me, ba - by, 'cause I need to know now. Oh, be - cause

𝄋 G7/B G7 E♭ Fm Gsus G
my lone - li - ness / My lone - li - ness is kill - ing me, and I, I must con - fess I still be - lieve (still be - lieve)

Cm G7/B A♭ B♭ E♭ **To Coda** 𝄌 1. Fm G Cm
that when I'm not with you I lose my mind. Give me a sign. Hit me, ba - by, one more time.

2. Fm G Cm N.C.
Hit me, ba - by, one more time. Oh, ba - by, ba - by. Oh, ba - by, ba - by.

Cm G7/B E♭ Fm Gsus G
Oh, ba - by, ba - by, how was I sup - posed to know?

A♭maj7 B♭ Fm7 A♭ B♭
Oh, pret - ty ba - by, I should - n't have let you go. I must con - fess

Cm G7/B G7 E♭ Fm Gsus G
that my lone - li - ness is kill - ing me now. Don't you know I still be - lieve

A♭ B♭ A♭maj7 E♭/G Fm N.C. **D.S. al Coda**
that you will be here and give me a sign. Hit me, ba - by, one more time.

CODA 𝄌

Fm G Cm G7/B G7 E♭
Hit me, ba - by, one more time.
I must con - fess that my lone - li - ness is kill - ing me now. Don't you

Fm Gsus G Cm G7/B A♭ B♭ E♭ Fm G Cm
know I still be - lieve that you will be here and give me a sign. Hit me, ba - by, one more time.

BAD BLOOD

Words and Music by NEIL SEDAKA and PHIL CODY

Moderately fast
It could-'ve been me, but it was you who went and bit off a lit-tle bit more than he could chew. You said you had it made, but you been had; the wom-an no good, no how, think-in' may-be the blood is bad.
stand it looks might-y strange how you let a wom-an like that treat you like small change. I don't un-der-stand what you're look-in' to find: the on-ly thing bad blood do is mess up a good man's mind.
Bad blood! The wom-an was born to lie, makes prom-is-es she can't keep with the wink of an eye. Bad blood! Brother, you've been de-ceived; it's bound to change your mind a-bout all you be-lieve.
Bad blood! The bitch is in her smile, the lie is on her lips; such an e-vil child. Bad blood is tak-in' you for a ride; the on-ly good thing a-bout bad blood is let-ting it slide.
To Coda
From where I
Do run do run di di dit dit run run, Do run do run di di dit dit run run, do run do run di di dit dit run run. Bad blood! Talk-in' 'bout bad blood.
D.S. al Coda (2nd verse)
CODA
The on-ly good thing a-bout bad blood is let-ting it slide.

BATDANCE

from the Motion Picture BATMAN

Words and Music by
PRINCE

Medium Funk
E♭7
N.C.
Choir: Bat - man.
Gemini: Get the funk up!
Choir: Bat - man.
Gemini: Get the funk up!
Joker: Go, go, go with a smile.
E♭7(6)
Choir: Bat - dance.
Gemini: Do it.
E♭5
Keep bustin'.
(Instrumental)
I've seen the fu - ture and it will be,
I've seen the fu - ture and it will be
Choir: Bat - man.
Bat - man.
Gemini: I've seen the fu - ture and it will be,
I've seen the fu - ture and it will be
Choir: Bat - man.
Joker: And where, and where is the Batman?
Gemini: Do it, do it.
Slightly slower Funk
Joker: Stop the press,
D♭9
stop the press. Who is that? Vicki: Vicki Vale, Vicki Vale. I like
Choir: Bat - man, Bat - man, Bat - man.
Vicki: Oh– bats
Bruce: Hi, Bruce Wayne. I've tried 2 avoid all this, but I can't.
Vicki: I've just gotta know, are we gonna try 2 love each other?
Joker: Stop the press– who is that? Vicki: Vicki Vale,
Bruce: She is great, isn't she?
Gemini: Ooh yeah, ooh yeah, I wan - na bust that bod - y, ooh
yeah, ooh yeah. I wan - na bust that bod - y right, ooh yeah, ooh yeah, I wan - na bust that bod - y, ooh yeah, ooh yeah.
Bruce: I'd like 2, but he's out there right now.

2 - night. Joker: Well, Miss Vale, ever dance with the devil in the pale moon - light? I always ask
that of all my prey. I just like the sound of it. Bruce: I've got 2 go 2 work.
Choir: Bat - man. Bruce: I've got 2 go 2 work. Choir: Bat - man. Gemini: If a man is con - sid - ered guilt -
Bruce: Work!
Gb/Db
Db9
y 4 what goes on in his mind, then gim-me the e-lec-tric chair 4 all my fu-ture crimes.
Work! Work! Work!
Prince: Hey Duckie, let me stick the 7 inch in the computer. Gemini: Ha, ha, ha, ha, ha, ha, ha, ha, ha, ha, ha, ha, ha, ha, ha.
Joker's Gang: Hey, we got the pow - er. Bat Dancers: Oh, we got the soul.
N.C.
Hey, we got the sho-'nuff get off 2 make the dev-il go, go.
Tempo I
Ebm7
N.C.
Joker: This town needs an enema. Joker's Gang: Pow - er Bat Dancers: Soul.
Batman: I'm gonna kill U. I'm not gonna kill U.
Gemini: Let's do it.
Ebm7
N.C.
Joker's Gang: Pow - er Bat Dancers: Soul.
I'm gonna kill U. I'm not gonna kill U. Gemini: Let's do it.
Eb7
Choir: Bat - man.
Batman: I'm Batman. Gemini: Don't stop dancin'. Batman: I'm Batman.
Eb7(6)#9
Choir: Bat - man. do it, do it. Joker's Gang: Power.
Gemini: Don't stop dancin'. Do it, do it
(See additional lyrics)
1
Choir: Bat - man, Bat - man, Bat - man.
Gemini: Don't stop dancin', let's, let's do it. Gemini: Don't stop, don't stop.
2
N.C.
Joker: Haven't U ever heard of the healing power of laughter? Gemini: Who's gonna stop 200 balloons? Choir: Batman Prince: Stop!

Aditional Lyrics for repeat

Gemini: Don't stop, don't stop, don't stop dancin'.

Don't stop dancin'. Let's do it, let's do it.
Don't stop dancin'. Let's do it.

Choir: Batman, Batman,

Gemini: Don't stop, don't stop. Let's do it.

Don't stop dancin'. Let's do it.

Choir: Batman.

BEAST OF BURDEN

Words and Music by MICK JAGGER
and KEITH RICHARDS

Slow beat

I'll nev-er be your beast of bur-den. My back is broad, but it's a-hurt-ing. All I want is for you to make love to me.
I'll nev-er be your beast of bur-den. I've walked for miles, my feet are hurt-ing. All I want is for you to make love to me.

Am I hard e-nough? Am I rough e-nough? Am I rich e-nough? I'm not too blind to see

I'll nev-er be your beast of bur-den.

So let's go home and draw the cur-tains, mu-sic on the ra-di-o. Come on, ba-by, make sweet love to me.

Am I hard e-nough? Am I rough e-nough? Am I rich e-nough? I'm not too blind to see.

Oh, lit-tle sis-ter, pret-ty, pret-ty, pret-ty, pret-ty girl.

(Instrumental) *(End instrumental)* You're a pret-ty, pret-ty, pret-ty, pret-ty, pret-ty, pret-ty girl. Pret-ty, pret-ty, such a pret-ty, pret-ty, pret-ty girl.

Come on, ba-by, please, please, please.

(Spoken) *I'll tell ya, you can put me out on the street.* Put me out with no shoes on my feet, *(Sung)* but put me out, put me out, put me out of mis-er-y, yeah.

E B/D♯ C♯m A E B/D♯ C♯m A E B/D♯ C♯m
All your sick - ness, I can suck it up. Throw it all at me, I can shrug it off. There's one thing that
A E E/G♯ A E B/D♯ C♯m
I don't un - der - stand. You keep on tell - ing me I ain't your kind of man. Ain't I rough e - nough?
A E B/D♯ C♯m A E B/D♯ C♯m
Oh! Ain't I tough e - nough? Ain't I rich e - nough, in love e - nough?
A E B/D♯ C♯m A
Ooh, ooh please.
E E/G♯ A E A
I'll nev - er be your beast of bur - den. I'll nev - er be your beast of bur - den.
I'll nev - er be your beast of bur - den. I've walked for miles and my feet are hurt - ing.
I won't need no beast of bur - den. I need no fuss - ing, I need no nurs - ing.
Repeat and Fade
E E/D♯ C♯m A E B/D♯ C♯m A A/B
Nev - er, nev - er, nev - er, nev - er, nev - er, nev - er, nev - er be.
All I want is you to make love to me.
Nev - er, nev - er, nev - er, nev - er, nev - er, nev - er, nev - er be.

BIRD DOG

Words and Music by
BOUDLEAUX BRYANT

Moderately
G G7 C
John - ny is a jok - er (He's a bird) a ver - y fun - ny jok - er (he's a bird) but when he jokes, my hon - ey,
C7 G D7 C7
(he's a dog) his jok - in' ain't so fun - ny. (what a dog.) John - ny is the jok - er that's a - try - in' to steal my ba - by. (He's a
G D7 G7 C7 G
bird dog.) Hey, bird dog, get a - way from my quail hey, bird dog, you're on the wrong trail.
D7 C7 G G7 C7
Bird dog, you'd bet - ter leave my lov - ey dove a - lone. Hey, bird dog, get a - way from my chick
G D7 C7 G
hey, bird dog, you'd bet - ter get a - way quick. Bird dog, you'd bet - ter find a Chick - en Lit - tle of your own.

BEAUTIFUL

Words and Music by
LINDA PERRY

Moderately slow
Ev - 'ry - day is so won - der - ful, then sud - den - ly,
To all your friends you're de - lir - i - ous. So con - sumed
it's hard to breathe.
in all your doom.
Now and then I get in - se - cure from all the pain, feel so a - shamed.
Try - ing hard to fill the emp - ti - ness. The piec - es gone, left the puz - zle un - done. Ain't that the way it is?
I am beau - ti - ful no mat - ter what they say. Words can't bring me down.
You are beau - ti - ful no mat - ter what they say. Words can't bring you down.
'Cause we are beau - ti - ful no mat - ter what they say. Words won't bring us down.
I am beau - ti - ful in ev - 'ry sin - gle way. Yes, words can't bring me down, oh no.
You are beau - ti - ful in ev - 'ry sin - gle way. Yes, words can't bring you down, oh no.
We are beau - ti - ful in ev - 'ry sin - gle way. Yes, words won't bring us down, oh no.
1, 3
To Coda
So don't you bring me down to - day.
So don't you bring me down
2
So don't you bring me down to - day. No mat - ter what we do. No mat - ter what we say.
We're the song in - side the tune full of beau - ti - ful mis - takes.
And ev - 'ry - where we go the sun will al - ways shine. on the oth - er side.
D.S. al Coda
(Take 1st Ending)

CODA
E♭
E♭/D♭
Cm
to - day.
B(♭5)
E♭
E♭/D♭
Don't you bring me down to - day, yeah, ooh.
Cm
B(♭5)
N.C.
E♭
Don't you bring me down um to - day.

(IT'S A) BEAUTIFUL MORNING

Words and Music by FELIX CAVALIERE and EDWARD BRIGATI, JR.

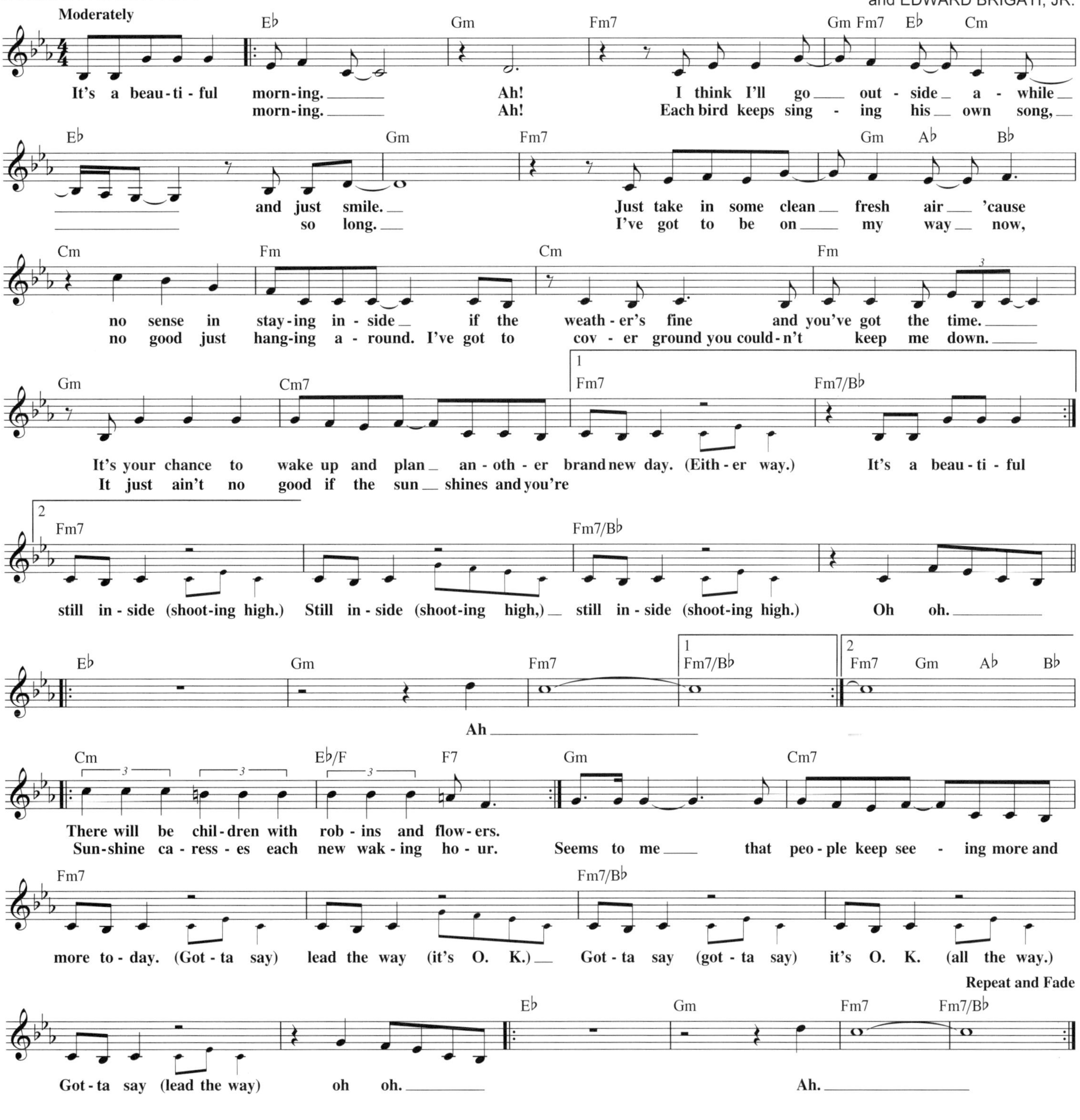

Moderately

E♭ Gm Fm7 Gm Fm7 E♭ Cm

It's a beau-ti-ful morn-ing. Ah! I think I'll go out-side a-while

morn-ing. Ah! Each bird keeps sing-ing his own song,

E♭ Gm Fm7 Gm A♭ B♭

and just smile. Just take in some clean fresh air 'cause

so long. I've got to be on my way now,

Cm Fm Cm Fm

no sense in stay-ing in-side if the weath-er's fine and you've got the time.

no good just hang-ing a-round. I've got to cov-er ground you could-n't keep me down.

Gm Cm7 1 Fm7 Fm7/B♭

It's your chance to wake up and plan an-oth-er brand new day. (Eith-er way.) It's a beau-ti-ful

It just ain't no good if the sun shines and you're

2 Fm7 Fm7/B♭

still in-side (shoot-ing high.) Still in-side (shoot-ing high,) still in-side (shoot-ing high.) Oh oh.

E♭ Gm Fm7 1 Fm7/B♭ 2 Fm7 Gm A♭ B♭

Ah

Cm E♭/F F7 Gm Cm7

There will be chil-dren with rob-ins and flow-ers.

Sun-shine ca-ress-es each new wak-ing ho-ur. Seems to me that peo-ple keep see-ing more and

Fm7 Fm7/B♭

more to-day. (Got-ta say) lead the way (it's O. K.) Got-ta say (got-ta say) it's O. K. (all the way.)

Repeat and Fade

E♭ Gm Fm7 Fm7/B♭

Got-ta say (lead the way) oh oh. Ah.

BAKER STREET

Words and Music by
GERRY RAFFERTY

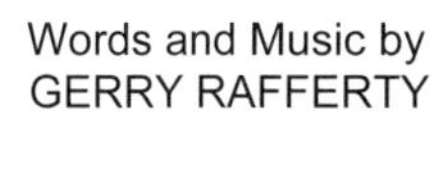

Moderately, with a steady beat
(Instrumental)
1. Wind - ing your way down on Bak - er Street, _
2. (See additional lyrics)
light in your head and _ dead _ on your feet. Well, an - oth - er cra - zy day. _ You'll
drink the night _ a - way _ and for - get a - bout ev - 'ry - thing. _ This cit - y des - sert makes you
feel so cold. _ He's got so man - y peo - ple _ but he's got no soul. _ And it's tak - ing so _ long _ to
find out you _ were wrong _ when you thought it held ev - 'ry - thing. _
You used to think that it was so eas - y. You used to see that it was so eas - y. But you're try - in', you're try - in' now. _
An - oth - er year and then you'll be hap - py. Just one more year and then you'll be hap - py. But you're cry - in', you're cry - in' now. _
(Instrumental)
To Coda
D.S. al Coda (with repeat)
CODA

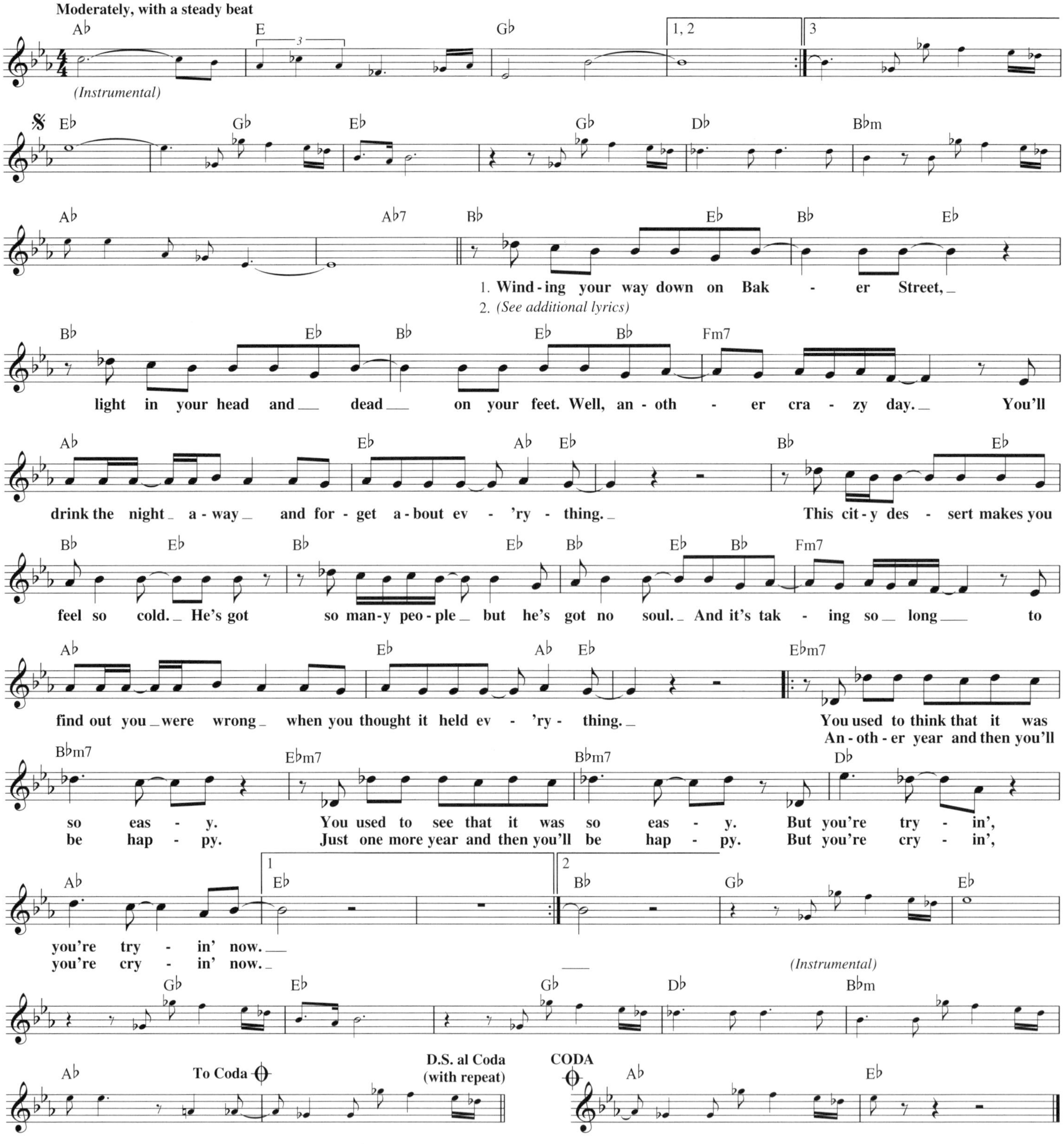

Additional Lyrics

2. Way down the street there's a lot in his place,
He opens his door he's got that look on his face
And he asks you where you've been
You tell him who you've seen and you talk about anything.

He's got this dream about buyin' some land, he's gonna
Give up the booze and the one night stands and
Then you'll settle down with some quiet little town
And forget about everything.

But you know you'll always keep movin'
You know he's never gonna stop movin'
'Cause he's rollin', he's the rollin' stone.

When you wake up it's a new mornin'
The sun is shinin', it's a new mornin'
And you're goin, you're goin' home.

BEACH BABY

Words and Music by JOHN CARTER
and GILL SHAKESPEARE

Shuffle-Beat
Ah ah ah ah
Do you re-mem-ber back in old L. A., oh oh,
Re-mem-ber danc-ing at the high school hop, oh oh,
We could-n't wait for grad-u-a-tion day, oh no,
when ev-'ry-bod-y drove a Chev-ro-let, oh oh? What-e-ver hap-pened to the
the dress I ru-ined with the so-da pop, oh oh? I did-n't rec-og-nize the
we took the car and drove to San Jo-sé oh oh. That's where you told me that you'd
boy next door, the sun-tanned, crew cut, All-A-mer-i-can male?
girl next door, the beat-up sneak-ers and the po-ny-tail.
wear my ring; I guess you don't re-mem-ber an-y-thing.
Beach ba-by, beach ba-by, give me your hand, give me some-thing that I can re-mem-ber.
Just like be-fore, we could walk by the shore in the moon-light. Beach ba-by, beach ba-by,
there on the sand from Ju-ly to the end of Sep-tem-ber, surf-ing was fun, we'd be out
in the sun ev-'ry day.
To Coda
Mm I nev-er thought that it would end.
Long hot days, blue sea haze, juke-box plays,
but now it's fad-ing a-way. Do do do do do do do do do do
D.S. al Coda
Ah ah ah ah
CODA
Ah ah ah ah
Beach ba-by, beach ba-by, beach ba-by, beach ba-by, beach ba-by, beach ba-by, do do do do do do
Repeat and Fade

BELIEVE WHAT YOU SAY

Words and Music by DORSEY BURNETTE
and JOHNNY BURNETTE

Fast Shuffle Rock
A D7
I be - lieve what you say when you say you're go - in' stead - y with no - bod - y else but
lieve what you say when you say you don't miss
A D E
me. I be - lieve what you say when you say ya don't kiss no - bod - y else but
A D7 A
me. I be - lieve, do be - lieve, I be - lieve, yeah be -
D A D7/E E A D
lieve, pret - ty ba - by, be - lieve you're go - in' stead - y with no - bod - y else but me.
A
Well, there's a - one thing ba - by, that I want you to know when you rock -
Well, when you kiss me ba - by, then you roll your eyes I get a
E A D
in' with me you don't a - rock too slow. A - move on in get toe to toe we're gon - na
fun - ny feel - in' that I'm hyp - no - tized. The chills run all up and down my spine a -
A N.C. A D7
rock 'til we can't rock no more. I be - lieve, do be - lieve,
tell - in' ev - 'ry - bod - y that you're mine all mine. I be - lieve,
E7 A D A
I be - lieve, yeah be - lieve, pret - ty ba - by, be - lieve you're go - in' stead - y with
To Coda
D7/E E A D.S. al Coda
no - bod - y else but me. Well, I be -
CODA
A
me. Oh, yeah well, I be -
D7 A D
lieve do be - lieve I be - lieve, well be - lieve, pret - ty ba - by, be -
A D7/E E7♯5 A
lieve you're go - in' stead - y with no - bod - y else but me.

BENNIE AND THE JETS

Words and Music by ELTON JOHN
and BERNIE TAUPIN

Slow Rock
Gmaj7
(Instrumental)
Fmaj7
Am7 D7 G G♯dim7
Hey kids shake it loose to-geth-er the spot-light's hit-ting some-thing that's been known to change the wea-ther.
Hey kids plug in-to the faith-less may-be they're blind-ed but Ben-nie makes them age-less.
Am7 D Em
We'll kill the fat-ted calf to-night so stick a-round. You're
We shall sur-vive let us take our-selves a-long. Where we
Am Bm C
gon-na hear e-lec-tric mu-sic sol-id walls of sound.
fight our par-ents out the streets to find who's right and who's wrong. Say
G Am C
Can-dy and Ron-nie have you seen them yet but they're so spaced out Ben-nie and the Jets.
G Am
But they're weird and they're won-der-ful oh, Ben-nie she's real-ly keen, she's got e-
C D Em Em7
lec-tric boots a mo-hair suit you know I read it in a mag-a-zine oh.
C B♭ D Gmaj7 G6 Gmaj7
Be-Be-Be-Ben-nie and the Jets. (Instrumental)
To Coda
Fmaj7 G7 Fmaj7 G7 Fmaj7 G7 Fmaj7 Am7
D.S. al Coda
CODA
Gmaj7
Ben-nie Ben-nie Ben-nie Ben-nie Ben-nie Ben-nie and the Jets.
Fmaj7 G7 Fmaj7 G7 Fmaj7 G7 Fmaj7 Am7
Repeat and Fade

BECAUSE OF YOU

Words and Music by ARNTOR BIRGISSON, CHRISTIAN KARLSSON, PATRICK TUCKER and ANDERS SVEN BAGGE

Moderately
C G/B Dm7(add4) C G/B Dm7(add4)
You're my sun - shine af - ter the rain. You're the cure a - gainst my fear and my pain 'cause I'm
To Coda
Am7 G F(add2) C/E Dm7 Gsus G Am G7/B
los - in' my mind when you're not a - round. It's all, (it's all,) it's all be - cause of you.
C G/B Dm7(add4) C G/B Dm7(add4)
You're my sun - shine, oh yeah.
Oh yeah, yeah.
Csus2 G/B Dm7 Csus2 G/B Dm7
Ba - by, I real - ly know by now. Since we met that day, you showed me the way. I
Hon - est - ly, could it be you and me like it was be - fore, nei - ther less or more? 'Cause when I
Am G F C/E Dm7
felt it, then you gave me love. I can't de - scribe how much I feel for you.
close my eyes at night I re - a - lize that no one else could ev - er take your place.
G Am7 G7/B C(add2) G/B Dm7(add4)
I said, "Ba - by, I should - 've known by now, should - 've
I still can feel and it's so un - real when you're touch -
C(add2) G/B Dm7(add4) Am G
been right there when - ev - er you gave me love." And if on - ly you were here
in' me, kiss - es end - less - ly. It's just a place in the sun where our love's
F C/E 1 Dm7 Gsus G Am7 G/B 2 Dm7
I'd tell you yes, I'd tell you, oh yeah, you're my
be - gun. I miss you. Yes, I miss
Gsus G Am7 G/B
you, oh babe. You're my
D.S. al Coda
CODA
Gsus G Am7 G7/B B♭(add2)
be - cause of you. If I knew how to tell
F(add2) Em7 A Bm7♭5 A7/C♯ Dm C6
you what's on my mind, make you un - der - stand, then I'd al - ways be there

right by your side. You're my sun-shine af-ter the rain. You're the cure a-gainst my fear and my pain 'cause I'm los-in' my mind when you're not a-round. It's all, (it's all,) it's all be-cause of you.

You're my sun-shine af-ter the rain. You're the cure a-gainst my fear and my pain 'cause I'm los-in' my mind when you're not a-round. It's all, (it's all,) it's all be-cause of you. You're my

Repeat and Fade

THE BIRDS AND THE BEES

Words and Music by
HERB NEWMAN

Moderately, with a beat

Let me tell ya 'bout the birds and the bees and the flow-ers and the trees and the moon up a-bove and a thing called love.

Let me tell ya 'bout the stars in the sky and a girl and a guy and the way they could kiss, on a night like this.

When I look in-to your big brown eyes it's so ver-y plain to see that it's time you learned a-bout the facts of life start-ing from "A" to "Z".

Let me tell ya 'bout the birds and the bees and the flow-ers and the trees and the moon up a-bove and a thing called love.

Let me tell ya 'bout the love.

BLACK DENIM TROUSERS AND MOTORCYCLE BOOTS

Words and Music by JERRY LEIBER
and MIKE STOLLER

Briskly
Cm G7
He wore black den - im trou - sers and mo - tor - cy - cle boots and a black leath - er jack - et with an
Cm G7
ea - gle on the back. He had a hopped - up cy - cle that took off like a gun. That
Cm Cm6/9 Cm(maj9)
fool was the ter - ror of high - way 1 0 1.
Cm G7
Well, he nev - er washed his face and he nev - er combed his hair. He had
Lou, poor girl, she plead - ed and she begged him not to leave. She
Cm
ax - le grease em - bed - ded un - der - neath his fin - ger - nails. On the mus - cle of his arm was a
said, "I've got a feel - ing if you ride to - night I'll grieve." But her tears were shed in vain, and her
Fm G7 Cm
red tat - too, a pic - ture of a heart say - ing, "Moth - er I love you." He
ev - 'ry word was lost in the rum - ble of his en - gine and the smoke from his ex - haust. He
G7
had a pret - ty girl - friend by the name of Mar - y Lou, but he treat - ed her just like he
took off like a dev - il, there was fi - re in his eyes. He said, "I'll go a thou - sand miles be -
Cm Fm
treat - ed all the rest. And ev - 'ry - bod - y pit - ied her 'cause ev - 'ry - bod - y knew he
fore the sun can rise. But he hit a scream - ing die - sel that was Cal - i - for - nia bound, and
G7 Cm
loved that dog - gone mo - tor - cy - cle best. He wore black den - im trou - sers and
when they cleared the wreck - age all they found. was his
G7 Cm
mo - tor - cy - cle boots and a black leath - er jack - et with an ea - gle on the back. He
But they
G7 1 Fm D♭
had a hopped - up cy - cle that took off like a gun, That fool was the ter - ror of
could - n't find the cy - cle that took off like a gun, and they

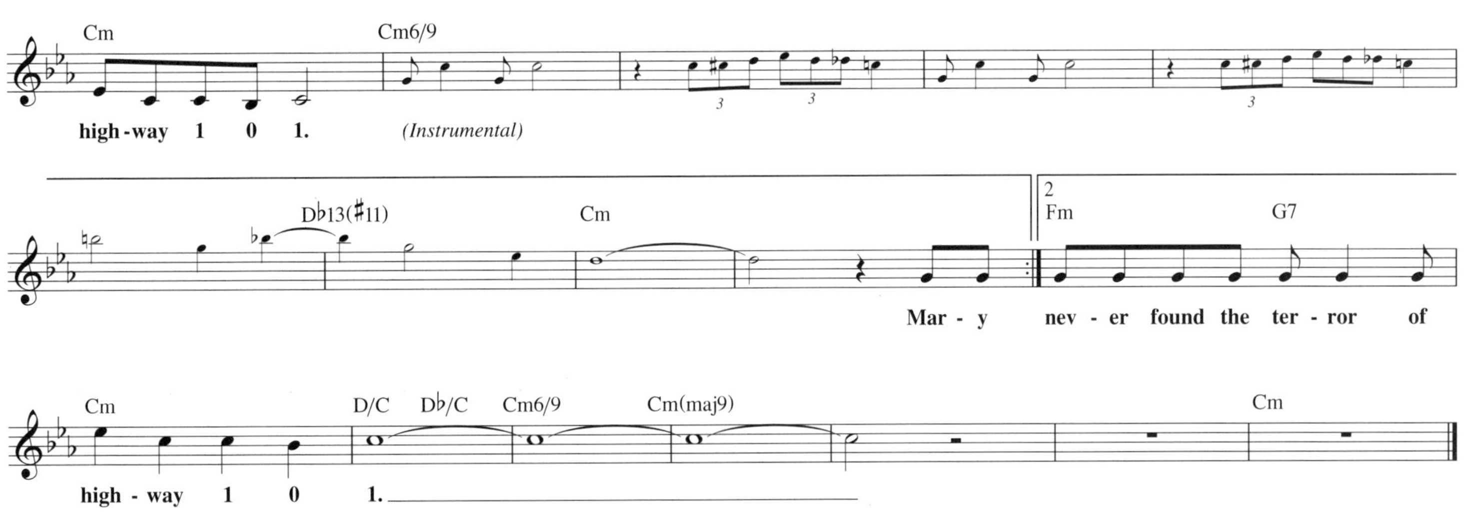

BIG GIRLS DON'T CRY

Words and Music by BOB CREWE
and BOB GAUDIO

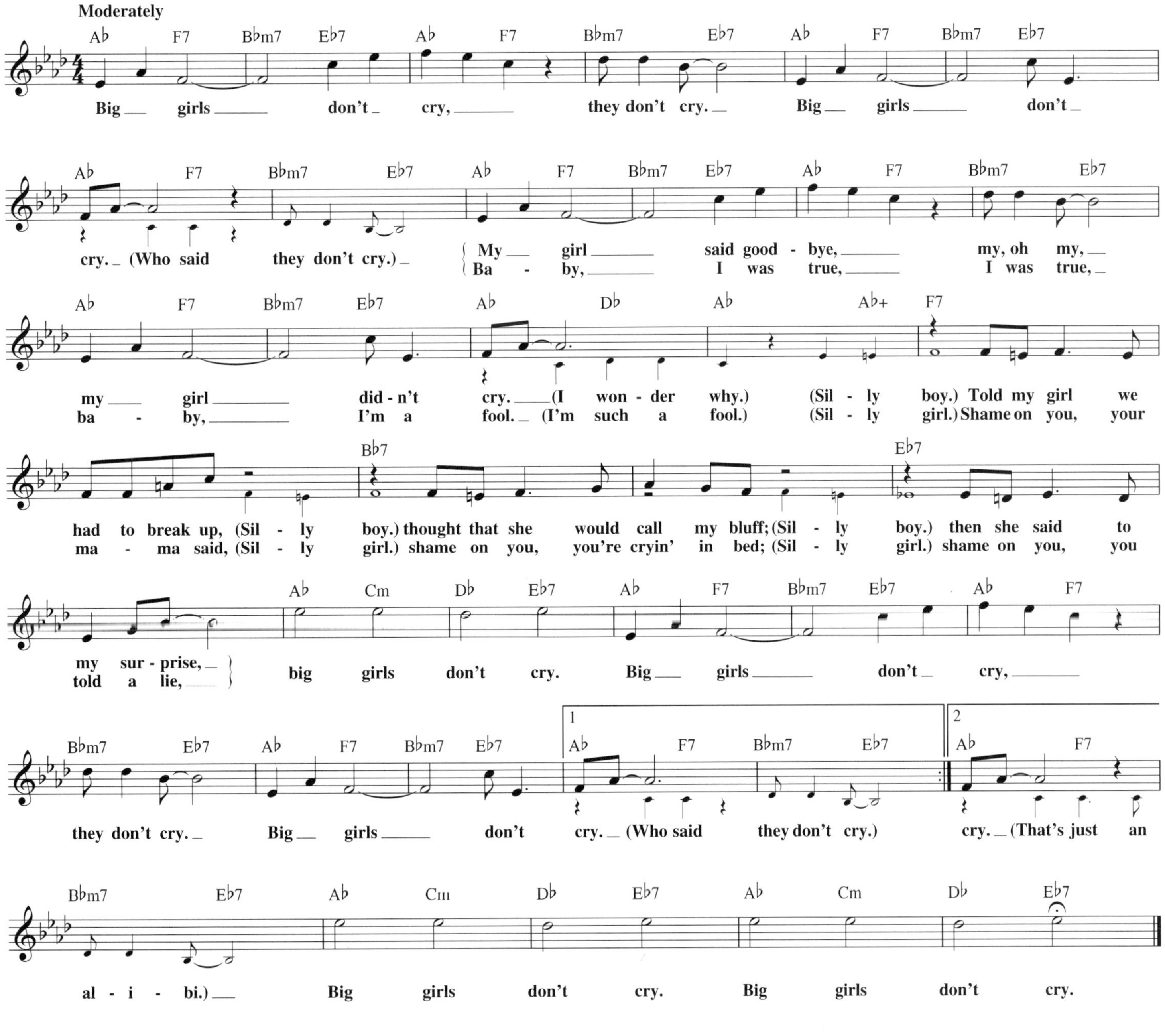

Moderately

A♭ F7 B♭m7 E♭7 A♭ F7 B♭m7 E♭7 A♭ F7 B♭m7 E♭7

Big girls don't cry, they don't cry. Big girls don't

A♭ F7 B♭m7 E♭7 A♭ F7 B♭m7 E♭7 A♭ F7 B♭m7 E♭7

cry. (Who said they don't cry.)
{ My girl said good - bye, my, oh my,
{ Ba - by, I was true, I was true,

A♭ F7 B♭m7 E♭7 A♭ D♭ A♭ A♭+ F7

my girl did - n't cry. (I won - der why.) (Sil - ly boy.) Told my girl we
ba - by, I'm a fool. (I'm such a fool.) (Sil - ly girl.) Shame on you, your

B♭7 E♭7

had to break up, (Sil - ly boy.) thought that she would call my bluff; (Sil - ly boy.) then she said to
ma - ma said, (Sil - ly girl.) shame on you, you're cryin' in bed; (Sil - ly girl.) shame on you, you

A♭ Cm D♭ E♭7 A♭ F7 B♭m7 E♭7 A♭ F7

my sur - prise, }
told a lie, }
big girls don't cry. Big girls don't cry,

B♭m7 E♭7 A♭ F7 B♭m7 E♭7 1 A♭ F7 B♭m7 E♭7 2 A♭ F7

they don't cry. Big girls don't cry. (Who said they don't cry.) cry. (That's just an

B♭m7 E♭7 A♭ Cm D♭ E♭7 A♭ Cm D♭ E♭7

al - i - bi.) Big girls don't cry. Big girls don't cry.

THE BIG HURT

Words and Music by
WAYNE SHANKLIN

Moderate Beguine tempo
F6 G♭6 F6
Now it be- gins now that you're gone, nee-dles and pins
G♭6 F6 D7 Gm B♭m
twi-light till dawn. Watch-ing that clock till you re - turn,
Am G♯dim7 Gm C7 F6
light-ing that torch and watch-ing it burn. Now it be- gins
G♭6 F6 G♭6
day af - ter day. This is my life tick-ing a - way.
F6 D7 Gm B♭m Am G♯dim7
Wait-ing to hear foot steps that say love will ap - pear
Gm C9 E♭9 A♭
and this time to stay. Oh, each time you go I try to pre- tend.
A♭m C7 C7♯5 C7 F6
It's o - ver at last, this time the big hurt will end. Now it be - gins
G♭6 F6 G♭6
now that you're gone, nee-dles and pins twi-light till dawn.
F6 D7 Gm B♭m Am G♯dim7
But if you don't come back a - gain, I won-der when,
Gm C7♭9 F G♭ F
oh, when will it end the big hurt.

BEST THING THAT EVER HAPPENED TO ME

Words and Music by
JIM WEATHERLY

Moderately
Amaj7
Bm7
I've _ had my share of life's ups and downs, but fate's
been times when times were hard, but al-ways
E7sus
E7
Amaj7
A7
Dmaj7
been kind. The downs have been few. I guess you could say _
some-how, I made it through. 'Cause for ev - 'ry mo - ment _
E
Amaj7
F♯m
F+
that I've _ been luck - y. _ Oh, I guess you could say _
that I've _ spent hurt - ing, _ there was a mo - ment _
A/E
B7
E7sus
E
D/E
E
Amaj7
A7
that it's all be - cause of you. _
that I've spent just lov - ing you. _
If an - y - one should ev - er write my life _
Dmaj7
Bm7
E7
Amaj7
sto - ry for what - ev - er rea - son there _ might be,
A7
Dmaj7
E7
E7sus
Amaj7
Dmaj7
oh, _ you'll be there be - tween each line of pain _ and glo - ry, 'cause
Bm7
E7
Amaj7
Dmaj7
you're the best thing _ that ev - er hap - pened to me. Oh, _
Bm7
E7
1
Amaj7
Bm7/A
you're the best thing _ that ev - er hap - pened to me. There _ have
2
Amaj7
Dmaj7
Bm7
E
me. you're the best thing that ev - er hap - pened _ To
A
A/G♯
A/G
D/F♯
Dmaj7
E7♭9
3
Amaj7
me. _ (Instrumental)

BITS AND PIECES

Words and Music by DAVE CLARK and MIKE SMITH

Moderately, with a driving beat
C F C F C F C F C
I'm in piec - es, bits and piec - es. Since you left me and you said good - bye.
I'm in piec - es, bits and piec - es. You said you loved me and you'd al - ways be mine.
F C F C F C F C
I'm in piec - es, bits and piec - es. All I do is sit and cry.
I'm in piec - es, bits and piec - es. We'd be to - geth - er till the end of time.
F C F C F C F C
I'm in piec - es, bits and piec - es. You went a - way and left me mis - er - y.
I'm in piec - es, bits and piec - es. Now you say it was just a game.
F C F C
I'm in piec - es, bits and piec - es and that's the way it - 'll al - ways be.
I'm in piec - es, bits and piec - es but all you're do - ing is leav - ing me pain.
1 N.C. 2 N.C. E7
Time goes by, it
A7 D7
goes so slow, It just does - n't seem true. On - ly just a
G7 N.C.
few days a - go you said you loved me, nev - er make me blue.
C F C F C F C
I'm in piec - es, bits and piec - es. Now you're gone and I'm
F C F C F C F C
all a - lone. I'm in piec - es, bits and piec - es. You're still way up there
F C F C F C F C
on your own. I'm in piec - es, bits and piec - es. Noth - ing seems to
F C F C F C
ev - er go right. I'm in piec - es, bits and piec - es. 'Cos night is day and
1 G7 2 C F C
day is night.

BLACK HOLE SUN

Words and Music by
CHRIS CORNELL

Slow Rock
G6 Bb6 F5 Em Eb Dsus
In my eyes, in - dis - posed, in dis - guise as no _ one knows, _ hides the face, _ lies the snake, and the
ing, cold and damp. Steal the warm wind, ti - red friend. _ Times are gone _ for hon - est men, and some - times
G6 Fdim Ab G6 Bb6 F5 Em
sun in my _ dis - grace. _ Boil - ing heat, sum - mer stretch. 'Neath the black, the sky _ looks dead. _ Call my name _
far too long _ for snakes. _ In my shoes, a walk - ing sleep, and my youth I pray _ to keep. _ Heav - en send _
Eb Dsus G6 Fdim Ab Ebsus Dsus
_ through _ the cream, and _ I'll hear you scream _ a - gain. _
_ hell _ a - way. No _ one sings like you _ an - y - more.
Black - hole sun, won't you come _ and
G G5/F Bb Eb D7 C
wash a - way _ the rain? _ Black hole sun, won't you come? _ Won't you come? _ Won't you come? _
D C Bb Ebsus D7sus G G5/F Bb
Stut - ter - _ Black hole sun, won't you come _ and wash a - way _ the rain? _ Black hole
Eb D7 C Bb D C Bb D
To Coda
sun, won't you come? _ Won't you come? _ Won't you come? _ Won't you come? _
C Bb D C Bb D N.C. G/F
6 times
Won't you come? _
(Instrumental)
F5 G5 G6 Bb6 F5 Em
D.S. al Coda
(take 2nd ending)
Hang my head, drown my fear, 'til you all just dis - ap - pear. _ Black hole
CODA
D C Bb D C Bb D
Won't you come? _ Won't you come? _ Won't you come? _
C Bb D C Bb D N.C. G/F F5 G5
Won't you come? _
(Instrumental)

BLUE VELVET

Words and Music by BERNIE WAYNE
and LEE MORRIS

Slowly, with tender expression
B♭ Dm Cm7 F7♭9
She wore blue vel - vet, blu - er than vel - vet was the
B♭ Cm7 F7 F7♯5 B♭maj7 G7♭9
night. Soft - er than sat - in was the light from the stars.
Cm F7 B♭ Dm Cm7 F7♭9
She wore blue vel - vet, blu - er than vel - vet were her
B♭ G7 Cm7 F7 F7♯5 Fm7 B♭7
eyes. Warm - er than May her ten - der sighs, love was ours.
E♭maj7 E♭m7 Dm7 Gm7 B♭7
Ours, a love I held tight - ly, feel - ing the rap - ture grow
E♭maj7 E♭m7 Dm7 D♭dim7 Cm7 F7
like a flame burn - ing bright - ly. But when she left, gone was the glow of
B♭ Dm Cm7 F7♭9 B♭ G7
blue vel - vet. But in my heart there'll al - ways be,
Cm7 F7 F7♯5 Fm7 B♭9
pre - cious and warm a mem - o - ry through the years and I
E♭maj7 F7♭9 1 B♭6 G7♭9 Cm F 2 B♭6
still can see blue vel - vet through my tears. She wore tears.

BLUE ON BLUE

Lyric by HAL DAVID
Music by BURT BACHARACH

Moderately

Blue on blue, heart-ache on heart-ache, blue on blue, now that we are through. Blue on blue, heart-ache on heart-ache and I find I

can't ___ get o-ver los-ing you. ______ I walk a - long the street we used to walk. Two by two lov-ers pass
lone - ly night we meet in dreams. As I run to your side

and as they're pass-ing by I could die 'cause you're not here with me. Now the trees are bare, there's sad-ness in the air and
you wait with o - pen arms; o - pen arms that now are closed to me. Through a vale of tears your vi - sion dis-ap-pears and

I'm as blue as I can be.
I'm as blue as I can be.
Blue on blue, heart-ache on heart-ache, blue on blue, now that we are through. Blue on blue,

heart-ache on heart-ache and I find I can't ___ get o-ver los-ing you. Night af - ter los-ing you. ______

BOBBY'S GIRL

Words and Music by GARY KLEIN
and HENRY HOFFMAN

Moderately

When peo - ple ask of me ___ what would you like to be, ___ now that you're not a kid ___ an - y - more? ___
Each night I sit at home ___ hop - ing that he will phone, ___ but I know Bob - by has ___ someone else. ___

I know just what to say, ___ I an - swer right a - way. ___ There's just one
Still in my heart I pray, ___ there soon will come a day ___ when I will

thing I've been ___ wishing for. ______
have him all ___ to my - self. ______
I wan - na be ___ Bob-by's girl, ___ I wan - na be ___ Bob-by's girl. ___

That's the most ___ im - por - tant thing ___ to me. ______ And if ___ I was ___ Bob-by's girl; ___ if ___ I was

___ Bob-by's girl, ___ what a faith - ful, thank - ful girl I'd be. ______

BONY MORONIE

Words and Music by
LARRY WILLIAMS

Bright Rock tempo
F F7 F
I got a girl named Bo - ny Mo - ro - nie. She's as skin - ny as a stick of mac - a -
told your ma - ma and your pa - pa, too just ex - act - ly what I'm gon - na
B♭7
ro - ni. Ought-a see her rock with her blue jeans on. She's
do. We'll get mar - ried on a night in June. And rock and
F F7 C B♭
not fat she's just skin and bones.
roll by the light of the sil - v'ry moon.
I love her, she loves me.
C B♭ F7 1 B♭ F
Oh, how hap - py now we can be. Mak - ing love un - der - neath the ap - ple tree. Well, I
2 B♭ F C B♭ A♭
I got a girl, I got a girl.
G G6 G7
She's my one, she's my on - ly she's my heart's de - sire, she's a
G G6 G7 C C7
real up - set - ter she's real live wire. Ev - 'ry - bod - y looks when she goes
G G7
by. She's a real good, good girl real - ly grabs your eyes.
D C D C G7
I love her, she loves me. Oh, how hap - py now we can be. Mak - ing love un - der - neath the
C G D D/G
ap - ple tree. I got a girl, I got a girl.

BOOGIE OOGIE OOGIE

Words and Music by JANICE MARIE JOHNSON
and PERRY KIBBLE

Moderate Disco

If you're think - ing you're too cool to boog - ie,
There's no time to waste, let's get this show on the road.

boy, oh boy, have I got news for you.
Lis - ten to the mu - sic and let your bod - y flow. The

Ev - ry - bod - y here to - night must boog - ie. Let me tell you,
soon - er we be - gin, the long - er we've got to groove.

you are no ex - cep - tion to the rule. Get on
Lis - ten to the mu - sic and let your bod - y move. Now get on

up on the floor 'cause we're gon - na boog - ie oog - ie oog - ie till we just can't boog - ie no more,

boog - ie no more. You can't boog - ie no more, boog - ie no more.

To Coda

Lis - ten to the mu - sic.
Lis - ten to my bass, yeah.

D.C. al Coda

(Ooh, ooh.)

CODA

Boog - ie!

Play 3 times

Boog - ie! Get down, boog - ie oog - ie oog - ie. Get down, boog - ie oog - ie oog - ie. Get down, boog - ie oog - ie oog - ie. Get down.

Boog - ie!

Repeat and Fade

Boog - ie!

BOHEMIAN RHAPSODY

Words and Music by
FREDDIE MERCURY

Slowly

B♭6 C7 B♭6 C7 F7 Cm7 F7 B♭ Cm7 B♭

Is this the real life? Is this just fan - ta - sy? Caught in a land - slide, No es - cape from re - al - i - ty.

Gm B♭7 E♭ Cm F7

O - pen your eyes, Look up to the skies and see, I'm just a poor boy, I need no sym - pa - thy, Be - cause I'm

B B♭ A B♭ B B♭ A B♭ E♭ B♭/D C♯dim7 F/C F

eas - y come, eas - y go, Lit - tle high, lit - tle low, An - y way the wind blows does - n't real - ly mat - ter to me, to

B♭ B♭ Gm Cm

me. Ma - ma just killed a man, Put a gun a - gainst his head, pulled my
Too late, my time has come, Sends shiv - ers down my spine, bod - y's

F B♭ Gm Cm7 B+ E♭/B♭

trig - ger, now he's dead. Ma - ma, life had just be - gun, But now I've gone and thrown it all a -
ach - ing all the time. Good - bye, ev - 'ry - bod - y I've got to go, Got - ta leave you all be - hind and face the

F/A Fm/A♭ E♭ B♭/D Cm Fm B♭

way. Ma - ma, ooh, Did - n't mean to make you cry. If I'm not back a - gain this time to -
truth. Ma - ma, ooh, I don't want to die, I some - times wish I'd nev - er been born at

1

E♭ B♭/D Cm A♭m E♭ A♭/E♭ E♭ E♭dim Fm7/E♭ B♭

mor - row, car - ry on, car - ry on as if noth - ing real - ly mat - ters.

2

E♭ B♭/D Cm Fm B♭7 E♭ Gm/D Cm Fm

all.

D♭ D♭/C B♭m

L'istesso tempo

A D/A A Adim A D/A A Adim A D/A A D/A A

I see a lit - tle sil - hou - et - to of a man, Scar - a - mouche, Scar - a - mouche, will you

Adim A D/A A D♭/A♭ A♭ C/G E A N.C.

do the Fan - dan - go? Thun - der - bolt and light - ning, ver - y, ver - y fright - 'ning me. (Gal - li - le - o.) Gal - li -

B B♭ A B♭

le - o. (Gal - li - le - o.) Gal - li - le - o, Gal - li - le - o Fig - a - ro Mag - ni - fi - co. I'm just a poor boy and

B B♭ A B♭ A♭/E♭ E♭ E♭dim E♭ A♭/E♭ E♭ E♭dim E♭ A♭ E♭/G F B♭
no - bod - y loves me. He's just a poor boy from a poor fam - i - ly. Spare him his life from this mon - stros - i - ty.
A♭ E♭/G F♯dim7 Fm7 B B♭ A B♭ B B♭ A B♭ E♭ B♭ E♭
Eas - y come, eas - y go, will you let me go, Bis - mil - lah? No, we will not let you go. (Let him go!)
B♭ E♭ B♭
Bis mil - lah! We will not let you go. (Let him go!) Bis - mil - lah! We will not let you go. (Let me go.)
G♭7 Bm A D D♭ G♭ B♭ E♭ N.C.
Will not let you go. Will not let you go. Ah. No, no, no, no, no, no, no. Oh ma-ma
(Let me go.) (Let me go.)
E♭ B♭ E♭ A♭ D Gm B♭
mi - a, ma-ma mi - a. Ma-ma mi - a, let me go. Be - el - ze - bub has a dev - il put a - side for me, for me, for
E♭ F7 B♭7 E♭/B♭ B♭ E♭
me. So you think you can stone me and spit in my
B♭ D♭ B♭7 E♭/B♭ B♭ E♭ A♭
eye. So you think you can love me and leave me to die.
Fm B♭ Fm B♭ Fm7 B♭ Fm7 B♭
Oh, ba - by, can't do this to me, ba - by, Just got - ta get out, just got - ta get right out - ta
E♭ B♭7 Slowly, a tempo E♭ B♭/D
here.
Cm G/B Cm G7/B Cm B♭7 E♭ D Gm A♭ E♭
Cm Gm Cm Gm Cm A♭m B♭11
Noth - ing real - ly mat - ters, An - y - one can see, Noth - ing real - ly mat - ters, Noth - ing real - ly mat - ters to
E♭ A♭/E♭ E♭ E♭dim7 B♭/D B♭m/D♭ C7 C7♭9 C7 F B♭ F/A A♭dim7 Gm7 F
me. An - y way the wind blows.

BOOGIE FEVER

Words and Music by FREDERICK PERREN and KENNETH ST. LEWIS

Moderately
F7
Boo - gie fe - ver, got to boo - gie down. she likes to boo - gie down.
She's got the Boo - gie fe - ver, I think it's go - in' a - round.
F7 Eb/F Bb/F
I took my ba - by to the drive - in show, she turned the speak - er down.
I took my ba - by to the piz - za par - lor, to get a bite to eat now.
I called the doc - tor on the tel - e - phone, say doc - tor, doc - tor, please:
Then she turned on the ra - di - o; I watched the si - lent mov - ie dig - gin' funk - y sounds. She's got the
I put some mon - ey in the juke - box for her; you know she ate her piz - za danc - in' to the beat. She's got the
I got this feel - in' rock - in' and a reel - in'. Tell me what can it be? Is it some new dis - ease. He called it
Gm7/C
Boo - gie fe - ver, she likes to boo - gie down. got to boo - gie down.
She's got the Boo - gie fe - ver, I think it's go - in' a - round.
To Coda
N.C.
G C/G
All night long we did the bump bump bump. (Yes, we did. Yes, we did, yeah!)
G C/G Gm7
We kept it go - in' strong, do - in' the bump bump bump, do - in' the bump bump, yeah!
D.S. al Coda
CODA
N.C.
Fe - ver! Fe - ver!
G C/G
All night long, we did the bump bump bump. (Yes, we did. Yes, we did. Yes, we did.)
G C/G G
We kept it go - in' strong, do - in' the bump bump bump.

Gm7/C
F7
Yeah, ev - 'ry - bod - y's got the Boo - gie fe - ver, got to
boo - gie down. She's got the Boo - gie fe - ver, I think it's
go - in' a - round.
F7
I (I) got the Boo - gie fe - ver! You (you) got the
Repeat and Fade
Boo - gie fe - ver! She's (she's) got the Boo - gie fe - ver! Ev - er - y - bod - y's got the Boo - gie fe - ver!

BREAD AND BUTTER

Words and Music by LARRY PARKS
and JAY TURNBOW

Moderate Rock
1. I like bread and but - ter. I like toast and jam. That's what my ba - by
2., 3. (See additional lyrics)
feeds me. I'm her lov - in' man. He likes bread and
but - ter. He likes toast and jam. That's what his ba - by feeds him.
1, 2
He's her lov - in' man.
3
with some oth - er man.

Additional Lyrics

2. She don't cook mashed potatoes,
Don't cook T-bone steak.
Don't feed me peanut butter.
She knows that I can't take
No more bread and butter,
No more toast and jam.
He found his baby eatin'
With some other man.

3. Got home early one mornin'
Much to my surprise,
She was eatin' chicken and dumplin's
With some other guy.
No more bread and butter,
No more toast and jam.
I found my baby eatin'
With some other man.

BORN TOO LATE

Lyric by FRED TOBIAS
Music by CHARLES STROUSE

With a slow, driving beat
C Am Dm7 G7 C Em7 Dm7 G7
Born too late for you to no - tice me, To you I'm just a kid that
C Am Dm7 G7 C Am Dm7 G7
you won't date, Why was I born too late?
C Am Dm G7 C Em7 Dm7 G7
Born too late to have a chance to win your love, Oh why, oh why was
C Am Dm7 G7 C F C C7
it my fate to be born too late? I
F C F C C7
see you walk with an - oth - er, I wish it could be me; I
F C D7 G7 N.C.
long to hold you and kiss you, But I know it nev - er can be. For I was
C Am Dm7 G7 C Em7
born too late for you to care, Now my heart cries be -
Dm7 G7 C Am 1 Dm7 G7 C Am
cause your heart just could - n't wait, Why was I born too late?
Dm7 G7 2 Dm7 G7 Gm6 A7
Why was I born too late?
Dm A7 Dm Dm7 G7 C F C
Why was I born too late?

BORN TO BE WILD

from EASY RIDER

Words and Music by
MARS BONFIRE

Moderate Rock beat
E♭
Get your mo - tor run - ning.
I like smoke and light - ning.
Head out on the high - way
Heav - y me - tal thun - der
look - ing for ad - ven - ture
rac - ing in the wind
in what - ev - er comes our way.
and the feel - ing that I'm un - der.
G♭ A♭ E♭ G♭ A♭
Yeah, dar - ling, gon - na make it hap - pen, take the world in a
E♭ G♭ A♭ E♭
love em - brace. Fire all of your guns at once and
G♭ A♭
ex - plode in - to space.
1, 3
E♭
2, 4
E♭
Like a true
na - ture child we were born,
G♭
born to be wild.
A♭ G♭
We have climbed so high, nev - er want to die.
E♭ D♭
Born to be wild,
E♭ D♭ E♭ D♭ E♭
born to be wild.
1
D♭
D.C.
(Lyric 1)
2
D♭
E♭ D♭ E♭ D♭
Born to be wild.
Repeat and Fade

BREAKAWAY

from THE PRINCESS DIARIES 2: ROYAL ENGAGEMENT

Words and Music by BRIDGET BENENATE,
AVRIL LAVIGNE and MATTHEW GERRARD

Moderately
Am G/B C Fsus2 Am G/B Fsus2
Dah, dah, dah, dah, dah. Dah, dah, dah, dah, dah. Dah, dah, dah, dah, dah, dah, dah.
Am G/B C Fsus2 Am G Fsus2
Dah, dah, dah, dah, dah. Dah, dah, dah, dah, dah. Dah, dah, dah, dah, dah, dah, dah.
Am G/B C Fsus2 Am G/B Fsus2
Grew up in a small town and when the rain would fall down, I'd just stare out my win - dow.
Am G/B C Fsus2 Am G Fmaj7
Dream - in' of what could be and if I'd end up hap - py. I would pray.
Am G/B C Fsus2 Am G/B
Try - ing hard to reach out but when I tried to speak out, felt like no one could
Wan - na feel the warm breeze. Sleep un - der a palm tree. Feel the rush of the
Fsus2 Am G/B C Fsus2 Am G
hear me. Want-ed to be - long here but some - thing felt so wrong here. So I'd
o - cean. Get on board a fast train. Trav - el on a jet plane far a -
Fsus2 Am G D F G
pray. (I would pray) I could break - a - way.
way and break - a - way.
C G Am Fsus2
I'll spread my wings and I'll learn how to fly. I'll do what it takes 'til I touch the sky. I'll
C G Am G Fsus2
make a wish. Take a chance. Make a change and break - a - way.
C G Am Fsus2
Out of the dark - ness and in - to the sun. But I won't for - get all the ones that I love. I'll
I got - ta

To Coda
C G Am G Fsus2
take a risk. Take a chance. Make a change and break - a - way.
Am G/B C Fsus2 Am G Fsus2
D.S. al Coda
Dah, dah, dah, dah, dah. Dah, dah, dah, dah, dah. Dah, dah, dah, dah, dah, dah, dah.
CODA
Am G Fsus2 G5 C5 F5
break - a - way. Build - ing with a hun - dred floors. Swing - ing 'round re - volv - ing doors.
G5 C5 F5 G5
May - be I don't know where they'll take me. But, got - ta keep mov - in' on,
C5 F5 D5 F5 G5 C
mov - in' on. Fly a - way, break - a - way. I'll spread my wings and I'll
G Am Fsus2
learn how to fly. Though it's not eas - y to tell you good - bye, got - ta
C G Am G Fsus2
take a risk. Take a chance. Make a change and break - a - way.
C G Am
Out of the dark - ness and in - to the sun. But I won't for - get the
Fsus2 C G Am G
place I come from. I got - ta take a risk. Take a chance. Make a change and break - a -
Fsus2 Am G Fsus2 Am G Fsus2
way, break - a - way, break - a - way.

A BOY NAMED SUE

Words and Music by
SHEL SILVERSTEIN

Moderately bright
B♭
E♭
(Spoken:) 1. "Well, my daddy left home when I was three, and he didn't leave much to Ma and me, just this
2.-5. (See additonal lyrics)
F7
B♭
old guitar and an empty bottle of booze. Now, I don't blame him because he
E♭
F7
run and hid, but the meanest thing that he every did was, before he left, he went and named me
B♭
Sue. Well, he must have thought it was quite a joke, and it
E♭
F7
B♭
got lots of laughs from a lot of folks. It seems I had to fight my whole life through.
E♭
F7
Some gal would giggle and I'd get red. And some guy would laugh and I'd bust his head. I tell you life ain't easy
1-4
B♭
5
B♭
for a boy named Sue.

Additional Lyrics

2. *Well, I grew up quick and I grew up mean;*
My fists got hard and my wits got keen.
Roamed from town to town to hide my shame,
But I made me a vow to the moon and stars,
I'd search the honky-tonks and bars,
And kill that man that give me that awful name.

Well, it was Gatlinburg in mid July,
And I had just hit town and my throat was dry.
I'd thought I'd stop and have myself a brew.
At an old saloon on a street of mud,
There at a table dealin' stud,
Sat the dirty, mangy dog that named me Sue.

3. *Well, I knew that snake was my own sweet dad*
From a worn-out picture that my mother had.
And I knew that scar on his cheek and his evil eye.
He was big and bent and gray and old,
And I looked at him and my blood ran cold,
And I said, "My name is Sue. How do you do?
Now you gonna die." Yeah, that's what I told him.

Well, I hit him hard right between the eyes,
And he went down, but to my surprise
He come up with a knife and cut off a piece of my ear.
But I busted a chair right across his teeth.
And we crashed through the wall and into the street,
Kickin' and a-gougin' in the mud and the blood and the beer.

4. *I tell you, I've fought tougher men,*
But I really can't remember when.
He kicked like a mule and he bit like a crocodile.
I heard him laugh and then I heard him cussin';
He went for his gun and I pulled mine first.
He stood there lookin' at me and I saw him smile.

And he said, "Son, this world is rough,
And if a man's gonna make it, he's gotta be tough.
And I know I wouldn't be there to help you along.
So I give you that name and I said, 'Goodbye.'
I knew you'd have to get tough or die.
And it's that name that helped to make you strong."

5. *Yeah, he said, "Now you just fought one helluva fight,*
And I know you hate me and you've got the right
To kill me now and I wouldn't blame you if you do.
But you ought to thank me before I die
For the gravel in your guts and the spit in your eye,
'Cause I'm the _____ that named you Sue."
Yeah, what could I do? What could I do?

I got all choked up and I threw down my gun,
Called him my pa and he called me his son.
And I come away with a different point of view.
And I think about him now and then,
Ev'ry time I try and ev'ry time I win.
And if I ever have a son, I think I'm gonna name him...
Bill or George. Anything but Sue.
I still hate that man. Yeah.

BRISTOL STOMP

Words and Music by KAL MANN
and DAVE APPELL

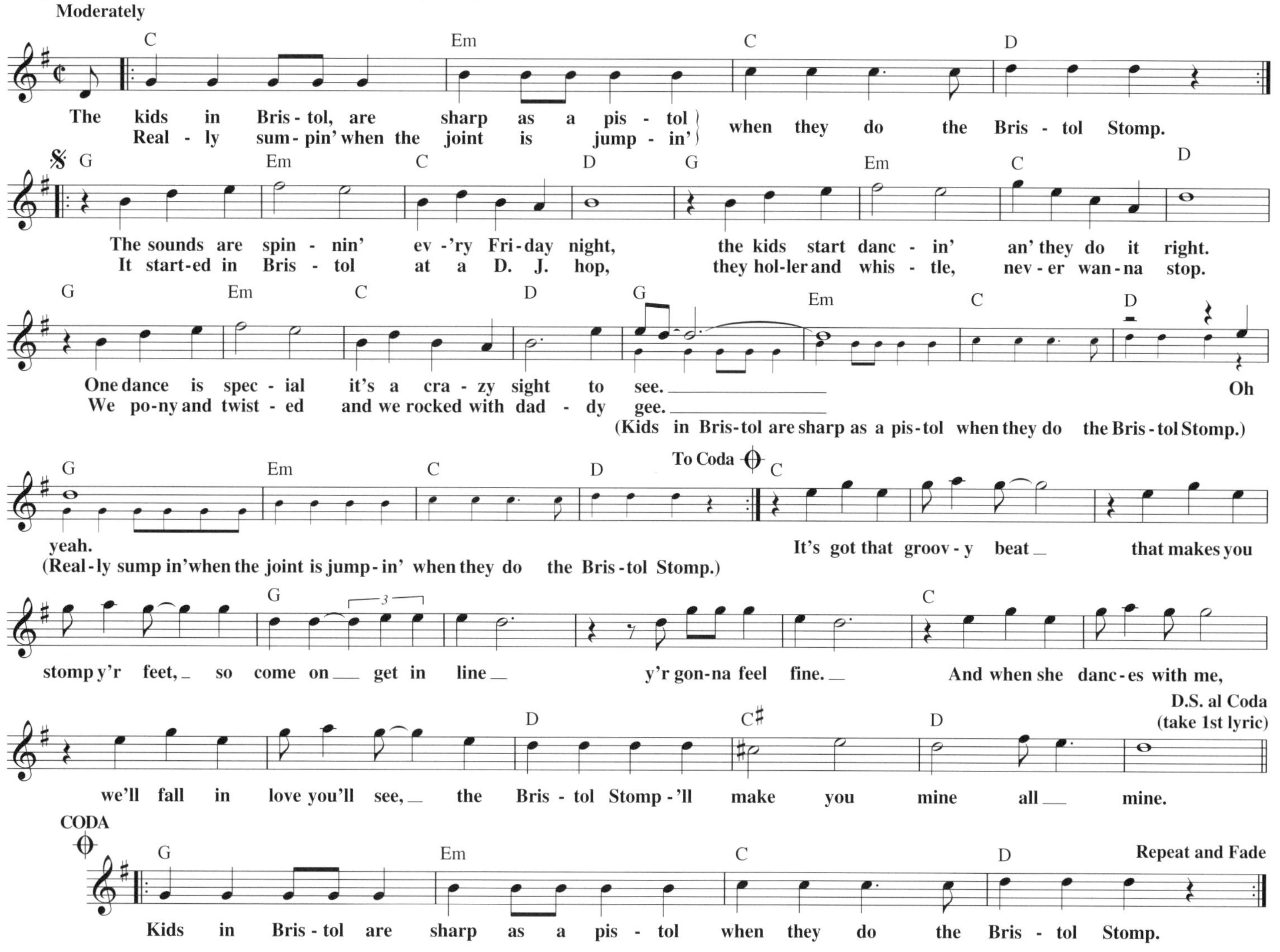

Moderately

C Em C D

The kids in Bris - tol, are sharp as a pis - tol
Real - ly sum - pin' when the joint is jump - in'
when they do the Bris - tol Stomp.

G Em C D G Em C D

The sounds are spin - nin' ev - 'ry Fri - day night, the kids start danc - in' an' they do it right.
It start - ed in Bris - tol at a D. J. hop, they hol - ler and whis - tle, nev - er wan - na stop.

G Em C D G Em C D

One dance is spec - ial it's a cra - zy sight to see. Oh
We po - ny and twist - ed and we rocked with dad - dy gee.
(Kids in Bris - tol are sharp as a pis - tol when they do the Bris - tol Stomp.)

G Em C D To Coda C

yeah.
(Real - ly sump in' when the joint is jump - in' when they do the Bris - tol Stomp.)
It's got that groov - y beat that makes you

G C

stomp y'r feet, so come on get in line y'r gon - na feel fine. And when she danc - es with me,

D C♯ D D.S. al Coda (take 1st lyric)

we'll fall in love you'll see, the Bris - tol Stomp - 'll make you mine all mine.

CODA

G Em C D Repeat and Fade

Kids in Bris - tol are sharp as a pis - tol when they do the Bris - tol Stomp.

BUSTED

Words and Music by
HARLAN HOWARD

Freely
C G7
My bills are all due and the ba - by needs shoes and I'm bust - ed.
went to my broth - er to ask for a loan 'cause I was bust - ed.
I am no thief, but a man can go wrong when he's bust - ed. The
C
Cot - ton is down to a quar - ter a pound, but I'm bust - ed. I got a cow that went dry and a
I hate to beg like a dog without his bone, but I'm bust - ed. My broth - er said there ain't a
food that we canned last sum - mer is gone, and I'm bust - ed. The fields are all bare and the
F G7
hen that won't lay, a big stack of bills that gets big - ger each day. The coun - ty's gon - na haul my be -
thing I can do, my wife and my kids are all down with the flu. And I was just think - in' about
cot - ton won't grow. Me and my fam - 'ly got to pack up and go, but I'll make a liv - ing, just
1, 2 C F C F C 3 C F C F C
long - ings a - way 'cause I'm bust - ed. I
call - in' on you and I'm bust - ed. Well,
where I don't know, 'cause I'm bust - ed.
(Spoken) I'm broke, no bread, I mean nothin', forget it!

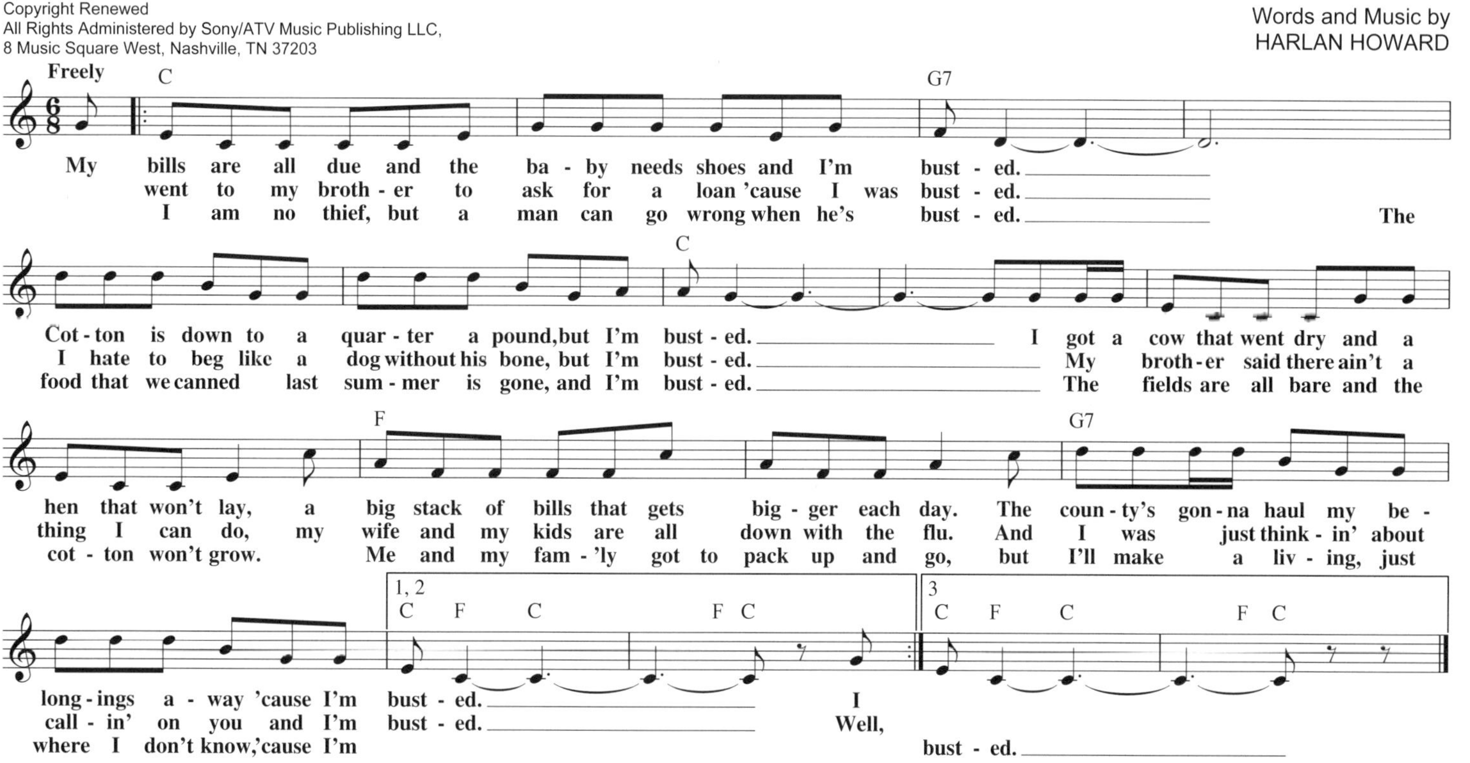

BROTHER LOUIE

Words and Music by ERROL BROWN
and ANTHONY WILSON

Tempo

Spoken: - 2nd time only
(Louie's papa:) What's going on here? (She:) Well, we're in love. (Louie's papa:) Now listen, let me tell you, I don't want no spook in my family. Get it, no spook in my family.

She was black __ as the night, __
(Sung:) See what I mean, __

Lou - ie was whit - er than white. __ Dan - ger, dan - ger when you taste brown sug - ar,
Lou - ie real - ly caused __ a scene, __ *(He did, I tell you.)* Ain't no dif - f'rence 'tween black or white, __

Lou - ie fell in love o - ver night. __ *(Spoken:) (Hey man, what's wrong with that?)*
Broth - er you know what I mean. __

To Coda

Noth - ing bad __ it was good. __
See what I mean __

Lou - ie had the best that he could. __ When she took him home __ to meet her ma - ma and pa - pa,
Lou - ie real - ly caused __ a scene. __ *(He did, I tell you now.)* Ain't no dif - f'rence 'tween black or white, __

Lou - ie knew just where he stood. __
Broth - ers, you know __ what I mean. __

Lou - ie, Lou - ie, Lou - ie, __ Lou - ie, Lou - ie, Lou I __ Lou - ie, Lou - ie, Lou - ie, __ Lou - ie you're gon - na cry. __

1

(Her papa:) All right, what's all this about? (Louie:) I love her, man. (Her papa:) Oh, yeah, Man, let me tell you, I don't want no honky in my family, do you dig? No honky in my family.

2

There he stood __ in the night, __ know - ing what's wrong from what's right. __ He took her home __ to his ma - ma and pa - pa, Lou - ie had a ter - ri - ble fright. __

D.C. al Coda

CODA

Lou - ie, Lou - ie, Lou - ie, __ Lou - ie, Lou - ie, Lou I __
Lou - ie, Lou - ie, Lou - ie, __ Lou - ie, you're gon - na cry. __

Repeat and Fade

BROWN EYED GIRL

Words and Music by
VAN MORRISON

Moderately
E♭ A♭ E♭ B♭7
1. Hey, where did we go? Days, when the rains came,
2., 3. (see additional lyrics)
E♭ A♭ E♭ B♭7
down in the hol - low play - in' a new game,
E♭ A♭ E♭ B♭7
laugh - ing and a - run - ning, hey, hey, skip - ping and a jump - ing.
E♭ A♭ E♭ B♭7
In the mis - ty morn - ing fog with our hearts a - thump - in', and
A♭ B♭7 E♭ Cm
you, my brown eyed girl.
A♭ B♭7 E♭ B♭7
You, my brown eyed girl. Do you re - mem -
Chorus
E♭ A♭
- ber when we used to sing: sha la la la la la la la
E♭ B♭7 E♭ A♭
la la la te da. Sha la la la la la la la
E♭ B♭7 E♭
1, 2
A♭
3
A♭ E♭
la la la te da la te da.

Additional Lyrics

2. Whatever happened to Tuesday and so slow
Going down the old mine with a transistor radio
Standing in the sunlight laughing
Hiding behind a rainbow's wall
Slipping and a-sliding
All along the water fall
With you, my brown eyed girl
You, my brown eyed girl.
Do you remember when we used to sing:
Chorus

3. So hard to find my way, now that I'm all on my own
I saw you just the other day, my, how you have grown
Cast my memory back there, Lord
Sometime I'm overcome thinking 'bout
Making love in the green grass
Behind the stadium
With you, my brown eyed girl
With you, my brown eyed girl.
Do you remember when we used to sing:
Chorus

BITCH

Words and Music by
MEREDITH BROOKS and SHELLY PEIKEN

Easy Rock
A5 D A5
I hate the world _ to - day. You're so good to me, _ I know, _ but I ___ can't change.
D F♯m Bsus2
Tried to tell _ you, but _ you look at me _ like may - be I'm _ an an - gel un - der - neath,
D A
in - no - cent and _ sweet. Yes - ter - day _ I cried. _
take me as ___ I am. ___
D/A A D/A
You must have been _ re - lieved _ to see _ the soft - er side. _ I can un - der - stand _ how you'd _
This may mean _ you'll have ___ to be ___ a strong - er man. _ Rest as - sured _ that when _ I start ___
F♯m Bsus2 D
___ be so ___ con - fused. ___ I don't en - vy you. _ I'm a lit - tle bit of ev - 'ry - thing
___ to make _ you ner - vous and I'm go - ing to ___ ex - tremes, to - mor - row I will change and to -
N.C. A E
all rolled in - to one. I'm a bitch. I'm a lov - er, I'm a child. I'm a moth - er. I'm a
day won't mean a thing.
Bsus2 D A
sin - ner. I'm a saint. I do not feel a - shamed. I'm your help. I'm your dream. I'm
E F♯m 1 D 2 D
noth - ing in be - tween. You know you would - n't want it an - y oth - er way. _ So, way. _
A E F♯m D(add 9)
Guitar solo
A E Bsus2 D
Solo ends
E5 F♯m
Just when you think you got me fig - ured out, the sea - son's al - read - y chang -
D E5 F♯m
ing. I think it's cool, you do what you do ___ and

D N.C. A
don't try to save me. I'm a bitch. I'm a lov - er. I'm a
bitch. I'm a tease. I'm a
E Bsus2 D
child. I'm a moth - er. I'm a sin - ner. I'm a saint. I do not feel a - shamed. I'm your
god - dess on my knees. When you hurt, when you suf - fer, I'm your an - gel un - der - cov - er. I've been
A E
help. I'm your dream. I'm noth - ing in be - tween. You know you
numb. I'm re - vived. Can't say I'm not a - live. You know I
1 F♯m D 2 F♯m D(add 9)
would - n't want it an - y oth - er way. I'm a would - n't want it an - y oth - er way.
A E F♯m D Repeat and Fade
Ooh, ooh, ooh. Ooh, ooh, ooh.

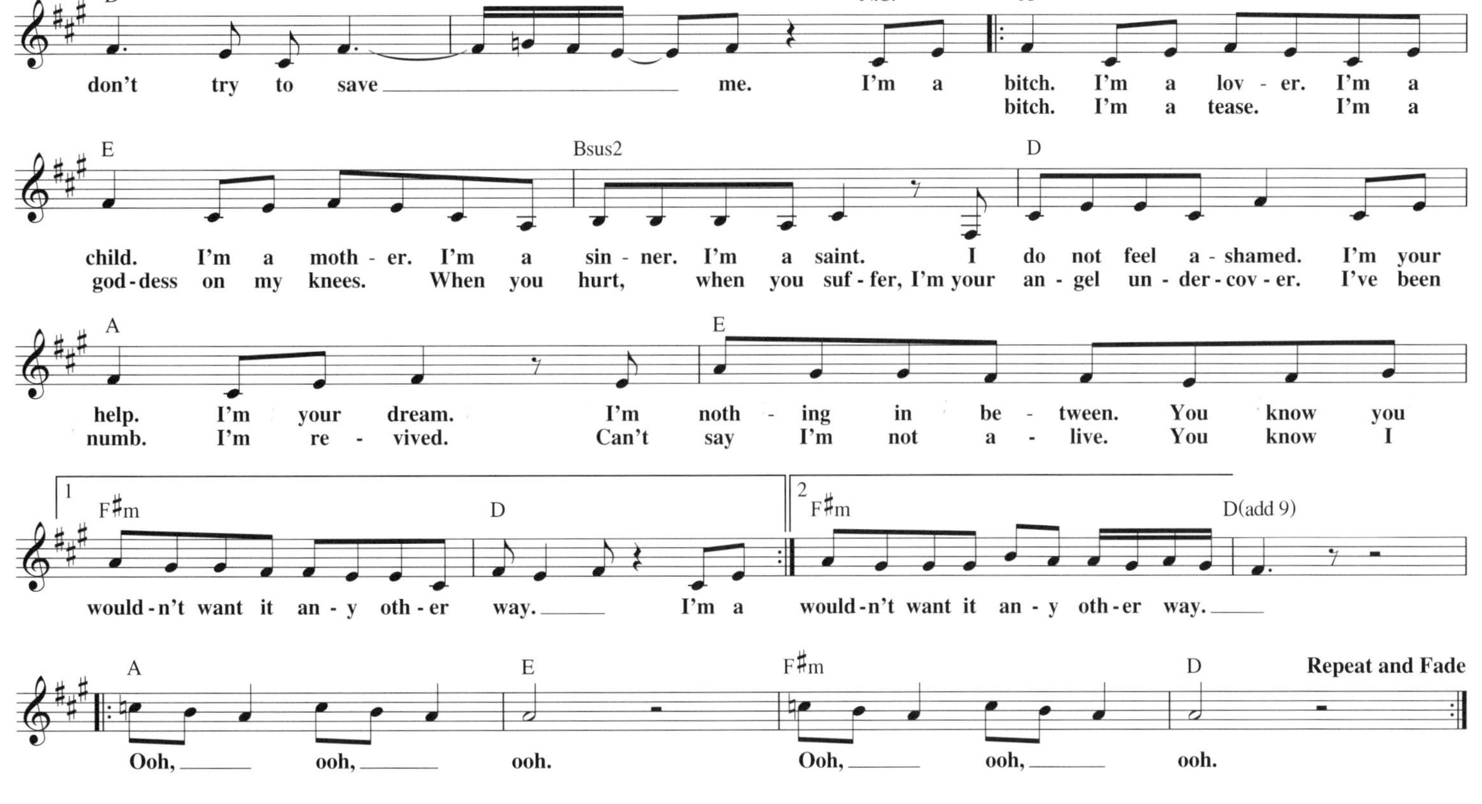

THE CANDY MAN

from WILLY WONKA AND THE CHOCOLATE FACTORY

Words and Music by LESLIE BRICUSSE
and ANTHONY NEWLEY

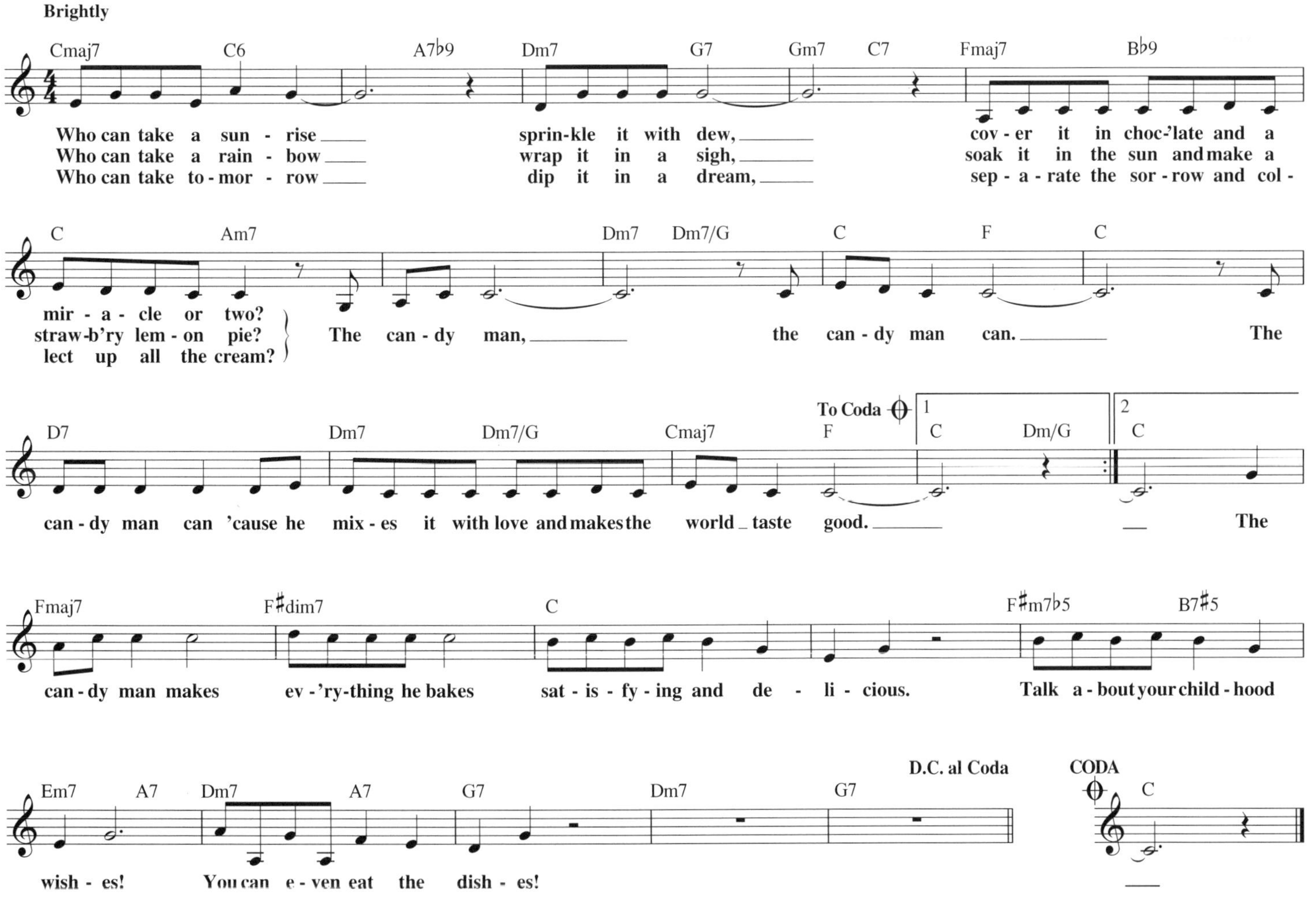
Brightly
Cmaj7 C6 A7♭9 Dm7 G7 Gm7 C7 Fmaj7 B♭9
Who can take a sun - rise sprin - kle it with dew, cov - er it in choc - 'late and a
Who can take a rain - bow wrap it in a sigh, soak it in the sun and make a
Who can take to - mor - row dip it in a dream, sep - a - rate the sor - row and col -
C Am7 Dm7 Dm7/G C F C
mir - a - cle or two?
straw - b'ry lem - on pie?
lect up all the cream?
The can - dy man, the can - dy man can. The
To Coda
D7 Dm7 Dm7/G Cmaj7 F 1 C Dm/G 2 C
can - dy man can 'cause he mix - es it with love and makes the world taste good. The
Fmaj7 F♯dim7 C F♯m7♭5 B7♯5
can - dy man makes ev - 'ry - thing he bakes sat - is - fy - ing and de - li - cious. Talk a - bout your child - hood
D.C. al Coda CODA
Em7 A7 Dm7 A7 G7 Dm7 G7 C
wish - es! You can e - ven eat the dish - es!

BURNING LOVE

Words and Music by
DENNIS LINDE

Moderate Boogie-rock
Lord Al-might - y, I feel my temp - 'ra-ture ris - ing, high - er, high - er, it's burn-ing thru to my soul.
Oo - ee I feel my temp - 'ra-ture ris - ing, help me I'm flam - in', it must be a hun-dred and nine.
It's com-in' clos - er, the flames are now lick - in' my bod - y, won't you help me? I feel like I'm slip-pin' a - way.
Girl, girl, girl, girl, you've gone and set me on fire, my brain is flam - in', I don't know which way to go.
Burn - in', burn - in', burn - in' and noth - in' can cool me, I just might turn to smoke but I feel fine.
It's hard to breathe and my chest is a - heav - in', Lord have mer - cy, I'm burn-in' a hole where I lay.
Your / Your / 'Cause your kiss - es lift me high - er, like the sweet song of a choir, and you light my morn - in' sky with burn - in' love.
1, 2
3
with burn - in' love. With just a hunk - a, hunk - a burn - in' love. With just a
Repeat and Fade

BUTTERFLY

Words and Music by KAL MANN
and BERNIE LOWE

Moderately

You tell me you love me, you say you'll be true, then you fly a - round with some - bod - y new, but I'm cra - zy a - bout you,

you but - ter - fly. You're treat - in' me mean, you're mak - in' me cry, I've

made up my mind to tell you good - bye, but I'm no good with - out you, you but - ter - fly.

I knew from the first time I kissed you that you were the trou - bl - in' kind, 'cause the

hon - ey drips from your sweet lips; One taste and I'm out of my mind. I love you so much, I

know what I'll do; I'm clip - pin' your wings, your fly - in' is through, 'cause I'm cra - zy a - bout you,

you but - ter - fly. You fly.

C'EST LA VIE

Words and Music by ROBBIE NEVIL,
MARK I. HOLDING and DUNCAN PAIN

Moderate Disco beat
Got a job, that's O. K. But they got me work - in' night to day. Punch - in' in, punch - in' out; is this real - ly what life's all a - bout?
all a - lone. Are you sad be - cause you're on your own? Get back up, qui - et down. There's so man - y in the round.
what you been do - in'? You say your car broke down, the thing just is - n't mov - in'. J. J. J., don't you know, when you're down there's just one way to go.
To Coda
What you gon - na do? What you gon - na feel? I don't know.
What you gon-na feel? What you gon - na do? Oh, don't tell me. What you gon-na say? What you gon - na do?
There's on - ly one thing left to say:
I guess there's just one thing to do.
C'est la vie. That's just the way it goes, oh, yeah.
That's right!
C'est la vie, c'est la vie. That's just the way it goes.
That's right!
Ba-by's gone, Hey, J. J.,
D.S. al Coda
CODA
C'est la vie. That's just the way it goes some - times.
That's right!
Repeat and Fade
C'est la vie, c'est la vie. That's just the way it goes.
That's right!

CANDLE IN THE WIND

Words and Music by ELTON JOHN
and BERNIE TAUPIN

In a slow 2
E
A
Good - bye, Nor - ma Jean. Though I nev - er knew you at all,
Lone - li - ness was tough, the tough - est role you ev - er played.
E/G♯
A
Asus
you had the grace to hold your - self while those a - round you crawled.
Holly - wood cre - at - ed a su - per - star and pain was the price you paid.
A
E
A
They crawled out of the wood - work and they whis - pered in - to your brain.
And e - ven when you died, oh, the press still hound - ed you.
E/G♯
A
Asus
They sent you on a tread - mill and they made you change your name.
All the pa - pers had to say was that Mar - i - lyn was found in the nude.
A
B
B7
E
And it seems to me you lived your life like a can - dle in the wind,
A
E
A/E
E
B
nev - er know - ing who to cling to when the rain set in.
Bsus
B
A
C♯m
And I would have liked to known you but I was just a kid. Your
To Coda
B
Bsus
B
A
E/G♯
F♯m7
can - dle burned out long be - fore your leg - end ev - er did.
E
A
E/G♯
F♯m7
E
B
B7
(Instrumental)
E
A
Good - bye Nor - ma Jean. Though I nev - er knew you at all, you had the grace to hold
E/G♯
A
Asus
A
your - self while those a - round you crawled.

E
Good-bye, Nor-ma Jean, from a young man in the twen-ty sec-ond row
A
who sees you as some-thing more
E/G♯
than sex-ual, more than just our Mar-i-lyn Mon-roe.
A
Asus A
D.S. al Coda
And it
CODA
E
E7/G♯
I
A
would have liked to known you, oh, but I
C♯m
was just a kid. Your can-dle burned out long
B
be-fore
Bsus B
A
your leg-end ev-er did.
E/G♯ F♯m7 E

CALL ME

from the Paramount Motion Picture AMERICAN GIGOLO

Words by DEBORAH HARRY
Music by GIORGIO MORODER

Medium Disco tempo

Dm
Col-or me your col-or, ba-by,
B♭7
col-or me your car.
Dm
Col-or me your col-or, dar-ling,
B♭7
I know who you are.
G
Come up off your col-
A
or chart,
G
I know where you're com-
A
ing from. Call me
Dm
on the line,
F
call me,
G
call me an-y,
B♭
an-y-time. Call me,
Dm
I love you,
F
can't you
G
call me an-y day
B♭
or night? Call me
Repeat and Fade

CAN'T SMILE WITHOUT YOU

Words and Music by CHRIS ARNOLD, DAVID MARTIN and GEOFF MORROW

Moderately, with a relaxed beat
G Em Am
You know, I can't smile with - out You. I can't smile with - out You. I can't laugh and I
D11 D7 G
can't sing. I'm find-ing it hard _ to do an - y - thing. You see, I feel sad when you're sad,
Em Am D11
I feel glad when you're glad. If you _ on-ly knew what I'm _ go-ing through; I just can't
G D11 Gmaj9 G Em7 Am7
smile _ without you. You came a - long _ just like a song _ and bright-ened my day. _
D11 D7 Gmaj9 G Em7 Am7
Who'd a be-lieved that you were part of a dream. _ Now it all seems light-years a - way.
D7 G Em Am
And now you know I can't smile with-out you. I can't smile with-out you. I can't laugh and I
D11 D♭ A♭
can't sing. I'm find ing it hard _ to do an - y - thing. _ You see, I feel sad when you're sad,
Fm B♭m E♭11
I feel glad when you're glad. If you _ on-ly knew what I'm _ go-ing through; I just can't
E♭m7 A♭11
smile. _ Now, some peo - ple say _ hap - pi - ness takes _ so _ ver - y long to find. _
D♭maj7 D♭m E♭7sus E7sus
Well, I'm find-ing it hard _ leav-ing your love be - hind _ me. And you see, I
A F♯m Bm
can't smile with - out you. I can't smile with - out you. I can't laugh and I can't sing. I'm
E11 E♭ B♭ Gm
find - ing it hard to do an - y - thing. You see, I feel glad when you're glad, I feel sad when
you. _
(Instrumental till fade)
Cm F11
you're sad. If you _ on - ly knew what I'm _ go - ing through; I just can't smile with - out
Repeat and Fade

CAR WASH

Words and Music by
NORMAN WHITFIELD

Moderately slow (with a double time feel)

C7

You might not ev - er get rich but let me tell ya it's bet-ter than dig-gin' a ditch.

There ain't no tell-in' who ya might meet. A mov - ie star or may-be e - ven a

In-di-an chief. / Work-in' at the car wash.

F7

work - in' at the / talk in' a-bout the car wash yeah!

Come on and sing it with me car wash. Get with the feel-in' y'all car wash yeah.

N.C.

1

Come sum-mer the work gets kind-a hard. This ain't no place to be if ya planned on be-ing a star. Let me tell you it's al - ways cool, and the boss don't mind some-times if ya act a fool.

2

At the (Work and work) well those cars nev-er seem to stop com-in'. (Work and work) keep those rags and ma-chines hum-min'. (Work and work) my fin-gers to the bone (work) at five I can't wait 'til it's time to go home.

F Em Dm

Hey, get your car washed to-day.

F Em Dm

Fill up and you don't have to pay.

F Em Dm

Come on and give us a play.

F G

Get a wash right a-way.

D.S. and Fade

CARRIE

Words and Music by JOEY TEMPEST
and MIC MICHAELI

Moderately
Em G/D C G/B Am7 G/B
When lights go down, I see no rea - son for you to cry. We've been through
mind, with no in - ten - tions of be - ing un - kind, I wish I
C D Em G/D C G/B Am7 G/B
this be - fore in ev -'ry time, in ev -'ry sea - son. God knows I've tried, so please don't
could ex - plain. It all takes time, whole lot of pa - tience. If it's a crime how come I
C D C D C Am D C D
ask for more. Can't you see it in my eyes? Well, this might be our last good - bye.
feel no pain?
G D/F♯ Em D C D Em Dsus D
Car - rie, Car - rie, things, they change, my friend, whoa.
To Coda
G D/F♯ Em D C D Em Dsus D
Car - rie, Car - rie. May - be we'll meet a -
Am7 G/B C G D/F♯ Dsus D C D
gain, some - where, a - gain. I read your meet a - gain.
Em D Em D/F♯ G C Em D
(Instrumental)
Em D E D/F♯ G C Em D
D.S. al Coda
Can't you
CODA
Dsus D Am7 G/B C
meet a - gain, oh, some - where a -
G Em D G C/G G
gain. When lights go down.

CARS

Words and Music by
GARY NUMAN

Synth Pop
A7
Here in my car, I feel saf-est of all, I can lock all my doors, it's the on-ly way to live in
Here in my car, where the im-age breaks down, will you vis-it me, please, if I o-pen my door in
G
cars.
cars?
A7
Here in my car, I can on-ly re-ceive, I can
Here in my car, I know I've start-ed to think a-bout
lis-ten to you, it keeps me sta-ble for days in
leav-ing to-night, al-though noth-ing seems right in
G
cars.
cars.
D7
(Instrumental)
A7
G
Repeat and Fade

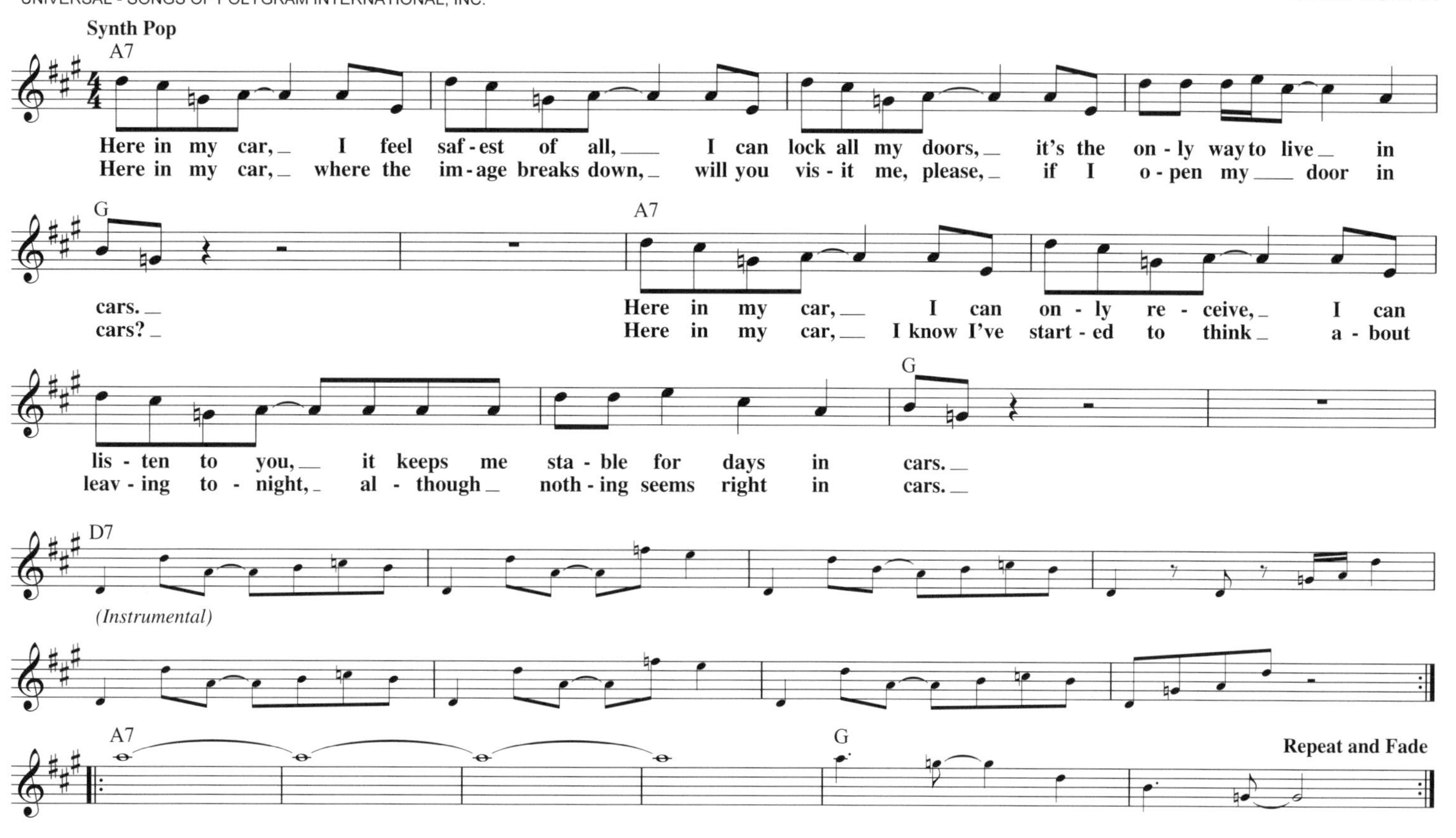

CATCH A FALLING STAR

Words and Music by PAUL VANCE
and LEE POCKRISS

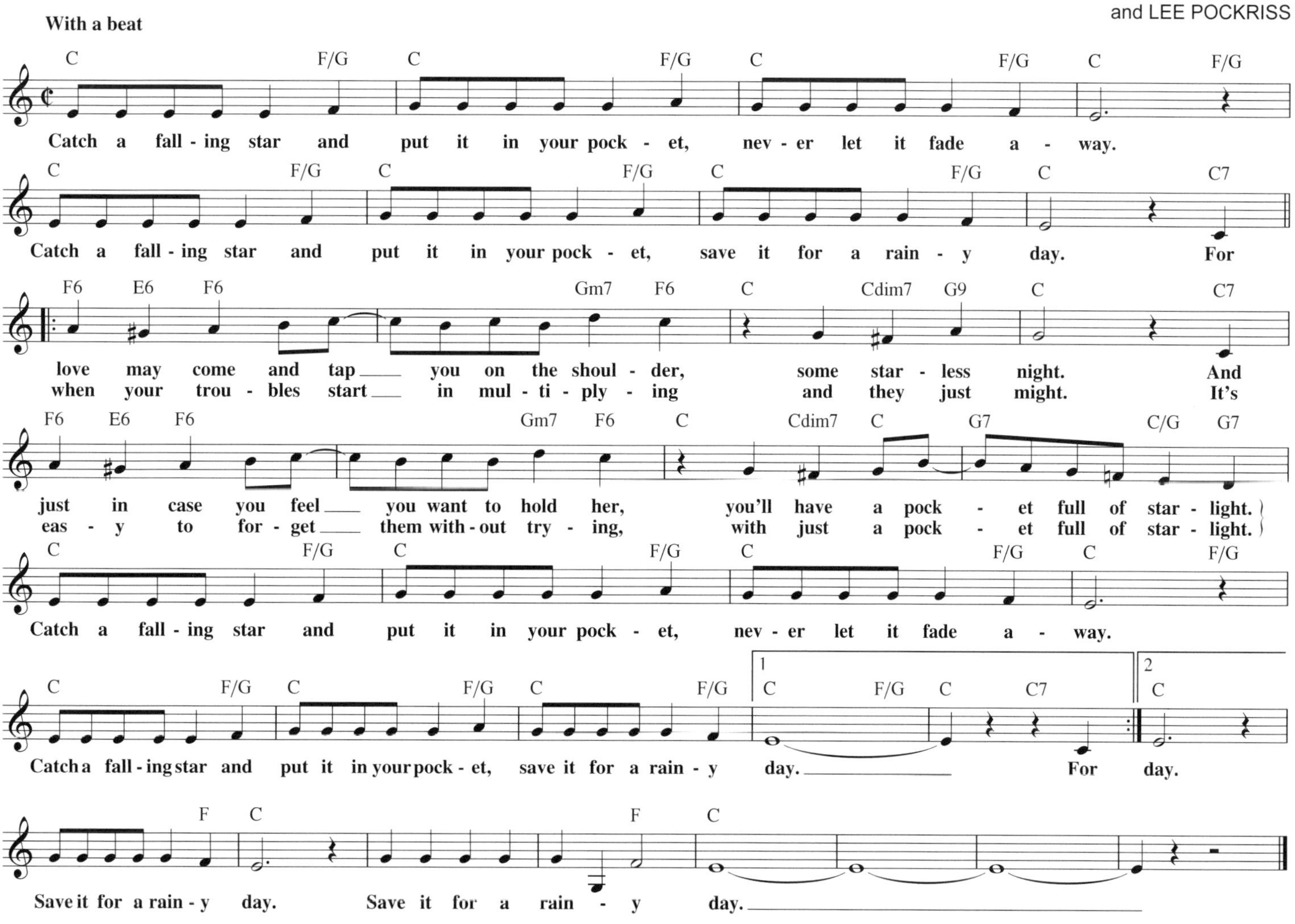
With a beat
C F/G C F/G C F/G C F/G
Catch a fall-ing star and put it in your pock-et, nev-er let it fade a-way.
C F/G C F/G C F/G C C7
Catch a fall-ing star and put it in your pock-et, save it for a rain-y day. For
F6 E6 F6 Gm7 F6 C Cdim7 G9 C C7
love may come and tap you on the shoul-der, some star-less night. And
when your trou-bles start in mul-ti-ply-ing and they just might. It's
F6 E6 F6 Gm7 F6 C Cdim7 C G7 C/G G7
just in case you feel you want to hold her, you'll have a pock-et full of star-light.
eas-y to for-get them with-out try-ing, with just a pock-et full of star-light.
C F/G C F/G C F/G C F/G
Catch a fall-ing star and put it in your pock-et, nev-er let it fade a-way.
C F/G C F/G C F/G 1 C F/G C C7 2 C
Catch a fall-ing star and put it in your pock-et, save it for a rain-y day. For day.
F C F C
Save it for a rain-y day. Save it for a rain-y day.

CLOCKS

Words and Music by GUY BERRYMAN, JON BUCKLAND,
WILL CHAMPION and CHRIS MARTIN

Moderately
E♭ B♭m Fm
Lights go out and I can't be saved. Tides that I tried to swim a - gainst
Con - fu - sion nev - er stops. Clos - ing walls and tick - ing clocks gon - na
E♭ B♭m Fm
brought me down up - on my knees. Oh I beg, I beg and plead. Sing - in',
come back and take you home. I could not stop that you now know. Sing - in',
E♭ B♭m Fm
come out of things un - said. Shoot an ap - ple off my head. And a
come out up - on my seas, curse missed op - por - tu - ni - ties. Am I
E♭ B♭m Fm
trou - ble that can't be named. A ti - ger's wait - ing to be tamed.
a part of the cure or am I part of the dis - ease? Sing - in',
E♭ B♭m Fm E♭
you are. You
B♭m Fm 1 E♭ B♭m
are. (Instrumental)
A♭6 E♭ B♭m
A♭6 2 E♭ B♭m
You

Fm Eb Bbm Fm
are. You are.
Eb Bbm Abmaj7
(Instrumental)
To Coda
Eb Bbm Abmaj7
You are.
Gbmaj7 Db 1, 2 Ab
And noth - ing else com - pares.
3 Gbmaj7 Eb/G
(Instrumental)
Bbm/F 1 Fm 2 Fm
D.S. al Coda
(with repeats)
CODA
Eb Bbm Ab6
Home, home, where I want - ed to go.
Eb Bbm Ab6 Eb
Home, home, where I want - ed to go.
(Instrumental)
Repeat and Fade
Optional Ending
Bbm Fm Eb

CHAINS

Words and Music by GERRY GOFFIN and CAROLE KING

Moderately

A, A7, D9, A, E9, D9, A, E7, A7, D, A, A7, D, E, E7, A

(1.,3.,4.) Chains, my ba - by's got me locked up in chains, and they ain't the kind that you can see. Wo, these chains of love got a hold on me, yeah.
(2.) Chains, well I can't break a - way from these chains, can't run a - round 'cause I'm not free. Wo, these chains of love won't let me be, yeah.

4th time to Coda

I wan - na tell you, pret - ty ba - by, I think you're fine. I'd like to love you, but dar - ling I'm im - pris - oned by these
Please be - lieve me when I tell you, your lips are sweet. I'd like to kiss them, but I can't break a - way from all of these

D.C. al Coda

CODA

Chains, chains of love.

Repeat and Fade

CINCO ROBLES
(Five Oaks)

Words by LARRY SULLIVAN
Music by DOROTHY WRIGHT

Moderate Waltz

E♭, B♭7, E♭, B♭7, E♭, E♭7, A♭, E♭, B♭m6, C7, Fm7, B♭7, E♭, E♭7, A♭, E♭, E♭7, E♭m, B♭, F7, Fm7, B♭7, E♭, B♭7, E♭, E♭7, A♭, B♭7, E♭, C♭

Cin - to Ro - bles, cin - co cer - ros, my sweet - heart Five oaks and five hills a - way. Cin - co Ro - bles, cin - co cer - ros, my lov - er. Five hills to trav - el to - day. One hill I'll think of your laugh - ter. One hill your cour - age in pain. One for your (beau - ty / kind - ness) and one for your smile. And the last hill to hold you a - gain. Cin - co Rou - bles, cin - co cer - ros, my dar - ling, Five oaks and five hills a - part. Cin - co Ro - bles, cin - co cer - ros. I'll count them As each brings me near - er your

1. heart. Cin - co
2. heart.

CHANCES ARE

Words by AL STILLMAN
Music by ROBERT ALLEN

Moderately, with great warmth
C6 G7♯5 C Cm6 G/D Bm7 E9 E7
Chanc - es are 'cause I wear a sil - ly grin, the mo - ment you come in - to view,
Am7 A7 D7 Am7/D D7 G E♭7/G G G7♯5
chanc - es are you think that I'm in love with you. Just be -
C6 G7♯5 C Cm6 G/D Bm7 E9 E7
cause my com - po - sure sort of slips, the mo - ment that your lips meet mine,
Am7 A7 D7 Am7/D D7 D7♭9 G E♭7/G G Gmaj7
chanc - es are you think my heart's your val - en - tine. In the mag - ic of
Cm Cm6 Gm
moon - light, when I sigh, "Hold me close, dear," chanc - es are you be -
Gm6 A7 E♭9 D9 G7♯5
lieve the stars that fill the skies, are in my eyes. Guess you feel you'll al - ways
C6 G7♯5 C Cm6 G Bm7 E9 E+
be the one and on - ly one for me. And if you think you could, well,
Am Bdim7 Am C♯dim7 1 Am7/D D7 D7♭9 G D7 G G7♯5 2 Am7/D D7
chanc - es are your chanc - es are aw - f'ly good. Chanc - es are aw - f'ly
Bm7♭5 E7 Am Am7/D D7 D7♭9 G E♭/G G
good; the chanc - es are your chanc - es are aw - f'ly good.

COLD-HEARTED

Words and Music by
ELLIOT WOLFF

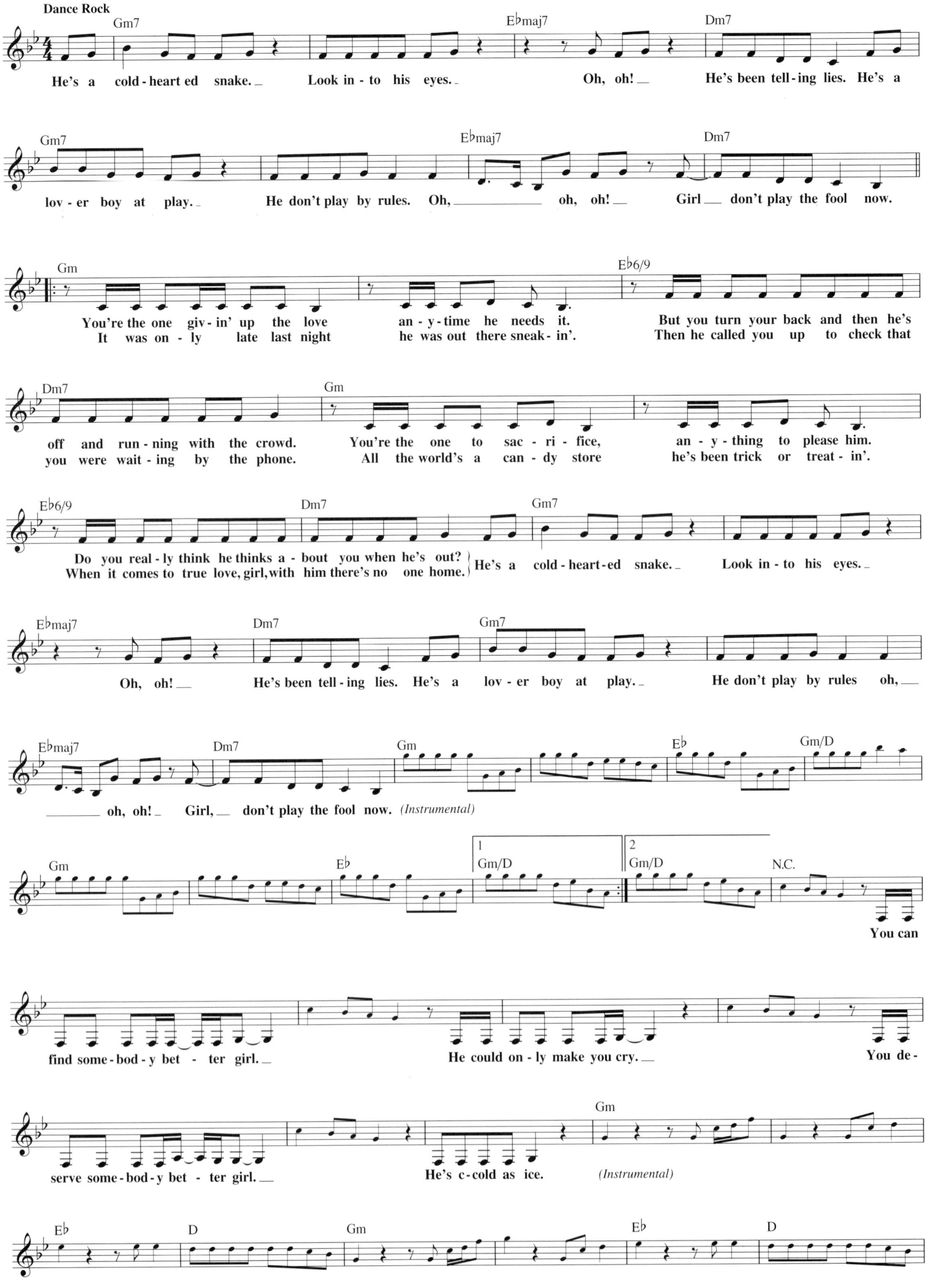

Dance Rock

Gm7 | E♭maj7 | Dm7

He's a cold-heart ed snake. Look in-to his eyes. Oh, oh! He's been tell-ing lies. He's a

Gm7 | E♭maj7 | Dm7

lov-er boy at play. He don't play by rules. Oh, oh, oh! Girl don't play the fool now.

Gm | E♭6/9

You're the one giv-in' up the love an-y-time he needs it. But you turn your back and then he's
It was on-ly late last night he was out there sneak-in'. Then he called you up to check that

Dm7 | Gm

off and run-ning with the crowd. You're the one to sac-ri-fice, an-y-thing to please him.
you were wait-ing by the phone. All the world's a can-dy store he's been trick or treat-in'.

E♭6/9 | Dm7 | Gm7

Do you real-ly think he thinks a-bout you when he's out?
When it comes to true love, girl, with him there's no one home.
He's a cold-heart-ed snake. Look in-to his eyes.

E♭maj7 | Dm7 | Gm7

Oh, oh! He's been tell-ing lies. He's a lov-er boy at play. He don't play by rules oh,

E♭maj7 | Dm7 | Gm | E♭ | Gm/D

oh, oh! Girl, don't play the fool now. *(Instrumental)*

Gm | E♭ | 1 Gm/D | 2 Gm/D | N.C.

You can

find some-bod-y bet-ter girl. He could on-ly make you cry. You de-

Gm

serve some-bod-y bet-ter girl. He's c-cold as ice. *(Instrumental)*

E♭ | D | Gm | E♭ | D

Gm
1
2
Co-co-co-cold-heart - ed ooh ah, ah. Co-co-co cold-heart - ed sss snake. sss snake. He's a
Gm7
Ebmaj7
Dm7
cold - heart - ed snake. Look in - to his eyes. Oh, oh! He's been tell - ing lies. He's a
Gm7
Ebmaj7
Dm7
Repeat and Fade
lov - er boy at play. He don't play by rules. Oh, oh, oh. Girl don't play the fool. He's a

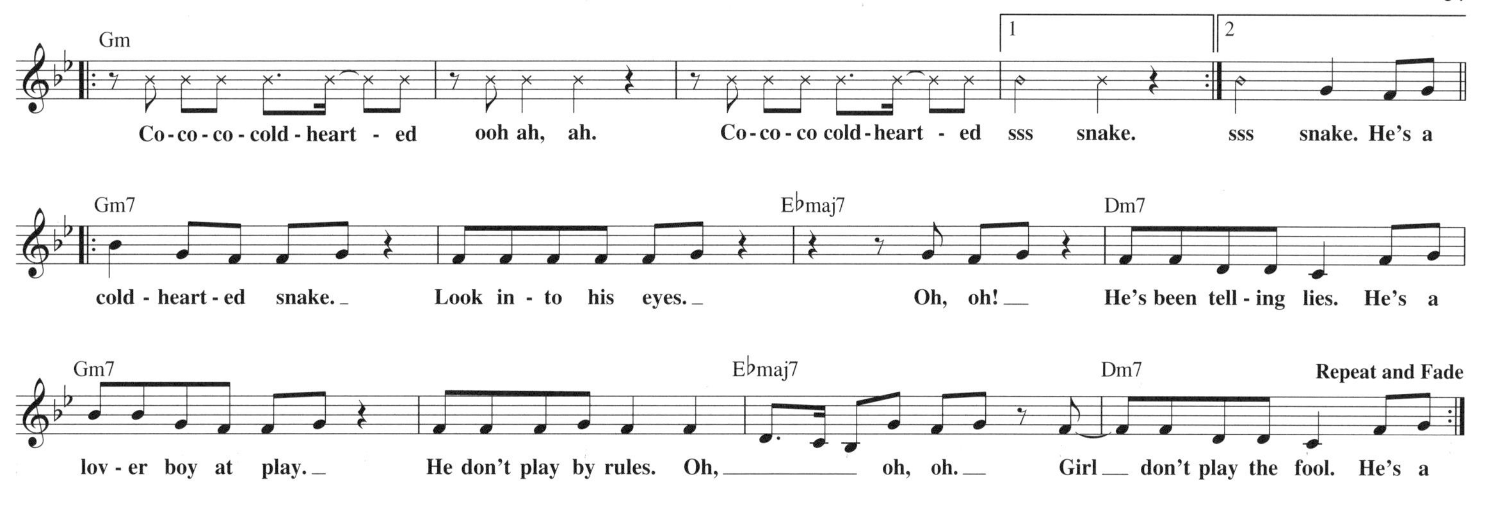

COME AND GET IT

Words and Music by
PAUL McCARTNEY

Quickly

Eb Ab6 Bb Eb

If you want it, here it is, come and get it. Mm, make your mind up fast. If you want it an - y time,

Ab6 Bb Cb Ebm

I can give it, but you bet-ter hur-ry 'cause it may not last. Did I hear you say that there must be a catch?

E Ebm Bb7 To Coda Eb

Will you walk a-way from a fool and his mon - ey? If you want it, here it is, come and get it but you bet-ter

Ab6 Bb7 Eb Bb D.S. al Coda CODA Eb

hur-ry 'cause it's go-ing fast. If you Son - ny, if you want it, here it is,

Ab6 Bb7 Eb Ab7 Bb7

come and get it, but you bet-ter hur - ry 'cause it's go - ing fast. You'd bet - ter hur - ry 'cause it's go - ing fast.

1 Cb Ebm7 Fb Eb Bb

Do. Fool and his mon - ey, Son - ny, if you

2 Eb Ab7 Bb7 Cb Eb

You'd bet - ter hur - ry 'cause it's go - ing fast.

COLD AS ICE

Words and Music by MICK JONES
and LOU GRAMM

Brightly, with a beat
Em(sus) Em Em(sus) Em C6 C C6 C Em(sus) Em
You're as cold as ice. You're will-ing to sac-ri-fice our love.
You never take advice
You want paradise.
Some-day you'll pay the price, I know.
I've seen it be-fore; it hap-pens all the time.
You're clos-ing the door; you leave the world be-hind.
You're dig-ging for gold yet throw-ing a-way a for-tune in feel-ings, but some-day you'll pay.
some-day you'll pay.
(Instrumental)
Cold as ice. You know that you are.
Cold (cold) as (as) ice.
Ooh, cold as, cold as
ice. Cold as, cold as
Lead vocal ad lib.
Repeat and Fade

THE CLOSER YOU GET

Words and Music by JAMES PENNINGTON
and MARK GRAY

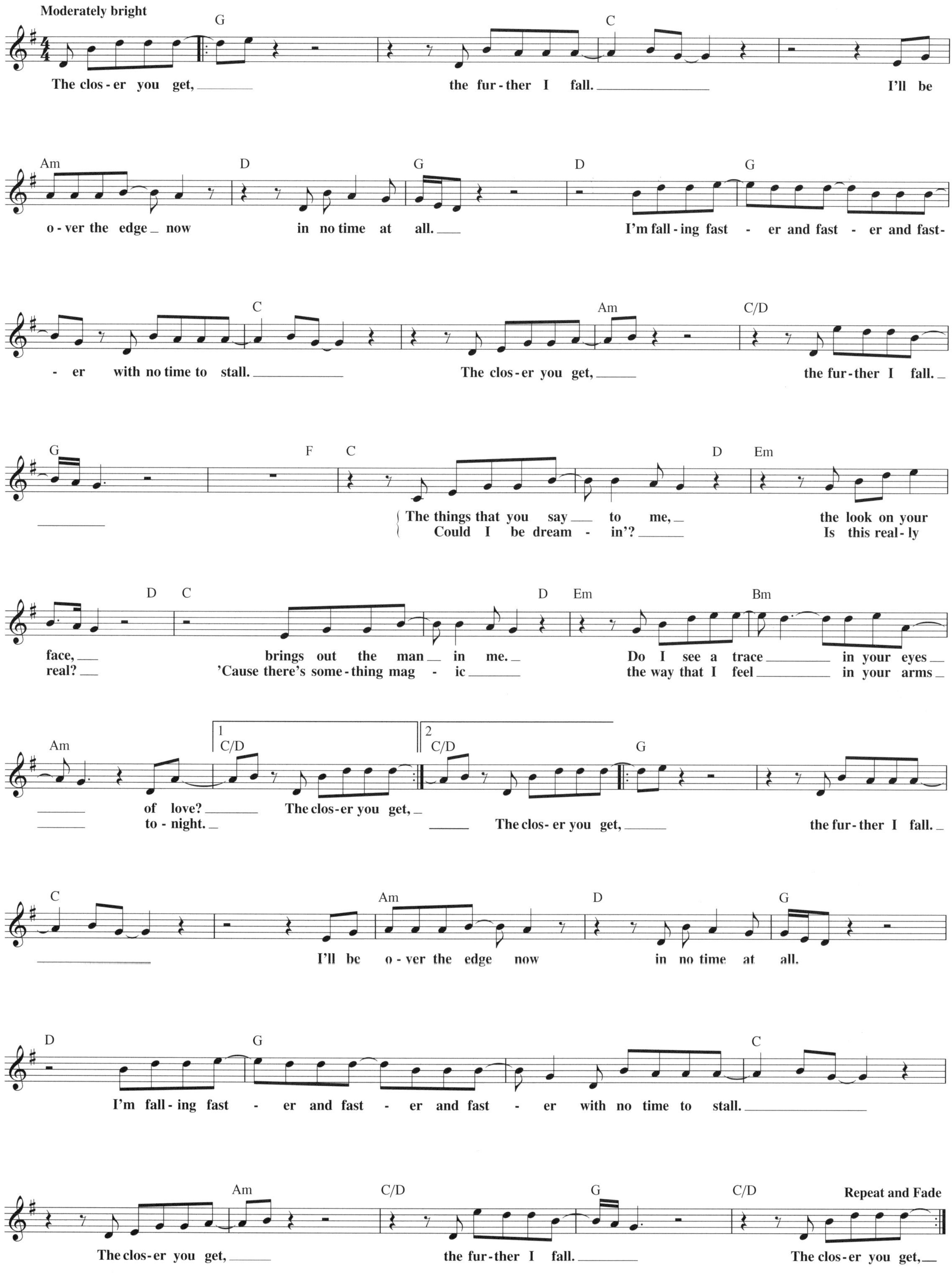
Moderately bright
G C
The clos - er you get, the fur - ther I fall. I'll be
Am D G D G
o - ver the edge now in no time at all. I'm fall - ing fast - er and fast - er and fast-
C Am C/D
- er with no time to stall. The clos - er you get, the fur - ther I fall.
G F C D Em
The things that you say to me, the look on your
Could I be dream - in'? Is this real - ly
D C D Em Bm
face, brings out the man in me. Do I see a trace in your eyes
real? 'Cause there's some - thing mag - ic the way that I feel in your arms
Am 1 C/D 2 C/D G
of love? The clos - er you get,
to - night. The clos - er you get, the fur - ther I fall.
C Am D G
I'll be o - ver the edge now in no time at all.
D G C
I'm fall - ing fast - er and fast - er and fast - er with no time to stall.
Am C/D G C/D
The clos - er you get, the fur - ther I fall. The clos - er you get,
Repeat and Fade

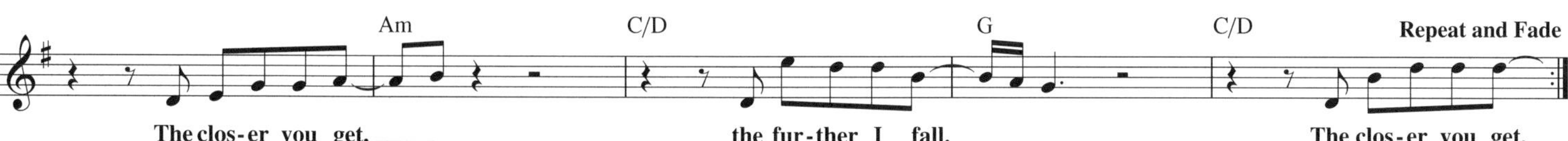

COMPLICATED

Words and Music by AVRIL LAVIGNE, LAUREN CHRISTY,
SCOTT SPOCK and GRAHAM EDWARDS

Moderate Pop
F
Dm
Chill out, what cha yell - in' for? Lay back, it's all been done be - fore.
You came o - ver un - an-nounced, dressed up like you're some - thing else.
B♭(add9)
C
And if you could on - ly let it be you will see.
Where you are ain't where it's at, you see. You're mak - in' me
F
Dm
I like you the way you are when we're driv - in' in your car
laugh out when you strike your pose. Take off all your prep - py clothes.
Lay back, it's all been done be - fore.
B♭(add9)
C
and you're talk - in' to me one on one but you be - come
You know you're not fool - in' an - y - one when you be - come
And if you could on - ly let it be you will see
B♭(add9)
Dm
To Coda
some - bod - y else 'round ev - 'ry - one else. You're watch - ing your back like you can't re - lax. You're
B♭(add9)
C5
try'n' to be cool. You look like a fool to me. Tell me,
D5
B♭5
F5
C5
why'd you have to go and make things so com - pli - cat - ed? See the way you're
D5
B♭5
F5
C5
act - ing like you're some - bod - y else, gets me frus - trat - ed. Life's like this, you,

D5 B♭5 F5 C5
you fall and you crawl and you break and you take what you get and you turn it in - to

Gm9 B♭ 1 F
hon - es - ty and prom - ise me I'm nev - er gon - na find you fake it, no, no, no.

2 F Dm B♭ Csus C F
D.S. al Coda
no, no, no, no, no, no, no, no, no, no, no, no, no, no, no, no. Chill out, what cha yell - in' for?

CODA
B♭(add9) C5 N.C.
try'n' to be cool. You look like a fool to me. Tell me

D5 B♭5 F5 C5
why'd you have to go and make things so com - pli - cat - ed? See the way you're

D5 B♭5 F5 C5
act - ing like you're some - bod - y else, gets me frus - trat - ed. Life's like this, you,

D5 B♭5 F5 C5
you fall and you crawl and you break and you take what you get and you turn it in - to

Gm9 1 B♭ 2 B♭
hon - es - ty. Prom - ise me I'm nev - er gon - na find you fake it, no, no, it, no, no, no.

COME ON EILEEN

Words and Music by KEVIN ROWLAND, JAMES PATTERSON and KEVIN ADAMS

Moderately
C Em F C G
Come on Ei - leen.
C Em F
Poor old John - ny Ray sound-ed sad up - on the ra - di - o; he moved a
These peo - ple 'round here wear beat - en down eyes sunk in smoke dried fac - es, re -
C G
mil - lion hearts in mon - o.
signed to what their fate is, but
1st time only
C Em F C G
Our moth - ers used to sing a - long; who'd blame them?
C Em F C G
You're grown. (You're grown up.) So grown. (So grown up.) Now I must say more than ev - er: Come on Ei-leen.
not us, no not us. We are far too young and clev - er. Re-mem - ber,
C Em F C G
Too ra, loo ra, too ra, loo rye aye. And we can sing just like our fa - thers.
too ra, loo ra, too ra, loo rye aye. Ei - leen, I'll hum this tune for - ev - er.
D A7
Come on Ei - leen, oh, I swear well he means at this mo -
Come on Ei - leen, oh, I swear well he means, ah, come on
Em G A D A7
- ment. You mean ev - 'ry-thing. With you in that dress, my thoughts I con - fess verge on dirt -
let's take off ev - 'ry - thing, that pret - ty red dress. Ei - leen, tell him less. Ah, come on,
Em
- y, ah, come on
let's, ah, come on
1
On D.S.
Repeat back to 𝄋
G A
Ei - leen.
2
G A D D
Ei - leen. Come on Ei - leen. Too loo rye
(2nd & 3rd time solo voice ad lib.)

F♯m
aye, come on Ei - leen, too loo rye
G
aye, too ra. Too ra, too loo ra.
End solo (2nd time)
1, 2
D
A
Oh Ei - leen.
Things won't e - ven change.
3
D
A
D.S. (take 1st ending)
Vocal ad lib. and Fade

COME TOGETHER

Words and Music by JOHN LENNON
and PAUL McCARTNEY

Moderately slow, with a double-time feeling

Dm7
Here come old flat - top, he come groov - ing up slow - ly, he got joo joo eye - ball, he one ho - ly rol - ler, he got
A
hair down to his knee.
G7 N.C.
Got to be a jok - er, he just do what he please.
Dm7
(Instrumental)

Dm7
He wear no shoe - shine, he got toe - jam foot - ball, he got mon - key fin - ger, he shoot
He Bag Pro - duc - tion, he got wal - rus gum - boot, he got O - no side - board, he one
He rol - ler - coast - er, he got ear - ly warn - ing, he got Mud - dy Wa - ter, he one

Co - ca Co - la, he say
A
"I know you, you know me."
G7 N.C.
One thing I can tell you is you got to be free.

spi - nal crack - er, he got feet down be - low his knee.
Hold you in his arm - chair, you can feel his dis - ease.

Mo - jo fil - ter, he say, "One and one and one is three."
Got to be good - look - ing 'cause he so hard to see.

Bm Bm/A G G/A N.C.
Come to - geth - er, right now, o - ver me.

Dm7
(Instrumental)
1, 2
3

Repeat and Fade
Come to - geth - er, Yeah!

COME BACK WHEN YOU GROW UP

Words and Music by
MARTHA SHARP

With a beat
C D7 G
Come back when you grow up, girl, you're still liv - in' in a pap - er doll world.
Am7 D7 Am7 D7 Am7 D7 Am7 D7
Liv - in' ain't ea - sy, Lov - in's twice as tough. Come back, Ba - by when we grow
G C D7
up You're look - in' real good like a wo - man now, your
G Am7 D7 Am7 D7
mind has - n't got - ten the mes - sage some - how. If you can't take it the go - in' gets rough,
Am7 D7 Am7 D7 G
come back, Ba - by when you grow up. I
G F G
want you girl but your wide eyed in - no - cence has real - ly messed up my mind Yeah! I'd
D7 G F A7 D7
rath - er you'd get your ve - ry first heart - break some - where else a - long the line.
C D7 G
Come back when you grow up girl you're still liv - in' in a pap - er doll world.
Am7 D7 Am7 D7 Am7 D7 Am7 D7
Some - day be a wo - man, rea - dy to love;
Liv - in' ain't ea - sy, lov - in's twice as tough;
come back, Ba - by when you grow
G C D7
up. Come back when you grow up girl, you've
G Am7 D7 Am7 D7
still got a lot of time left in the world. Some - day be a wo - man, read - y to love;
Am7 D7 Am7 D7 G
come back, ba - by when you grow up.

COME AS YOU ARE

Words and Music by
KURT COBAIN

Heavy Rock

Come as you are, as you were, as I want you to be, as a friend, as a friend, as an old en - e - my.
Take your time, hur - ry up, the choice is yours, don't be late. Take a rest as a friend, as an old mem - o - ry.
Come doused in mud, served in bleach, as I want you to be. As a trend, as a friend, as an old mem - o - ry.

Mem - o - ry. Mem - o - ry. Mem - o - ry.

To Coda

D.C. al Coda

CODA

Well, I swear that I don't have a gun. No, I don't have a gun. No, I don't have a gun.

(Instrumental)

Ry. Mem - o - ry. Mem - o - ry. Mem - o - ry.

Well, I swear that I don't have a gun. No, I don't have a gun. No, I don't have a gun. No, I don't

Mem - o - ry.

Mem - o - ry.

COVER GIRL

Words and Music by
MAURICE STARR

Driving Rock
D G Asus D
I get up in the morn - ing and I see your face, girl. You're
G Asus D
look - ing so good, ev - 'ry - thing's in place. Don't
G Asus D
you know I could nev - er leave your side, girl. Won't you
look through the pag - es of a mag - a - zine. Still,
G A D A/C♯
stay here with me and be my bride? Don't you
your pret - ty face is the pret - ti - est I've seen.
Bm A G A
know you're my kind, you're just what I like, girl. You're ev - 'ry - thing, don't you know you're al - right.
Don't you know I on - ly want to be with you.
Bm A G
The on - ly girl I've al - ways need - ed for so long.
No oth - er girl could make me feel the way you do. You're my ev - er - y - thing.
D G A D G A D
Oh, oh, she's my cov - er girl. Oh, oh, oh, oh,
G A D G 1 A D
oh, oh, she's my cov - er girl. Oh, oh, oh, oh. When I
2 A D G A D G
oh, oh, oh, oh, she's my cov - er girl. Oh, oh,
A D G A D G
oh, oh, oh, oh, she's my cov - er girl. Oh, oh,
A D G A D G A D G
oh, oh. Bass! It's al - right. Oh, yeah, it's out of sight.
A D G A D G A D
Let me say it's al - right. Ah. Yeah! (Instrumental)
G A D G A D G

A D Bm A
Don't you know I on-ly want to be with you.
Bm A G A♭
No oth-er girl could make me feel the way you do. You're my ev-er-y-thing.
E♭ A♭ B♭ E♭ A♭ B♭ E♭
Repeat ad. lib and Fade
Oh, oh, she's my cov-er-girl. Oh, oh, oh, oh.

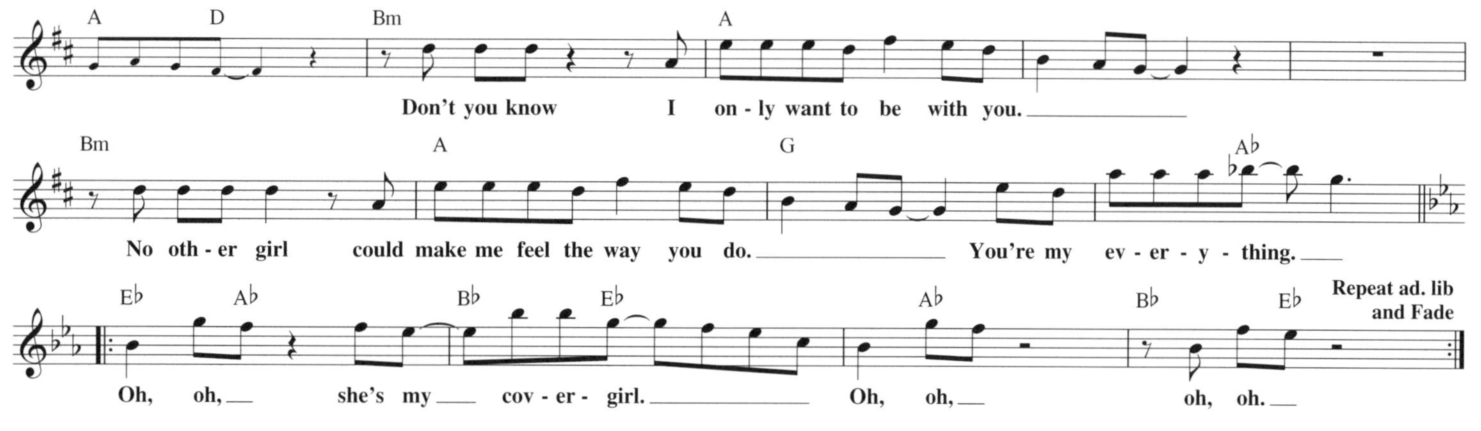

CRACKLIN' ROSIE

Words and Music by
NEIL DIAMOND

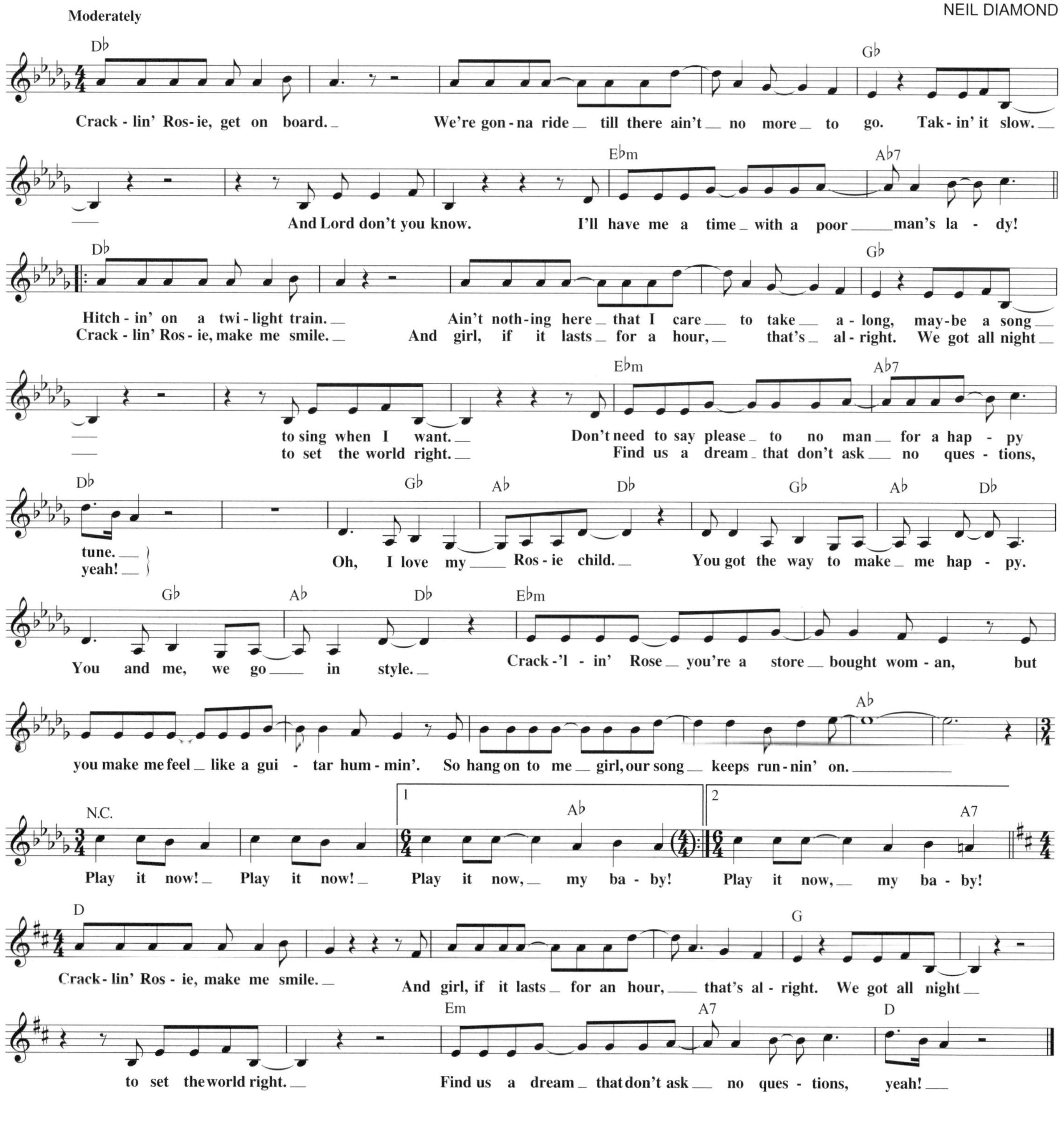
Moderately
D♭ G♭
Crack-lin' Ros-ie, get on board. We're gon-na ride till there ain't no more to go. Tak-in' it slow.
E♭m A♭7
And Lord don't you know. I'll have me a time with a poor man's la-dy!
D♭ G♭
Hitch-in' on a twi-light train. Ain't noth-ing here that I care to take a-long, may-be a song
Crack-lin' Ros-ie, make me smile. And girl, if it lasts for a hour, that's al-right. We got all night
E♭m A♭7
to sing when I want. Don't need to say please to no man for a hap-py
to set the world right. Find us a dream that don't ask no ques-tions,
D♭ G♭ A♭ D♭ G♭ A♭ D♭
tune.
yeah!
Oh, I love my Ros-ie child. You got the way to make me hap-py.
G♭ A♭ D♭ E♭m
You and me, we go in style. Crack-'l-in' Rose you're a store bought wom-an, but
A♭
you make me feel like a gui-tar hum-min'. So hang on to me girl, our song keeps run-nin' on.
N.C. 1 A♭ 2 A7
Play it now! Play it now! Play it now, my ba-by! Play it now, my ba-by!
D G
Crack-lin' Ros-ie, make me smile. And girl, if it lasts for an hour, that's al-right. We got all night
Em A7 D
to set the world right. Find us a dream that don't ask no ques-tions, yeah!

COWARD OF THE COUNTY

Words and Music by ROGER BOWLING
and BILLY EDD WHEELER

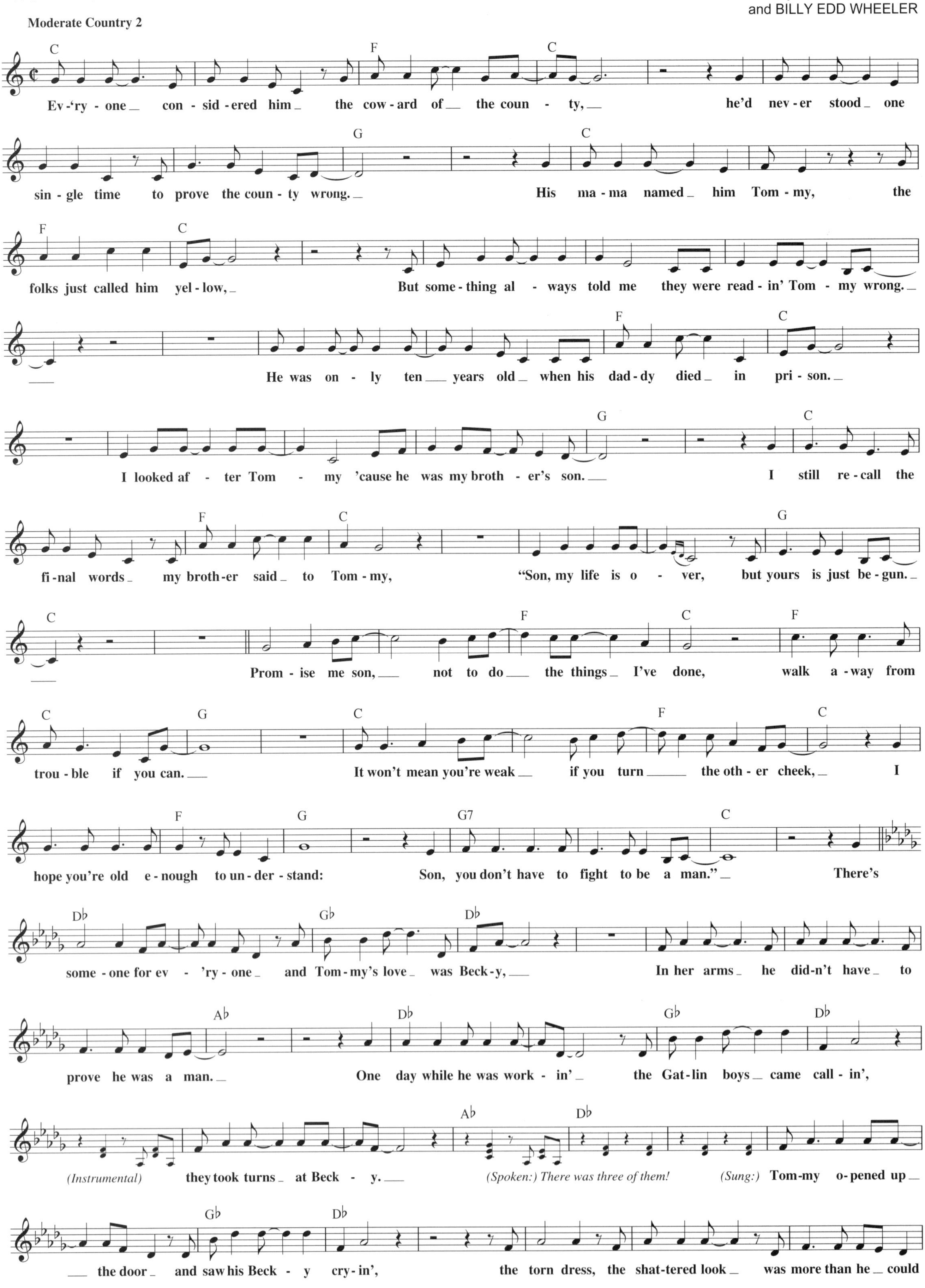
Moderate Country 2
C F C
Ev-'ry-one con-sid-ered him the cow-ard of the coun-ty, he'd nev-er stood one
G C
sin-gle time to prove the coun-ty wrong. His ma-ma named him Tom-my, the
F C
folks just called him yel-low, But some-thing al-ways told me they were read-in' Tom-my wrong.
F C
He was on-ly ten years old when his dad-dy died in pri-son.
G C
I looked af-ter Tom-my 'cause he was my broth-er's son. I still re-call the
F C G
fi-nal words my broth-er said to Tom-my, "Son, my life is o-ver, but yours is just be-gun.
C F C F
Prom-ise me son, not to do the things I've done, walk a-way from
C G C F C
trou-ble if you can. It won't mean you're weak if you turn the oth-er cheek, I
F G G7 C
hope you're old e-nough to un-der-stand: Son, you don't have to fight to be a man." There's
D♭ G♭ D♭
some-one for ev-'ry-one and Tom-my's love was Beck-y, In her arms he did-n't have to
A♭ D♭ G♭ D♭
prove he was a man. One day while he was work-in' the Gat-lin boys came call-in',
A♭ D♭
(Instrumental) they took turns at Beck-y. (Spoken:) There was three of them! (Sung:) Tom-my o-pened up
G♭ D♭
the door and saw his Beck-y cry-in', the torn dress, the shat-tered look was more than he could

stand. He reached a - bove the fire - place and took down his dad - dy's pic - ture. As his
tears fell on his dad - dy's face, he heard these words a - gain: "Prom - ise me son, not to do
the things I've done, walk a - way from trou - ble if you can. It won't mean you're weak
if you turn the oth - er cheek, I hope you're old e - nough to un - der - stand:
Son, you don't have to fight to be a man." The Gat - lin boys just laughed at him when he
walked in - to the bar - room. One of them got up and met him half - way 'cross the floor.
When Tom - my turned a - round they said, "Hey look! Ol' yel - low's leav - in'." (Spoken:) But you coulda heard a pin
drop when Tommy stopped and blocked the door. (Sung:) Twen - ty years of crawl - in' was bot - tled up in -
side him, he was - n't hold - in' noth - in' back he let 'em have it all. When
Tom - my left the bar - room not a Gat - lin boy was stand - in', He said, "This one's for Beck - y," as he
watched the last one fall. (Spoken:) And I heard him say, (Sung:) "I prom - ised you, Dad, not to do the things you done, I
walk a - way from trou - ble when I can. Now please don't think I'm weak, I did - n't turn the oth - er cheek,
and, Pop - pa, I sure hope you un - der - stand: Some - times you got - ta fight when you're a man."
Ev - 'ry - one con - sid - ered him the cow - ard of the coun - ty.

CORRINE CORRINA

Words and Music by J.M. WILLIAMS
and BO CHATMAN

Moderately
A E7 A A7
I love Cor - ri - na, tell the world I do. I love Cor -
dar - lin', where you been so long? Oh, lit - tle
ri - na way a - cross the sea. Oh me, I left Cor -
D A E/G♯ F♯m7 E7
ri - na, tell the world I do. I pray ev - 'ry night
dar - lin', where you been so long? I ain't had no lov - in'
ri - na way a - cross the sea. If you see Cor - ri - na,
A A7 D
she'll learn to love me, too.
since you've been gone.
send her home to me.
Cor - ri - na, Cor - ri - na,
D7 A E7
Cor - ri - na, Cor - ri - na, Cor - ri - na, Cor - ri - na,
To Coda
1 A 2
I love you so. Oh, lit - tle I love you
A E
so. (Instrumental)
A A7 D E
A
D.S. al Coda
I left Cor -
CODA
I love you
A A7 D D7
so. Cor - ri - na, Cor - ri - na, Cor - ri - na, Cor -
A E7
-ri - na, Cor - ri - na, Cor - ri - na, I love you
A E7 A E7
Repeat and Fade
so. Oh, dar - lin', Dar - lin', don't you know, I love you

CRADLE OF LOVE

Words and Music by JACK FAUTHEREE
and WAYNE GRAY

Bright Rock
G Em
Well, rock - a - bye ba - by in the tree - top;
G Em
when the wind blows the cra - dle will rock.
C6 D7
So rock - a - bye ba - by in the tree - top,
G Em G
when the wind blows. Blows.
Em
Well, Jack be nim - ble, Jack be quick. Jack jumped o - ver the
Hi - did - dle did - dle, the cat and the fid - dle, the cow jumped o - ver the
Jack and Jill went up the hill to get a pail of
B7
can - dle - stick. He jumped so high up a - bove, he land - ed in the
moon. And on her way down she met a tur - tle - dove, said let's go rock - in' in the
wa - ter, Jack fell for Jill and gave her a shove and land - ed in the
Em D7 N.C. G
cra - dle of love.
cra - dle of love.
cra - dle of love. Well, rock - a - bye ba - by
Em G
in the tree - top; when the wind blows
Em C6
the cra - dle will rock. So rock - a - bye ba - by
D7 G
in the tree - top, when the wind blows.
Em 1, 2 G Em 3 G Em
Blows. Blows.

CRY LIKE A BABY

Words and Music by DAN PENN and SPOONER OLDHAM

Moderately bright
G
C/G
1., 3. When I think a - bout the good love you gave me, I cry like a ba - by.
2. (See additional lyrics)
To Coda
Liv - ing with - out you is driv - ing me cra - zy; I cry like a ba - by.
C
D
Well, I know now, that you're not a play - thing; not a toy, or a pup - pet on a string.
B
C/G G N.C.
Am
Em
To - day we passed on the street, and you just walked on by;
C7
how my heart just fell to my feet, and like a fool I be - gan to cry.
D.S. al Coda
Oh,
CODA
C G N.C.
Repeat ad lib. and Fade
1. I know now that you're not a play - thing;
2. Ev - er - y road is a lone - ly street.
3., 4., etc. (See additional lyrics)
I cry like a ba - by, cry like a ba - by.

Additional Lyrics

2. As I look back on a love so sweet,
I cry like a baby.
Oh, every road is a lonely street;
I cry like a baby.
I know now that you're not a plaything;
Not a toy, or a puppet on a string.

Vocal ad lib 3:
Living without you is driving me crazy;
I cry like a baby, cry like a baby.

Vocal ad lib 4:
I cry, I cry, I cry,
I cry, I cry like a baby. *(etc.)*

CUTS LIKE A KNIFE

Words and Music by BRYAN ADAMS
and JIM VALLANCE

Moderate Rock
D G C(add2) D
Driv - in' home this eve - nin' I could - a sworn we had it all worked out.
G C(add2) D G C(add2) D
You had this boy be - liev - in' way be - yond the shad - ow of a doubt.
G C(add2) D G C(add2) D
Well, I heard it on the street, I heard you might have found some - bod - y new.
times I've been mis - tak - en, there's times I thought I've been mis - un - der - stood.
G C(add2) D G C(add2) D
Well, who is he, ba - by? Who is he and tell me what he means to you. I
So wait a min - ute dar - lin', can't you see we did the best we could? This
A Bm C(add2)
took it all for grant - ed, but how was I to know that you'd be let - ting go?
would - n't be the first time that things have gone a - stray. Now you've thrown it all a - way.
G To Coda D G C(add2) D G C(add2) D
Now it cuts like a knife, but it feels so right. Oh, it cuts like a knife,
G C(add2) 1 D G C(add2) 2 D G C(add2)
but it feels so right. There's right. Oh, and it cuts like a
(Na na na na na na na na na na.)
D G C(add2) D G C(add2) D G C(add2)
knife. And it feels so right, ba - by. Oh, and it cuts like a knife.
(Na na na na na na na na na na.)
D G C(add2) D 1 G C(add2)
(Instrumental)
2 D.S. (lyric 1) al Coda
I
CODA
D
knife, but it feels so right. And it cuts like a knife,
Repeat and Fade
D G C(add2) D G C(add2)
but it feels so right. Na na na na na na na na na na. (Instrumental)

CREEQUE ALLEY

Words and Music by JOHN PHILLIPS
and MICHELLE PHILLIPS

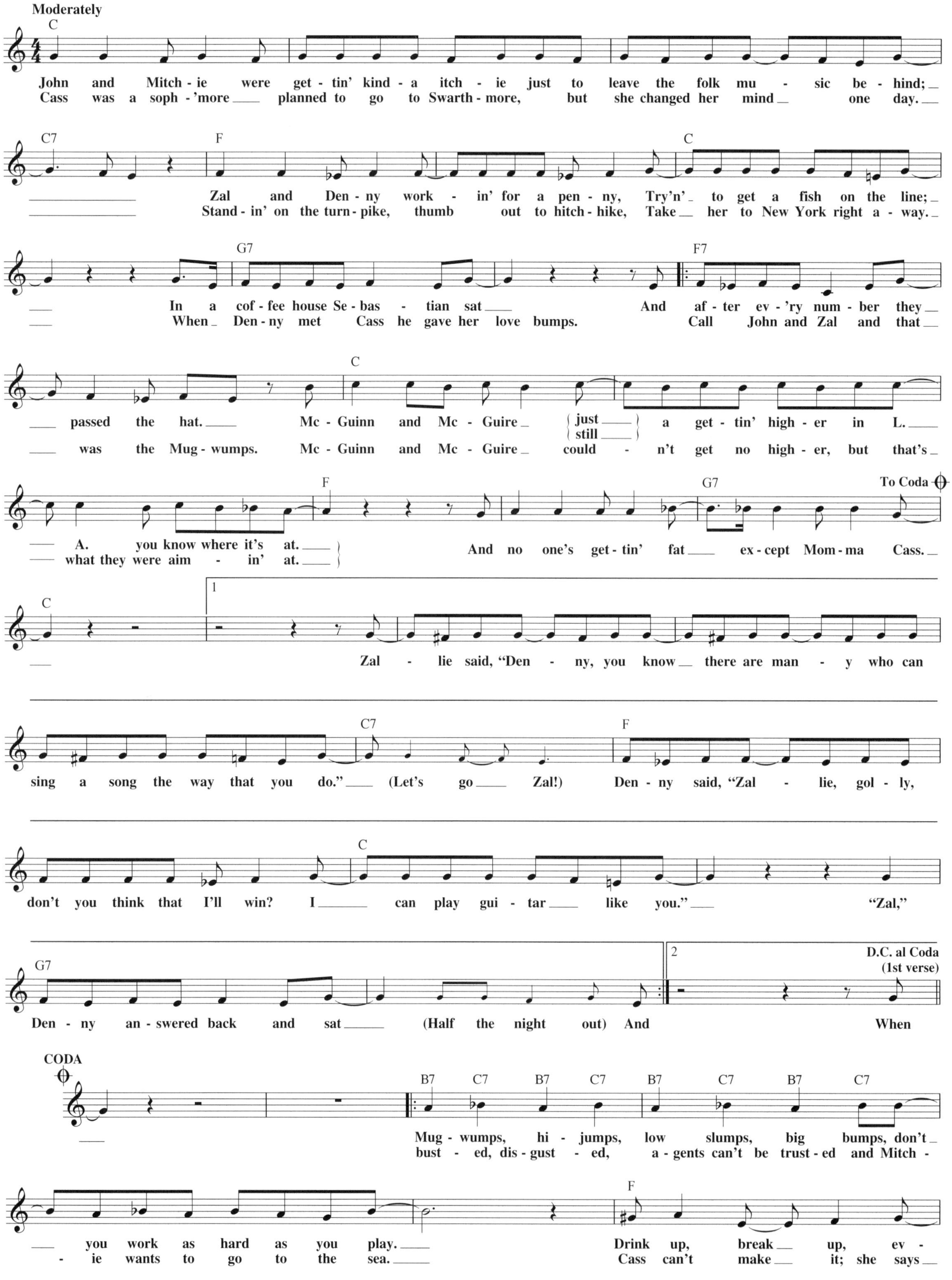
Moderately
C
John and Mitch - ie were get - tin' kind - a itch - ie just to leave the folk mu - sic be - hind;
Cass was a soph - 'more planned to go to Swarth - more, but she changed her mind one day.
C7 F C
Zal and Den - ny work - in' for a pen - ny, Try'n' to get a fish on the line;
Stand - in' on the turn - pike, thumb out to hitch - hike, Take her to New York right a - way.
G7 F7
In a cof - fee house Se - bas - tian sat And af - ter ev - 'ry num - ber they
When Den - ny met Cass he gave her love bumps. Call John and Zal and that
C
passed the hat. Mc - Guinn and Mc - Guire just / still a get - tin' high - er in L.
was the Mug - wumps. Mc - Guinn and Mc - Guire could - n't get no high - er, but that's
F G7 To Coda
A. you know where it's at.
what they were aim - in' at.
And no one's get - tin' fat ex - cept Mom - ma Cass.
C 1
Zal - lie said, "Den - ny, you know there are man - y who can
C7 F
sing a song the way that you do." (Let's go Zal!) Den - ny said, "Zal - lie, gol - ly,
C
don't you think that I'll win? I can play gui - tar like you." "Zal,"
G7 2 D.C. al Coda (1st verse)
Den - ny an - swered back and sat (Half the night out) And When
CODA
B7 C7 B7 C7 B7 C7 B7 C7
Mug - wumps, hi - jumps, low slumps, big bumps, don't
bust - ed, dis - gust - ed, a - gents can't be trust - ed and Mitch -
you work as hard as you play.
ie wants to go to the sea.
F
Drink up, break up, ev -
Cass can't make it; she says

C
- 'ry - thing is shake up. Guess it had to be that way. Se -
we'll have to fake it; we knew she'd come e - ven - tu - al - ly
G7 F7
bas - tian and Zal formed the Spoon - ful, Mi - chelle, John and Den - ny get -
Greas - in' on A - mer - i - can Ex - press card. Tents, low rents and keep -
C
- tin' ver - y tune - ful, Mc - Guinn and Mc - Guire just a - catch - in' fire in
- in' out the heat's hard. Duf - fy's good vi - bra - tions and our i - mag - i - na - tions
F
L. A., you know where that's at. And ev - 'ry - bod - y's get - tin' fat
can't go on in - def - i - nite - ly. And "Cal - i - for - nia Dream - in'" is be -
G7 1 C C7 2 C
ex - cept Mom - ma Cass. Broke,
com - ing a re - al - i - ty.

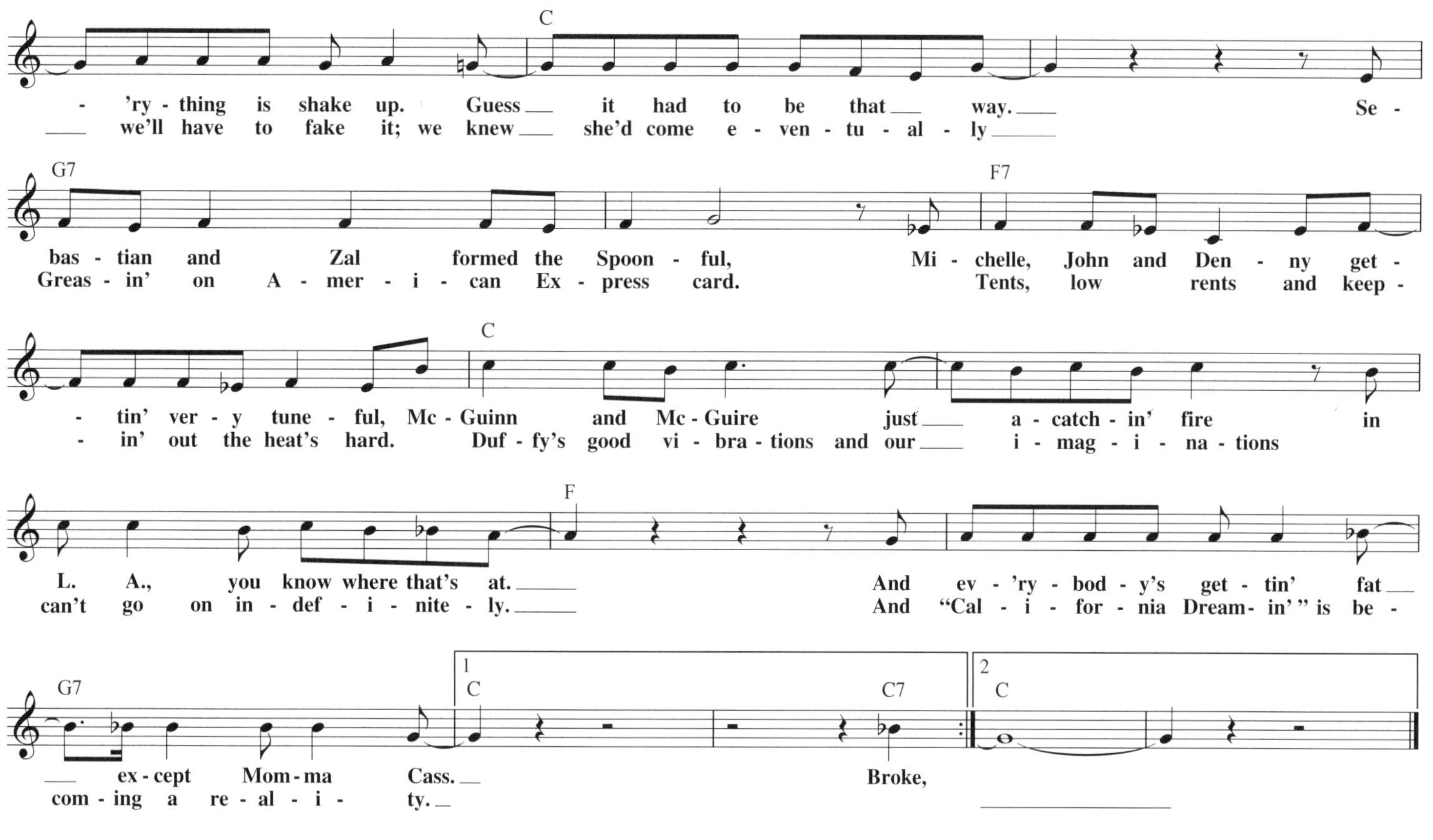

DAYDREAM BELIEVER

Words and Music by
JOHN STEWART

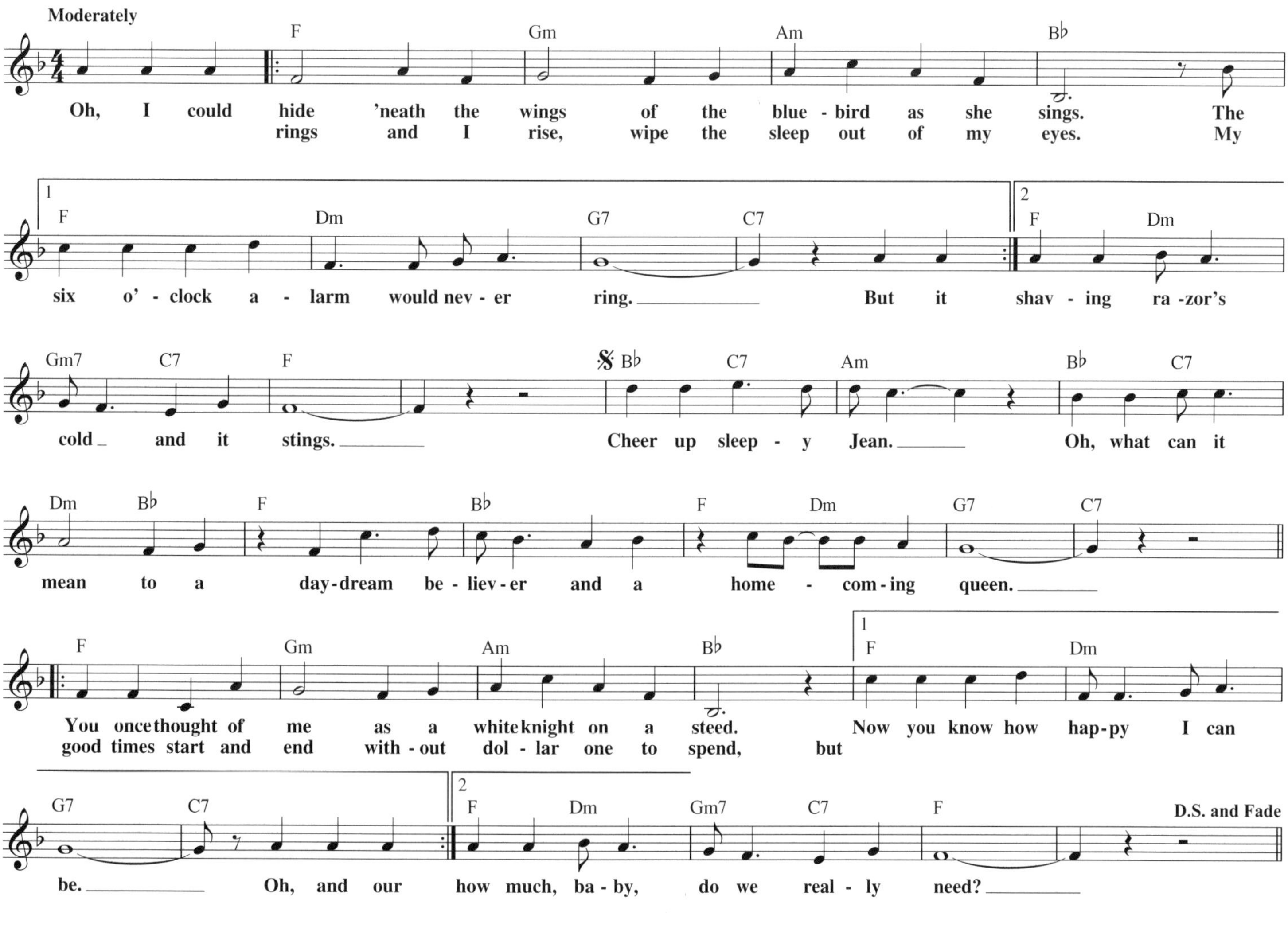

Moderately

F Gm Am B♭
Oh, I could hide 'neath the wings of the blue - bird as she sings. The
rings and I rise, wipe the sleep out of my eyes. My

1 F Dm G7 C7 2 F Dm
six o' - clock a - larm would nev - er ring. But it shav - ing ra - zor's

Gm7 C7 F 𝄋 B♭ C7 Am B♭ C7
cold and it stings. Cheer up sleep - y Jean. Oh, what can it

Dm B♭ F B♭ F Dm G7 C7
mean to a day - dream be - liev - er and a home - com - ing queen.

F Gm Am B♭ 1 F Dm
You once thought of me as a white knight on a steed. Now you know how hap - py I can
good times start and end with - out dol - lar one to spend, but

G7 C7 2 F Dm Gm7 C7 F D.S. and Fade
be. Oh, and our how much, ba - by, do we real - ly need?

CYCLES

Words and Music by
GAYLE CALDWELL

Moderately
D A G A7sus A7 D A G A7sus A7 G F♯m Em7 A7sus A7
So I'm down, and so I'm out, but so are man - y oth - ers, So I feel like try'n' to hide my head 'neath these cov - ers. Life is like the sea - sons, af - ter win - ter comes the spring.
I've been told, and I be - lieve that life is meant for liv - in'. E - ven when my chips are low, there's still some left for giv - in'. I've been man - y plac - es, may - be not as far as you.
But I'll keep my head up high, al - though I'm kind - a tired. My gal / man just up and left last week; Fri - day, I got fired. You know, it's al - most fun - ny, but things can't get worse than now.
D A To Coda G A7
So I'll keep this smile a - while, and see what to - mor - row
So I think I'll stay a - while, and see if some dreams come
So I'll keep on try'n' to sing, but
D 1 2 G
brings.
true.
There is - n't
F♯m Bm G A7 D
much that I have learned through all my fool - ish years, ex -
G F♯m Bm G
cept that life keeps run - nin' in cy - cles. First, there's
A7sus A7 D.C. al Coda
laugh - ter, then there's tears.
CODA
G A7sus A7 D
please, just don't ask me now.

DANIEL

Words and Music by ELTON JOHN
and BERNIE TAUPIN

Moderately bright
C Dm
Dan - iel is trav - 'ling to - night on a plane
They say Spain is pret - ty 'though I've nev - er been
G E7 Am
I can see the red tail - lights head - ing for Spain. Oh and
well Dan - iel says it's the best place he's ev - er seen. Oh and
F G Am
I can see Dan - iel wav - ing good - bye God it looks
he should know he's been there e - nough Lord I
F G7 F
To Coda
like Dan - iel must be the clouds in my eyes.
miss Dan - iel oh I miss him so much.
1
C G7
(Instrumental)
2
C F
Oh Dan - iel my broth - er you are
C F
old - er than me do you still feel the pain of the scars
C Am
that won't heal. Your eyes have died but
F Fm C A7
you see more than I. Dan - iel you're a star in the face of the sky.
Dm7 G7
D.C. al Coda
(Verse 1)
CODA
C F
Oh God it looks like Dan - iel
G7 F C F C
must be the clouds in my eyes.

DANCE WITH ME

Words and Music by PETER BROWN
and ROBERT RANS

Moderately
Cm7 F/C Cm7
(Got-ta keep on mak-in' me high; _ you got-ta keep on mak - in' me high. _
Got-ta keep on mak - in' me high; _ you got - ta
F/C Cm7 F/C Cm7
keep on mak-in' me high.) _
1.,3. If you're feel-ing sad and blue, _ come on _ and dance with _ me.
2. La - dies, get up off your seats; _ come on _ and dance with _ me.

F/C Cm7 F/C Cm7 1 F/C
I can make your dreams come _ true; ___
Gen - tle - men, get on your _ feet; ___
come on _ and dance with _ me. _

2, 3 F/C Eb6 F Abmaj7 F7 Bb7sus N.C. Cm
Say the _ word ___ and I'll sum - mon the _ band _ with my _ hand.

Eb F Abmaj7 F7 Bb7sus N.C. To Coda
Let your _ mind ___ and your bod - y be _ free, _ dance with _ me.

Cm7 F/C Cm7 F/C
(Got-ta keep on mak-in' me high, _ you got - ta keep on mak-in' me high.) _

Cm7 F/C Cm7 F/C

Cm7 F/C Eb F Abmaj7 F7 Bb7sus N.C.
If you're _ free ___ and you like what you _ see, ___ dance with _ me.

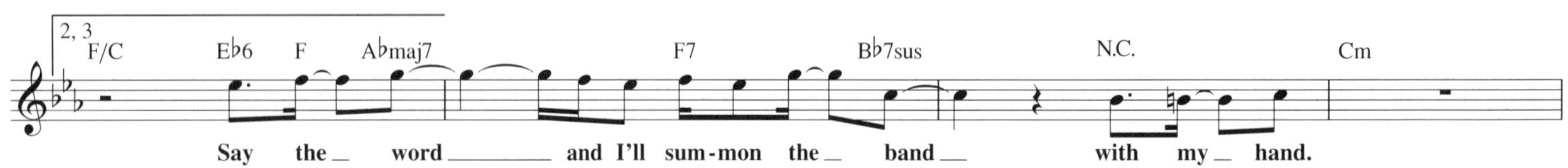

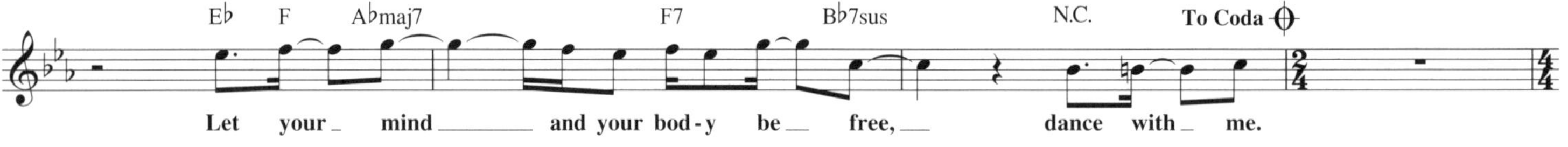

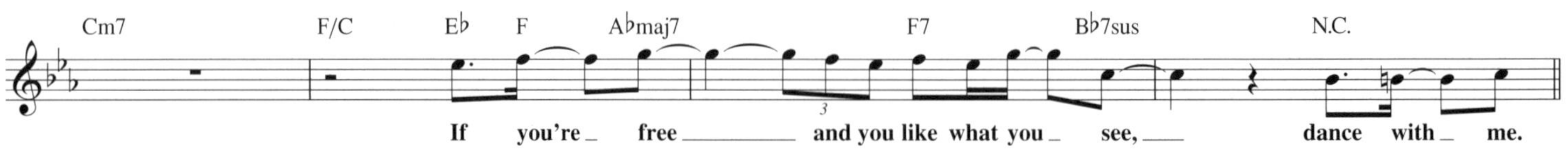

1
2
Female: You
Cm7
got to keep danc - in', 'cause it's mak - in' me high; you got - ta keep, keep danc - in'. You
(You got - ta keep on mak - in' me high; you got - ta keep on mak - in' me high.)
got to keep danc - in' 'cause it's mak - in' me high; you got - ta keep, keep danc - in'. You
1-3
(You got - ta keep on mak - in' me high; you got - ta keep on mak - in' me high.)
got to keep danc - in' 'cause it's mak - in' me high; you got - ta keep, keep danc - in'. You
4
E♭ F A♭maj7 F7 B♭7sus N.C.
keep on mak - in' me high.)
keep, keep danc - in', yeah.
Cm7 F/C
D.S. al Coda
(Got - ta keep on mak - in' me high; you got - ta keep on mak - in' me high.)
CODA
Cm7
(Got - ta keep on mak - in' me high; you got - ta
F7/C Cm7 F7/C E♭ F7 A♭maj7
keep on.) (Got - ta keep on mak - in' me high; you got - ta keep on.) Let your mind
F7 B♭7sus N.C. Cm
and your bod - y be free; dance with me. Ha!

DANCING WITH MYSELF

Words and Music by BILLY IDOL
and TONY JAMES

Very Fast Rock
E5
A5
1. On the floors of To - ky - o - o, or down in Lon - don town to go - go, oh, with the
2., D.S. looked all o - ver the wo - orld, and there's ev - 'ry type of gi - irl. But, your

B5
A5
rec - ord se - lec - tion and the mir - ror's re - flec - tion, I'm a - danc - in' with my - se - elf. Oh, when there's
emp - ty eyes seem to pass me by, and leave me danc - in' with my - se - elf. So let's

E5
A5
To Coda
no one else in si - ight, and in the crowd - ed, lone - ly ni - ight, well, I
sink an - oth - er dri - ink, 'cause it - 'll give me time to thi - ink. If I

B5
A5
wait so long for my love vi - bra - tion, and I'm danc - in' with my - se - elf.
had the chance, I'd ask the world to dance, and I'd be danc - in' with my - se - elf.
Oh, oh, oh,

E5
A5
danc - in' with my - se - elf. Oh, oh, oh, danc - in' with my - se - elf. Well, there's

B5
A5
noth - in' to lose, and there's noth - in' to prove, when I'm danc - in' with my - se - elf, oh, oh, oh,

1
E
oh. If I
2
E
A
oh. Oh, oh, oh, oh, oh.

E
B
Oh, oh, oh, oh, oh, oh, oh, oh.

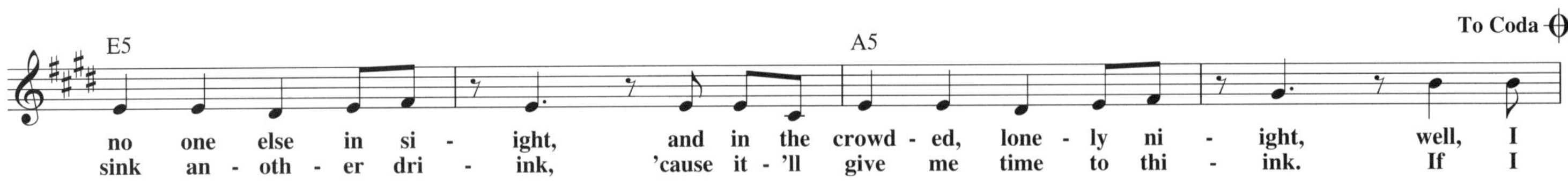

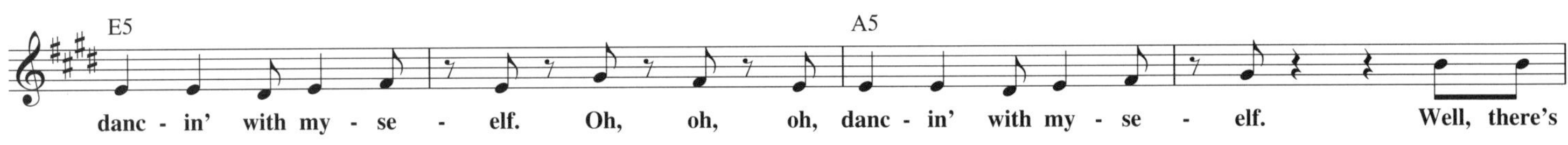

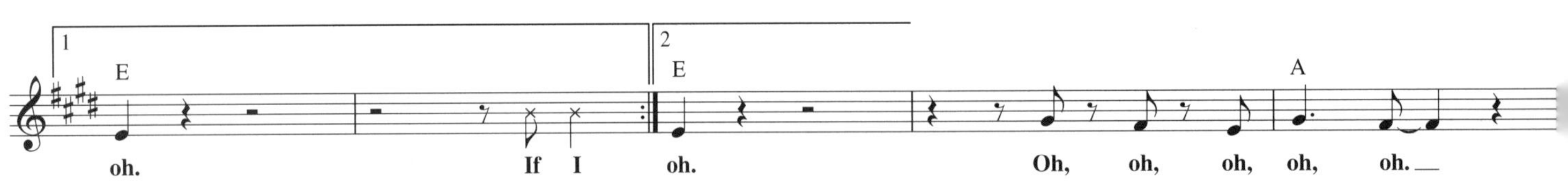

B5
E5
B5
D.S. al Coda
Well, if I
CODA
B5
A5
had the chance, I'd ask the world to dance, and I'd be danc - in' with my - se -
elf. Oh, oh, oh, danc - in' with my - se - elf. Oh, oh, oh,
E5
A5
B5
danc - in' with my - se - elf. If I had the chance, I'd ask the
world to dance, and if I had the chance, I'd ask the world to dance, if I
had the chance, I'd ask the world to dance.
Oh, oh, oh, oh. Oh, oh, oh, oh. Oh, oh, oh,
E5
A5
Repeat and Fade
vocal ad lib. to end
(Danc - in' with my - se - elf. Oh, oh, oh, danc - in' with my - se - elf. Oh, oh, oh)

DARLING, BE HOME SOON

Words and Music by
JOHN SEBASTIAN

Moderately

G C G
Come, and talk of all the things we did to-day. Hear, and

C G C G/B Am7 G
laugh a-bout our fun-ny lit-tle ways while we have a few min-utes to breathe. Then I

C G/B Am7 G 𝄋 Csus C
know that it's time you must leave. But, dar-ling, be home soon. I

Csus C G Csus C
could-n't bear to wait an ex-tra min-ute if you daw-dled. My dar-ling, be home soon.

Csus C G
It's not just these few hours, but I've been wait-ing since I tod-dled for the great

C G/B Am7 G To Coda
re-lief of hav-ing you to talk to. And now a

C/G G C/G G
quar-ter of my life is al-most past. I think I've come to see my-self at last. And I

C G/B Am7 G C G/B Am7 G
see that the time spent con-fused was the time that I spent with-out you. And I

C G/B Am7 D D.S. al Coda CODA
feel my-self in bloom. So,

C/G G
(Instrumental)
C/G G C G/B Am7 D
So,
Csus C Csus2 C Csus C
dar - ling, my dar - ling, be home soon. I could - n't bear to wait an ex - tra
G Csus C Csus C
min - ute if you daw - dled. My dar - ling, be home soon. It's
Csus C G C G/B Am7
not just these few hours, but I've been wait - ing since I tod dled for the great re - lief of hav - ing you to
G C/G G
talk to. Go and beat your cra - zy head a - gainst the sky.
C/G G
Try and see be - yond the hous - es in your eyes. It's o -
C G/B Am7 D Csus C
kay to shoot the moon. But, dar - ling, be home soon.
Csus2 C Csus C G
I could - n't bear to wait an ex - tra min - ute if you daw - dled. My
Csus C Csus2 C Csus C G
dar - ling, be home soon. It's not just these few hours, but I've been wait - ing since I tod - dled
C G/B Am7 G
for the great re - lief of hav - ing you to talk to.

DE DO DO DO, DE DA DA DA

Words and Music by
STING

Moderately
Asus2 F♯m7(add4) C♯m7
Don't think me un - kind.
Asus2 F♯m7(add4) C♯m7
Words are hard to find.
Asus2 F♯m7(add4) C♯m7
They're on - ly cheques I've left un - signed
Asus2 F♯m7(add4) C♯m7
from the banks of cha - os in my mind.
D/A E
And when their el - o - quence es - capes me,
'Cause when their el - o - quence es - capes you,
D/A E D
their log - ic ties me up and rapes me.
their log - ic ties you up and rapes you.
De
Asus2 A Asus(add2) A Esus2 E Esus2 D
do do do, de da da da is all I want to say to you. De
To Coda
1, 3
Asus2 A Asus(add2) A Esus2 E Esus2 D
do do do, de da da da, their in - no - cence will pull me through. De
the mean - ing - less and all
2
Esus2 D Asus2 F♯m7(add4) C♯m7
that's true. Po - ets, priests and pol - i - ti - cians

Asus2
F♯m7(add4)
C♯m7
have words to thank for their po - si - tions.
Asus2
F♯m7(add4)
C♯m7
Words that scream for your sub - mis - sion,
Asus2
F♯m7(add4)
C♯m7
and no one's jam - ming their trans - mis - sion.
D.S. al Coda
(with repeat)
CODA
Esus2
D
Bmaj7
Gmaj7
that's true.
Oh.
Amaj7
Emaj7
Bmaj7
Gmaj7
A6
G/A
D/E
E
D
De
Asus2
A
Asus(add2)
Esus2
do do do, de da da da, is all I want to say to you. De
do do do, de da da da,
their in - no - cence will pull me through. De
the mean - ing - less and all that's true.
Repeat and Fade

DEJA VU

Copyright © 1979 by Rightsong Music Inc. and Universal Music - Careers
Lyric by ADRIENNE ANDERSON
Moderately Slow
Emaj7 G G♯m7
This is in-sane; all you did was say hel-lo, speak my name.
How can it be? You're a dif-f'rent space and time, come to me.
C♯7(♯9) Dmaj7 F
Feel-ing your love, like a love I used to know,
Feel like I'm home in a place I used to know,
Cmaj7 1,3 C♯m7 2,4 A B
long a-go.
long a-go,
Chorus
F♯m7 C♯m7
de-ja vu, could you be the dream that I once knew. Is it you?
could you be the dream that might come true, shin-ing through?
1 De-ja vu,
2 G♯m7
I keep re-mem-ber-ing me, I keep re-
F♯m7 C♯m7 B♭ To Coda A D.C. al Coda
mem-ber-ing you, de-ja vu.
CODA
A F♯m9 1-3 4 A D.S. and Fade
De-ja vu. De-ja vu,
DIANA
Copyright © 1957 Chrysalis Standards, Inc.
Copyright Renewed
All Rights Administered by BMG Rights Management (US) LLC
Words and Music by
PAUL ANKA
Medium Rock
E♭ Cm Fm7 B♭7 E♭ Cm
I'm so young and you're so old. This my dar-ling I've been told. I don't care just what they say
Fm7 B♭7 E♭ Cm Fm7 B♭7 E♭
'cause for-ev-er I will pray you and I will be as free as the birds up in the trees. Oh
Cm Fm7 B♭7 E♭ Fm7 B♭7 E♭ Fm7 B♭7 E♭ Cm
please stay by me, Di-an-a. Thrills I get when you hold me close.
Fm7 B♭7 E♭ Cm Fm7 B♭7
Oh my dar-ling you're the most. I love you but do you love me? Oh Di-an-a, can't you see

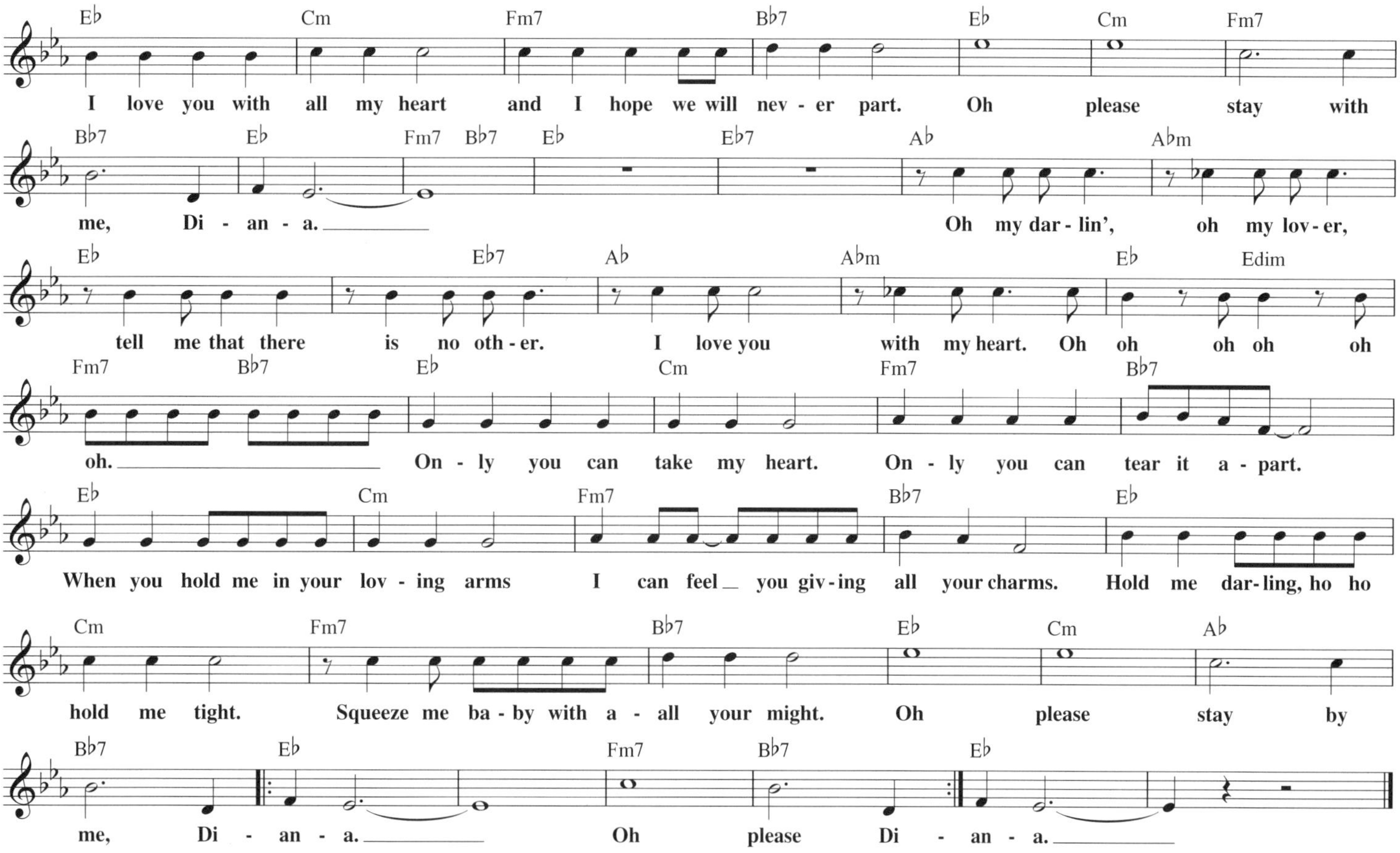

E♭ Cm Fm7 B♭7 E♭ Cm Fm7
I love you with all my heart and I hope we will nev - er part. Oh please stay with

B♭7 E♭ Fm7 B♭7 E♭ E♭7 A♭ A♭m
me, Di - an - a. Oh my dar - lin', oh my lov - er,

E♭ E♭7 A♭ A♭m E♭ Edim
tell me that there is no oth - er. I love you with my heart. Oh oh oh oh oh

Fm7 B♭7 E♭ Cm Fm7 B♭7
oh. On - ly you can take my heart. On - ly you can tear it a - part.

E♭ Cm Fm7 B♭7 E♭
When you hold me in your lov - ing arms I can feel you giv - ing all your charms. Hold me dar - ling, ho ho

Cm Fm7 B♭7 E♭ Cm A♭
hold me tight. Squeeze me ba - by with a - all your might. Oh please stay by

B♭7 E♭ Fm7 B♭7 E♭
me, Di - an - a. Oh please Di - an - a.

DETROIT CITY

Words and Music by DANNY DILL
and MEL TILLIS

Moderately
D A7 D A7
Last night I went to sleep in De - troit cit - y and I dreamed a - bout the cot - ton fields and
Home folks think I'm big in De - troit cit - y, from the let - ters that I write they think I'm
D D7 G D E7 To Coda
home; I dreamed a bout my moth - er, dear old pa - pa, sis - ter and broth - er and I dreamed a - bout the
fine. But by day I make the cars, by night I make the bars; if on - ly they could
A7 D D7 G C G
girl who's been wait - ing for so long. I wan - na go home, I wan - na go home;
D A7 D G D D.S. al Coda
Oh, how I wan - na go home.
CODA
A7
read be - tween the lines. I wan - na go
D D7 G C G D A7 D G D
home, I wan - na go home; Oh, how I wan - na go home.

Recitation

'Cause you know I rode a freight train north to Detroit city.
And after all these years I find I've just been wasting my time
So I just think I'll take my foolish pride and put it on the south-bound freight and ride
And go on back to the loved ones, the ones that I left waiting so far behind,
I wanna go home, I wanna go home; Oh, how I wanna go home.

DO YOU KNOW WHAT I MEAN

Copyright © 1971 ALMO MUSIC CORP. and LA BREA MUSIC
Copyright Renewed
All Rights Controlled and Administered by ALMO MUSIC CORP.
Words and Music by
LEE MICHAELS
Bluesy Rock
Been for - ty days since I don't know when, I just saw her with my best friend, do you know what I mean? Do you know, know what I mean?
Her and Bob - by were step - ping out, her and Bob - by did - n't know I found out, do you know what I mean? Do you know, know what I mean?
I just saw her yes - ter - day, I just saw her, asked her to stay, do you know what I mean? Lord, do you know what I mean?
So I asked her if she still cared, she did - n't hear me, she just stared, do you know what I mean? Lord, do you know what I mean?
And then she said:
Lee, you have - n't loved me in near - ly four years. You have - n't no - ticed that I held back my tears.
And now you have, but it's real - ly too late, bet - ter find your - self an - oth - er girl.
Bet - ter find an - oth - er girl, bet - ter find, uh, an - oth - er place. Woo!
She just left me yes - ter - day, she just left me, had noth - ing to say, do you know what I mean? Oh, do you know what I mean?
for - ty days since I don't know when, I just saw her with my best friend, do you know what I mean? Lord, do you know what I mean?
She's a dan - dy, yes in - deed, she's a dan - dy, but now she's free, do you know what I mean? Lord, do you know what I mean? Yeah. Been
I just saw her yes - ter - day, I just saw her learn how to stay, do you know what I mean? Lord, do you know what I
mean? Yeah, here it comes now. Woo! Help me! (Whistle)

DO YOU KNOW WHERE YOU'RE GOING TO?

Theme from MAHOGANY

Words by GERRY GOFFIN
Music by MICHAEL MASSER

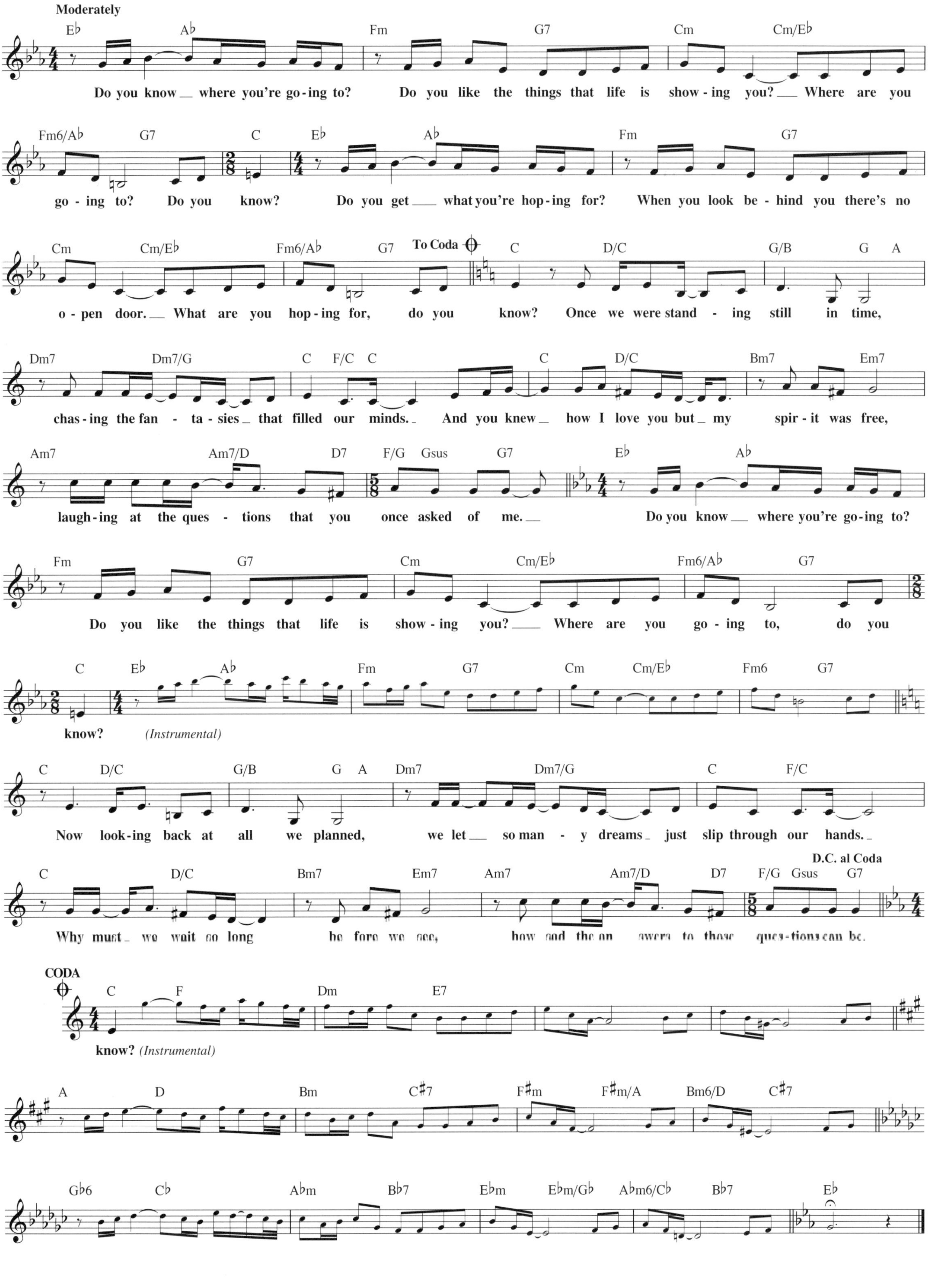
Moderately
E♭ A♭ Fm G7 Cm Cm/E♭
Do you know where you're go-ing to? Do you like the things that life is show-ing you? Where are you
Fm6/A♭ G7 C E♭ A♭ Fm G7
go-ing to? Do you know? Do you get what you're hop-ing for? When you look be-hind you there's no
Cm Cm/E♭ Fm6/A♭ G7 To Coda C D/C G/B G A
o-pen door. What are you hop-ing for, do you know? Once we were stand-ing still in time,
Dm7 Dm7/G C F/C C C D/C Bm7 Em7
chas-ing the fan-ta-sies that filled our minds. And you knew how I love you but my spir-it was free,
Am7 Am7/D D7 F/G Gsus G7 E♭ A♭
laugh-ing at the ques-tions that you once asked of me. Do you know where you're go-ing to?
Fm G7 Cm Cm/E♭ Fm6/A♭ G7
Do you like the things that life is show-ing you? Where are you go-ing to, do you
C E♭ A♭ Fm G7 Cm Cm/E♭ Fm6 G7
know? (Instrumental)
C D/C G/B G A Dm7 Dm7/G C F/C
Now look-ing back at all we planned, we let so man-y dreams just slip through our hands.
D.C. al Coda
C D/C Bm7 Em7 Am7 Am7/D D7 F/G Gsus G7
Why must we wait so long be-fore we see, how sad the an-swers to those ques-tions can be.
CODA
C F Dm E7
know? (Instrumental)
A D Bm C♯7 F♯m F♯m/A Bm6/D C♯7
G♭6 C♭ A♭m B♭7 E♭m E♭m/G♭ A♭m6/C♭ B♭7 E♭

DO YOU REALLY WANT TO HURT ME

Words and Music by GEORGE O'DOWD,
JON MOSS, MICHAEL CRAIG and ROY HAY

Freely
G D/F# Em G
Give me time to re - al - ize my crime. Let me love
D/F# Em G D/F#
and steal. I have danced
Em G D/F# Em
in - side your eyes. How can love be real?
Moderate Reggae
G D/F# Em G D/F#
Do You Real - ly Want To Hurt Me? Do you real - ly want to
Em C G Am7 Bm
make me cry? Pre - cious kiss - es, words that burn me. Lov - ers nev - er ask you
Bm/E G D/F# Em G D/F#
why. In my heart the fire's burn - ing. Choose my col - or, find a
Em C G Am7 Bm
star. Pre - cious peo - ple al - ways tell me that's a step a step
Bm/E G D/F# Em G D/F#
too far. Do You Real - ly Want To Hurt Me? Do you real - ly want to
Em C G Am7 Bm
make me cry? Do You Real - ly Want To Hurt Me? Do you real - ly want to
G B♭maj7 A♭maj7
make me cry? (Instrumental)
To Coda
Gm G D/F# Em G D/F#
Words of you I have spo - ken. I could waste a thou - sand
You've been talk - in' but be - lieve me, if it's true you do not
Em C G Am7 Bm
years. Wrapped in sor - row, words are to - ken. Come in - side and catch
know. This by law's with - out a rea - son, I'm pre - pared to let you

1 Bm/E | 2 Bm/E | C | D | C
my tears. go. If it's love that you want from me, then take it a-

D | C | D | C | D — D.S. al Coda
way. Ev-'ry-thing's not a what you see. It's o-ver a-gain.

CODA
Gm — Play 4 times — G D/F# Em
Do You Real-ly Want To Hurt Me?

G D/F# Em C G Am7 Bm
Do you real-ly want to make me cry? Do You Real-ly Want To Hurt Me? Do you real-ly want to

G Bbmaj7 G Em
make me cry? Do You Real-ly Want To Hurt Me?

G D/F# Bbmaj7
Do you real-ly want to make me cry? *(Instrumental)*

DO YOU WANNA MAKE LOVE

Words and Music by
PETER McCANN

Moderately

Ab Db Ab Eb Ab/Bb
Do you wan-na make love, or do you just wan-na fool a-round?

Eb Eb/Bb Bb Ab/C Bb/D Eb Ab/Bb
I guar-an-tee it will bring you down if you try to fool your-self.

Eb N.C. Ab Db/Eb Ab Eb Ab/Bb
Do you wan-na make love, or do you just wan na fool a-round?

Eb Eb/Bb Bb Fm7 Ab/Bb Eb
You can take it ser-i-ous-ly, or take it some-where else.

N.C. Bbsus Bb Eb Ab/Bb Eb
But, if you wan-na get close to me, you could do it so eas-i-ly. Is it love that I see

Gm Cm Ab/Bb Eb N.C. — D.S. and Fade
when I look in your eyes or just an-oth-er emp-ty lie? Do you wan-na make

DOCTOR! DOCTOR!

Words and Music by TOM BAILEY,
ALANNAH CURRIE and JOE LEEWAY

Steady Rock beat
C
I saw you there just stand - ing there
and I thought I was on - ly dream - ing yeah. I
Eb Dm
C
kissed you then then once a - gain
(D.S.) Ships at night give such de - light
Eb Dm
C
you said you would come and dance with me.
we all leave be - fore the morn - ing light.
Eb Dm F
Dance with me a - cross the sea
Please don't go no please don't go
Ab Bb C
and we could feel the mo - tion of a thou - sand dreams.
'cause I don't want to stay here on my own. Oh
Eb Dm Ab Fm7
Doc - tor, Doc - tor, can't you see I'm
Bb Gm Ab Fm7 Bb
burn - ing, burn - ing; oh Doc - tor, Doc - tor, is this love I'm feel -
1 Gsus G 2, 3 Gsus G Ab Fm7 Bb
ing? ing? Doc - tor, Doc - tor, can't you see I'm burn - ing, burn - ing;
Gm Ab Fm7 Bb Gsus G
To Coda
oh Doc - tor, Doc - tor, is this love I'm feel - ing?
Ab Bb Ab
Fe - ver breathe your love on me, take a - way my name. Fe - ver lay your hands
Bb G C Eb Dm
D.S. al Coda
on me, nev - er be the same. Oh

CODA
C
Come with me ___ and make ___ be - lieve ___
E♭ Dm
C
we can trav - el to ___ e - ter - ni - ty.
E♭ Dm
C
Repeat and Fade
E♭ Dm

DON'T

Words and Music by JERRY LEIBER
and MIKE STOLLER

Moderately

F C7 F F7 B♭ C7 F Am Dm

Don't, don't, that's what you say each time that I hold you ___ this

Don't, don't leave my em - brace, for here in my arms is ___ your

Gm7 C7 N.C. F F7 B♭ Gm7 C7 | 1. F Dm Gm7 C7

way. ___ When I feel like this and I want to kiss you, ba - by, don't say don't. ___

place. ___ When the night grows cold and I want to hold you, ba - by, don't say

| 2. F F7 B♭ A A7 B♭ C7 F B♭ F

don't. ___ If you think that this is just a game I'm play - ing, ___

G7 C7 Bdim C7 F C7 F F7

if you think that I don't mean ev - 'ry word I'm say - ing, ___ don't, don't, don't feel that

B♭ C7 F Am Dm Gm7 C7 N.C. F F7

way. I'm your love and yours I ___ will stay. ___ This you can be - lieve; I will nev - er

B♭ Gm7 C7 F Dm Gm7 C7sus C7 | 1. F B♭7 F C7 D.C. | 2. F B♭7 F

leave you, heav - en knows I won't. ___ Ba - by, don't say don't. don't. ___

DON'T WORRY, BE HAPPY

Words and Music by
BOBBY McFERRIN

Brightly
Whistle
add higher notes on repeat
Here's a lit - tle song I wrote you might want to sing it note for note. Don't wor - ry, be hap - py.
Ain't got no place to lay your head. Some - bod - y came and took your bed. Don't wor - ry, be hap - py.
Ain't got no cash, ain't got no style. Ain't got no gal to make you smile. Don't wor - ry, be hap - py.
In ev - 'ry life we have some trou - ble but when you wor - ry you make it dou - ble. Don't wor - ry, be hap - py. Don't wor - ry, be hap - py now.
The land - lord say your rent is late, he may have to lit - i - gate. Don't wor - ry, be hap - py. Spoken: Look at me — I'm happy.
'Cause when you worry your face will frown, and that will bring ev'ry - bod - y down. Don't wor - ry, be hap - py. Don't wor - ry, be hap - py now.
Oo. Oo. Don't wor - ry. Oo. Be hap - py. Oo.
Don't wor - ry, be hap - py.
Spoken: Here, I give you my phone number. When you worry, call me, I make you happy.
Don't wor - ry, be hap - py.
Oo. Oo. Don't wor - ry. Oo. Be hap - py. Oo. Don't wor - ry, be hap - py.

Bb Eb Bb Cm
Don't wor - ry, be hap - py. Oo. Oo.
Eb6 Bb
Repeat and Fade
Oo. Oo.

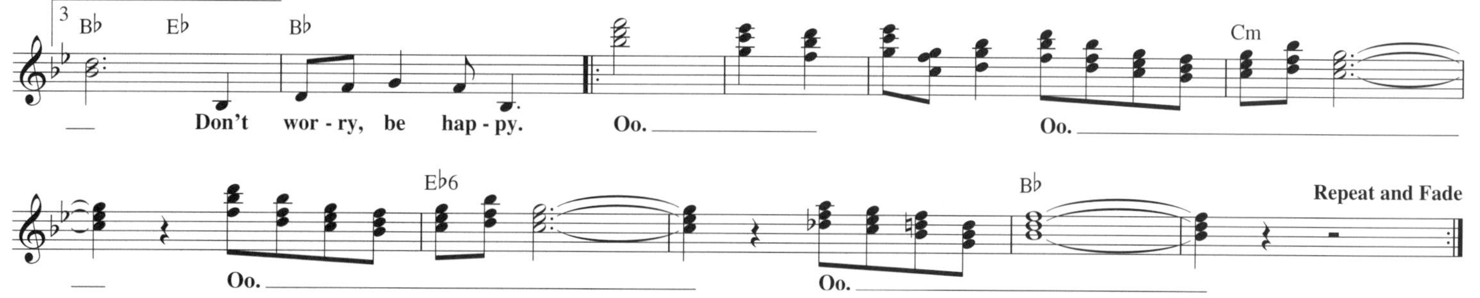

Additional Lyrics

Spoken ad lib. over repeat and fade:

Don't worry. Don't worry. Don't do it.
Be happy. Put a smile on your face.
Don't bring everybody down. Don't
Worry. It will soon pass, whatever it is.
Don't worry. Be happy. I'm not worried.
I'm happy.

DON'T LET THE SUN CATCH YOU CRYING

Words and Music by GERARD MARSDEN,
FRED MARSDEN, LES CHADWICK and LES MAGUIRE

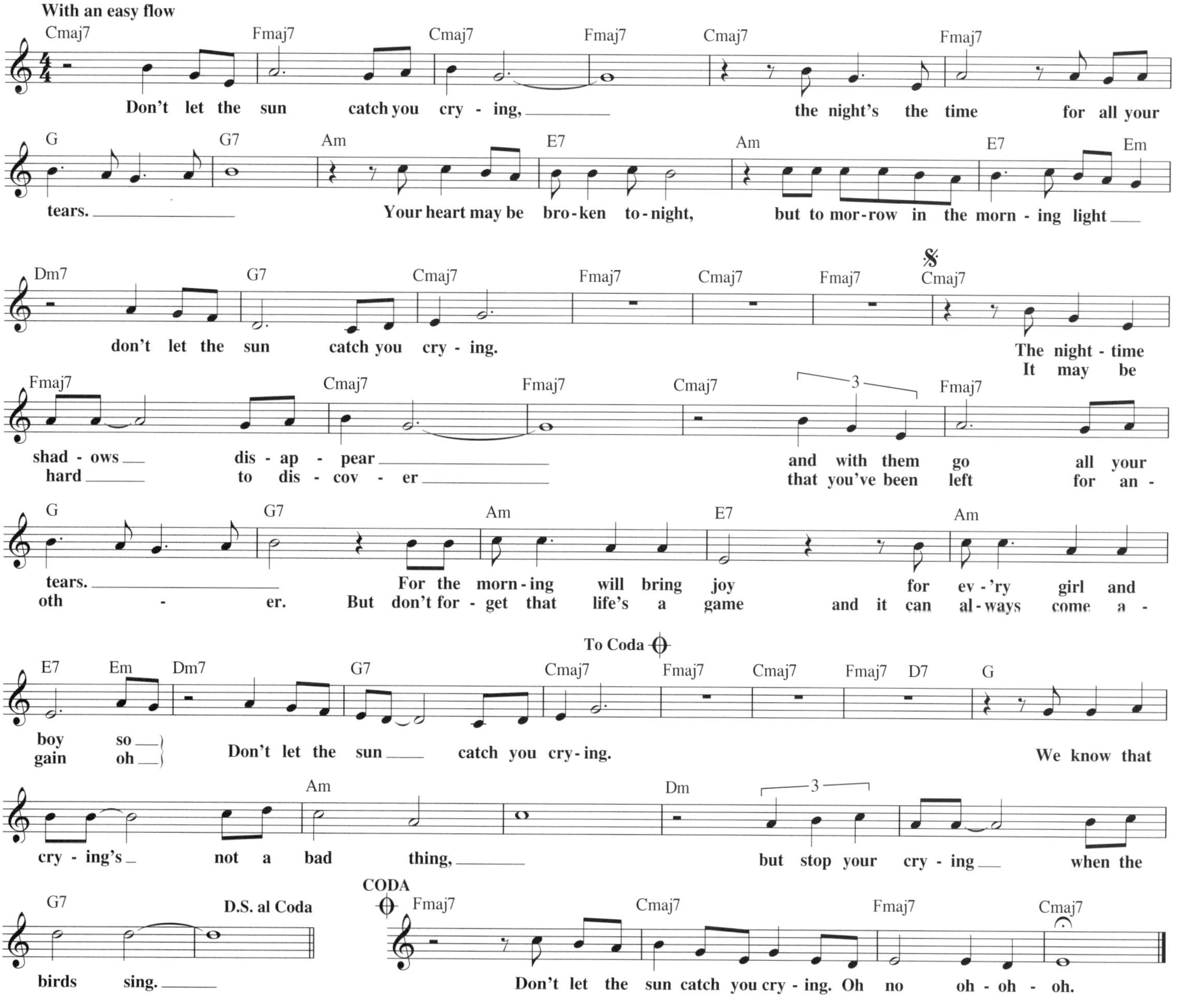

With an easy flow

Cmaj7 Fmaj7 Cmaj7 Fmaj7 Cmaj7 Fmaj7
Don't let the sun catch you cry - ing, the night's the time for all your

G G7 Am E7 Am E7 Em
tears. Your heart may be bro - ken to - night, but to mor - row in the morn - ing light

Dm7 G7 Cmaj7 Fmaj7 Cmaj7 Fmaj7 𝄋 Cmaj7
don't let the sun catch you cry - ing. The night - time / It may be

Fmaj7 Cmaj7 Fmaj7 Cmaj7 Fmaj7
shad - ows dis - ap - pear and with them go all your / hard to dis - cov - er that you've been left for an -

G G7 Am E7 Am
tears. For the morn - ing will bring joy for ev - 'ry girl and / oth - er. But don't for - get that life's a game and it can al - ways come a -

E7 Em Dm7 G7 Cmaj7 Fmaj7 Cmaj7 Fmaj7 D7 G
To Coda 𝄌
boy so / gain oh Don't let the sun catch you cry - ing. We know that

Am Dm
cry - ing's not a bad thing, but stop your cry - ing when the

G7
D.S. al Coda
birds sing.

CODA
𝄌 Fmaj7 Cmaj7 Fmaj7 Cmaj7
Don't let the sun catch you cry - ing. Oh no oh - oh - oh.

DON'T LOSE MY NUMBER

© 1984 PHILIP COLLINS LTD. and HIT & RUN MUSIC (PUBLISHING) LTD.
All Rights Controlled and Administered by EMI APRIL MUSIC INC.
Words and Music by
PHIL COLLINS
Moderately fast
Cm Bb/C Ab/C
1., 3. They came at night leav-ing fear be - hind, shad-ows all on the ground.
2. Search-ing through the day and in-to the night, they would-n't stop till they found him.
Cm Bb/C Ab/C
No-bod - y knew where to find him; no ev - i - dence was found. "I'm
They did - n't know him and they did - n't un - der-stand; they nev - er asked him why. "Get
Cm Bb/C Ab/C
nev - er com-ing back," they heard him cry, and I be - lieve him. Well,
out of my way," they heard him shout, then a blind - ing light, and
Cm Bb/C Fm Ab Bb
he nev - er meant to do an - y - thing wrong, but it's gon - na get worse if he waits too long.
all they could see was him run - ning down the street, out of the shad-ows and in-to the night.
Eb Fm7 Db Ab
Bil - ly, Bil - ly, don't you lose my num - ber 'cause you're not
Cm Bb Db
an - y - where that I can find you. Oh, now
Eb Fm7 Db Ab
Bil - ly, Bil - ly, don't you lose my num - ber 'cause you're not
Cm Bb Db
an - y - where that I can find you. Oh,
1
Cm Bb/C Cm Bb/C
no.

2
Gm F/G E♭/G F/G
don't give up, keep run - ning, keep hid - ing.
Gm F/G E♭/G F/G
Don't give up, Bil - ly, if you know you're right.
Gm F/G E♭/G F/G
Don't give up, you know that I am on your side.
Gm F/G E♭/G F/G
Don't give up, oh, Bil - ly, you bet - ter, you
G
bet - ter, you bet - ter run for your life.
Cm B♭/C Cm B♭/C
E♭ Fm7 D♭ A♭
Bil - ly, Bil - ly, don't you lose my num - ber 'cause you're not
Cm B♭ D♭
an - y - where that I can find you. Oh, now
E♭ Fm7 D♭ A♭
Bil - ly, Bil - ly, don't you lose my num - ber 'cause you're not
D.C. and Fade
Cm B♭ D♭
an - y - where that I can find you. Oh.

DON'T YOU WANT ME

Words and Music by PHIL OAKEY,
ADRIAN WRIGHT and JO CALLIS

Moderately fast
F Gsus G F C G
1. You were work - ing as a wait - ress in a cock - tail bar when I met you.
2. five years lat - er on you've got the world at your feet. Suc - cess has been so eas - y for you.
3., 4. (See additional lyrics)
F Gsus G F C G
I picked you out, I shook you up and turned you a - round, turned you in - to some - one new.
But don't for - get it's me who put you where you are now, and I can put you back there too.
1, 3
Now
2, 4
Am Em F
Don't, don't you want me? You know I can't be - lieve it when I
Dm Gsus G Am Em F
hear that you won't see me. Don't, don't you want me? You know I don't be - lieve you when you
Dm Gsus G A Bdim
say that you don't need me. It's much too late to find when you think you've changed your mind. You'd
Am/C E F G F G
bet - ter change it back or we will both be sor - ry. Don't you want me, ba - by? Don't you want me, oh?
F G F To Coda G D.S. al Coda (take repeat)
Don't you want me, ba - by? Don't you want me, oh? (3.) I was
CODA
G Am F Am 1 Em/A 2 Em/A
oh?
F G F G Repeat and Fade
Don't you want me, ba - by? Don't you want me, oh?

Additional Lyrics

3. I was working as a waitress in a cocktail bar,
   That much is true.
   But even then I knew I'd find a much better place
   Either with or without you.

4. The five years we had have been such good times,
   I still love you.
   But now I think it's time I live my life on my own.
   I guess it's just what I must do.

DON'T GIVE UP ON US

Words and Music by
TONY MACAULAY

Ballad
A Amaj7/G♯ D E/D
Don't give up on us, ba - by, don't make the wrong seem right, the
up on us, ba - by, we're still worth one more try, and
C♯m F♯m7 D A/C♯ To Coda
fu - ture is - n't just one night, it's writ - ten in the moon - light
tho' we put a last one by, just for a rain - y eve - ning
1 D A/C♯ Bm7 D/E 2 D
and paint - ed on the stars, we can't change ours. Don't give when may - be stars are
C♯sus C♯ Bm7 Dmaj7/A D/E A A7
few. Don't give up on us, I know we can still come through. I
F Fmaj9 Bm(add4) Bm7 A C♯/G♯
near - ly lost my head last night, you've got a right to stop be - liev - ing. There's still a lit - tle
F♯m D/E F Esus D/E A
love left e - ven so. Don't give up on us, ba - by,
Amaj7/G♯ D E/D C♯m F♯m7
Lord knows we've come this far, why can't we stay the way we are?
D A/C♯ D C♯sus C♯ Bm7
The an - gel and the dream - er who some - times plays a fool. Don't give up on us, I know
D/E A Amaj7/G♯ Dmaj7/F♯ A/E D E/D
we can still come through. (Instrumental)
C♯m7 F♯m7 D A/C♯ D
It's writ - ten in the moon - light and paint - ed on the stars,
A/C♯ D/A Bm7 D/E D.S. al Coda (2nd verse) CODA D C♯sus C♯
we can't change ours. Don't give when may - be stars are few. Don't give
Bm7 Dmaj7/A D/E A Amaj7/G♯ Dmaj7/F♯
up on us, I know we can still come through. Don't give up on us, ba - by,
A/E D D/E A(add9)
don't give up on us, ba - by. (Instrumental)

DON'T TALK TO STRANGERS

Words and Music by
RICK SPRINGFIELD

Moderately
When you were just a young girl and still in school, how come you never learned the
golden rule? Don't talk to strange men, don't be a fool, I'm hearin' stories, I don't
think that's cool!
N.C.
Why don't you tell me someone isn't lovin' you, 'cause you're my
Now who's this, Don Juan I've been hearin' of?
girl, some say it's no longer true. You're seein' some slick contin-
Love hurts when only one's in love. Did you fall at first sight did you
nental dude.
need a shove?
I'm beggin' you, please don't talk to strangers, (baby don't you talk). Don't talk to strangers (you know he'll only use you up).
Don't talk, don't talk, don't talk, don't talk, don't talk, don't talk to them don't talk,
To Coda
don't talk.
N.C.
Now tell me, how's life in the
big city? I hear the competition's tough, baby, that's a pity, and ev'ry
man's an actor, ev'ry girl is pretty. I don't like what's gettin' back to me.
D.S. al Coda

CODA

C♯m7 B A E/G♯

Fais l'a-mour a-vec moi (What she say?)

B A E/G♯ B A E/G♯ A B

I ask you now

Vien dor-mir mon a-mour Don-nes moi ton coeur ce soir I'm beg-gin' you:

B/E E B/C♯ E/C♯ B/E E B/C♯

Don't talk to stran-gers, (ba-by don't you talk) don't talk to stran-

E/C♯ B/A E/A B/A E/A C♯m

-gers (you know he'll on-ly use you up.)

Don't talk, don't talk, don't talk

B/C♯ E/C♯ B/C♯ E/C♯ B/A E/A B/A E/A

Repeat and Fade

don't talk, don't talk to, don't talk, don't talk.

DON'T STOP

Words and Music by
CHRISTINE McVIE

Medium Rock beat

E D A E D A

If you wake up and don't want to smile; if it takes just a lit-tle while,
Why not think a-bout times to come, and not a-bout the things that you've done.
All I want is to see you smile, if it takes just a lit-tle while.

E D A B

o-pen your eyes and look at the day. You'll see things in a dif-f'rent way.
If your life was bad to you, just think what to-mor-row will do.
I know you don't be-lieve that it's true. I nev-er meant an-y harm to you.

E D/E A E D/E A

Don't stop think-ing a-bout to-mor-row. Don't stop. It-'ll soon be here.

E D/E A B 1, 2

It-'ll be bet-ter than be-fore. Yes-ter-day's gone. Yes-ter-day's gone.

3 E D/E A E D/E A

Repeat and Fade

-ter-day's gone. Ooh, don't you look back.

DON'T KNOW WHY

Words and Music by
JESSE HARRIS

Moderately slow
B♭maj7 B♭7 E♭maj7 D+ Gm7 C7 F7sus B♭
I wait - ed till I saw the sun.
Some - thing has to make you run.
I don't know why I did - n't come.
B♭maj7 B♭7 E♭maj7 D+ Gm7 C7 F7sus B♭
I left you by the house of fun.
I feel as emp - ty as a drum.
I don't know why I did - n't come, I
Gm7 C7 To Coda F7sus B♭ F7sus B♭maj7 B♭7 E♭maj7 D+
don't know why I did - n't come.
When I saw the break of day,
Gm7 C7 F7sus B♭ B♭maj7 B♭7 E♭maj7 D+
I wished that I could fly a - way
'stead of kneel - ing in the sand
Gm7 C7 F7sus B♭ Gm7 C7
catch - ing tear - drops in my hand.
My heart is drenched in wine,
F7 Gm7 C7
(Instrumental)
but you'll be on my mind
F7 F7/E♭ B♭/D F/C B♭maj7 B♭7 E♭maj7 D+
for - ev - er.
Out a - cross the end - less sea,
Gm7 C7 F7sus B♭ B♭maj7 B♭7 E♭maj7 D+
I would die in ec - sta - sy.
But I'll be a bag of bones
Gm7 C7 F7sus B♭ Gm7
driv - ing down the road a - lone.
My heart is drenched
C7 F7 Gm7
in wine,
(Instrumental)
but you'll be on
C7 F7 D.S. al Coda
my mind for - ev - er.
CODA
F7 B♭ Gm7 C7 F7sus B♭
come.
I don't know why I did - n't come.

DOWNTOWN

Words and Music by
TONY HATCH

Medium Rock
G Gmaj7 C D7 G
When you're a - lone and life is mak - ing you lone - ly, you can al - ways go
Don't hang a - round and let your prob - lems sur - round you, there are mov - ie shows
(Instrumental)
C D G Gmaj7 C D7
down - town. When you've got wor - ries, all the noise and the hur - ry seems to
down - town. May - be you know some lit - tle plac - es to go to where they
G C D G
help, I know. Down - town. Just lis - ten to the mu - sic of the
nev - er close. Down - town. Just lis - ten to the rhy - thm of a
And you may find some - bod - y kind to
Em G
traf - fic in the cit - y. Lin - ger on the side - walk where the
gen - tle Bos - sa No - va. You'll be danc - ing with 'em too be -
help and un - der - stand you. Some - one who is just like you and
Em Bm C
ne - on signs are pret - ty. How can you lose? The lights are much
fore the night is o - ver, hap - py a - gain.
needs a gen - tle hand to guide them a - long. So, may - be I'll
Em7 A Em7 A G Gmaj7
bright - er there, you can for - get all your trou - bles, for - get all your cares. So go down - town
see you there, we can for - get all our trou - bles, for - get all our cares. So go down - town
Am7 D6 D9 G Gmaj7 Am7 D6 D9
things - 'll be great when you're down - town no fin - er place for sure
where all the lights are bright down - town wait - ing for you, to - night
things - 'll be great when you're down - town don't wait a min - ute more
G Gmaj7 Am7 D6 D9 1, 2 G Am7 Gmaj7 Am7 Gmaj7 Am7
down - town. Ev - 'ry - thing's wait - ing for you. Down - town.
down - town. You're gon - na be al - right now. Down - town.
down - town. Ev - 'ry - thing's wait - ing for
Gmaj7 Am7 3 G Am7 G Am7 G Am7 G Am7 Gmaj7
you. Down - town. Down - town.

DRIFT AWAY

Words and Music by
MENTOR WILLIAMS

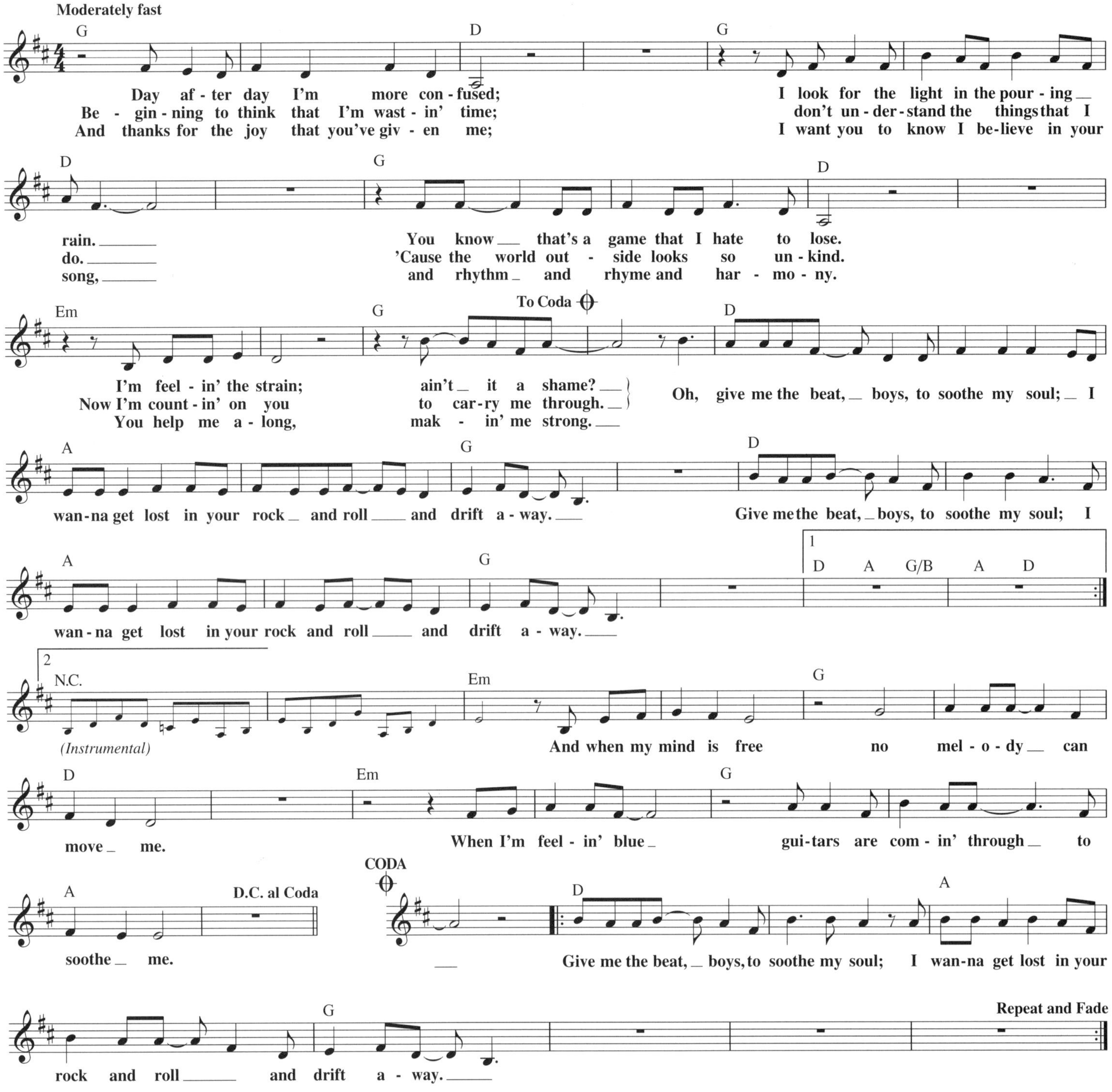

Moderately fast

G D G

Day af - ter day I'm more con - fused; I look for the light in the pour - ing
Be - gin - ning to think that I'm wast - in' time; don't un - der - stand the things that I
And thanks for the joy that you've giv - en me; I want you to know I be - lieve in your

D G D

rain. You know that's a game that I hate to lose.
do. 'Cause the world out - side looks so un - kind.
song, and rhythm and rhyme and har - mo - ny.

Em G To Coda D

I'm feel - in' the strain; ain't it a shame?
Now I'm count - in' on you to car - ry me through.
You help me a - long, mak - in' me strong.
Oh, give me the beat, boys, to soothe my soul; I

A G D

wan - na get lost in your rock and roll and drift a - way. Give me the beat, boys, to soothe my soul; I

A G 1 D A G/B A D

wan - na get lost in your rock and roll and drift a - way.

2 N.C. Em G

(Instrumental) And when my mind is free no mel - o - dy can

D Em G

move me. When I'm feel - in' blue gui - tars are com - in' through to

A D.C. al Coda

soothe me.

CODA D A

Give me the beat, boys, to soothe my soul; I wan - na get lost in your

G Repeat and Fade

rock and roll and drift a - way.

DREAMER

Words and Music by RICK DAVIES
and ROGER HODGSON

Moderately fast
D A7sus A7 D A7sus A7
Dream - er, you know you are a dream - er. Well, can you put your
you're noth - ing but a dream - er. Well, can you put your
you stu - pid lit - tle dream - er. So now you put your
C 1 Fmaj7 G 2 Fmaj7 G Fmaj7 G
hands in your head, oh no! I said no! I said
hands in your head, oh
head in your hands, oh

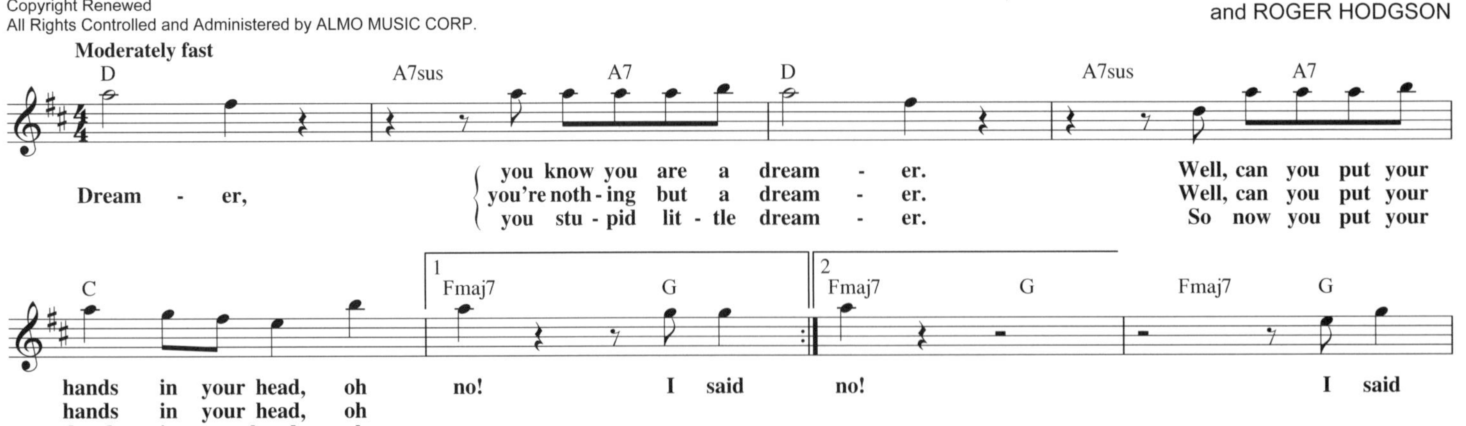

A♭ B♭(add9) Gm C A♭
"Far out, what a day, a year, a laugh it is." You
D.C. al Coda
(take 2nd ending)
B♭(add9) Gm C To Coda Gm C
know well you know you had it com-in' to you, now there's not a lot I can do.
CODA
Gm C
now there's not a lot I can do. If I could see some-thing...
B♭/C C B♭/C
(You can see an-y-thing you want, boy.) If I could be some-one. (You can be an-y-one.
C
Cel-e-brate, boy.) Well, if I can do some-thing... (Well, you can do some-thing.) If
B♭/C
I could do an-y-thing...
(But can you do some-thing out of this world?)
C
(Ah.) Take a dream on a
Gm7/C C
Sun-day. (Instrumental) I'll take a life, take a hol-i-day. (Instrumental)
Gm7/C
Take a lie, take a dream-er. (Instrumental) Dream, (dream,) dream, (dream,) dream, (dream,) dream, dream a-
C F/C C F/C C F/C C F/C C B♭maj7 C/B♭ B♭ C/B♭ B♭ C/B♭ B♭ C/B♭ B♭
long...
C
Dream-er. (Dream-er, dream a-long. Come on, you dream-er, dream a-long.) Roll it on.
B♭maj7 D A7sus A7 D
(Come on, you dream-er, dream a-long. Dream-er, you know you are a dream-er.
A7sus A7 C Fmaj7 G Fmaj7 G Fmaj7 G
Can you put your hands in your head, oh no! I said, no! Oh no! (Instrumental)
N.C.
Fade out

EARLY IN THE MORNING

Words and Music by MIKE LEANDER
and EDDIE SEAGO

Moderately

Gm Cm Cm6 F7 Gm F7/A B♭
Eve - ning is the time of day I find noth - ing much to
Night - time is - n't clear to me. I find noth - ing near to

Gm Edim7 E♭7 D7 C/E D7/F♯ Gm D7sus G Am G/B
say. Don't know what to do, but I come to when it's
me. Don't know what to do, but I come to when it's

Cm Cm7 F7 B♭ B♭maj7 E♭maj7
(1., D.S.) ear - ly in the morn - ing. O - ver by the win - dow, day is dawn - ing. When I feel the
(2.) ear - ly in the morn - ing. Ver - y, ver - y ear - ly, with - out warn - ing, I can feel a

Am7 D7 Gm D7 G Am G/B
air, I feel that life is ver - y good to me, you know. In the
new - ly born vi - bra - tion sneak - ing up on me a - gain. There's a

Cm Cm7 F7 B♭ B♭maj7 E♭maj7
sun, there's so much yel - low. Some - thing in the ear - ly morn - ing mead - ow tells me that to -
song - bird on my pil - low, I can see the fun in weep - ing wil - low, I can see the

Am7 D7 To Coda 1 Gm D7/F♯ Gm
day you're on your way and you'll be com - ing home, home to me.
sun. You're on your way and you'll be com - ing

F D7/F♯ 2 Gm D7 G Am G/B D.S. al Coda
home to me. When it's
CODA Gm D7/F♯
home, home to me, home to

Gm F D7/F♯ Gm
me.

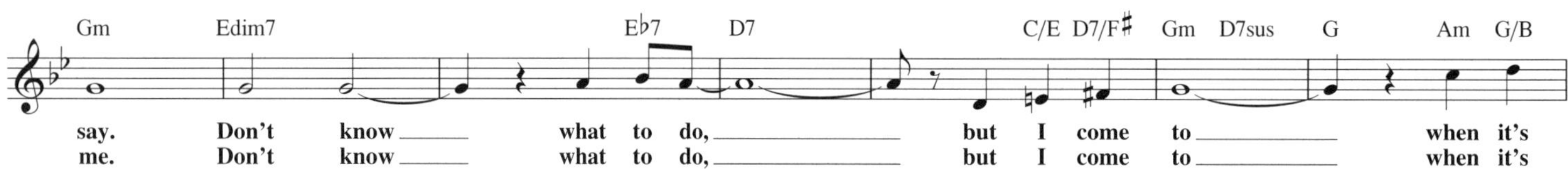

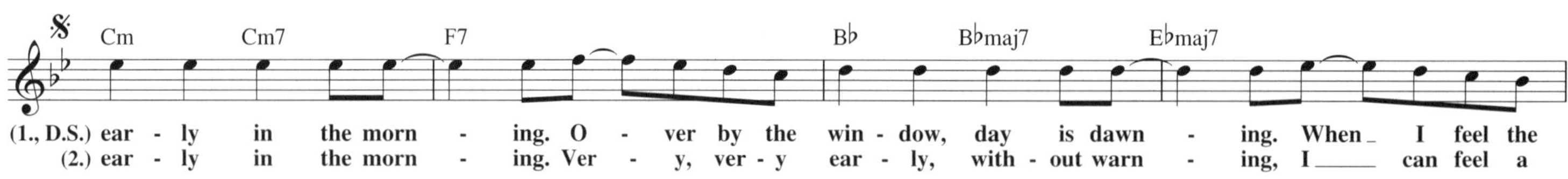

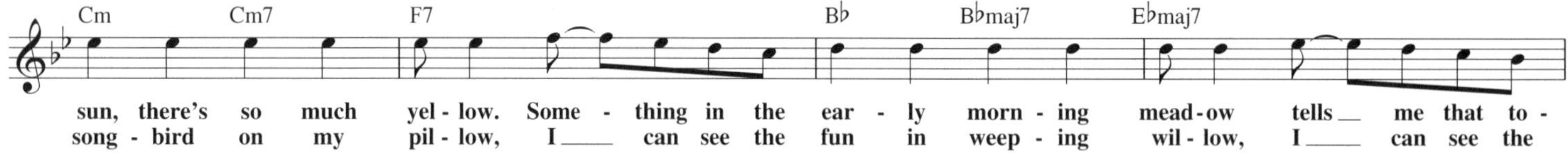

EBONY AND IVORY

Words and Music by
PAUL McCARTNEY

Moderately
E F#m7 E F#m7
Eb - o - ny and i - vo - ry live to - geth - er in per - fect har - mo - ny, side by
E F#m7 A B E C#m B G#m A F#m7
side on my pian - o key - board, oh Lord, why don't we?
E C#m B A E
We all know that peo - ple are the same wher - ev - er you go. There is good and bad in ev -
B D6 Ddim7 C#7 F#m
- 'ry - one, we learn to live we learn to give each oth - er what we need to sur - vive to -
A E F#m7 E
geth - er a - live. Eb - o - ny and i - vo - ry live to - geth - er in per - fect
F#m7 E F#7 B A B E To Coda
har - mo - ny, side by side on my pian - o key - board, oh Lord, why don't we?
Double tempo
C#sus C# F# G#7sus C#
Eb - o - ny, i - vo - ry, liv - ing in per - fect har - mo - ny,
F# A D.S. a Tempo I CODA C#sus C#
Eb - o - ny, i - vo - ry, ooh. Side by
F#m7 B A B E F#m7
side on my pian - o key - board, oh Lord, why don't we?
Double tempo Repeat and Fade
E F#m7 E F#m7 B
Eb - o - ny, i - vo - ry, liv - ing in per - fect har - mo - ny.

EDDIE MY LOVE

Words and Music by AARON COLLINS,
MAXWELL DAVIS and SAUL SAM LING

Slowly
C Am7 Dm7 G7 C Am7
Ed - die my love, I love you so. How I want - ed for you,
Dm7 C Am Dm7 G7
You'll nev - er know. Please, Ed - die, don't make me wait too
C Am7 Dm7 G7 C Am7 Dm7 G7
long. Ed - die please write. me one line.
C Am7 Dm7 C Am7
Tell me your love is still on - ly mine. Please, Ed - die,
Dm7 G7 C F C G7 F
don't make me wait too long. You left me last Sep -
C F C F
tem - ber to re - turn to me be - fore long. But all I do is cry
C Dm7 G7
my - self to sleep, Ed - die, since you've been go - o - one.
C Am7 Dm7 G7 C Am7
Ed - die my love, I'm sink - ing fast, The ver - y next day
Dm7 C Am7 Dm7 G7
might be my last. Please, Ed - die, don't make me wait too
1 C F C C7 2 C
long. You lo - o - ong.

ERES TU/TOUCH THE WIND

Words and Music by
JUAN C. CALDERON

Slowly
I woke up this morn - ing, and my mind fell a - way, look-ing back sad - ly from to -
mor - row. As I heard an ech - o from the past soft - ly say, come
back, come back, won't you stay?
Want - ed to reach you, let you know I still care.
And on - ly for - ev - er can I say I love you.
I'm lost in the si - lence of my sor - row. And I put a prom - ise in the
And on - ly for - ev - er have I lost you. But, on - ly a dream - er could wake
wind, on the air, to fly a - way to you there.
up, as I do, and hope it's still yes - ter - day.
Touch the wind, catch my love as it goes sail - ing. Touch the wind, and I'll be
close to you I'll be eas - y to find, oo
on the wings of the morn - ing I'll go sail - ing. I'll be eas - y to find,
oo and I'll be, ba - by, I'll be close to you. you.

867-5309/JENNY

Words and Music by ALEX CALL
and JAMES KELLER

Moderately bright four
Jen - ny, Jen - ny, who can I turn to?
Jen - ny, Jen - ny, you're the girl for me.
You give me some-thing I can hold on to.
You don't know me but you make me so hap - py.
I know you'll think I'm like the oth - ers be - fore,
I tried to call you be - fore but I lost my nerve. I
who saw your name and num - ber on the wall.
tried my i - mag - i - na - tion but I was dis - turbed.
Jen - ny, I've got your num - ber, I need to make you mine.
Jen - ny, don't change your num - ber. Eight six sev - en five three "o" nine,
(I've called)
eight six sev - en five three "o" nine, eight six sev - en five three "o" nine,
To Coda
eight six sev - en five three "o" nine. I got it, I got it,
(I got it.)
I got your num - ber on the wall. I got it, I got it for a
(I got it.)
good time, for a good time call.

B♭ C Gm E♭/G B♭ C
D.S. al Coda
CODA
Gm E♭/G B♭ C
Jen - ny, Jen - ny, who can I turn to?
Gm E♭/G B♭ C Gm E♭/G B♭ C
3
3
Eight six sev - en five three "o" nine
For the price of a dime I can al - ways turn to
Gm E♭/G B♭ C Gm E♭/G B♭ C
Repeat and Fade
Eight six sev - en five three "o" nine, eight six sev - en five three "o" nine.
you.

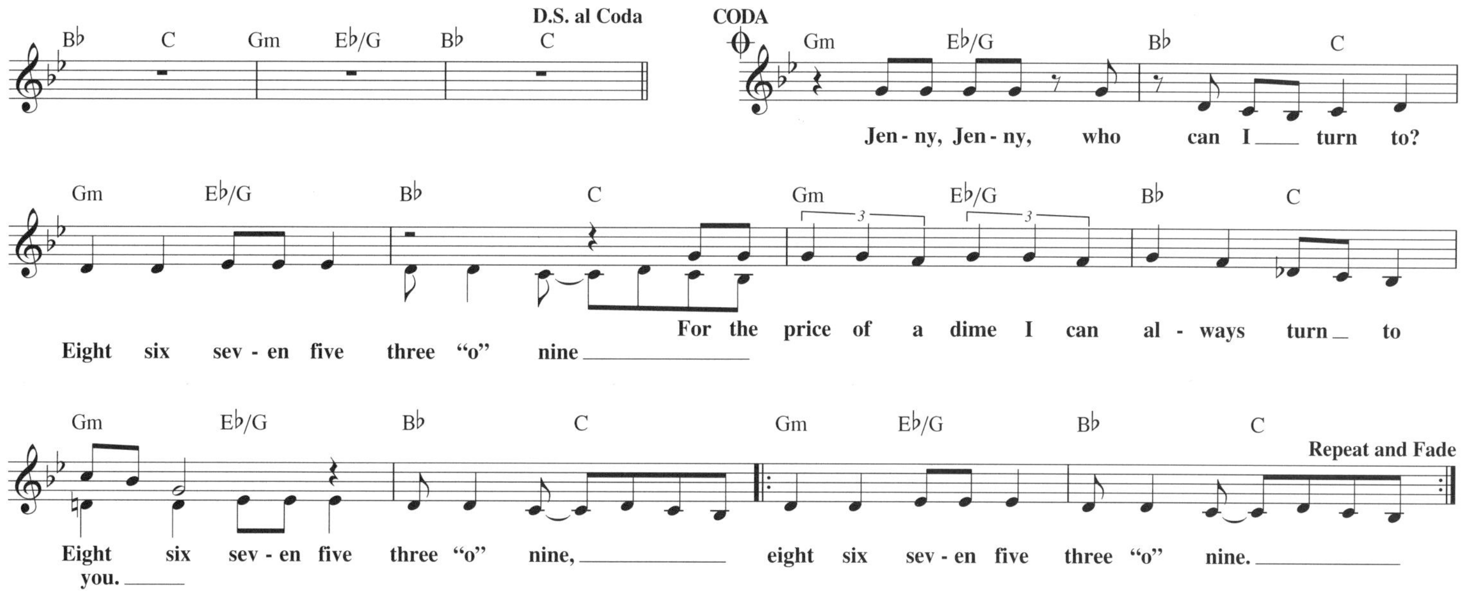

ENDLESSLY

Words and Music by CLYDE OTIS
and BROOK BENTON

Brightly
F B♭ F B♭ F B♭ Bdim7
High - er than the high - est moun - tain and deep - er than the deep - est sea, that's how I will
Soft - er than the gen - tle breez - es and strong - er than a wild oak tree, that's how I will

F Dm F B♭ F B♭ F
3
love you, dar - ling, end - less - ly.
hold you, dar - ling, end - less - ly.
Oh, my love, you are my heav - en, you are my

Gm C7 F B♭ Am Dm G7
king - dom, you are my crown. Oh, my love, you're all I prayed for, you were made for

3
C7 F B♭ F B♭
these arms to sur - round. Faith - ful as a morn - ing sun - rise and sa - cred as a love can

F B♭ Bdim7 F Dm F B♭ F
Repeat and Fade
be, that's how I will love you, dar - ling, end - less - ly. End - less -

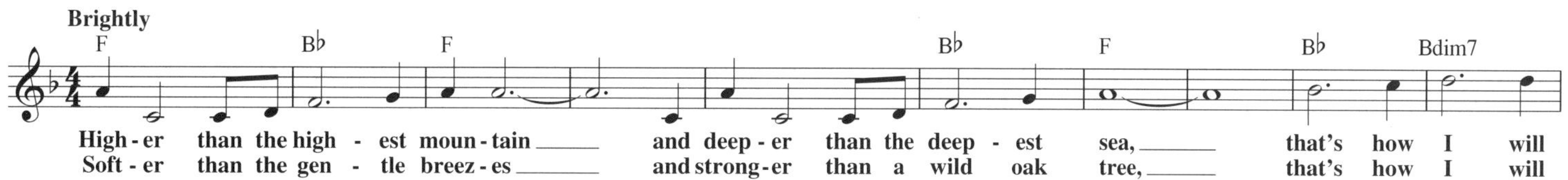

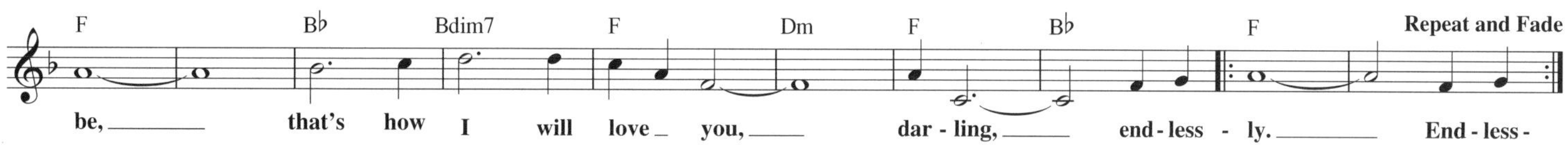

EVE OF DESTRUCTION

Words and Music by P.F. SLOAN
and STEVE BARRI

Moderately, with intensity
1. The East - ern world it is ex - plod - in', vi - o - lence flar - in' and bul - lets load - in'. You're
3. (See additional lyrics)
old e - nough to kill, but not for vot - in'. You don't be - lieve in war, but what's that gun you're tot - tin'? And
e - ven the Jor - dan Riv - er has bod - ies float - in'! But you tell me o - ver and o - ver and o -
- ver a - gain, my friend, ah, you don't be - lieve we're on the eve of des -
truc - tion.
(Instrumental)
2. Don't you un - der - stand what I'm try'n to say? Can't you feel the fears that I'm feel - in' to - day? If the
4. (See additional lyrics)
but - ton is pushed, there's no run - ning a - way. There'll be no one to save with the
world in a grave. Take a look a - round you, boy, it's bound to scare you, boy. And you tell me
o - ver and o - ver and o - ver a - gain, my friend, ah, you don't be - lieve we're on the eve of des -
truc - tion.

2
D G A
Yeah, my You don't be - lieve we're on the eye of des -
D G D
truc - tion.
(Instrumental)

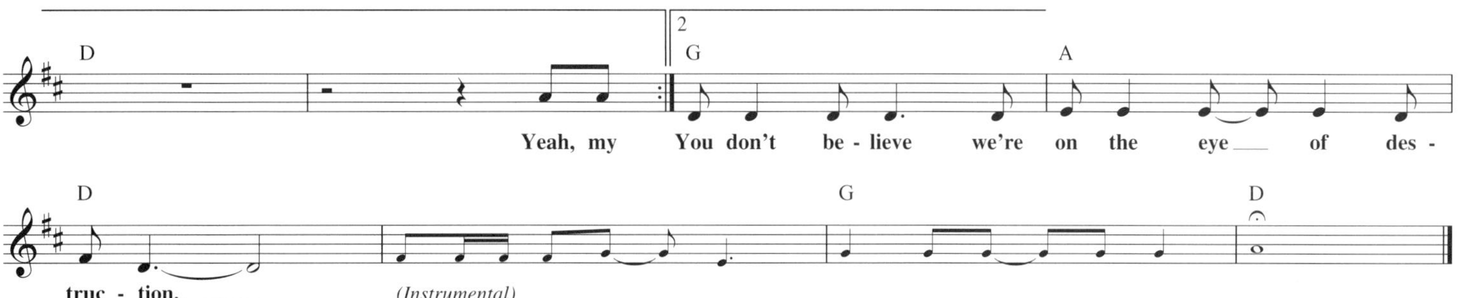

Additional Lyrics

3. Yeah, my blood's so mad feels like coagulatin'
I'm sittin' here just comtemplatin'
You can't twist the truth it knows no regulatin'
And a handful of senators don't pass legistlation
Marches alone can't bring integration
When human respect is disintegratin
This whole crazy world is just too frustratin'.

4. Think of all the hate there is in Red China
Then take a look around to Selma, Alabama!
You may leave here for four days in space
But when you return, it's the same old place,
The pounding drums, the pride and disgrace
You can bury your dead, but don't leave a trace
Hate your next door neighbor, but don't forget to say grace.

EVERYBODY LOVES SOMEBODY

Words by IRVING TAYLOR
Music by KEN LANE

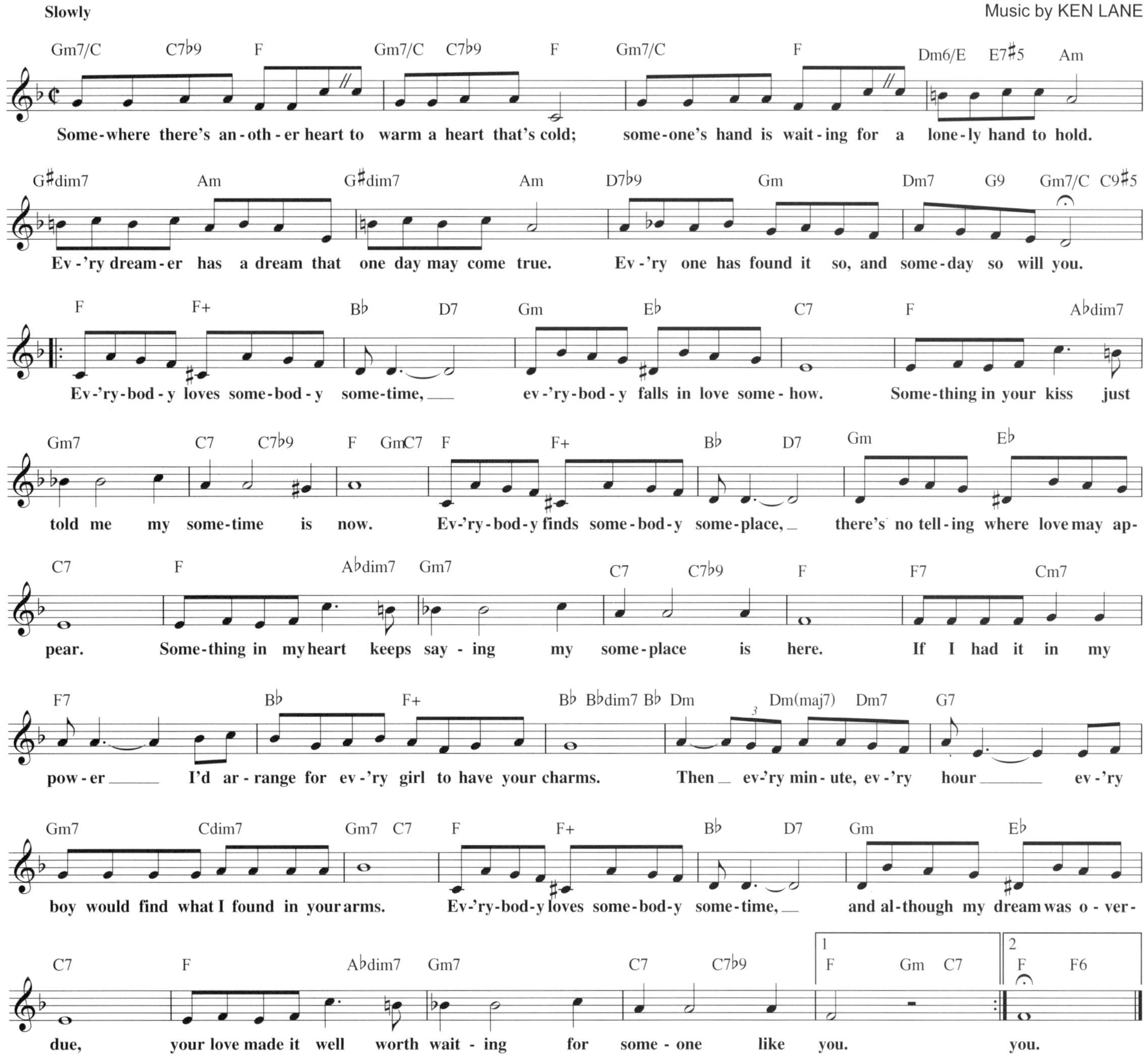
Slowly
Gm7/C C7♭9 F Gm7/C C7♭9 F Gm7/C F Dm6/E E7♯5 Am
Some-where there's an-oth - er heart to warm a heart that's cold; some-one's hand is wait - ing for a lone - ly hand to hold.
G♯dim7 Am G♯dim7 Am D7♭9 Gm Dm7 G9 Gm7/C C9♯5
Ev - 'ry dream - er has a dream that one day may come true. Ev - 'ry one has found it so, and some - day so will you.
F F+ B♭ D7 Gm E♭ C7 F A♭dim7
Ev-'ry-bod - y loves some-bod - y some-time, ev - 'ry-bod - y falls in love some - how. Some-thing in your kiss just
Gm7 C7 C7♭9 F Gm C7 F F+ B♭ D7 Gm E♭
told me my some-time is now. Ev-'ry-bod-y finds some-bod-y some-place, there's no tell-ing where love may ap-
C7 F A♭dim7 Gm7 C7 C7♭9 F F7 Cm7
pear. Some-thing in my heart keeps say - ing my some-place is here. If I had it in my
F7 B♭ F+ B♭ B♭dim7 B♭ Dm Dm(maj7) Dm7 G7
pow - er I'd ar - range for ev - 'ry girl to have your charms. Then ev-'ry min- ute, ev - 'ry hour ev - 'ry
Gm7 Cdim7 Gm7 C7 F F+ B♭ D7 Gm E♭
boy would find what I found in your arms. Ev-'ry-bod-y loves some-bod-y some-time, and al-though my dream was o - ver-
C7 F A♭dim7 Gm7 C7 C7♭9 1 F Gm C7 2 F F6
due, your love made it well worth wait - ing for some - one like you. you.

ELI'S COMIN'

Words and Music by
LAURA NYRO

Freely
N.C. Cm7 Gm7 A♭maj7
E - li's com - in', E - li's a - com - in'! Whoa, you bet - ter hide your heart, your
Gm7 Fm7/B♭ Bright Gospel Rock F7 Fm7 C
lov - in' heart. E - li's a - com - in' and the cards say bro - ken heart, oh, bro - ken heart!
C7 F Fm7 B♭/F Fm7
E - li's com - in', hide your heart, girl, E - li's com - in', hide your heart girl.
F Fm7 B♭/F E♭/F F
Girl, E - li's a - com - in', bet - ter hide. Girl, E - li's a - com - in', bet - ter hide your heart! Your
Fm7 B♭/F Fm7 F Fm7 B♭/F
heart! E - li's com - in', hide your heart! You bet - ter, bet - ter hide your heart!
E♭/F Fm7
E - li's com - in', bet - ter walk, walk, but you'll nev - er get a - way, so you'll nev - er get a - way from the burn and the heart - ache,
E - li's com - in', bet - ter walk, cry, but he's nev - er gon - na hear, no, he's nev - er gon - na hear, and he ain't gon - na fol - low,
Gm7 Gm7/C C Fm Fm7/B♭
I walked to A - pol - lo and the bay and ev - 'ry - where I go, whoa!
I cried at the cor - ners of the square, and ev - 'ry - where I go, whoa!
E - li's a -
com - in', E - li's a - com - in', E - li's a - com - in' and he's com - in' to get me, ma - ma!
1 G5 G F Fm7 B♭/C A♭/C 2 G5 G
I'm down on my knees. E - li's com - in', hide it! I'm down on my knees.
G5 Dm7/G G(N.C.) Cm
I'm down on my knees. Oh, no, no, no!
F(♯9) Fm7 B♭/F Fm7 F(♯9) Fm7
Hide it! Whoa, hide it! Hide it! Hide it! Hide it! Whoa, hide it!
B♭/F Cm7 Freely F(N.C.) A♭(N.C.)
Hide it! E - li's com - in'. E - li's a - com - in'. Bet - ter
Gm7 Slowly (a tempo) Fm7 Gm7 Fm7 Repeat and Fade
hide! E - li's com - in', bet - ter hide your heart, girl. E - li's com - in', bet - ter hide your heart, girl.

EVERY ROSE HAS ITS THORN

Words and Music by BOBBY DALL, BRETT MICHAELS,
BRUCE JOHANNESSON and RIKKI ROCKETT

Moderately

G C(add9)
We both lie si - lent - ly still __ in the dead of the night. __ Al - though we
lis - ten to our fa - vor - ite song ____ play - ing on the ra - di - o, ____ hear the

G C(add9)
both lie close to - geth - er __ we feel miles a - part __ in - side. ___ Was it
D. J. say love's a game of eas - y come __ and eas - y go. __ But I

G C(add9) G C(add9)
some - thing I said or some - thing I did? Did my words not come out right? __ Though I
won - der does he know, ____ has he ev - er felt __ like this? And I

D C G
tried not to hurt you, __ though I tried. But I guess that's why __ they say, }
know that you'd be here right now if I __ could - 've let you __ know some - how. __ I guess }
ev - 'ry rose has its

C(add9) G C(add9) G D
thorn, just like ev - 'ry night has its dawn. ____ Just like ev - 'ry cow - boy __ sings his

C G | 1 C G C(add9) | 2 C(add9)
sad, sad __ song, ev - 'ry rose has its thorn. I thorn.

Em D C G
Though it's been a - while __ now I can still feel so much pain. __

Em D C G
Like the knife that cuts __ you, the wound heals, but the scar, that scar re - mains.

C(add9) G C(add9) G
I know I could have saved our love that night __ if I'd

C(add9) G C(add9)
known what to say. __ In - stead of mak - ing love __ we both made our sep - 'rate ways. __ Now I

G C(add9) G C
hear you've found some - bod - y new __ and that I nev - er meant that much to you. __ To

D C G
hear that tears me up in - side __ and to see you cuts me like a knife. I guess ev - 'ry rose has its

C(add9) G C(add9) G D
thorn, just like ev - 'ry night has its dawn. ____ Just like ev - 'ry cow - boy __ sings his

C(add9) G C(add9) D G
sad, sad __ song, ev - 'ry rose has its thorn.

EASY

Words and Music by
LIONEL RICHIE

Moderately

A♭ Cm7 B♭m7 B♭m7/E♭
Know it sound fun - ny, but I just can't stand the pain; __

A♭ Cm7 B♭m7 B♭m7/E♭ A♭ Cm7
girl, I'm leav - ing you __ to - mor - row. ________ Seems to me, _ girl, you know I've done all _

B♭m7 B♭m7/E♭ A♭ Cm7 B♭m7
— I can. You see, I begged, stole __ and I bor - rowed, _ yeah. _

B♭m7/E♭ 𝄋 A♭ Cm7 B♭m7 B♭m7/E♭
Ooh, that's why I'm eas - y. _____ I'm eas - y like Sun - day morn -

A♭ Cm7 B♭m7 B♭m7/E♭ A♭ Cm7
- ing. That's why I'm eas - y. ________________

B♭m7 B♭m7/E♭ G♭ D♭/F D♭/E♭ To Coda 𝄌 A♭
— I'm eas - y like Sun - day morn - ing.

Cm7 B♭m7 B♭m7/E♭
Why in the world _ would an - y - bod - y put chains __ on me? __

A♭ Cm7 B♭m7 B♭m7/E♭
I've paid __ my dues __ to make it. ______________________

A♭ Cm7 B♭m7 B♭m7/E♭
Ev - 'ry - bod - y wants _ me to be ___ what they want ___ me to be. ___

A♭ Cm7 B♭m7 B♭m7/E♭ D.S. al Coda
I'm not hap - py when I try to fake __ it, ________ no. _ Ooh, _____ that's why I'm eas -

CODA 𝄌
A♭ G♭maj7 Fm7 E♭m7 E♭m7/A♭ D♭/F
ing. I wan - na be high, ___________ so _________ high. I wan - na be

G♭maj7 Fm7 E♭m7 E♭m7/A♭ D♭ G♭maj7 Fm7
free to know _ the things _ I do _ are right. ______________ I wan - na be free, __ just ____

E♭m7 E♭m7/A♭ C♭/G♭ G♭/D♭ C♭/E♭ D♭ A♭ Cm7
me, oh, ____________ babe. *(Instrumental)*

B♭m7 B♭m7/E♭ A♭ Cm7 1 B♭m7 B♭m7/E♭ 2 B♭m7
That's why I'm eas -
A♭ Cm7 B♭m7 B♭m7/E♭ A♭ Cm7 B♭m7 B♭m7/E♭
- y. I'm eas - y like Sun - day morn - ing. That's why I'm eas -
Repeat and Fade
A♭ Cm7 B♭m7 B♭m7/E♭ A♭ Cm7 B♭m7 B♭m7/E♭
- y. I'm eas - y like Sun - day morn - ing. 'Cause I'm eas -

EYE OF THE TIGER

Theme from ROCKY III

Words and Music by FRANK SULLIVAN
and JIM PETERIK

Medium Rock beat

Cm A♭/C B♭/C Cm
Ris - in' up, back on the street, did my time, took my chanc - es.

A♭/C B♭/C Cm
Went the dis - tance. Now I'm back on my feet, just a man and his will to sur - vive.

A♭/C B♭/C Cm
So man - y times it hap - pens too fast. You trade your pas - sion for glo - ry.
Face to face, out in the heat, Hang - in' tough, stay - in' hun - gry.
Ris - in' up, straight to the top. Had the guts, got the glo - ry.

A♭/C B♭/C
Don't lose your grip on the dreams of the past. You must fight just to keep them a - live.
They stack the odds, still we take to the street for the kill with the skill to sur - vive.
Went the dis - tance. Now I'm not gon - na stop, just a man and his will to sur - vive.

Cm B♭ Cm7 Fm E♭/G B♭ Cm7 Fm
It's the eye of the ti - ger. It's the thrill of the fight, ris - in' up to the chal-lenge of our

Cm B♭ Cm7 Fm E♭/G B♭ Cm7 Fm E♭/G
ri - val. And the last known sur-vi - vor stalks his prey in the night, and he's watch-in' us all with the

1, 2 A♭ Cm 3 A♭ Cm
eye of the ti - ger. eye of the ti - ger.

FEELS LIKE THE FIRST TIME

Words and Music by
MICK JONES

Moderate Rock beat

G F/G Am/G G

I would climb an - y moun - tain, sail a - cross a storm - y sea, __
I have wait - ed a life - time, spent my time so fool - ish - ly. __

F/G Am/G G

if that's _ what it takes me, ba - by, to show how much you mean _ to me, __
But now __ that I've found _ you, ____ to - geth - er we'll make his - to - ry. __

D/A A D/A A

And I guess it's just the wom - an in __ you __ that brings out the man in __ me. ____
And I know it must be the wom - an in __ you __ that brings out the man in __ me. ____

E/B B E/B To Coda B C G

I know _ I can't help my - self; you're all __ in the world to me. ____
I know _ I can't help my - self; you're all ____ my eyes can see. _

F/G Am/G G

It feels _ like the first time; _ it feels _ like the ver - y first _ time.

F/G Am/G G D.C. al Coda

It feels _ like the first time; _ it feels _ like the ver - y first time. _

CODA

B N.C. Em D C

__ And it feels like the first __ time, like it

B Em D C

nev - er __ did be - fore. Feels like the first __ time, like we've

B Em D C

o - pened _ up the door. Feels like the first ___ time, like it

B C

nev - er will a - gain, ____ nev - er a - gain. _

G F/G Am/G G Repeat and Fade

It feels _ like the first time; _ it feels _ like the ver - y first _ time.

FIELDS OF GOLD

Music and Lyrics by
STING

Flowing, moderately
You'll re - mem - ber me when the west wind moves up - on the fields of bar - ley. You'll for -
stay with me, will you be my love a - mong the fields of bar - ley? We'll for -
get the sun in his jeal - ous sky as we walk in fields of gold.
get the sun in his jeal - ous sky as we lie in fields of gold.
So she took her love for to gaze a - while up - on the fields of bar - ley. In his
See the west wind move like a lov - er so up - on the fields of bar - ley. Feel her
arms she fell as her hair came down a - mong the fields of gold. Will you
bod - y rise when you kiss her mouth a - mong the fields of gold.
I nev - er made prom - is - es light - ly and there have been some that I've bro - ken, but I swear in the
days still left we'll walk in fields of gold. We'll walk in fields of gold.
(Instrumental)
Man - y years have passed since those sum - mer days a -
mem - ber me when the west wind moves up -
mong the fields of bar - ley. See the chil - dren run as the sun goes down a - mong the fields of gold.
on the fields of bar - ley. You can tell the sun in his jeal - ous sky when we walked in fields of gold,
You'll re - when we walked in fields of gold, when we walked in fields of gold.
(Instrumental)

FERNANDO

Words and Music by BENNY ANDERSSON,
BJORN ULVAEUS and STIG ANDERSON

Moderately
A
Can you hear the drums, Fer - nan - do?
They were clos - er now, Fer - nan - do.
Now we're old and grey, Fer - nan - do,
I re - mem - ber long a -
Ev - 'ry ho - ur, ev - 'ry
and since man - y years I
F♯m
go an - oth - er star - ry night like this.
min - ute seemed to last e - ter - nal - ly.
have - n't seen a ri - fle in your hand.
In the fi - re - light, Fer -
I was so a - fraid, Fer -
Can you hear the drums, Fer -
Bm
nan - do,
nan - do,
nan - do?
you were hum - ming to your - self and soft - ly strum - ming your gui -
we were young and full of life and none of us pre - pared to
Do you still re - call the fright - ful night we crossed the Ri - o
E
tar. I could hear the dis - tant drums and sounds of bu - gle calls were
die. And I'm not a - shamed to say the roar of guns and can - nons
Grande? I can see it in your eyes how proud you were to fight for
1
A
com - ing from a - far.
2, 3
al - most made me cry.
free - dom in this land.
A
E7
There was some - thing in the air that night, the stars
were bright, Fer - nan - do.
They were shin - ing there for you and me, for lib -
er - ty, Fer - nan - do.
Gdim7
F♯
Though we nev - er thought that we could lose, there's no re - gret.
B7
If I had to do the same a - gain, I would, my friend, Fer - nan - do.
To Coda
If I had to do the same a - gain, I would, my friend, Fer - nan - do.
D
(Instrumental)
D.C. al Coda
(take 2nd ending)

CODA
A
E7
A
There was some-thing in the air that night, the stars were bright, Fer-nan - do.
E7
A
They were shin-ing there for you and me, for lib - er - ty, Fer-nan - do. Though we
Gdim7
F♯
B7
nev - er thought that we could lose, there's no re - gret.
If I had to do the
E7
A
Repeat and Fade
same a - gain, I would, my friend, Fer-nan - do.
If I had to do the

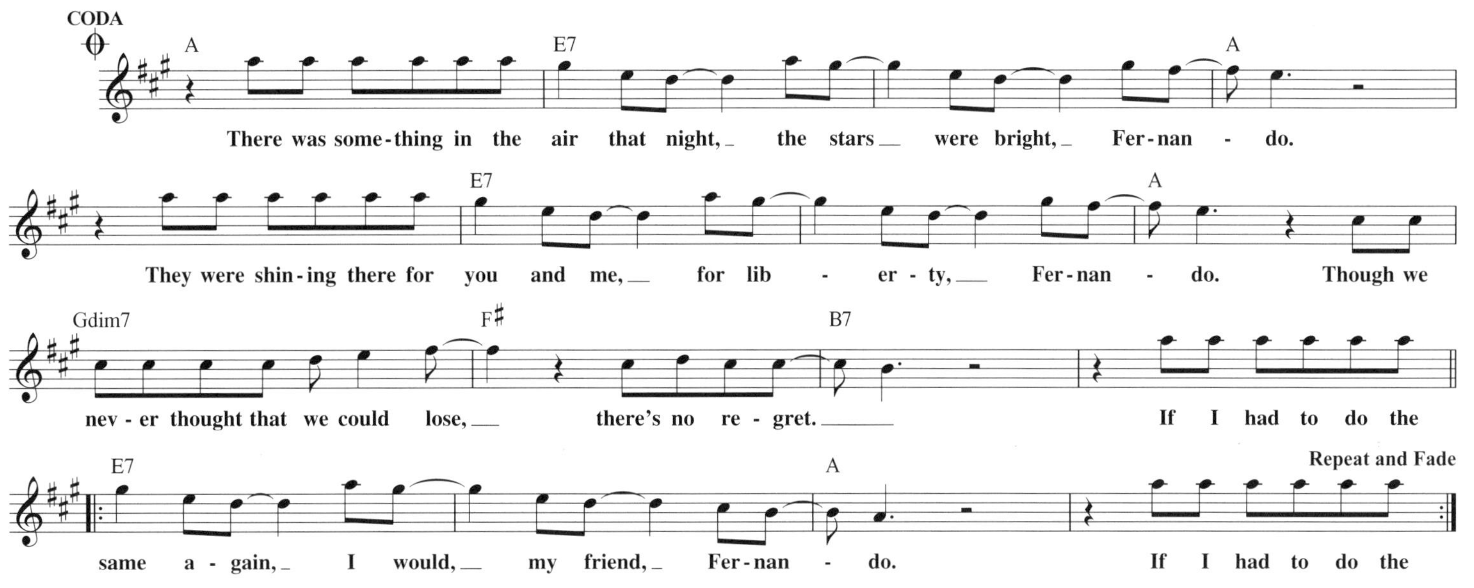

FEEL LIKE MAKIN' LOVE

Words and Music by
EUGENE McDANIELS

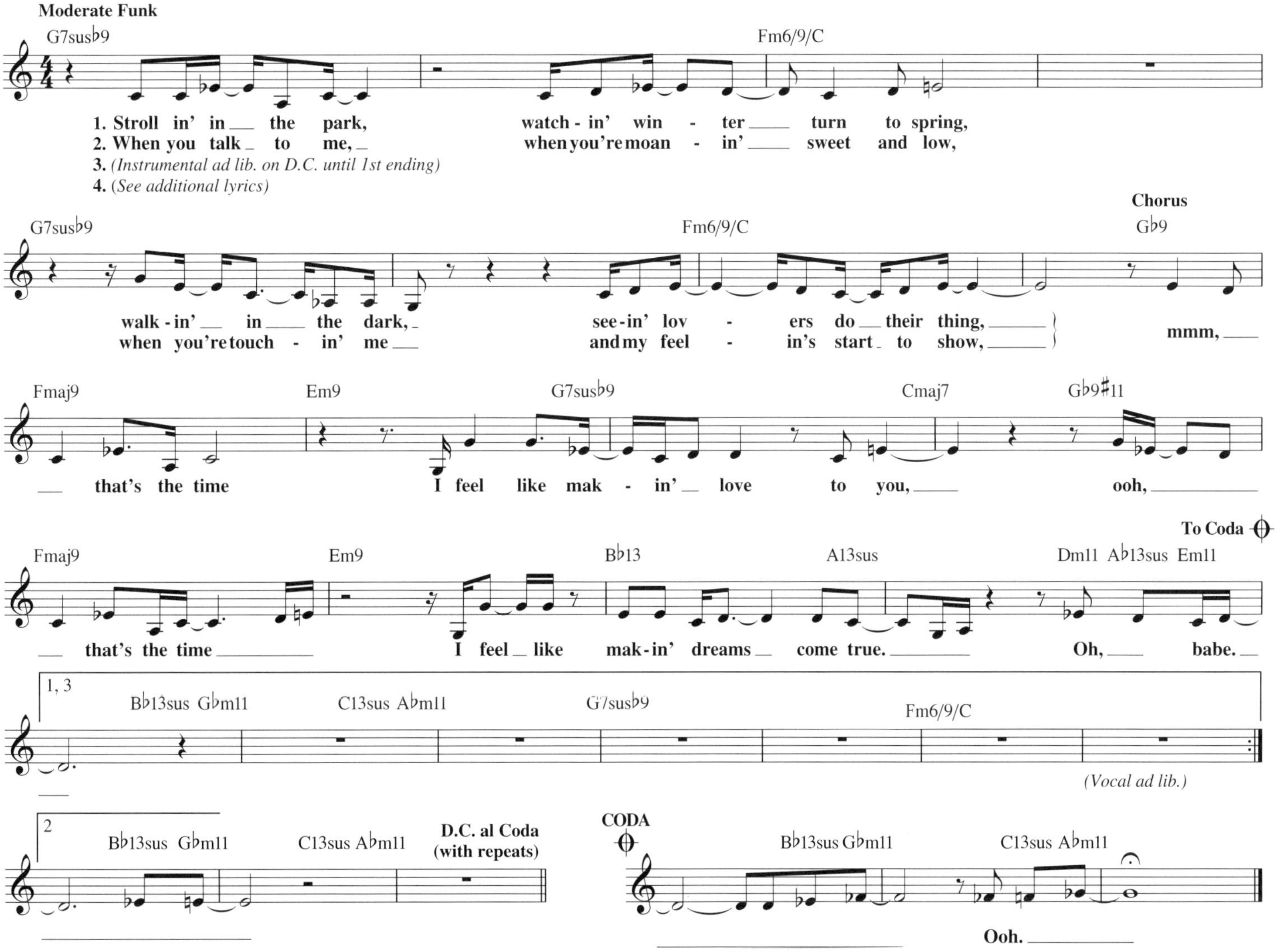
Moderate Funk
G7sus♭9
Fm6/9/C
1. Stroll in' in the park, watch - in' win - ter turn to spring,
2. When you talk to me, when you're moan - in' sweet and low,
3. (Instrumental ad lib. on D.C. until 1st ending)
4. (See additional lyrics)
G7sus♭9
Fm6/9/C
Chorus
G♭9
walk - in' in the dark, see - in' lov - ers do their thing,
when you're touch - in' me and my feel - in's start to show,
mmm,
Fmaj9
Em9
G7sus♭9
Cmaj7
G♭9♯11
that's the time I feel like mak - in' love to you, ooh,
To Coda
Fmaj9
Em9
B♭13
A13sus
Dm11 A♭13sus Em11
that's the time I feel like mak-in' dreams come true. Oh, babe.
1, 3
B♭13sus G♭m11
C13sus A♭m11
G7sus♭9
Fm6/9/C
(Vocal ad lib.)
2
B♭13sus G♭m11
C13sus A♭m11
D.C. al Coda
(with repeats)
CODA
B♭13sus G♭m11
C13sus A♭m11
Ooh.

Additional Lyrics

4. In a restaurant,
Holdin' hands by candlelight,
While I'm touchin' you,
Wanting you with all my might,
Chorus

FIGHT FOR YOUR RIGHT

(To Party)

Words and Music by RICK RUBIN,
ADAM HOROVITZ and ADAM YAUCH

Driving Rock
A♭5
A♭m7 D♭/A♭ A♭5 A♭m7 D♭/A♭ A♭5
You wake up late for school, man, you don't wan - na go. You
pops _ caught you smok - in', man, he says, "No _ way."
A♭m7 D♭/A♭ A♭5 A♭m7 D♭/A♭ A♭5
ask your mom, "please," but she still says no. You
That _ hyp - o - crite smokes _ two packs a day. Man,
A♭m7 D♭/A♭ A♭5 A♭m7 D♭/A♭ A♭5
missed two class - es and no home - work, but your
liv - in' at home _ is such a drag. Now your
A♭m7 D♭/A♭ A♭5
teach - er preach - es class like you're some kind - a jerk.
mom _ threw a - way your best _ porn - o mag. (Spoken:) Busted.
You got - ta fight _
D♭ E♭ A♭5 A♭m7 D♭/A♭ A♭5 A♭m7 D♭/A♭ A♭5
_ for your right _ to par - ty. _
A♭m7 D♭/A♭ A♭5
1
A♭m7 E♭m A♭5
Your
2, 3
A♭m7 D♭/A♭ E♭
To Coda
You got - ta fight.
A♭5 A♭m7 D♭/A♭ A♭5
Guitar solo
A♭m7 D♭/A♭ A♭5 A♭m7 D♭/A♭ A♭5 A♭m7 E♭m A♭5
Solo ends
Don't step out of this house if that's the
A♭m7 D♭/A♭ A♭5 A♭m7 D♭/A♭ A♭5
clothes you're gon - na wear. I'll kick you out of my home if you don't
A♭m7 D♭/A♭ A♭5 A♭m7 D♭/A♭ A♭5
cut that hair. Your mom bust - ed in and said,
A♭m7 D♭/A♭ A♭5 A♭m7 D♭/A♭ A♭5
"What's that noise?" "Oh, Mom, you're just jeal - ous, it's the
A♭m7 D♭/A♭ A♭5 D♭
Beast - ie Boys." You got - ta fight _ for your right _

D.S. al Coda (take 2nd ending)
Eb Ab5 Abm7 Db/Ab Ab5 Abm7 Db/Ab Ab5 Abm7 Db/Ab Ab5 Abm7 Db/Ab
to par - ty. You got - ta fight
CODA
Eb5 Ab5 Abm7 Db/Ab Ab5 Abm7 Db/Ab Ab5 Abm7 Db/Ab Ab5 Abm7 Db/Eb
Par - ty,
Ab5 Abm7 Db/Ab Ab5 Abm7 Db/Ab Ab5 Abm7 Db/Ab Ab5 Abm7 Ebm Ab5
par - ty.

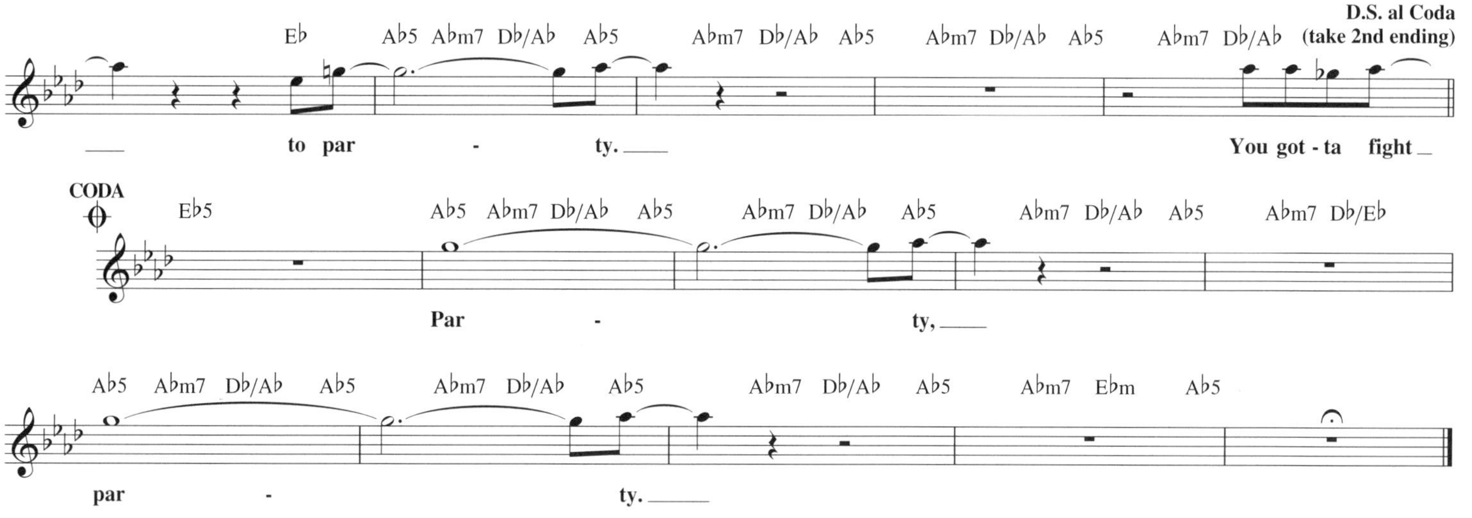

THE FIRST TIME EVER I SAW YOUR FACE

Words and Music by
EWAN MacCOLL

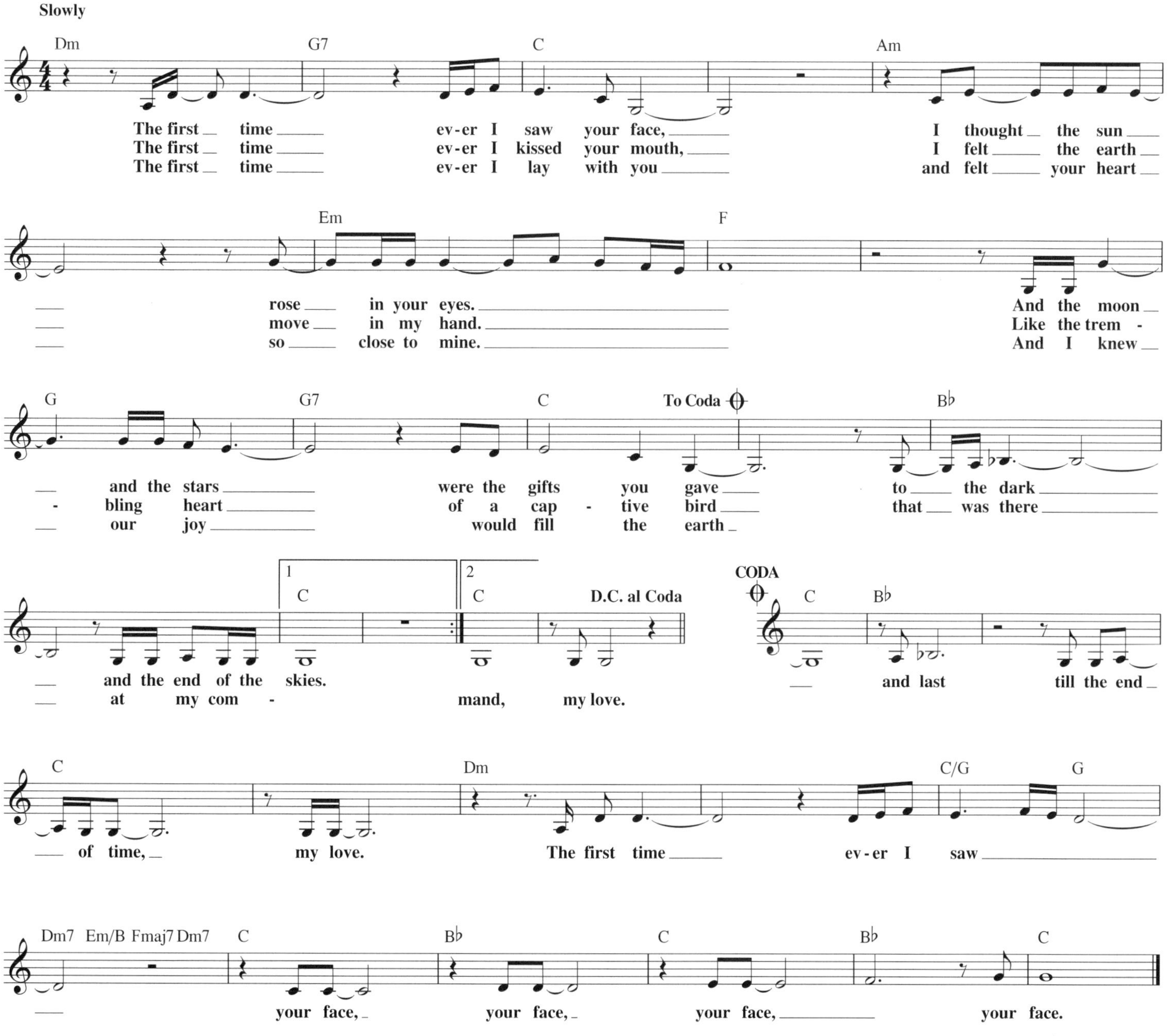
Slowly
Dm G7 C Am
The first time ev-er I saw your face, I thought the sun
The first time ev-er I kissed your mouth, I felt the earth
The first time ev-er I lay with you and felt your heart
Em F
rose in your eyes. And the moon
move in my hand. Like the trem -
so close to mine. And I knew
G G7 C To Coda Bb
and the stars were the gifts you gave to the dark
- bling heart of a cap - tive bird that was there
our joy would fill the earth
1 C 2 C D.C. al Coda
and the end of the skies.
at my com - mand, my love.
CODA
C Bb
and last till the end
C Dm C/G G
of time, my love. The first time ev-er I saw
Dm7 Em/B Fmaj7 Dm7 C Bb C Bb C
your face, your face, your face, your face.

FOOLISH HEART

Words and Music by RANDY GOODRUM
and STEVE PERRY

Moderately
Fmaj9 G/F F(add9) G/F Fmaj9 G/F F(add9) G/F
I need a love that grows. I don't want it un - less I know. With each
C7 C9 Am7 Am7(add4) Am7 D7sus D7 F/G
pass - ing hour, some - one, some - how will be there read - y to share. I
Fmaj9 G/F F(add9) G/F Fmaj9 G/F F(add9) G/F
need a love that's strong. I'm so ti - red of be - ing a - lone. But will my
Feel - ing that feel - ing a - gain. I'm play - ing a game I can't win. Love's knock - ing
C7 C9 Am7 Am7(add4) Am7 D7sus D7 F/G
lone - ly heart play the part of the fool a - gain be - fore I be - gin?
on the door of my heart once more. Think I'll let her in be - fore I be - gin.
Fool - ish heart,
Fsus2 G/B C Fmaj9 G/B C
hear me call - ing. Stop be - fore you start fall - ing. Fool - ish heart
Fsus2 G/B C G/B 1 Am7 D7sus4 D7 F/G
heed my warn - ing. You've been wrong be - fore; don't be wrong an - y - more.
Fmaj9 G/F F G/F Fmaj9 G/F F G/F
2 Am7 D7sus D7 F/G Fmaj9 G/B C
wrong be - fore; don't be wrong an - y - more. Fool - ish heart.
Fmaj9 G/B C Fmaj9 G/B C G/B
Fool - ish, fool - ish heart. You've been
Am7 D7sus D7 F/G N.C.
wrong be - fore.
(Instrumental)

Fmaj9 G/B C Fmaj9
Fool - ish heart, hear me call - ing. Stop be - fore you start
G/B C Fsus2 G/B C G/B Am7 D7sus D7
fall - ing. Fool - ish heart, heed my warn - ing. You've been wrong be - fore; don't be
F/G Fsus2 G/B C Fmaj9
wrong an - y - more. Fool - ish heart. Oh,
G/B C Fsus2 G/B C G/B Am7 D7sus D7
fool - ish, fool - ish heart. You've been wrong be - fore.
F/G Fsus2 G/B C Fmaj9 G/B C Repeat and Fade
Vocal ad lib...

(NOW AND THEN THERE'S) A FOOL SUCH AS I

Words and Music by
BILL TRADER

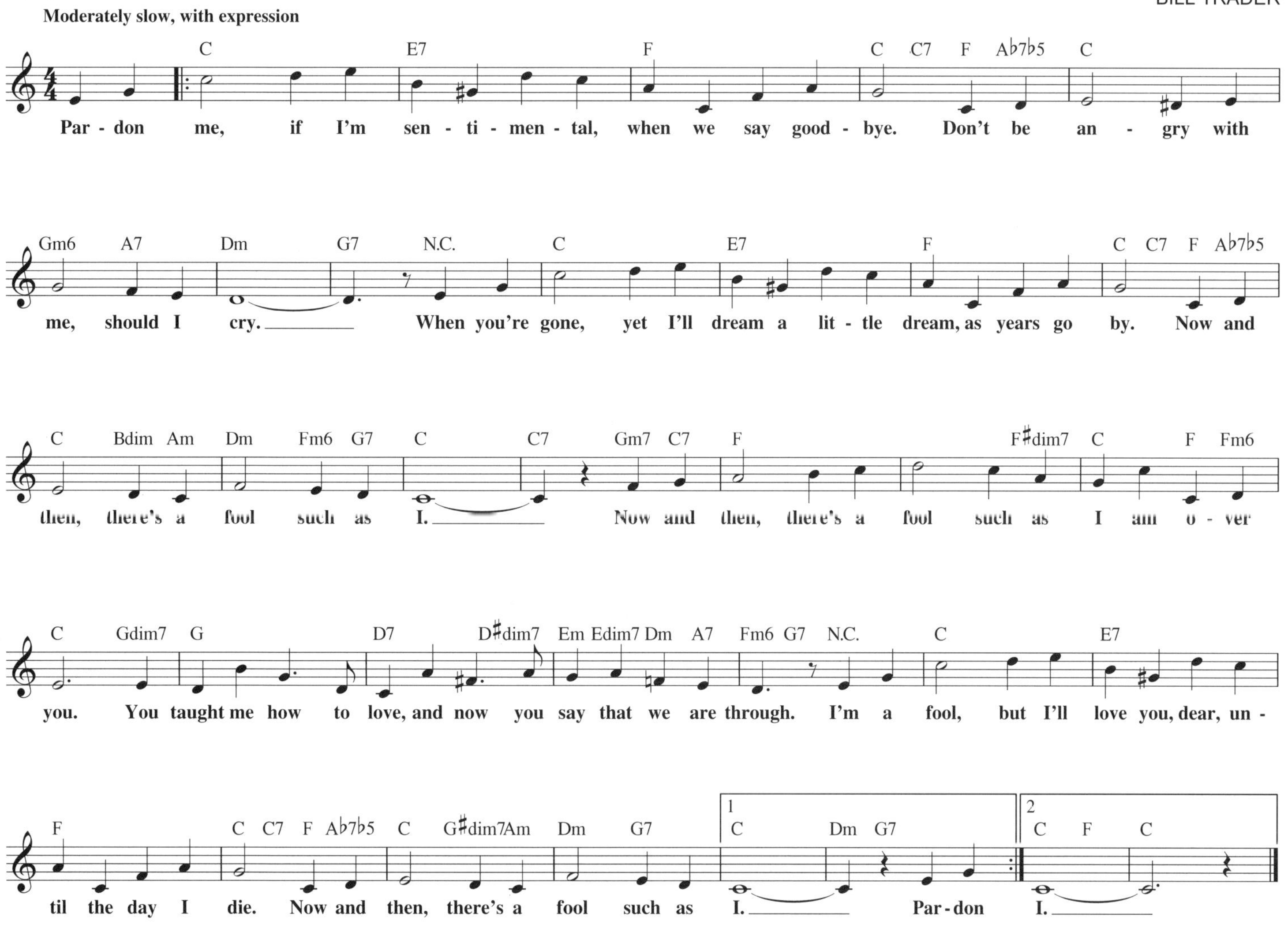

Moderately slow, with expression

C E7 F C C7 F A♭7♭5 C
Par - don me, if I'm sen - ti - men - tal, when we say good - bye. Don't be an - gry with

Gm6 A7 Dm G7 N.C. C E7 F C C7 F A♭7♭5
me, should I cry. When you're gone, yet I'll dream a lit - tle dream, as years go by. Now and

C Bdim Am Dm Fm6 G7 C C7 Gm7 C7 F F♯dim7 C F Fm6
then, there's a fool such as I. Now and then, there's a fool such as I am o - ver

C Gdim7 G D7 D♯dim7 Em Edim7 Dm A7 Fm6 G7 N.C. C E7
you. You taught me how to love, and now you say that we are through. I'm a fool, but I'll love you, dear, un -

F C C7 F A♭7♭5 C G♯dim7 Am Dm G7 1 C Dm G7 2 C F C
til the day I die. Now and then, there's a fool such as I. Par - don I.

FOREVER YOUNG

Words and Music by ROD STEWART, JIM CREGAN, KEVIN SAVIGAR and BOB DYLAN

Driving beat
E A E A E F♯m7 C♯m7 A/E F♯m B
(Instrumental)
May the good Lord be with you down ev - er - y road you roam. (Instrumental) And may sun - shine and hap - pi - ness sur - round you when you're far from home. (Instrumental) And may you
grow to be proud, dig - ni - fied and true. (Instrumental) And do un - to oth - ers as you'd have done to you. (Instrumental) Be cou - ra - geous and be brave.
for - tune be with you, may your guid - ing light be strong, build a stair - way to heav - en with a prince or a vag - a - bond. And may you nev - er love in vain.
fi - n'lly fly a - way, I'll be hoping that I served you well. For all the wis - dom of a life - time, no one can ev - er tell. But what - ev - er road you choose,
And in my heart you'll al - ways stay
And in my heart you will re - main
I'm right be - hind you win or lose,
for - ev - er young, (for - ev - er young,) for - ev - er young, (for - ev - er young.) May good young.)
For - ev - er young. (Instrumental)
For - ev - er young. (Instrumental)
To Coda

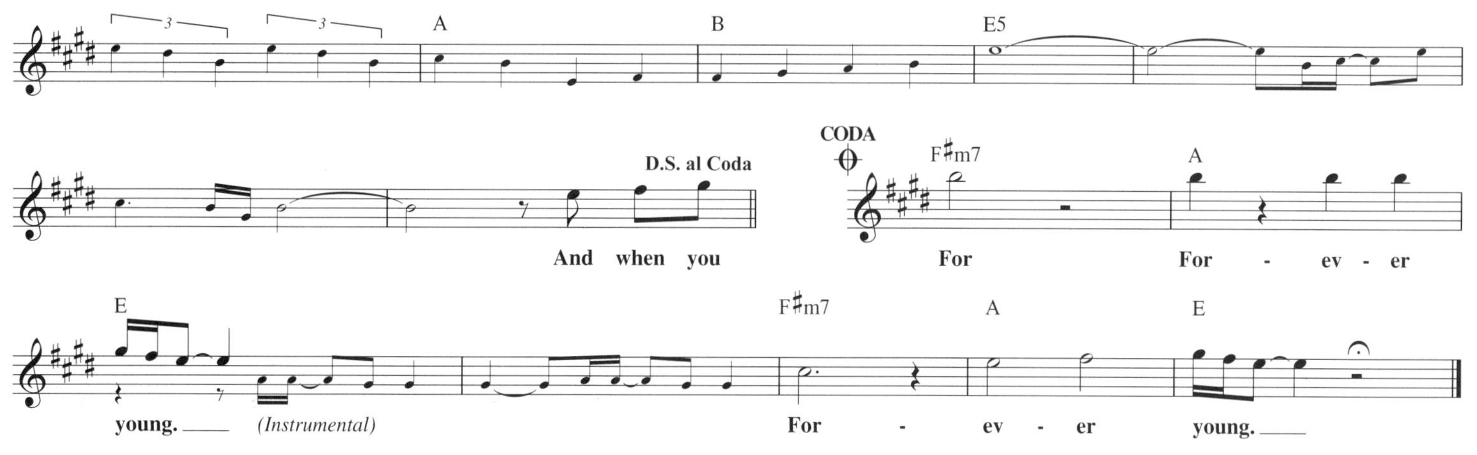

FOR YOUR LOVE

Words and Music by
GRAHAM GOULDMAN

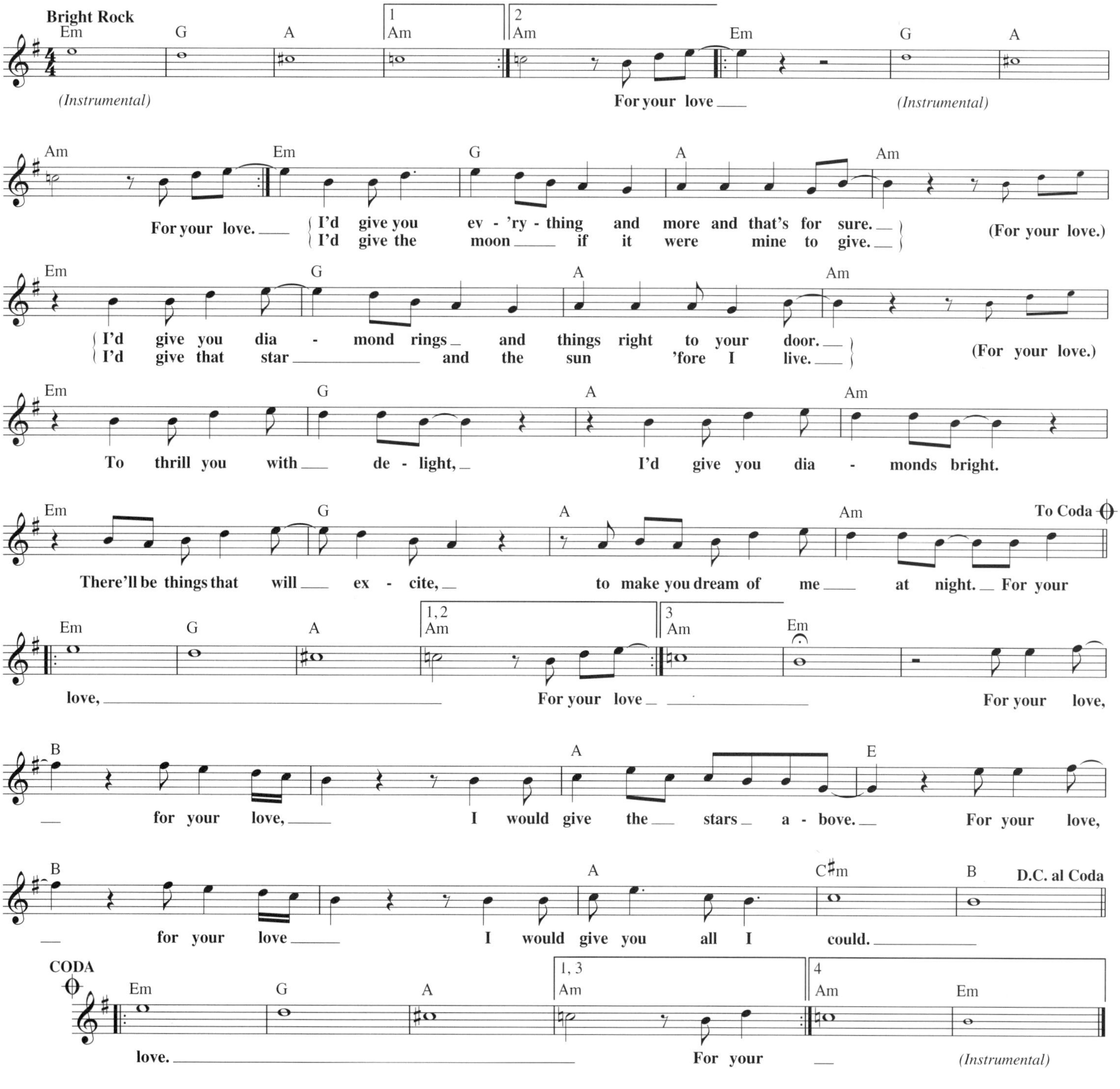

Bright Rock

Em G A | 1 Am | 2 Am Em G A
(Instrumental) For your love ___ (Instrumental)

Am Em G A Am
For your love. ___ { I'd give you ev - 'ry - thing and more and that's for sure. ___ / I'd give the moon ___ if it were mine to give. ___ } (For your love.)

Em G A Am
{ I'd give you dia - mond rings ___ and things right to your door. ___ / I'd give that star ___ and the sun 'fore I live. ___ } (For your love.)

Em G A Am
To thrill you with ___ de - light, ___ I'd give you dia - monds bright.

Em G A Am To Coda
There'll be things that will ___ ex - cite, ___ to make you dream of me ___ at night. ___ For your

Em G A | 1, 2 Am | 3 Am Em
love, ___ For your love ___ For your love,

B A E
___ for your love, ___ I would give the ___ stars ___ a - bove. ___ For your love,

B A C♯m B D.C. al Coda
___ for your love ___ I would give you all I could. ___

CODA
Em G A | 1, 3 Am | 4 Am Em
love. ___ For your ___ (Instrumental)

THE FOOL ON THE HILL

Words and Music by JOHN LENNON and PAUL McCARTNEY

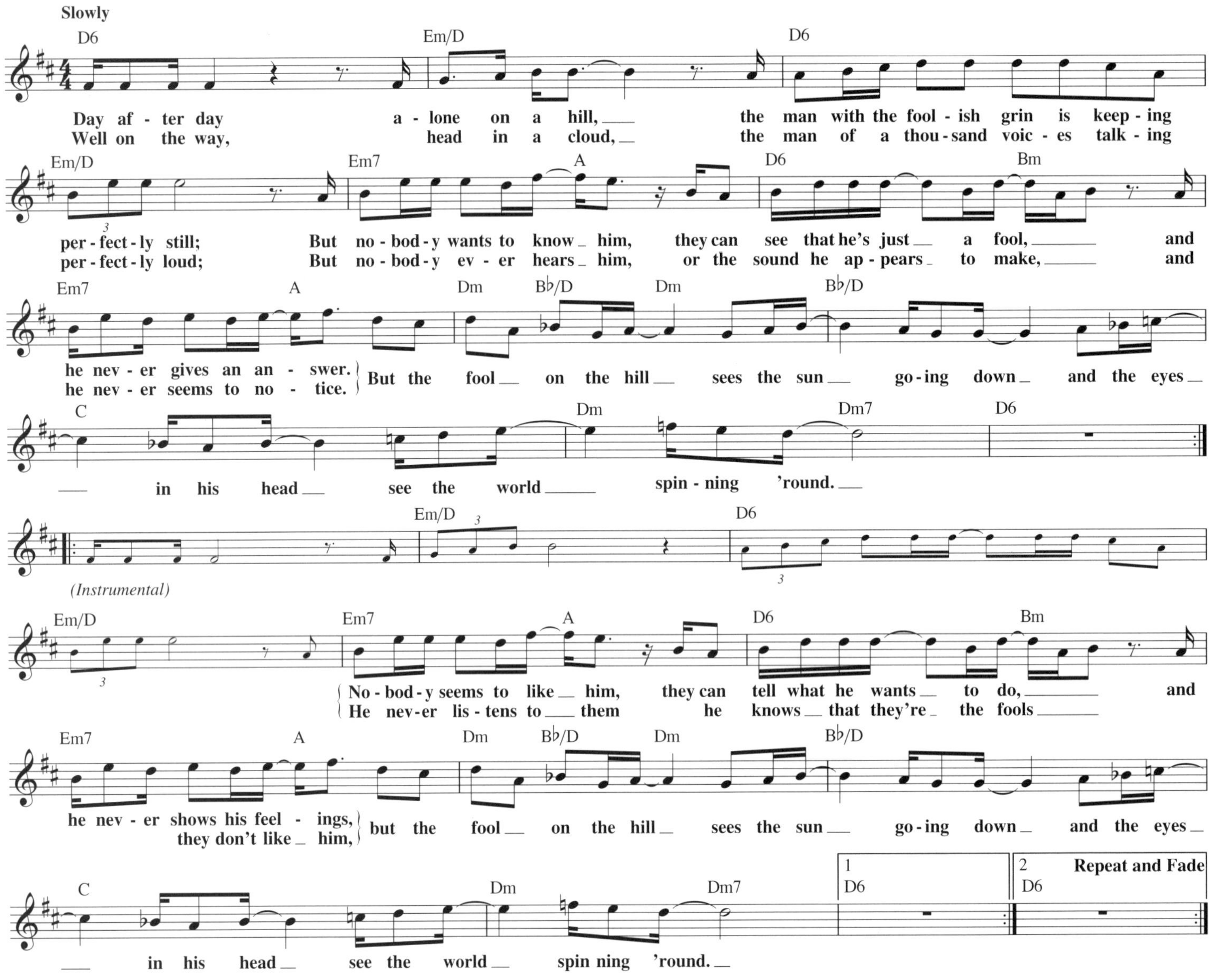

Slowly

D6 Em/D D6 Em/D Em7 A D6 Bm Em7 A Dm B♭/D Dm B♭/D C Dm Dm7 D6

Day af - ter day a - lone on a hill, the man with the fool - ish grin is keep - ing per - fect - ly still; But no - bod - y wants to know him, they can see that he's just a fool, and he nev - er gives an an - swer. But the fool on the hill sees the sun go - ing down and the eyes in his head see the world spin - ning 'round.

Well on the way, head in a cloud, the man of a thou - sand voic - es talk - ing per - fect - ly loud; But no - bod - y ev - er hears him, or the sound he ap - pears to make, and he nev - er seems to no - tice.

(Instrumental)

Em/D D6 Em/D Em7 A D6 Bm Em7 A Dm B♭/D Dm B♭/D C Dm Dm7 1 D6 2 D6 Repeat and Fade

No - bod - y seems to like him, they can tell what he wants to do, and he nev - er shows his feel - ings, but the fool on the hill sees the sun go - ing down and the eyes in his head see the world spin ning 'round.

He nev - er lis - tens to them he knows that they're the fools they don't like him,

FOOLISH LITTLE GIRL

Words and Music by HOWARD GREENFIELD and HELEN MILLER

Moderate Rock
Fool - ish lit - tle girl. Fick le lit - tle girl. You did - n't want him when he want - ed you. He's
found an - oth - er love; it's her he's dream - ing of, and there's not a sin - gle thing that you can do.
Solo: But I love him. Group: No you don't, it's just your pride that's hurt. Group: It's too late to have a change of heart. Solo: I still love him. Group: To -
Group: If you got him back a - gain, you'd go right out and do him hurt.
mor - row is his wed - ding day, and you'll keep qui - et if you're smart.

Dm Gm Dm Gm Cm F6 B♭ Dm Gm

(Instrumental)

Dm Gm Cm F6 B♭ Dm Gm Dm Gm

You fool - ish lit - tle girl. Fick - le lit - tle girl. You

Cm F6 B♭6 Dm Gm Dm Gm

did n't want him when he want - ed you. ___ He's found an - oth - er love; it's her he's dream - ing of, and there's

Cm F6 B♭6 Cm F6 B♭6

not a sin - gle thing that you can do. Just for - get him 'cause he don't be - long to you.

(But I love him.) (I still love him.)

Cm F6 B♭6 Cm F6

Repeat and Fade

It's too late, he's found some - bod - y new. There's not a sin - gle thing that you can

(Oh I love him.)

FREE RIDE

By DAN HARTMAN

With energy

A D A D A

The moun - tain is high, ___ the val - ley is low, ___ and you're con - fused ___ on which way to go. ___ So,

o - ver the coun - try I've seen it the same; ___ no - bod - y's win - ning at this kind of game. ___ We've

(Instrumental)

D A D A

I've come here ___ to give you a hand ___ and lead you in - to the prom - ised land. ___

got - ta do bet - ter, it's time to be - gin. ___ You know all the an - swers must come from with - in, *(End Instrumental)* } So,

F♯m G A F♯m G D F♯m G D To Coda

come on ___ and take a free ride, ___ (free ride.) ___ Come on ___ and sit here by my side. ___ Come on ___ and take a free ride.

N.C. A G D G D A D A G D 1 G D A D

(Instrumental)

A G D G D A D A G D G D A 2 A D.S. al Coda

(End instrumental) All, Yeah, yeah, yeah, yeah.

CODA

A D G/A A G/A D/A A Repeat and Fade

Come on ___ and take a free ride. Yeah, yeah, yeah, yeah.

FREE FALLIN'

Words and Music by TOM PETTY
and JEFF LYNNE

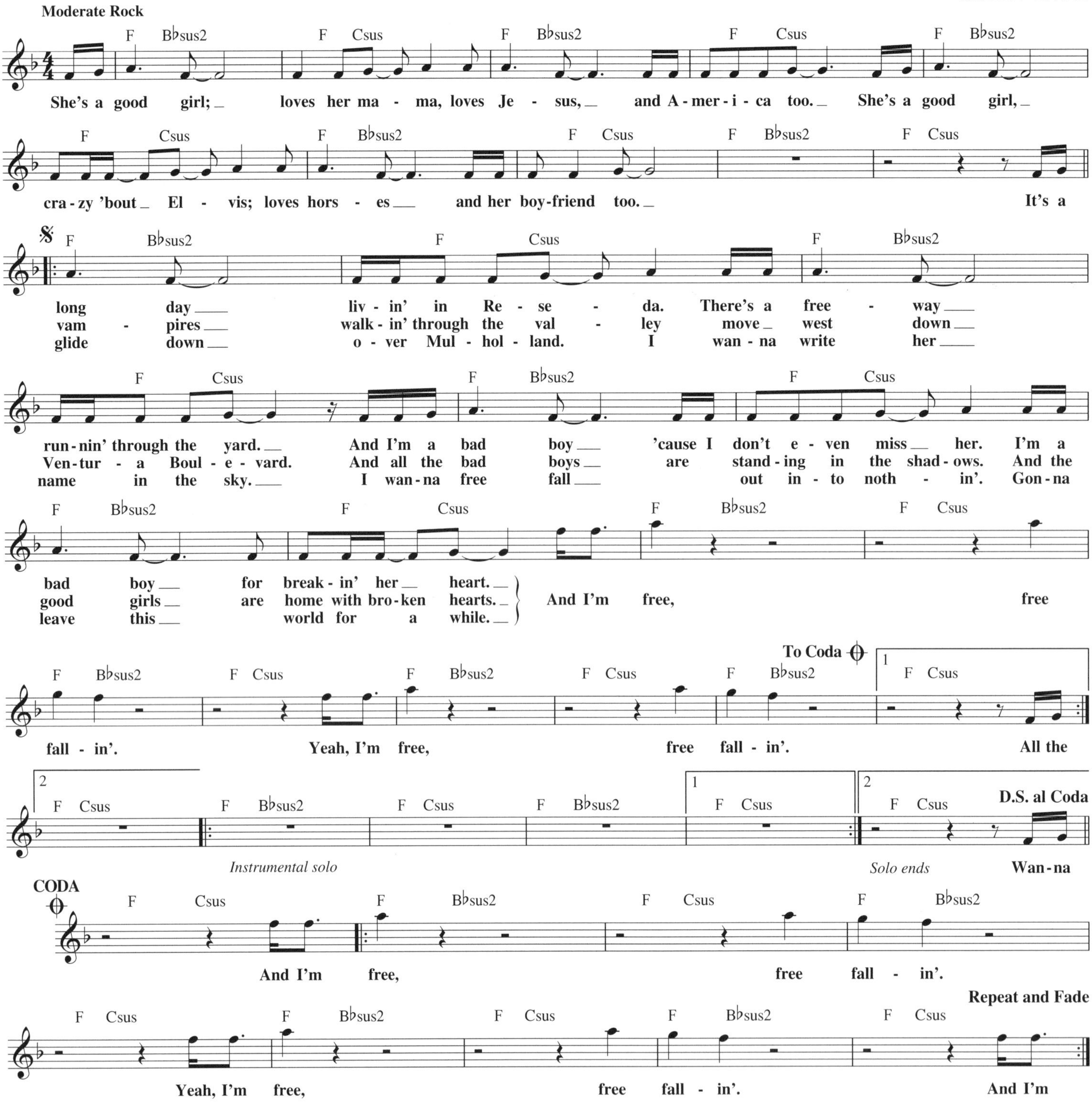

Moderate Rock

F Bb♭sus2 F Csus F B♭sus2 F Csus F B♭sus2

She's a good girl; loves her ma - ma, loves Je - sus, and A - mer - i - ca too. She's a good girl,

F Csus F B♭sus2 F Csus F B♭sus2 F Csus

cra - zy 'bout El - vis; loves hors - es and her boy-friend too. It's a

1. long day liv - in' in Re - se - da. There's a free - way run - nin' through the yard. And I'm a bad boy 'cause I don't e - ven miss her. I'm a bad boy for break - in' her heart.
2. vam - pires walk - in' through the val - ley move west down Ven - tur - a Boul - e - vard. And all the bad boys are stand - ing in the shad - ows. And the good girls are home with bro - ken hearts.
3. glide down o - ver Mul - hol - land. I wan - na write her name in the sky. I wan - na free fall out in - to noth - in'. Gon - na leave this world for a while.

And I'm free, free fall - in'. Yeah, I'm free, free fall - in'.

To Coda — 1. All the — 2. — Instrumental solo — 1. — 2. Solo ends — D.S. al Coda — Wan - na

CODA

And I'm free, free fall - in'. Yeah, I'm free, free fall - in'. And I'm

Repeat and Fade

GALVESTON

Words and Music by
JIM WEBB

Moderately
F B♭ C F Fmaj7 F7
Gal - ves - ton, oh, Gal - ves - ton, I still hear your sea - winds
Gal - ves - ton, oh, Gal - ves - ton, I still hear your sea - waves
B♭ Am Gm7 C F B♭ Gm7 C
blow - ing; I still see her dark eyes glow - ing. She was twen - ty - one,
crash - in', while I watch the can - nons flash - in'. I clean my gun,

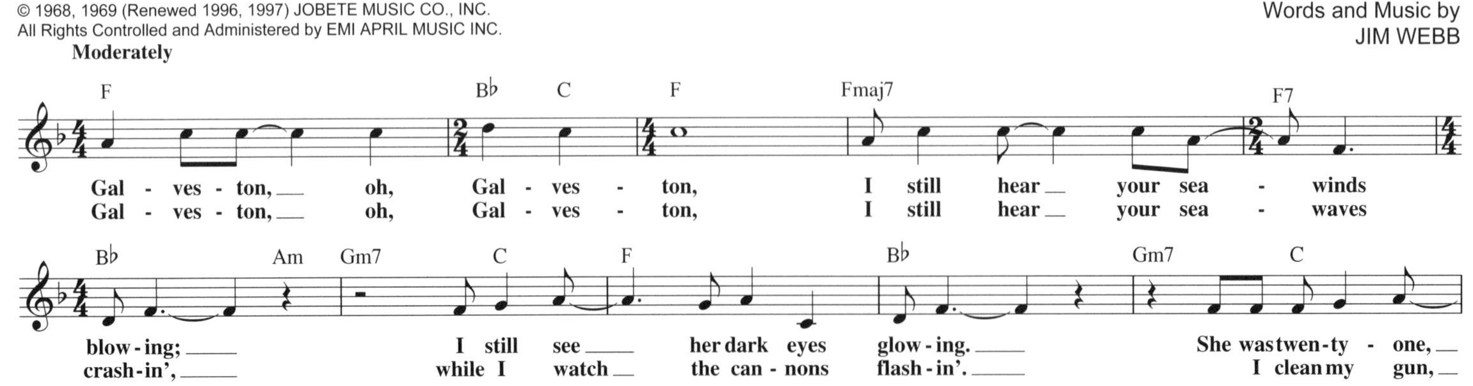

when I left Gal - ves - ton.
and dream of Gal - ves - ton.

I still see her stand - ing by the wa - ter, stand - ing there

look - ing out to sea. And is she wait - ing there for me, on the beach where we used to

run? Gal - ves - ton, oh! Gal - ves - ton,

I am so a - fraid of dy - ing, be - fore I dry the tears she's

cry - ing, be - fore I watch your sea birds fly - ing in the sun

at Gal - ves - ton, at Gal - ves - ton.

GENTLE ON MY MIND

Words and Music by
JOHN HARTFORD

Moderately bright
It's know - ing that your door is al - ways o - pen and your path is free to walk,
that makes me tend to leave my sleep - ing bag rolled up and stashed be - hind your couch.
And it's know - ing I'm not shack - led by for - got - ten words and bonds, and the
ink stains that have dried up - on some line; that keeps you in the
back - roads by the riv - ers of my mem - 'ry that keeps you ev - er Gen - tle On My Mind.

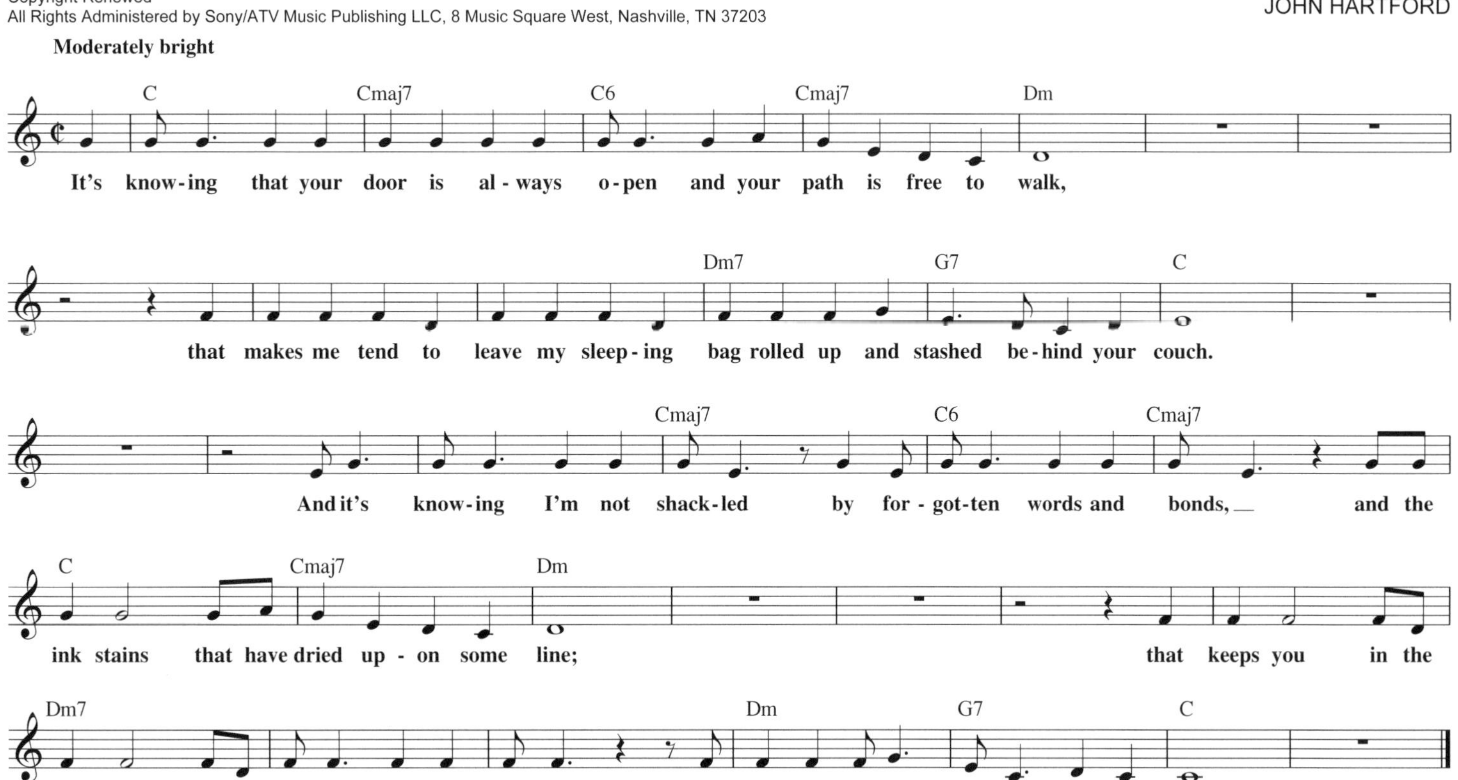

FOOLISH BEAT

Words and Music by
DEBORAH GIBSON

With a steady beat, not too fast
Am Fmaj7 Dm7 G Em
There was a time when broken hearts and broken dreams were over.
Am Fmaj7 Dm7 Esus E
There was a place where all you could do was wish on a four leaf clover. But
when I was sorry it was too late to turn around and tell you so.
Am Fmaj7 1 Dm7 Esus E
now is a new time, there is a new place where dreams just can't come true. It
There was no reason, there was no reason,
F E To next strain 2 Dm Esus E
started the day when I left you. Oh, just a foolish beat of my heart. Ah.
Am G Fmaj7 G Am
1.,2. I could never love again the way I loved you. Oh, I could never cry again.
D.S. (Instrumental)
G Fmaj7 G Am Fmaj7
like I did when I left you and when we said goodbye. Oh, the look in your eyes just left me beside
G Esus E Fmaj7 Em Dm Em To Coda
myself, without your heart. I could never love again now that we're apart.
(Instrumental ends)
1 F G 2 F G Am G
Oh, Oh, can't you see I'm not fooling nobody. Don't you see the tears are fallin'
Fmaj7 Em7 E Am G
down my face. since you went away. Break my heart, you slipped away, didn't know I was wrong.
Fmaj7 E7sus E7 D.S. al Coda
Never meant to hurt you, now you're gone.
CODA
F G Am G Dm7 Em7
(Now that we're a-
Fmaj7 Em7 Dm7 Em7 F G A(add9)
part) I could never love again now that we're apart.

GOT TO GET YOU INTO MY LIFE

Words and Music by JOHN LENNON
and PAUL McCARTNEY

Very steady
G
F/G
N.C.
(Instrumental)
I was a - lone, I took a ride, I did - n't know what I would find there.
You did - n't run, you did - n't lie, you knew I want - ed just to hold you.
What can I do, what can I be, when I'm with you I want to stay there.
An - oth - er road, where may - be I could see an - oth - er kind of mind there.
And had you gone you knew in time we'd meet a - gain for I'd have told you.
If I'm true I'll nev - er leave and if I do I know the way there.
Bm
Bm/A♯
D/A
G♯m7♭5
C
C/B
Am7
D
Ooh, then I sud - den - ly see you. Ooh, did I tell you I need you ev - 'ry sin - gle day of my life?
Ooh, you were meant to be near me. Ooh, and I want you to hear me say we'll be to - gether ev - 'ry day.
Ooh, then I sud - den - ly see you. Ooh, did I tell you I need you ev - 'ry sin - gle day of my life?
To Coda
1
2
Got to get you in - to my life!
C/D
D.S. al Coda
CODA
Got to get you in - to my life! (Instrumental)
F
Got to get you in - to my life! (Instrumental)
Repeat and Fade

GARDEN PARTY

Words and Music by
RICK NELSON

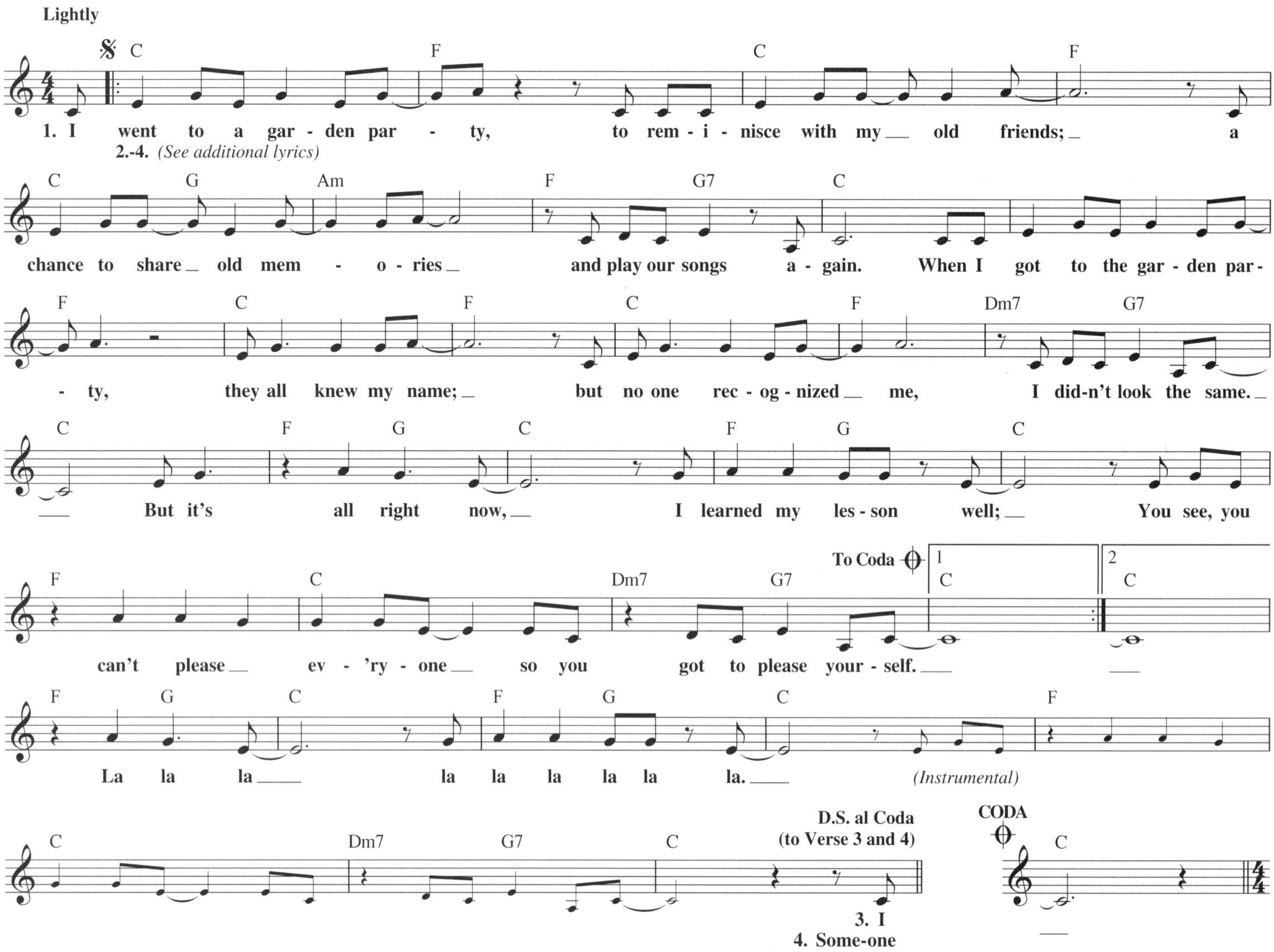

Lightly

C F C F
1. I went to a gar - den par - ty, to rem - i - nisce with my old friends; a
2.-4. *(See additional lyrics)*

C G Am F G7 C
chance to share old mem - o - ries and play our songs a - gain. When I got to the gar - den par -

F C F C F Dm7 G7
- ty, they all knew my name; but no one rec - og - nized me, I did-n't look the same.

C F G C F G C
But it's all right now, I learned my les - son well; You see, you

F C Dm7 G7 To Coda 1 C 2 C
can't please ev - 'ry - one so you got to please your - self.

F G C F G C F
La la la la la la la la la. *(Instrumental)*

C Dm7 G7 C D.S. al Coda (to Verse 3 and 4) CODA C
3. I
4. Some-one

Additional Lyrics

2. People came for miles around, everyone was there;
Yoko brought her walrus, there was magic in the air.
And over in the corner, much to my surprise,
Mr. Hughes hid in Dylan's shoes, wearing his disguise.
Chorus

3. I played them all the old songs, I thought that's why they came;
No one heard the music, we didn't look the same.
I said hello to Mary-Lou, she belongs to me;
When I sang a song about a honky-tonk, it was time to leave.
Chorus

4. Someone opened up a closet door and out stepped Johnny B. Goode;
Playing guitar like a-ringin' a bell, and lookin' like he should.
If you gotta play at garden parties, I wish you a lotta luck;
But if memories were all I sang, I'd rather drive a truck.
Chorus

GIVE ME JUST A LITTLE MORE TIME

Words and Music by EDYTHE WAYNE
and RONALD DUNBAR

Steady beat

Cmaj7 Am7 Em F
Give me just a lit - tle more time and our love will sure - ly grow. Give
Cmaj7 Am7 Em F
me just a lit - tle more time and our love will sure - ly grow.

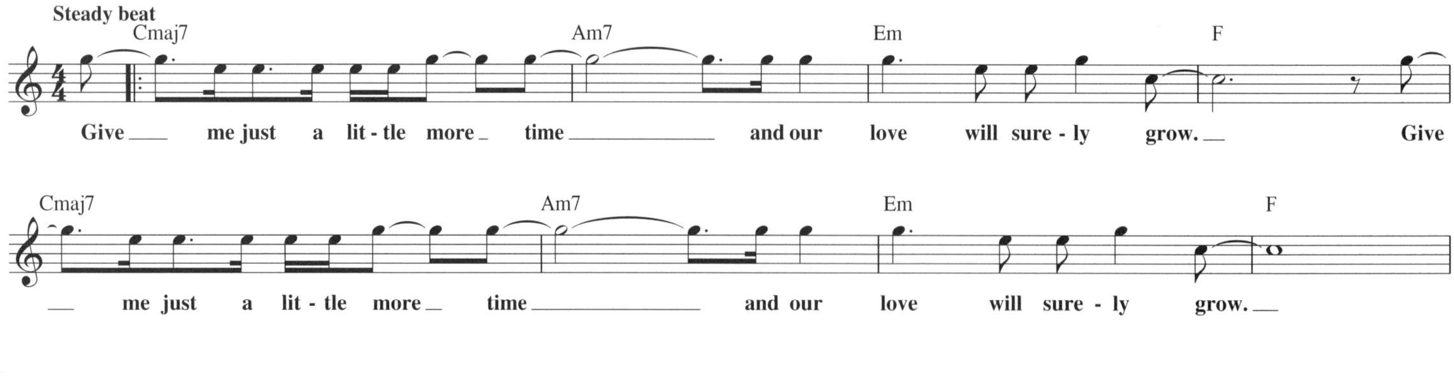

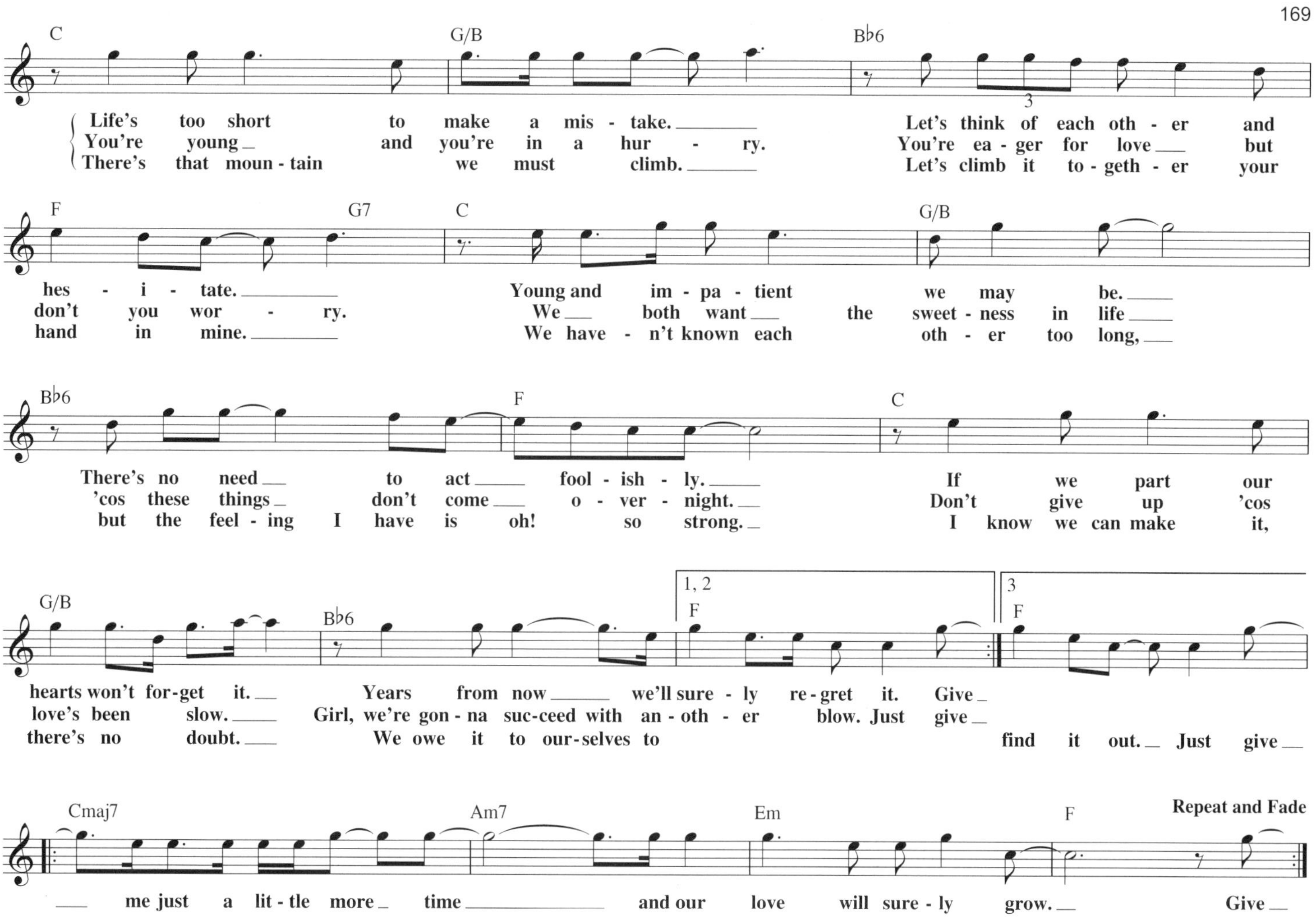
C G/B B♭6
Life's too short to make a mis - take. Let's think of each oth - er and
You're young and you're in a hur - ry. You're ea - ger for love but
There's that moun - tain we must climb. Let's climb it to - geth - er your
F G7 C G/B
hes - i - tate. Young and im - pa - tient we may be.
don't you wor - ry. We both want the sweet - ness in life
hand in mine. We have - n't known each oth - er too long,
B♭6 F C
There's no need to act fool - ish - ly. If we part our
'cos these things don't come o - ver - night. Don't give up 'cos
but the feel - ing I have is oh! so strong. I know we can make it,
G/B B♭6 1, 2 F 3 F
hearts won't for - get it. Years from now we'll sure - ly re - gret it. Give
love's been slow. Girl, we're gon - na suc - ceed with an - oth - er blow. Just give
there's no doubt. We owe it to our - selves to find it out. Just give
Cmaj7 Am7 Em F Repeat and Fade
me just a lit - tle more time and our love will sure - ly grow. Give

THE GODFATHER

(Love Theme)

from the Paramount Picture THE GODFATHER

By NINO ROTA

Slowly and expressively

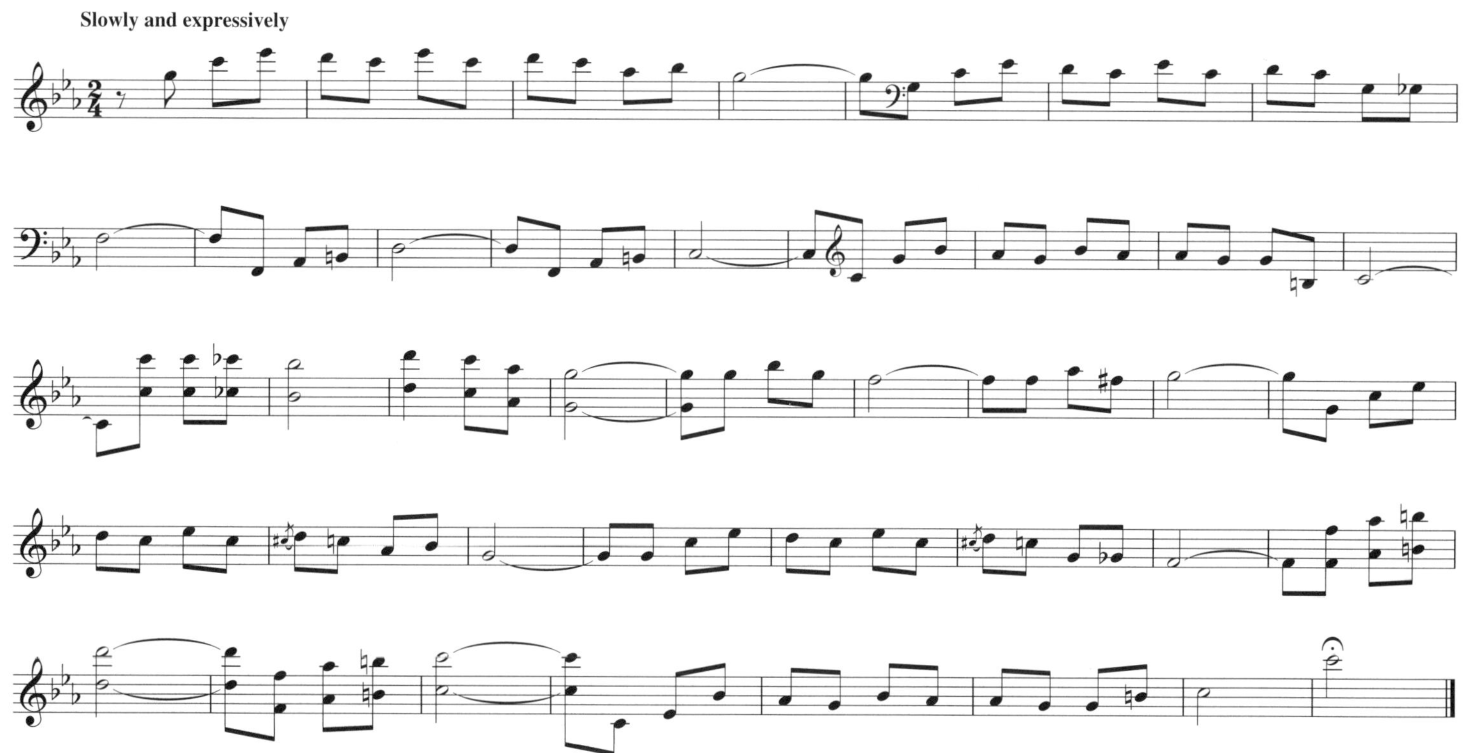

GET READY

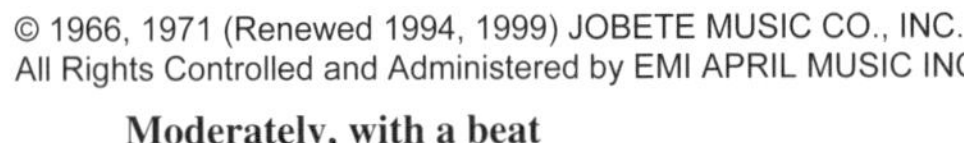

Words and Music by
WILLIAM "SMOKEY" ROBINSON

Moderately, with a beat

Em A G Em

I never met a girl who makes __ me feel __ the way that you do (it's al -
wan - na play hide and seek __ with love __ let me re - mind you (it's al -
All my friends should - n't want me to __ I un - der - stand it (it's al -

A G Em A G

right.) __ When - ev - er I'm asked __ who makes my dreams real __ I say that
right.) __ The lov - ing you're gon - na miss and the time __ it takes to
right.) __ I hope I'll get __ to you be - fore they do __ the way I

Em A G Em

you __ do (you're out - ta sight.) __ So fee fi __
find __ you (it's out - ta sight.) __ So fid - dle - lee - dee __
planned __ it (Be out - ta sight.) __ So twid - dle - dee - dee __

A G Em A G

fo __ fum __ / fid - dle-lee dum __ / twid - dle dee - dum __ look out ba - by 'cause here I come. And I'm bring - ing you a

C Am7 D7 G C

love that's true __ so get read - y so get read - y. I'm gon - na try to make love to you so get

Am7 D7 D11 Em 1, 2 A G Em

read - y so get read - y here __ I come. __ I'm on my way. __

3 A G Em Em Repeat and Fade

If you I'm on my way. __ Get read - y 'cause here I come, boy.

GIMME SOME LOVIN'

Words and Music by SPENCER DAVIS,
MUFF WINWOOD and STEVE WINWOOD

Moderately bright
E A/E E A/E A/E
Well, my tem - p'ra ture's ris - ing and my feet on the floor. Twen - ty peo - ple knock - in' 'cause they're
feel so good; __ ev - 'ry - thing is sound - ing hot. Bet - ter take it eas - y, 'cause the
feel so good; __ ev - 'ry - bod - y's get - tin' high. Bet - ter take it eas - y, 'cause the
E A/E E A/E E A/E
want - ing some more. Let me in, ba - by. I don't know what you've got. But you'd
place is on fire. Been a hard day, __ and I don't know what to do.
place is on fire. Been a hard day, __ noth - in' went too good. Now I'm
E A/E E A/E E G A C
bet - ter take it eas - y. This __ place is hot.
Wait a min - ute ba - by. It could hap - pen to you.
gon - na re - lax, hon - ey. Ev - 'ry - bod - y should. __
So glad __ we made __ it, so glad __ we made __ it. You got - ta

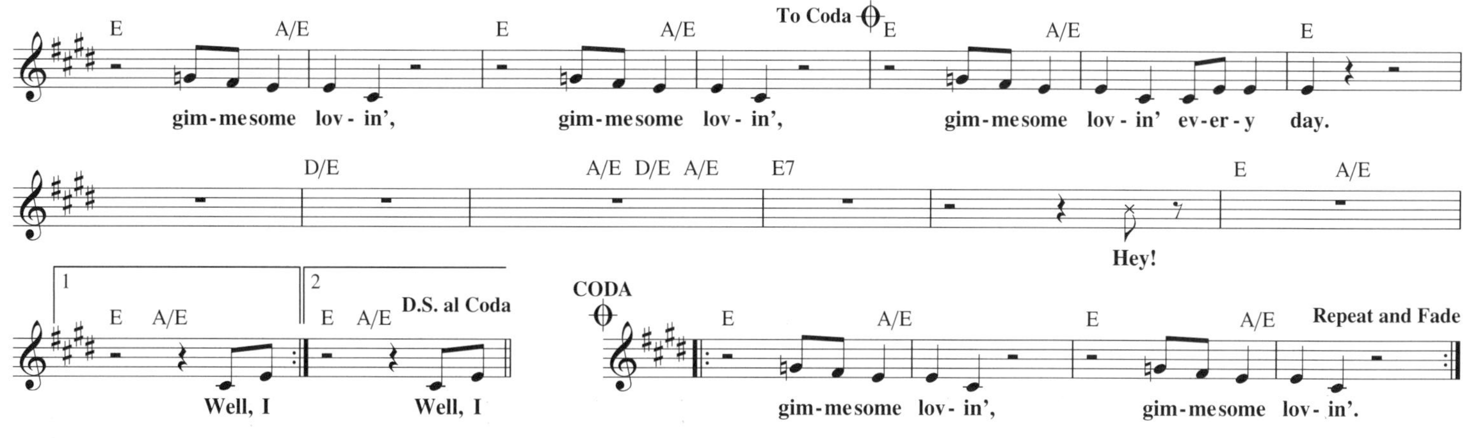

GOT TO BE THERE

Words and Music by
ELLIOTT WILLENSKY

Moderately

B♭ B♭maj7 E♭maj7 E♭ A♭5 B♭/A♭

Got to be there, got to be there in the morn - ing, when she says hel-lo to the world.
Got to be there, got to be there when she needs some-one to keep her thru the night.

Gm Gm/F B♭ B♭maj7 E♭maj7 E♭

Got to be there, got to be there, bring her good times and
Got to be there, got to be there, to take her hand and

A♭5 B♭/A Gm Gm/F Cm7(add4) E♭/F B♭maj7

show her that she's my girl.
lead her in - to my life.
Oh, what a feel - ing there'll be the

E♭/F B♭maj7 Dm7 Gm7 E♭/F

mo-ment I know she loves me. 'Cause when I look in her eyes, I re-al-ize

Amaj7 E♭/F B♭

I need her shar - ing the world be-side me.
So, I've got to be there, got to
That's why I've got to be there, got to

B♭maj7 E♭maj7 E♭ A♭5 B♭/A♭ Gm Gm/F A♭5 B♭/A♭ Gm

be there in the morn - ing, and wel-come her in - to my world, and show her that she's my girl. When
be there where love begins and that's ev - 'ry - where she goes. I've got to be there so she knows that

A♭5 B♭7/A♭ 1 E♭/F B♭maj7 E♭/F 2 E♭/F

she says hel - lo world, go to be there. she's
when she's with me

B♭maj7 C7sus/B♭ B♭maj7 C7sus/B♭ B♭maj7 E♭/F Repeat and Fade

home. Got to be there, got to be there, got to be there.

GUITAR BOOGIE SHUFFLE

By ARTHUR SMITH

Moderately bright Shuffle

E♭6 A♭7

E♭6 B♭7 To Coda E♭6

A♭7 E♭6 B♭7

E♭6

A♭7 E♭6

B♭7 A♭maj7 B♭7 D.C. al Coda E♭6

CODA E♭6

GYPSY

Words and Music by
STEVIE NICKS

Moderately bright
Fmaj7 F6 F B♭maj7
So I'm back to the vel - vet un - der - ground, back to the floor
C B♭maj7 C F Fmaj7
that I love; to a room with some lace
F6 F B♭maj7 C B♭maj7
and pap - er - flow - ers; back to the gyp - sy that I was,
C B♭maj7 C F Fmaj7 F6
to the gyp - sy that I was.
F B♭maj7 C B♭maj7 C F
(Instrumental)
And it all
Fmaj7 F6 F B♭maj7 C
comes down to you. Well, you know that it does. Well, ligh - ning strikes, may - be once,

maybe twice. Ah, and it lights up the night.
And you see your gypsy. You see your
gypsy. To the
gypsy that remains, faces freedom
with a little fear, I have no fear. I have only
love. And if I was a child, and the child was enough,
enough for me to love, enough to love,
She is dancing away from me now. She was just a wish.
She was just a wish. And a memory is all that is
left for you now. You see your gypsy. You see your
gypsy.
(Instrumental)
Repeat (vocal ad lib) and Fade

Vocal ad lib.

Lightning strikes, maybe once, maybe twice.
And it all comes down to you.
I still see your bright eyes.
And it all comes down to you.

GUILTY

Words and Music by BARRY GIBB,
ROBIN GIBB and MAURICE GIBB

Moderately
Cmaj7
Shad - ows fall - ing ba - by. We stand a - lone out on the street. An - y - bod - y you meet got a heart
ache of their own.
Am Em7 Am Em7
Make it a crime to be lone - ly or sad.
Am Em7 Am B♭maj7
You got a rea - son for liv - ing. You bat - tle on with the love you're liv - in on, you got - ta be
D Gm D Gm D C
mine. We take it a - way. It's got - ta be night and day just a mat - ter of time,
D Cmaj7
and we got noth - ing to be guil - ty of. Our love will climb an - y moun - tain
G11 Cmaj7
near or far we are and we nev - er let it end. We are de - vo -
Am Cmaj7
tion and we got noth - ing to be sor - ry for. Our love is one in a mil - lion.
G11 Cmaj7
Eyes can see that we got a high - way to the sky. I don't wan - na hear
Am To Coda Cmaj7 Dm G11 Fmaj7
your good - bye. Pul - se's rac - ing dar - ling
how grand we are. Lit - tle by lit - tle we meet in the mid - dle there's dan - ger in the dark.
Dm Am Dm Am Dm Am Dm
Make it a crime to be out in the cold. You got a rea - son for liv - in'. You bat -

E♭maj7 D Gm
- tle on with the love you're build - in' on you got-ta be mine. We take it a - way.
D Gm D C D
D.S. al Coda
It's got-ta be night and day just a mat-ter of time, and we got noth-ing to be
CODA
Cmaj7 Am
bye. Don't wan-na hear your good -
Cmaj7 Am D11
D.S. and Fade
bye, I don't wan-na hear your. And we got noth-ing, and we got noth-ing to be

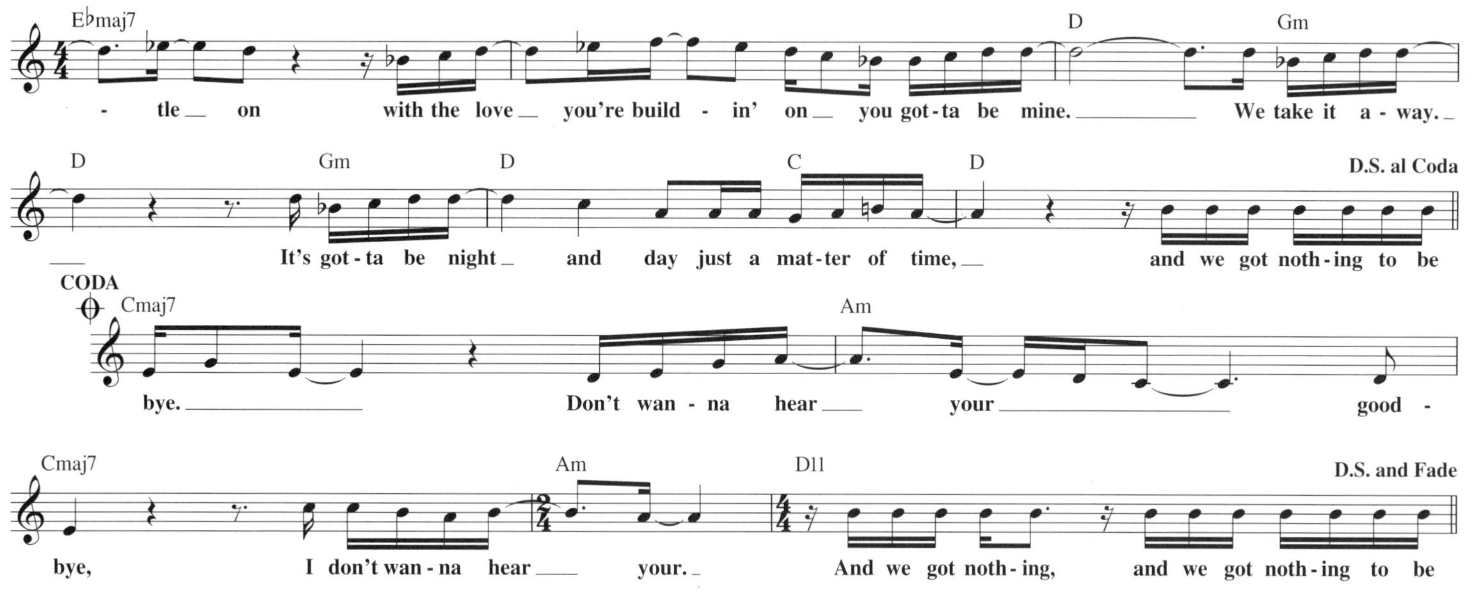

GREENBACK DOLLAR

Words and Music by HOYT AXTON
and KEN RAMSEY

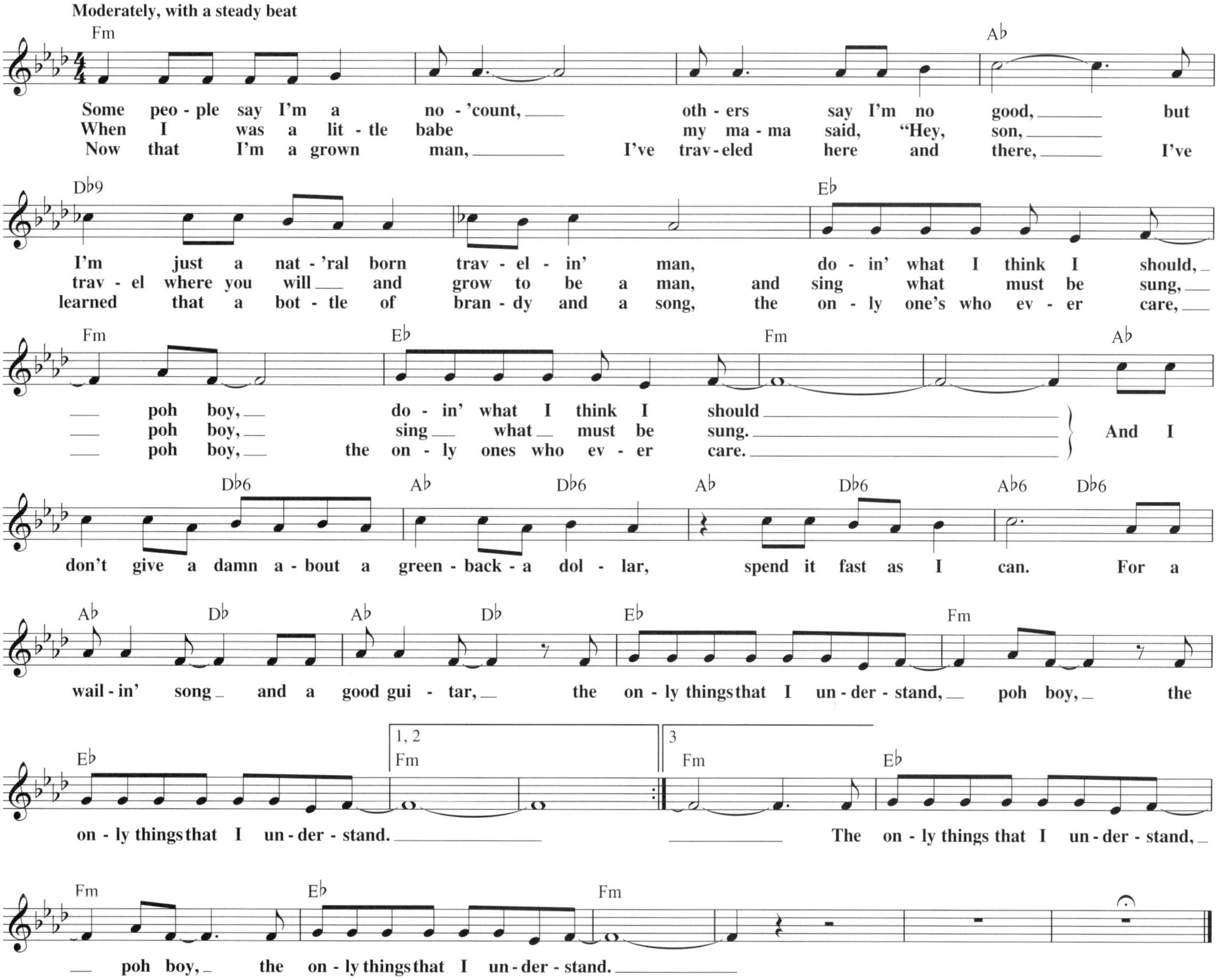
Moderately, with a steady beat
Fm A♭
Some peo-ple say I'm a no-'count, oth-ers say I'm no good, but
When I was a lit-tle babe my ma-ma said, "Hey, son,
Now that I'm a grown man, I've trav-eled here and there, I've
D♭9 E♭
I'm just a nat-'ral born trav-el-in' man, do-in' what I think I should,
trav-el where you will and grow to be a man, and sing what must be sung,
learned that a bot-tle of bran-dy and a song, the on-ly one's who ev-er care,
Fm E♭ Fm A♭
poh boy, do-in' what I think I should
poh boy, sing what must be sung.
poh boy, the on-ly ones who ev-er care.
And I
D♭6 A♭ D♭6 A♭ D♭6 A♭6 D♭6
don't give a damn a-bout a green-back-a dol-lar, spend it fast as I can. For a
A♭ D♭ A♭ D♭ E♭ Fm
wail-in' song and a good gui-tar, the on-ly things that I un-der-stand, poh boy, the
E♭ 1, 2 Fm 3 Fm E♭
on-ly things that I un-der-stand. The on-ly things that I un-der-stand,
Fm E♭ Fm
poh boy, the on-ly things that I un-der-stand.

GREENFIELDS

Words and Music by TERRY GILKYSON, RICHARD DEHR and FRANK MILLER

Slowly, with a steady beat

Cm Fm Cm G7 Cm Fm Cm G7

Once there were green-fields kissed by the sun; once there were val-leys where riv-ers used to run;
Green-fields are gone now, parched by the sun; gone from the val-leys where riv-ers used to run;

Ab Bb7#5 Gm7 C7#5 C7 Fm7 Bb7 Cm G7#5 G7

once there was blue sky with white clouds high a-bove; once they were part of an ev-er-last-ing love.
gone with the cold wind that swept in-to my heart; gone with the lov-ers who let their dreams de-part.

Cm Fm Cm G7 Cm Fm Cm G7 Ab Bb9

We were the lov-ers who strolled through green-fields,
Where are the green-fields that we used to roam? I'll nev-er know what

Fm7 Bb7 Eb Cm7 Fm7 Bb9 Fm7 Bb7 Eb G7 Cm

made you run a-way. How can I keep search-ing when dark clouds hide the day? I on-ly know there's

Ab Fm Cm Fm Fm6 G7b5 G7 Cm Fm

noth-ing here for me, noth-ing in this wide world left for me to see, but I'll keep on wait-in'

Cm G7 Cm Fm Cm G7 Ab Bb7#5

'til you re-turn. I'll keep on wait-ing un-til the day you learn you can't be hap-py while

Gm7 C7#5 C7 Fm7 Bb7 Cm G7#5 G7 Cm Fm

your heart's on the roam. You can't be hap-py un-til you bring it home, home to the green-fields and

To Coda — D.C. al Coda (verse 1 with repeat)

Cm G7 Cm Fm Cm G7

me once a-gain.

CODA

Cm Fm Cm G7

gain.

Ab Fm7 Cm6 Ab7 G7 Cm

Home to the green-fields and me once a-gain.

HAPPY BIRTHDAY SWEET SIXTEEN

Words and Music by HOWARD GREENFIELD and NEIL SEDAKA

Moderately
F A7 Dm
To-night's the night, I've wait-ed for, Be-cause you're not a ba-by
What hap-pened to that fun-ny face? My lit-tle tom-boy now wears
if I should smile with sweet sur-prise, It's just that you've grown up be-
F7 Bb Bdim7 F/C D7
an-y-more. You've turned in-to the pret-ti-est girl I've ev-er seen.
sat-ins and lace. I can't be-lieve my eyes; you're just a teen-age dream.
fore my ver-y eyes, you've turned in-to the pret-ti-est girl I've ev-er seen.

G7
1
C7
2
C7
F
Fine
Hap - py birth-day sweet six - teen.
birth-day sweet six - teen.
C7
F
C7
When you were on-ly six,
I was your big broth-er;
Then when you were ten,
F
D7
Gm7
we did-n't like each oth-er.
When you were thir-teen, you were my fun-ny val-en-tine.
G7
C7
Gm7
C7
D.C. al Fine
But since you've grown up your fu-ture is sewn up, from now on, you're gon-na be mine; So,

HARD HEADED WOMAN

Words and Music by
CLAUDE DEMETRIUS

Bright Rock
B♭ N.C.
Well, a hard head-ed wom-an a soft heart-ed man Been the cause of trou-ble ev-er since the world be-gan.
A-dam told Eve: Lis-ten here to me; Don't you let me catch you mess-in' 'round that ap-ple tree.
Oh,
E♭7
B♭
F7
yeah, Ev-er since the world be-gan. Uh-huh-huh. A hard head-ed wom-an been a thorn in the side of
1
2
G♭7
man. Now man. Now
Sam-son told De-li-lah loud and clear:
heard 'bout a king who was do-in' swell
I got a wom-an a head like a rock.
Keep your cot-ton-pick-in' fin-gers out my curl-y hair.
Till he start-ed play-in' with that e-vil Jez-e-bel.
If she ev-er went a-way I'd cry a-round the clock.
Oh, yeah, Ev-er since the world be-gan.

B♭
F7
E♭7
1, 2
G♭7
3
Uh-huh-huh. A hard head-ed wom-an been a thorn in the side of man. I man.

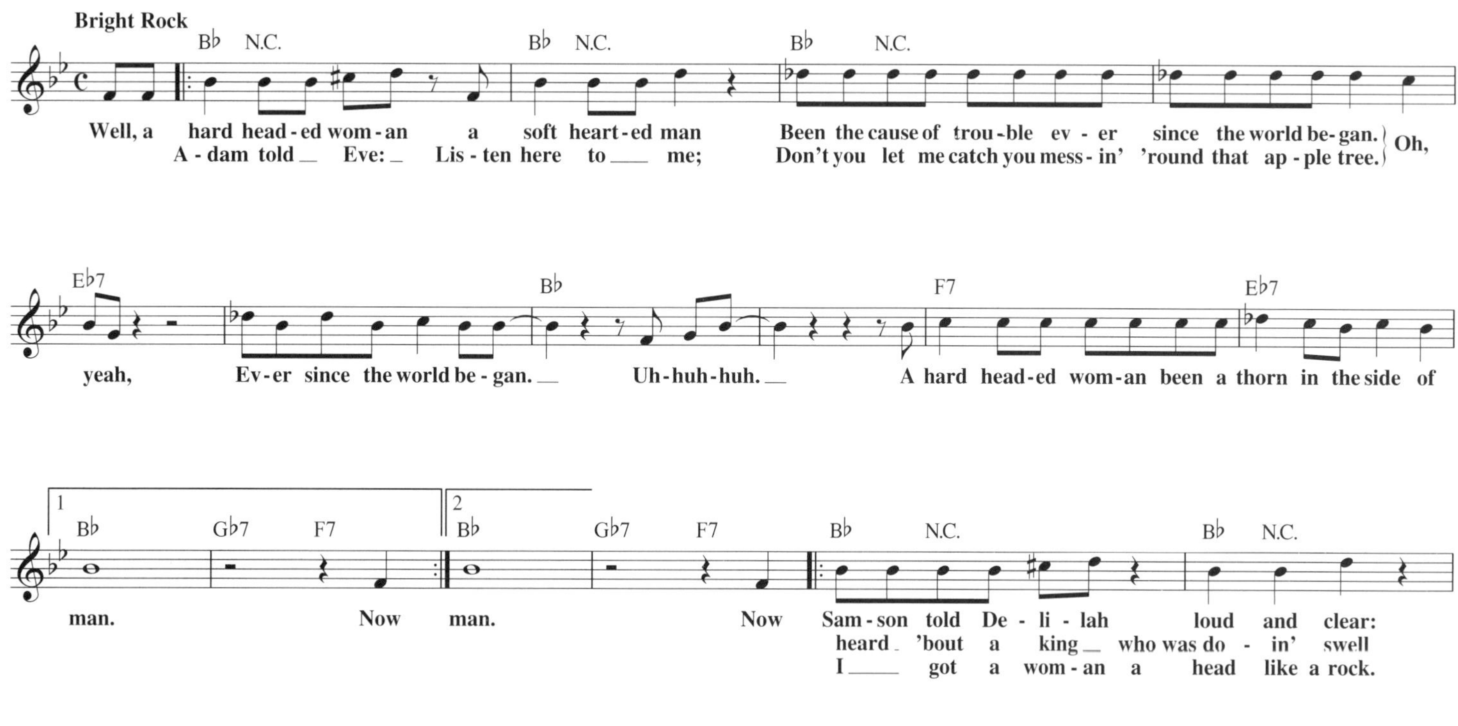

GOOD THING

Words by ROLAND GIFT
Music by DAVID STEELE

Bright Rock Shuffle
E G Bm A E G Bm A
The one good thing in my life
Peo - ple say I should for - get.
E G Bm A E G Bm A
has gone a - way, I don't know why.
There's plen - ty more. Don't get up - set.
E G Bm A E G Bm A
She's gone a - way, I don't know where.
Peo - ple say she's do - ing fine,
she came back.
E G Bm A E G Bm A
Some - where I can't fol - low her.
mu - tual friends I see her some - times.
I was so hap - py that I did - n't ask.
F♯m B
You would - n't think I stayed too long.
That's not why I have wan - dered here.
Morn - in' came in, in - to my room.
To Coda
G♯m C♯ B A
My back was turned and she was gone.
I want her here, she wants me near.
God, you treat me like a fool.
E G Bm A E G D6 A
Good thing, where have you gone? My
E G Bm A E G 1 D6 A 2 D6 A
good thing, you've been gone too long.
D.S. al Coda
E G Bm A E G Bm A E G Bm A
(Good thing.) Then one day
CODA
E G Bm A E G D6 A
Good thing. Good thing. My my
Repeat and Fade
E G Bm A E G D6 A
my my good thing, where have you gone? My

HAVEN'T GOT TIME FOR THE PAIN

Words and Music by CARLY SIMON
and JACOB BRACKMAN

Moderate Rock
All those crazy nights when I cried myself to sleep; now melodrama never makes me weep anymore. 'Cause I haven't got time for the pain, I haven't got room for the pain, I haven't the need for the pain, not since I've known you. You showed me how, how to leave myself behind, how to turn down the noise in my mind. Now I
haven't got time for the pain, I haven't got room for the pain, I haven't the need for the pain, not since I've known you. I pain.
Suffering was the only thing made me feel I was alive, thought that's just how much it cost to survive in this world. 'Til you showed me how, how to fill my heart with love, how to open up and drink in all that white light pouring down from the heaven. I
haven't got time for the pain, I haven't got room for the pain, I haven't the need for the pain, not since I've known you. I haven't got time / got room / the need for the pain. I
Repeat and Fade

HARLEM SHUFFLE

Written by BOB RELF and EARL NELSON

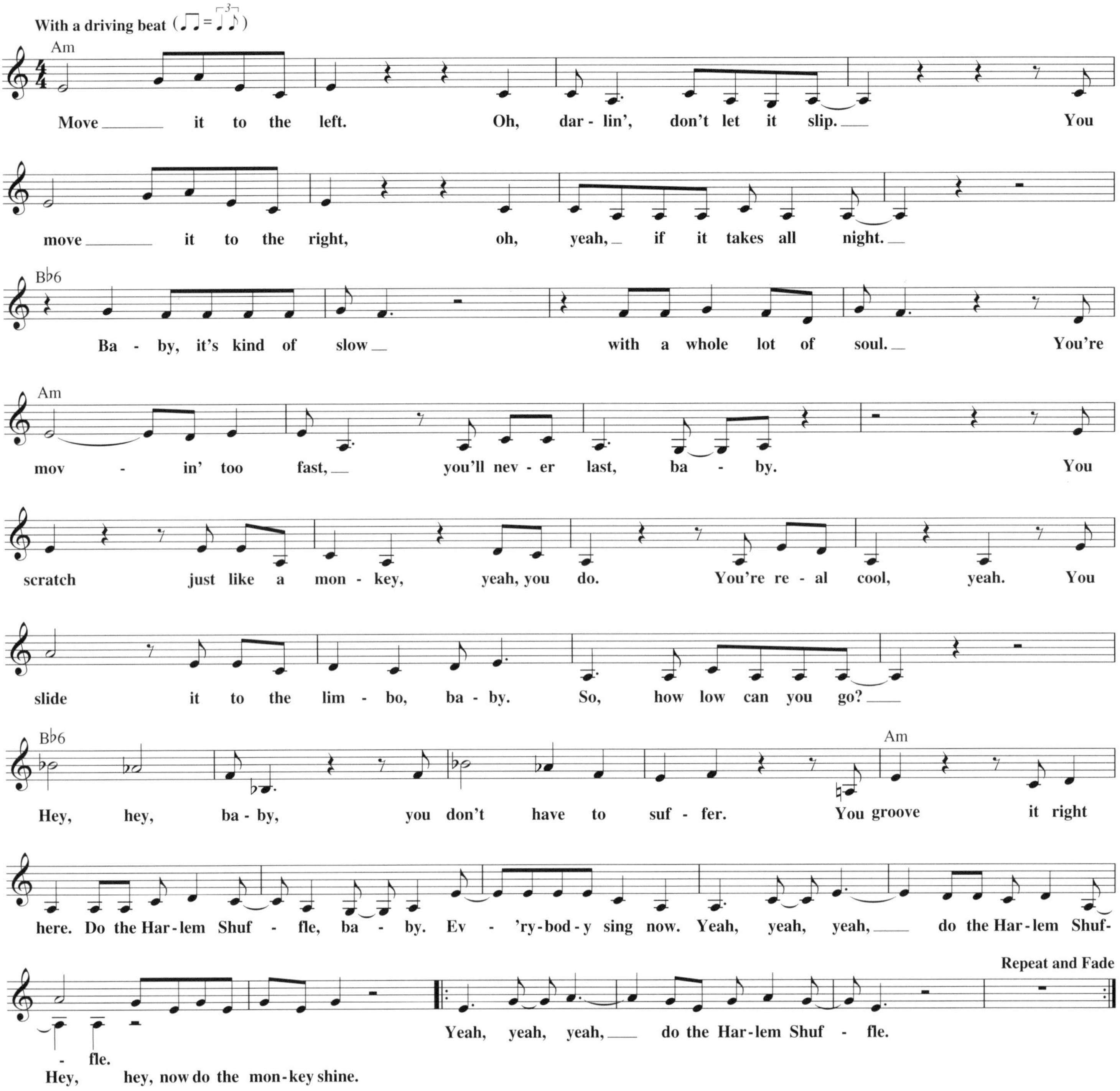

With a driving beat

Am

Move it to the left. Oh, dar - lin', don't let it slip. You move it to the right, oh, yeah, if it takes all night.

B♭6

Ba - by, it's kind of slow with a whole lot of soul. You're

Am

mov - in' too fast, you'll nev - er last, ba - by. You scratch just like a mon - key, yeah, you do. You're re - al cool, yeah. You slide it to the lim - bo, ba - by. So, how low can you go?

B♭6

Hey, hey, ba - by, you don't have to suf - fer. You groove

Am

it right here. Do the Har - lem Shuf - fle, ba - by. Ev - 'ry - bod - y sing now. Yeah, yeah, yeah, do the Har - lem Shuf - fle.

Hey, hey, now do the mon - key shine.

Yeah, yeah, yeah, do the Har - lem Shuf - fle.

Repeat and Fade

HAVE I TOLD YOU LATELY THAT I LOVE YOU

Words and Music by SCOTT WISEMAN

Ballad
C
C♯dim7
G7
Have I told you late - ly that I love you? Could I tell you
told you late - ly how I miss you when the stars are
told you late - ly when I'm sleep - ing ev - 'ry dream I
C
F
once a - gain some - how? Have I told with all my heart and
shin - ing in the sky? Have I told you why the nights are
dream is you some - how? Have I told you who I'd like to

C C♯dim7 G7 C Fm C C7♯5
soul how I a - dore you? Well, dar - ling, I'm tell - ing you now.
long when you're not with me? Well, dar - ling, I'm tell - ing you now.
share my love for - ev - er? Well, dar - ling, I'm tell - ing you now.
This heart would
F C C♯dim7 G7
break in two if you re - fuse me. I'm no good with - out you an - y -
C C7♯5 F C C♯dim7
how. Dear, have I told you late - ly that I love you? Well,
G7 1, 2 C Fm C Dm7 G7 3 C Fm C
dar - ling, I'm tell - ing you now.
Have I
Have I
now.

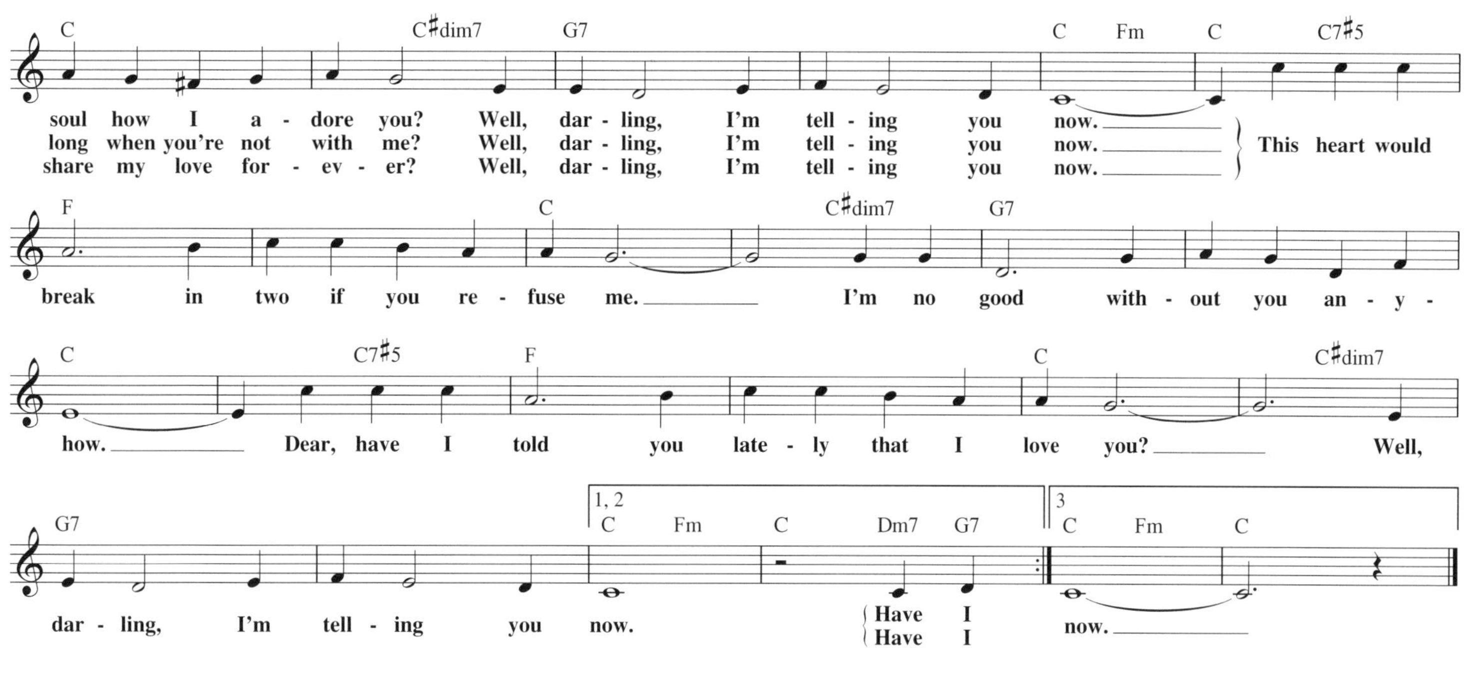

HE'LL HAVE TO GO

Words and Music by JOE ALLISON
and AUDREY ALLISON

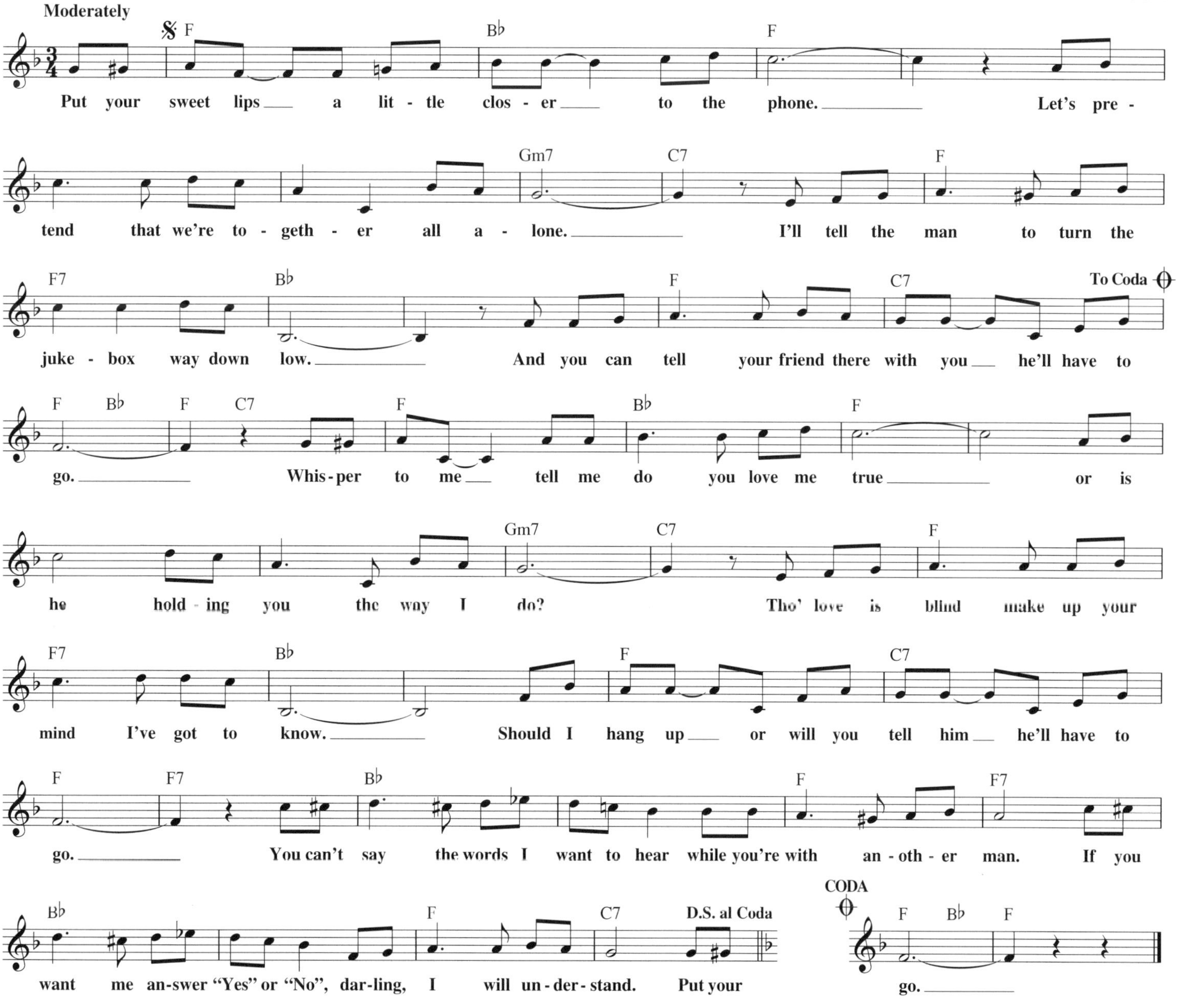

Moderately
F B♭ F
Put your sweet lips a lit - tle clos - er to the phone. Let's pre -
Gm7 C7 F
tend that we're to - geth - er all a - lone. I'll tell the man to turn the
F7 B♭ F C7 To Coda
juke - box way down low. And you can tell your friend there with you he'll have to
F B♭ F C7 F B♭ F
go. Whis - per to me tell me do you love me true or is
Gm7 C7 F
he hold - ing you the way I do? Tho' love is blind make up your
F7 B♭ F C7
mind I've got to know. Should I hang up or will you tell him he'll have to
F F7 B♭ F F7
go. You can't say the words I want to hear while you're with an - oth - er man. If you
B♭ F C7 D.S. al Coda
want me an - swer "Yes" or "No", dar - ling, I will un - der - stand. Put your
CODA
F B♭ F
go.

HEAD OVER HEELS

Words and Music by ROLAND ORZABAL
and CURT SMITH

Moderately
A9 A Cmaj7 C A9 A Cmaj7 C
1. I want-ed to be with you a - lone _ and talk a - bout the weath - er, but tra -
2. (See additional lyrics)
A9 A Cmaj7 C A9 A Cmaj7 C
di - tions I can trace a - gainst the child in your face _ won't es - cape my at - ten - tion.
A9 A Cmaj7 C A9 A Cmaj7 C
You keep your dis - tance with a sys - tem of touch _ and gen - tle per - sua - sion. I'm
A9 A Cmaj7 C A9 A Cmaj7 C
lost in ad - mir - a - tion, could I need you this much? _ Oh you're just wast - ing my time, _ you're _ just, just, just wast - ing time.
Chorus
G Em G Em
Some - thing hap - pens and I'm head o - ver heels I nev - er find _ out till I'm head o - ver heels. _
G Em Dm7
Some - thing hap - pens and I'm head o - ver heels. _ Ah _ don't take my heart, don't break my heart, don't, don't, don't throw it a - way.
A9 A Cmaj7 C A9 A Cmaj7 C
Throw it a - way. _ Throw it a - way. _ (Instrumental) This is my
D C D
four _ leaf _ clo - ver. _ I'm _ on the line, _ o - pen mind. This is my four _ leaf _
C D
_ clo - ver. _ La la la la la la la la la la la la _ la _ la la la
C D
In _ my _ mind's _ eye, _
C D
one _ lit - tle boy, _ one lit - tle man, fun - ny how time flies.

Additional Lyrics

2. I made a fire and watching it burn
Thought of your future
With one foot in the past now just how long will it last
No, no, no have you no ambition
My mother and my brothers used to breathing clean air
And dreaming I'm a doctor
It's hard to be a man when there's a gun in your hand
Oh I feel so...
Chorus

HEARTBREAKER

Words and Music by CLIFF WADE
and GEOFF GILL

Moderately
Your love is like a tidal wave spin-nin' o-ver my head,
Your love has set my soul on fire burn-in' out of con-trol.
drown-in' me in your prom-is-es bet-ter left un-said.
You taught me the ways of de-sire, now it's tak-en its toll.
You're the right kind of sin-ner to re-lease my in-ner fan-ta-sy,
the in-vin-ci-ble win-ner and you know that you were born to be.
You're a heart-break-er, dream mak-er, love tak-er, don't you
mess a-round with me! You're a heart-break-er, dream mak-er, love tak-er, don't you
mess a-round, no, no, no!
To Coda
(Instrumental)
D.S. al Coda
(End instrumental)
CODA
mess a-round with me! You're a heart-break-er, dream mak-er, love tak-er, don't you
mess a-round with me! You're a love tak-er, heart-break-er.
(Instrumental)

HEART OF GLASS

Words and Music by DEBORAH HARRY
and CHRIS STEIN

Moderately fast
E C♯m
Once I had a love and it was a gas. Soon turned out, had a heart of glass.
E C♯
Seemed like the real thing, on-ly to find
C♯m E5
mu-cho mis-trust, love's gone be-hind.
E C♯m
Once I had a love and it was di-vine. Soon found out, I was los-in' my mind.
Once I had a love and it was a gas. Soon turned out to be a pain in the ass.
E C♯
Seemed like the real thing, but I was so blind.
Seemed like the real thing, on-ly to find
C♯m E5 A
Mu-cho mis-trust, love's gone be-hind.
mu-cho mis-trust, love's gone be-hind.
In be-tween,
E
what I find is pleas-ing and I'm feel-ing fine. Love is so con-fus-ing; there's no
A F♯ B To Coda
peace of mind, yet I fear I'm los-ing you. It's just no good, you teas-ing like you do.
A E
(Instrumental)
A F♯ B E5

E
C♯m
E
Once I had a love and it was a gas. Soon turned out, had a heart of glass. Seemed
C♯
C♯m
like the real thing, on-ly to find mu-cho mis-trust, love's gone be-hind.
E5
A
Lost in-side a-dor-a-ble il-lu-sion and I
E
A
can-not hide. I'm the one you're us-ing; please don't push me a-side. We
E
A
could-'ve made it cruis-ing, yeah.
(Instrumental)
E
A
E
A
E
A
1
E
2
F♯
B
Yeah, rid-ing high on love's true blu-ish light.
E5
Ooh, whoa. Ooh, whoa.
D.S. al Coda
CODA
A
E
A
F♯
B
Repeat and Fade

HEAVEN HELP US ALL

Words and Music by
RONALD MILLER

Moderately
A♭ A♭7 D♭ A♭ A♭7
Heav-en help the child who nev-er had a home. Heav-en help the girl who
D♭ A♭ A♭7 D♭
walks the streets a - lone. Heav-en help the ros - es if the bombs be - gin to fall.
E♭7 D♭ A♭ A♭7
Heav - en help us all. Heav-en help the black man if he
D♭ A♭ A♭7 D♭
strug - gles one more day. Heav-en help the white man if he turns his back a - way.
A♭ D♭ E♭7 D♭
Heav-en help the man who kicks the man who has to crawl. Heav - en help us
A♭ B♭m7 A♭7 D♭ E♭7 A♭ B♭m7 A♭7 D♭ E♭7
all; heav-en help us all; heav - en help us all, help us all.
A♭ B♭m A♭ B♭m C7 Fm Fm7 B♭7
Heav - en help us, Lord hear our call when we call.
E♭7 E7 A A7 D
Oh yeah, heav - en help the boy who won't reach twen - ty - one.
A A7 D A A7
Heav - en help the man who gave that boy a gun. Heav-en help the peo - ple with their
D E7 D A D/A
backs a - gainst the wall. Lord, heav - en help us all; heav en help us all.
A D/A A Bm7 A7 D E7 A Bm7 A7 D
Heav - en help us all. Heav - en help us all.
E7 A Bm A Bm C♯7 F♯m F♯m7
Help us all; heav - en help us; Lord, hear our call. When we call

B7
E7
A
D/A
A
D/A
help us all.
A
D/A
A
(Spoken:) Now I lay me down before I go to sleep in a troubled world, I pray
D/A
A
D/A
the Lord to keep, keep hatred from the mighty and the mighty from the
D.S. and Fade
E7
D
A
3
Bm7
A7
D
small. Heaven help us all
Oh, oh, oh, yeah
heav - en help us all.

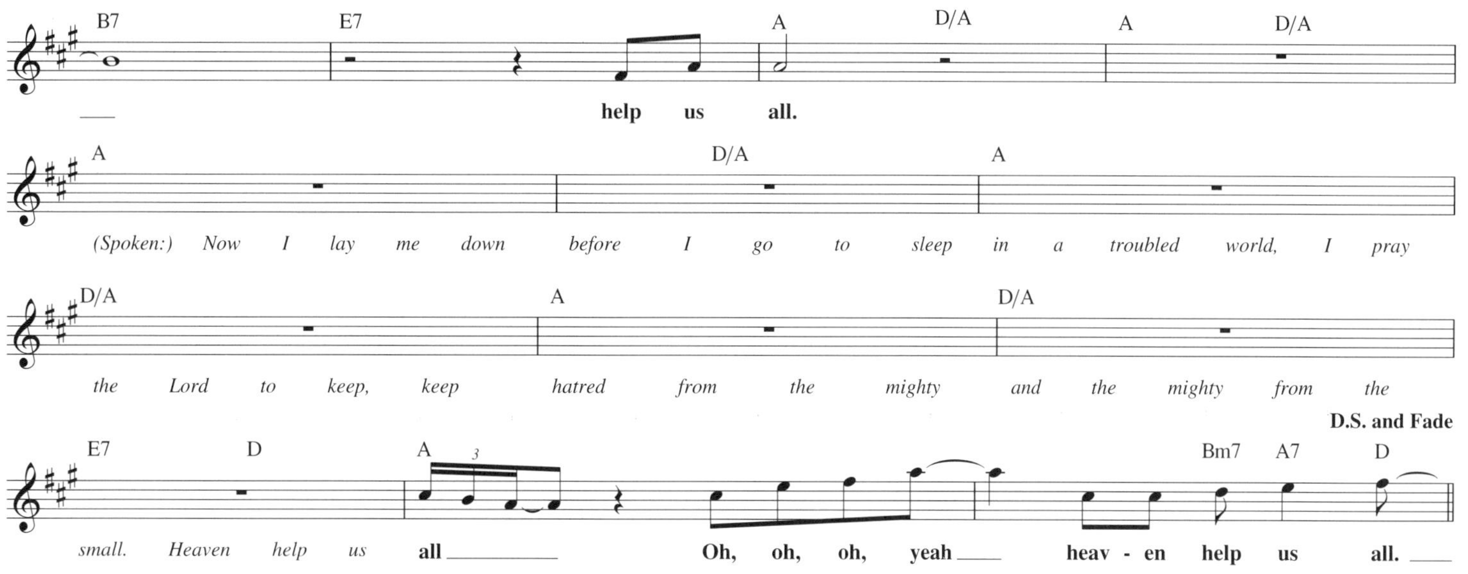

HELP!

Words and Music by JOHN LENNON
and PAUL McCARTNEY

Moderately, with a driving beat

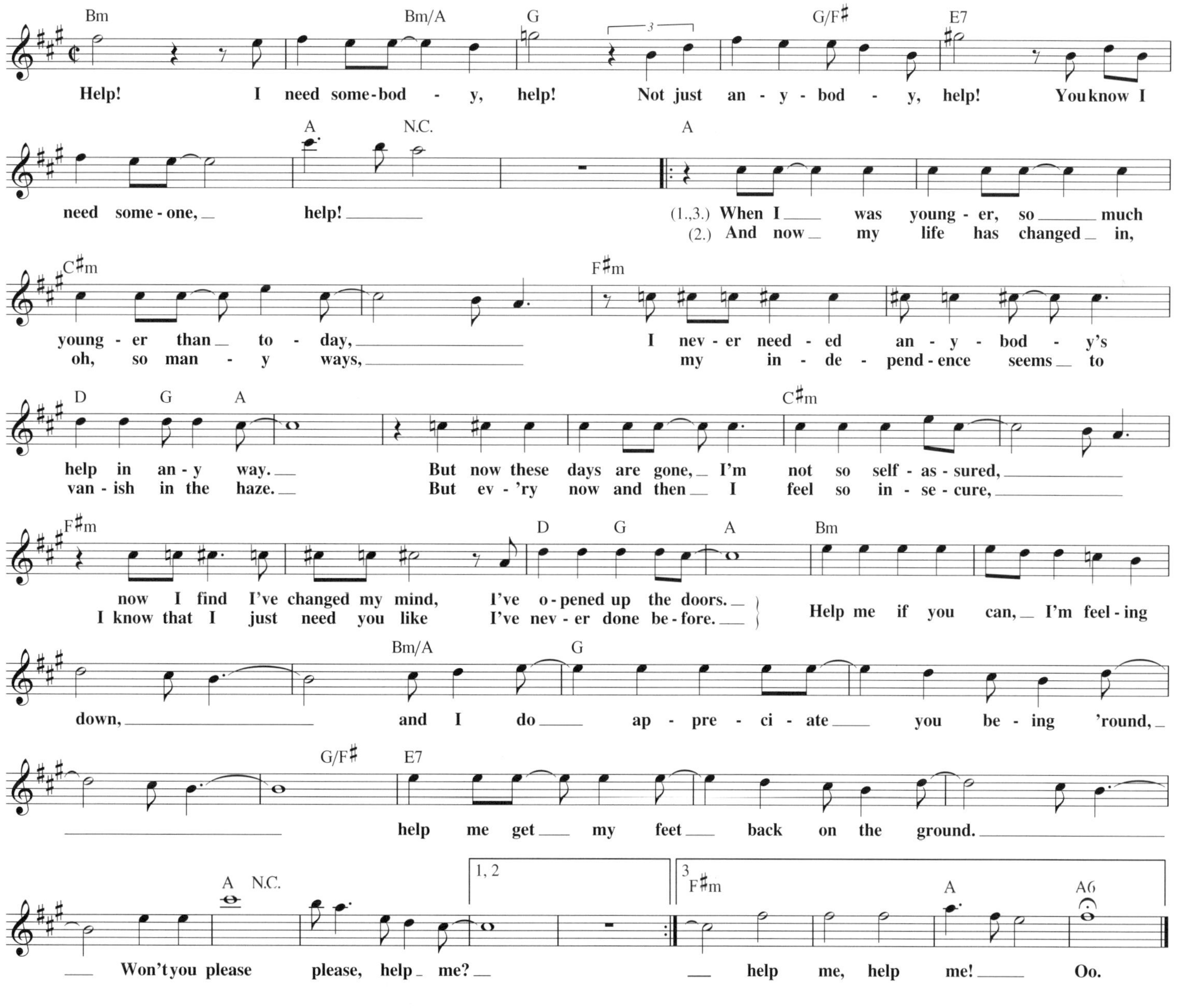

Bm Bm/A G G/F♯ E7

Help! I need some-bod - y, help! Not just an - y - bod - y, help! You know I

A N.C. A

need some - one, help!

(1.,3.) When I was young - er, so much

(2.) And now my life has changed in,

C♯m F♯m

young - er than to - day, I nev - er need - ed an - y - bod - y's

oh, so man - y ways, my in - de - pend - ence seems to

D G A C♯m

help in an - y way. But now these days are gone, I'm not so self - as - sured,

van - ish in the haze. But ev - 'ry now and then I feel so in - se - cure,

F♯m D G A Bm

now I find I've changed my mind, I've o - pened up the doors.

I know that I just need you like I've nev - er done be - fore.

Help me if you can, I'm feel - ing

Bm/A G

down, and I do ap - pre - ci - ate you be - ing 'round,

G/F♯ E7

help me get my feet back on the ground.

A N.C. 1, 2 3 F♯m A A6

Won't you please please, help me? help me, help me! Oo.

HELP ME MAKE IT THROUGH THE NIGHT

Words and Music by
KRIS KRISTOFFERSON

Moderately

D G D G

Take the rib-bon from your hair, shake it loose and let it fall,
Come and lay down by my side till the ear-ly morn-in' light.
Yes-ter-day is dead and gone and to-mor-row's out of sight,

Em A7 To Coda 1. D G

lay-in' soft up-on my skin, like the shad-ows on the wall.
All I'm tak-in' is your time.
and it's sad to be a-lone.

2. D G D

Help me make it through the night. I don't care what's right or

G D

wrong, I don't try to un-der-stand. Let the

E7 A7 D.C. al Coda

dev-il take to-mor-row. Lord, to-night I need a friend.

CODA

D G D

Help me make it through the night.

HEY THERE LONELY GIRL

(Hey There Lonely Boy)

Words and Music by EARL SHUMAN
and LEON CARR

Moderately
Cmaj7 Bm7 Am7 Gmaj7 G
Hey there, lone-ly girl, lone-ly girl, let me make your bro-ken heart like new. Hey there,
Cmaj7 Bm7 Am7 G C
lone-ly girl, lone-ly girl, don't you know this lone-ly boy loves you?
G Bm C D
Ev-er since he broke your heart, you seem so lost each time you pass my way.
lips can kiss your lips and make your heart stand still:
N.C. Bm C D
Oh how I long to take your hand, and say don't cry, I'll kiss your tears a-way.
But once you're in my arms you'll see no one can kiss your lips the way I will.
Hey there,

Cmaj7 Bm7 Am7 Gmaj7 G Cmaj7
lone - ly girl, lone - ly girl, let me make your bro - ken heart like new. Hey there, lone - ly girl,
Bm7 Am7 1 G C G N.C. 2 G
lone - ly girl, don't you know this lone - ly boy loves you? You think that on - ly his two you? Hey there,
Cmaj7 Bm7 Am7 G C G
lone - ly girl, lone - ly girl, don't you know this lone - ly boy loves you?

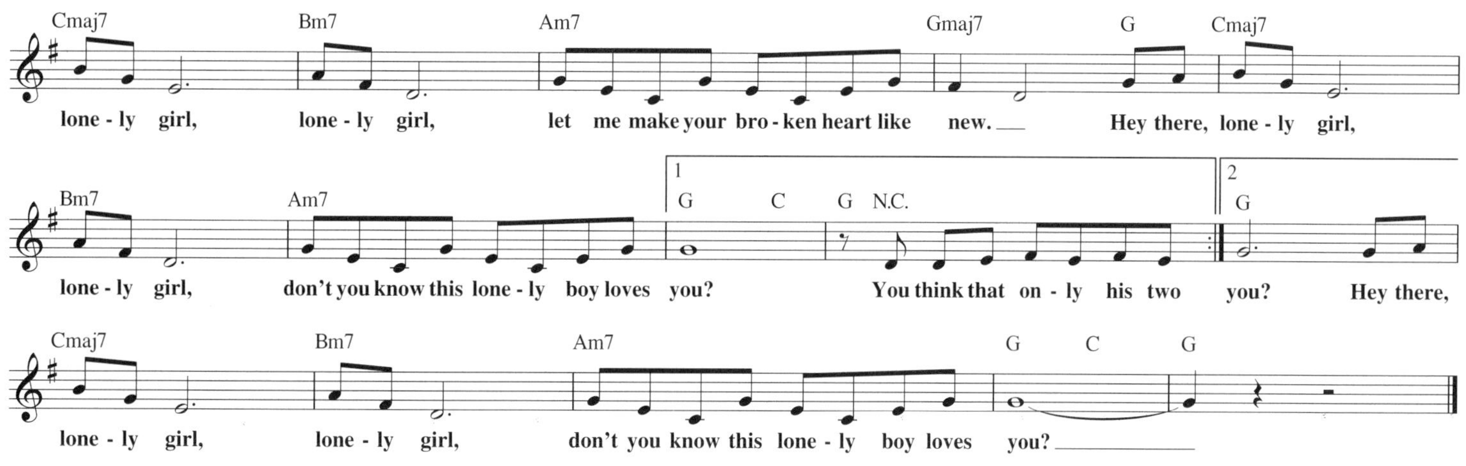

(HEY, WON'T YOU PLAY) ANOTHER SOMEBODY DONE SOMEBODY WRONG SONG

Words and Music by LARRY BUTLER
and CHIPS MOMAN

Easy Swing

F Bb Am F
It's lone - ly out to - night and the feel - in' just got right for a brand - new love song,

Bb F F Fmaj7
some - bod - y done some - bod - y wrong song. Hey, won't you play an - oth - er

F7 Bb F
some - bod - y done somebod - y wrong song? And make me feel at home

Gm C7 F
while I miss my ba - by, while I miss my ba - by. So, play, play for

A7 D7 G7
me a sad mel - o - dy, so sad that it makes ev - 'ry - bod - y cry.

C7 F D7
A real hurt - in' song a - bout a love that's gone wrong 'cause

G7 C C7 **D.S. and Fade**
I don't want to cry all a - lone.

HEARTACHE TONIGHT

Words and Music by JOHN DAVID SOUTHER,
DON HENLEY, GLENN FREY and BOB SEGER

Moderate Blues beat

G Em G Em
Some - bod - y's gon - na hurt some - one before the night is through.

G Em G D
Some - bod - y's gon - na come un - done; there's noth - in' we can do.

G5 Em G5 Em
Ev - 'ry - bod - y wants to touch some - bod - y, if it takes all night.

G5 C5 G5 D5
Ev - 'ry - bod - y wants to take a lit - tle chance, make it come out right.

C7 G7
There's gon - na be a heart - ache to - night, a heart - ache to - night, I know.

C7 To Coda A
There's gon - na be a heart - ache to - night, a heart - ache to - night, I know. Lord, I

D G Em G Em
know. Some peo - ple like to stay out late. Some folks can't hold out that long. But

G C G D5
no - bod - y wants to go home now; there's too much go - in' on.

G Em G Em
The night is gon - na last for - ev - er. Last all, last all sum - mer long.

G C G D
Some - time be - fore the sun comes up the ra - di - o is gon - na play that song.

C7 G7
There's gon - na be a heart - ache to - night, a heart - ache to - night, I know.

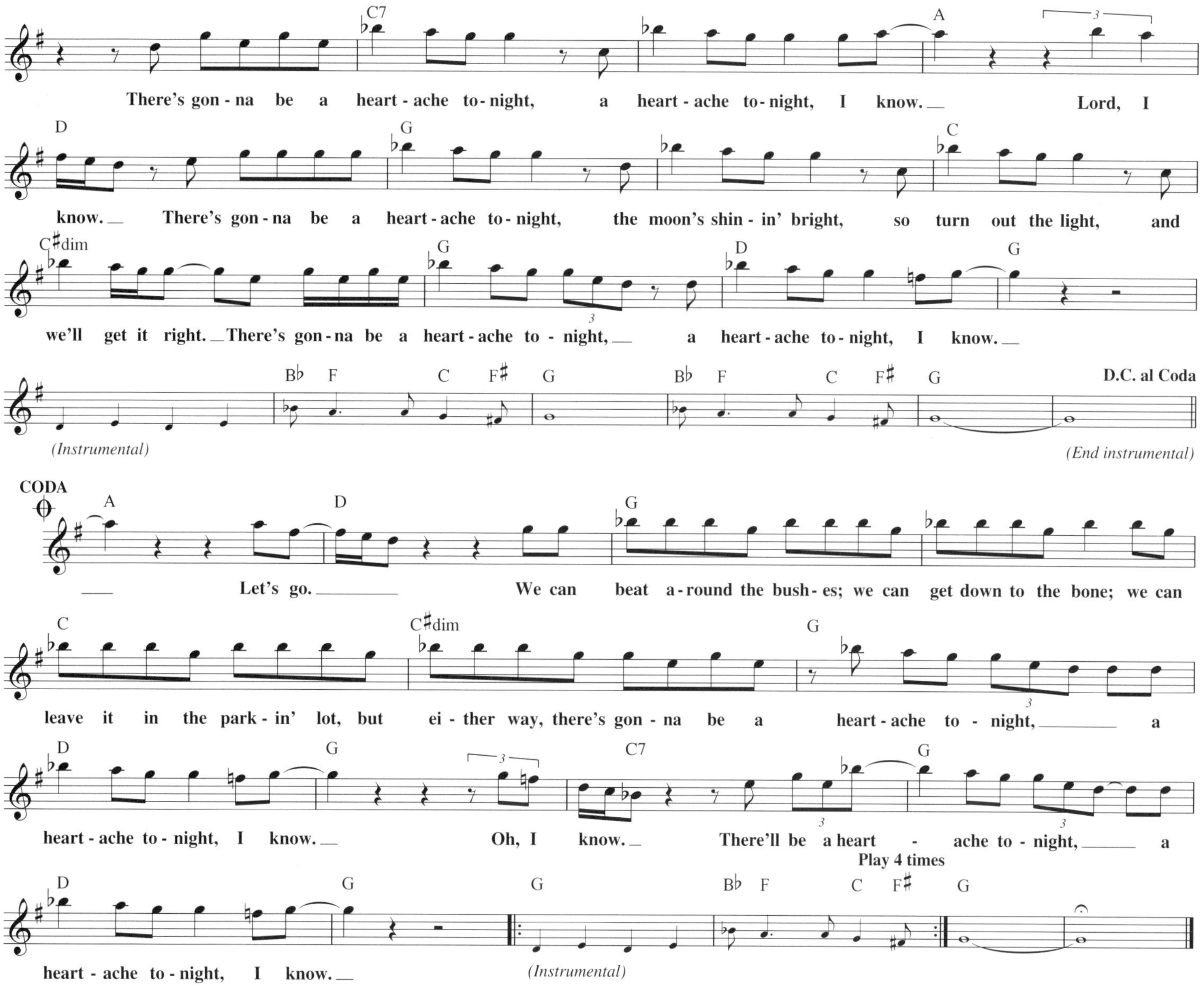

C7
A
3
There's gon - na be a heart - ache to - night, a heart - ache to - night, I know. __ Lord, I
D
G
C
know. __ There's gon - na be a heart - ache to - night, the moon's shin - in' bright, so turn out the light, and
C♯dim
G
D
G
we'll get it right. __ There's gon - na be a heart - ache to - night, __ a heart - ache to - night, I know. __
B♭ F C F♯ G B♭ F C F♯ G
D.C. al Coda
(Instrumental)
(End instrumental)
CODA
A
D
G
__ Let's go. ________ We can beat a - round the bush - es; we can get down to the bone; we can
C
C♯dim
G
leave it in the park - in' lot, but ei - ther way, there's gon - na be a heart - ache to - night, ______ a
D
G
C7
G
heart - ache to - night, I know. __ Oh, I know. __ There'll be a heart - ache to - night, ______ a
Play 4 times
D
G
G
B♭ F C F♯ G
heart - ache to - night, I know. __
(Instrumental)

HILL STREET BLUES THEME

from the Television Series

By MIKE POST

Moderately
E♭ B♭/E♭ E♭ A♭maj9 B♭/A♭ A♭maj9 E♭/B♭ B♭ E♭/B♭ B♭ E♭ B♭/E♭ E♭
A♭maj7 A♭ B♭9 E♭ B♭/E♭ E♭
To Coda
F/A F7/A E♭/B♭ E♭+/B
C A/C♯ D Gm Cm/G Gm7 A♭/B♭ A♭maj7/B♭ B♭7
D.C. al Coda
CODA
A♭maj7 Gm7 Fm7 A♭maj7 Gm7 Fm7 A♭maj7 Gm7 Fm7 A♭/B♭ E♭ B♭/E♭ E♭ B♭/E♭ E♭/B♭ B♭/A♭ E♭

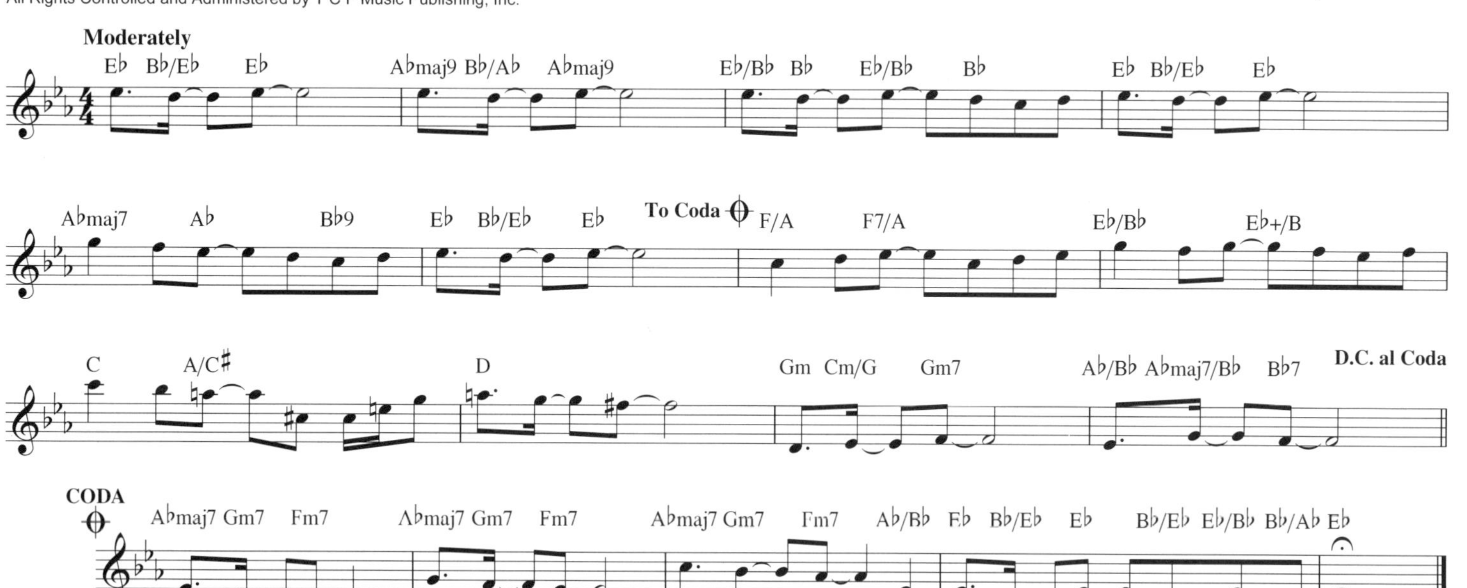

HERE YOU COME AGAIN

Words by CYNTHIA WEIL
Music by BARRY MANN

Moderately
Here you come a - gain, just when I've be-gun to get my - self to - geth - er, you
Here you come a - gain, just when I'm a-bout to make it work with - out you, you
waltz right in the door, just like you've done be-fore and wrap my heart 'round your lit - tle fin - ger.
look in - to my eyes and lie those pret-ty lies and
pret-ty soon I'm won-d'rin how I came to doubt you. All you got-ta do is smile that smile and
there go all my de - fens - es. Just leave it up to you and in a lit - tle while you're
mess-in' up my mind and fill-in' up my sens - es. Here you come a - gain
Instrumental
look-in' bet - ter than a bod - y has a right to; and shak-in' me up so that all I real-ly know is
here you come a-gain and here I go.
End instrumental
All you got-ta do is smile that smile and
there go all my de - fens - es. Just leave it up to you and in a lit - tle while you're
mess-in' up my mind and fill-in' up my sens - es. Here you come a - gain,
look-in' bet - ter than a bod - y has a right to and shak-in' me up so that all I real-ly know is
here you come a - gain and here I go,
Repeat and Fade
here I go,

HIGH HOPES

Words by SAMMY CAHN
Music by JAMES VAN HEUSEN

Moderately, with a beat (♫ = ♩♪ [triplet 3])

F6 F♯dim7 Gm7

Next time you're found with your chin on the ground, there's a lot to be learned,
When trou - bles call and your back's to the wall, there's a lot to be learned;
Instrumental solo

C9 F Dm Gm7 C13 F B♭

so look a - round. Just what makes that lit - tle ol' ant
that wall could fall. Once there was a sil - ly ol' ram,

C7 F F♯dim7 Gm7 G♯dim7

think he'll move that rub - ber tree plant. An - y - one knows an ant can't
thought he'd punch a hole in a dam. No one could make that ram scram;

Gm7 C7 F6 F7 B♭ Bdim7

move a rub - ber tree plant. But he's got high hopes, he's got
he kept butt - in' that dam, 'cause he had high hopes, he had
Solo ends So keep your high hopes, keep your

F/C F Dm7 G7 Dm7 G7 Dm7/G G7

high hopes, he's got high ap - ple pie in the
high hopes, he had high ap - ple pie in the
high hopes, keep those high ap - ple pie in the

C7 F F7

sky hopes. So an - y - time you're get - tin' low, 'stead of let - tin' go,
sky hopes. So an - y - time you're feel - in' bad, 'stead of feel - in' sad,
sky hopes. A prob - lem's just a toy bal - loon, they'll be burst - ing soon,

B♭ Bdim7 F6 F♯dim7 Gm7 C

just re - mem - ber that ant. Oops! There goes an - oth - er rub - ber tree
just re - mem - ber that ram. Oops! There goes a bil - lion kil - o - watt
they're just bound to go, "Pop!" Oops! There goes an - oth - er prob - lem, ker -

F6 F♯dim7 Gm7 C7 F6 F♯dim7

(Oops! There goes an - oth - er rub - ber tree plant.)
(Oops! There goes a bil - lion kil - o - watt dam.)
(Oops! There goes an - oth - er prob - lem, ker - plop!)

plant. Oops! There goes an -
dam. Oops! There goes a
plop! Oops! There goes an -

Gm7 C | 1,2 F F♯dim7 Gm7 C | 3 F C7 F F6/9

oth - er rub - ber tree plant.
bil - lion kil - o - watt dam.
oth - er prob - lem, ker - plop! Ker - plop!

HIGHER GROUND

Words and Music by
STEVIE WONDER

Moderate Rock

Eb7 Gb Ab Eb7 Gb Ab Gb Ab Eb7

Peo-ple keep on learn in'. Sol-diers keep on
Pow-ers keep on ly-in', While your peo-ple keep on
Lov-ers keep on lov-in', Be-liev-ers keep on be-

Gb Ab Eb7 F7 Ab Bb F7 G7 Ab7 Db7 Eb7 Gb Ab

war-rin', World keep on turn-in' 'cause it won't be too long.
dy-in'. World keep on turn-in' 'cause it won't be too long.
liev-in'. Sleep-ers just stop sleep-in' 'cause it won't be too long.

Eb7 Eb Gb Ab 1 Eb7 2, 3 Eb7 Ab7 Eb7

I'm so darn glad
I'm so darn glad
he let me try it a-gain, 'cause my

Ab7 Eb7 Ab7 Eb7

last time on earth I lived a whole world of sin. I'm so glad that I know more than I knew then, gon-na keep

F7 Bb7#9 Eb7 Gb Ab Eb7 To Coda Gb Ab Eb7

D.C. al Coda
(Take 2nd ending)

on try-in' till I reach (the / my) high-est ground.

CODA

Gb Ab Eb7 Gb Ab Eb7 Gb Ab

Repeat and Fade

Till I reach my high-est ground. No
one's gon-na bring me down. Till

HOLD ON LOOSELY

Words and Music by JEFF CARLISI,
DON BARNES and JIM PETERIK

Moderately
E B/D# D A/C# B A E B/D#
You see it all a-round you: good lov-in' gone bad. And you be-lieve it's
So damn eas-y when your feel-ings are such, to o-ver-pro-
D A/C# C
too late when you re-al-ize what you had.
tect her, to love her too much.
And my mind goes back to a girl that I left
D E E/D# E/D A/C#
some years a-go, who told me: Just hold on loose-ly, but don't let go.
D E E/D# E/D A/C#
If you cling too tight-ly, you're gon-na lose con-trol.

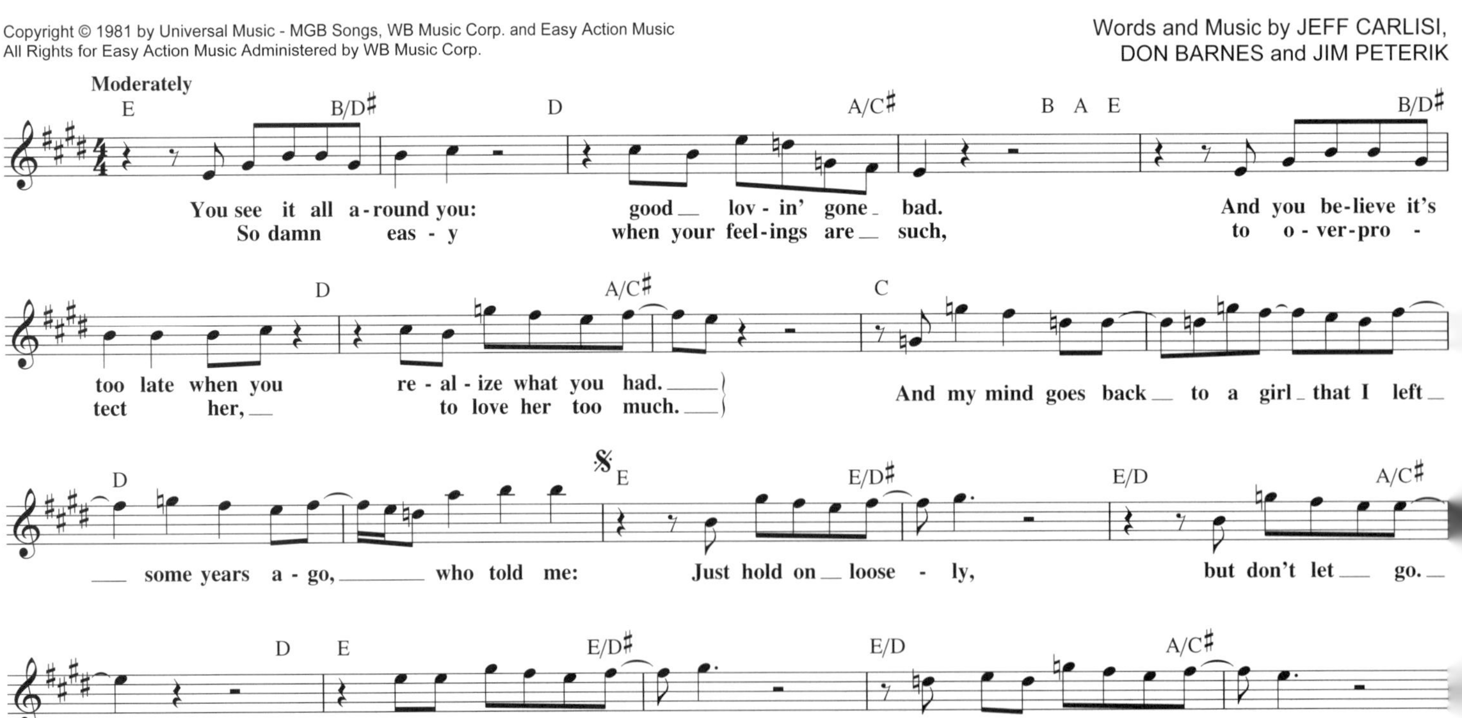

F♯m
B
F♯m
A
G/A
D/A
G/A
D/A
B
D.S. and Fade
Your ba-by needs some - one to be-lieve in _ and a whole lot of space to breathe _ in. _ to breathe _ in. _
Don't let her slip a - way. Sen - ti - men-tal fool. _
Don't let your heart get in _ the _ way. _

HOT ROD LINCOLN

Words and Music by W.S. STEVENSON
and CHARLEY RYAN

Bright Rock
My pappy said, "Son, you're gonna drive me to drinkin', if you don't stop drivin' that hot rod Lincoln."
E
A
(Bass)
B7
E
To Next Strain
(Spoken:) Have you
Fine
E
A
1. heard the sto - ry of the hot rod race, when the Fords and Lin-colns was set- tin' the pace. That
2.-13. (See additional lyrics)
B7
D.C. al Fine
sto - ry is true, I'm here to say, _ 'Cause I was a-driv- in' that mod-el "A". _ It's got a

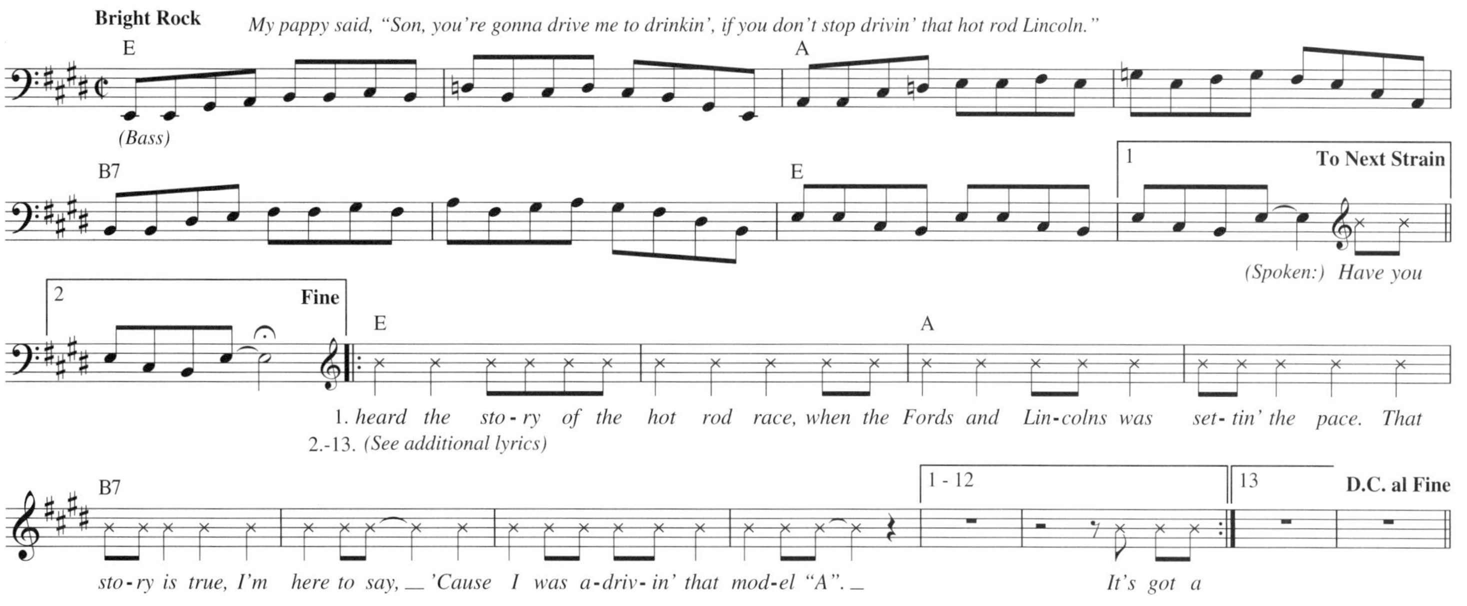

Additional Lyrics

2. *It's got a Lincoln motor and it's really souped up,*
   That model "A" body makes it look like a pup.
   It's got 8 cylinders and uses 'em all,
   Got overdrive, just won't stall.

3. *With a 4-barrel carb and dual exhaust,*
   With 4-11 gears you can really get lost.
   It's got safety tubes but I ain't scared.
   The brakes are good, the tires, fair.

4. *Pulled out of San Pedro late one night,*
   The moon and the stars were shining bright.
   We was drivin' up Grapevine Hill,
   Passin' cars like they was standin' still.

5. *All of a sudden, in the wink of an eye,*
   A Cadillac sedan passed us by.
   I said, "Boys, that's a mark for me."
   By then the tail-light was all you could see.

6. *Now the fellas ribbed me for bein' behind,*
   So I thought I'd make the Lincoln unwind.
   Took my foot off the gas and man-a-live,
   I shoved it on down into overdrive.

7. *I wound it up to a hundred and ten,*
   My speedometer said that I hit top then.
   My foot was glued like lead to the floor.
   That's all there is and there ain't no more.

8. *Now the boys all thought I lost my sense.*
   Them telephone poles looked like a picket fence.
   They said, "Slow down, I see spots.
   The lines on the road, just look like dots."

9. *Took a corner, sideswiped a truck,*
   I crossed my fingers just for luck.
   My fenders was clickin' the guard-rail posts,
   The guy beside me was white as a ghost.

10. *Smoke was comin' from out of the back,*
    When I started to gain on that Cadillac.
    I knew I could catch him, I thought I could pass.
    Don't you know by then we'd be low on gas.

11. *They had flames comin' from out of the side.*
    You can feel the tension, man, what a ride!
    I said, "Look out, boys, I got a license to fly."
    And that Caddy pulled over and let us by.

12. *Now all of a sudden she started to knockin',*
    Down in a dip she started to rockin'.
    I looked in the mirror, a red light was blinkin',
    The cops was after my hot rod Lincoln.

13. *They arrested me and they put me in jail,*
    I called my pappy to throw my bail.
    He said, "Son, you're gonna drive me to drinkin',
    If you don't stop drivin' that hot rod Lincoln."

HOLDING BACK THE YEARS

Words by MICK HUCKNELL
Music by MICK HUCKNELL and NEIL MOSS

Moderately slow
Dm9 G9 Dm9 G9
Hold - ing back the years, think - ing of the fear I've had so long.
Hold - ing back the years, chance for me es - cape from all I've known.
Dm9 G9 Dm9 G9
When some - bod - y hears, lis - ten to the fear that's gone.
Hold - ing back the tears 'cause noth - ing here has grown.
tight. Instrumental ad lib.
Dm9 G9 Dm9
Instrumental ends
Stran - gled by the wish - es of pa - ter, hop - ing for the
(2., D.S.) I've wast - ed all my tears, wast - ed all those
G9 Dm9 G9
arms of ma - ter, get to meet her soon - er or lat - er, oh.
years. Noth - ing had the
Dm9 G9 Dm9 G9 G9
I'll keep hold - ing on. I'll keep hold - ing on.
2, 3
chance to be good.
Dm9 G9 Dm9 G9
Noth - ing ev - er could, yeah, oh. I'll keep hold - ing on.
Dm9 G9 Dm9 G Dm9
I'll keep hold - ing on. I'll keep hold - ing on. I'll keep
To Coda
G9
D.S. al Coda
hold - ing on so
CODA
G9
hold - ing on, hold - ing, hold - ing, hold - ing. Ah,
Dm9 G9 Dm9 G9
la, la, la, la, la, la. I said ooh, yeah.
Dm9 G9 Dm9 G9 Dm9 G9
Repeat and Fade
That's all I have to pay. It's all I have to say.

HOW DO YOU TALK TO AN ANGEL

Words and Music by STEVE TYRELL,
STEPHANIE TYRELL and BARRY COFFING

Moderate rock
I hear a voice in my mind, I know her face by heart.
Heav-en and earth are mov-ing in my soul, I don't know where to start.
At night I dream that she is there, and I can feel her in the air.
Tell me, tell me the words to de-fine the way I feel a-bout some-one so fine.
How do you talk to an an-gel? How do you hold her close to where you are?
How do you talk to an an-gel? It's like try-ing to catch a fall-ing star.
star.
1. Guitar solo ad lib.
2.,3. How do you talk to an an-gel? How do you hold her close to where you are? How do you talk to an an-gel?
Solo ends
It's like try-ing to catch a fall-ing...
It's like try-ing to catch a fall-ing star.
Yeah.
Yeah.

HONKY CAT

Words and Music by ELTON JOHN
and BERNIE TAUPIN

Brightly

D7 — G
When _ I look back, boy, I must _ have been green, _ bop-pin' in the coun-

D7
-try. fish-in' in ___ a stream. _ Look-in' for an an - swer,

G
try-in' to find _ a sign, ___ un-til I saw your cit-y lights, _ hon-ey I ___ was blind. _

𝄋 B7
___ They said, get back, hon-ky cat, bet-ter get back to the woods, _ well, I

E7
quit those days ___ and _ my red - neck ways ___ and _ a,

D7 — Am7/D — D7 — G
(hmm, _ hmm, hmm, hmm, hmm,) oh, the change _ is gon-na do me good. ___
(oo, ___ oo, ___ oo, oo, ___ oo,)

B7
You bet-ter get back, hon-ky cat, liv-in' in the cit-y ain't _

E7
where it's at, it's like try'n' _ to find gold ___ in ___ a sil - ver mine, _

D7 — Am7/D — D7 — To Coda 𝄌
___ it's _ like try'n' _ to drink whis-key, oh, ___ from a bot-tle of wine. _

G — D7
___ Well I read _ some books and I

G
read some mag - a - zines ___ a - bout those high - class la - dies down _ in

D7
New Or - leans, and all the folks back home, well, they said I was a fool.
G
They said, oh, be - lieve in the Lord is the gold - en rule. They said,
B7
E7
get back, hon - ky cat, bet - ter get back to the woods well, I quit those days
D7
and my red - neck ways and (oo, oo, oo, oo, oo,)
Am7/D
D7
G
1
oh, the change is gon - na do me good. They said,
2
D7
They said, stay at home, boy, you got - ta tend the farm,
G
liv - in' in the cit - y, boy, is, is gon - na break your heart. But
D7
Am7/D
how can you stay, when your heart says no, ah, ah,
G
D.S. al Coda
how can you stop, when your feet say go. You bet - ter
CODA
G
D7
Get back, hon - ky cat, get
G
Repeat and Fade
back, hon - ky cat, get back, ooh.

HOW CAN I FALL?

Words and Music by DAVID GLASPER, MARCUS LILLINGTON, IAN SPICE and MICHAEL DELAHUNTY

Moderate ballad

A(add9) F♯m7(add4)

Give me time to care. The moment's here for us to share,
Could I lie to you, I'm just too weak to face the truth.
When all faith is gone, I fight myself to carry on.
Now I hold this line. I know the choice to leave is mine.

E(add9) D(add9) C♯m7 1 Bm7

still my heart is not always there.
Now I know I should make a move.
Yes I know of the harm I do.
I can't help what I feel inside.

What more can I say to you?

2 Bm7 A(add9)

say? How can I fall, how can I fall when you

To Coda
D.C. al Coda (with repeat)
D(add9) C♯m7 D(add9) C♯m7 Bm7 D C♯m7 Bm7 D/E
just won't give me reasons, when you just won't give me reasons at all?

CODA
Bm7 D C♯m7 Bm7 A(add9) F♯m7 C♯m7 Dmaj7
all? I'll follow through I'll see I do when the

C♯m7 D C♯m7 Bm7 A(add9) F♯m7 C♯m7 Dmaj7
time is far more right for you I'll make that move and when I do will I

C♯m7 D C♯m7 Bm7 A(add9)
doubt again the way I do? How can I fall, how can I fall when you

Repeat and Fade
D(add9) C♯m7 D(add9) C♯m7 Bm7 D C♯m7 Bm7
just won't give me reasons, when you just won't give me reasons at all?

HOW SWEET IT IS (TO BE LOVED BY YOU)

Words and Music by EDWARD HOLLAND,
LAMONT DOZIER and BRIAN HOLLAND

Moderate Rock beat

Cmaj7 Bm7 Am7 D11 G | 1 | 2 Am7 D11

How sweet it is to be loved by you.

G Em D7 D♭7

I need-ed the shel-ter of some-one's arms; there you
I close my eyes at night won-der-ing where would I be with-out
(Instrumental)

C7 G Em

were. I need-ed some-one to un-der-stand my ups and downs;
you in my life. Ev-'ry-thing I did was just a bore;

D7 D♭7 C7 G

there you were with sweet love and de-
ev-'ry-where I went, seems I'd been there be-fore. But you bright-en up for me
(Instrumental ends) You were bet-ter to me than I

C7 Em C7 C♯dim7

vo-tion deep-ly touch-ing my e-mo-tion.
all of my days with a love so sweet in so man-y ways. } I want to
was to my-self; for me there's you and there ain't no-bod-y else. }

G C7 G N.C.

stop and thank you, ba-by; I want to stop and thank you,

G F Em Dm Cmaj7 Bm7 Am7 D11

ba-by. How sweet it is to be loved by

G Cmaj7 Bm7 Am7

you. How sweet it is

D11 G | 1, 2 Am7 D11

to be loved by you.

3 | Cmaj7 Bm7 Am7 D11 G

How sweet it is to be loved by you.

Repeat and Fade

HURDY GURDY MAN

Words and Music by
DONOVAN LEITCH

Slowly

G Bm C D7

Thrown like a star in my vast sleep I o - pen my eyes to take a peep
His - tor - ies of ag - es past un - en - light - ened shad - ows cast

G Bm C D7

to find that I was by the sea gaz - ing with tran - quil - i - ty. 'Twas
down through all e - ter - ni - ty, the cry - ing of hu - man - i - ty. 'Tis

F C G

then when the hur - dy gur - dy man came sing - ing songs of love,
then when the hur - dy gur - dy man comes sing - ing songs of love,

F C G

then when the hur - dy gur - dy man came sing - ing songs of love.
then when the hur - dy gur - dy man comes sing - ing songs of love.

F C G

Hur - dy gur - dy hur - dy gur - dy hur - dy gur - dy, gur - dy, he sang.

F C G

Hur - dy gur - dy hur - dy gur - dy hur - dy gur - dy gur - dy, he sang.

F C G

Hur - dy gur - dy hur - dy gur - dy hur - dy gur - dy gur - dy, he sang.

F C | 1. G N.C. | 2. G | F C

(Instrumental)

Hur - dy gur - dy hur - dy gur - dy hur - dy

G F C

gur - dy gur - dy, he sang. Here comes the ro - ly po - ly man and he's

G F C G **Repeat and Fade**

sing - ing songs of love. Ro - ly po - ly ro - ly po - ly po - ly ro - ly po - ly, he sang.

HURT SO BAD

Words and Music by TEDDY RANDAZZO, BOBBY WEINSTEIN and BOBBY HART

Slowly
Gm7 Fm7 E♭maj7
I know you don't know what I'm go - ing through,
you've been mak - in' out O. K.
B♭m7 Cm7 F7 Gmaj7
stand - ing here look - ing at you. Well, let me tell you that it
She's in love; don't stand in her way. But let me tell you that it
A♭maj7 Gm7 A♭maj7
hurt so bad. It makes me feel so bad.
hurt so bad. It makes me feel so bad.
Gm7 A♭maj7 Gm7
It makes me hurt so bad to see you a - gain,
It's gon - na hurt so bad if you walk a - way.
Cm 1 Fm7
like nee - dles and pins. Peo - ple say
2 A♭maj7 Gm7
Why don't you stay and let me make it up to you?
A♭maj7 Gm7 Cm Gm7
Stay, I'll do an - y - thing you want me to. You loved me be - fore, please
A♭maj7 B♭7 A♭6 Gm7 Fm7 B♭7
love me a - gain. I can't let you go back to him. Please don't go, please don't
A♭maj7 Gm7 A♭maj7
go. It hurt so bad. Come back, it hurt so bad.
Gm7 A♭maj7 Gm7 Cm
Don't make it hurt so bad, I'm beg - gin' you please.
Fm7 B♭7 E♭
Please don't go, please don't go.

I CAN SEE FOR MILES

Words and Music by
PETER TOWNSHEND

Bright Rock
E5 G5 A5 E5 G5 A5 E5
I know you've de - ceived me, now here's a sur - prise. I know that you have, 'cause there's
G5 A5 E5 E Em7 A/E C/E
mag - ic in my eyes. I can see for miles and miles and miles and
Asus/E E5 Em E E5
miles and miles. Oh yeah. Oh yeah.
If you think that I
You took ad - van - tage of my
The Eif - fel Tow - er and the
G5 A5 E5 G5 A5 E5
don't know a - bout the lit - tle tricks you play, and nev - er see you when de -
trust in you when I was so far a - way. I saw you hold - ing lots of
Taj Ma - hal are mine to see on clear - er days. You thought that I would need a
G5 A5 E
lib - 'rate - ly you put things in my way. Well, here's a
oth - er guys and now you got the nerve to say that you
crys - tal ball to see right through the haze. Well, here's a
A B A
poke at you. You're gon - na choke on it too. You're gon - na lose that smile,
still want me. Well, that's as may be, but you got - ta stand trial,
poke at you. You're gon - na choke on it too. You're gon - na lose that smile,
be -
B A A/B E
cause all the while, I could see for miles and miles. I could see for
A A/B E Em7 A/E
miles and miles. I could see for miles and miles and
To Coda
C/E Asus/E E5
miles and miles and miles. Oh
Em E 1 2 D.S. al Coda
yeah. I
CODA
E
miles and miles and miles and miles.
A A/B E Repeat and Fade
I could see for miles and miles. I could see for

I CAN'T GET NEXT TO YOU

Words and Music by BARRETT STRONG
and NORMAN WHITFIELD

Moderately
Cm7 A♭(add9) Cm7
1. I can turn the grey sky blue and I can make it rain when-
2., 3. (See additional lyrics)
A♭(add9) B♭ Cm7 A♭(add9)
ev - er I want it to. And I can build a cas - tle from a sin - gle grain of sand and
Cm7 A♭(add9) B♭/D Fm Cm To Coda
I can make a ship sail on dry land, but my life is in - com - plete and I'm so blue. 'Cause
Fm Cm Fsus
I can't get next to you, I can't get next to you. babe, I can't get next to you, I
Cm 1 Fsus Cm7 A♭(add9)
can't get next to you babe, I can't get next to you. (Instrumental)
Cm7 A♭(add9) B♭/D 2 Fsus Cm7
(End instrumental) can't get next to you. I can't get next to you babe, I
Fsus Cm7 A♭(add9) B♭
can't get next to you. (Instrumental)
Cm7 A♭(add9) B♭ Cm7
A♭(add9) B♭ Cm7 A♭(add9) B♭
D.C. al Coda
(End instrumental)
CODA
Fm Cm F B♭/F Fm7 F A♭maj7
man, you're the key to my hap - pi - ness, 'cause I can't get next to
Cm7 Fsus F Cm7
you, you're blow - ing my mind 'cause I can't get next to
you, it's you that I need I got - ta get next to
you. Can't you see these tears I'm cry -
Fsus F Cm7 F7 Play 4 times Cm7
ing, can't get next to you. Ah ah ah ah ah ah.
I can't get next to you.

Additional Lyrics

2. I can fly like a bird in the sky
And I can buy anything that money can buy.
I can turn a river into a raging fire
I can live forever if I so desire.
I don't want it, all these things I can do
'Cause I can't get next to you.

3. I can turn back the hands of time — you better believe I can
I can make the seasons change just by waving my hand.
I can change anything from old to new
The thing I want to do the most I'm unable to do.
I'm an unhappy woman with all the powers I possess
'Cause man, you're the key to my happiness.

I CAN'T STAND IT

Words and Music by
ERIC CLAPTON

Slowly
Dm7 Am7 G7
You've been told, so may - be it's time you learned. You've been sold;
I feel like I'm be - in' used. Make it plain,
time for me to let you know. Ain't no crime,
Dm7 Am7 G7 Am7
may - be it's time that you earned. I can't stand it. Your
so you don't get con - fused. I can't stand it. Your
no crime to let your feel - ings show. I can't stand it. Your
F G7 Am7 F G7 Am7
fool - ing a - round, I can't stand it. Your run - ning a - round, I won't stand it. You're
fool - ing a - round, I won't stand it. Your run - ning a - round, I can't stand it. You're
run - ning a - round, I can't stand it. Your play - ing a - round, I can't stand it. Your
To Coda
F G7 Am7
fool - ing a - round with my heart. I'll ex - plain,
fool - ing a - round with my heart.
fool - ing a - round, I can't stand
Dm7 Am G7 Dm7
(Instrumental)
Am7 G7
I can't stand
Am7 F G7 Am7
it. Your fool - ing a - round, I won't stand it. Your
F G7 Am7 F G7
run - ning a - round, I can't stand it. Your fool - ing a - round with my heart.
Am7
D.S. al Coda
It was time,
CODA
Am7
it. Your
F G7 Am7
Play 3 times
run - ning a - round, I won't stand it, Your
fool - ing a - round, I won't stand it, Your
play - ing a - round, I won't stand it, Your
F G7 Am7
Repeat and Fade
run - ning a - round, I won't stand it. You're
run - ning a - round with my heart. Your

I DIDN'T MEAN TO TURN YOU ON

Words and Music by
JAMES HARRIS III & TERRY LEWIS

Moderately Fast
Fm9 Bbm9 Eb9sus Fm9 To Coda
1. When I took you out, I knew what you were all a - bout; but when I did, I did-n't mean to turn you on.
2.,4. (See additional lyrics)
Now I bring you home, you tell me good-night's not e-nough for you; I'm sor - ry ba - by, I did-n't mean to turn you on.
Oh, I did-n't mean to turn you on. You
3. I told you twice: I was on-ly tryin' to be nice, on-ly tryin' to be nice; ooh, I did-n't mean to turn you on.
Babe, now why should I feel guil-ty 'cos I won't give, guil-ty 'cos I won't give in? I did-n't mean to turn you on.
Ooh, I did-n't mean to turn you on.
D.S. al Coda
4. When I
CODA
Ooh, I did-n't mean to turn you on.
Did-n't mean to turn you on. I did-n't mean to turn you on. I
Repeat and Fade

Additional Lyrics

2. You read me along,
I wasn't tryin' to lead you on;
But, like, you're vain.
I didn't mean to turn you on.

I know you expected anyone
Might stand in; I refused,
I knew you wouldn't understand.
I'm sorry baby,
I didn't mean to turn you on.

4. When I took you out,
I knew what you were all about;
But when I did,
I didn't mean to turn you on.
Ooh, I didn't mean to turn you on.

I didn't mean to turn you on, etc.

I DON'T WANT TO WAIT

Words and Music by
PAULA COLE

Strongly
Gsus2/F Gsus2/E Gsus2/D Gsus2/C
So o - pen up your morn - ing light and say a lit - tle prayer for I. You know that
Gsus2/F Gsus2/E Gsus2/D Gsus2/C G(add2)
if we are to stay a - live, then see the peace in ev - 'ry eye. Du du du du du,
C6/9 G(add2)
du du du du du, du du du du du du. She had two ba - bies, / He showed up all wet
C6/9
one was six months, one was three, in the war of for - ty four. / on the rain - y front step wear - ing shrap - nel in his skin.
G(add2)
Ev - 'ry tel - e - phone ring, ev - 'ry heart beat sting - ing when she / And the war he saw lives in - side him still. It's so
Em7 D Cmaj9 Em D6
thought it was God call - ing her. Oh, would her son grow to know his fa - / hard to be gen - tle and warm. The years pass by, and now he has grand -
C(add9) G(add2) D(add4)/F♯ Em11 Dsus
ther? / daugh - ters. I don't want to wait for our lives to be o - ver. I want
C6 G(add2)/B Dsus/A Dsus G(add2) D(add4)/F♯
to know right now, what will it be? I don't want to wait for our lives
Em11 Dsus C6 G(add9)/B 1 Dsus/A
to be o - ver. Will it be yes, or will it be sor - ry?
G(add2) C6/9
Du du du du du, du du du du du, du du du du du du.
2 Dsus/A G7(add4)
Oh. so you look at me from a - cross the room. You're

Am9♭13
wear - ing your an - guish a - gain.
B♭(add2)
Be - lieve me, I know the feel - ing; it sucks
Fsus
you in - to the jaws of an - ger.
C(add9)
G7(add4)
Oh, so breathe a lit - tle more deep - ly, my
love. All we have is this ver - y mo - ment, and
Am9♭13
B♭(add2)
I don't want to do what his fa - ther and his fa - ther and his fa - ther did. I want to be here now.
Fsus
Gsus2
Gsus2/F
Gsus2/E
So o - pen up your morn - ing light and
Gsus2/E
Gsus2/C
Gsus2/F
Gsus2/E
say a lit - tle prayer for I. You know that if we are to stay a - live, then
Gsus2/D
Gsus2/C
G(add2)
D(add4)/F♯
Em11
Dsus
see the peace in ev - 'ry eye. I don't want to wait for our lives to be o - ver. I want
C6
G(add9)/B
Dsus/A
Dsus
G(add2)
D(add4)/F♯
to know right now, what will it be? I don't want to wait for our lives
Em11
Dsus
C6
G(add9)/B
1 Dsus/A Dsus
2 Dsus/A
to be o - ver. Will it be yes, or will it be... sor - ry?
G(add2)
C6/9
Du du du du du, du du du du du, du du du du du du.
1
2
Gsus2/F
Gsus2/E
So o - pen up your morn - ing light and
Gsus2/D
Gsus2/C
Gsus2/F
Gsus2/E
say a lit - tle prayer for I. You know that if we are to stay a - live, then
Gsus2/D
Gsus2/C
F(add2)
Repeat and Fade
see the love in ev - 'ry eye.

I DON'T KNOW HOW TO LOVE HIM
from JESUS CHRIST SUPERSTAR

Words by TIM RICE
Music by ANDREW LLOYD WEBBER

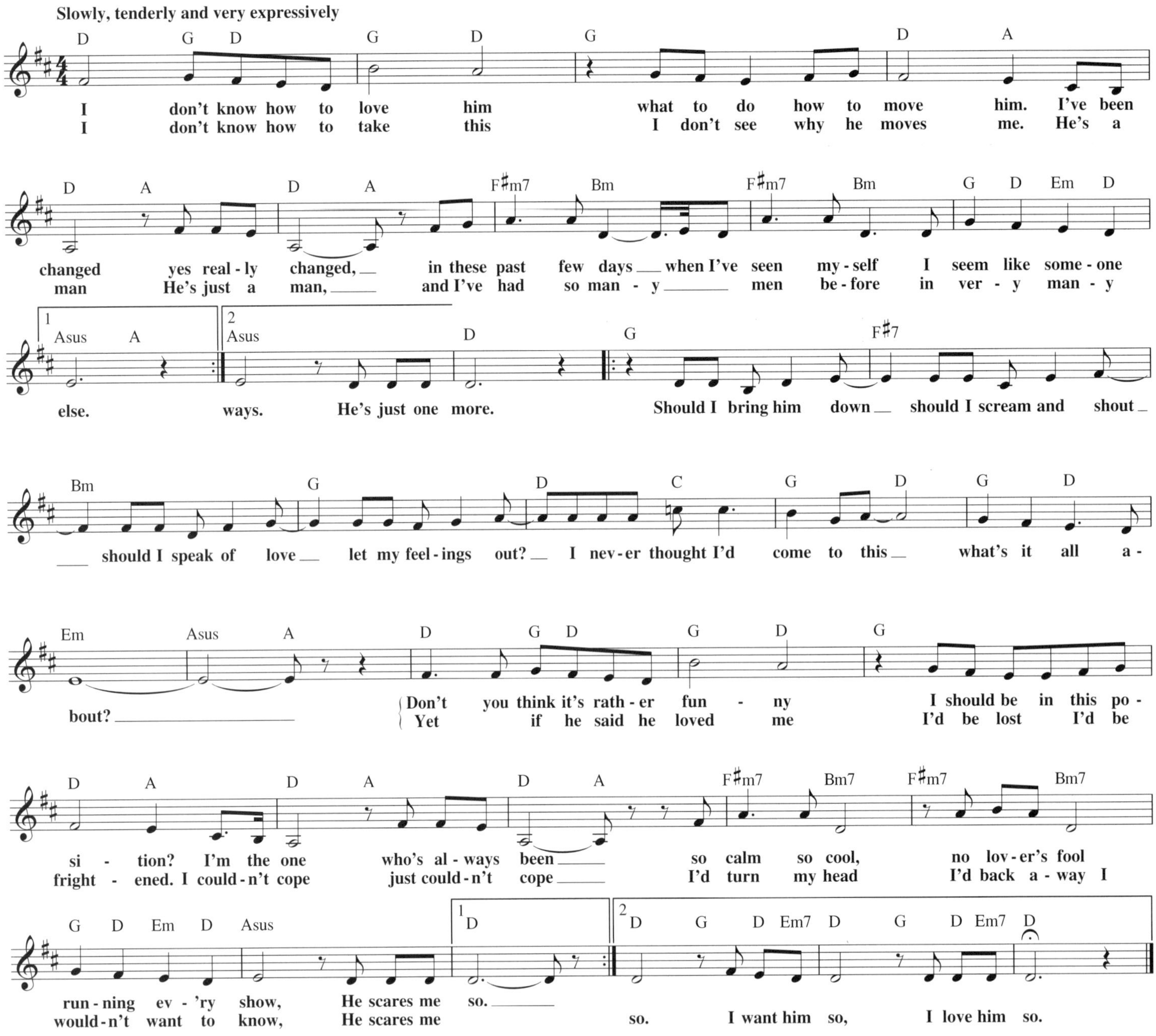
Slowly, tenderly and very expressively
D G D G D G D A
I don't know how to love him what to do how to move him. I've been
I don't know how to take this I don't see why he moves me. He's a
D A D A F♯m7 Bm F♯m7 Bm G D Em D
changed yes real-ly changed, in these past few days when I've seen my-self I seem like some-one
man He's just a man, and I've had so man-y men be-fore in ver-y man-y
1 Asus A 2 Asus D G F♯7
else. ways. He's just one more. Should I bring him down should I scream and shout
Bm G D C G D G D
should I speak of love let my feel-ings out? I never thought I'd come to this what's it all a-
Em Asus A D G D G D G
bout? Don't you think it's rath-er fun-ny I should be in this po-
Yet if he said he loved me I'd be lost I'd be
D A D A D A F♯m7 Bm7 F♯m7 Bm7
si-tion? I'm the one who's al-ways been so calm so cool, no lov-er's fool
fright-ened. I could-n't cope just could-n't cope I'd turn my head I'd back a-way I
G D Em D Asus 1 D 2 D G D Em7 D G D Em7 D
run-ning ev-'ry show, He scares me so.
would-n't want to know, He scares me so. I want him so, I love him so.

I LIKE DREAMIN'

Words and Music by
KENNY NOLAN

Moderately slow
G Am D Am D
I like dream-in' 'cause dream-in' can make you mine. I like dream in' clos-in' my
G Dm G Cmaj7 Bm7 Am7 G7
eyes and feel-in' fine. When the lights go down, I'm hold-in' you so tight,
Cmaj7 Bm7 Em7 Am7 D7
got-cha in my arms and it's par-a-dise 'til the morn-in' light.

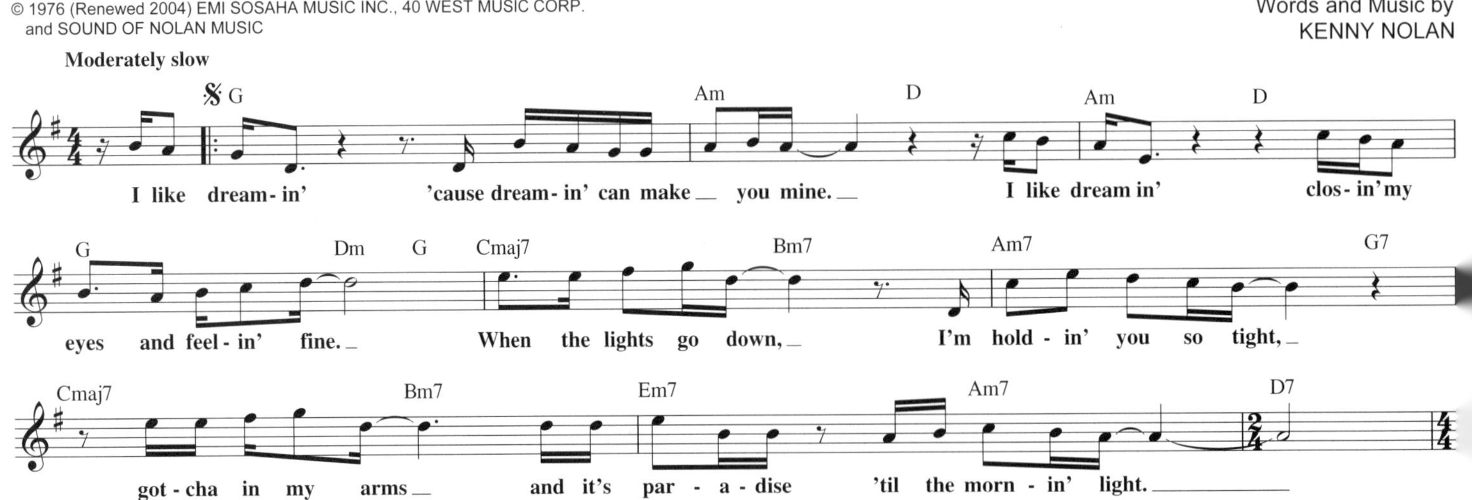

G Em7 Am7

I see us on the shore be-neath the bright sun-shine,
Through each dream how our love has grown,

D7 C G

we walked a-long Saint Thom-as beach a mil-lion times. Hand in hand,
I see us with our chil-dren and our hap-py home, lit-tle smiles,

Em Bm7 Am7 D

two bare-foot lov-ers kiss-in' in the sand. Side by
so warm and ten-der, look-in' up at us. Blessed by

Em Bm7 C

side, the tide rolls in, I'm touch-in' you, you're touch-in' me, if
love, the world we share. Un-til I wake I reach for you

Cmaj7 1 D7sus D7 2 D7sus D7 D.S. and Fade

on-ly it could be. I like
and you're just not there. I like

I LOVE A RAINY NIGHT

Words and Music by EDDIE RABBITT,
EVEN STEVENS and DAVID MALLOY

Moderately bright

C7

(1., 3.) Well, I love a rain-y night; I love a rain-y night. I
(2., 4.) a rain-y night; it's such a beau-ti-ful sight. I love to
(5.) *Instrumental solo ad lib.*

F

love to hear the thun-der; watch the light-ning when it lights up the sky.
feel the rain on my face; taste the rain on my lips,

C7 1, 3 2, 4, 5 Fine G

You know it makes me feel good. 2.,4. Well, I love (1., 3.) Show-ers wash all my
in the moon-light shad-ows. (2.) Puts a song in this

Am G F G C

cares a-way; I wake up to a sun-ny day, 'cause I love a rain-y night.
heart of mine; puts a smile on my face ev-'ry time,

F G C F G C F G

Yeah, I love a rain-y night. Well, I love a rain-y night. Well, I love

1, 2 C F G D.S. after repeat 3, 4 C F G D.S. al Fine after repeat

a rain-y night, ooh, oh. I love a rain-y night. Well, I love

('TIL) I KISSED YOU

Words and Music by
DON EVERLY

Moderately

G Em G Em G
Nev - er felt like this __ un - til I kissed you. How did
Things have real - ly changed __ since I kissed you. My life's

Em G Em G
I ex - ist __ un - til I kissed you? Nev - er had you on my mind, __
not the same _ now that I kissed you. Mmm, _ you got a way a - bout _ you,

D7 G Em G
now __ you're there all the time. __
now __ I can't live with - out you.
Nev - er knew what I missed un - til I kissed you.

Em 1 G Em 2 G Em
Uh huh, I kissed you, oh yeah. kissed you, oh yeah.

G Em
You don't re - al - ize __ what you do to me, __ and I did - n't

G
re - al - ize __ what a kiss could be. __ Mmm, _ you got a way a - bout _ you,

D7 G Em G
now __ I can't live with - out you. Nev - er knew what I missed un - til I kissed you.

Em G Em G
Uh huh, I kissed you. Oh yeah, I kissed you.

I SAY A LITTLE PRAYER

Lyric by HAL DAVID
Music by BURT BACHARACH

Moderately
Gm7 Cm7 F B♭
The mo - ment I wake up be - fore _ I put on my make - up ______ I
I run _ for the bus, dear, while rid - ing I think of us, dear. ______ I
Am7 D7 Gm7 Cm7
say a lit - tle prayer for you. __ While comb - ing my hair now and won - d'ring what
say a lit - tle prayer for you. __ At work _ I just take time and all __ through my
F B♭ Am7 D7 E♭ F/E♭
dress to wear now ______ I say a lit - tle prayer for you. __
cof - fee break time ______ I say a lit - tle prayer for you. __
For - ev - er, for - ev - er you'll

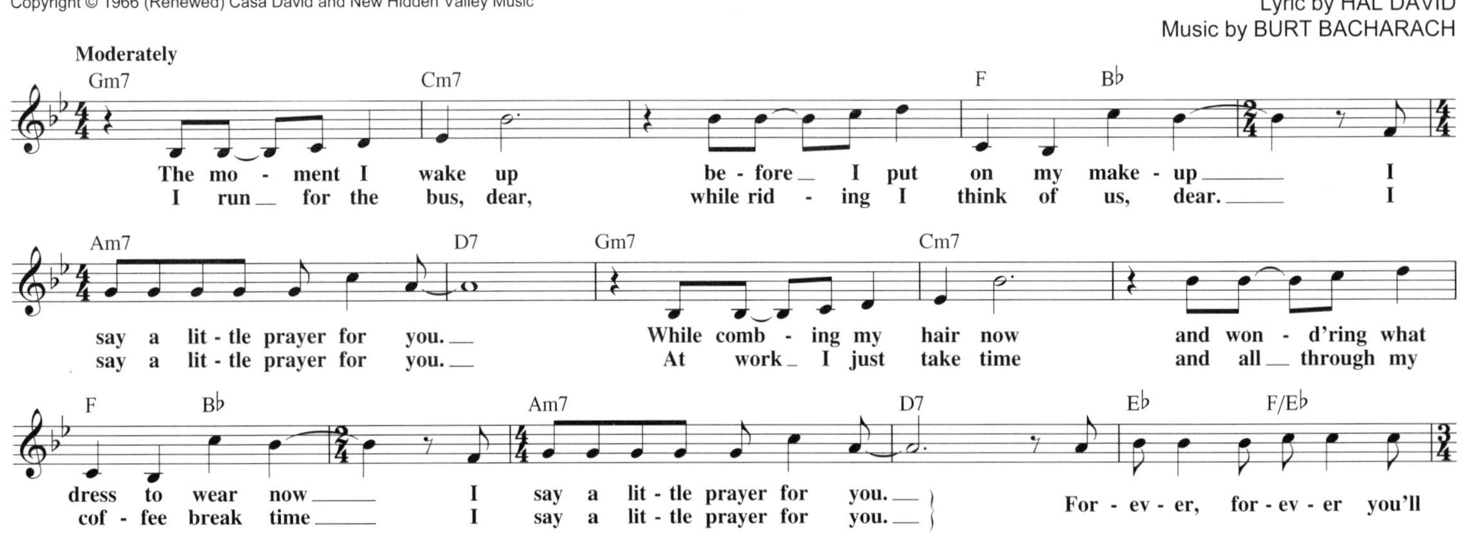

Dm7 Bb Ab/Bb Bb/C Bb9/D Eb Eb/F Dm7
stay in my heart and I will love you for-ev-er and ev-er. We nev-er will part. Oh,
Ab/Bb Bb Bb9 Bb Bb/D Eb Eb/F Dm7 Bb Ab Bb/C Bb9/D
how I'll love you. To-geth-er, to-geth-er, that's how it must be, to live with-out you would
Eb F/Eb D Gm7 Cm7
on-ly mean heart-break for me. My dar-ling, be-lieve me, for me there is
Eb/F Bbmaj7 F9 Bbmaj7 F9sus
no one but you. Please love me too. I'm in love with
Bbmaj7 F9sus Bbmaj7 F9sus Bbmaj7
you. An-swer my prayer. Say you love me too.

I SHOT THE SHERIFF

Words and Music by
BOB MARLEY

Moderately slow, with a beat

Gm7 Cm7 Gm
1. I shot the sher - iff, but I did not shoot the dep - u - ty.
2.-4. *(See additional lyrics)*

Gm7 Cm7 Gm
I shot the sher - iff, but I did - n't shoot the dep - u - ty.

Ebmaj7 Dm7 Gm Ebmaj7 Dm7 Gm
All a-round in my home town, they're try-ing to track me down. They

Ebmaj7 Dm7 Gm Ebmaj7 Dm7 Gm Ebmaj7 Dm7
say they want to bring me in guilt - y for the kill-ing of a dep - u - ty, for the life of a dep - u -

Gm N.C. 1-3 4 D.C and Fade
ty. But I say: *(Instrumental)*

Additional Lyrics

2. I shot the sheriff, but I swear it was in self-defense.
I shot the sheriff, and they say it is a capital offense.
Sheriff John Brown always hated me; for what, I don't know.
Every time that I plant a seed, he said, "Kill it before it grows."
He said, "Kill it before it grows." But I say:

3. I shot the sheriff, but I swear it was in self-defense.
I shot the sheriff, but I swear it was in self-defense.
Freedom came my way one day, and I started out of town.
All of a sudden, I see Sheriff John Brown aiming to shoot me down.
So I shot, I shot him down. But I say:

4. I shot the sheriff, but I did not shoot the deputy.
I shot the sheriff, but I didn't shoot the deputy.
Reflexes got the better of me, and what is to be must be.
Every day, the bucket goes to the well, but one day the bottom will drop out.
Yes, one day the bottom will drop out. But I say:

I TOUCH MYSELF

Words and Music by BILLY STEINBERG, TOM KELLY, CHRISTINE AMPHLETT and MARK McENTEE

Moderate Rock
C Dm Bb C Am7 Dm
I (1., D.S.) love my - self, I want you to love me. When I feel down, I
(2.) close my eyes and see you be - fore me. Think I would die if you were
Bb C Dm Bb C
want you a - bove me. I search my - self, I want you to find me. I for -
to ig - nore me. A fool could see how much I a - dore you I'd get
To Coda
Am7 Dm Bb C Bb C F
get my - self, I want you to re - mind me.
down on my knees, I'd do an - y - thing for you.
I don't want an -
Bb C F Bb C F
- y - bod - y else. When I think a - bout you, I touch my - self. Oh, I don't want an -
Bb C
1
Cm
- y - bod - y else, oh no, oh no, oh no. You're the one who
Eb F7
makes me come run - nin'. You're the sun who makes me shine. When you're a - round, I'm
Ab N.C.
2
al - ways laugh - in'. I wan - na make you mine. I yeah.
Cm7 F/C
(Instrumental)
Ab/C
D.S. al Coda
I
CODA
to re - mind me.
Bb C F Bb C F
I don't want an - y - bod - y else. When I think a - bout you, I touch my - self. Oh,
Bb C F/A Bb C
I don't want an - y - bod - y else, oh no, oh no, oh no.

F C7/B♭ C F
(Spoken:) I want you I don't want anybody else. And when I think a-bout you, I touch my-self. Ooh.
C7/B♭ C F C7/B♭ C F
Ooh. Ooh ooh. Ah.
B♭ C F B♭ C F
Repeat and Fade
I don't want an-y-bod-y else. When I think a-bout you, I touch my-self. Oh,

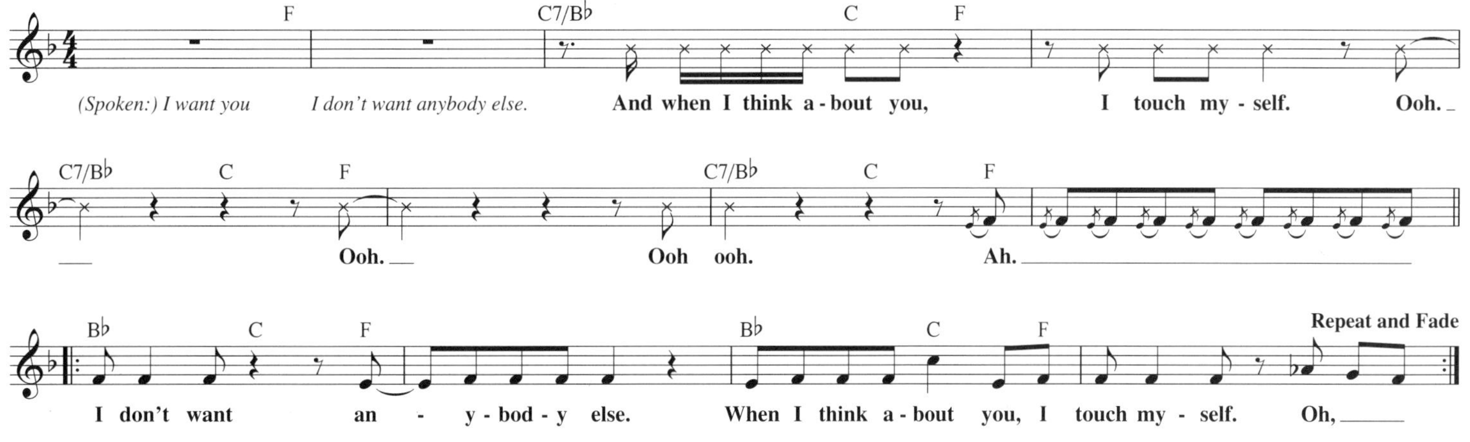

I WANT TO HOLD YOUR HAND

Words and Music by JOHN LENNON
and PAUL McCARTNEY

Moderately, with a beat

C G7 Am Em
Oh yeah, I'll tell you some - thing I think you'll un - der - stand. When
please say to me you'll let me be your man, and

C G7 Am Em
I say that some - thing, I want to hold your hand.
please say to me you'll let me hold your hand.

F G7 C Am
I want to hold your hand,
Now, let me hold your hand,

1. F G7 C
I want to hold your hand. Oh

2. F G7 C
I want to hold your hand.

Gm7 C7 F Dm
And when I touch you, I feel hap-py in-side.

Gm7 C7 F G7 F G7 F G7
It's such a feel-ing that my love I can't hide, I can't hide I can't hide.

C G7 Am Em C
Yeah, you got that some-thing, I think you'll un-der-stand. When I {say / feel} that

G7 Am Em F G7 C Am
some - thing, I want to hold your hand, I want to hold your hand,

1. F G7 C
I want to hold your hand.

2. F G7 E F G7 F C
I want to hold your hand. I want to hold your hand.

I FEEL THE EARTH MOVE

Words and Music by
CAROLE KING

Moderately
Cm7 F Cm7/F
I feel the earth move under my feet; I feel the sky tumbling down;
F Cm7
I feel my heart start to tremblin' whenever you're around.
F/C Bb Ebmaj7 Eb6 Abmaj7 Ab6 Fm7
Ooh, baby, when I see your face mellow as the month of May,
Ab/Bb Ebmaj7 Eb6 Abmaj7 Fm7
oh, darlin', I can't stand it when you look at me that way.
Ab/Bb F/G Cm7 F7 Cm7/F
I feel the earth move under my feet; I feel the sky tumbling down;
F Cm7
I feel my heart start to tremblin' whenever you're around.
F/C Cm7 F Bb Ebmaj7 Eb6
Ooh, darlin', when I'm near
Abmaj7 Ab6 Fm7 Ab/Bb Ebmaj7 Eb6
you and you tenderly call my name, I know that my emo-
Abmaj7 Fm7 Ab/Bb F/G
tions are something I just can't tame. I just got to have you,
Cm7 F7 Cm7 F Cm7 F Cm7/F F
baby. Aah! Aah! Yeah, I feel the
Repeat and Fade
Cm7 F7 Cm7/F F7 Cm7/F
earth move under my feet; I feel the sky tumblin' down, tumblin' down. I feel the

I GUESS THAT'S WHY THEY CALL IT THE BLUES

Words and Music by ELTON JOHN,
BERNIE TAUPIN and DAVEY JOHNSTONE

Slow beat
1. Don't wish it a-way, don't look at it like it's for-ev-er.
2. Just stare in-to space; pic-ture my face in your hands.
3. (Instrumental)
Be-tween you and me, I could hon-est-ly say, that things can on-ly get bet-ter.
Live for each sec-ond with-out hes-i-ta-tion, and nev-er for-get I'm your man.
(Instrumental ends)
And while I'm a-way, bust out the de-mons in-side, and it won't be long be-fore you and me run, to the place in our hearts where we hide.
Wait on me, girl, cry in the night if it helps, but more than ev-er I sim-ply love you, more than I love life it-self.
Wait on me, girl, cry in the night if it helps, but more than ev-er I sim-ply love you, more than I love life it-self.
And I guess that's why they call it the blues. Time on my hands could be time spent with you, laugh-ing like chil-dren, liv-ing like lov-ers, roll-ing like thun-der un-der the cov-ers, and I guess that's why they call it the blues.
1, 2
3
blues, laugh-ing like chil-dren, liv-ing like lov-ers, and I guess that's why they call it the blues.
And I guess that's why they call it the blues.

I WANT IT THAT WAY

Words and Music by MARTIN SANDBERG
and ANDREAS CARLSSON

Moderately
You are my fire, the one desire. Believe when I say I want it that way. But we
are two worlds apart. Can't reach to your heart when you say that I want it that way.
your fire, your one desire? Yes, I know it's too late, but I want it that way.
Tell me why. Ain't nothin' but a heartache. Tell me why. Ain't nothin' but a mistake. Tell me why. I never wanna hear you say
To Coda
I want it that way. Am I
D.S. al Coda
CODA
that way.
Now I can see that we've fallen apart from the way that it used to be, yeah.
No matter the distance, I want you to know that deep down inside of me you are my fire, the one desire. You are, you are, you are, you are.
Don't wanna hear you say...
Ain't nothin but a heartache. Ain't nothin but a mistake. I never wanna hear you say I want it that way.
Tell me why. Ain't nothin' but a heartache. Tell me why. Ain't nothin' but a mistake. Tell me why. I never wanna hear you say I want it that way. Tell me
that way. 'Cause I want it that way.

I WISH YOU LOVE

English Words by ALBERT BEACH
French Words and Music by CHARLES TRENET

Moderately

Fm7 B♭7 Fm7 B♭7 E♭maj7 E♭6 E♭maj7 E♭6
I wish you blue - birds in the Spring, to give your heart a song to sing; And then a

Fm7 B♭7 E♭6 Edim7
kiss, but more than this I wish you love. And in Ju -

Fm7 B♭7 Fm7 B♭7 E♭maj7 E♭6 E♭maj7 E♭6
ly, a lem - on - ade, to cool you in some leaf - y glade; I wish you

Fm7 B♭7 E♭7
health and more than wealth, I wish you love. My break - ing

A♭ A♭m6 E♭ B♭m6/D♭ C7
heart and I a - gree that you and I could nev - er be, so with my

Fm F9 B♭7
best, my ver - y best, my ver - y best, I set you free.

Edim7 Fm7 B♭7 Fm7 B♭7
I wish you shel - ter from the storm, a co - zy

E♭maj7 E♭6 E♭maj7 E♭6 Fm7
fire to keep you warm; But most of all, when snow - flakes

1.
B♭7 E♭ Edim7
fall, I wish you love. I wish you

2.
B♭7 E♭
fall, I wish you love.

I WILL ALWAYS LOVE YOU

Words and Music by
DOLLY PARTON

Freely
N.C.
If I should stay, I would on - ly be in your

way. So I'll go, but I know I'll think of

Slowly
A F♯m Dmaj7 E
you ev'ry step of the way. And I will al-ways

A F♯m Dmaj7 E A(add2)
love you. I will al-ways love you.

D A/C♯ Bm7 A/E Bm/E
You, my dar-ling, you. Hmm. Bit-ter -

A Bm/A A E/G♯ F♯m C♯m/E
1. sweet mem - o - ries that is all I'm tak - ing with
2. (Instrumental)
3. hope life treats you kind. And I hope you have all you've

D E A E/A A E/G♯
me. So, good - bye. Please, don't cry. We both
dreamed of And I wish to you joy and hap - pi - ness. But a - bove

To Coda
F♯m C♯m/E
1 Dmaj7 E To Next Strain
2 Dmaj7 E D.S. al Coda
know I'm not what you, you need. And I I
all this I wish you

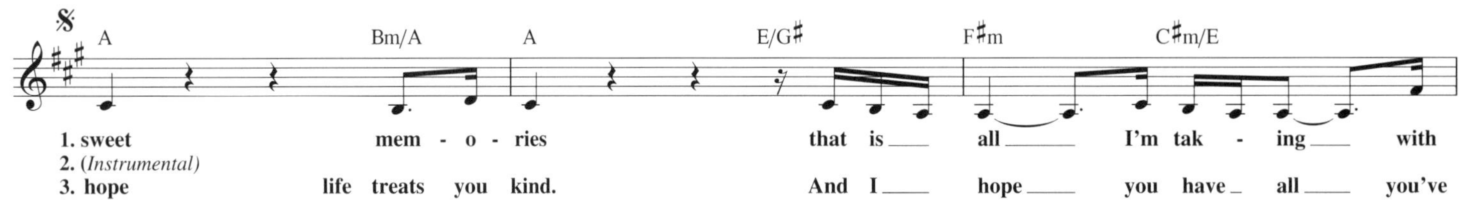

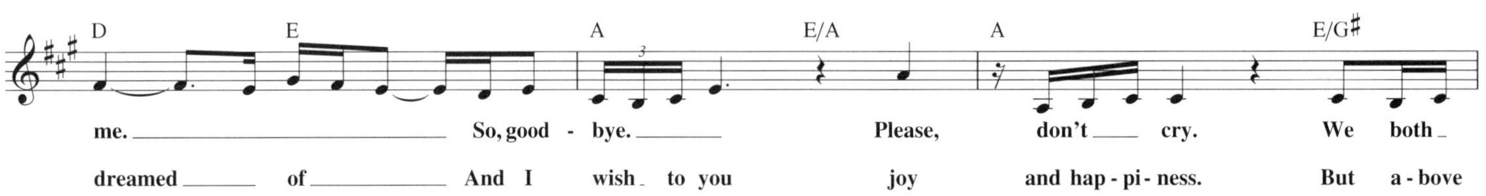

A F♯m D E A F♯m
will al - ways love you. I
D E A D/A A C♯m/E Cm/E Bm/E
D.S.
will al - ways love you.
CODA
Dmaj7 E B G♯m
love. And I
Emaj7 F♯ B G♯m C♯m7 F♯
will al - ways love you. I will al - ways love
B G♯m Emaj7 F♯ B G♯m
you. I will al - ways love you. I will al -
C♯m7 F♯ B G♯m Emaj7 F♯
- ways love you. I will al - ways love
B G♯m E F♯
you. I, I will al - ways love
N.C. Emaj7 B/D♯
you. You, dar - ling, I love you. Ooh, I'll
E/F♯ F♯ B(add2)
al - ways, I'll al - ways love you.

I WILL FOLLOW HIM

(I Will Follow You)

featured in the Motion Picture SISTER ACT

English Lyrics by NORMAN GIMBEL and ARTHUR ALTMAN
French Words by JACQUES PLANTE
Music by J.W. STOLE and DEL ROMA

Slowly
B♭
Dm
I will fol - low him, fol - low him wher - ev - er he may go. And

Gm
Dm
E♭
F
B♭
near him I al - ways will be, for noth - ing can keep me a - way. He is my des - ti - ny.

Gm
B♭
Dm
I will fol - low him. Ev - er since he touched my heart I knew. There

Gm
Dm
E♭
Cm7
F
B♭
is - n't an o - cean too deep, a moun - tain so high it can keep, keep me a - way,

Gm
F
B♭
Moderately fast Rock
N.C.
a - way from his love. (Instrumental) I

B♭
Gm
F♯
love him, I love him, I love him. And where he goes I'll fol - low, I'll fol - low, I'll fol - low, I will fol - low

B
D♯m
G♯m
him, fol - low him wher - ev - er he may go. There is - n't an o - cean too

D♯m
E
F♯
B
G
deep, a moun - tain so high it can keep, keep me a - way. I will fol - low

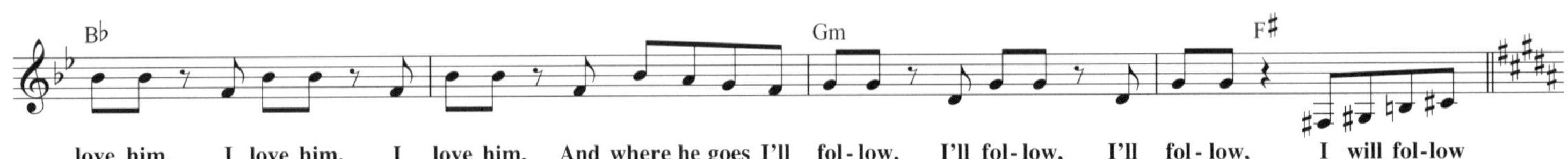

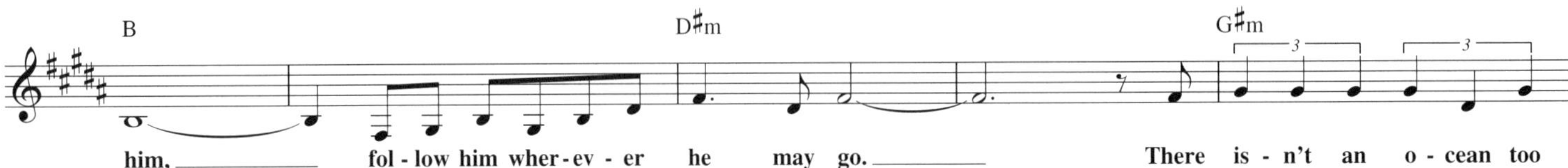

C Em Am
him, fol - low him wher - ev - er he may go. There is - n't an o - cean too

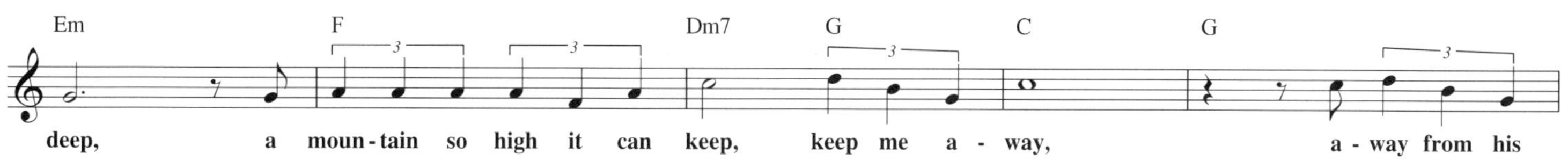
Em F Dm7 G C G
deep, a moun - tain so high it can keep, keep me a - way, a - way from his

C G C Am
love. (I love him,) oh, yes, I love him. (I'll fol - low,) I'm gon - na

C Am
fol - low. (True love,) he'll al - ways be my true love. (For - ev - er,) from now un - til for -

C Am
ev - er. I love him, I love him, I love him. And where he goes I'll fol - low, I'll fol - low, I'll

C Am
fol - low. He'll al - ways be my true love, my true love, my true love from now un - til for - ev - er, for - ev - er, for -

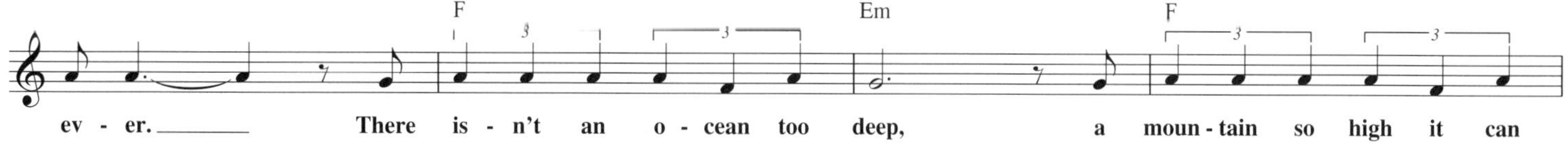
F Em F
ev - er. There is - n't an o - cean too deep, a moun - tain so high it can

Dm7 G C Am G F C
keep, keep me a - way, a - way from his Love.

I'LL BE THERE FOR YOU

Words and Music by JON BON JOVI
and RICHIE SAMBORA

Slow
N.C. Em G D
I guess this time you're real-ly leav-ing. I heard your suit-case say good-bye.
Em G D
Well, as my bro-ken heart lies bleed-ing, you say true love, it's su-i-cide.
Em G D
You say you've cried a thou-sand riv-ers, but now you're swim-ming for the shore.
Em G A
You left me drown-ing in my tears, and you won't save me an-y-more. I'm
D Bm
pray-ing to God you'll give me one more chance, girl. I'll be there for you. These five words I swear to you. When you
G A C D/G D
breathe, I want to be the air for you. I'll be there for you. I'd live and I'd die for you.
Bm G A C D/G To Coda
I'd steal the sun from the sky for you. Words can't say what love can do. I'll be there for
N.C. Em
you. I know you know we've had some good times;
G D Em
now they have their own hid-ing place. Well, I can prom-ise you to-mor-row,
G A G
but I can't buy back yes-ter-day. Yeah, ba-by, you know my hands are dirt-y,
A D A/C♯ Bm G
but I want-ed to be your val-en-tine. I'll be the wa-ter when you get thirst-y, ba-by.

CODA
D.S. al Coda
A
When you get drunk, I'll be the wine. Oh!
D Bm
you. Guitar solo
G A D Dmaj7 Bm G A
G A D A/C#
I was-n't there when you were hap - py, and I was-n't there when you were down, child.
Bm G
Did-n't mean to miss your birth-day, ba - by. I wish I'd seen you blow those can-dles
A N.C. D Bm
out. Oh, yeah! I'll be there for you. These five words I swear to you. When you
G A C D/G D
breathe, I want to be the air for you. I'll be there for you. I'd live and I'd die for you.
Bm G A C D/G
I'd steal the sun from the sky for you. Words can't say what love can do. I'll be there for,
E C#m A
I'll be there for you. These five words I swear to you. When you breathe, I want to be the air for you.
B D E/A E C#m
I'll be there for you. I'd live and I'd die for you. I'd steal the sun from the sky for you.
A B D E/A E C#m
Words can't say what love can do. I'll be there for you. Oh,
A B D A E C#m A
oh. Oh, oh, oh.
B D A E N.C.
(Instrumental)

I'LL BE HOME

Words and Music by FERDINAND WASHINGTON and STAN LEWIS

Slowly

I'll be home, my dar-ling, please wait for me. We'll stroll a-long to-geth-er.
Once more our love will be free. At the cor-ner drug store, each Sat-ur-day we would meet;
I'd walk you home in the moon-light, all of these things we'll re-peat. So dar-ling, as I write this
let-ter, here's hop-ing you're think-ing of me; my mind's made up, so long, un-til I'll
be home to start serv-ing you. I'll be home, my dar-ling, please wait for me.
I'll walk you home in the moon-light, once more our love will be free. I'll be free.

I'M LEAVING IT UP TO YOU

Words and Music by DON HARRIS and DEWEY TERRY, JR.

Slow Rock tempo

I'm leav-in' it all up to you. You de-cide what you're gon-na do. Now do you want my
love, or are we through? That's why I'm leav-in' it up to I've got my heart in my
hand. I, I, I don't un-der-stand, what have I done wrong?
I wor-ship the ground you walk on. That's why I'm leav-in' it up to you.
You de-cide what you're gon-na do. Now do you want my love, or are we
through? Or are we through? Or are we through?

I'LL WAIT

Words and Music by DAVID LEE ROTH,
EDWARD VAN HALEN, ALEX VAN HALEN
and MICHAEL McDONALD

Medium Rock beat
You got me cap-tured. I'm un-der your spell. I guess I'll nev-er learn.
I wrote a let-ter and told her these words. That meant a lot to me.
You can't i-mag-ine what your im-age means. The pag-es come a-live.
I have your pic-ture. Yes, I know it well. An-oth-er page is turned.
I nev-er sent it. She would-n't have heard. Her eyes still fol-low me.
Your mag-ic free to ev-'ry-one who reads. Heart-break-in' mo-tor drive.
Play 1st time only
Are you for real? It's so hard to tell from just a mag-a-zine.
Yeah, you just smile and the pic-ture sells. Look what that does to me.
And while she watch-es I can nev-er be free. Such good pho-tog-ra-phy.
Yeah, you just smile and the pic-ture sells. Look what it does to me.
I'll wait till your love comes down. I'm com-ing straight for your heart.
No way you can stop me now, as fine as you are.
To Coda
as fine as you are.
D.C. al Coda
CODA
as fine as you are.
D.S. and Fade

I'M SO EXCITED

Words and Music by TREVOR LAWRENCE,
JUNE POINTER, RUTH POINTER and ANITA POINTER

Bright Disco feel

Gm7 Bb/C Eb/C
To - night, to - night we're gon - na make it hap - pen, To - night
(Instrumental)

Bb/Eb Eb Eb/Bb Bb Gm7
we'll put all oth - er things a - side. Get in this time and

Bb/C Eb/C Bb/Eb Eb Eb/Bb Bb
show me some af - fec - tion, We're go - in' for those pleas - ures in the night.
(End instrumental)

Am7 Gm7 Dm
(Sing both times) I want to love you, feel you, wrap my - self a - round you. I want to

Am7 Gm7 Cm7
squeeze you, please you, I just can't get e - nough. And if you move real slow,

Bb/D Cm7/F **Chorus** Gm Eb
I'll let it go. I'm so ex - cit - ed, and I just can't hide it,

F Gm
I'm a - bout to lose con - trol and I think I like it! I'm so ex - cit - ed,

Eb F
and I just can't hide it, And I know, I know I know, I know, I know I

Gm Bb/C Eb/C
want you. We should - n't e - ven think a - bout to - mor - row,

Bb/Eb Eb Eb/Bb Bb
Sweet mem - o - ries will last a long, long time.

Bb/A Gm7 Bb/C Eb/C
We'll have a good time, ba - by, don't you wor - ry, And if

Bb/Eb Eb Eb/Bb Bb Gm
we're still play - in' a - round, boy, that's just fine. Let's get ex - cit - ed,

Eb F
we just can't hide it, I'm a - bout to lose con - trol and I think I like

Gm
Eb
it! I'm so ex-cit - ed and I just can't hide it,
F
Gm
D.S. and Fade on Chorus
And I know, I know, I know, I know, I know I want you, I want you!
Instrumental

I'M IN YOU

Words and Music by
PETER FRAMPTON

Light Rock

F Em7 F6 G6 F

I don't care where I go when I'm with you. When I cry,
don't pre - tend, we make love. I can't feel
when you think of last fall. You can't buy

Em7 F6 G6 C

you don't laugh, 'cause you know me.
an - y more than I'm sing - ing.
what we made, you and I.
I'm in you,

C6 Gm F C Am Gm

you're in me. I'm in you, you're in me.

F Abmaj7/Eb Bb/F To Coda C F/C C F/C

'Cause you gave me the love, love that I nev-er had. Yes, you

Abmaj7/Eb Bb/F G C/G 1. G F 2. G C/G

gave me the love, love that I nev - er had. You and I

G C/G G Bb/F F Bb/F F C Bb/C C Bb/C

Bb/F F Bb/F F Am G Am G Am/G G G7sus

D.S. al Coda F CODA C F/C C F/C Abmaj7/Eb Bb/F

Come so far Yes, you gave me the love, love that I nev - er had.

C F/C C F/C Abmaj7/Eb Bb/F G C/G G C/G G7 G7sus

You gave me the love, love that I nev - er had.

G7 F Em7 Dm7 Dm7/G Dm/G Cmaj7

I don't care where I go when I'm with you.

I'M A BELIEVER

Words and Music by
NEIL DIAMOND

Moderately
E B7 E B7
I thought love was on - ly true in fair - y tales, meant for some - one else but not for
I thought love was more or less a giv - in' thing; seems the more I gave the less I
E A E A
me. Love was out to get me. That's the way it seemed.
got. What's the use in try - in'? All you get is pain.
E A E B7
Dis - ap - point - ment haunt - ed all my dreams.
When I need - ed sun - shine, I got rain.
Then I saw her
E A E A E A E A E A
face; now I'm a be - liev - er! Not a trace
E A E A E A E A
of doubt in my mind. I'm in love, and I'm a be -
To Coda
E D B7 N.C. N.C.
liev - er! I could - n't leave her if I tried.
(Instrumental)
D.S. al Coda
(1st verse)
CODA
E A E A
Saw her face; now I'm a be-
E A E A E A E A E A
liev - er! Not a trace of doubt in my mind.
Repeat and Fade
E A E A E A E A E A
I'm in love, and I'm a be - liev - er! I'm in
(I'm a be - liev - er!) (I'm a be - liev - er!)

I'M NOT IN LOVE

Words and Music by ERIC STEWART
and GRAHAM GOULDMAN

Moderately
B♭ B♭m F/A A7 Dm
(1.,3.) I'm not in love, so don't for - get it, it's just a sil - ly phase I'm go - ing through.
(2.) I like to see you, but then a - gain, that does - n't mean you mean that much to me.
B♭ B♭m F/A A7 Dm
And just be - cause I call you up, don't get me wrong, don't think you've got it made.
So if I call you, don't make a fuss, don't tell your friends a - bout the two of us.
To Coda
B♭ C C7 F B♭ B♭11 B♭
I'm not in love, no, no! It's be - cause
F F6/9
cause. Be quiet, big boys don't cry, big boys don't cry, big boys don't cry, big boys don't cry, big boys don't cry, big boys don't cry,
A7 B♭ B♭m F/A
I keep your pic - ture up-on the wall, it hides a
A7 Dm B♭ B♭m
nas - ty stain that's ly - ing there. So don't you ask me to give it
F/A A7 Dm B♭
back. I know you know it does - n't mean that much to me. I'm not in
C9 C7 F B♭m7 E♭7 A♭
love, no, no! It's be - cause. Ooh, you'll wait a long time for me.
Fm7 A♭/E♭ B♭m7 E♭7 F11 F D.C. al Coda F
Ooh, you'll wait a long time.
CODA
B♭
I'm not in
B♭m C11 C
love, I'm not in love.
Repeat and Fade

I'VE TOLD EV'RY LITTLE STAR
from MUSIC IN THE AIR

Lyrics by OSCAR HAMMERSTEIN II
Music by JEROME KERN

Gracefully
F C7 C11 Fmaj7 C7 C11 Fmaj7 Bdim C11 C7♭9
I've told ev - 'ry lit - tle star just how sweet I think you are. Why have - n't I told
F C11 F C7 C11 Fmaj7 C7 C11 Fmaj7 A♭dim
you? I've told rip - ples in a brook, made my heart an o - pen book, Why have - n't
Gm7 C7♭9 F Fm C G7 C
I told you? Friends ask me; Am I in love? I al - ways an - swer
Cdim G7 Am Dm7 G7 C7 F
"Yes." Might as well con - fess. If I don't they guess. May - be
Gm7 C11 B♭m Fmaj7 F♯dim Gm7 B♭m6 F A♭dim Gm7 C7♭9 F
you may know it too, oh, my dar - ling if you do. Why have - n't you told me?

ICE ICE BABY

Words and Music by VANILLA ICE, EARTHQUAKE, M. SMOOTH, BRIAN MAY, FREDDIE MERCURY, ROGER TAYLOR, JOHN DEACON and DAVID BOWIE

Moderate Rap beat
FIGURE A
N.C.
(See rap lyrics)
FIGURE B
G5 D5 G5
(Spoken:) Ice Ice Baby, Vanilla Ice Ice Baby.
D5 G5 D5
Ice Ice Baby, Vanilla Ice Ice Baby.
BRIDGE
D5 N.C.
(Spoken:) Yo man let's get out of here! Word to your mother!
ENDING
N.C.
(Instrumental)
1-3
4

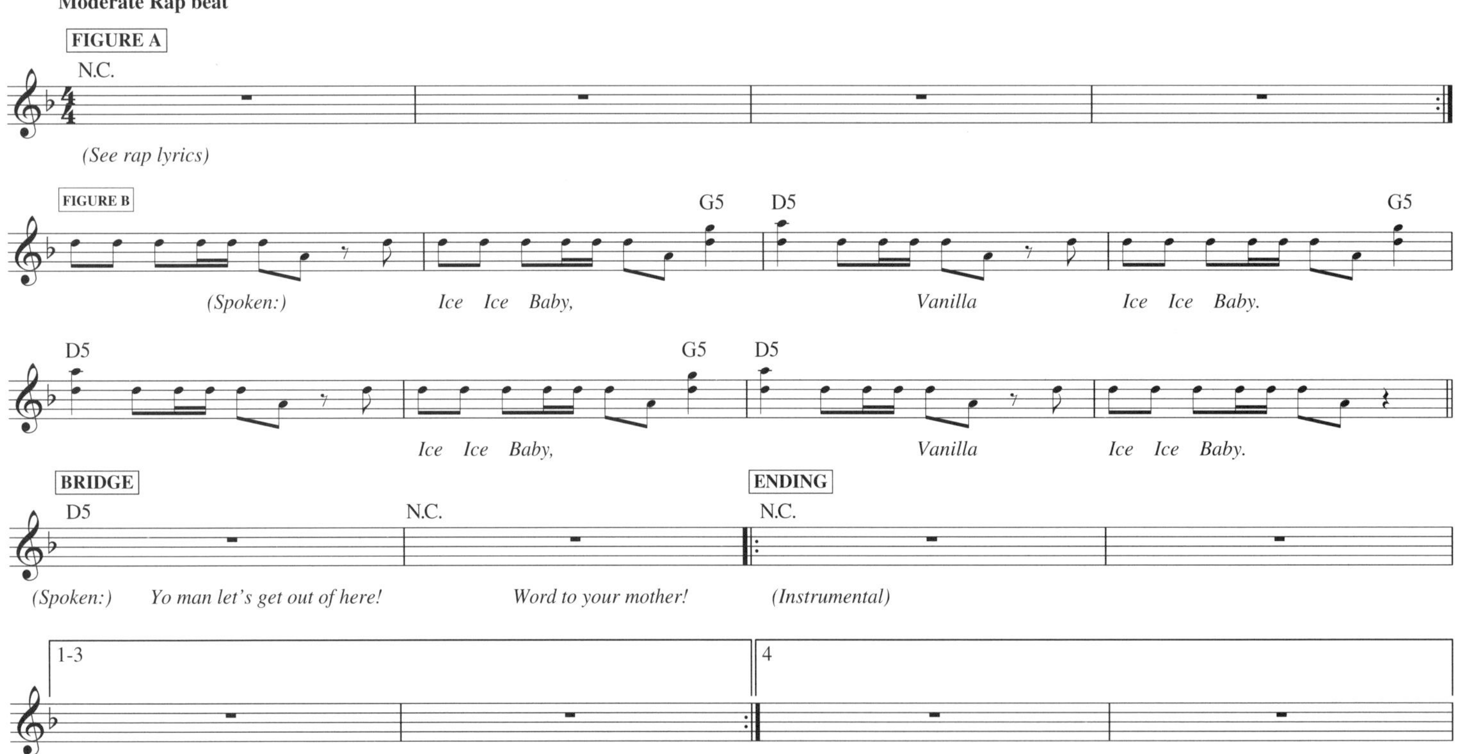

with **FIGURE A**

1. All right stop. Collaborate and listen
Ice is back with my brand new invention
Something grabs ahold of me tightly
Then I flow like a harpoon daily and nightly
Will it ever stop? Yo - I don't know
Turn off the lights and I'll glow
To the extreme I rock a mic like a vandal
Light up a stage and wax a chump like a candle.

Dance. Burn rush the speaker that booms
I'm killing your brain like a poisonous mushroom
Deadly, when I play a dope melody
Anything less than the best is a felony
Love it or leave it. You better gain way
You better hit the bull's eye. The kid don't play
If there was a problem, Yo, I'll solve it
Check out the hook while my DJ revolves it.

with **FIGURE A**

2. Now that the party is jumping
With the bass kicked in, the Vegas are pumpin'
Quick to the point, to the point no faking
I'm cooking MC's like a pound of bacon
Burning them if they're not quick and nimble
I go crazy when I hear a cymbal
And a hi hat with a souped up tempo
I'm on a roll and it's time to go solo
Rollin' in my 5.0
With my ragtop down so my hair can blow
The girlies on standby. Waving just to say Hi
Did you stop? No - I just drove by
Kept on pursuing to the next stop
I busted a left and I'm heading to the next block
That block was dead
Yo - so I continued to A1A Beachfront Ave.
Girls were hot wearing less than bikinis
Rockman lovers driving Lamborghinis
Jealous 'cause I'm out getting mine
Shay with a guage and Vanilla with a nine
Reading for the chumps on the wall
The chumps acting ill because they're so full of eight balls
Gunshots ranged out like a bell
I grabbed my nine - All I heard were shells
Falling on the concrete real fast
Jumped in my car, slammed on the gas
Bumper to bumper the avenue's packed
I'm trying to get away before the jackers jack
Police on the scene. You know what I mean
They passed me up, confronted all the dope fiends
If there was a problem, Yo, I'll solve it
Check out the hook while my DJ revolves it.

with **FIGURE B**

Ice Ice Baby, Vanilla Ice Ice Baby
Ice Ice Baby, Vanilla Ice Ice Baby

with **FIGURE A**

3. Take heed, 'cause I'm a lyrical poet
Miami's on the scene just in case you didn't know it
My town, that created all the bass sound
Enough to shake and kick holes in the ground
'Cause my style's like a chemical spill
Feasible rhymes that you can vision and feel
Conducted and formed, This is a hell of a concept
We make it hype and you want to step with this
Shay plays on the fade, slice like a ninja
Cut like a razor blade so fast, Other DJ's say, "damn"
If my rhyme was a drug, I'd sell it by the gram
Keep my composure when it's time to get loose
Magnetized by the mic while I kick my juice
If there was a problem, Yo - I'll solve it!
Check out the hook while Deshay revolves it.

with **FIGURE B**

Ice Ice Baby, Vanilla Ice Ice Baby
Ice Ice Baby, Vanilla Ice Ice Baby

with **FIGURE B**

Ice Ice Baby Too cold, Ice Ice Baby Too cold Too cold
Ice Ice Baby Too cold Too cold, Ice Ice Baby Too cold Too cold

IF YOU LEAVE
from PRETTY IN PINK

Words and Music by PAUL HUMPHREYS,
ANDY McCLUSKEY and MARTIN COOPER

Moderate Rock

F Dm B♭ C F
If you leave, don't leave now, please don't take my heart a-way. Prom-ise me just

Dm Am B♭ F Dm
one more night, then we'll go on our sep-'rate ways. When hours have time on our sides,

B♭ C F Dm B♭
now it's fad-ing fast. Ev-'ry sec-ond, ev-'ry mo-ment, we've got to, got to

C D D/G A G
make it last. Touch you once, / touch you once, I touch you twice, I won't let go at an-y price. I

D D/G A To Coda G D
need you now like I need you then, you al-ways said we'd still be friends some-day.

D/G G Em C D
If you leave, I won't cry, I won't waste one sin-gle day. But

G Em Bm C G
if you leave, don't look back, I'll be run-ning the oth-er way. Sev-en years went

Em C D G Em
un-der the bridge like time stand-ing still. Heav-en knows what hap-pens now, you've

C D E E/A B
got to, you've got to make it last. Touch you once, I touch you twice, I won't let go at

A E E/A B A
an-y price. I need you now like I need you then, you al-ways said we'd meet a-gain.

C A Dm(add2) B♭ C A F G D.S. al Coda
(Instrumental) I

CODA

G E E/A B A
still be friends. I touch you once, I touch you twice, I won't let go at an-y price. I

E E/A B A E A
need you now like I need you then, you al-ways said we'd meet a-gain some-day.

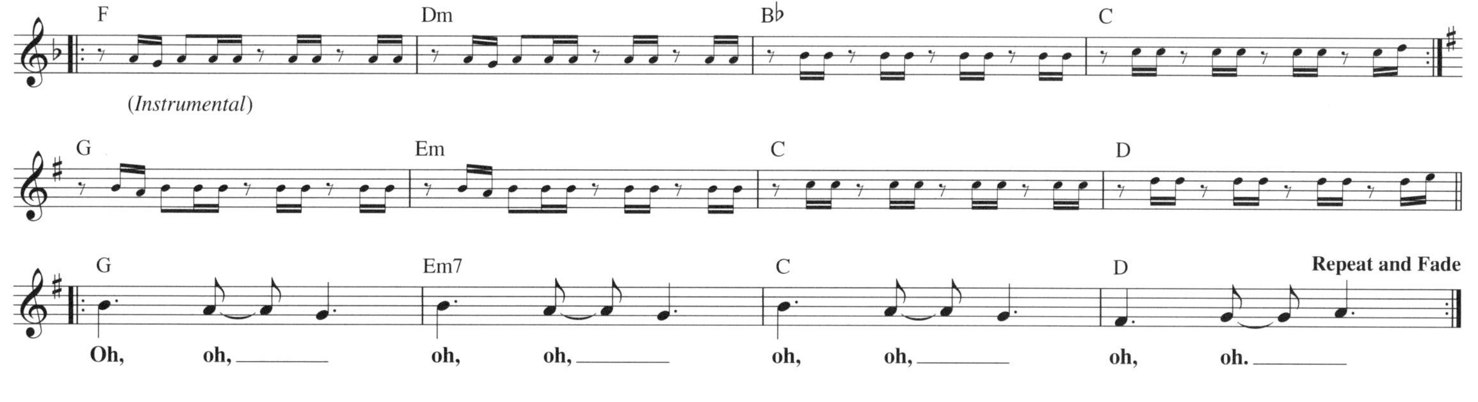

IF YOU GO AWAY

French Words and Music by JACQUES BREL
English Words by ROD McKUEN

Am Dm
If you go a - way on this sum - mer day then you might as well take the sun a -
way, as I know you will, you must tell the world to stop turn - ing
way, as I know you must, there'll be noth - ing left in the world to

G7 C
way; All the birds that flew in the sum - mer sky, when our love was new and our hearts were
till you re - turn a - gain, if you ev - er do, for what good is love with - out lov - ing
trust; Just an emp - ty room, full of emp - ty space, like the emp - ty look I see on your

Dm6 E7 Am
high; When the day was young and the night was long, and the moon stood still for the night - bird's
you; Can I tell you now, as you turn to go, I'll be dy - ing slow - ly till the next hel -
face; I'd have been the shad - ow of your shad - ow if I thought it might have kept me by your

Am7 F6 E7 Am Dm To Coda
song. / lo. / side. If you go a - way, if you go a - way, if you go a - way, if you go a -
(Last time) please don't go a -

Am Am7 Am6 E7♭9 Am
way. But if you stay, I'll make you a day like no day has been, or will be a - gain; We'll sail the
But if you stay, I'll make you a night, like no night has been, or will be a - gain; I'll sail on your

Am7 Am6 G7 C E7 Am
sun, we'll ride on the rain, we'll talk to the trees and wor - ship the wind. Then if you go, I'll un - der -
smile, I'll ride on your touch, I'll talk to your eyes, that I love so much. But if you go, go, I won't

B♭ Dm6 E7 Am C Dm Dm6
stand, leave me just e - nough love to fill up my hand.
cry, though the good is gone from the word, "good - bye."
If you go a - way, if you go a - way, if you go a -

E7 Dm6 E7 Dm6 E7 Dm6 E7 E7 D.S. al Coda
way, if you go a - way. 1. If you go a - 2. If you go a -

CODA
way.

IN YOUR ROOM

Words and Music by SUSANNA HOFFS,
BILLY STEINBERG and TOM KELLY

Bright Rock
E
I love it in your room at night. You're the on - ly one who gets through to me.
I love it in your room all day. When you've gone, I like to try on all your clothes.
I love it in your room at night. You're the on - ly one who gets through to me.
In the warm of the can - dle - light, oh, I know what you're gon - na do to me.
You won't re - gret it if you let me stay. Teach you ev - 'ry - thing that a boy should know.
In the warm of the can - dle - light, oh, I know what you're gon - na do to me.
B
E/B
I'm a - live when I'm with you. I'll do an - y - thing you want me to
I'm a - live when I'm with you. Gon - na make your dreams come true
I'll do an - y - thing you want me to. I on - ly wan - na be with you
To Coda
1
2
in your room.
Feel good in your room. Let's lock the world out.
D
A
Feels so good when we kiss. No - bod - y ev - er made me cra - zy like this.
C
B7
(Instrumental)
D.C. al Coda
CODA
In your room. Feel good in your room.
A/B
Let's lock the world out. Feels so good when we kiss.
No - bod - y ev - er made me cra - zy like this.
Repeat and Fade
In your room, in your room.

I'M SORRY

Words and Music by RONNIE SELF
and DUB ALBRITTEN

Slowly
C B7 C C♯dim7 Dm7 G7
I'm sor - ry, so sor - ry that I was such a fool. I did - n't know
Dm7 G7 C C♯dim7 Dm7 G7♯5 C B7
love could be so cruel. You tell me mis - takes
C C♯dim7 Dm7 G7 C C♯dim7
are part of be - ing young, but that does - n't right the wrong that's been done.
Dm7 G7♯5 C B7 C C♯dim7
I'm sor - ry, so sor - ry please ac - cept my a - pol - o - gy. But
Dm7 G7 Dm7 G7 1 C A♭7 G7 2 C F7 C
love is blind and I was too blind to see. see.
I'VE GOTTA GET A MESSAGE TO YOU
Copyright © 1968 by Universal Music Publishing International MGB Ltd.,
Warner-Tamerlane Publishing Corp. and Crompton Songs LLC
Copyright Renewed
All Rights for Universal Music Publishing International MGB Ltd.
in the U.S. and Canada Administered by Universal Music - Careers
Words and Music by BARRY GIBB,
ROBIN GIBB and MAURICE GIBB
Moderately slow, with a beat
B♭ Cm F
The preach - er talked with me and he smiled, said, "Come and walk with me, come and
I told him I'm in no hur - ry, but if I broke her heart, then won't you
laughed but that did - n't hurt, and it's on - ly her love that keeps me
B♭ Cm
walk one more mile. Now for once in your life you're a - lone, but you
tell her I'm sor - ry. And for once in my life I'm a - lone, and I
wear - ing this dirt. Now I'm cry - ing but deep down in - side, well, I
F G C
ain't got a dime, there's no time for the phone."
got - ta let her know just in time be - fore I go.
did it to him, now it's my turn to die.
I've just got - ta get a mes - sage to you;
Dm F G C
hold on, hold on. One more hour and my life will be through;
Dm F G 1, 2 C F 3 C G
D.S. and Fade
hold on, hold on. Well, I I've just

IN MY HOUSE

Words and Music by
RICK JAMES

Dance funk
N.C.
Boy, you can just best be - lieve I'm the on - ly girl in your life. I'll be your
time day or night when you call me I will be there. Just call me
su - gar in the morn - ing and the sweet stuff you need at night. And you can
up on the phone when you need some - one round to care. And when you
just best be - lieve when it comes down to mak - ing love, I'll sat - is -
feel sad and blue, you just come see me an - y - time, I'll kiss a -
fy your ev - 'ry need and ev - 'ry fan - ta - sy you think up.
way all your tears and your fears you can leave be - hind. So when you
Em9
need a lit - tle piece of mind come on o - ver, boy, an - y - time. I'll keep you
hap - py and so sat - is - fied in my house, in my house. So, when you
need some love and ten - der - ness and it's me, ba - by, that you miss here's the key to un - lock the door
to my house, my house.
To Coda
Em
Ooo, in my house. Ooo,
ooo, in my house. Ooo.
D.S. al Coda
Boy, an - y
CODA
house.
N.C.
(Instrumental)
Em
Ooo, in my house. Ooo,
ooo, in my house. Ooo.
Repeat and Fade

THE ISRAELITES

Words and Music by
DESMOND DEKKER

Moderately

B♭
E♭
Get up in the morn-ing slav - ing for bread sir so that ev - 'ry mouth can be fed poor

F
B♭
D♭
B♭
me the Is - rael - ite Aah!
Get up in the morn - ing slav - ing for bread sir
wife and my kids they packed up and leave me
Shirt them ah tear up trous - ers are gone I
Af - ter a storm there must be a calm they

E♭
F
B♭
so that ev - 'ry mouth can be fed
darling she said I was yours to be seen
don't want to end up like Bon - nie and Clyde
catch me in the farm you sound the a - larm
poor me the Is - rael - ite Aah!

1-3
4
D♭
E♭
F
B♭
Repeat and Fade
(2.) My Poor me the Is - rael - ite I
won - der who I'm work - ing for
look a - down and out sir

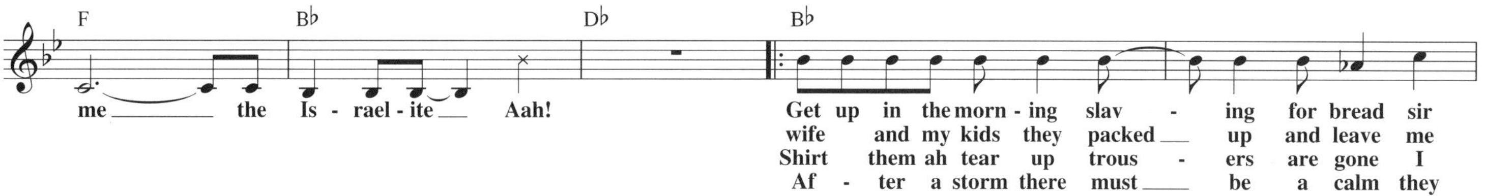

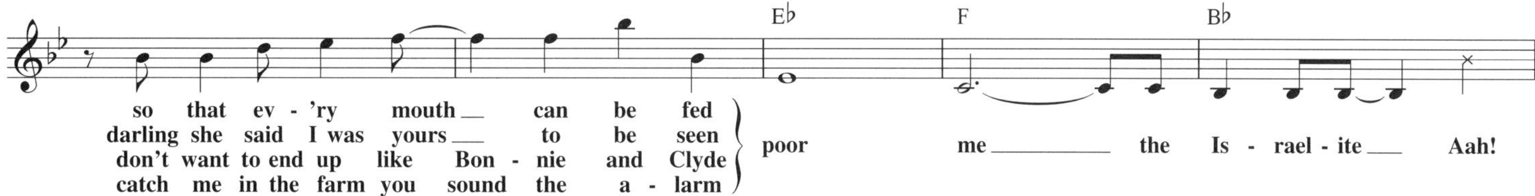

IT'S ALMOST TOMORROW

Words and Music by WADE BUFF
and GENE ADKINSON

Moderately

B♭
Dm
E♭
B♭
It's al - most to - mor - row, but what do I do? Your

E♭
B♭
C7
F7
kiss - es all tell me that your love is un - true. I'll

B♭
Dm
E♭
B♭
love you for - ev - er till stars sease to shine, and

E♭
B♭
C7
F7
1
B♭
2
B♭
hope some - day, dar - ling, that you'll al - ways be mine. It's mine.

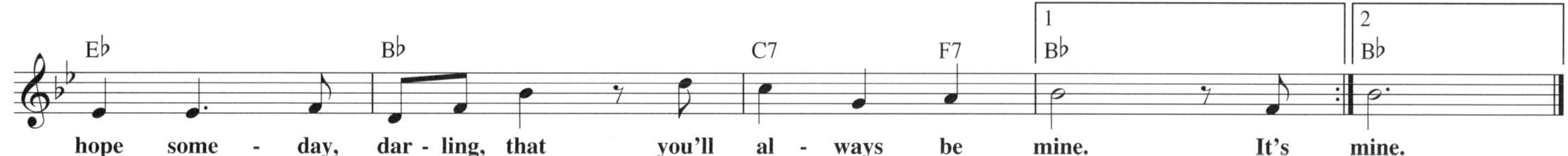

IN MY ROOM

Words and Music by BRIAN WILSON
and GARY USHER

Moderately slow
C Bb Dm7 Bb G G7 To Coda
There's a room where I can go and tell my se - crets to,
In this world I lock out all my wor - ries and my cares
Now it's dark and I'm a - lone but I won't be a - fraid,
in my room, in my
C Bb C
room. In my room.
Am G
Do my dream - ing and my schem - ing,
Am G Am G C Am G Dm7 G7 D.C. al Coda
lie a - wake and pray. Do my cry - ing and my sigh - ing, laugh at yes - ter - day.
CODA
room. In my room, in my room, in my room, in my room, in my room.
Room.

INSTANT KARMA

Words and Music by
JOHN LENNON

Moderately

A A/G♯ F♯m A A/G♯ F♯m

In - stant kar - ma's gon - na get you, gon - na knock you right on the head.
In - stant kar - ma's gon - na get you, gon - na look you right in the face.
In - stant kar - ma's gon - na get you, gon - na knock you off your feet.

A A/G♯ F♯m F G A

You bet - ter get your self to - geth - er. Pret - ty soon you're gon - na be dead.
You bet - ter get your self to - geth - er, dar - lin'. Join the hu man race.
Bet - ter rec - og - nize your broth - ers, ev - 'ry - one you meet.

D D/C♯ Bm To Coda D D/C♯ Bm

What in the world you think - ing of? Laugh - ing in the face of love,
How in the world you gon - na see? Laugh - in' at fools like me,
Why in the world are we here?

C C/B Am7 D 1. E9

what on earth you try'n to do? It's up to you, yeah, you.
who on earth d'you think you are, a su - per - star? Well, al -

2. E9 G Bm Em G Bm

right, you are. Well, we all shine on like the moon and the stars and the

Em G Bm Em D E9 D.C. al Coda

sun. Well, we all shine on. Ev - 'ry - one, come on.

CODA

D D/C♯ Bm C C/B Am

Sure-ly not to live in pain and fear. Why on earth are you there when you're

D Em7 G Bm Em

ev-'ry-where? Come and get your share. Well, we all shine on like the

G Bm Em G Bm Em D

moon and the stars and the sun. Well, we all shine on. Come on and on and on, / On and on and on and

1. E7 A A/G♯ F♯m A A/G♯ F♯m

on, yeah yeah, al - right, ah ha,

A A/G♯ F♯m C G A

ah. Well, we

2. E9

on and on. Well, we / you, more

G Bm Em G Bm Em

all shine on like the moon and the stars and the sun. Well, we / than I love life it - self.

Repeat and Fade

IT WAS ALMOST LIKE A SONG

Lyric by HAL DAVID
Music by ARCHIE JORDAN

Slowly

C F/C Fm C G/B Am Dm Dm7

Once in ev-'ry life, some-one comes a long, and you came to me. / You were in my arms, just where you be-long, we were so in love.

F/G C Fmaj7 Em7 Dm7 G7

It was al-most like a song. Jan-u-ar-y through De-cem-ber, we had such a per-fect

C G/B Am Em Dm7 B♭maj7 G7sus G7

year. Then the flame be-came a dy - ing em-ber; all at once you weren't there.

C F/C Fm C G/B Am

Now my bro-ken heart cries for you each night. It's al-most like a

Dm 1. G7sus G7 C 2. G7 A♭dim7 Am C+/G♯

song, but it's too sad to write. but it's too sad to write.

Am/G D7/F♯ Dm7 Dm7/G C F/C C

It's too sad to write.

IT'S MY TURN

from IT'S MY TURN

Words and Music by CAROLE BAYER SAGER
and MICHAEL MASSER

Moderately
G♯m7 C♯m7 F♯m7 F♯m7/B G♯m7 C♯m7 F♯m7 B7
I can't cov-er up my feel-ings in the name of love, or play it safe, for a while that was eas-y; and if
G♯m7 C♯m7 F♯m7 F♯m7/B A♯m7♭5 Amaj7 G♯m7 Amaj9
liv-ing for my-self is what I'm guilt-y of, go on and sen-tence me, I'll still be free.
G Em Am7 D G Em Am7 D7
It's my turn to see what I can see, I hope you'll un-der-stand, this time's just for me, be-cause it's
Emaj9 C♯m7 F♯m7 B7 E C♯m7 F♯m7 B7
my turn, with no a-pol-o-gies, I've giv-en up the truth to those I've tried to please, but now it's
E G♯m7 Amaj9 B7 E G♯m7 Amaj9 B7
my turn; if I don't have all the an-swers, at least I know I'll take my share of chanc-es.
G♯7sus G♯m7 C♯m7 C♯m7/F♯ E G♯m7
Ain't no use in hold-in' on when noth-in' stays the same,
ain't no use in hold-in' on when noth-in' stays the same,
so I'll let it rain, 'cause the
Amaj9 A F♯m7/B E G♯m7 Amaj9 A F♯m7/B B7
rain ain't gon-na hurt me, and I'll let you go, 'though I know it won't be eas-y.
Gmaj9 Em Am7 D7 G Em
It's my turn, with no more room for lies; for years I've seen my life through
It's my turn, to see what I can see, I hope you'll un-der-stand,
Am7 D7 Emaj9 C♯m7 F♯m7 B7 E C♯m7
some-one else-'s eyes and now it's my turn to try and find my way, and if I should get lost, at
this time's just for me, be-cause it's my turn to turn and say good-bye, I sure would like to know that
1
F♯m7 B7 Emaj9 G♯m7 A A/B B7 E G♯m7 Amaj9 B7
least I'll own to-day. It's my turn, yes, it's my turn. And there
2
F♯m7 B B7 G Em7 Am7 D7 G Em Am7 D
you're still on my side, be-cause it's my turn, it's my turn.
E C♯m7 F♯m7 B7 E C♯m7 F♯m7 B B7
it's my turn to start from num-ber one, try-ing to un-do some dam-age that's been done, and now it's

G Gmaj9 Em Am7 D7 G Em Am7 D7
my turn to reach and touch the sky; no one's gon - na say at least I did - n't try.
E C#m7 F#m7 B7 E C#m7 F#m7 B7
It's my turn, yes, it's my turn,
Repeat and Fade
G Em Am7 D7 G Em Am7 D
it's my turn, my turn.

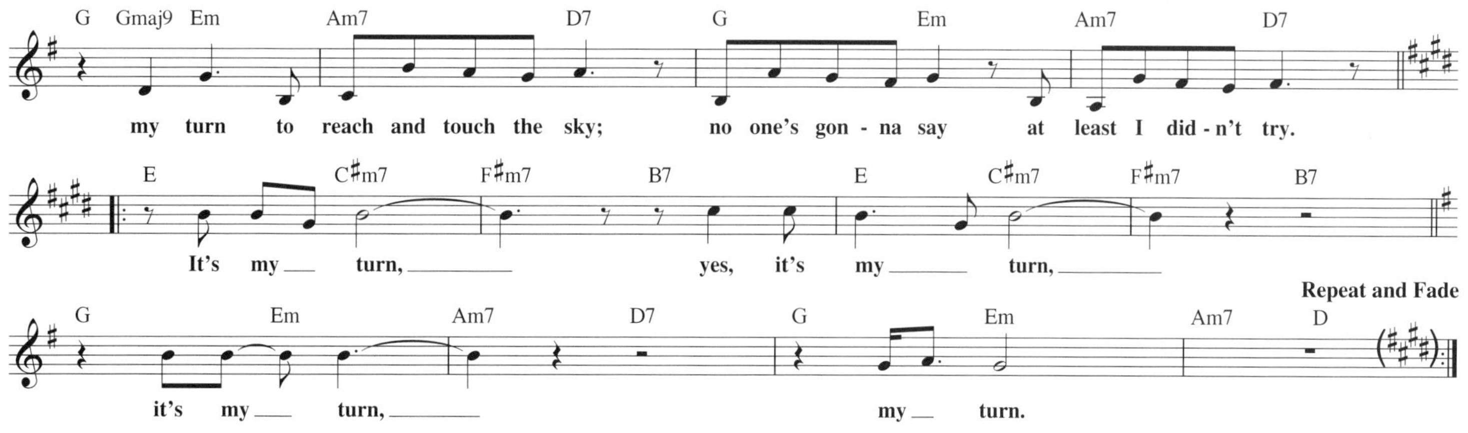

IT DON'T MATTER TO ME

Words and Music by
DAVID GATES

Moderately

C G7/B B♭
It don't mat-ter to me if you real - ly feel that you need some time
And it don't mat-ter to me if you take up with some - one who's bet -
It don't mat-ter to me if your search - in' brings you back to - geth -

Fm/A♭ C/G C
to be free, time to go out search - ing for your - self hop -
- ter than me, 'cause your hap - pi - ness is all I want for
- er with me, 'cause there'll al - ways be an emp - ty room wait -

Dm7/G G7 **To Coda** C/E C E♭
ing to find, time to go to find.
you to find, peace, your peace of mind.
ing for you,

1 G7 | 2 B♭maj7 E♭maj7 B♭maj7
Lot - ta peo - ple have an e - go hang - up 'cause they want to be the on - ly one.

E♭maj7 B♭maj7 E♭maj7 B♭maj7 E♭maj7
How man - y came be - fore? It real - ly does - n't mat - ter just as long as you're the last,

Cmaj7 Fmaj7 Cmaj7 Fmaj7 **D.C. al Coda**
ev - 'ry - bod - y run - nin' 'round and try'n' to find out what's been miss - in' in the past.

CODA

C Dm7/G G7 C/E
an o - pen heart wait - ing for you, time

C E♭ G7 C
is on my side, 'cause it don't mat - ter to me.

INDIAN RESERVATION

Words and Music by
JOHN D. LOUDERMILK

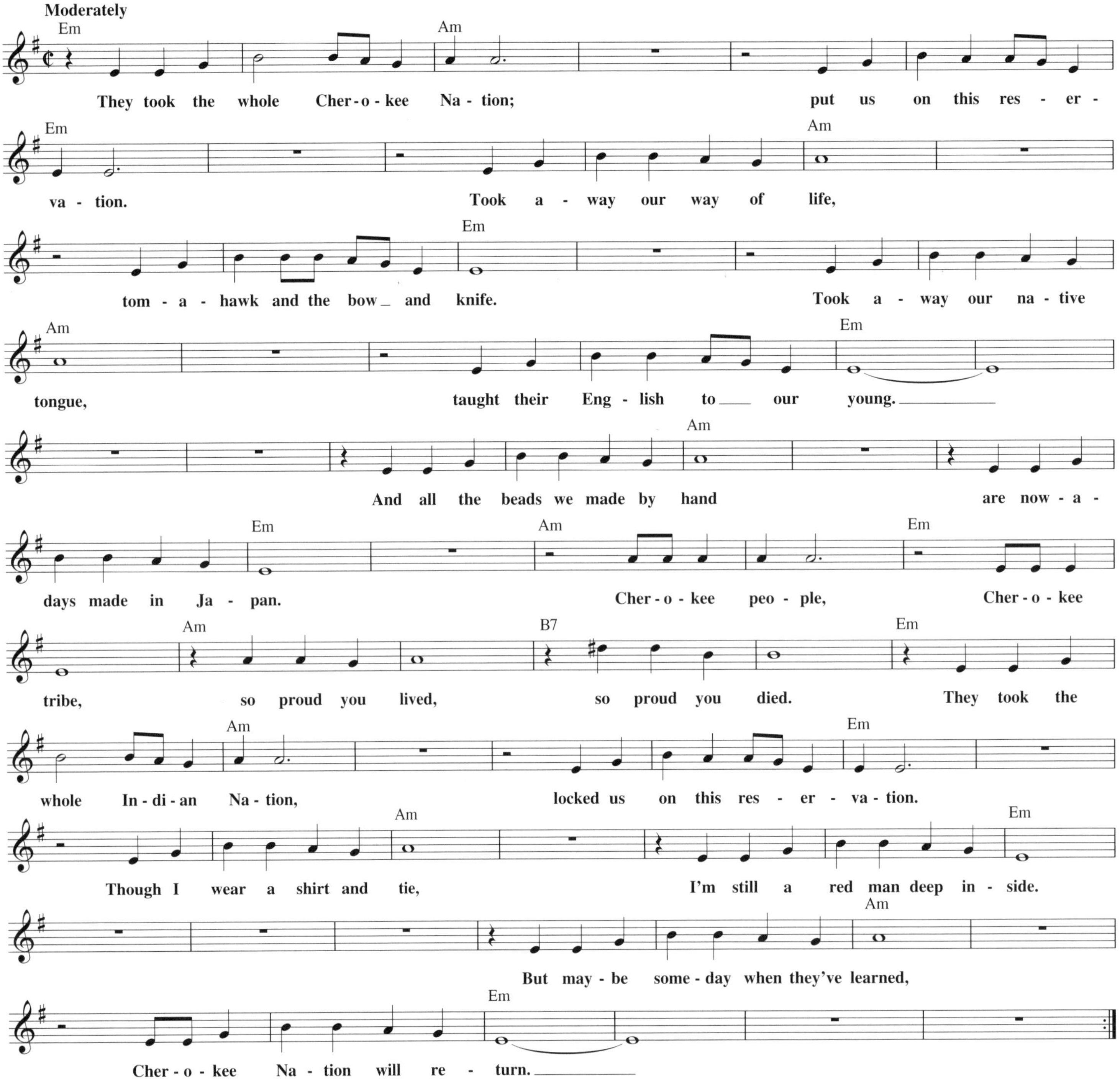

Moderately

Em Am
They took the whole Cher-o-kee Na-tion; put us on this res-er-

Em Am
va-tion. Took a-way our way of life,

Em
tom-a-hawk and the bow and knife. Took a-way our na-tive

Am Em
tongue, taught their Eng-lish to our young.

Am
And all the beads we made by hand are now-a-

Em Am Em
days made in Ja-pan. Cher-o-kee peo-ple, Cher-o-kee

Am B7 Em
tribe, so proud you lived, so proud you died. They took the

Am Em
whole In-di-an Na-tion, locked us on this res-er-va-tion.

Am Em
Though I wear a shirt and tie, I'm still a red man deep in-side.

Am
But may-be some-day when they've learned,

Em
Cher-o-kee Na-tion will re-turn.

IT'S NOT UNUSUAL

Words and Music by GORDON MILLS
and LES REED

With a strong beat
G
Am7
D7
It's not un-u-su-al to be loved by an-y-one.
It's not un-u-su-al to go out at an-y-time,
It's not un-u-su-al to be mad with an-y-one.
G
Am7
It's not un-u-su-al to have fun with an-y-one.
but when I see you out and a-bout it's such a crime.
It's not un-u-su-al to be sad with an-y-one.

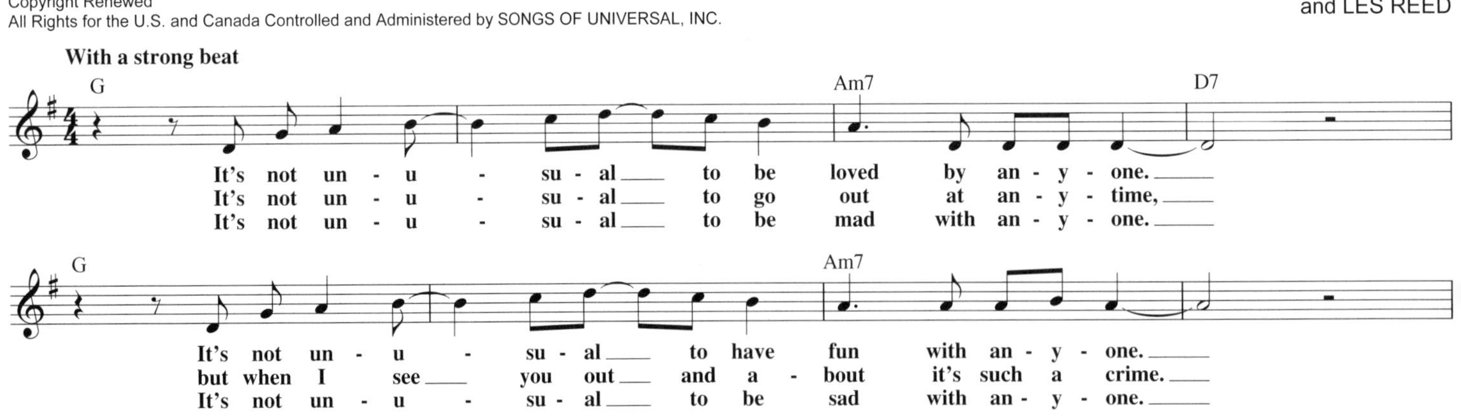

Bm Am7

But when I see you hang-ing a-bout with an-y-one,
If you should ev-er wan-na be loved by an-y-one,
But if I ev-er find that you've changed at an-y-time,

D7 To Coda 1. G D7

It's not un-u-su-al to see me cry. I wan-na die.
It's not un-u-su-al, it
It's not un-u-su-al to

2. G Am7 D7

hap-pens ev-'ry day. No mat-ter what you say, you'll find it

G

hap-pens all the time. Love will nev-er do

Am7 D7 Bm7 B♭7

what you want it to. Why can't this cra-zy love be mine?

Am7 D7 D.C. al Coda

CODA

G Am7 D7 G

find that I'm in love with you.

IT'S TOO LATE

Words and Music by CAROLE KING and TONI STERN

Slowly

Am7 D6 Am7 D6

Stayed in bed all morn-in' just to pass the time. There's some-thin' wrong here, there can be no de-ny-in'.
used to be so eas-y liv-ing here with you; you were light and breez-y and I knew just what to do. Now
There'll be good times a-gain for me and you; but we just can't stay to-geth-er, don't you feel it, too?

Am7 Gm7 Fmaj7 B♭maj7

One of us is chang-in' or may-be we've just stopped try-in'.
you look so un-hap-py and I feel like a fool.
Still I'm glad for what we had and how I once loved you.
And it's too late, ba-by now,

Fmaj7 B♭maj7 Fmaj7 B♭maj7 Fmaj7

it's too late, though we real-ly did try to make it. Some-thin' in-side has died and I can't hide

1, 2 Dm7 Fmaj7 E7sus Em7 Am7 D6 Am7 D6

and I just can't fake it. It

3 Dm7 Fmaj7 G7sus G7 Cmaj7 Fmaj7

and I just can't fake it. It's too late, ba-by, it's too late

Cmaj7 Fmaj7 Cmaj7

now, dar-lin', it's too late.

IT'S RAINING MEN

Words and Music by PAUL JABARA
and PAUL SHAFFER

Moderate Dance
Fm Bb Fm Bb
Hu - mid - i - ty's ris - ing. Ba - rom - e - ter's get - ting low. Ac -
Fm Bb C7sus C7
cord - ing to all sourc - es the street's the place to go. 'Cause to -
Fm Bbm C7sus
night for the first time at just a - bout half past ten, for the first time in his -
To Coda C7 N.C. Db
- to - ry, it's gon - na start rain - ing men. It's rain - ing men, hal - le - lu -
Eb C7sus C7 Fm Db Eb
- jah, it's rain - ing men. A - men! It's rain - ing men, hal - le - lu - jah, it's rain - ing men.
C7sus C7 Fm Fm7 Fm6 Dbmaj7/F N.C. D.S. al Coda
A - men! Hu -
CODA
C7 N.C. Db Eb
It's rain - ing men, hal - le - lu - jah, it's rain - ing men.
C7sus C7 Fm Db Bbm
A - men! I'm gon - na go out. I'm gon - na let my - self get
C7sus C7 N.C. Db Eb
ab - so - lute - ly soak - ing wet. It's rain - ing men, hal - le - lu - jah, it's rain - ing men.
C7sus C7 Fm Db Ab/C Bbm
Ev - 'ry spec - i - men! Tall, blond, dark and mean.

C7sus C7 D♭ E♭
Rough and tough and strong and lean. God bless Moth-er Na - ture.
C7sus Fm D♭ E♭
She's a sin-gle wom - an, too. She took on a heav - en
C7sus Fm D♭ E♭ C7sus C7
and she did what she had to do. She taught ev-'ry an - gel to re-ar-range the sky
Fm B♭m A♭/C D♭ B♭/D C/E Fm C/G
so that each and ev - 'ry wom - an could find the per - fect guy.
Fm/A♭ C7sus C7 N.C. Fm Fm7
It's rain - ing men.
Spoken: Go get yourself wet, girl! I
Fm6 D♭maj7/F N.C. Fm A♭/E♭
know you want to.
I feel storm - y weath - er mov - ing
D♭ C7sus C7 Fm
3
in, a - bout to be - gin. Hear the thun - der,
A♭/E♭ D♭ C7sus
don't you lose your head. Rip off the roof and stay
C7 C7sus C7 N.C. D♭ E♭
in bed. It's rain - ing men, hal - le - lu - jah, it's rain - ing men.
C7sus C7 Fm D♭ E♭
A - men! It's rain - ing men, hal - le - lu - jah, it's rain - ing men.
C7sus C7 1 Fm 2 Fm D♭
A - men! It's rain - ing men. It's rain-ing men. It's rain-ing men.
E♭ C7sus C7 Fm Repeat and Fade
It's rain - ing men. It's rain - ing men. It's rain - ing men.

IT'S THE SAME OLD SONG

Words and Music by EDWARD HOLLAND,
LAMONT DOZIER and BRIAN HOLLAND

Moderately

C Dm F G

You're sweet_ as a hon-ey bee but like a hon-ey bee stings,_ you've gone and left my heart in pain._ All you
fool___ am I to hear an old love song______ and wan-na cry,________ but the

C Dm F G

left is our fa - vor - ite song, the one__ we danced_ to all___ night long._ It used to
melody keeps haunt - ing me re - mind - ing me how___ in love___ we used to be. Keep

C Dm F G

bring_ sweet mem - o - ries of a ten - der love_ that used to be,__ now it's the
hear - ing the part that used to touch our heart say - ing to - geth - er for - ev - er. Break - ing up nev - er, it's the

𝄋 C G Dm G F

same old__ song_ but with a dif - f'rent mean - ing since - a you been gone._ Now it's the

Instrumental

C G Dm G F **To Coda** 𝄌

same, same old song but with a dif - f'rent mean - ing since - a you been gone._

(3rd time) Pre - cious

1. C 2. **(D.S. Instrumental)** 3.

I, oh__ I,___ sen - ti - men - tal *(Instrumental)* mem - o - ries keep - a

Dm F G C

lin - ger - ing on,__ ev - 'ry - time I hear_ our__ fa - vor - ite song,_ now you're gone, left this

Dm F G C

emp - ti - ness, I on - ly re - mi - nisce. The hap - pi - ness we spent, we used to dance to the mu - sic make ro -

Dm F **D.S. al Coda**

mance_ to the mu - sic, now it's the

CODA 𝄌 C

I oh,__ I can't bear to hear it, it's the

G Dm G F **Repeat and Fade**

same old song but with a dif - f'rent mean - ing since you been gone;_____ it's the

JAZZMAN

Words and Music by DAVID PALMER
and CAROLE KING

Moderately
Gm Am7 B♭ E♭maj7 Gm A♭maj7
Lift me, won't you lift me a - bove the old rou - tine? Make it nice,
A♭/B♭ F/G B♭/C (clap) C B♭/C
play it clean, jazz - man.
Alto solo
C B♭/C Am7/C B♭/C
Solo ends
When the jazz - man's tes - ti - fy - in' a faith - less man be - lieves.
gos - pel kind of feel - in', a touch of Geor - gia slide,
When the jazz - man's sig - ni - fy - in', and the band is wind - in' low,
fill a room with sad - ness as he fills his horn with tears.
Fmaj9 B♭/C Am7/C 1,3 B♭/C
He can sing you in - to par - a - dise or bring you to your knees.
a song of pure re - vi - val and a style
it's the late night side of morn - ing in the dark - ness of his soul.
He can cry like a fall - len an - gel when ris -
G/A 2,4 B♭/C Am7/C Dm F/G
It's a that's sanc - ti - fied.
He can - in' time is near.
B♭/C C F/G Fm/C C B♭/C C
Jazz - man, take my blues a - way. Make my pain the same as yours with
B♭/C To Coda Fmaj9 A♭/B♭ F/G
ev - er - y change you play. Jazz - man, oh, jazz - man.
D.S. al Coda
CODA
Fmaj7 Gm Am7 B♭ F
Oh, lift me, won't you lift me with
E♭maj7 Gm A♭maj7 A♭/B♭
ev - 'ry turn - a - round? Play it sweet - ly, take me down, oh,
F/G B♭/C (clap) C
Repeat and Fade
jazz - man.
Alto solo

JEREMY

Music by JEFF AMENT
Lyric by EDDIE VEDDER

Alternative Rock
A5 A7 A5 A7 A5 A7 A5 A7
At home, drawing pictures of mountaintops with him on top, lemon yellow sun.
A5 A7 A5 A7 A5 A7 A5 A7
Arms raised in a V, the dead lay in pools of maroon below.
A5 G5/A D/A G5/A A5 A7
Daddy didn't give attention, oh, to the fact that Mommy didn't
Daddy didn't give affection, no. And the boy was something that Mommy wouldn't
A5 A7 D/A G5/A A5 A
care.
wear.
King Jeremy The Wicked, oh, ruled his world.
Fmaj7 Dm7 Em7 Fmaj7 A
Jeremy spoke in class today.
Fmaj7 Dm7 Em7 Fmaj7/C A
To Coda
Jeremy spoke in class today.
A5 A7 A5 A7 A5 A7
Clearly I remember picking on the boy. Seemed a harmless
A5 A7 A5 A7 A5 A7
little fuck. Oh, but we unleashed a lion; gnashed
A5 A7 A5 A7 A5 A7
his teeth and bit the recess lady's breast. How could I forget? And he hit me with a
A5 A7 A5 A7 A5 A7
surprise left, my jaw left hurting, oh, dropped wide open,

A5
A7
A5
A7
A5
A7
Asus
A
D.S. al Coda
just like the day,
oh, like the day I heard
CODA
Fmaj7
Dm7
Em7
Fmaj7
A
Je - re - my spoke in class to - day.
N.C.
Ooh ooh ooh ooh ooh ooh ooh ooh ooh ooh oooh ooh ooh ooh. Try to for-get
this, try to for-get this. Try to e-rase this, try to e-rase this from the black -
Fmaj7
Dm7
Em7
Fmaj7
Am
board.
F/G
Dm7
Em7
Fmaj7
A
Je - re - my spoke in class to - day.
Fmaj7
Dm7
Em7
Fmaj7/C
A
Je - re - my spoke in class to - day.
F/G
Dm7
Em7
Am
Je - re - my spoke in, spoke in... Je - re - my spoke in, spoke in...
F
G
A5
Am
Je - re - my spoke in class to - day.
Repeat and ad lib. as required
F
G
Am
Ooh ooh ooh ooh ooh ooh ooh ooh ooh ooh ooh ooh ooh ooh ooh ooh
A7(no3)
D/A
Asus
Am
G/A
Am
1
G/A
Am
2
G/A
A7(no3)
(Instrumental)

JET

Words and Music by
PAUL and LINDA McCARTNEY

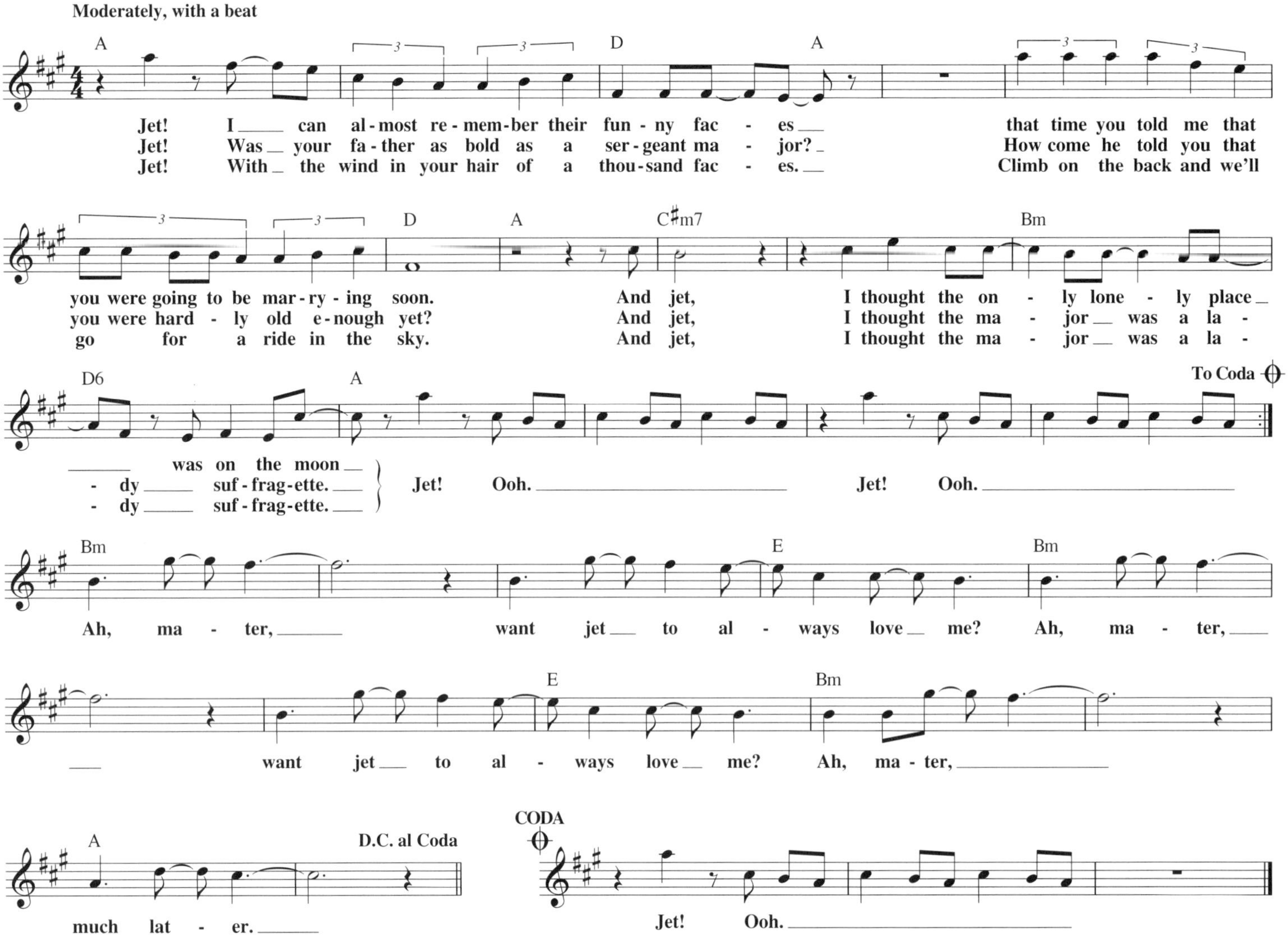

Moderately, with a beat
A D A
Jet! I can al-most re-mem-ber their fun-ny fac-es that time you told me that
Jet! Was your fa-ther as bold as a ser-geant ma-jor? How come he told you that
Jet! With the wind in your hair of a thou-sand fac-es. Climb on the back and we'll
D A C♯m7 Bm
you were going to be mar-ry-ing soon. And jet, I thought the on-ly lone-ly place
you were hard-ly old e-nough yet? And jet, I thought the ma-jor was a la-
go for a ride in the sky. And jet, I thought the ma-jor was a la-
D6 A To Coda
was on the moon
-dy suf-frag-ette.
-dy suf-frag-ette.
Jet! Ooh. Jet! Ooh.
Bm E Bm
Ah, ma-ter, want jet to al-ways love me? Ah, ma-ter,
E Bm
want jet to al-ways love me? Ah, ma-ter,
A D.C. al Coda
much lat-er.
CODA
Jet! Ooh.

JUST THE TWO OF US

Words and Music by RALPH MacDONALD,
WILLIAM SALTER and BILL WITHERS

Moderately
E♭maj7 D7 Gm Fm7 B♭7 E♭maj7 D7 Gm7
I see the crys-tal rain-drops fall, and the beau-ty of it all is when the sun comes shin-ing through
We look for love; no time for tears. Wast-ed wa-ter's all that is, and it don't make no flow-ers grow.
I hear the crys-tal rain-drops fall on the win-dow down the hall, and it be-comes the morn-ing dew.
E♭maj7 D7 Gm Fm7 B♭7 E♭maj7 D7
to make those rain-bows in my mind when I think of you some-time, and I want to spend some time with
Good things might come to those who wait not for those who wait too late. We've got to go for all we
And, dar-ling, when the morn-ing comes and I see the morn-ing sun. I want to be the one with
Gm E♭maj7 D7 Gm7 F♯m7 Fm7 B♭7 E♭maj7 D7
you.
know.
you.
Just the two of us, we can make it if we try. Just the two of us. (Just the two

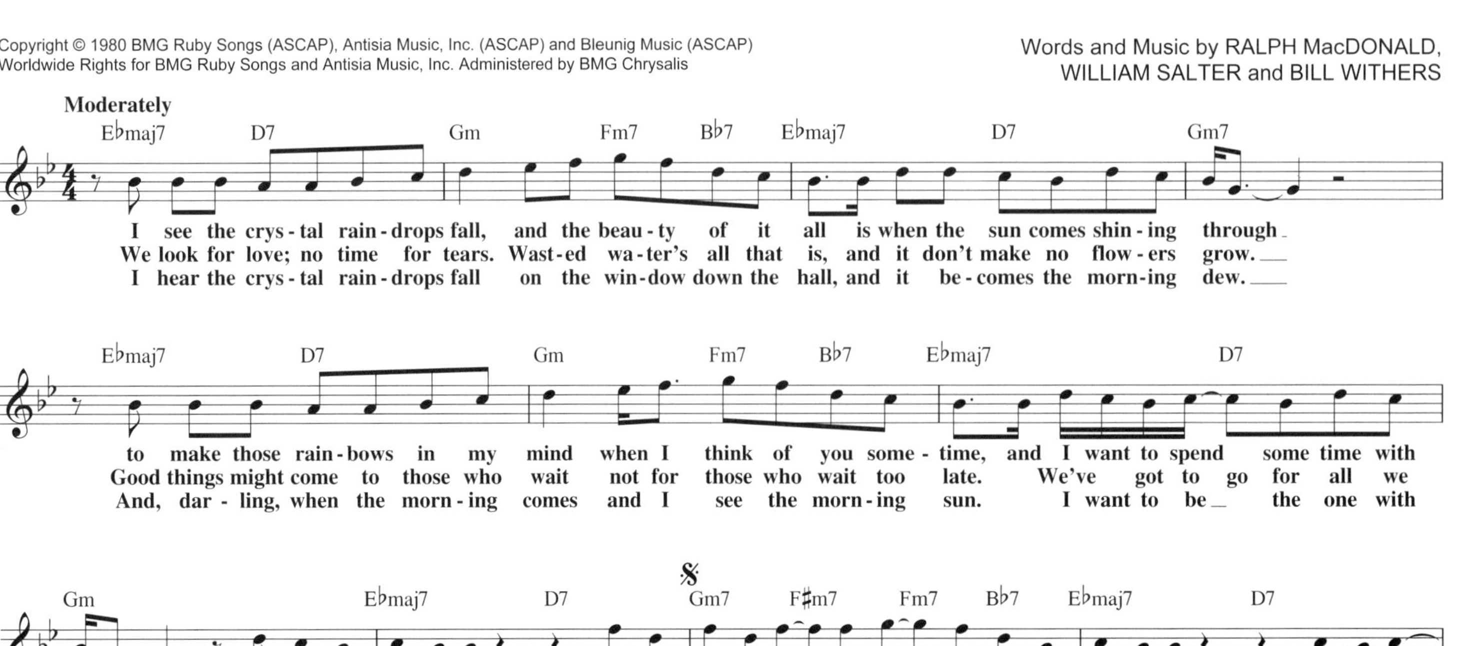

To Coda
of us.) Just the two of us building castles in the sky. Just the two of us, you and I.
D.C. al Coda
CODA
D.S. and Fade
Just the
JIMMY MACK
© 1966, 1967 (Renewed 1994, 1995) JOBETE MUSIC CO., INC.
All Rights Controlled and Administered by EMI BLACKWOOD MUSIC INC.
on behalf of STONE AGATE MUSIC (A Division of JOBETE MUSIC CO., INC.)
Words and Music by BRIAN HOLLAND,
LAMONT DOZIER and EDWARD HOLLAND
Moderately
1. My arms are missing you my lips feel the same way, too. I tried so hard to be true like I
2. (See additional lyrics)
promised to do; but this boy keeps coming around he's trying to wear my resistance down. Hey, Jimmy, Jimmy, oh Jimmy Mack, when are you coming back? Jimmy, Jimmy, oh Jimmy Mack, you better
hurry back. hurry back, need your loving, need your loving.
To Coda
D.S. al Coda (take 2nd ending)
CODA
Repeat and Fade
loving. Hey, Jimmy Mack, you better hurry back. / when are you coming back? Hey,

Additional Lyrics

2. He calls me on the phone about three times a day
Now my heart's just listening to what he has to say.
But this loneliness I have within
Keeps reaching out to be his friend.
Hey Jimmy, Jimmy, oh Jimmy Mack,
When are you coming back?
Jimmy, Jimmy, oh Jimmy Mack, you better hurry back.

JUDY IN DISGUISE (WITH GLASSES)

Words and Music by ANDREW BERNARD and JOHN FRED GOURIER

With a beat
C
G7
C
G
C F C
1
N.C.
2
F
B♭ G
F
E♭
F
G N.C.
(Instrumental)
C
G7
C
G7
C
3
Ju - dy in dis - guise, well, that's what you are, lem - on - ade pie with a brand new car. Can - ta - lope eyes come to me to - night
brace - lets and your new ra ra, cross your heart with your liv - ing bra. Chim - ney sweep spar - row with guise
Ju - dy in dis - guise with glass - es.
Keep a - wear - ing your glass - es.
Come to me to - night. Come to me to - night.
Tak - ing ev - 'ry - thing in sight, ex - cept for the strings on my kite.
Ju - dy in dis - guise. well, what you aim - ing for, a cir - cus of hor - rors, yeah. Well, that's what you are
You made me a life of ash - es. I guess I'll just take your glass - es!

JUST ONCE

Words by CYNTHIA WEIL
Music by BARRY MANN

Slowly

C(add9) Fmaj7 Em7 Am9
Dm7 G/F Em7 Am(add9) Am Dm7 Gsus G

I did my best, but I guess my best was - n't good e - nough 'cause here we are back where we were be - fore.
I gave my all, but I think my all may have been too much 'cause Lord knows we're not get - ting an - y - where.
Seems noth - ing ev - er chang - es, we're
It seems we're al - ways blow - in' what

E7sus E7 Am(add9) Am/G Dm7 C(add9)/E F(add9)
back to be - ing stran - gers won-d'ring if we ought to stay or head on out the door.
ev - er we've got go - in' and it seems at times with all we've got we have-n't got a prayer.
F/G G F/G G C G/C Gm7/C C7/E Fmaj7 C/E
Just once can't we fig - ure out what we keep do - in' wrong?
Just once can't we fig - ure out what we keep do - in' wrong?
Dm7 G/F Em7 Am(add9) Am Dm7 F/G G
Why we nev - er last for ver - y long? What are we do - in' wrong?
Why the good - times nev - er last for long? Where are we go - ing wrong?
C G/C Gm7/C C7/E Fmaj7 C/E
Just once can't we find a way to fi - n'lly make it right? To
Just once can't we find a way to fi - n'lly make it right? To
Dm7 G/F Em7 Am(add9) Am Dm7
make the mag - ic last for more than just one night? If we could just get to it, I
make the mag - ic last for more than just one night? I know we could break through it if
F/G F/G A♭(add9)
know we could break through it. we could just get to it. Just once I want to
Fm7 B♭m7 D♭/E♭ A♭(add9) A♭
un - der - stand why it al - ways comes back to good - bye.
B(add9) G♯m7 C♯m7 B(add9)/D♯ E(add9) B(add9)/D♯
Why can't we get our - selves in hand and ad - mit to one an - oth - er we're no good with - out each oth - er?
C♯m7 B(add9)D♯ Em7 G/A A
Take the best and make it bet - ter, find a way to stay to - geth - er.
D A/D Am7/D D7/F♯ Gmaj7 D/F♯
Just once can't we find a way to fi - n'lly make it right? Oh, to
Em7 A/G F♯m7 Bm(add9) Bm Em7
make the mag - ic last for more than just one night? I know we could break through it if
G/A D A/D G/D A/D D A/D
we could just get to it just once. Whoa, we can
Gm/B♭ G/A D Em/D Dmaj7/F♯ Gmaj9 Gmaj9/A G/A B(add9)
get to it just once.

JUMP (FOR MY LOVE)

Words and Music by MARTI SHARRON, GARY SKARDINA and STEPHEN MITCHELL

Moderate Rock
Closed eyes tell me how you want me. I can feel it in your heart - beat.
Hold me, I'll give you all that you need. Wrap your love a - round me.
You told me I'm the on - ly wom-an for you. No - bod - y does you like I do.
I know you like what you see.
You're so ex - cit - ed I can feel you get - tin' hot - ter, oh, ba - by! I'll take you down,
Then make the move be - fore you turn to go much far - ther, oh, ba - by! You are the one,
I'll take you down where no one's ev - er gone be - fore,
you are the one, and heav - en waits here at my door,
and if you want more, if you want more, more, more, then jump for my love. Jump in and feel my touch.
Jump, if you wan - na taste my kiss - es in the night, then jump for my love. Jump!
I know my heart can make you hap - py. Jump in. You know these arms can fill you up. Jump!
If you wan - na taste my kiss - es in the night, then jump for my love.
To Coda
(Instrumental)
D.C. al Coda
CODA
When you are next to me, Oh, I come a - live. Your love burns in - side.
Oh, it feels so right. Come to me if you want me to - night.
Jump! Jump in if you wan - na taste my kiss - es in the night, then
jump, jump, jump. Ooh yeah. You know my heart can make you hap - py. Jump! You know these arms can
fill you up. Jump in. You wan - na taste my kiss - es in the night, then jump, jump for my love. Jump!
Repeat and Fade

JUMP, JIVE AN' WAIL

Words and Music by
LOUIS PRIMA

Moderately fast Swing
B♭ E♭ B♭ F7/C F7 B♭ B♭ E♭7 B♭ F7/C E♭7/F B♭ E♭ B♭ F7/C F7 B♭ D♭9♯11 C♯m7 F♯13 B E B Dm7 C♯m7 F♯7♯9 B13 G♯m7 C♯m7 G7♭9(add13) E/F♯ C7♯9 B E7 B F♯7 E7 B B E7 B F♯7/C♯ E7/F♯ B A♭13 Dm7 G13
Ba - by, ba - by, it looks like it's gon-na hail. Ba - by, ba - by, it looks like it's gon-na hail.
Pa-pa's in the ice-box look-ing for a can of ale. Pa-pa's in the ice-box looking for a can of ale.
You bet-ter come in - side and let me teach you how to jive and wail.
Ma-ma's in the back yard learn-ing how to jive and wail.
Oh, you got - ta jump, jive, and then you wail. You got - ta jump, jive, and then you wail. You got - ta jump, jive, and then you wail. You got - ta jump, jive, and then you wail. You got - ta jump, jive and then you wail a - way.
1 2
A wom-an is a wom-an and a man ain't noth-in' but a male. Wom - an is a wom-an and a man ain't noth-in' but a male. One good thing a-bout him; he knows how to jive and wail.
Jack and Jill went up the hill to get a pail. Jack and Jill went up the hill to get a pail. Jill stayed up; she wants to learn how to jive and wail.
Jump, jive, and then you wail. You got - ta jump, jive, and then you wail. You got - ta jump, jive, and then you wail. You got - ta jump, jive, and then you wail. You got - ta jump, jive, and then you wail a - way.
You got - ta jump, jive, and then you wail. You got - ta jump, jive, and then you wail. You got - ta jump, jive, and then you wail. You got - ta jump, jive, and then you wail. You got - ta jump, jive, and then you wail a - way.
Oh, you got - ta
Repeat and Fade

JUST DROPPED IN
(To See What Condition My Condition Was In)

Words and Music by
MICKEY NEWBURY

Moderately
Em A7 Em
I woke up this morn - ing with the sun-down shin - ing in.
B7 Em
Found my mind in a brown pa-per bag but then I tripped on a cloud and fell
G A7 Em
eight miles high, I tore my mind on a jag-ged sky. I just dropped in to
B7♯9 Em D Em
see what con - di - tion my con - di - tion was in. Yeah! Yeah! Oh yeah! My con - di - tion, my con -
Fm B♭7
di - tion was in. I pushed my soul in a deep dark hole and then I
Fm
fol-lowed it in. Watched my - self crawl-ing out as I was
C7 Fm A♭
crawl - ing in, I got up so tight I could-n't un - wind, I
B♭7 Fm C7♯9
saw so much I broke my mind. I just dropped in to see what con - di - tion my con -
Fm E♭ Fm
di - tion was in. Yeah! Yeah! Oh, yeah! My con - di - tion, my con -
F♯m B7
di-tion was in. Some - one pain-ted "Ap - ril Fool" in big black let-ters on a
F♯m
dead-end sign. I kept my foot on the gas as I left the road, blew

C♯7 F♯m A
out my mind. Eight miles out of Mem-phis and I've got no spare, eight
B7 F♯m C♯7♯9
miles straight up down-town some-where. I just dropped in to see what con-di-tion my con-
F♯m C♯7
di-tion was in. Said, I just dropped in to see what con-di-tion my con-
F♯m E/F♯ F♯m E/F♯ Bm/F♯ F♯m
di-tion was in. Yeah! Yeah! Whoa. Yeah!

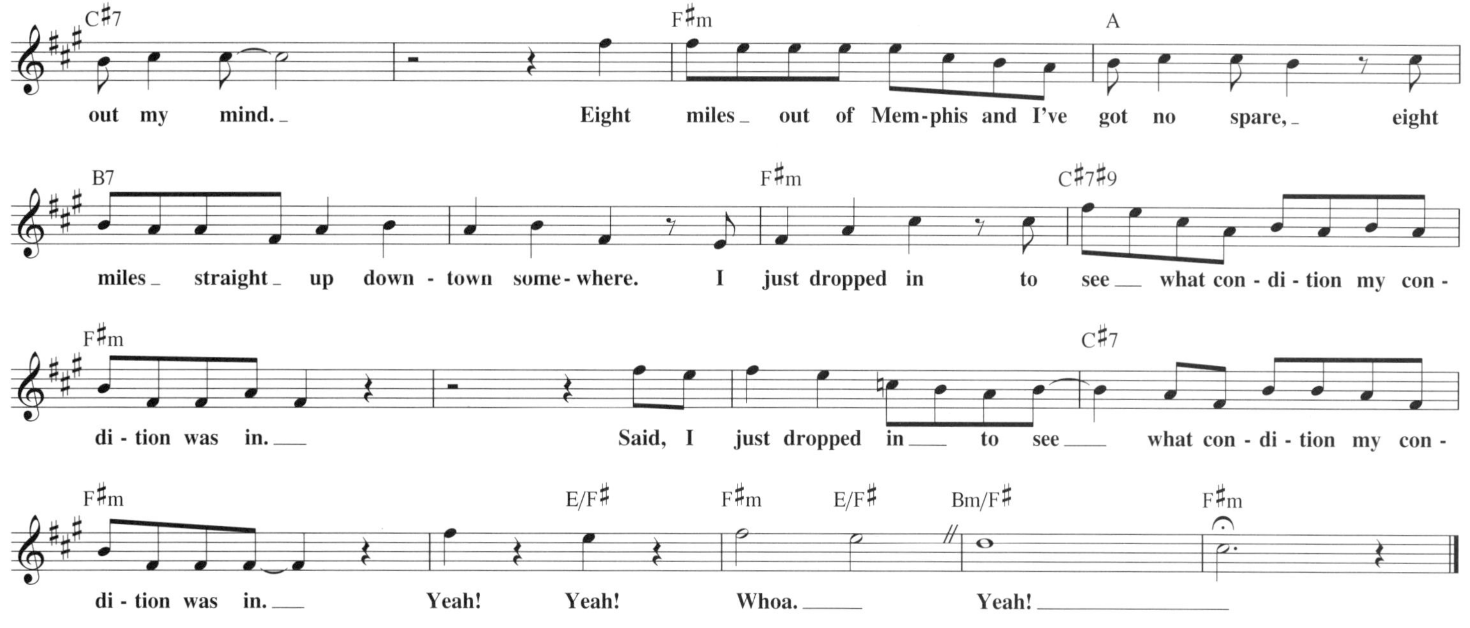

KISSES SWEETER THAN WINE

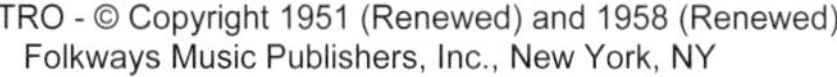

Words by RONNIE GILBERT, LEE HAYS,
FRED HELLERMAN and PETE SEEGER
Music by HUDDIE LEDBETTER

Moderately slow
B♭ F Gm Dm F Dm G
1. When I was a young man and nev-er been kissed, I got to think-in' o-ver what I had missed. I
2. asked me to mar-ry and be his sweet wife, and we would be so hap-py all of our life. He
3.-5. (See additional lyrics)
B♭ F Gm Dm F Dm G
got me a girl, I kissed her and then, Oh, Lord, I kissed her a-gain.
begged and he plead-ed like a nat-ur-al man and then, Oh, Lord, I gave him my hand.

B♭ Dm Gm7 D7 G
Oh, kiss-es sweet-er than wine.

B♭ Dm Gm7 D7 G
1–4 5
Oh, kiss-es sweet-er than wine. He

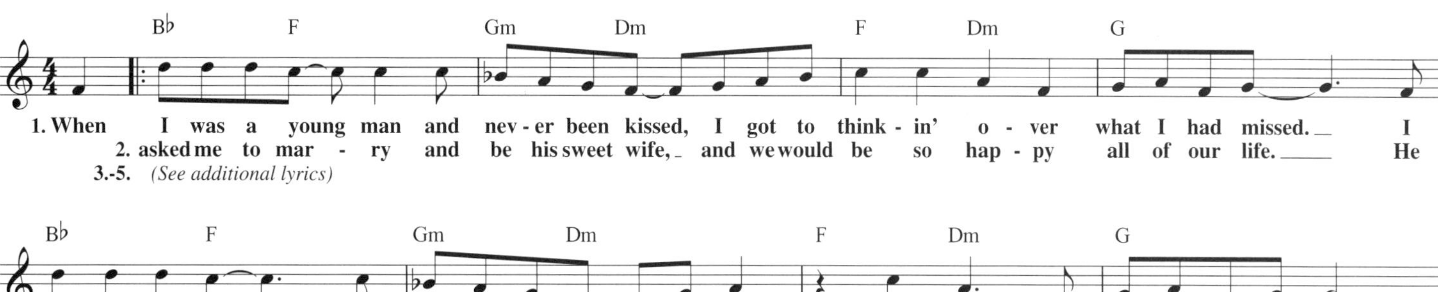

Additional Lyrics

3. I worked mighty hard and so did my wife,
   A-workin' hand in hand to make a good life.
   With corn in the fields and wheat in the bins,
   And then, oh, Lord, I was the father of twins.
   Chorus

4. Our children numbered just about four,
   And they all had sweethearts knock on the door.
   They all got married, and they didn't wait.
   I was, oh, Lord, the grandfather of eight.
   Chorus

5. Now we are old and ready to go.
   We get to thinkin' what happened a long time ago.
   We had lots of kids and trouble and pain,
   But, oh, Lord, we'd do it again.
   Chorus

JUST TO SEE HER

Words and Music by JIMMY GEORGE and LOU PARDINI

Moderate Rock Ballad
Just to see her, just to touch her, just to hold her in my arms again one more time.
If I could feel her warm embrace, see her smilin' face.
Can't find anyone to take her place. I've got to see her again.
it, no. I can't fight it, oh. It's so hard to live without the love she gave to me.
Doesn't she know it? I tried hard not to show it, oo.
Can't I make her realize that she really needs me again?
I would do anything. I would go anywhere.
There's nothing I wouldn't do just to see her again.
I can't hide
She brightened / brightens up my ev'ry day, made / makes me feel so good in ev'ry way.
If I could have her back to stay, (today) I've got to see her again.
To Coda
(Instrumental solo)
Oo
Oo
N.C.

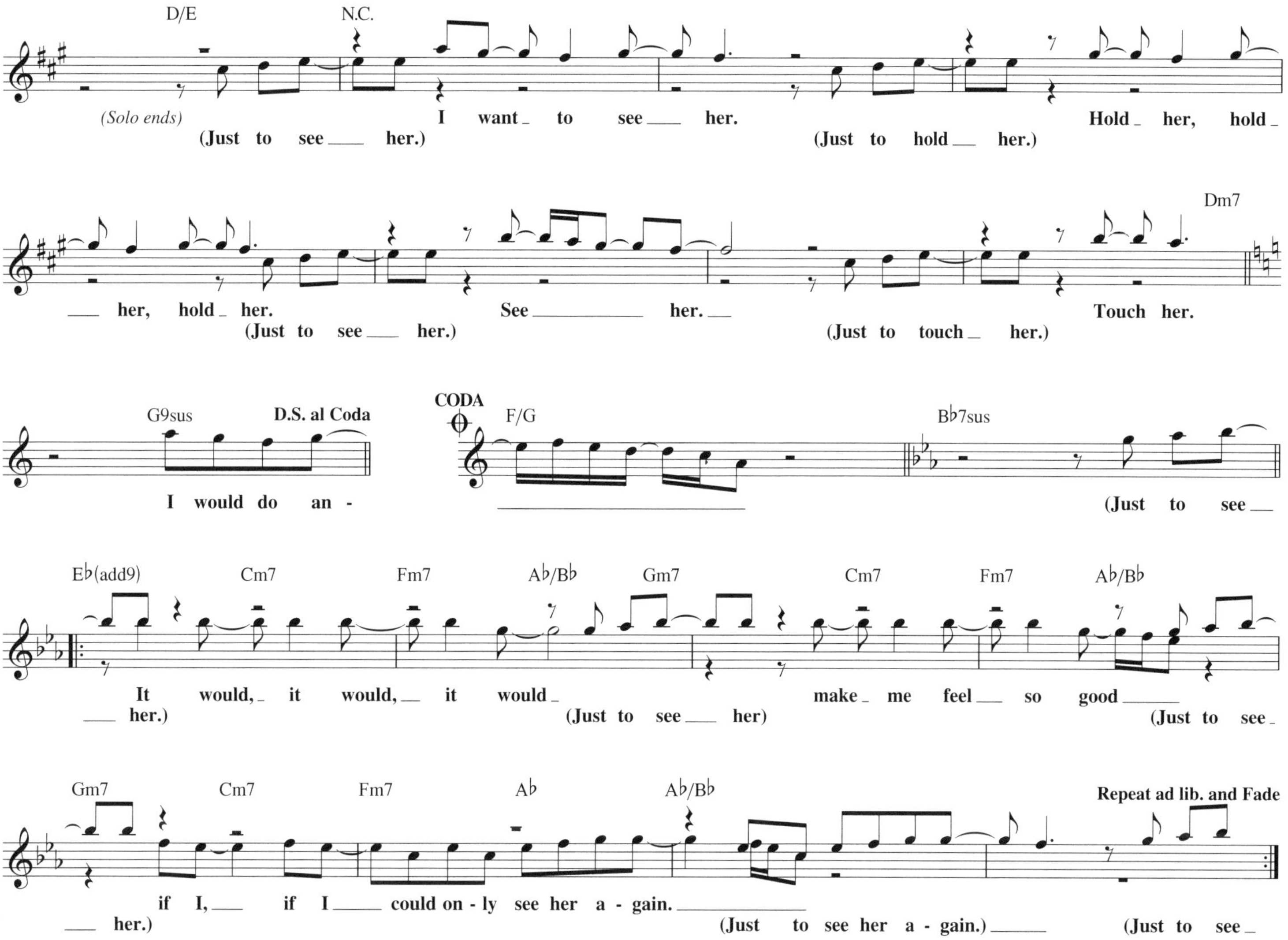

D/E N.C.

(Solo ends) I want to see her. Hold her, hold
(Just to see her.) (Just to hold her.)

Dm7

her, hold her. See her. Touch her.
(Just to see her.) (Just to touch her.)

G9sus **D.S. al Coda** **CODA** F/G B♭7sus

I would do an - (Just to see

E♭(add9) Cm7 Fm7 A♭/B♭ Gm7 Cm7 Fm7 A♭/B♭

It would, it would, it would make me feel so good
her.) (Just to see her) (Just to see

Gm7 Cm7 Fm7 A♭ A♭/B♭ **Repeat ad lib. and Fade**

if I, if I could on - ly see her a - gain.
her.) (Just to see her a - gain.) (Just to see

KEEP A-KNOCKIN'

Words and Music by
RICHARD PENNIMAN

Moderately
A♭
Keep a-knock-in' and you can't come in. Keep a-knock-in' and you can't come in.
E♭
Keep a-knock-in' and you can't come in.
A♭
Come back to-mor-row night and try it a - gain.
You said you loved me and you can't come in. You said you loved me and you can't come in.
E♭
You said you loved me and you can't come in.
A♭
Come back to-mor-row night and try it a - gain.

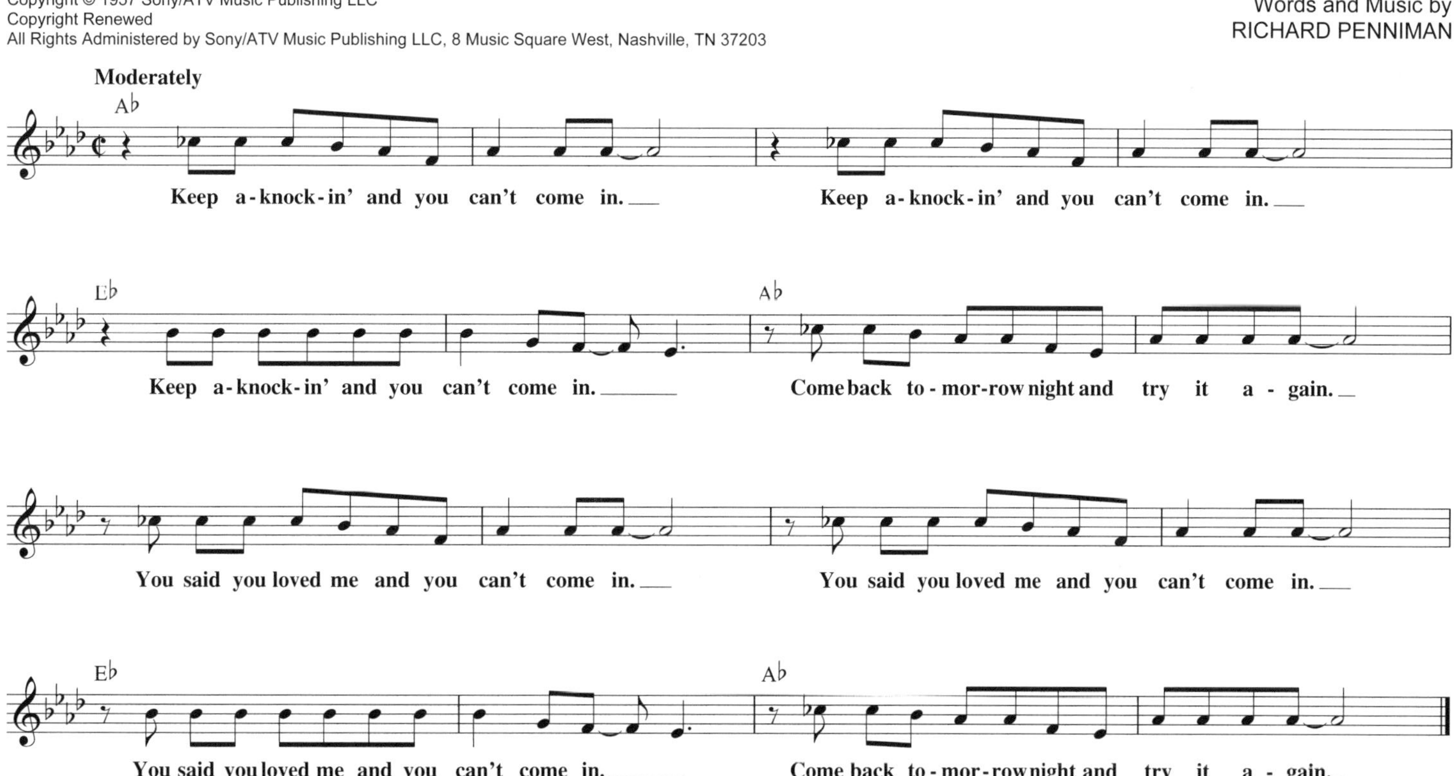

KEEP ON LOVING YOU

Words and Music by
KEVIN CRONIN

Moderately
You should have seen by the look in my eyes, ba - by, there was some - thin' miss - in'.
You should have known by the tone of my voice, may - be, but you did - n't lis - ten.
You played dead, but you nev - er bled. In - stead you laid still in the grass
all coiled up and hiss - in'. And though I know all a -
(Instrumental)
bout those men, still I don't re - mem - ber. 'Cause it was us, ba - by,
way be - fore them, and we're still to - geth - er. And I meant
(Instrumental ends)
ev - 'ry word I said. When I said that I love you, I meant that I'll love you for - ev - er.
And I'm gon - na keep on lov - in' you, 'cause it's the on - ly thing I wan - na do.
I don't wan - na sleep. I just wan - na keep on lov - in' you.
Ba - by, I'm gon - na keep on lov - in' you, 'cause it's the on -
- ly thing I wan - na do. I don't wan - na sleep. I just wan - na keep on lov -
- in' you.

KUNG FU FIGHTING

Words and Music by
CARL DOUGLAS

Moderately
D
Em7
Bm7
A7
Ev - 'ry - bod - y was Kung Fu fight - ing, Those cats were fast as light - ning. In fact it was a lit - tle bit fright - 'ning, but they fought with ex - pert tim - ing.
There were funk - y Chi - na - men from funk - y Chi - na - town. They were chop - ping them up, they were chop - ping them down. 'Tis an an - cient Chi - nese art and ev - 'ry - bod - y knew their part. From a feint - ing to a slip and a kick - ing from the hip. Ev - 'ry - bod - y was
There was funk - y Bill - ly Chin and lit - tle Sam - my Chung. He said here comes the big boss, let's get it on. He took a bow and made a stand. Start - ed sway - ing with the hand. A sud - den mo - tion made me skip now we're in - to a brand new trip. Ev - 'ry - bod - y was
Kung Fu fight - ing, Those cats were fast as light - ning. In fact it was a lit - tle bit fright 'ning, but they fought with ex - pert tim - ing.
Oh ho ho hoo. Oh ho ho hoo. Oh ho ho hoo. Oh ho ho hoo.
Repeat and Fade
Ev - 'ry - bod - y was

LAND OF CONFUSION

Words and Music by TONY BANKS,
PHIL COLLINS and MIKE RUTHERFORD

Driving Rock
D♭ E♭ G♭ A♭
I must - 've dreamed a thou - sand dreams, been hun - ted by a
Now did you read the news to - day? They say that dan - ger's
Oh su - per - man, where are you now? Well ev - 'ry - thing's gone
I won't be com - ing home to - night. My gen-er - a - tion will
C♭ D♭
mil - lion screams. But I can hear the march - ing feet
gone a - way, but I can see the fire's still a - light,
wrong some - how. The men of steel the men of power
put it right. We're not just mak - ing prom - is - es
E♭m 1 D♭ 2-4
they're mov - ing in - to the street.
burn - ing in - to the night. There's
are los - ing con - trol by the hour.
that we know we'll nev - er keep. There's
D♭ E♭m E♭m7 A♭ D♭ E♭m
too man - y men, too man - y peo - ple mak - ing too man - y prob - lems
This is the time, this is the place, so we look for the fu - ture
too man - y men, too man - y peo - ple mak - ing too man - y prob - lems
E♭m7 D♭ E♭m E♭m7 A♭
and not much love to go round. Can't you see this is a
but there's not much love to go round. Tell me why this is a
and not much love to go round. Can't you see this is a
D♭ E♭m7 D♭ E♭m7 C♭ D♭ B♭m E♭m C♭
land of con - fu - sion?
land of con - fu - sion.
land of con - fu - sion?
(1.-3.) This is the world we live in and these are the
(D.S.) for. This is the world we live in and these are the
D♭ B♭m E♭m C♭ D♭ B♭m E♭m C♭ To Coda I
hands we're giv - en. Use them and let's start try - ing to make it a
hands we're giv - en. Stand up and let's start show - ing just where our
To Coda II 1 D.C. (take 3rd ending)
D♭ B♭m A♭ A♭m D♭
place worth liv - ing in.
lives are go - ing to.
(Instrumental)
2
Cm A♭maj7/C
E♭ Gm/D Cm F Cm
I re-mem - ber long a - go,

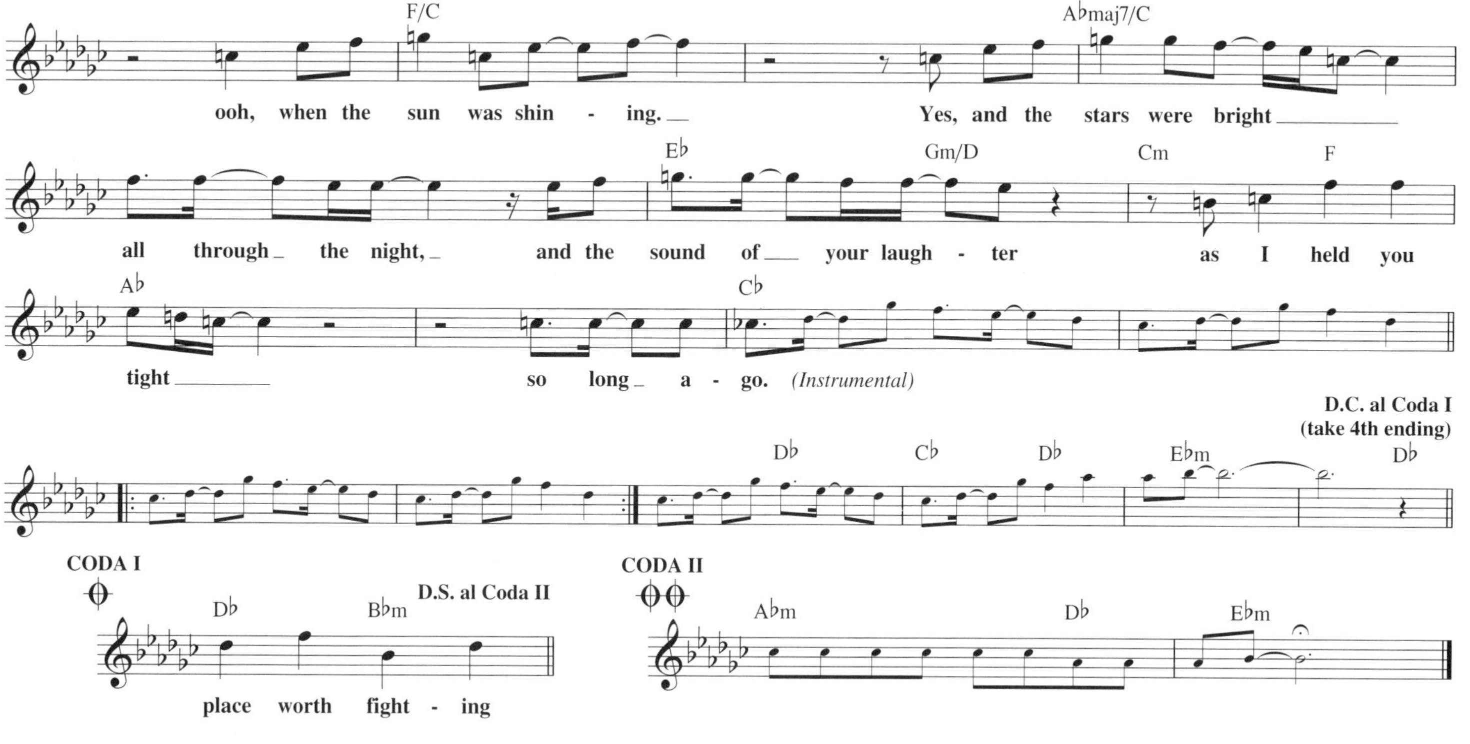

KISS AND SAY GOODBYE

Words and Music by
WINFRED LOVETT

Moderately slow

C N.C. G G7 C

I had to meet you here to - day, there's just so man - y things to say.

G G7 C

Please don't stop me till I'm through, this is some-thing I hate to do.

N.C. F C

We've been meet - ing here so long, I guess what we done was wrong.

G G7 C

Please, dar - ling, don't you cry. Let's just kiss and say good - bye.

N.C. G G7 C

Man - y months have passed us by, I'm gon - na miss you I can't lie.

G G7 C

I've got ties and so do you, I just think this is the thing to do.

N.C. F C

It's gon - na hurt me I can't lie, may - be you'll meet an - oth - er guy.

G G7 C F C Dm7 C

Un - der - stand me won't you try, try, try. Let's just kiss and say good - bye.

LADY MARMALADE

Words and Music by BOB CREWE
and KENNY NOLAN

Moderately
Em A Em A
Met Mar-ma-lade down in ol' New Or-leans, strut-tin' her stuff on the street. She say,
Am7 Bm7 Em A
"Hel-lo, hey Joe, ya wan-na give it a go?" 'N' get chor get chor ya da da.
Em A Em A Am
Get chor get chor ya ya he ya. Mo-cha cho-co-la-ta ya ya. Cre-ole La-dy Mar-ma-lade.
Em Em7 A Em7
To Coda
"Vou-lez vous cou-cher a-vec mois ce soir? Vou-lez vous cou-cher a-vec mois?"
A Em A Em
1
Sat in her bou-doir while she fresh-ened up. 'N' I drank her mag-no-lia wine.
A Am7 Bm7 Em
2
Up-on her black sat-in sheets, I swear I start-ed to freak when she said: Touch of her skin feel-in' silk-
A Em A Am7 Bm7
-y smooth, col-or of ca-fé au lait; made the sav-age beast in-side roar un-til it cried
B7 Em A Em
more, more, more. Now I'm back home do-in' ol' nine-to-five, liv-in' my gray flan-nel
A Am7 Bm7 B7
life. But when I turn off to sleep, I get mem-'ries that keep a-com-in' more, more, more.
D.S. al Coda
CODA
A Em7 A
Repeat ad lib. and Fade
Get chor get chor ya, ya da da.
Get chor get chor ya, ya he ya.

LE FREAK

Words and Music by NILE RODGERS
and BERNARD EDWARDS

Medium Disco beat
Am7 D C Am7 1 D C
Freak out! Le Freak, c'est chic. Freak out! Freak
2 D C Am7 D C6
Have you heard a - bout the new dance craze?
All that pres - sure got you down;
Am7 D C6 Am7
Lis - ten to us. I'm sure you'll be a - mazed. Big fun to be
has your head spin - ning all a - round. Feel the rhy - thm.
D C6 Am7 D C6
had by ev - 'ry - one. It's up to you. It sure - ly can be done.
Chant the rhyme. Come on a - long and have a real good time.
Am7 D C6 Am7
Young and old are do - in' it, I'm told. Just one try and
Like the days of stomp - in' at the Sa - voy, now we Freak.
D C6 Am7 D C6
you, too, will be sold. It's called "Le Freak." They're do - in' it night and day.
Oh, what a joy. Just come on down to the Fif - ty - four.
Am7 D C6 Am7
Al - low us, we'll show you the way.
Find a spot out on the floor.
Freak out! Le
D C Am7 1 D C 2 D C
Freak, c'est chic. Freak out! Freak
Am7 D C Am7 D C
Repeat and Fade
out! Le Freak, c'est chic. Freak out! Freak

LEADER OF THE BAND

Words and Music by
DAN FOGELBERG

Gently
Ab Db/Ab Ab Cm Db
An on - ly child a - lone and wild a cab - 'net mak - er's son,
A qui - et man of mu - sic de - nied a sim - pler fate,
Bbm Fm Bbm Db Eb
his hands were meant for dif - f'rent work and his heart was known to none.
he tried to be a sol - dier once but his mu - sic would - n't wait.
Ab Db/Ab Ab Cm Db
He left his home and went his lone and sol - i - tar - y way and he
He earned his love through dis - ci - pline a thun - d'ring vel - vet hand, his
Bbm Fm Bbm Eb7 1 Ab Db/Ab Ab Db/Ab
gave to me a gift I know I nev - er can re - pay. (Instrumental)
gen - tle means of sculpt - ing souls took me years to un - der -
Ab Db/Ab Ab 2 Ab Db Cm
stand. The lead - er of the band is tired and his
Db Ab Bbm Fm Bbm
eyes are grow - ing old. But his blood runs through my in - stru - ment and his song is in my
Gb Eb Db Cm Db Ab
soul. My life has been a poor at - tempt to im - i - tate the man, I'm
Bbm Fm Bbm Db Ab Db/Ab Ab Db/Ab
just a liv - ing leg - a - cy to the lead - er of the band. (Instrumental)
Ab Db/Ab Ab Db/Ab Ab Cm
My broth - ers' lives were dif - f'rent for they heard an - oth - er call.
I thank you for the mu - sic and your sto - ries of the road,
Db Bbm Fm Bbm Db Eb
One went to Chi - ca - go and the oth - er to St. Paul.
I thank you for the free - dom when it came my time to go.
Ab Db/Ab Ab Cm Db
And I'm in Col - o - ra - do when I'm not in some ho - tel
I thank you for the kind - ness and the times when you got tough and,
To Coda
Bbm Fm Bbm Eb7 Ab Db/Ab Ab
liv - ing out this life I've chose and come to know so well. (Instrumental)
pa - pa, I don't think I said, 'I love you' near e -

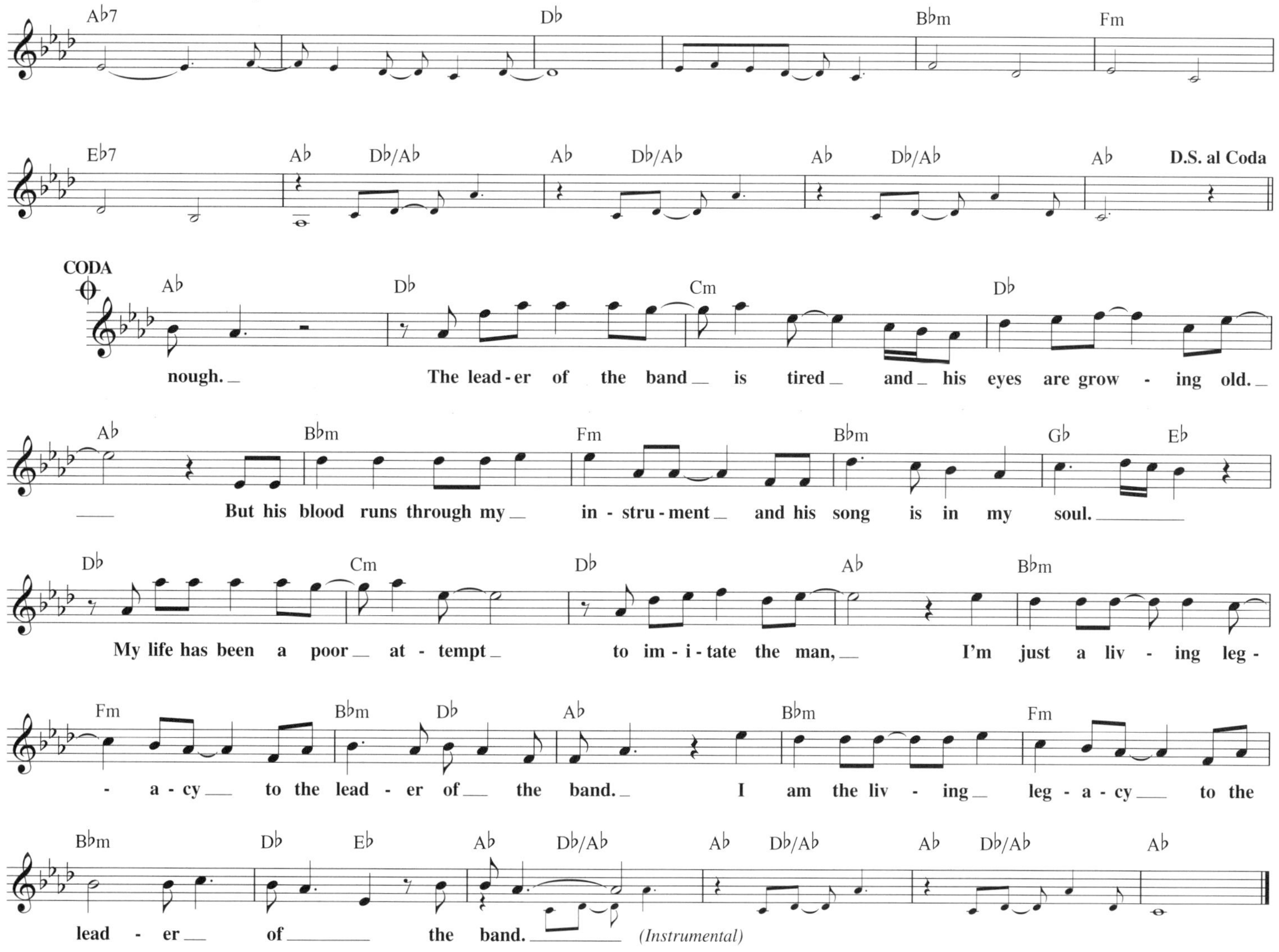

A♭7 D♭ B♭m Fm

E♭7 A♭ D♭/A♭ A♭ D♭/A♭ A♭ D♭/A♭ A♭ **D.S. al Coda**

CODA

A♭ D♭ Cm D♭

nough. The lead-er of the band is tired and his eyes are grow-ing old.

A♭ B♭m Fm B♭m G♭ E♭

But his blood runs through my in-stru-ment and his song is in my soul.

D♭ Cm D♭ A♭ B♭m

My life has been a poor at-tempt to im-i-tate the man, I'm just a liv-ing leg-

Fm B♭m D♭ A♭ B♭m Fm

-a-cy to the lead-er of the band. I am the liv-ing leg-a-cy to the

B♭m D♭ E♭ A♭ D♭/A♭ A♭ D♭/A♭ A♭ D♭/A♭ A♭

lead-er of the band. *(Instrumental)*

LET 'EM IN

Words and Music by
PAUL and LINDA McCARTNEY

Moderately
B♭maj7 B♭6 B♭maj7
Some-one's knock-in' at the door. Some-bod-y's ring-in' the bell. Some-one's knock-in' at the door.
B♭6 F7 E♭ To Coda
Some-bod-y's ring-in' the bell. Do me a fa-vor, o-pen the door and let 'em in.
B♭maj7 B♭6 Fm B♭ Fm
Sis-ter Su-zie, broth-er John, Mar-tin Lu-ther,
B♭ Fm B♭ Fm
Phil and Don, Broth-er Mi-chael, Un-cle Er-nie, Aunt-ie Gin, o-pen the door and
F Fmaj7 F7 F6 F D.C. al Coda
let 'em in, oh yeah.
CODA
B♭maj7 B♭6

LEATHER AND LACE

Words and Music by
STEVIE NICKS

Moderately slow, in 2
(Female) Is love so frag - ile? And the hearts so hol - low shat - ter with
words im - pos - si - ble to fol - low. You're say - in' I'm frag - ile.
I try not to be. I search on - ly for some - thin' I can't see.
I have my own life, and I am strong - er than you
know. But I car - ry this feel - in'
when you walked in - to my house that you won't be walk - in' out the door.
Still I car - ry this feel - in' when you walked in -
to my house that you won't be walk - in' out the door.
Lov - ers for - ev - er, face to face, my cit - y or
moun - tains. Stay with me, stay. I need you to love me. I
need you to - day. Give to me your leath - er. Take from me my
To Coda
lace. (Male) You in the moon - light with your
sleep - y eyes, could you ev - er love a man like me?

E♭ E♭/D♭ A♭/C E♭/B♭
And you were right: _ when I walked in - to your house, _

A♭ E♭/G B♭7sus E♭
I knew I'd nev - er want _ to leave. ___ Some - times I'm a

E♭/D♭ A♭/C E♭/B♭ A♭ E♭/G
strong man, some - times cold and scared, _ and some - times I cry. _

B♭7sus E♭ E♭/D♭ A♭/C
But that time I saw ___ you, I knew with you _ to light _

E♭/B♭ A♭ E♭/G B♭7sus
___ my nights, _____ some - how I'd __ get __ by. __

D.S. *(Male and Female sing)* **al Coda**

CODA

B♭7sus A♭ E♭/G B♭7sus
lace. Take from me __ my lace. Take

Repeat and Fade

LET IT BE ME
(Je t'appartiens)

English Words by MANN CURTIS
French Words by PIERRE DeLANOE
Music by GILBERT BECAUD

Moderately

F C7 C♯dim7 Dm Am B♭
I bless the day I found you, I want to stay a-round you, and so I
If for each bit of glad - ness, some - one must taste of sad - ness, I'll bear the

F Gm7 C7♭9 F C7 C♯dim7 Dm
beg you, let it be me. Don't take this heav - en from one, if you must
sor - row, let it be me. No mat - ter what the price is, I'll make the

Am B♭ F Gm7 C7♭9 F B♭
cling to some - one, now and for - ev - er, let it be me. Each time we
sac - ri - fic - es, through each to - mor - row, let it be me. To you I'm

Am B♭ F Gm7 F B♭
meet love, I find com - plete love, with - out your sweet love, what would life
pray - ing, hear what I'm say - ing, please let your heart beat for me, just

A F C7 C♯dim7 Dm Am
be? So nev - er leave me lone - ly, tell me you'll love me on - ly,
me. And nev - er leave me lone - ly, tell me you'll love me on - ly,

B♭ F Gm7 C7♭9 1 F 2 F
and that you'll al - ways let it be me.
and that you'll al - ways let it be me.

LET IT BE

Words and Music by JOHN LENNON
and PAUL McCARTNEY

Slowly
C G Am G F C G
When I find my-self in times of trou-ble Moth-er Mar - y comes to me, speak-ing words of wis - dom, let it
Instrumental
F C/E Dm7 C G Am G F
be. And in my hour of dark - ness she is stand-ing right in front of me,
C G F C/E Dm7 C Am G
speak-ing words of wis - dom, let it be. Let it be, let it be, let it be,
Instrumental ends
F C G F C/E Dm7 C
let it be, whis-per words of wis - dom, let it be. And when
And when
G Am G F C G
the bro - ken-heart-ed peo-ple liv-ing in the world a-gree, there will be an an - swer, let it
the night is cloud-y there is still a light that shines on me, shine un - til to-mor - row, let it
F C/E Dm7 C G Am G F
be. For though they may be part - ed there is still a chance that they will see,
be. I wake up to the sound of mu-sic, Moth-er Mar - y comes to me,
C G F C/E Dm7 C Am G
there will be an an - swer, let it be. Let it be, let it be, let it be,
speak-ing words of wis - dom, let it be.
F C G F C/E Dm7 C G
let it be, there will be an an - swer, let it be. Let it be,
Am G F C G To Coda
let it be, let it be, let it be, whis-per words of wis-dom, let it be.
there will be an an-swer, let it be.
F C/E Dm7 C F Em Dm7 C B♭ F/A G F C F C G F C D.S. al Coda
(Instrumental)

CODA
F C/E Dm7 C Am G F C
Let it be, let it be, let it be, let it be.
G F C/E Dm7 C F Em Dm7 C B♭ F/A G F C
Whis-per words of wis - dom, let it be.
(Instrumental)

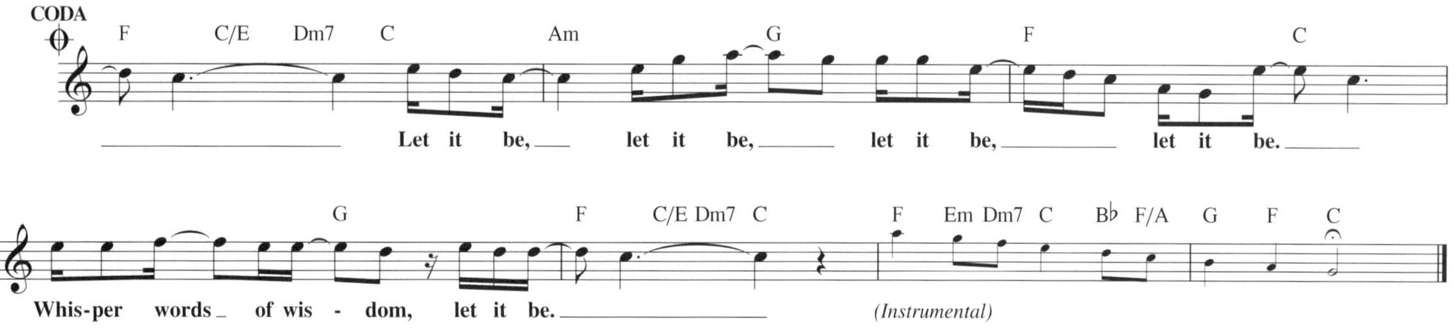

LET THE GOOD TIMES ROLL

Words and Music by LEONARD LEE
and SHIRLEY GOODMAN

Medium Bounce

F
(1.,3.) Come on, ba - by, let the good times roll, come on, ba - by, let me thrill your soul.
(2.) Come on, ba - by, gon - na have a ball, put your trou bles up a - gainst the wall.

B♭ F G7 C7
Come on, ba - by, let the good times roll, roll on and on.

F
Come on, ba - by, let me hold you tight, tell me ev - 'ry-thing is right to - night.
Come on, ba - by, let us paint the town, don't let noth - in' ev - er bring us down.
Let's go, ba - by, on a cra - zy fling, love can be such a swing in' thing.

B♭ F C7 1 F 2, 3 F
Come on, ba - by, let the good times roll, roll on and on. on.

B♭ F C7 F B♭ F
Feel so good in my arms, sug - ar ba - by,
Feel so good when you're close, sug - ar ba - by,

G7 C7
you're my good luck charm.
I dig you the most.

F
Come on, ba - by, let the good times roll,

come on, ba - by, let me thrill your soul.

B♭
Come on, ba - by, let the

F F7 To Coda F D.C. al Coda
good times roll, roll on and on.

CODA
F
on.

LET'S GO CRAZY

Words and Music by
PRINCE

Slowly and freely
G
Gsus
G
(Spoken:) Dearly beloved, we r gathered here today 2 get through this thing called life. Electric word, "life"; it means forever, and

Em
Bm/D
Cmaj7
C
that's a mightly long time. But I'm here 2 tell u there's something else: the afterworld, a world of never-ending happiness; u can

D7
D7sus
G
always see the sun, day or night. So when u call up that shrink in Beverly Hills, u know the one, Dr. Everything'll be alright,

Gsus2
G
Gsus
G
instead of asking him how much of your time is left, ask him how much of your mind, baby. 'cuz in this life things r much harder than in the

Fast Rock beat
G
C
afterworld. In this life you're on your own.

G
C
G
C
G
And if de el - e - va - tor tries 2 bring u down, go cra - zy;

C
G
C
G
C
punch a high - er floor.

G
C
G
C
If u don't like the world you're liv - in' in,
all ex - cit - ed, but we don't know why.

G
C
G
C
take a look a - round u; at least u got friends. U see, I
May - be it's 'cuz we're all gon - na die. And

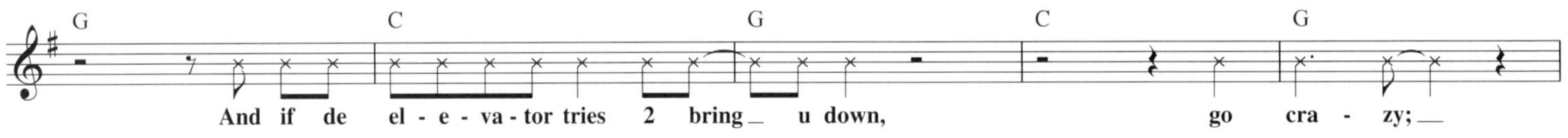

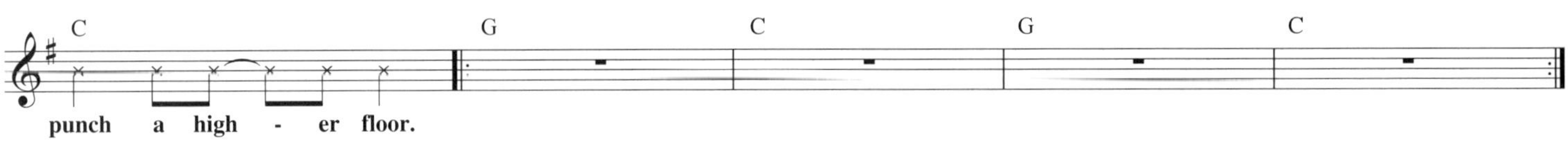

G C G C
called my old la - dy 4 a friend - ly word. She just
when we do, what's it all 4? U
G C G C
picked up the phone, dropped it on the floor. Sex, sex is all I heard.
bet - ter live now be - fore the grim reap - er comes knock - ing on your door. Tell me,
D Em C D N.C.
R we gon - na let de el - e - va - tor bring us down? Oh no! Let's go!
G C G C
Let's go cra - zy. Let's get nuts. Let's
G C G C To Coda
look 4 the pur - ple ba - nan - a 'til they put us in the truck. Let's go!
G Dm7 G 1 Dm7 2 Dm7 D.S. al Coda
(Instrumental) We're
CODA
G C G C
Doc - tor Ev - 'ry - thing - 'll be al - right - 'll make ev - 'ry - thing go wrong.
G C G C
Pills and thrills and daf - fo - dils will kill. Hang tough, chil - dren.
G Dm7 G Dm7 G Dm7
He's com - ing, he's com - ing, he's
G Dm7 G Dm7 G Dm7 Repeat and Fade
com - ing. (Instrumental)

LET YOUR LOVE FLOW

Words and Music by
LARRY E. WILLIAMS

Moderately
C F/G
There's a rea - son for the sun - shine sky. There's a
rea - son for the warm sweet nights. There's a
C F/G G7
rea - son why I'm feel - in' so high. Must be the sea - son when that
rea - son for the can - dle - lights. Must be the sea - son when those
C F/G C
love light shines all a - round us. So let that feel - ing grab you
love rites shine all a - round us. So let the won - der take you
F/G C F/G
deep in - side and send you reel - ing where your love can't hide and then go
in - to space and lay you un - der its lov - ing em - brace. Feel the
G7 C
steal - ing through the sum - mer nights with your lov - er.
thun - der as it warms your face; you can't hold back.
C7 F
Just let your love flow like a moun - tain stream; and let your
C G7
love grow with the small - est of dreams and let your love show. And you'll
C C7
know what I mean; it's the sea - son. Let your
F C
love fly like a bird on the wing. And let your love bind you to all
G7 To Coda
liv - ing things, and let your love shine and you'll know what I mean, that's the rea -
1 C F/G 2 C C7 D.S. al Coda
- son. There's a - son. Let your

CODA

C C7 F

- son. ___ Let your love flow ___ like a

C

moun - tain _ stream; ___ (and) let your love grow _ with the small - est of dreams _ and let your

G7 C

love show. _ And you'll know what I mean; ______ it's the sea - son. _

C7 F

Let your love fly _____ like a bird on the wing. _____ (And) let your

C G7

love bind _ you to all ___ liv - ing things, _ and let your love shine _ and you'll

C C7 Repeat and Fade

know what I mean, ________ that's the rea - son. _____ Let your

LET'S TWIST AGAIN

Words by KAL MANN
Music by DAVE APPELL and KAL MANN

Lively

C Am F

Let's twist a - gain, _ like we did last sum - mer. ____ Yeah, let's twist a - gain, _

G C

like we did last year. _____ Don't - cha re - mem - ber when things were real - ly

Am F G C C7

hum - min'? ___ Yeah, let's twist a - gain, _ twist - in' time is here. _ Ee ah

F C F

'roun' 'n a - roun' 'n a up 'n down we go _______ a - gain. Oh ba - by, make me

F♯ G7 C

know you love me so, ________ an' _____ then let's twist a - gain, _ like we did last

Am F G C

sum - mer. ____ Yeah, let's twist a - gain, _ like we did last year. ___________

LIKE A ROCK

Words and Music by
BOB SEGER

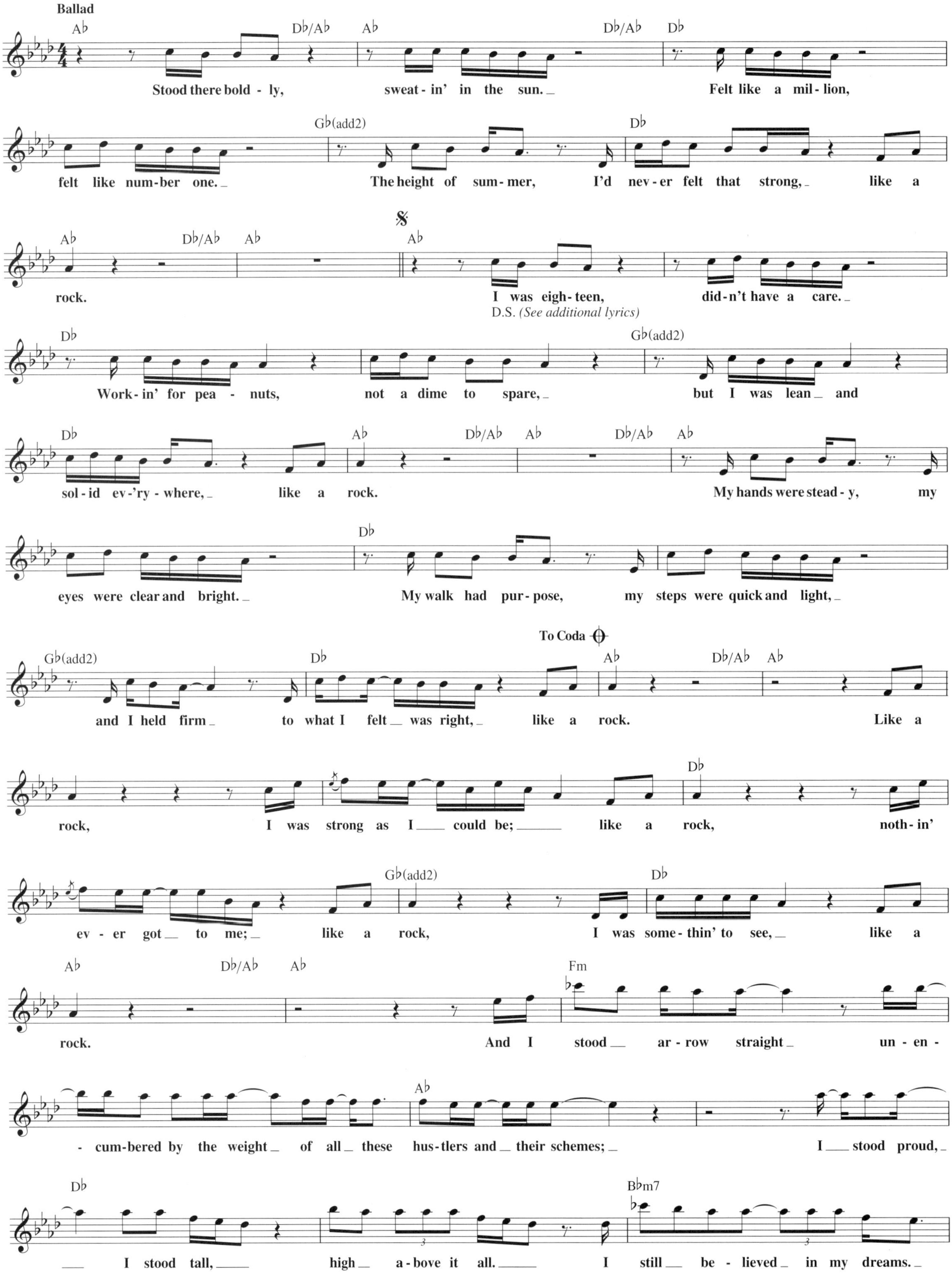

Ballad

A♭ D♭/A♭ A♭ D♭/A♭ D♭
Stood there bold - ly, sweat - in' in the sun. Felt like a mil - lion,

G♭(add2) D♭
felt like num - ber one. The height of sum - mer, I'd nev - er felt that strong, like a

A♭ D♭/A♭ A♭ 𝄋 A♭
rock. I was eigh - teen, did - n't have a care.
D.S. *(See additional lyrics)*

D♭ G♭(add2)
Work - in' for pea - nuts, not a dime to spare, but I was lean and

D♭ A♭ D♭/A♭ A♭ D♭/A♭ A♭
sol - id ev - 'ry - where, like a rock. My hands were stead - y, my

D♭
eyes were clear and bright. My walk had pur - pose, my steps were quick and light,

To Coda 𝄌
G♭(add2) D♭ A♭ D♭/A♭ A♭
and I held firm to what I felt was right, like a rock. Like a

D♭
rock, I was strong as I could be; like a rock, noth - in'

G♭(add2) D♭
ev - er got to me; like a rock, I was some - thin' to see, like a

A♭ D♭/A♭ A♭ Fm
rock. And I stood ar - row straight un - en -

A♭
- cum - bered by the weight of all these hus - tlers and their schemes; I stood proud,

D♭
B♭m7
I stood tall, high a - bove it all. I still be - lieved in my dreams.

Eb (let ring) Ab
(Instrumental)
Db Gb/Db Db Gb(add2) Db
Ab Bbm/Ab
1 Ab
2 Ab (let ring)
D.S. al Coda
Ab Ab/Db Ab Ab/Db Ab Ab/Db Ab Ab/Db
CODA
Ab
call. I re-call like a rock, stand-in' ar-row straight like a rock,
rock, the sun up-on my skin like a rock,
Db
Gb(add2) Db Ab
Repeat and Fade
charg-in' from the gate like a rock, car-ry-in' the weight like a rock. Oh, like a
hard a-gainst the wind like a rock, I see my-self a-gain like a rock.

Additional Lyrics

Twenty years now; where'd they go?
Twenty years; I don't know.
I sit and wonder sometimes where they've gone.

And sometimes late at night,
When I'm bathed in the firelight,
The moon comes callin' a ghostly white, and I recall.

LITTLE DARLIN'

Words and Music by
MAURICE WILLIAMS

Brightly
C6 Am Dm7
Lit-tle dar-lin', my lit-tle dar-lin', oh, where
G7 C6 Am
are you? My love, I was wrong
Dm7 G7 C6
to try to love two, know-ing well
Am Dm7 G7
that my love was just for you,
1 C Dm7 G7
2. C F9 C
on-ly you. Lit-tle you.

Additional Lyrics

(May be spoken over repeat of Chorus)

My dear, I need your love to call my own
And never do wrong; and to hold in mine your little hand.
I'll know too soon that I'll love again.
Please come back to me.

LEGS

Words and Music by BILLY F GIBBONS,
DUSTY HILL and FRANK LEE BEARD

Moderate Rock
E5
She got legs. She knows how to use them. She never
hair down to her fanny. She's kind-a
legs. She knows how to use them. She never
C♯5
begs. She knows how to choose them. She holdin'
jet-set. Try undo her panties. Ev-'ry time she's
begs. Knows how to choose them. She got a
E5
leg, won-d'rin' how to feel them. Would you get be-
dancin' she knows what to do. Ev-'rybody
dime all of the time. Stays out at
C♯5
hind them if you could only find them? She's my ba-
wants to see, see if she can use it. She's so
night, movin' through time. Whoa, I want
A5
-by, B5 she's my baby. To Coda Yeah, it's all
fine. She's all mine. Girl, you got it
her. Shit, I got to have her. The girl is all
1 E5
right. Oh, yeah. She's got
2 E5
right. (Instrumental)
D.S. al Coda
She got
CODA
E5
right.
She's all right. (Instrumental)
Play 3 times
C♯5
Guitar solo ad lib.
E5
Repeat and Fade

LET'S HEAR IT FOR THE BOY

from the Paramount Motion Picture FOOTLOOSE

Words by DEAN PITCHFORD
Music by TOM SNOW

Moderately bright
C Am7 F G C Am7 F G
1. My ba - by, he don't talk sweet; he ain't got much to say. But he
2. (See additional lyrics)
C Am7 F G C Am7 F Dm/G
loves me, loves me, loves me; I know that he loves me an - y - way. And
C Am7 F G C Am7 F G
may - be he don't dress fine, but I don't real - ly mind. 'Cause
B♭maj9 C(add2) G D G/B
ev - 'ry time he pulls me near
Ev - 'ry time he pulls me near
I just wan - na cheer; let's hear it for the boy,
C(add2) G/A D G/B C(add2) G/A D G/B
let's give the boy a hand, let's hear it for my ba - by,
C(add2) G/A D G/B C G/A Em7
you know you got - ta un - der - stand. Oh, may be he's no Ro-me-o, but
To Coda
F♯m7 G C G/B A7sus D F F/C C G/A G
he's my lov-in' one - man show. Oh whoa, whoa, whoa, let's hear it for the boy.
1
F G C F G
2 D.S. al Coda
D G
2. My
CODA
A7sus
whoa, let's hear it for the boy,
D G/B C G/A D G/B C G/A
Repeat ad lib. and Fade
Let's hear it for my man. Let's hear it for the boy.
(Bkgd.) Let's hear it for the boy. Let's hear it for my ba - by.

Additional Lyrics

2. My baby may not be rich;
He's watchin' ev'ry dime.
But he loves me, loves me, loves me.
We always have a real good time.
And maybe he sings off key,
But that's all right by me, yeah.
But what he does, he does so well.
Makes me wanna yell.
Chorus

LITTLE LIES

Words and Music by CHRISTINE McVIE
and EDDY QUINTELA

Moderately
F♯m F♯m7/E
1., 3. If I could turn the page in time then I'd re - ar - range just a
2. Al-though I'm not mak - ing plans, I hope that you un - der - stand there's a
D E/D Dmaj7 E/D Dmaj7 E/D A
day or two. (Close my, close my, close my eyes.)
rea - son why. (Close your, close your, close your eyes.)
F♯m F♯m7/E
But, I could - n't find a way, so I'll set - tle for one day to be -
No more bro - ken hearts. we're bet - ter off a - part, let's give
D E/D Dmaj7 E/D Dmaj7 E/D A
lieve in you.
it a try.
(Tell me, tell me, tell me lies.)
F♯m A6/9 A D F♯m7/E
Tell me lies, tell me sweet lit - tle lies. (Tell me lies.)
(Tell me, tell me lies.)
To Coda
F♯m A6/9 A D F♯m7(addB)/E
Oh no, no you can't dis - guise. (You can't dis - guise.
(No you can't dis-guise.)
F♯m A6/9 A D F♯m7/E
Tell me lies, tell me sweet lit - tle lies.
Dmaj7 E Dmaj7 E Dmaj7 E Dmaj7 E
(Instrumental)
D.C. al Coda
Dmaj7 E Dmaj7 E Dmaj7 E Dmaj7 Dmaj7/E
CODA
F♯m A6/9 A D F♯m7/E
Tell me lies, tell me sweet lit - tle lies. (Tell me lies.)
(Tell me, tell me lies.)
Repeat and Fade
F♯m A6/9 A D F♯m7(addB)/E
Oh no, no you can't dis - guise. (You can't dis - guise.)
(No you can't dis-guise.)

LITTLE WILLY

Words and Music by MICHAEL CHAPMAN
and NICKY CHINN

Moderately
North side, East side, lit - tle Wil - ly, Wil - ly wears the crown, he's the king a - round town.
Up - town, down - town, lit - tle Wil - ly, Wil - ly drives them wild with his run - a - round style.
Danc - ing, glanc - ing, Wil - ly drives them sil - ly with his star shoe shim - my shuf - fle down. 'Way
In - side, out - side, Wil - ly sends them sil - ly with his star - shine shim - my shuf - fle smile. Ma -
past one, and feel - ing al - right 'cos when lit - tle Wil - ly's 'round they can last all night.
- ma done chase Wil - ly down thru the hall, but laughs Wil - ly laugh, he don't care at all.
Lay down, stay down, stay down, down. 'Cos
lit - tle Wil - ly, Wil - ly won't go home. But you can't push Wil - ly 'round, Wil - ly won't go. Try
tell - in' ev - 'ry - bod - y but, oh no, lit - tle Wil - ly, Wil - ly won't go home.
Lit - tle Wil - ly, Wil - ly won't, Wil - ly won't, Wil - ly won't, lit - tle Wil - ly, Wil - ly won't, Wil - ly won't, Wil - ly won't,
lit - tle Wil - ly, Wil - ly won't, Wil - ly won't, Wil - ly won't, lit - tle Wil - ly, Wil - ly won't, Wil - ly won't, Wil - ly won't.
Lit - tle Wil - ly, Wil - ly won't go home. But you can't push Wil - ly 'round, Wil - ly won't go. Try
Repeat and Fade
tell - in' ev - 'ry - bod - y but, oh no, lit - tle Wil - ly, Wil - ly won't go home.

LIKE A PRAYER

Words and Music by PATRICK LEONARD
and MADONNA CICCONE

Medium dance groove
Dm C/D Gm/D Dm C/D Gm/D Dm
Life is a mys - ter - y. Ev - 'ry - one must stand a - lone.
C/E F/A F/C C
I hear you call my name and it feels like
Dm
home.
F C B♭
When you call my name it's like a lit - tle prayer. I'm down on my knees,
F/A F/D Gm/D F C
I wan - na take you there. In the mid - night hour I can feel your pow -
B♭ F/A F/D Gm/D B♭ F
er just like a prayer. You know I'll take you there. I hear your voice,
there. Like a child
C Dm B♭ F
it's like an an - gel sigh - ing. I have no choice, I hear your
you whis - per soft - ly to me. You're in con - trol. Just like a
C B♭ F
voice, feels like fly - ing. I close my eyes.
child, now I'm danc - ing. It's like a dream,
C Dm B♭ F
Oh God, I think I'm fall - ing out of the sky. I close my
no end and no be - gin - ning. You're here with me, it's like a
C F C
eyes. Heav - en help me.
dream. Let the choir sing.
When you call my name it's like a lit - tle prayer.
B♭ F/A F/D Gm/D F
I'm down on my knees, I wan - na take you there. In the mid - night hour

C Bb 1 F/A F/D Gm/D
I can feel your pow - er just like a prayer. You know I'll take you
2 F/A F/D Gm/D F C
You know I'll take you there. When you call my name it's like a lit - tle prayer.
there. In the mid - night hour I can feel your pow -
Bb F/A F/D Gm/D Dm C/D
I'm down on my knees, I wan - na take you
er just like a prayer. You know I'll take you there.
Dm C/D Dm C/D Dm
Life is a mys - ter - y. Ev - 'ry - one must
C/D Dm C/E Gm/Bb F/A Bb
stand a - lone. I hear you call my name and it
F/C C Dm C/D
feels like home. Just like a prayer your voice can take me there.
Dm C/D Dm
Just like a muse to me. You are a mys - ter - y. Just like a dream
C Gm/Bb F/A Bb F/C C
you are not what you seem. Just like a prayer, no choice, your voice can take me
F C N.C. Bb F/A
there. (Just like a prayer I'll take you there. It's like a dream to me.)
1-3 Dm 4 Dm Dm C/D
(there.) Just like a prayer your voice can take me there.
Dm C/D Dm
Just like a muse to me. You are a mys - ter - y. Just like a dream,
C/E Gm/Bb F/A Bb F/C C
you are not what you seem. Just like a prayer, no choice, your voice can take me
Dm C/D Dm C/D Repeat and Fade
there. Your voice can take me there. Take me

LIVE TO TELL

Words and Music by MADONNA CICCONE
and PAT LEONARD

Moderately
C F Gm F C Dm
I have a tale to tell. Some-
know where beau-ty lives. I've
C F Gm F C Dm
times it gets so hard to hide it well.
seen it once, I know the warmth she gives.
C F Gm F C Dm
I was not read-y for the fall. Too
The light that you could nev-er see. It
C F Gm F C
blind to see the writ-ing on the wall.
shines in-side, you can't take that from me.
A
Gm7/F F Gm7/F Am B♭(add2)
man can tell a thou-sand lies; I've learned my les-son well. Hope I live to tell
Gm7/F F Dm B♭(add2)/D C(add2)/E Dm C
the se-cret I have learned. Till then, it will burn in-side of me.
1 B♭ C 2 B♭ C Dm11 Gm7/F
I The truth is nev-er far
F Gm7/F Am B♭(add2) Gm7/F
be-hind; you kept it hid-den well. If I live to tell the se-cret I
F Dm B♭(add2)/D C(add2)/E Dm C B♭ C To Coda
knew then, will I ev-er have the chance a-gain?
D5 Slowly Dm11
Tempo I
N.C. B♭ C Dm
If I ran a-way, I'd nev-er have the strength to go ver-y far.

Am7
B♭
C
Am7
How would they hear the beat - ing of my heart?
B♭
C
Dm
Will it grow cold, the se - cret that I hide? Will I grow old?
Am7
B♭
C(add2)
Dm
How will they hear, when will they learn, how will they know?
C
F
Gm7
F
C
D.S. al Coda
(take 2nd ending)
A
CODA
D5
Dm11

LONELY DAYS

Words and Music by BARRY GIBB,
ROBIN GIBB and MAURICE GIBB

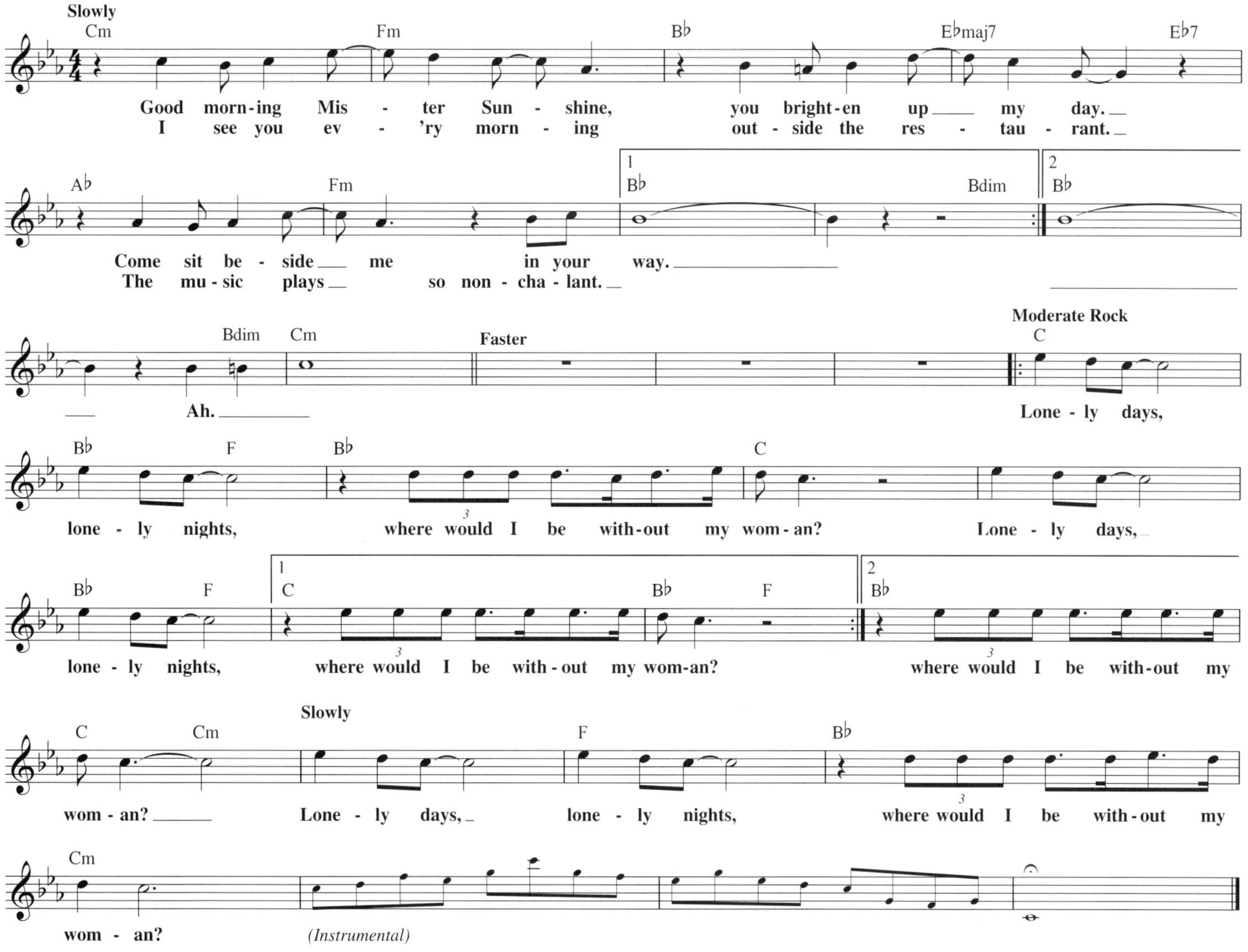

Slowly

Cm Fm B♭ E♭maj7 E♭7

Good morn-ing Mis - ter Sun - shine, you bright-en up my day.
I see you ev - 'ry morn - ing out - side the res - tau - rant.

A♭ Fm 1 B♭ Bdim 2 B♭

Come sit be - side me in your way.
The mu - sic plays so non - cha - lant.

Bdim Cm **Faster** **Moderate Rock** C

Ah. Lone - ly days,

B♭ F B♭ C

lone - ly nights, where would I be with - out my wom - an? Lone - ly days,

B♭ F 1 C B♭ F 2 B♭

lone - ly nights, where would I be with - out my wom - an? where would I be with - out my

C Cm **Slowly** F B♭

wom - an? Lone - ly days, lone - ly nights, where would I be with - out my

Cm

wom - an? *(Instrumental)*

LITTLE BIT O' SOUL

Words and Music by JOHN SHAKESPEARE
and KENNETH LEWIS

Moderately slow
Now when you're feel - in' low and the fish won't bite,
girl has gone and you're broke in two,
(Instrumental)
you need a lit - tle bit o' soul to
you need a lit - tle bit o' soul to
put you right.
see you through.
(Instrumental)
You got - ta
And when you
make like you wan - na kneel and pray,
raise the roof with your rock and roll,
(Instrumental)
and then a lit - tle bit o' soul will come your way.
you'll get a lot more kicks with a lit - tle bit o' soul.
(Instrumental)
1
2
Now when your
And if your
par - ty falls 'cause there's no - bod - y groov - in',
(Instrumental)
a
lit - tle bit o' soul and it real - ly starts mov - in'.
Yeah!
(Instrumental)
Now when you're
in a mess and you feel like cry - in',
(Instrumental)
just re - mem - ber this lit - tle song of mine.

C D7 G C
(Instrumental) And as you walk through life tryin' to
D7 G C C6 D7 G
reach your goal, (Instrumental) re - mem - ber
C D7 G C
what I say 'bout a lit - tle bit o' soul. (Instrumental)
Repeat and Fade
D7 G C D7 G
A lit - tle bit o' soul, a lit - tle bit o' soul. A

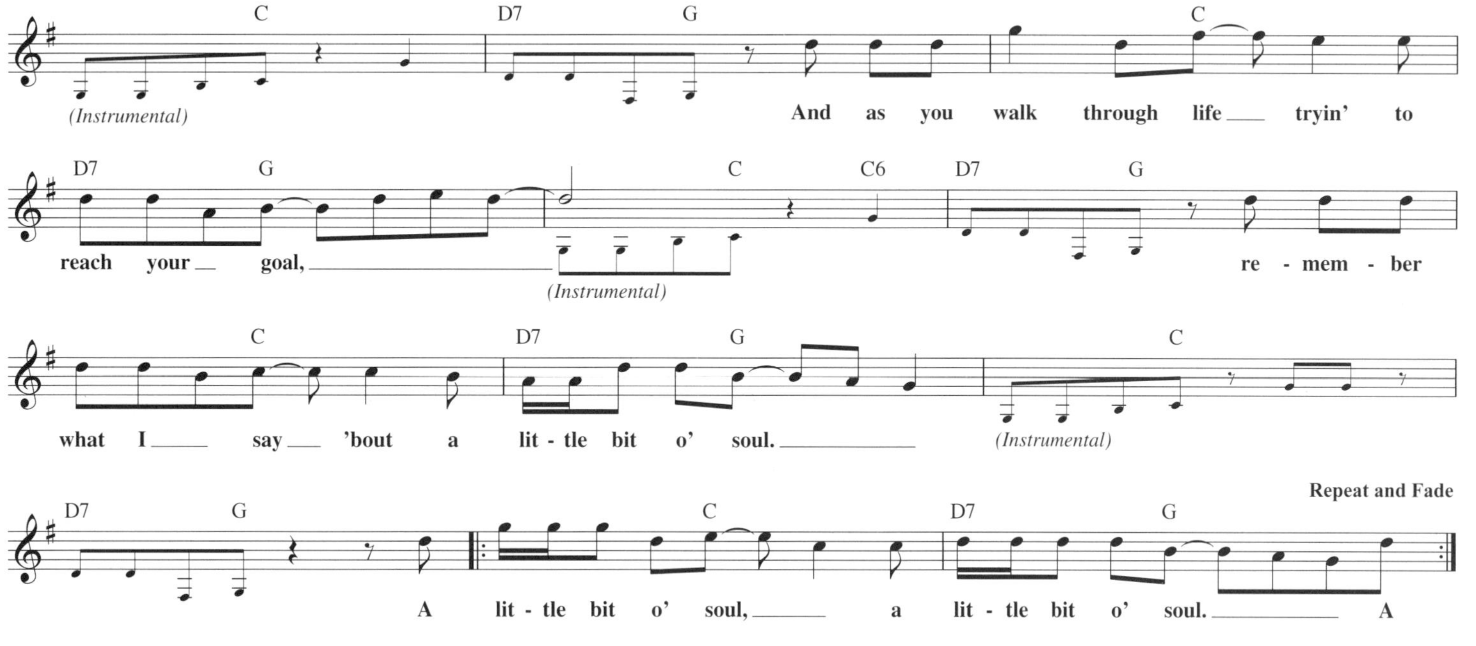

LONELY TEARDROPS

Words and Music by BERRY GORDY,
GWEN GORDY FUQUA and TYRAN CARLO

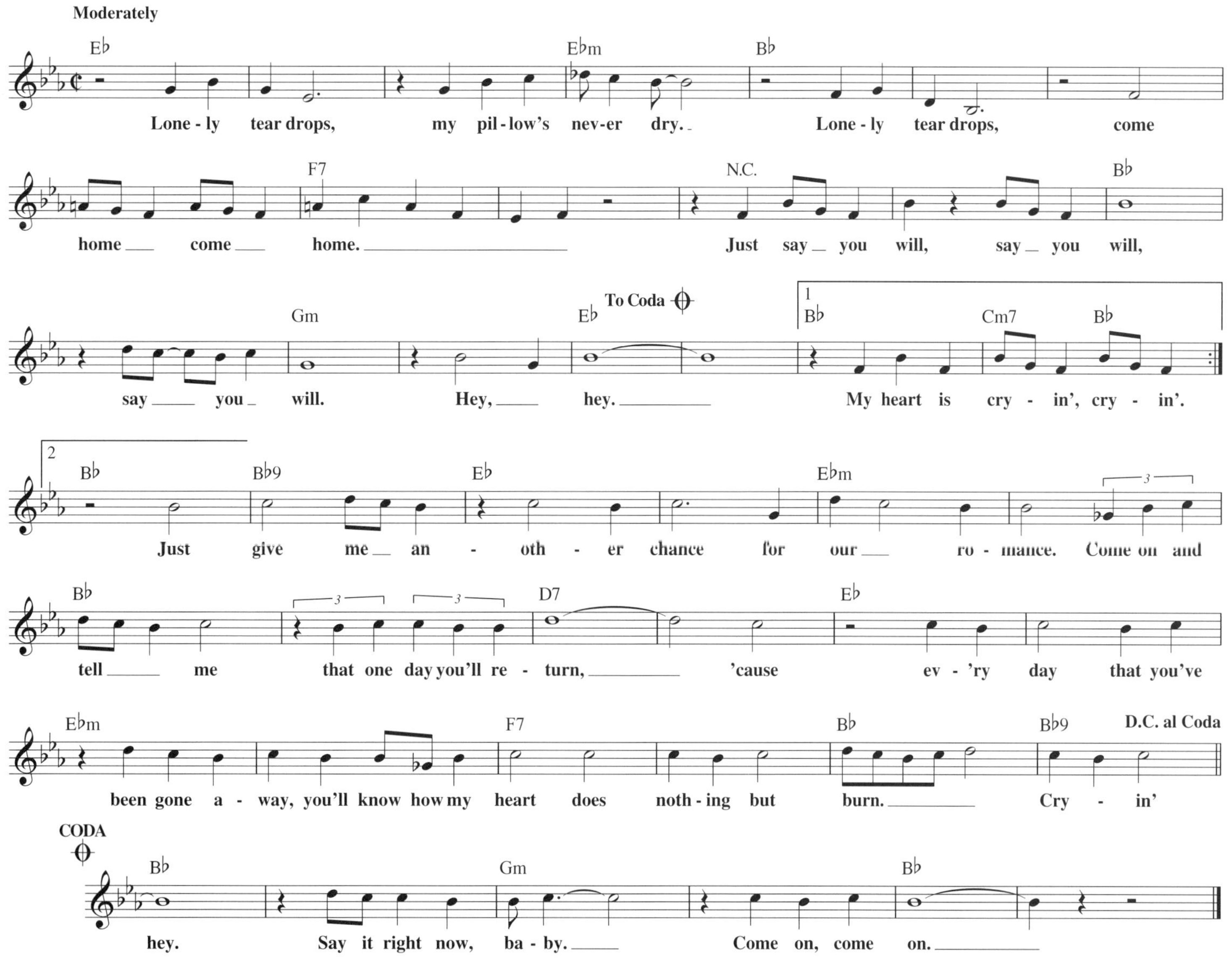

Moderately
E♭ E♭m B♭
Lone - ly tear drops, my pil - low's nev - er dry. Lone - ly tear drops, come
F7 N.C. B♭
home come home. Just say you will, say you will,
Gm E♭ To Coda
1 B♭ Cm7 B♭
say you will. Hey, hey. My heart is cry - in', cry - in'.
2 B♭ B♭9 E♭ E♭m
Just give me an - oth - er chance for our ro - mance. Come on and
B♭ D7 E♭
tell me that one day you'll re - turn, 'cause ev - 'ry day that you've
E♭m F7 B♭ B♭9 D.C. al Coda
been gone a - way, you'll know how my heart does noth - ing but burn. Cry - in'
CODA
B♭ Gm B♭
hey. Say it right now, ba - by. Come on, come on.

LONELY OL' NIGHT

Words and Music by
JOHN MELLENCAMP

Moderately
E Esus E
She calls me up and says, "Ba - by, it's a lone - ly ol' night."
Ra - di - o play - in' soft - ly some sing - er's sad, sad song.
Esus E
I don't know, I'm just so scared and lone - ly all at the same time.
He's sing - in' a - bout stand - in' in the shad - ows of love. I guess he feels aw - f'lly a - lone.
A Asus A
No - bod - y told us it was gon - na work out this way, no no
She says, "I know ex - act - ly what he means, yeah yeah
Asus E Esus
no no no. I guess they knew we'd work it out in our own way.
yeah yeah yeah." And it's a sad, sad feel - in' when you're liv - in' on those
E Esus E Esus E D A
in - be - tweens, but it's o - kay.
It's a lone - ly ol' night.
D A D A
Can I put my arms a - round you? It's a lone - ly ol' night,
E Esus E To Coda Esus
cus - tom - made for two lone - ly peo - ple like me and you.
1 2
E A/E E A/E
E A/E E A/E
She calls me ba - by. She calls ev - 'ry - bod - y ba - by.
E A/E E A/E E Esus
It's a lone - ly ol' night, but ain't they all?
E Esus D.S. al Coda
CODA
Yeah, like me
E Esus E Esus E
and you. Yeah, like me and you.

LONESOME TOWN

Words and Music by
BAKER KNIGHT

Moderately slow
C E7 F G9
There's a place where lov - ers go to cry their trou - bles a -
C F Fm C Am
way. And they call it Lone - some Town,
Dm7 G7 C G7 C
where the bro - ken hearts stay. (Lone - some Town.) You can buy a
E7 F G9 C
dream or two to last you all through the years.
F Fm C Am Dm7 G7
And the on - ly price you pay is a heart full of
C F Em
tears. (Full of tears.) Go - in' down to Lone - some Town,
Dm7 G7 C F
where the bro - ken hearts stay; go - in' down to
Em D7 G7
Lone - some Town, to cry my trou - bles a - way.
C E7 F G9
In the town of bro - ken dreams the streets are paved with re -
C F Fm C Am
gret; may - be down in Lone - some Town
Dm7 G7 C F Fm C Am
I can learn to for - get. (To for - get.) May - be down in Lone - some Town
Dm7 G7 C Fm/C C
I can learn to for - get. (Lone - some Town.)

LONGFELLOW SERENADE

Words and Music by
NEIL DIAMOND

Bright Rock tempo
E A/E E A
Long - fel - low se - re - nade, such were the plans I'd made. For
Long - fel - low se - re - nade, such were the plans I made. But
E
she was a la - dy, and I was a dream - er with on - ly words to trade. You know that I was
she was a la - dy as deep as the riv - er, and through the night we stayed. And in my way, I
A
born for a night like this, warmed by a sto - len kiss. For I was
loved her as none be - fore, loved her with words and more. For she was
E B7 E
lone - ly, and she was lone - ly.
lone - ly, and I was lone - ly.
Ride,
Emaj7 E7 A E
come on ba - by, ride. Let me make your dreams come
B7 E Emaj7
true. I'll sing my song; let me sing my song.
E7 A E B7
Let me make it warm for you. I'll
E A
weave his web of rhyme up - on the sum - mer night. We'll
B7 E
leave this world - ly time on his wing - ed flight. Then
A
come, and as we lay be - side this sleep - y glade, there I will sing
E B7 E Fine D A/C♯ E/B A D.C. al Fine
to you my Long - fel - low se - re - nade. (Instrumental)

LOOK IN MY EYES PRETTY WOMAN

Words and Music by DENNIS LAMBERT
and BRIAN POTTER

Bright Rock beat
Time is on my side tho' the world keeps get - tin' cold - er, 'cause I've got you, girl to ease my trou - bled mind.
You're my guid - ing star you're my faith, my hope, my pow - er, when I just can't find a rea - son to be - lieve.
I'm a dif - f'rent man when your head is on my shoul - der, I can find the an - swers in me that I nev - er tho't I'd find.
Touch my hand with love and you light my dark - est hour, I can feel the warm re - turn - ing and my pain a - bout to leave.
'Cause when you
look in my eyes pret - ty wom - an, the world is a peace - ful place.
All I can see when there's you and there's me is love up - on your face.
Stand by me, ba - by, and we'll find the way be - fore our day is done.
Look in my eyes pret - ty wom - an, and we'll o - ver - come.
D.S. and Fade

LOOKIN' FOR LOVE

from URBAN COWBOY

Words and Music by WANDA MALLETTE, PATTI RYAN and BOB MORRISON

Moderately fast
Gmaj7 D G
Well, I've spent a life - time look-in' for you; sin-gles bars and
And I was a - lone then, no love in sight; and I did ev - 'ry -
D A Gmaj7 D
good time lov-ers were nev - er true. Play-in' a fool's game, hop-in' to win;
thing I could to get me through the night. Don't know where it start - ed where it might end;
G D A A/G A/F♯ A/E
and tell - in' those sweet lies and los - in' a - gain. I was
I turned to a stran - ger just like a friend. I was
D F♯m
look - in' for love in all the wrong plac - es, look - in' for love in too man - y fac - es,
look - in' for love in all the wrong plac - es, look - in' for love in too man - y fac - es,
look - in' for love in all the wrong plac - es, look - in' for love in too man - y fac - es,
G Em F♯m G A D
search-in' their eyes and look-in' for trac - es of what I'm dream-in' of. Hop-in' to find a friend
search-in' their eyes and look-in' for trac - es of what I'm dream-in' of. Hop-in' to find a friend
search-in' their eyes and look-in' for trac - es of what I'm dream-in' of. Now that I've found a friend
F♯m To Coda G Em A
and a lov - er; I'll bless the day I dis - cov - er an - oth - er heart look-in' for love.
and a lov - er; I'll bless the day I dis - cov - er an - oth - er heart look-in' for love.
and a lov - er; I'll bless the day I dis - cov - ered
1 D 2 D G
Then you came a knock - in' at my heart's door; you're
Em F♯m G A D.S. al Coda
ev - 'ry - thing I've been look - in' for. No more
CODA G
you, oh
Em A D F♯m
you. Look-in' for love in all the wrong plac - es; in too man - y fac - es,
G Em F♯m G A D
search-in' their eyes and look in' for trac - es of what I'm dream- in' of. Now that I've found a friend
F♯m G Em A Repeat and Fade
and a lov - er, I bless the day I dis-cov ered you, oh you. Look-in' for love

LOST IN LOVE

Words and Music by
GRAHAM RUSSELL

Moderately
G(add9) G G(add9) G Cmaj9 C6
(1.) I re - al - ize the best part of love is the thin - nest slice and it don't
(2.,3.) Lost in love and I don't know much. Was I think - ing a - loud and fell
Cmaj9 C6 Am9 Am7 Am9 Am7
count for much. But I'm not let - ting go. I be - lieve there's too much to be - lieve
out of touch? But I'm back on my feet and ea - ger to be what you want -
G(add9) G G(add9) G G(add9) G G(add9) G
in. (1.,2.) So lift your eyes if you feel you can. Reach
- ed. (3.) (Instrumental)
Cmaj9 C6 Cmaj9 C6 Am9 Am7
for a star and I'll show you a plan. I've fig - ured it out: what I need -
Am9 Am7 G(add9) G Am7
- ed was some - one to show me. (Instrumental ends) You know you can't
Bm7 C G Em
fool me. I've been lov - ing you too long. It start - ed so eas -
Am7 A7/C# C
- y. You want to car - ry on, car - ry on.
1, 2
3
G(add9) G G(add9) G
Lost in love lost in love and I don't know much. Was I think -
Cmaj9 C6 Cmaj9 C6 Am9 Am7
- ing a - loud and fell out of touch? But I'm back on my feet,
Repeat ad lib. and Fade
Am9 Am7 G(add9) G G(add9) G
ea - ger to be what you want - ed. Now I'm

LOVE IS A BATTLEFIELD

Words and Music by MIKE CHAPMAN
and HOLLY KNIGHT

Moderate Rock
(Spoken:) We are young. Heart-ache to heart-ache we stand; no prom-is-es, no de-mands. Love is a bat-tle-field.
We are strong. No one can tell us we're wrong, search-ing our heart for so long; both of us know-ing love is a bat-tle-field.
You're beg-ging me to go, then mak-ing me stay. Why do you hurt me so bad? It would help me to know do I stand in your way, or am I the best thing you've had? Be-lieve me, be-lieve me, I can't tell you why, but I'm trapped by your love and I'm chained to your side.
los-ing con-trol, will you turn me a-way, or touch me deep in-side? And when all this gets old, will it still feel the same? There's no way this will die. But if we get much clos-er I could lose con-trol and if your heart sur-ren-ders you'll need me to hold.
We are young. Heart-ache to heart-ache we stand; no prom-is-es, no de-mands. Love is a bat-tle-field.
We are strong. We are strong.

Am B♭ Dm C Am B♭
No one can tell us we're wrong, search - ing our hearts for so
Dm C Am B♭ To Coda
long; both of us knowing - ing love is a bat - tle - field.
Dm C/D D.S. al Coda
When I'm
CODA
Dm C/D B♭/D Repeat and Fade
(Instrumental)

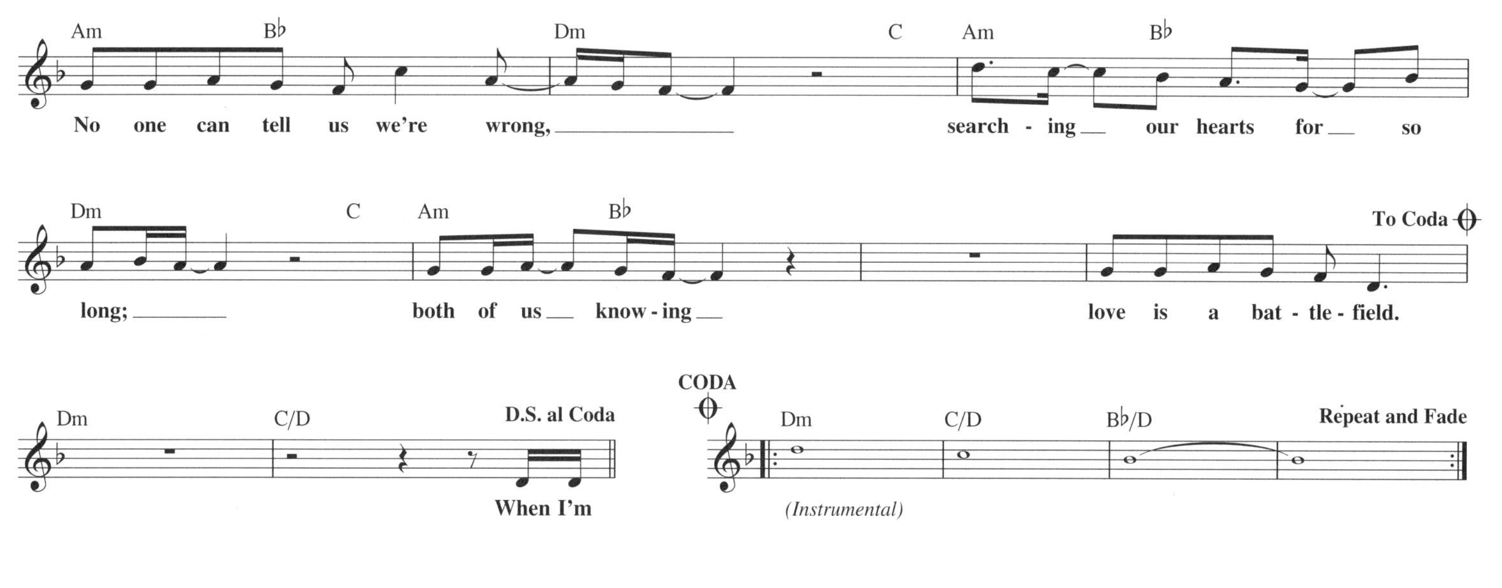

LOVE IS THICKER THAN WATER

Words and Music by BARRY GIBB
and ANDY GIBB

Moderately, with a beat

Dmaj7 C♯m7 F♯m E F♯m
Love is high - er than a moun - tain. Love is thick - er than wa - ter.

Dmaj7 C♯m7 F♯m E F♯m E F♯m
You are this dreamer's on - ly dream: heav - en's an - gel, dev - il's daugh - ter.

Bm9 Amaj7
Say, my mind, should I go with her on si - lent nights, she'll drive me cra - zy
Say, my thought, should I find out she don't care at all, she'll leave me cry - ing

Dmaj7 Bm9
in the end and I should leave this par - a - dise, but I can't leave her
in the end, wan - der - ing through the af - ter - glow, but I can't leave her

F♯m
while I need her more than she needs you. That's what I'm liv - ing for.
while I need her more than she needs you. That's what I'm pray - ing for.

Dmaj7 C♯m7 F♯m E F♯m
Love is high - er than a moun - tain. Love is thick - er than wa - ter.

Repeat and Fade
Dmaj7 C♯m7 F♯m E F♯m E F♯m
You are this dreamer's on - ly dream: heav - en's an - gel, dev - il's daugh - ter.

LOVE GROWS (WHERE MY ROSEMARY GOES)

Words and Music by TONY MACAULAY
and BARRY MASON

Slow beat
G C
She ain't got no mon - ey her clothes are kind - a fun - ny her hair is kind - a wild and free.
G Bm Em G C
Oh, but love grows where my Rose - ma - ry goes and no - bod - y knows like
D G C
me. She talks kin - da la - zy peo - ple say she's cra - zy and her life's a my - ster - y.
G Bm Em G C Am
Oh, but love grows where my Rose - ma - ry goes and no - bod - y knows
D7 G G7 C D
like me. There's some - thing a - bout her hand hold - ing mine,
G Am D7 G
it's a feel - ing that's fine and I've just got to say: Hey she's
C D G Em A7
real - ly got a mag - i - cal spell and it's work - ing so well that I can't get a - way.
D G
I'm a luck - y fel - la and I just got - ta tell her that I
C 3 G Bm
I love her end - less - ly be - cause love grows where my
Em G C Am D7
Rose - mar - y goes and no - bod - y knows like
1 G G7 2 G Bm Em G C D7 D9 G
me. There's me. (Instrumental)

LOVE IS ALL AROUND

Words and Music by
REG PRESLEY

Moderately
1. I feel it in my fin-gers, I feel it in my toes. The love that's all a-round me
2. (See additional lyrics)
and so the feel-ing grows. It's writ-ten on the wind, it's ev-'ry-where I go,
so if you real-ly love me, come on and let it show.
You know I love you, I al-ways will, my mind's made up by the
way that I feel. There's no be-gin-ning, there'll be no end, 'cause on my love you
can de-pend. (Instrumental)
2. I Got to keep it mov-ing. It's
writ-ten in the wind oh ev-'ry-where I go. So
if you real-ly love me, come on and let it show. Come on and let it
show.
Come on and let it, come on and let it, come on and let it show.
Repeat and Fade

Additional Lyrics

2. I see your face before me
As I lay on my bed;
I cannot get to thinking
Of all the things you said.
You gave your promise to me
And I gave mine to you;
I need someone beside me
In everything I do.
Chorus

LOVE ME DO

Words and Music by JOHN LENNON
and PAUL McCARTNEY

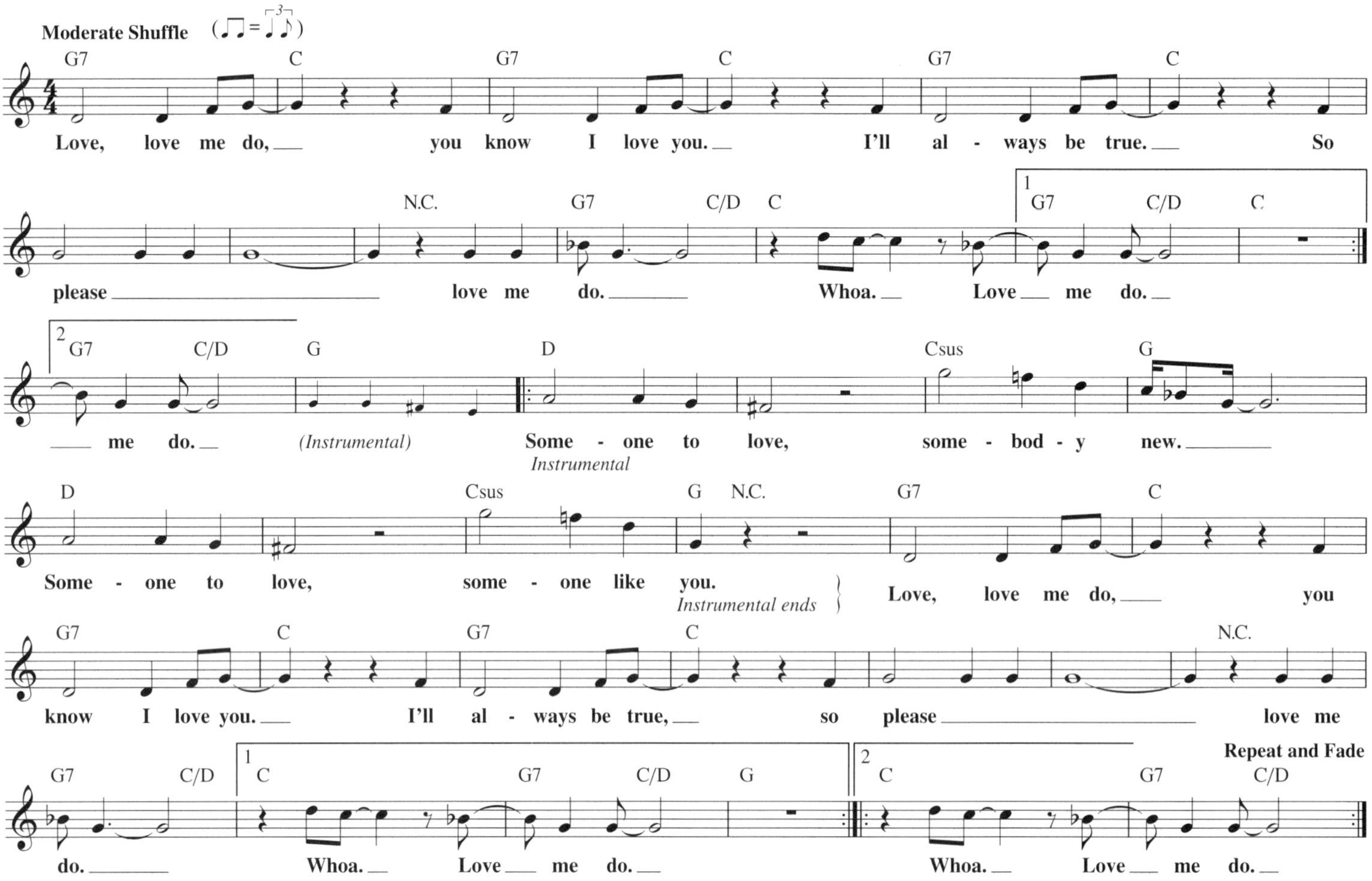

Moderate Shuffle

G7 C G7 C G7 C
Love, love me do, you know I love you. I'll al - ways be true. So

N.C. G7 C/D C G7 C/D C
please love me do. Whoa. Love me do.

G7 C/D G D Csus G
me do. *(Instrumental)* Some - one to love, some - bod - y new.
Instrumental

D Csus G N.C. G7 C
Some - one to love, some - one like you. Love, love me do, you
Instrumental ends

G7 C G7 C N.C.
know I love you. I'll al - ways be true, so please love me

G7 C/D C G7 C/D G C G7 C/D
do. Whoa. Love me do. Whoa. Love me do.
Repeat and Fade

LOVE ROLLERCOASTER

Words and Music by RALPH MIDDLEBROOKS,
JAMES WILLIAMS, MARSHALL JONES, LEROY BONNER,
CLARENCE SATCHELL, WILLIAM BECK and MARVIN PIERCE

Moderate Funk
C Bb A Bb C Bb A Bb C
Roll - er - coast - er of love, roll - er - coast - er, ooh, ooh, ooh, ooh! Roll - er -
Bb C To Coda G7
ooh, ooh, ooh! Your love is like a roll - er - coast - er, ba - by, ba - by. All you do is ride.
Why don't you ride, child? Your love is like a roll - er - coast er, ba - by, ba - by. All you do is ride,
G Ab A C Bb A Bb C Bb A Bb C Bb C
D.S. (take repeats) D.S. al Coda (take repeats)
ride! Roll-er - Roll-er -
CODA
G7
Repeat and Fade
Your love is like a roll - er - coast - er, ba - by, ba - by. All you do is ride.

LOVE ON THE ROCKS

from the Motion Picture THE JAZZ SINGER

Words and Music by NEIL DIAMOND
and GILBERT BECAUD

Moderately slow Ballad

Am F G Em7
Love on the rocks ain't no sur-prise. Pour me a drink, and I'll tell you some lies.

F B7 E Am
Got noth-in' to lose, so you just sing the blues all the time. Gave you my heart,

F G Em7 F
gave you my soul. You left me a-lone here with noth-ing to hold. Yes-ter-day's gone,

B7 E E/D A/C♯ E/B 𝄋 A
now all I want is a smile. First they say they want you,

Amaj7 G/A D/A F G
how they real-ly need you. Sud den-ly, you find you're out there walk-ing in a storm.

A Amaj7 A7 D6/A Dm6/A
When they know they have you, then they real-ly have you. Noth-ing you can do or say. You've

A G9 E To Coda Am C/G
got to leave, just get a-way. We all know the song. You need what you need,

F G G/F Em7
you can say what you want. Not much you can do when the feel-ing is gone. May be

F B7 E E/D A/C♯ E/B D.S. al Coda
blue skies a-bove, but it's cold when your love's on the rocks.

CODA

Am F G
Love on the rocks ain't no sur-prise. Pour me a drink, and I'll

Em7 F B7 E Am
tell you some lies. Yes-ter-day's gone, and now all I want is a smile.

LOVE YOU INSIDE OUT

Words and Music by BARRY GIBB,
ROBIN GIBB and MAURICE GIBB

Moderately
Em9
Ba - by, I can't fig - ure it out, your kiss - es taste like hon - ey.
Sweet lies don't gim - me no rise on; oh, what you try - ing to do?
Dmaj7
Liv - in' on your
Am7 B7 Em9
cheat - in', and the pain grows in - side me; it's e - nough to leave me cry - ing in the rain.
A7sus Dmaj7
Love you for ev - er but you're driv - ing me in - sane and I'm hang - ing on. Oh.
B7♭9 Em9
Oh, I'll win, I'll nev - er give in, our love has got the pow - er,
Wrap my - self up and take me home a - gain,
too man - y lov - ers in one life - time ain't good for you.
too man - y heart - aches in one life - time ain't good for me.
Dmaj7
You treat me like a vi -
I fig - ure it's the love
Am7 B7 Em7
- sion in the night, some - one there to stand be - hind you when your world ain't work - ing right.
that keeps you warm, let this mo - ment be for - ev - er we won't ev - er feel the storm.
A7sus Em7 A7 Em7 F♯m7 Bm7
I ain't no vi - sion, I'm the man who loves you in - side and out,
A7sus Dmaj7 Em7 F♯m7 Bm7
back - wards and for - wards with my heart hang - ing out. I love no oth - er way.
Em7 A7sus D7
What am I gon - na do if we lose that fire? Don't try to tell me it's all
o - ver, I can't hear a word, I can't hear a line.
No man could love you more and that's what I'm cry - in' for. You can't change the way I feel
G F
in - side. You are the rea - son for my laugh - ter and my sor - row,

Em7
A7
Dmaj7
Blow out the can - dle I will burn a - gain to - mor - row.
No man on earth can stand be -
Am7
B7
Em9
tween my love and I, and no mat - ter how you hurt me I will love you till I die.
A7sus
Em7
A7
Em7
F♯m7
Bm7
I ain't no vi - sion, I'm the man who loves you in - side and out,
A7sus
Dmaj7
Em7
F♯m7
back - wards and for - wards with my heart hang - ing out.
I love
Bm7
Em7
A7sus
Repeat and Fade
no oth - er way.
What am I gon - na do if we lose that fire?

LOVING YOU

Words and Music by JERRY LEIBER
and MIKE STOLLER

Slowly, with a beat

F C7
I will spend my whole life through lov - ing you, lov - ing you. Win - ter, sum - mer,

F F7 B♭
spring - time, too. lov - ing you, lov - ing you. Makes no dif - f'rence where I go or

F Cm6 D7 G7 C7 G7 C7 F
what I do. You know that I'll al - ways be lov - ing you. If I'm seen with

C7
some - one new, don't be blue, don't be blue. I'll be faith - ful I'll be true,

F F7 B♭ F Cm6
al - ways true, true to you. There is on - ly one for me, and you know

D7 G7 1 C7 F C7 2 C7 F
who. You know that I'll al - ways be lov - ing you. lov - ing you.

LOVE'S GROWN DEEP

Words and Music by
KENNY NOLAN

Freely
E♭ E♭maj7 A♭6/E♭ E♭maj7 E♭6 E♭maj7
Some-where back in time you be-came a friend of mine, and day by day we've grown
Fm7/E♭ E♭ E♭maj7
a lit-tle clos-er. You're my spir-it to be strong, a
A♭6/E♭ A♭m6/E♭ E♭ Cm9
friend when things go wrong, so I've writ-ten down these words to let you
B♭m7 E♭7sus E♭7
know.
Moderately, with a beat
A♭maj7 B♭7 E♭maj7
Love's grown deep, deep in-to the heart of me,
Cm7 Fm7 B♭7sus B♭7 E♭maj7 E♭9
you've be-come a part of me. Let us plant a seed and watch it grow.
A♭maj7 B♭7 Gm7 Cm7 B♭7sus
Love's grown deep, deep in-to the heart of me, you've be-come a part of me.
To Coda
E♭ Cm7 Fm7 B♭7sus B♭7
As we trav-el down the road, side by side we'll share the load.
Instrumental
E♭maj7 Cm7 Fm7 B♭7 E♭
Hand in hand we'll see each oth-er through. Though we've on-ly just be-gun,
Instrumental ends
As the sea-sons slip a-way,
Cm7 Fm7 B♭7sus B♭7 E♭maj7 E♭6
let's count our bless-ings one by one. I thank God for life,
for-ev-er lov-ers we will stay, to-geth-er, do or die,
Cm7 B♭m7 E♭7
2nd time D.S. al Coda
I thank God for you.
with all our heart.
CODA
A♭maj7 Gm7
Ah, ah,
Fm7 E♭maj7 A♭maj7 Gm7 Fm7 B♭7
Repeat and Fade
ah, oh, oh. Ah, ah, ah.

LOW RIDER

Words and Music by SYLVESTER ALLEN, HAROLD R. BROWN, MORRIS DICKERSON, JERRY GOLDSTEIN, LEROY JORDAN, LEE OSKAR, CHARLES W. MILLER and HOWARD SCOTT

Moderately

G7

All my friends know the low rid - er. The
Low rid - er drives a lit - tle slow - er.
Low rid - er knows ev - 'ry street, yeah.
Low rid - er don't use no gas, now.

low rid - er is a lit - tle high - er.
low rid - er He's a real go - er.
low rid - er is the one to meet, yeah.
low rid - er don't drive too fast.

(Instrumental)

Play 4 times

1 2 **D.S. and Fade**

Take a lit - tle trip, take a lit - tle trip, take a lit - tle trip and see. ___ / with me. ___

MAGIC CARPET RIDE

Words and Music by JOHN KAY and RUSHTON MOREVE

Heavy Metal Rock

D C G D C G D C G D C G

I like __ to dream ___ right be - tween __ my sound ma - chine. __ On a

D C G D C G D G D C G

cloud of sound __ I drift in the night, __ an - y place it goes __ is right; goes far, flies near, to the stars a - way __ from here. Well,

D C G D C G D C G D C G

you __ don't know what we __ can find. Oh, why don't you come with me __ lit - tle girl on a mag - ic car - pet ride. Well,

D C G D C G D C G D C G

you __ don't know what we can see. Why don't you tell your dreams to me, fan - tas - y __ will set you free.

B♭ C G7sus

Close your eyes girl, look in - side girl, let the sound take you a - way. Last

D C G D C G D C G

night I owned __ Al - lad - in's lamp __ and so I wished that I could stay. Be - fore the thing could an - swer me,

D C G D G D C G **D.S. and Fade**

some - one came and took the lamp a - way. I looked a - round a lous - y can - dle is all I found. Well,

MacARTHUR PARK

Words and Music by
JIMMY WEBB

Moderately

Dm Dm/C E♭/B♭
Spring was nev-er wait - ing ___ for us, girl, it ran _ one ___ step a - head as we fol - lowed in ___ the
I re-call _ the yel-low cot-ton dress foam - ing like a wave on the ground _ a-round your

Gm B♭/F A♭ B♭/E♭ Gm A♭/E♭ (♪ = ♪) D♭/E♭ E♭/F
dance. Be -
knees. The

(♪ = ♪) Dm Dm/C E♭/B♭
tween the part-ed pag - es ___ and were pressed in love's _ hot fe-vered i - ron ___ like a strip-ed pair _ of
birds like ten-der ba - bies ___ in your hands and the old man play-ing cheq - uers by the

Gm B♭/F A♭ B♭ C
pants.
trees.
Mac - Ar-thur's Park is melt - ing in the dark, _

Cmaj7 Gm7/C F
___ all the sweet green ic - ing flow - ing down. _ Some-one left the cake _ out ___ in the rain; _

Fmaj7 C/E Dm7
___ I don't _ think that I ___ can take it 'cause it took so long to bake _ it and I'll

C/E Fmaj7 E♭ 1 Cm
nev-er have _ that rec - i - pe ___ a - gain, oh, no. ___

D♭ A♭maj7 Cm/F D♭ 2 Cm A♭ E♭maj9 Dm7 Cmaj7 Am7 Fmaj9 Bm7 Fmaj7 B♭maj7 E♭
___

A♭ A♭maj7 A♭7 D♭ E♭/B♭ F
(Instrumental)

Fmaj7 B♭maj7 B♭6
There will be an - oth - er song _ for me for I will sing ___ it, ___

B♭dim7 Fsus9/A F Fmaj7
there will be an - oth - er dream for me, some-one will bring ___ it. ___ I will

B♭maj7 Em7♭5 Am7
drink the wine _ while it is warm ___ and nev - er let ___ you catch _ me look-ing at the sun, _

D7sus D7 C D7 Gm7 Gm7/C C7♭9 Fmaj7 F
and af - ter all the loves of my life, af - ter all the loves of my
B♭maj7 E♭maj7 Gm7/C C7 F
life you'll still be the one. I will take my life in - to my
Fmaj7 B♭maj7 B♭6 B♭dim7
hands and I will use it. I will win the wor - ship in their
Fsus9/A F B♭maj7
eyes and I will lose it. I will have the things that I de - sire
Em7♭5 Am7 D7sus D7 C D7 Gm7
and my pas - sion flow like riv - ers to the sky, and af - ter all the loves of my
Gm7/C C7♭9 Fmaj7 B♭maj7 E♭maj7
life, oh, af - ter all the loves of my life I'll be think - ing of you
Csus Dm Dm/C E♭/B♭ Gm B♭/F
and wonder ing why.
(Instrumental)
A♭ B♭/E♭ Gm A♭/E♭ D♭/E♭ E♭/F Am/D C/F N.C.
(Instrumental ends)
F Fmaj7
Mac - Ar - thur's Park is melt - ing in the dark, all the sweet green ic - ing
Cm7 Cm7/F F7♭9 B♭ B♭maj7 C6
flow - ing down. Some - one left the cake out in the rain; I don't
Dm F/C Bm7♭5
think that I can take it 'cause it took so long to bake it and I'll nev - er have that rec - i - pe a -
B♭m F A♭ Fm
gain, oh, no. Oh, no,
G♭ B♭sus B♭ B♭sus Fsus B♭
no, no, no, oh, no.

MAKE ME LOSE CONTROL

Words and Music by ERIC CARMEN
and DEAN PITCHFORD

Moderately
E A B A B E A B A E/B
I run a comb through my hair ___ and step out in the street, _ and the
We put the top down and park ___ 'neath the moon in the sky, ___ and the
E A B E/B E A B A E/G♯ Amaj7
cit - y's the col - or of green ___ in the mid-sum - mer heat, _ oh, yeah. ___
wind is so hard in our hair ___ like a fire in Ju - ly, ___ oh, yeah. ___
A Emaj7/G♯ C♯m7
Jen - ni - fer's got her dad - dy's car, _ she's play - in' "Up - town" on the ster - e - o. ___ We go
Jen - ni - fer's sing - in' "Stand By Me" _ and she knows ev - 'ry sin - gle word by heart. ___ Was love
F♯m7sus F♯m7 B7sus B7 A/B B7 E
cruis - in' so close, the way they did _ long a - go. ___ My dar - lin', turn the ra - di - o up
al - ways this good or could this be just the start? ___ Oh, dar - lin',
A B7 E A B7 E
for that sweet sound; _ hold me close, nev - er let me go. ___ Keep the spir - it a - live,
Keep this feel - in' a - live,
A B7 E A B7 E
make me lose con - trol, ___ ba - by, ba - by. ___ When I look in your eyes,
A B7 E A B7 E A
I go cra - zy; ___ fe - ver's high with the lights down low. ___ So take me o - ver the edge,
B7 1 E A B A B E A B
make me lose con - trol. ___
2 N.C.
When my ba - by comes home _
_ and we're mov - in' in time, _ and the heat from your touch makes me
E/B E A B
feel like I'm los - in' my mind, _ oh, yeah. _ And then they play "Back In My Arms A - gain"; _

E/B E A B E/B E A B

we close our eyes, we start re-mem-ber-in' when. We start to kiss and now the feel-in's in-tense,

E/B E 3 A B

and we just pray that this night nev-er ends, whoa, oh. My dar-lin',

E A B7 E A B7

turn the ra-di-o up for that sweet sound; hold me close, nev-er let me go.

E A B7 E A B7

Take me o-ver the edge, make me lose con-trol, ba-by, ba-by.

E A B7 E A B7

When I look in your eyes, I go cra-zy; fe-ver's high with the lights down low. So

Repeat and Fade

E A B7 E A B7

take me o-ver the edge, make me lose con-trol. Ba-by, ba-by,

MAYBE BABY

By NORMAN PETTY
and CHARLES HARDIN

Moderate Country beat

E C♯m E C♯m E

May-be, ba-by, I'll have you. May-be, ba-by, you'll be true. May-be, ba-by,

To Coda

A B E A E B E C♯m E

I'll have you for me. { It's fun-ny, hon-ey, you don't care. You nev-er lis-ten
{ *(Instrumental)*

C♯m E A B E A E

to my prayer. May-be, ba-by, you will love me some-day. Well,

A E A

you are the one that makes me sad, and you are the one that makes me glad. When some-day

D.C. al Coda (2nd time)

CODA

B E

you want me, I'll be there. Just wait and see. me.

(Instrumental ends)

MAKING LOVE OUT OF NOTHING AT ALL

Words and Music by
JIM STEINMAN

Moderately slow
G Bm/F♯ Em Em/D
I know just how to whis - per and I know just how to cry. I
C D C/D G Bm/F♯
know just where to find the an - swers, and I know just how to lie. I know just how to fake it, and I
Em Em/D C D
know just how to scheme. I know just when to face the truth, and then I know just when to dream. And I
G G/F♯ Em C
know just where to touch you, and I know just what to prove. I know when to pull you clos - er, and I
D G
know when to let you loose. And I know the night is fad - ing, and I
make the run or stum - ble. I can
Em Em7 Cmaj7
know that time's gon - na fly, and I'm nev - er gon - na tell you ev - 'ry - thing I've got to tell you, but I
make the fi - nal block. And I can make ev - 'ry tac - kle at the sound of the whis - tle, I can
Cmaj7/D D7 G
know I've got to give it a try. And I know the roads to rich - es, and I
make all the sta - di - ums rock. I can make to - night for - ev - er or I can
Em Em7 Cmaj7
know the ways to fame. I know all the rules and then I know how to break 'em and I
make it dis - ap - pear by the dawn. And I can make you ev - 'ry prom - ise that has ev - er been made and I can
Cmaj7/D D7 C F C F G
al - ways know the name of the game. But I don't know how to leave you, and I'll nev - er let you fall.
make all your de - mons be gone. But I'm nev - er gon - na make it with - out you. Do you real - ly wan - na see me crawl?
Am Em C D
And I don't know how you do it, mak - ing love out of noth - ing at
And I'm nev - er gon - na make it like you do,
G Em
(Mak - ing love) (Mak - ing love)
all. out of noth - ing at all. out of noth - ing at

To Coda
C
Dsus
D7
G
(Mak-ing love)
all.
out of noth-ing at
all.
(Mak-ing love)
out of noth-ing at
Em
C
D7
G
(Mak-ing love)
all..
out of noth-ing at
all.
(Mak-ing love)
out of noth-ing at
all.
C
D/F♯
G
C
Ev-'ry time I see you all the rays of the sun are stream-ing through the waves in your hair, and ev-'ry
Am7
Bm
Em
star in the sky is tak-ing aim at your eyes like a spot - light The
C
D/F♯
G
beat-ing of my heart is a drum and it's lost and it's look-ing for a rhy-thm like
C
Am7
D/F♯
you. You can take the dark-ness from the pit of the night and turn in-to a
G
C
bea-con burn-ing end-less-ly bright. I've got to fol-low it, 'cause
Am7
C/D
G
ev-'ry-thing I know, well, it's noth-ing till I give it to you.
(Instrumental)
Em
C
C/D
D7
D.S. al Coda
I can
CODA
Dsus
D7
G
(love)
out of noth-ing at
all.
(Mak-ing love)
out of noth-ing at
Em
C
C/D
D7
Repeat and Fade
(Mak-ing love)
all.
out of noth-ing at
all.
(Mak-ing love, love, love.)
out of noth-ing at

MAMBO NO. 5
(A Little Bit Of...)

Original Music by DAMASO PEREZ PRADO
Words by LOU BEGA and ZIPPY

Relaxed two-beat feel
N.C.
One, two, three, four, five. Ev-'ry-bod-y in the car. So, come on, let's ride to the
li-quor store a-round the cor-ner. The boys say they want some gin and juice, but I real-ly don't wan-na.
B♭7 E♭
Beer bust like I had last week. I must stay deep 'cause talk is cheap. I like
B♭7 E♭ E♭5/B♭
An-gel-a, Pam-el-a, San-dra and Rit-a and as I con-tin-ue you know they're get-tin' sweet-er.
B♭7 E♭
So, what can I do? I real-ly beg you my Lord. To me flirt-in' is just like a sport.
B♭7 E♭ N.C.
An-y-thing fly, it's all good. Let me dump it, please set in the trum-pet. A lit-tle bit of
B♭7 E♭
Mon-i-ca in my life, a lit-tle bit of Er-i-ca by my side, a lit-tle bit of
B♭7 E♭
Rit-a's all I need. A lit-tle bit of Tin-a's what I see. A lit-tle bit of
B♭7 E♭
San-dra in the sun, a lit-tle bit of Mar-y all night long, a lit-tle bit of
To Coda
B♭7 E♭ N.C.
Jes-si-ca, here I am, a lit-tle bit of you makes me your man.
B♭7 1-3 4 E♭6
(Instrumental)
B♭7 E♭
Jump up and down and move it all a-round. Shake your head to the sound, put your

Bb7
Eb
hands on the ground. Take one step left and one step right, one to the front and one to the side.
D.S. al Coda
Clap your hands once and clap your hands twice and if it looks like this then you do-in' it right.
A lit-tle bit of
CODA
I do all to fall in love with a girl like you 'cause
you can't run and you can't hide. You and me gon-na touch the sky.
1-3
4
Eb6
(Instrumental)
Last time (Spoken:)
Mambo Number Five.

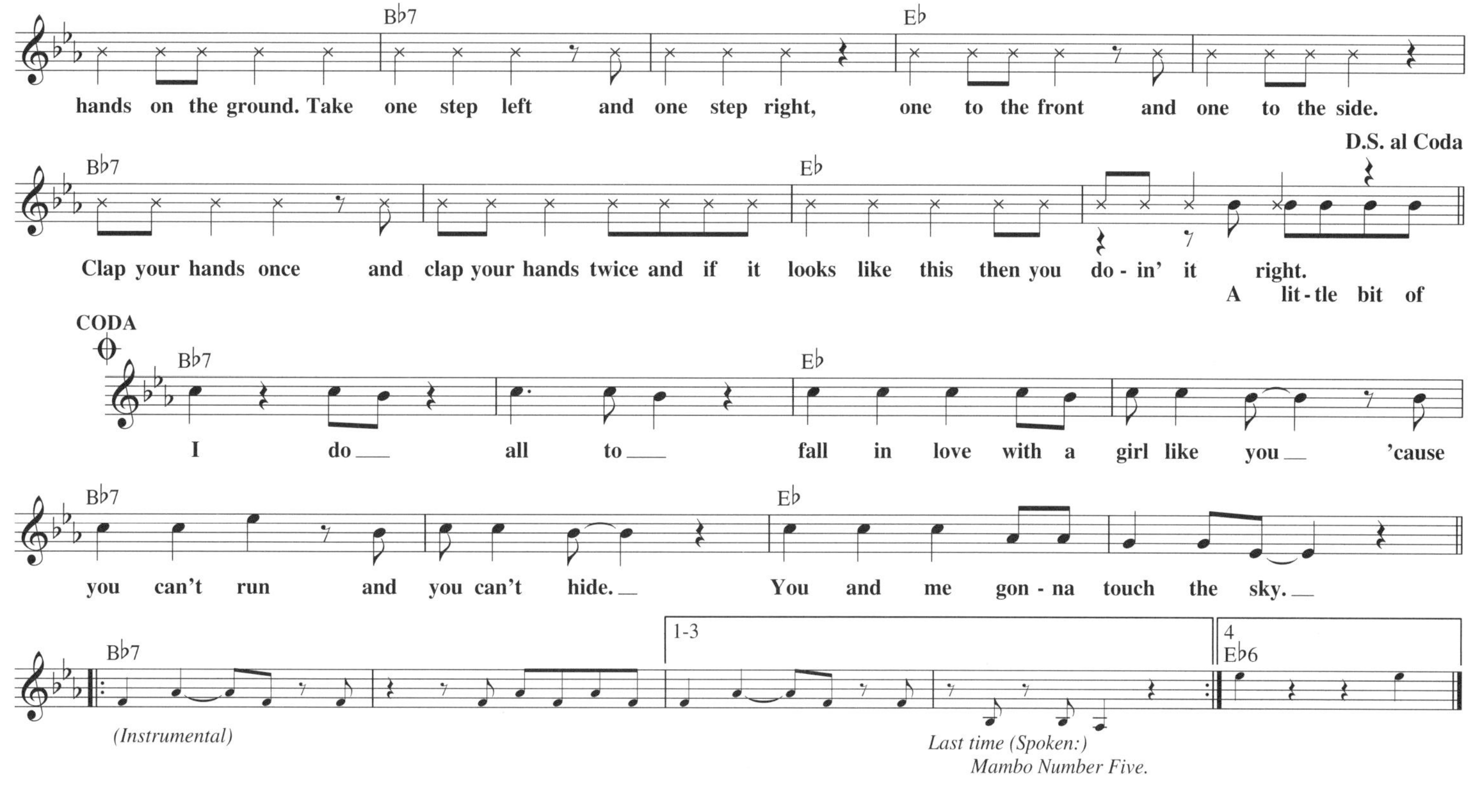

MARY IN THE MORNING

Words and Music by JOHNNY CYMBAL
and MIKE LENDELL

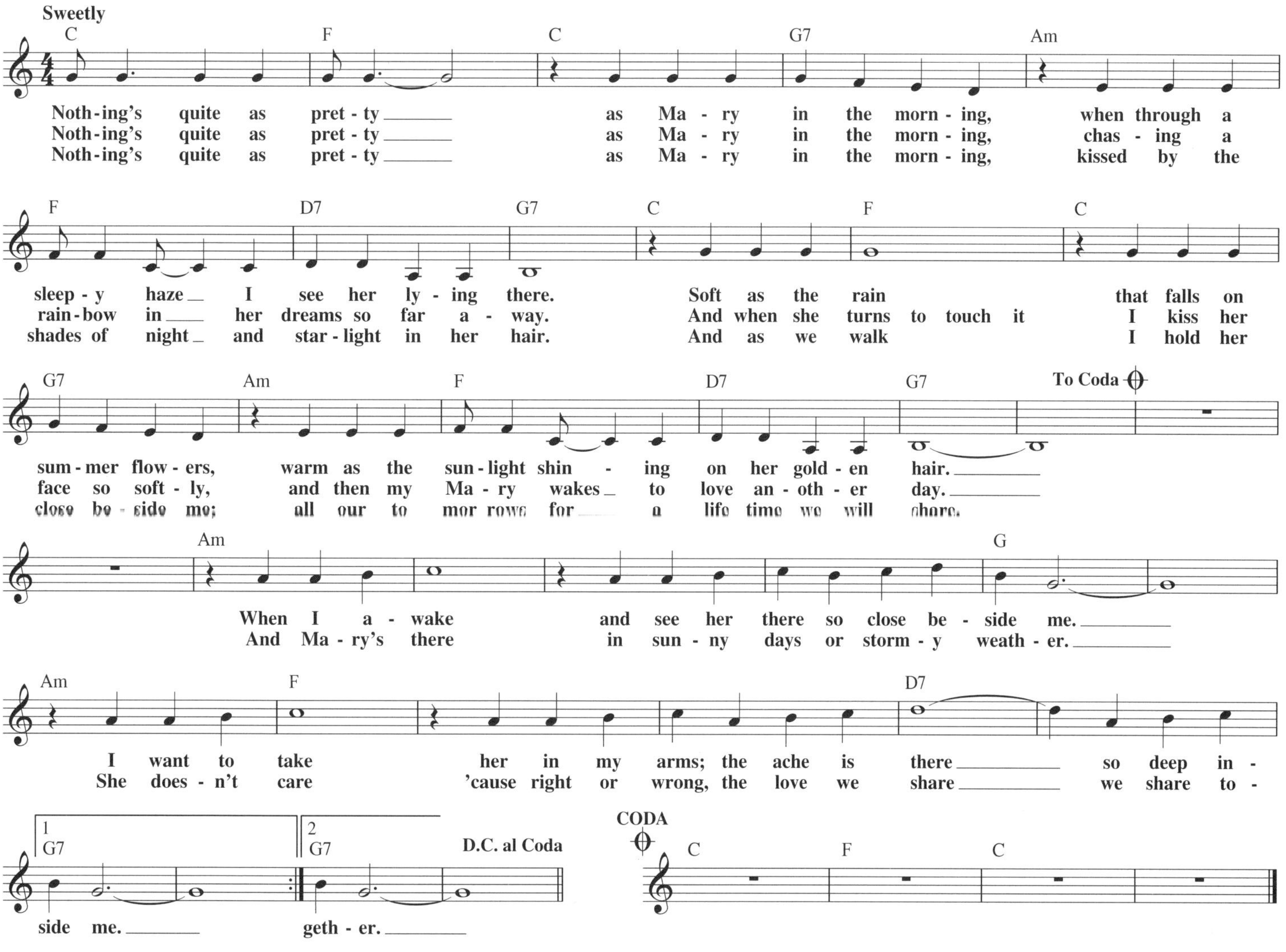

Sweetly
C F C G7 Am
Noth-ing's quite as pret-ty as Ma-ry in the morn-ing, when through a
Noth-ing's quite as pret-ty as Ma-ry in the morn-ing, chas-ing a
Noth-ing's quite as pret-ty as Ma-ry in the morn-ing, kissed by the
F D7 G7 C F C
sleep-y haze I see her ly-ing there. Soft as the rain that falls on
rain-bow in her dreams so far a-way. And when she turns to touch it I kiss her
shades of night and star-light in her hair. And as we walk I hold her
G7 Am F D7 G7
To Coda
sum-mer flow-ers, warm as the sun-light shin-ing on her gold-en hair.
face so soft-ly, and then my Ma-ry wakes to love an-oth-er day.
close be-side me; all our to-mor-rows for a life-time we will share.
Am G
When I a-wake and see her there so close be-side me.
And Ma-ry's there in sun-ny days or storm-y weath-er.
Am F D7
I want to take her in my arms; the ache is there so deep in-
She does-n't care 'cause right or wrong, the love we share we share to-
1 G7
2 G7
D.C. al Coda
side me.
geth-er.
CODA
C F C

MAYBE I'M AMAZED

Words and Music by
PAUL McCARTNEY

Slowly, with a beat
B♭ F/A C G/C
Ba - by I'm a - mazed at the way you love me all the time,
May - be I'm a - mazed at the way you're with me all the time.
B♭ F/A C
and may - be I'm a - fraid of the way I love you. (Instrumental)
May - be I'm a - fraid of the way I need you.
B♭ F/A C G B♭ F/A
Ba - by, I'm a - mazed at the way you pulled me out of time. You hung me on a line.
Ba - by, I'm a - mazed at the way you help me sing my song, right me when I'm wrong.
A♭ E♭/G C To Coda D A/D
Ba - by, I'm a - mazed at the way I real - ly need you. Ba - by, I'm a man, may - be I'm a
Ba - by, I'm a - mazed at the way I real - ly need you.
Am/D D9/F♯ G
lone - ly man who's in the mid - dle of some - thing that he does - n't real - ly un - der - stand.
D7 D7♯9 D A/D
(Instrumental) Ba - by, I'm a man, and may - be you're the
Am/D C/D D9/F♯ G
on - ly wom - an who could ev - er help me. Ba - by, won't you help me to un - der - stand.
D/F♯ Dm/F Em7 A7 B♭ F/A C G/C
(Instrumental)
B♭ F/A C B♭ F/A
C G B♭ F/A A♭ E♭/G C
D A/D Am/D D9/F♯
Ba - by, I'm a man, and may - be I'm a lone - ly man who's in the mid - dle of some - thing
G D7 D7♯9
that he does - n't real - ly un - der - stand.

D A/D Am/D C/D D9/F#
Ba - by, I'm a man, and may - be you're the on - ly wom - an who could ev - er help me.
D.C. al Coda
G D/F# Dm/F Em7 A7
Ba - by, won't you help me to un - der - stand.
(Instrumental)
CODA
D A/D Am/D C/D D9/F# G D7#9 D A/D
(Instrumental)
Am/D C/D D9/F# G D/F# Dm/F Em7 A7 Bb F/A
C G Bb F/A C Bb F/A
C G Bb F/A Ab Eb/G C
Repeat and Fade
MONDAY, MONDAY
Copyright © 1966 UNIVERSAL MUSIC CORP.
Copyright Renewed
Words and Music by
JOHN PHILLIPS
Steady Rock
G
Mon - day, Mon - day, so good to me. Mon - day morn -
- day, can't trust that day. Mon - day, Mon -
F Bb
- in', it was all I hoped it would be. Oh, Mon - day morn - in' Mon - day morn -
- day, some - times it just turns out that way. Oh, Mon - day morn - in', you gave me no warn -
D7 G Gsus
- in' could n't guar - an - tee, that Mon - day e - v'nin' you would still be here with
- in' of what was to be, oh, Mon - day, Mon - day how could you leave and not take
1 G 2 G Ab
me. Mon - day, Mon - me. Ev - 'ry oth - er day, ev - 'ry
F Ab
oth - er day, ev - 'ry oth - er day of the week is fine, yeah! But when - ev - er Mon - day comes,
F D N.C.
D.S. and Fade
but when - ev - er Mon - day comes you can find me cry'n, yeah! Mon - day, Mon -

A MAN WITHOUT LOVE

(Quando M'Innamoro)

English Lyric by BARRY MASON
Original Words and Music by D. PACE, M. PANZERI and R. LIVRAGHI

Moderately

D A7
I can re-mem-ber when we walked to - geth - er, shar - ing a love I thought ___ would last for -

D A7
ev - er. Moon - light to show the way ___ so we can fol - low. Wait - ing in - side her

D E♭ B♭7
eyes ___ was my to - mor - row. Then some - thing changed her mind, her kiss - es told me.

E♭
I had no lov - ing arms ___ to hold me. Ev - 'ry day I wake up, then I start to break up,

B♭7
{ lone - ly is a man with - out love. ___ }
{ know - ing that it's cloud - y a - bove. ___ }
Ev - 'ry day I start out, then I cry my heart out.

1 E♭ 2 E♭ D
Lone - ly is a man with - out love. ___ ___

D A7
I can - not face this world that's fall - en down on me. So, if you see my girl ___ please send her

D A7
home to me. Tell her a - bout my heart ___ that's slow - ly dy - ing.

D
Say I can't stop my - self ___ from cry - ing. Ev - 'ry day I wake up, then I start to break up,

A7
lone - ly is a man with - out love. ___ Ev - 'ry day I start out, then I cry my heart out.

D B♭7 E♭
Lone - ly is a man with - out love. ___ Ev - 'ry day I wake up, then I start to break up,

B♭7
{ know - ing that it's cloud - y a - bove. ___ }
{ lone - ly is a man with - out love. ___ }
Ev - 'ry day I start out, then I cry my heart out.

1 E♭ 2 (opt.) E♭
Lone - ly is a man with - out love. ___ Lone - ly is a man ___ with - out love. ___

MIAMI VICE

Theme from the Universal Television Series

By JAN HAMMER

MERCY, MERCY ME
(The Ecology)

Words and Music by
MARVIN GAYE

Moderately
Emaj7 C♯m7
Woo ah mer - cy, mer - cy me. Ah, things
2. (See additional lyrics)
F♯m7
ain't what they used to be. No, no, where did all the blue skies go,
Amaj7/B Emaj7
poi - son is the wind that blows from the north and south and east. Woo mer-
Amaj7/B Emaj7 Emaj7 C♯m7
mer - cu - ry, Ah. 3. Oh mer - cy, mer - cy me. Ah things
4. (See additional lyrics)
F♯m7
ain't what they used to be. No, no, no, ra - di - a - tion un - der - ground and in the
Amaj7/B E Emaj7
sky; an - i - mals and birds who live near - by are dy - ing. Oh,
Amaj7/B Emaj7
land how much more a - buse from man can she stand? Oh na, na,
D♭m7 F♯m7
my sweet Lord, no, no, na, na, na,
Amaj7/B
my, my Lord my sweet Lord.

Additional Lyrics

2. Ah things ain't what they used to be, no, no
Oil wasted on the ocean and upon
Our seas fish full of mercury, Ah.

4. Ah things ain't what they used to be
What about this overcrowded land
How much more abuse from man can she stand?

MIDNIGHT CONFESSIONS

Words and Music by
LOU JOSIE

Moderately, with a heavy beat
Fm Eb
The sound of your foot - steps tell - ing me that you're near.
Stag - ger - ing through the day - time, your im - age on my mind.
Gm Cm
Your soft, gen - tle mo - tion, babe, brings out a need in me that
Pass - ing so close be - side you, babe, some - times the feel - ings are so
Bb Eb Bb Fm
no one can hear, ex - cept in my mid - night con - fes - sions,
hard to hide, but, in my mid - night con - fes - sions,
In my mid - night con - fes - sions,
when I tell all the world
Bb Eb Bb
that I love you. In my mid - night con - fes - sions,
To Coda
Fm
when I say all the things
Bb Db
that I want to; I love you. But a lit - tle gold ring
Ab Eb Bb Db
you wear on your hand makes me un - der - stand. There's an - oth - er be - fore
Ab Eb C
me, you'll nev - er be mine, I'm wast - ing my time.
1
2
D.S. al Coda
CODA
Fm Bb
when I say all the things that I want to.
Eb Bb Db Ab
Repeat ad lib. and Fade
La la la la la la la la. La la la la la la la la.

MISSISSIPPI QUEEN

Words and Music by LESLIE WEST,
FELIX PAPPALARDI, CORKY LAING and DAVID REA

Moderately

F

Mis - sis - sip - pi Queen, _ if you know _ what I mean

Mis - sis - sip - pi Queen, _ she taught me ev - 'ry - thing.

B♭

Way down _ a - round Bicks - burg, a - round Lou - i - si - an - a way, _

F

lives a Ca - jun la - dy called the Mis - sis - sip - pi Queen.

C7 B♭7

You know _ she was a danc - er, she moved bet - ter on wine. While the

F To Coda

rest of them dudes was _ get - tin' their kicks, bud - dy, beg your par - don, I was get - tin' mine.

Mis - sis - sip - pi Queen, _ if you know _ what I mean

B♭

Mis - sis - sip - pi Queen, _ she taught me ev - 'ry - thing. This la - dy, she _ asked me,

F

if I would be her man. _____ You know _ that I told her

C7

I'd do ____ what I can to keep ___ her look - in' pret - ty,

B♭7 F

buy her dress - es that shine. While the rest of them dudes was _ mak - in' their bread, _

C7 D.S. al Coda

bud - dy, beg your par - don, I was los - in' mine. You know _

CODA

F

Hey, Mis - sis - sip - pi Queen.

MR. BIG STUFF

Words and Music by RALPH WILLIAMS,
JOSEPH BROUSSARD and CARROL WASHINGTON

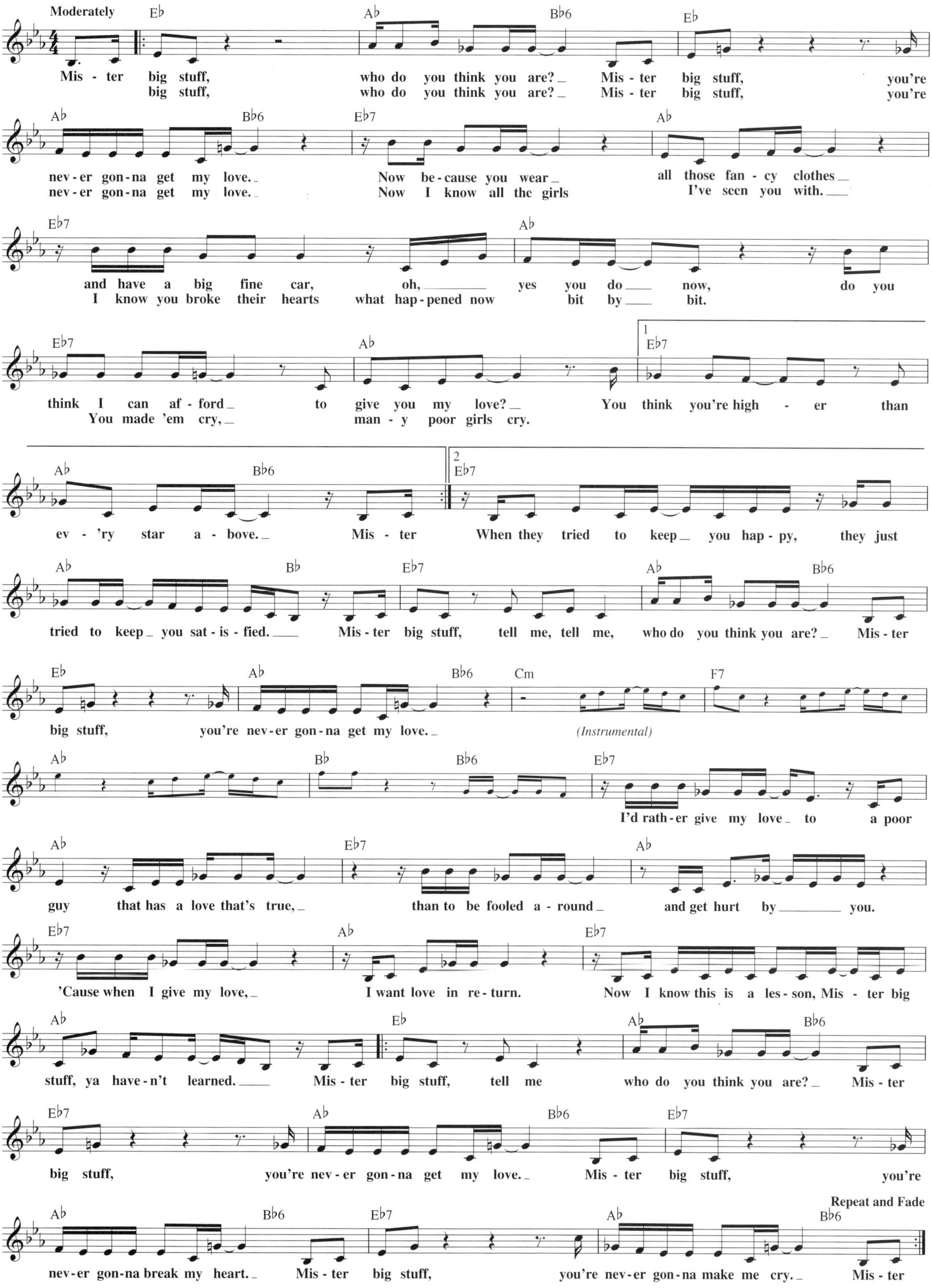
Moderately
E♭ A♭ B♭6 E♭
Mis - ter big stuff, who do you think you are? _ Mis - ter big stuff, you're
big stuff, who do you think you are? _ Mis - ter big stuff, you're
A♭ B♭6 E♭7 A♭
nev - er gon - na get my love. _ Now be - cause you wear _ all those fan - cy clothes _
nev - er gon - na get my love. _ Now I know all the girls I've seen you with. ___
E♭7 A♭
and have a big fine car, oh, ____ yes you do ___ now, do you
I know you broke their hearts what hap - pened now bit by ___ bit.
E♭7 A♭ 1 E♭7
think I can af - ford _ to give you my love? _ You think you're high - er than
You made 'em cry, _ man - y poor girls cry.
A♭ B♭6 2 E♭7
ev - 'ry star a - bove. _ Mis - ter When they tried to keep _ you hap - py, they just
A♭ B♭ E♭7 A♭ B♭6
tried to keep _ you sat - is - fied. ____ Mis - ter big stuff, tell me, tell me, who do you think you are? _ Mis - ter
E♭ A♭ B♭6 Cm F7
big stuff, you're nev - er gon - na get my love. _ (Instrumental)
A♭ B♭ B♭6 E♭7
I'd rath - er give my love _ to a poor
A♭ E♭7 A♭
guy that has a love that's true, _ than to be fooled a - round _ and get hurt by ________ you.
E♭7 A♭ E♭7
'Cause when I give my love, _ I want love in re - turn. Now I know this is a les - son, Mis - ter big
A♭ E♭ A♭ B♭6
stuff, ya have - n't learned. ____ Mis - ter big stuff, tell me who do you think you are? _ Mis - ter
E♭7 A♭ B♭6 E♭7
big stuff, you're nev - er gon - na get my love. _ Mis - ter big stuff, you're
A♭ B♭6 E♭7 A♭ B♭6
Repeat and Fade
nev - er gon - na break my heart. _ Mis - ter big stuff, you're nev - er gon - na make me cry. _ Mis - ter

MMM MMM MMM MMM

Words and Music by
BRAD ROBERTS

Moderately

Cm Bbsus Eb Ab Eb Bb Eb Ab Bbsus Eb Bb Eb Ab Eb Bb Cb Eb Cb Bb7/Ab Ab Gm7 Dm7

Once there was this kid who got in - to an ac - ci - dent and could - n't come to school. But when he fi - n'lly came back, his hair had turned from black in - to bright white. He said that it was from when the cars had smashed so hard.

Once there was this girl who would - n't go and change with the girls in the change room. And when they fi - n'lly made her, they saw birth-marks all o - ver her bod - y. She could - n't quite ex - plain it. They'd al - ways just been there.

then there was this boy whose par - ents made him come di - rect - ly home right af - ter school. And when they went to their church, they shook and lurched all o - ver the church floor. He could - n't quite ex - plain it. They'd al - ways just gone there.

Mmm mmm mmm mmm. Mmm mmm mmm mmm.

Gm7 Dm7 Ab(add9) Bbsus 1 Ab(add9) Bbsus 2, 3 Ab(add9) Bbsus

Gm7 Dm7 Gm7 Dm7 Ab(add9) Bbsus Ab(add9) Bbsus Fm

Mmm mmm mmm mmm. Mmm mmm mmm mmm.

To Coda

But both girl and boy were glad that one kid had it worse than that. 'Cause

Eb Bb Fm Eb Bb Ab(add9)

D.C. al Coda (take 2nd ending)

CODA

Ab(add9) Bbsus Fm Eb Bb Fm Eb Bb Ab(add9) Eb Repeat and Fade

MISUNDERSTANDING

Words and Music by
PHIL COLLINS

Moderately
Dm Em7 F6 Am G Dm Em7 F6 Am G
There must be some mis - un - der - stand - ing. There must be some kind of mis - take. I
Dm Em7 F6 Am G C Dm Em7 F6 Am G
wait - ed in the rain for hours, and you were late. Now, it's not like me to say the right
must be some mis - un - der - stand -

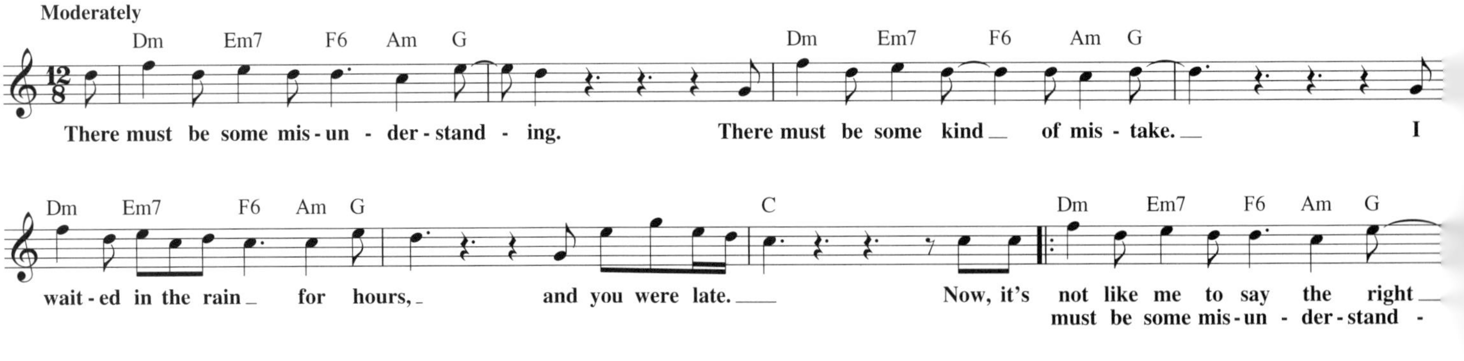

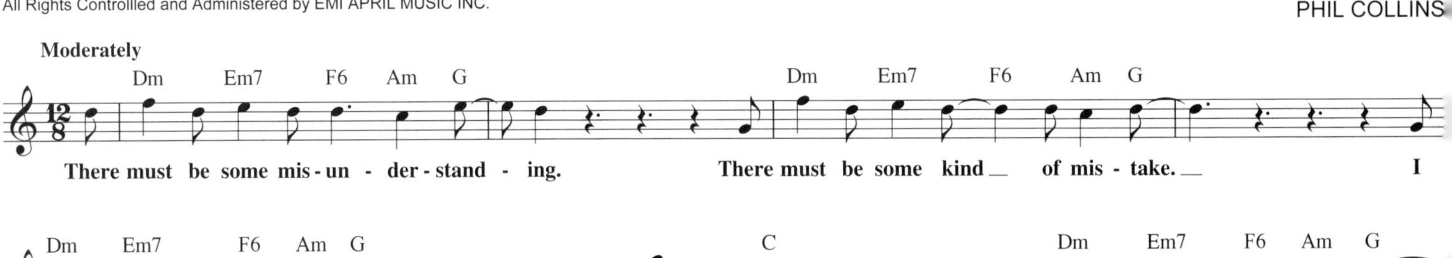

Dm Em7 F6 Am G Dm Em7 F6 Am G

___ thing, but you could have called _ to let me know. _ I checked your num-ber twice. _ Don't un-der-stand _
- ing. There must be some _ kind of mis - take. _ I wait - ed in the rain _ for hours, _

C Ab Bb/Ab

___ it. So I went home. ___ Well, I'd been wait - ing ___
_______ and you were late. _____ Since then, I've been run-ning a-round

Abmaj7 Bb/Ab Ab Bb/Ab Abmaj7 Bb/Ab

for this _ week - end. I thought that may - be we could see _ a show.
trying to ___ find _ you. I went to the plac - es that you al - ways go. _

Gm7 Fm7 Gm7 Fm7

Nev - er dreamed I'd have this feel - ing. Ah, but see-ing you _ is be - liev - ing. ___
I rang your house, but got no an - swer. Jumped in my car. I went round there. _

Gm7 1 A 2 A

That's why I don't know why _ you did - n't show up that night. _ There
I still don't be-lieve it. ___ He was just leav - ing. _ Oh, there

Dm Em7 F6 Am G Dm Em F6 Am G **Repeat and Fade**

must be some mis - un - der stand - ing. There must be some kind _ of mis - take. _ There

MONEY

Words and Music by
ROGER WATERS

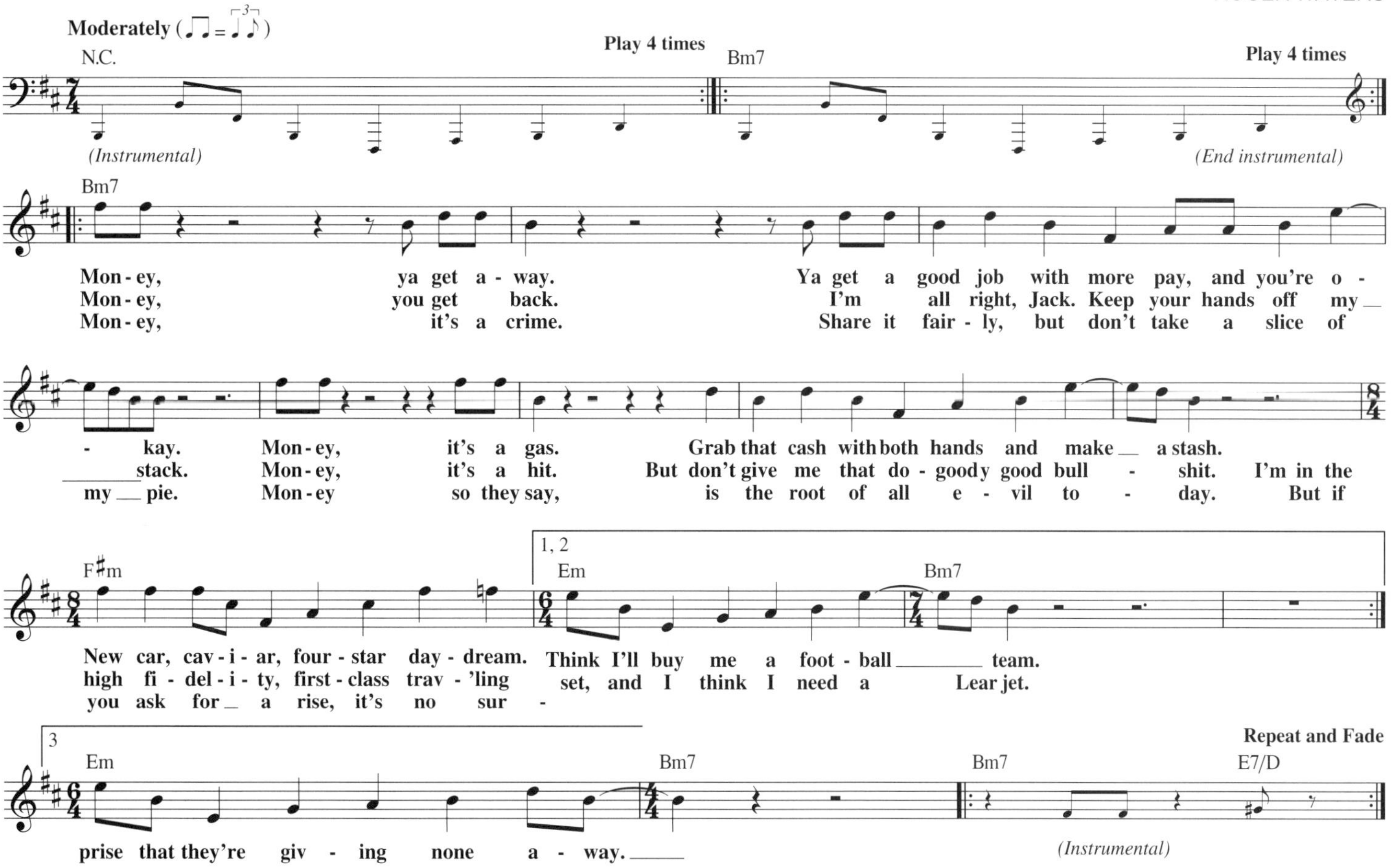

Moderately (♫ = ♩♪ triplet)

N.C. **Play 4 times** Bm7 **Play 4 times**

(Instrumental) *(End instrumental)*

Bm7

Mon - ey, ya get a - way. Ya get a good job with more pay, and you're o -
Mon - ey, you get back. I'm all right, Jack. Keep your hands off my _
Mon - ey, it's a crime. Share it fair - ly, but don't take a slice of

- kay. Mon - ey, it's a gas. Grab that cash with both hands and make _ a stash.
_______ stack. Mon - ey, it's a hit. But don't give me that do - goody good bull - shit. I'm in the
my _ pie. Mon - ey so they say, is the root of all e - vil to - day. But if

F#m 1, 2 Em Bm7

New car, cav - i - ar, four - star day - dream. Think I'll buy me a foot - ball ________ team.
high fi - del - i - ty, first - class trav - 'ling set, and I think I need a Lear jet.
you ask for _ a rise, it's no sur -

3 Em Bm7 Bm7 E7/D **Repeat and Fade**

prise that they're giv - ing none a - way. _____ *(Instrumental)*

MR. JONES

Words by ADAM DURITZ
Music by ADAM DURITZ and DAVID BRYSON

Bright Rock
Am F Dm G Am F
I was down at the New Am - ster-dam star-ing at this yel-low-haired girl._ Mis-ter Jones_ strikes up a con-ver-sa-
G Am F Dm
- tion with this black - haired fla-men - co danc-er. You know, she__ danc-es while his fa-ther plays gui-tar.
G Am F G
She's sud-den-ly beau - ti - ful. Well, we all__ want some - thing beau - ti - ful. Man, I wish I was beau-
Am F Dm G
ti - ful. So, come dance this si - lence down_through the morn - ing. Sha-la - la - la - la - la - la - la,_
Am F G Am F
__ yeah. Uh huh, yeah.____ Cut up, Ma-ri - a!
will paint my pic-ture,
Dm G Am F
Show me some of them_ Span - ish danc - es. Pass____ me a bot - tle, Mis - ter Jones.
paint my-self in blue and red and black and gray. All of the beau-ti-ful col - ors are ver - y, ver - y
G Am F Dm
Be-lieve_ in me. Help me be-lieve in an-
mean-ing-ful. Yeah, well you know gray is my fav - 'rite col-or. I_____ felt so sym -
G Am F G
y-thing 'cause I____ want to be some-one who be-lieves. Yeah._
bol - ic yes - ter - day. If I knew Pi - cas-so I would buy__ my - self__ a gray__
C F G
__ Mis - ter Jones and_ me tell each oth-er fair - y tales____ and we
__ gui - tar__ and play. Mis - ter Jones and_ me look in-to the fu-ture and we
C F G
stare at the beau-ti-ful wom-en. "She's look-ing at you. Ah, no, no, she's look-ing at me."_
stare at the beau-ti-ful wom-en. "She's look-ing at you. Oh, I don't think so. She's look-ing at me."_
C F G
__ Smil - ing in the bright__ lights, com - ing through in ster - e - o. When
__ Stand - ing in the spot - light, I bought my-self a gray gui-tar. When

C F 1 G
ev - 'ry - bod - y loves you, you can nev - er be lone - ly. Well, I
ev - 'ry - bod - y loves me,
2 G Am Fmaj7
I will nev - er be lone - ly. I will nev - er be lone - ly.
Am G
Said, I'm nev - er gon - na be lone - ly.
Am Fmaj7
I want to be a li - on. Yeah, ev - 'ry - bod - y wants to pass as cats.
Am G Am
We all want to be big, big stars, yeah but, we got dif - f'rent rea - sons for that. Be - lieve in me
Fmaj7 Am
be - cause I don't be - lieve in an - y - thing and I want to be some - one to be - lieve,
G C F G
to be - lieve, to be - lieve, yeah. Mis - ter Jones and me stum - bling through the bar -
Mis - ter Jones and me star - ing at the vid -
C F G
ri - o. Yeah, we stare at the beau - ti - ful wom - en. "She's per - fect for you. Man, there's got
e - o. When I look at the tel - e - vi - sion I want to see me
C F G
to be some - bod - y for me." I want to be Bob Dyl - an. Mis - ter Jones wish - es he was some - one just
star - ing right back at me. We all want to be big stars, but we don't know why and we don't
C F G
a lit - tle more funk - y. Where ev - 'ry - bod - y loves you, ah, son, that's just a - bout as funk -
know how. But when ev - 'ry - bod - y loves me, I'm going to be just a - bout as hap -
Freely
C F G
- y as you can be. Mis - ter Jones and me, we're gon - na be big stars...
- py as I can be.

MY MARIA

Words and Music by DANIEL L. MOORE
and B.W. STEVENSON

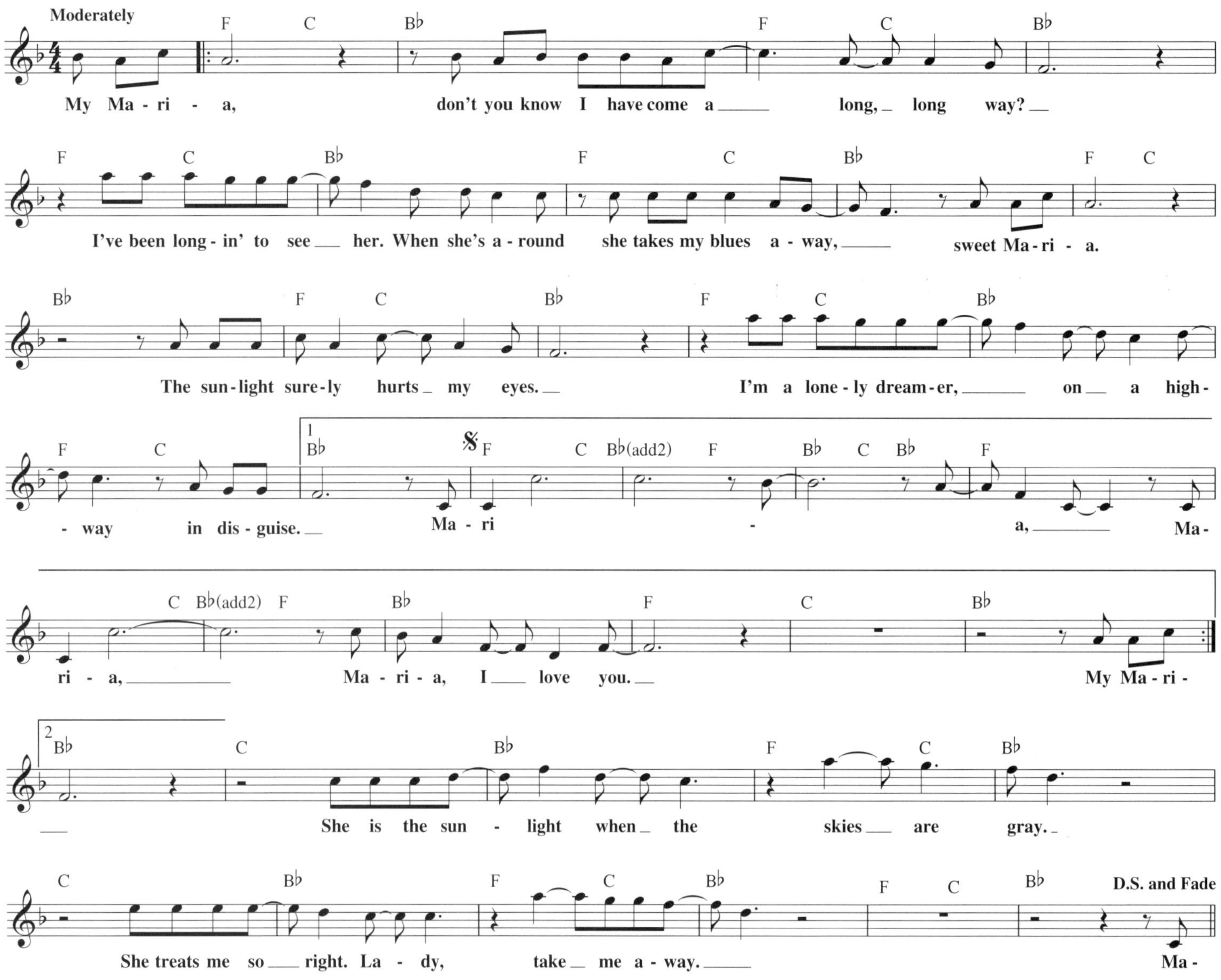

Moderately

F C B♭ F C B♭
My Ma - ri - a, don't you know I have come a long, long way?

F C B♭ F C B♭ F C
I've been long - in' to see her. When she's a - round she takes my blues a - way, sweet Ma - ri - a.

B♭ F C B♭ F C B♭
The sun - light sure - ly hurts my eyes. I'm a lone - ly dream - er, on a high -

F C 1 B♭ 𝄋 F C B♭(add2) F B♭ C B♭ F
- way in dis - guise. Ma - ri - a, Ma -

C B♭(add2) F B♭ F C B♭
ri - a, Ma - ri - a, I love you. My Ma - ri -

2 B♭ C B♭ F C B♭
She is the sun - light when the skies are gray.

C B♭ F C B♭ F C B♭ D.S. and Fade
She treats me so right. La - dy, take me a - way. Ma -

MY PRAYER

Music by GEORGES BOULANGER
Lyric and Musical Adaptation by JIMMY KENNEDY

Moderately
F Fdim7 G7 B♭m6 B♭m
My prayer is to lin - ger with you at the end of the day in a dream that's di -
F F♯dim7 C7 C7♯5 F Fdim7 G7
vine. My prayer is a rap - ture in blue with the world far a -
B♭m6 C7 C7♯5 F B♭m
way and your lips close to mine. To - night while our hearts are a -

Fm Fm7 B♭m G7 C7 C7♯5
glow, oh! tell me the words that I'm long-ing to know. My
F6 Fdim7 G7 B♭m6
prayer and the an-swer you give may they still be the same for as long as we
F Am Gm7 C7 1 F C7♯5 2 F
live, that you'll al-ways be there at the end of my prayer. My prayer.

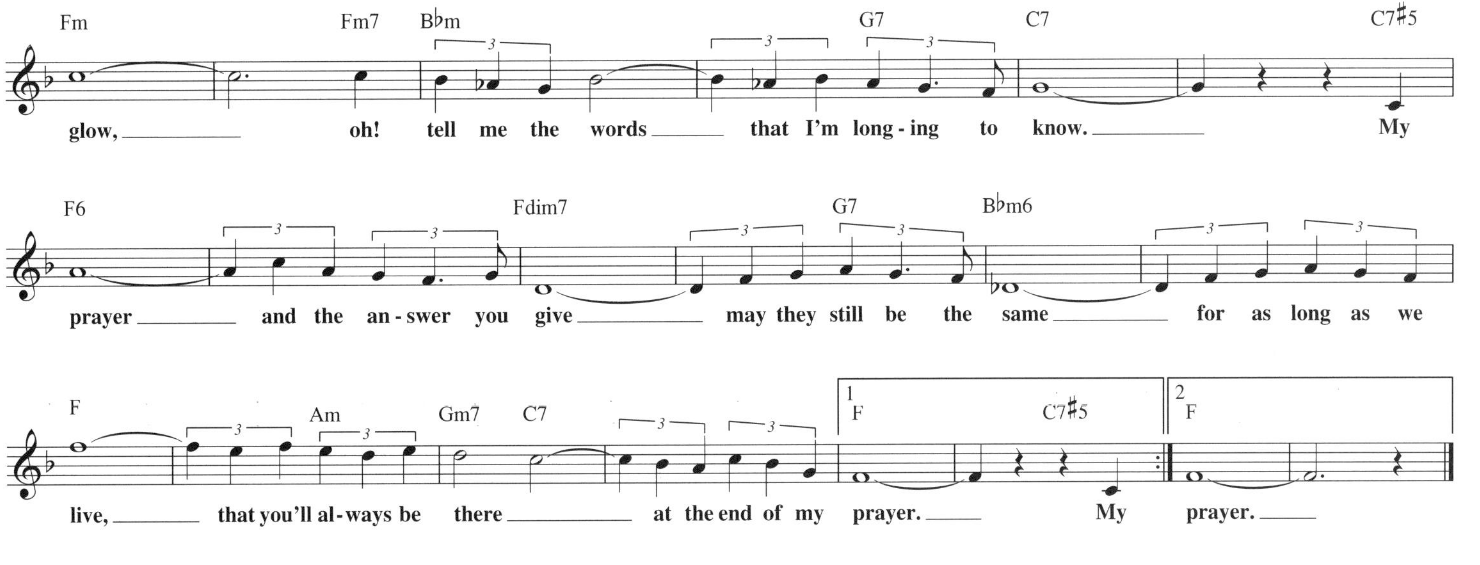

MY WAY

English Words by PAUL ANKA
Original French Words by GILLES THIBAULT
Music by JACQUES REVAUX and CLAUDE FRANCOIS

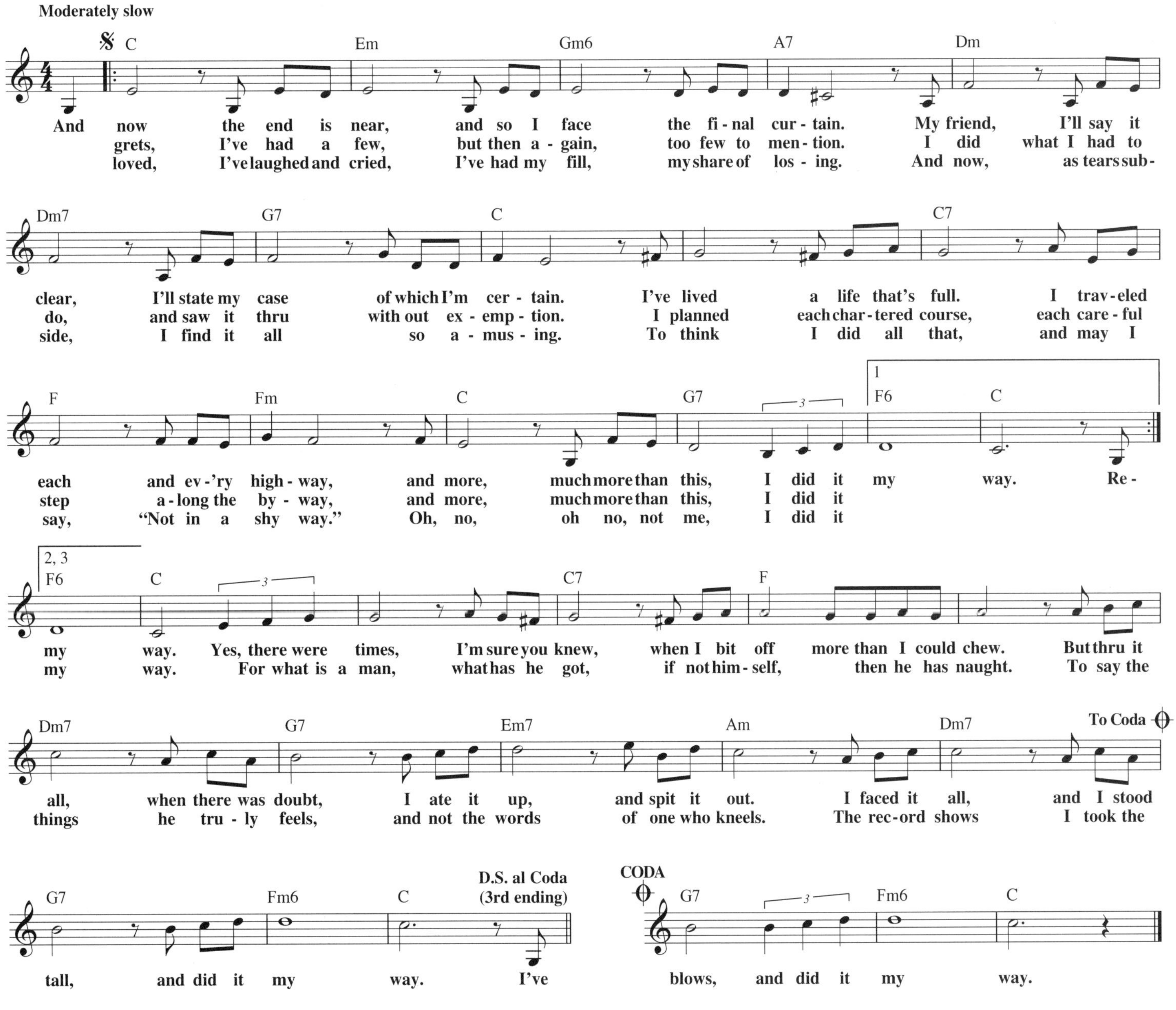
Moderately slow
C Em Gm6 A7 Dm
And now the end is near, and so I face the fi-nal cur-tain. My friend, I'll say it
grets, I've had a few, but then a-gain, too few to men-tion. I did what I had to
loved, I've laughed and cried, I've had my fill, my share of los-ing. And now, as tears sub-
Dm7 G7 C C7
clear, I'll state my case of which I'm cer-tain. I've lived a life that's full. I trav-eled
do, and saw it thru with out ex-emp-tion. I planned each char-tered course, each care-ful
side, I find it all so a-mus-ing. To think I did all that, and may I
F Fm C G7 1 F6 C
each and ev-'ry high-way, and more, much more than this, I did it my way. Re-
step a-long the by-way, and more, much more than this, I did it
say, "Not in a shy way." Oh, no, oh no, not me, I did it
2, 3 F6 C C7 F
my way. Yes, there were times, I'm sure you knew, when I bit off more than I could chew. But thru it
my way. For what is a man, what has he got, if not him-self, then he has naught. To say the
Dm7 G7 Em7 Am Dm7 To Coda
all, when there was doubt, I ate it up, and spit it out. I faced it all, and I stood
things he tru-ly feels, and not the words of one who kneels. The rec-ord shows I took the
G7 Fm6 C D.S. al Coda (3rd ending)
tall, and did it my way. I've
CODA G7 Fm6 C
blows, and did it my way.

MY LOVE

Words and Music by
LIONEL RICHIE

Slow and steady
I've been through so man-y chang-es in my life, wom-an, it's a won-der I ain't lost my mind.
And I ain't nev-er said how much I need you, sug-ar, but I sho' need you by my side.
My love, just think-in' a-bout you, ba-by, just blows my mind.
My love, just think-in' a-bout you, ba-by, just blows my mind all the time.
Life with me I know for sure it ain't been eas-y but you stayed with me an-y-way.
And e-ven though you ain't gon-na lose too much by leav-ing I'm so glad you stayed.
My love, just think-in' a-bout you, ba-by, just blows my mind.
My love, just think-in' a-bout you, ba-by, just blows my mind all the time.
To Coda

D♭ D♭/E♭ A♭
You've been my friend and you've been my lov - er, oh Lawd,
D♭ D♭/E♭ A♭ D♭ D♭/E♭
hon-ey, you're ev-'ry-thing I need. You've made my love so strong, now I
A♭ Cm/G Cdim7/G♭ F7 B♭m7 Cm7 D♭maj7
know where I be-long. Oh girl, you'll nev-er have to wor - ry, oh
D♭maj7/E♭ A♭(add2) E♭m/A♭ D♭(add2) D♭m(add2)
ba - by, an-y-more, an-y - more. My love,
D.S. al Coda
CODA
A♭ E♭/A♭ D♭(add2) D♭/E♭ A♭
time. Oh yeah.

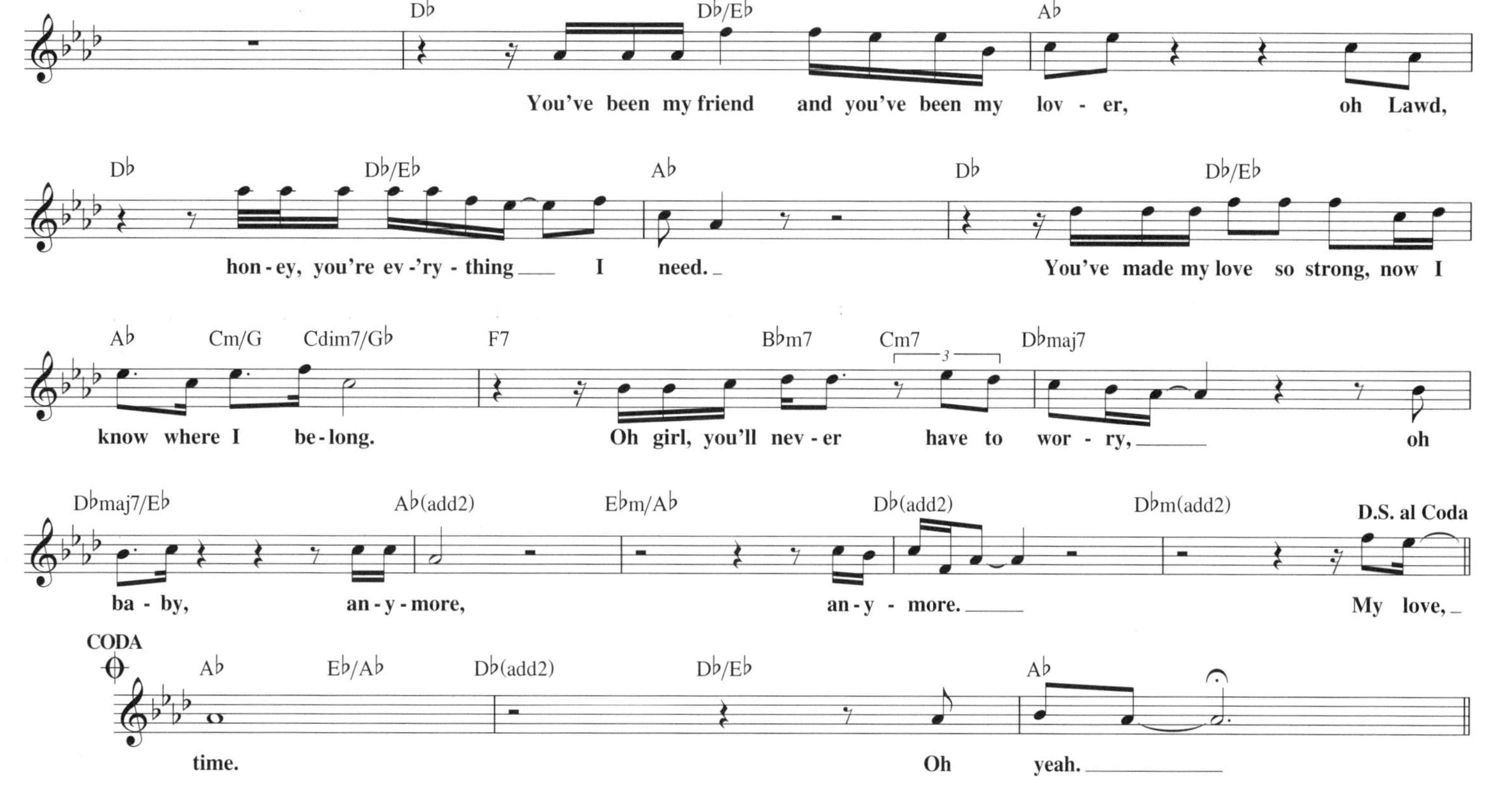

MY EMPTY ARMS

Words and Music by AL KASHA
and HANK HUNTER

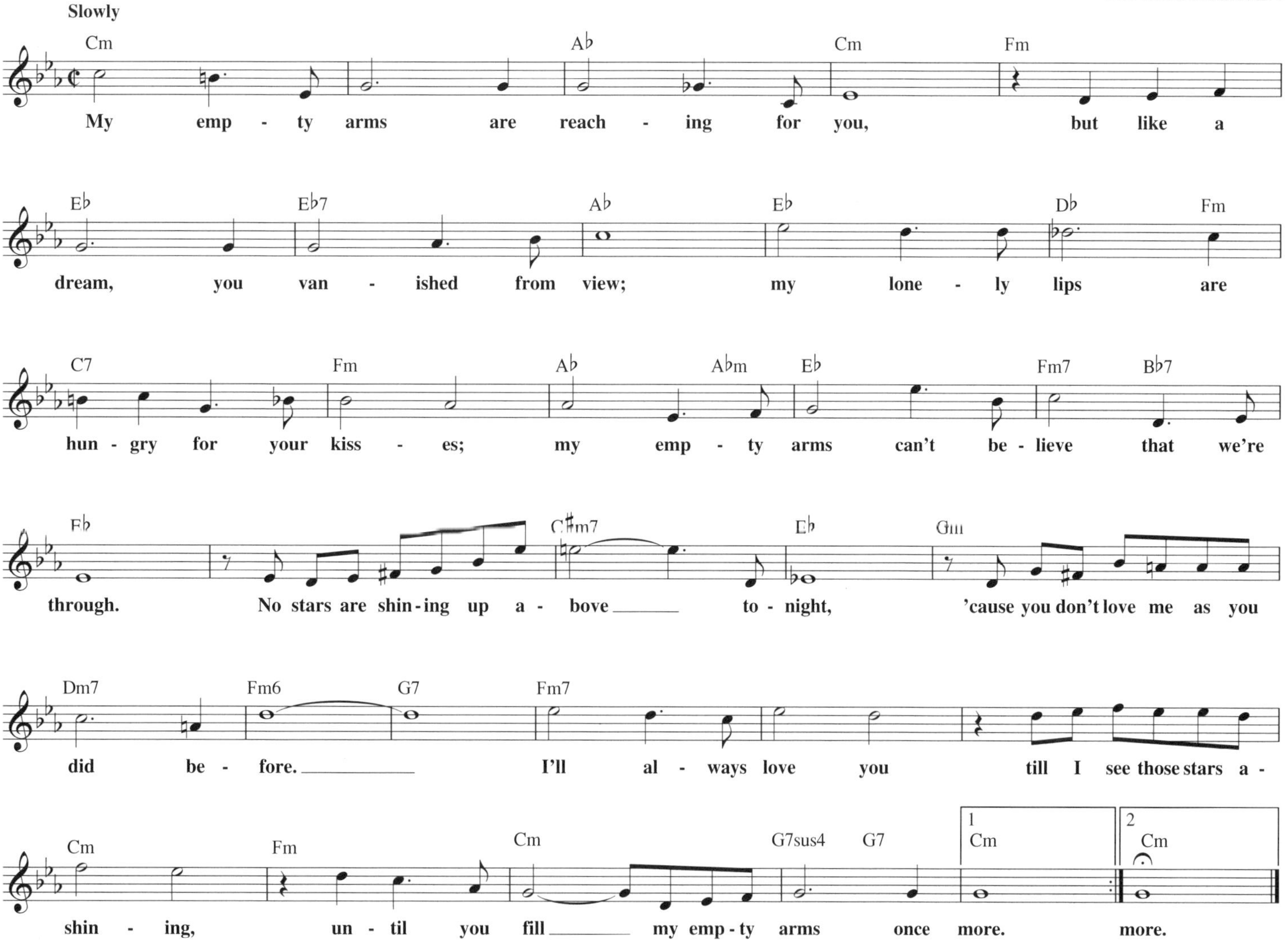

Slowly
Cm A♭ Cm Fm
My emp - ty arms are reach - ing for you, but like a
E♭ E♭7 A♭ E♭ D♭ Fm
dream, you van - ished from view; my lone - ly lips are
C7 Fm A♭ A♭m E♭ Fm7 B♭7
hun - gry for your kiss - es; my emp - ty arms can't be - lieve that we're
E♭ C♯m7 E♭ Gm
through. No stars are shin-ing up a - bove to - night, 'cause you don't love me as you
Dm7 Fm6 G7 Fm7
did be - fore. I'll al - ways love you till I see those stars a -
Cm Fm Cm G7sus4 G7 1 Cm 2 Cm
shin - ing, un - til you fill my emp-ty arms once more. more.

MOONLIGHT FEELS RIGHT

Words and Music by
MICHAEL BLACKMAN

Moderately fast

Em7 C6 Cmaj7

The wind blew some luck in my di - rec - tion; I caught it in my hands to - day. I
lay back and ob - serve the con - stel - la - tions and watch the moon smil - in' bright. I'll
see the sun come up on Sun - day morn - ing and watch it fade the moon a - way. I

Em7 C6 Cmaj7

fi - n'lly made a trick - y French con - nec - tion; you winked and gave me your O. K. I'll
play the ra - di - o on south - ern sta - tions, 'cause south - ern belles are hell at night. You
guess you know I'm giv - ing you a warn - ing, 'cause me and moon are itch - ing to play. I'll

A/B Cmaj7

take you on a trip be - side the o - cean and drop the top at Ches - a - peake Bay. Ain't
say you came to Bal - ti - more from Old Miss, a class of sev - en four gold ring. The
take you on a trip be - side the o - cean and drop the top at Ches - a - peake Bay. Ain't

A/B F/G G7sus To Coda

noth - ing like the sky to dose a po - tion; the moon - 'll send you on your way.
east - ern moon looks read - y for a wet kiss to make the tide rise a - gain.
noth - ing like the sky to dose a po - tion; the moon - 'll send you on your way.
Moon - light

Cmaj7 G7sus

feels right. Moon - light

Cmaj7 G7sus 1 2 D.S. al Coda

feels right. We'll We'll

CODA

Cmaj7 G7sus Repeat and Fade

feels right. Moon - light

MY LOVE

Words and Music by
PAUL and LINDA McCARTNEY

Slowly
B♭maj7
Am7
And when I go a - way I know my heart can stay with my love, it's un - der -
And when the cup - board's bare I'll still find some - thing there with my love, it's un - der -
Don't ev - er ask me why I nev - er say good - bye to my love, it's un - der -
D9
Gm7
Am7
B♭maj7
Dm
F
stood it's in the hands of my love.
stood it's ev - 'ry - where with my love.
stood it's ev - 'ry - where with my love.
And my love does it good, wo - wo wo - wo, wo - wo
Gm7
B♭
To Coda
1
F
2
F
Gm7
C7
wo - wo, my love does it good.
Wo - wo I love, oh wo,

F F+ B♭ C7 F F+ Gm7 C7
my love, on-ly my love holds the oth-er key to me. Oh wo, my love, oh,
F F+ B♭ C7 F Dm F Gm7
my love, on-ly my love does it good to me. Wo-wo wo-wo, wo-wo wo-wo,
B♭ F D.C. al Coda
my love does it good.
CODA
F Gm7 C7 F F+
Wo-wo, I love, oh wo, my love, on-ly
Gm7 C7 F F+ B♭ C13 F
my love does it good to me. Wo wo wo wo wo wo wo.

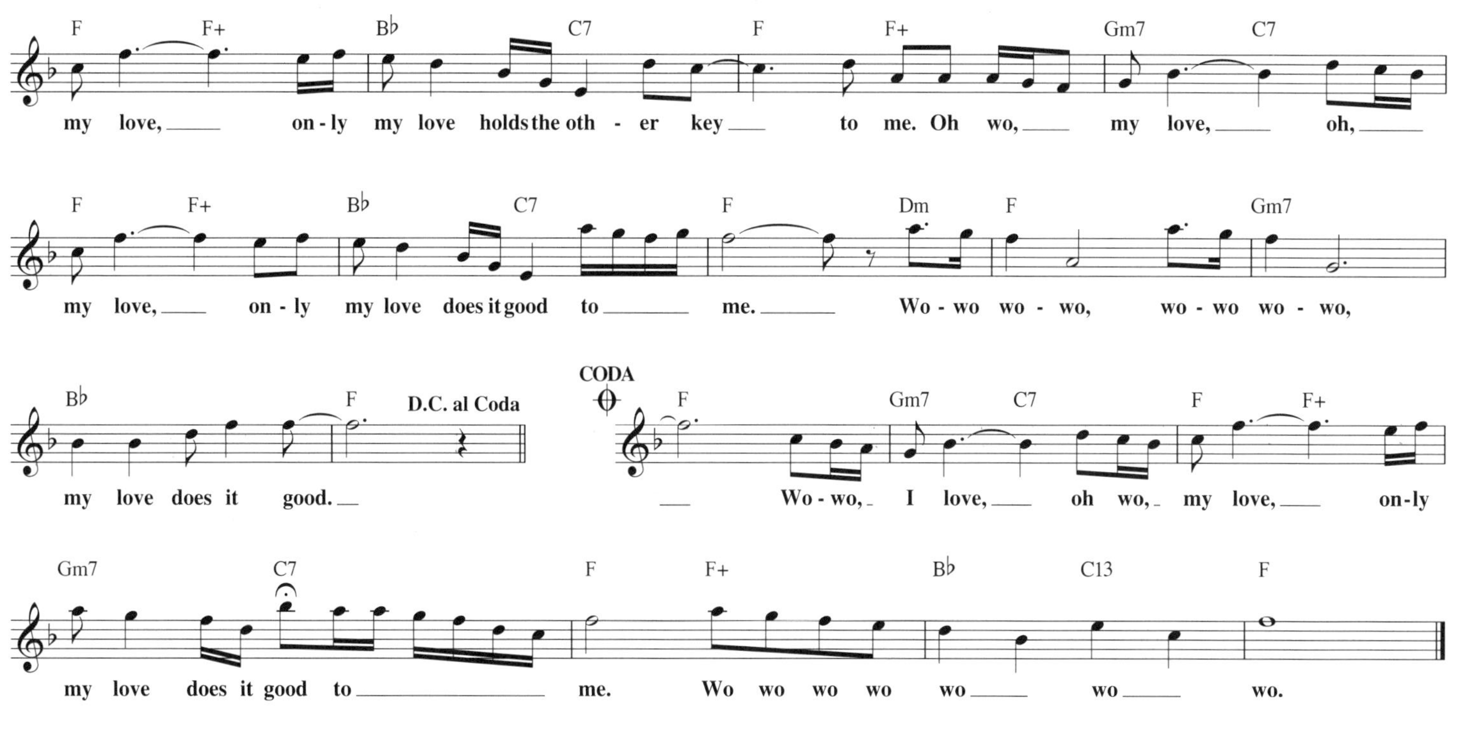

NIGHT

Words and Music by JOHNNY LEHMANN
and HERB MILLER

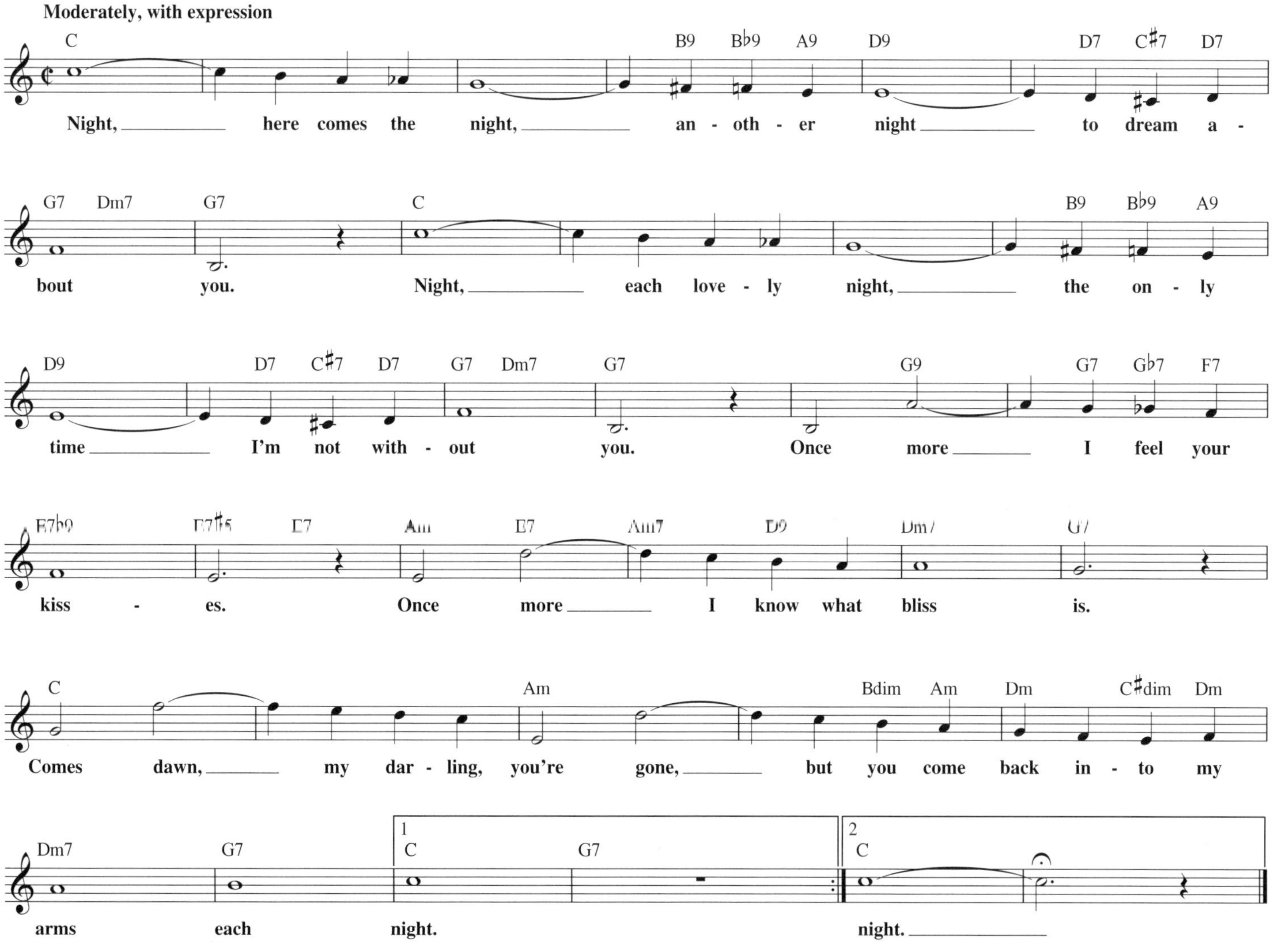

Moderately, with expression
C B9 B♭9 A9 D9 D7 C♯7 D7
Night, here comes the night, an-oth-er night to dream a-
G7 Dm7 G7 C B9 B♭9 A9
bout you. Night, each love-ly night, the on-ly
D9 D7 C♯7 D7 G7 Dm7 G7 G9 G7 G♭7 F7
time I'm not with-out you. Once more I feel your
E7♭9 E7♯5 E7 Am E7 Am7 D9 Dm7 G7
kiss-es. Once more I know what bliss is.
C Am Bdim Am Dm C♯dim Dm
Comes dawn, my dar-ling, you're gone, but you come back in-to my
Dm7 G7 1 C G7 2 C
arms each night. night.

MORE TODAY THAN YESTERDAY

Words and Music by
PAT UPTON

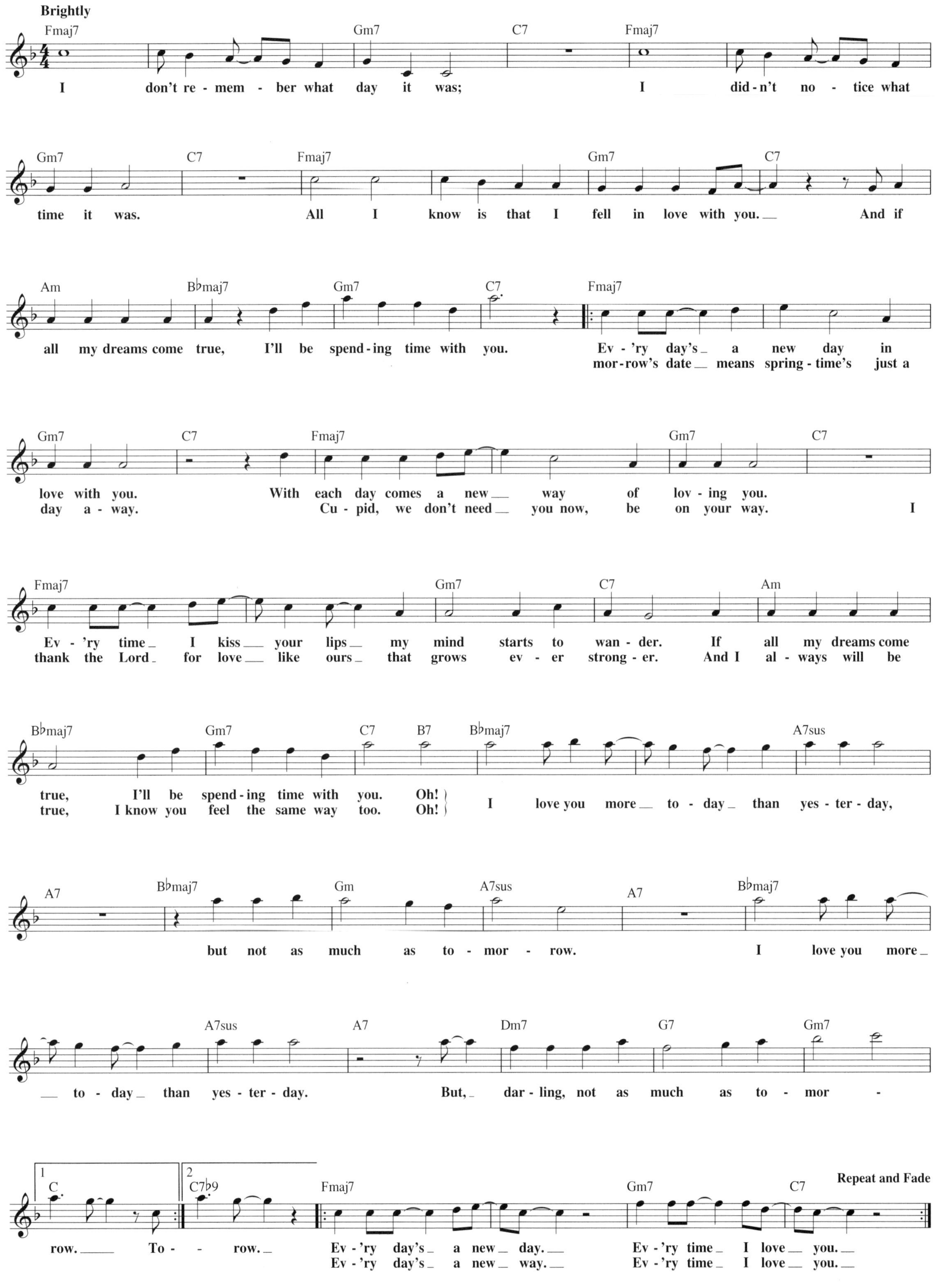
Brightly
Fmaj7 Gm7 C7 Fmaj7
I don't re - mem - ber what day it was; I did - n't no - tice what
Gm7 C7 Fmaj7 Gm7 C7
time it was. All I know is that I fell in love with you. And if
Am B♭maj7 Gm7 C7 Fmaj7
all my dreams come true, I'll be spend - ing time with you. Ev - 'ry day's a new day in
mor - row's date means spring - time's just a
Gm7 C7 Fmaj7 Gm7 C7
love with you. With each day comes a new way of lov - ing you.
day a - way. Cu - pid, we don't need you now, be on your way. I
Fmaj7 Gm7 C7 Am
Ev - 'ry time I kiss your lips my mind starts to wan - der. If all my dreams come
thank the Lord for love like ours that grows ev - er strong - er. And I al - ways will be
B♭maj7 Gm7 C7 B7 B♭maj7 A7sus
true, I'll be spend - ing time with you. Oh!
true, I know you feel the same way too. Oh!
I love you more to - day than yes - ter - day,
A7 B♭maj7 Gm A7sus A7 B♭maj7
but not as much as to - mor - row. I love you more
A7sus A7 Dm7 G7 Gm7
to - day than yes - ter - day. But, dar - ling, not as much as to - mor -
1 C 2 C7♭9 Fmaj7 Gm7 C7 Repeat and Fade
row. To - row. Ev - 'ry day's a new day. Ev - 'ry time I love you.
Ev - 'ry day's a new way. Ev - 'ry time I love you.

NEITHER ONE OF US (WANTS TO BE THE FIRST TO SAY GOODBYE)

Words and Music by
JIM WEATHERLY

Slowly
It's sad to think we're not gon-na make it, and it's got-ten to the point
where we just can't fake it, but for some un-god-ly rea-son, we
just won't let it die. I guess nei-ther one of us wants to be the first to say good-
bye. I keep won-d'ring what I'll do with-out you. And I
guess you must be won-der-ing that same thing too. So we go on to-
geth-er, liv-ing a lie, be-cause nei-ther one of us
wants to be the first to say good-bye. Ev-'ry time I find the nerve to say I'm leav-in',
old mem-o-ries get in the way. Lord knows it's on-ly me
that I'm de-ceiv-ing; when it comes to say-ing good-bye, that's a word I just can't
say. There can be no way this can have a hap-py end-ing. So we
just go on hurt-ing and pre-tend-ing, and con-vinc-ing our-selves to
give it just one more try. Be-cause nei-ther one of us wants to be the one to say good-
bye; Be-cause nei-ther one of us wants to be the first to say good-bye.

NEVER GONNA LET YOU GO

Words and Music by BARRY MANN
and CYNTHIA WEIL

Slowly
Gm7 Cm7 F(add2) B♭maj7/D
I was as wrong as I could be to let you get a-way from me.
Look-ing back, now it seems so clear. I had it all when you were here.
E♭(add2) B♭(add2)/D E♭/A♭ E♭/F F/G
I'll re-gret that move for as long as I'm liv-in'.
Oh, you gave it all and I took it for grant-ed.
Em7 Am7 D(add2) Gmaj7/B
But now that I've come to see the light, all I wan-na do is make things
But if there's some feel-ing left in you, some flick-er of love that still shines
C(add2) G(add2)/B C/D
right. So just say the word and tell me that I'm for-giv-en. And
through, let's talk it out. Let's talk a-bout sec-ond chanc-es. And
B♭(add2) F(add2)/A Gm7 C7/E C/F F
you and me, we're gon-na be bet-ter than we were be-fore. I
wait and see, it's gon-na be sweet-er than it was be-fore. I
C(add2) G(add2)/B F♯m7 B(add4)
loved you then but now I in-tend to o-pen up and love you e-ven more.
gave some then but now I in-tend to ded-i-cate my-self to giv-in' more.
B/E E B/E E D♯m7♭5 D♯m7♭5/G♯ Fm7
This time you can be sure.
This time you can be sure.
I'm nev-er gon-na let you go.
B♭m7 E♭(add2) A♭maj7/C D♭(add2)
I'm gon-na hold you in my arms for-ev-er. Gon-na try and make up for the times
G7 C(add2) B♭/C C/D F♯m7 Bm7
I hurt you so. Gon-na hold your bod-y close to mine. From this day on,

E(add2) Amaj7/C♯ D(add2) E(add2) F♯(add2)
we're gon-na be to-geth - er. Oh, I swear this time, I'm nev-er gon-na let you go.
F♯(add2) Fm7(add4) B♭7 B♭/E♭ E♭ Dm7(add4) G7(add4)
Oh, so if you just say you want me to, I'm
Em7 Am7 D(add2) Gmaj7/B
nev-er gon-na let you go. I'm gon-na hold you in my arms for-ev - er. Gon-na try
C(add2) F♯7 B(add2) A/B B/C♯ Fm7
and make up for the times I hurt you so. Gon - na hold your bod-y close to mine.
B♭m7 E♭(add2) A♭maj7/C D♭(add2)
From this day on, we're gon-na be to-geth - er. Oh, I swear this time, I'm
E♭(add2) F E♭/F F/G B♭m7 E♭m7
nev-er gon-na let you go. Nev-er gon-na let you go.
A♭(add2) D♭maj7/F G♭(add2) C7
Hold you in my arms for-ev - er. Gon-na try and make up for the times I hurt you so.
F E♭/F F/G B♭m7 E♭m7 A♭(add2)
Hold your bod-y close to mine. Al-ways gon-na be to-geth-
Repeat and Fade
D♭maj7/F G♭(add2) A♭(add2) B♭(add2) E♭/F F/G
- er. Oh, I swear this time, I'm nev-er gon-na let you go.

1999

Words and Music by
PRINCE

Moderately
I was dream - in' when I wrote this, for - give me if it goes a - stray,
dream - in' when I wrote this, so sue me if I go 2 fast,
but when I woke up this morn - ing, I could-'ve sworn it was judg - ment day.
but life is just a par - ty, and par - ties weren't meant 2 last.
The sky was all pur - ple, there were peo - ple run - nin' ev - 'ry - where;
War is all a - round us, my mind says pre - pare 2 fight.
try - in' 2 run from the de - struc - tion, and U know I did - n't e - ven care.
So if I got - ta die, I'm gon - na lis - ten 2 my bod - y 2 - night.
'Cuz they say two thou - sand, ze - ro, ze - ro, par - ty o - ver, oops, out of time.
So 2 - night I'm gon - na par - ty like it's nine - teen nine - ty - nine.
To Coda
I was
If U did - n't come 2 par - ty, don't both - er knock - in' on my door.
I got a li - on in my pock - et and, ba - by, he's read - y 2 roar.
Ev - 'ry - bod - y's got a bomb, we could all die an - y day. But be -
fore I let that hap - pen, I'll dance my life a - way. 'Cuz they say two
D.S. al Coda

CODA
F6 Gm/F F6 Gm/F F6 Gm/F
Nine - teen nine - ty - nine. Don't U wan-na
F6 Gm/F F6 Gm/F F6 Gm/F F6
Repeat and Fade
go? Nine - teen nine - ty - nine. Don't U wan na go? Nine - teen nine - ty - nine.

THE NIGHT OWLS

Words and Music by
GRAHAM GOBLE

Shuffle

C Em
1. There's a bar right a-cross the street, he's got a need he just can't beat,
2.,3. *(See additional lyrics)*

C Em
out on the floor he shuf - fles his feet a - way,

C Em
he'll get the girl 'cause he looks so fine, he's gon - na win her ev - 'ry - time, he knows

C B7 Em
he will, he's dressed to kill, he's a night owl. Move on,

C Em C
there's a heart of a night owl call - ing, to be - long,

Em C
she's cry - in' in the night, be strong, find the heart of the

Em C To Coda Am B7
night owl fall - ing, stay up till dawn, un - til the night has gone.

1 Em | 2 C B7 Em D.C. al Coda

CODA
B7 Em
til the night has gone.

Additional Lyrics

2. What will become of the restless kind,
Where do they go when they've done their time,
Wearin' their hearts out on the line for all to see,
Must be the gipsy in their soul,
They have a need to rock 'n' roll,
They always will, they're out there still,
They're The Night Owls.
To Chorus:

3. There's a bar right across the street,
He's got a need he just can't beat,
Out on the floor he shuffles his feet away, yeah, yeah,
He'll get the girl 'cause he looks so fine,
He's gonna win her every time,
He knows he will, he's out there still,
He's a night owl.
To Chorus:

THE NIGHT CHICAGO DIED

Music by MITCH MURRAY
Lyrics by PETER CALLENDER

Moderately
Dm
G7
In the heat of a sum - mer night in the land of the dol - lar
rang through the streets of the old east
C
Dm
G7
bill When the town of Chi - ca - go died And they talk a - bout it
side Till the last of the hood - lum gang had sur - ren - dered up or
all but the clock up - on the
C
Dm
G7
C
still when a man named Al Ca - pone tried to make that town his own And he called his gang to
died There was shout - ing in the street and the sound of run - ning feet And I asked some - one who
wall Then the door burst o - pen wide and my Dad - dy stepped in - side and he kissed my Ma - ma's
Dm
G7
To Coda
N.C.
C
war with the forc - es of the law
said "Bout a hun - dred cops are dead"
face and he brushed her tears a -
I heard my Ma - ma cry. I heard her pray the night Chi -
Dm
G7
ca - go died Broth - er what a night it real - ly was
C
broth - er what a fight it real - ly was Glo - ry be I heard my Ma - ma cry
Dm
I heard her pray the night Chi - ca - go died.
G7
Broth - er what a night the peo - ple saw broth - er what a fight the peo - ple saw
C
1
2
D.S. al Coda
Yes in - deed And the sound of the bat - tle Then there was no sound at
CODA
C
Dm
way the night Chi - ca - go died The night Chi -
G7
ca - go died Broth - er what a night the peo - ple saw
Broth - er what a night it real - ly was
C
N.C.
Repeat and Fade
broth - er what a fight the peo - ple saw yes in - deed
broth - er what a fight it real - ly was glo - ry be
The night Chi -

NO MATTER WHAT

Written by
PETER HAM

Medium Power Rock

A Bm D E D E A E N.C.

No mat-ter what you are, I will al-ways be with you. Does-n't mat-ter what you do, girl. Ooh, girl, want you. No mat-ter where you

A Bm D E D E A

go, I will al-ways be a-round. Won't you tell me what you found, girl? Ooh, girl, want you.

F♯m7 B7 E A D7 Bm A

Knock down the old gray wall. Be a part of it all. Noth-ing to say, noth-ing to see, noth-ing to do.

F♯m7 B7 E A D7 Bm G E N.C.

If you would give me all, as I would give it to you, noth-ing would be, noth-ing would be, noth-ing would be.

A Bm D E D E To Coda A

{No mat-ter where you go, there will al-ways be a place. Can't you see it in my face, girl?
{No mat-ter what you are, I will al-ways be with you. Does-n't mat-ter what you do, girl.}

Ooh, girl, want you.

Bm D E D E A D.S. al Coda

(Instrumental)

CODA

A D E D E A D E D E A

you. Ooh, girl, you, girl, want you. Ooh, girl, you, girl, want you.

NO NO SONG

Words and Music by HOYT ARTON
and DAVID JACKSON, JR.

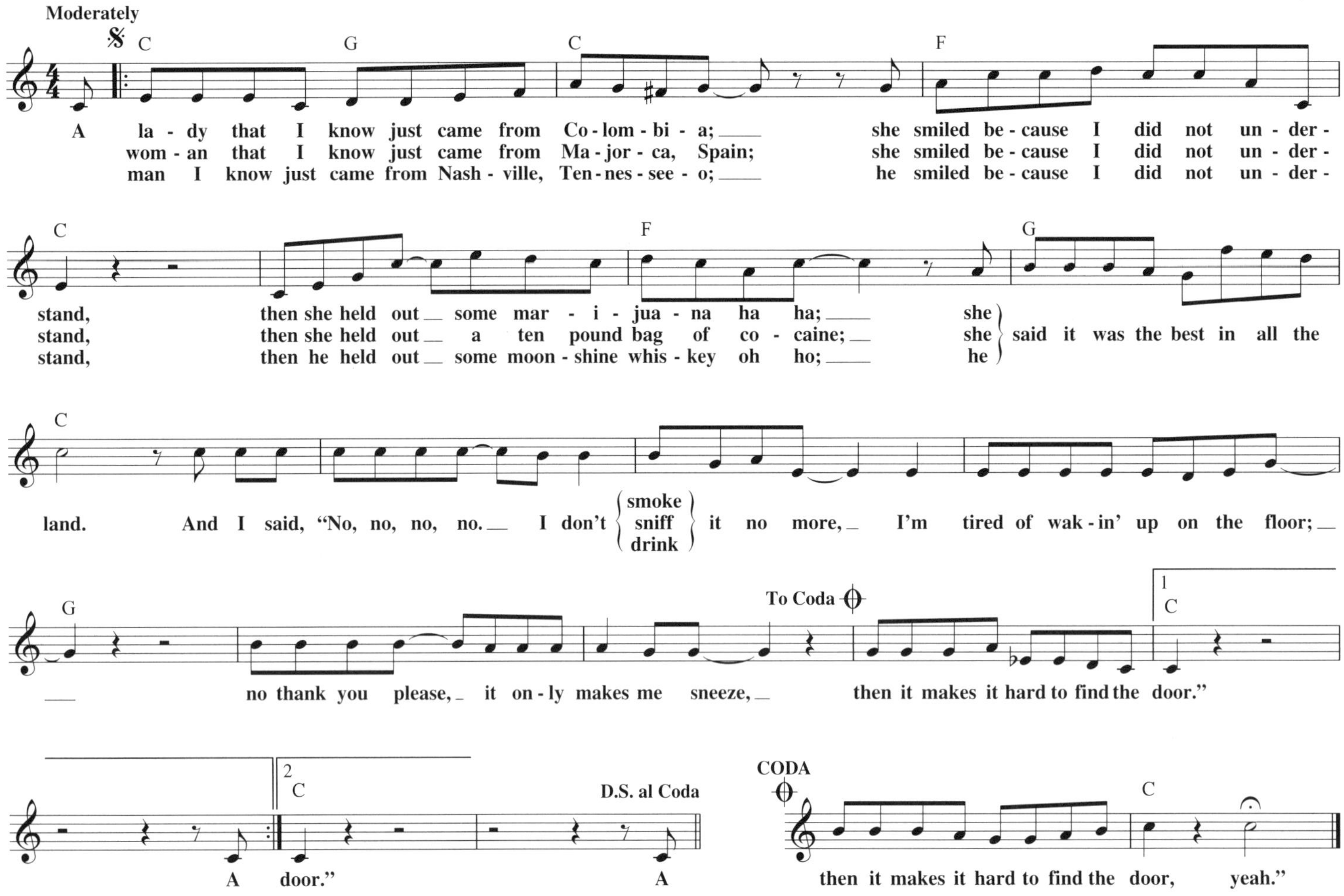

Moderately

C G C F
A la - dy that I know just came from Co - lom - bi - a; she smiled be - cause I did not un - der -
wom - an that I know just came from Ma - jor - ca, Spain; she smiled be - cause I did not un - der -
man I know just came from Nash - ville, Ten - nes - see - o; he smiled be - cause I did not un - der -

C F G
stand, then she held out some mar - i - jua - na ha ha; she said it was the best in all the
stand, then she held out a ten pound bag of co - caine; she
stand, then he held out some moon - shine whis - key oh ho; he

C
land. And I said, "No, no, no, no. I don't {smoke / sniff / drink} it no more, I'm tired of wak - in' up on the floor;

G To Coda 1 C
no thank you please, it on - ly makes me sneeze, then it makes it hard to find the door."

2 C D.S. al Coda CODA C
A door." A then it makes it hard to find the door, yeah."

NO, NOT MUCH!

Words by AL STILLMAN
Music by ROBERT ALLEN

Moderately slow
E♭ A♭dim7 E♭/G Edim7 Fm7 B♭7 Fm7 B♭7 B♭7♭9 E♭ A♭dim7
I don't want my arms a - round you no, not much! I don't bless the
I don't care to hug and kiss you When you're gone I
E♭ Edim7 Fm7 B♭7 Fm7 B♭7 B♭7♭9 E♭7 G7 G♯5
day I found you no, not much! I don't need you like the stars don't
nev - er miss you Like a ten cent so - da does - n't
A♭dim7 A♭ F7 Cm7 F7 Fm7 B♭7
need the sky I won't love you long - er than the day I die.
cost a dime. I don't want you near me, on - ly all the time.
E♭ A♭dim7 E♭ Edim7 Fm7 B♭7 Fm7 B♭7 A♭7♭5
You don't please me when you squeeze me no, not much! My
You don't thrill me when you hold me My

Bbm6 Bbm7 C7 Fm Ab
head's the light - est from your ver - y slight - est touch,
brain gets haz - y from your cool and cra - zy touch,
ba - by, if you
Abm Gm7b5 C7 Fm Bb7 Fm7/Bb Bb7b9
ev - er go, could I take it? May - be so. Ah, but would I like it? No, not
1 Eb Fm7 Bb9
much!
2 Gm7b5 C7b9 Fm7 E7 Eb
much! No, not much!

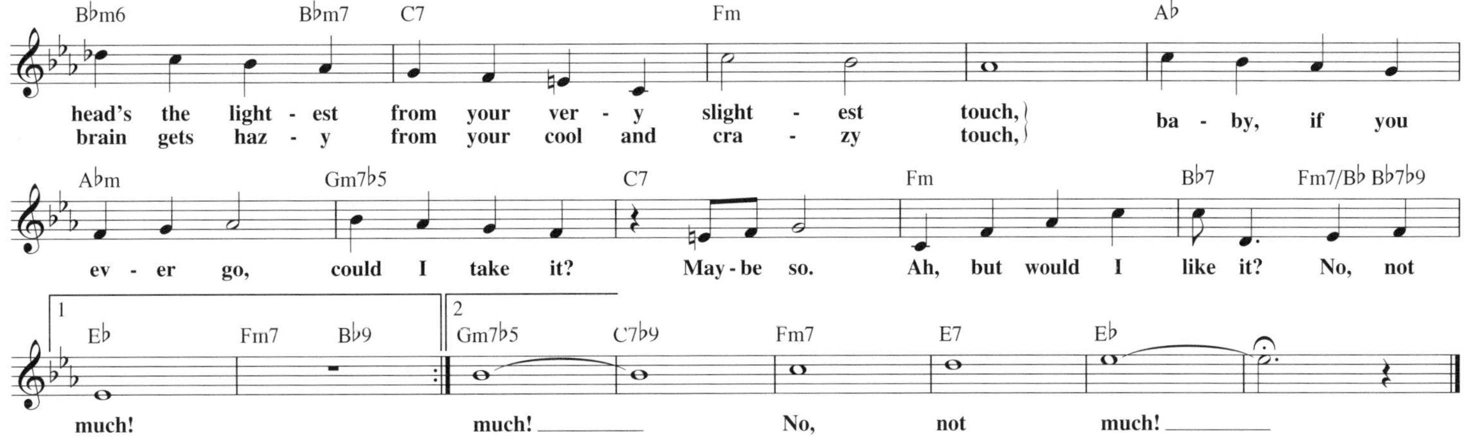

NORMAN

Words and Music by
JOHN D. LOUDERMILK

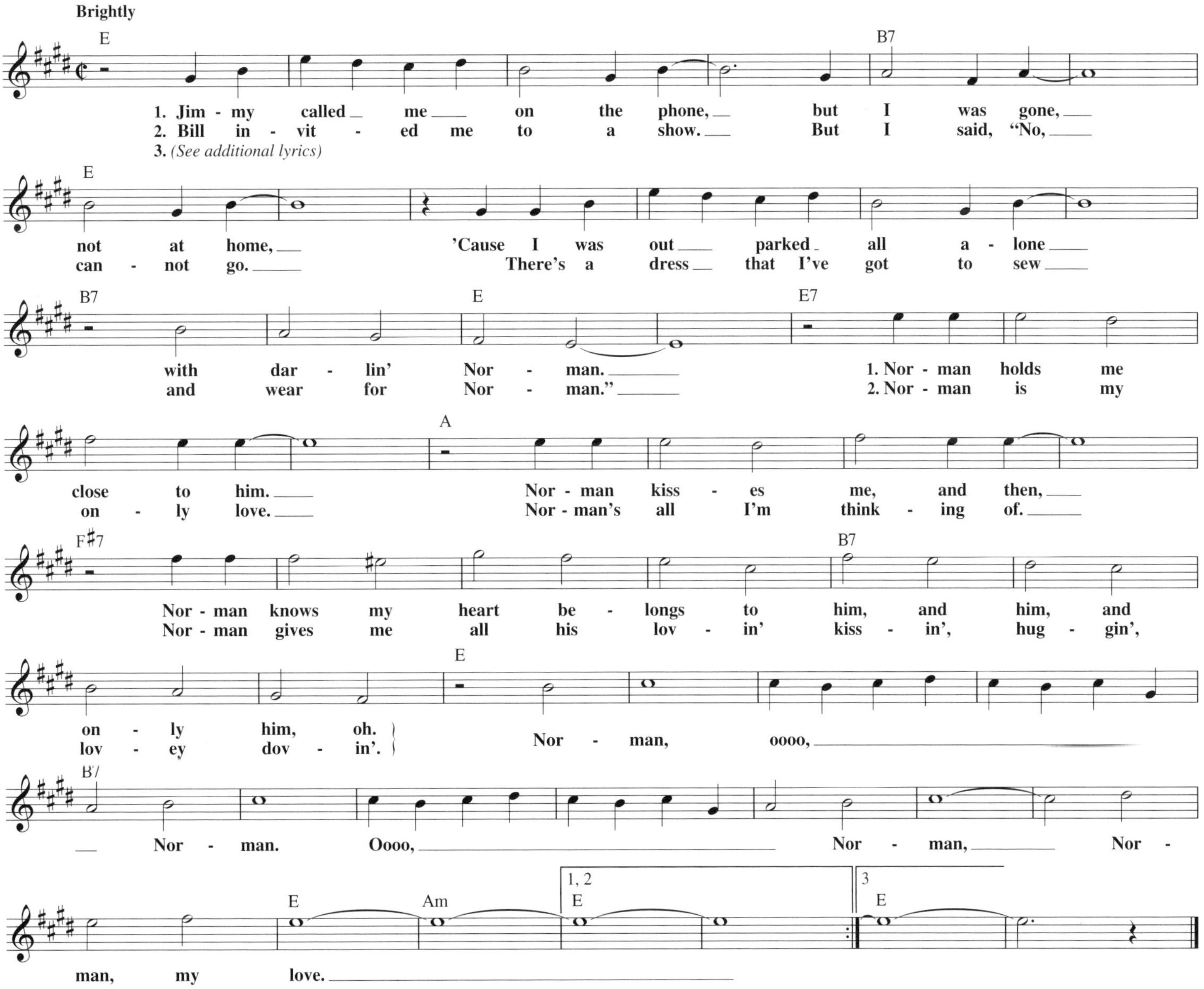

Brightly
E B7
1. Jim - my called me on the phone, but I was gone,
2. Bill in - vit - ed me to a show. But I said, "No,
3. (See additional lyrics)
E
not at home, 'Cause I was out parked all a - lone
can - not go. There's a dress that I've got to sew
B7 E E7
with dar - lin' Nor - man.
and wear for Nor - man."
1. Nor - man holds me
2. Nor - man is my
A
close to him. Nor - man kiss - es me, and then,
on - ly love. Nor - man's all I'm think - ing of.
F#7 B7
Nor - man knows my heart be - longs to him, and him, and
Nor - man gives me all his lov - in' kiss - in', hug - gin',
E
on - ly him, oh.
lov - ey dov - in'.
Nor - man, oooo,
B7
Nor - man. Oooo, Nor - man, Nor -
E Am 1, 2 E 3 E
man, my love.

Additional Lyrics

3. Joey asked me for a date.
He wanted to take me out to skate.
But I told Joey he would have to make
Arrangements with Norman.
Chorus (take 2nd Verse)

#9 DREAM

Words and Music by
JOHN LENNON

Moderate Rock Ballad

C Em F E7 Fmaj7
So long a - go was it dream?

C7 Fmaj7 G7
Was it just a dream? I know

C Em F E7
yes, I know it seemed so ve - ry

Fmaj7 D7 Fmaj7 G7
real. It seemed so real to me.

Took a walk down the street

through the heat whis - pered trees I thought I could

Em9 C7 Em9 B♭9 Em9 C7
hear, hear, hear,

Em9 A7 Em7 A7
hear some - bo - dy call out my name

Em7 A7 Em7 A7
as it start - ed to rain. Two spir - its danc - ing so strange.

Gm7 C7 Play 3 times D7
An Bow - a Ka Wa - pous - sé, pous - sé

To Coda
G7 C Em F
Dream dream a - way;

E7 Fmaj7 D7 Fmaj7 G7
ma - gic in the air, was ma - gic in the air
C Em F E7
I be - lieve yes, I be - lieve; more I can - not
Fmaj7 D7 Fmaj7 G7
say. What more can I say?

On a riv - er of sound
through the mir - ror go round and round
I thought I could feel,
Em9
A7
feel,
feel,
Em7
A7
Em7
feel,
mus - ic touch - ing my
A7
soul.
Em7
Some - thing warm; sud - den cold.
A7
Em7
The spi - rit dance was un -
A7
D.S. al Coda
fold - ing.
CODA
Gm7
C7
Repeat and Fade
Ah! Bow - a Ka Wa - pous - sé, pous - sé

NOWHERE MAN

Words and Music by JOHN LENNON
and PAUL McCARTNEY

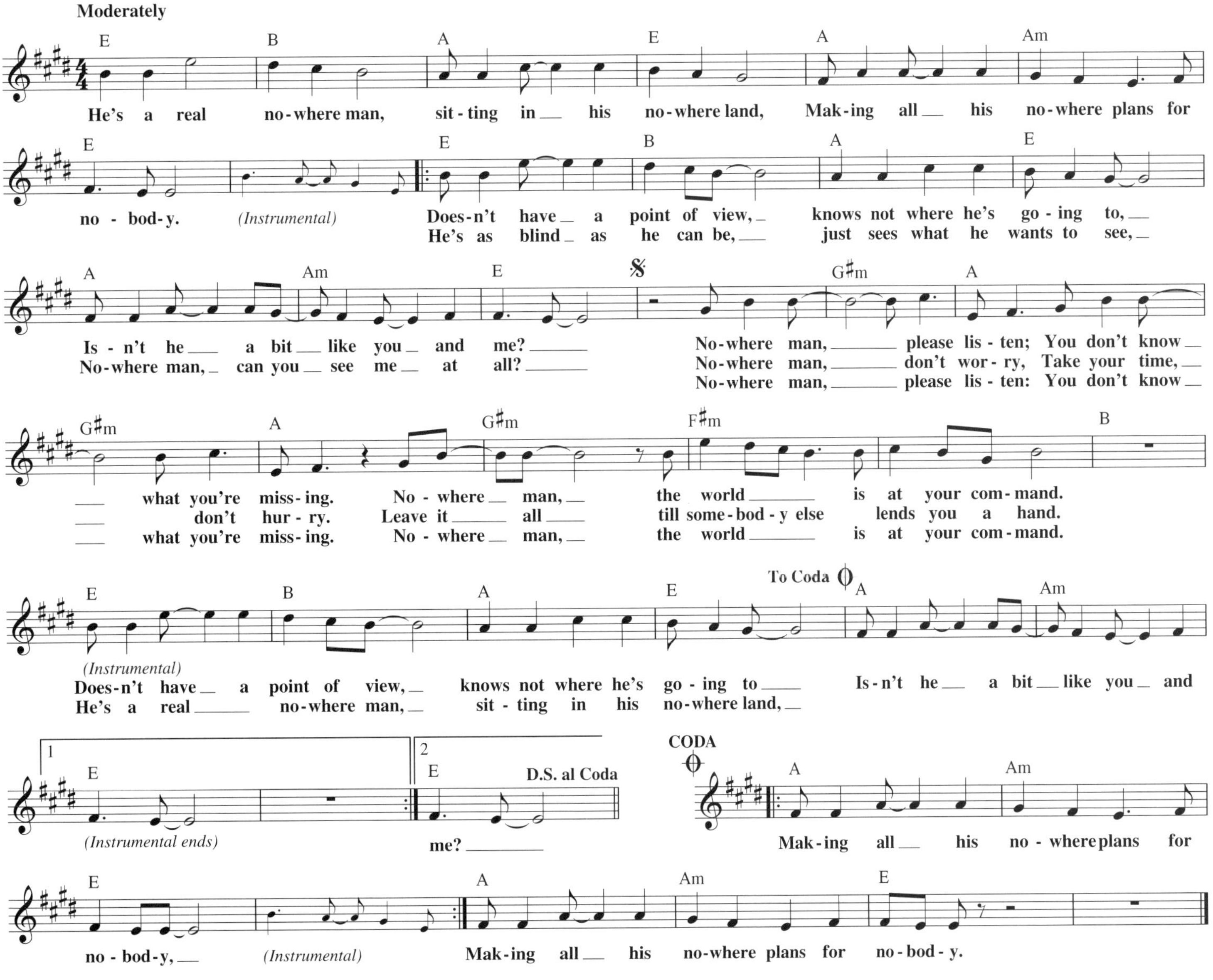

Moderately

E B A E A Am
He's a real no - where man, sit - ting in his no - where land, Mak - ing all his no - where plans for

E E B A E
no - bod - y. *(Instrumental)* Does - n't have a point of view, knows not where he's go - ing to,
He's as blind as he can be, just sees what he wants to see,

A Am E 𝄋 G♯m A
Is - n't he a bit like you and me? No - where man, please lis - ten; You don't know
No - where man, can you see me at all? No - where man, don't wor - ry, Take your time,
No - where man, please lis - ten: You don't know

G♯m A G♯m F♯m B
what you're miss - ing. No - where man, the world is at your com - mand.
don't hur - ry. Leave it all till some - bod - y else lends you a hand.
what you're miss - ing. No - where man, the world is at your com - mand.

E B A E To Coda A Am
(Instrumental)
Does - n't have a point of view, knows not where he's go - ing to Is - n't he a bit like you and
He's a real no - where man, sit - ting in his no - where land,

1. E *(Instrumental ends)*
2. E D.S. al Coda
me?

CODA
A Am
Mak - ing all his no - where plans for

E A Am E
no - bod - y, *(Instrumental)* Mak - ing all his no - where plans for no - bod - y.

NO RAIN

Words and Music by
BLIND MELON

Moderately fast
E D A G E
All I can say is that my life is pret-ty plain, I like watch-in' the pud - dles gath - er rain.
D A G
And all I can do is just pour some tea for two and speak my point of view but it's not
E D E D
sane. It's not sane. I just want some - one to say to me, oh,
E D E D E D
I'll al-ways be there when you wake, yeah. You know I'd like to keep
E D
my cheeks dry to-day.
To Coda
E D E D
So stay with me and I'll have it made.
E D A G
And I don't un-der-stand why I sleep all day and I start to com-plain that there's no
E D A
rain. And all I can do is read a book to stay a-wake, and it rips my life a-way
G E
but it's a great es - cape. Es - cape, es - cape, es - cape.
E D E D
Play 4 times
Guitar solo ad lib.
E D
All I can say is that my life is pret-ty plain,
A G E
you don't like my point of view, you think that I'm in - sane. It's not
D.S. al Coda
sane, it's not sane.
CODA
E
and I'll have it made.

OH BOY!

Words and Music by SUNNY WEST,
BILL TILGHMAN and NORMAN PETTY

Bright tempo

G

1., 3. All of my love, all of my kiss - in', you don't know what you been miss - in', oh boy!
2. All of my life I been wait - in', to - night there'll be no hes - i - tat - in', oh boy!

C G C♯dim7 D7 To Coda

(Oh boy!) When you're with me, oh boy! (Oh boy!) The world can see that you were meant for

1. G C D7 — me.
2. G C G D7 — me.

Stars ap - pear and shad - ows fall - in',

G C

you can hear my heart call - in'. A lit - tle bit o' lov - in' makes ev - 'ry - thing right, an'

D7 D.C. al Coda

I'm gon - na see my ba - by to - night!

CODA

G C6 G

me.

ONLY LOVE CAN BREAK A HEART

Lyric by HAL DAVID
Music by BURT BACHARACH

Moderately slow

B♭ B♭7 E♭ F7 B♭ A♭ G7 E♭6 F

Last night I hurt you, but dar - lin', re - mem - ber this, on - ly love can break a heart,
sor - ry, I'll prove it with just one kiss, on - ly love can break a heart,

E♭6 F F7

on - ly love can mend it a -
on - ly love can mend it a -

1. B♭ B♭7 — gain. You know I'm
2. B♭ F7 B♭ B♭7 — gain. Give me a

E♭ Cm B♭ B♭7 E♭ C7

chance to make up for the harm I've done. Try to for - give me and let's keep the

F7 E♭ F7 N.C. E♭ F7 B♭

two of us one! Please let me hold you and love you for al - ways and

G7 E♭6 F E♭6 F F7 B♭ E♭ B♭

al - ways, on - ly love can break a heart, on - ly love can mend it a - gain.

ONCE BITTEN TWICE SHY

Words and Music by
IAN HUNTER

Moderate Rock beat
C
G5
Well, the times are get - tin' hard for you, lit - tle girl. I'm a hum - min' and a strum - min' all
mid - dle of the night on the o - pen road. The heat - er don't work and it's,
wom - an, you're a mess, gon - na die in your sleep. There's blood on my amp and my
(Instrumental)
Dm
C5
o - ver God's world. You can't re - mem - ber when you had your last meal,
oh, so cold. You're look - in' tired, you're look - in' kind - a beat. The
Les Paul's beat. Can't keep you home, you're mess - in' a - round. My
G5
Dm
B♭5
and you don't know just how a wom - an feels. You did - n't know what
rhy - thm of the street sure knocks you off your feet. You did - n't know how
best friend told me you're the best lick in town. You did - n't know that
(Instrumental ends)
I did - n't know you had a
E♭
rock and roll was un - til you met my drum - mer on the Grey tour bus. I
rock and roll looked un - til you caught your sis - ter with the guys from the group. Half -
rock and roll burned so you bought a can - dle and you lived and you learned.
rock and roll rec - ord un - til I saw your pic - ture on an - oth - er guy's jacket.
B♭5
E♭
got there in the nick of time, be - fore he got his hands a - cross
- way home in the park - ing lot, by the look in her eye, she was
You got the rhy - thm. You got the speed. Ma - ma's lit - tle ba - by likes it
You told me I was the on - ly one. But look at you now, it's as
To Coda
1
C5
your state line. Yeah.
giv - in' what she got. I said
short and sweet. I said
dark as it's gone. I said...
(Instrumental)
2, 3
C
F
Now, it's the my, my, my, I'm once bit - ten twice shy, babe. ba - by.
C
F
My, my, my, I'm once bit - ten twice shy, ba - by. babe.
C
F
My, my, my, I'm once bit - ten twice shy, ba - by.
G5
1
2
D.S. al Coda
Oh, Al - right!

CODA
C F5
My, my, my, I'm once bit - ten twice shy, babe.
C F5
My, my, my, I'm once bit - ten twice shy, ba - by.
C5 F5
My, my, my, I'm once bit - ten twice shy, ba - by.
C F5
Repeat and Fade
My, my, my, I'm once bit - ten twice shy.

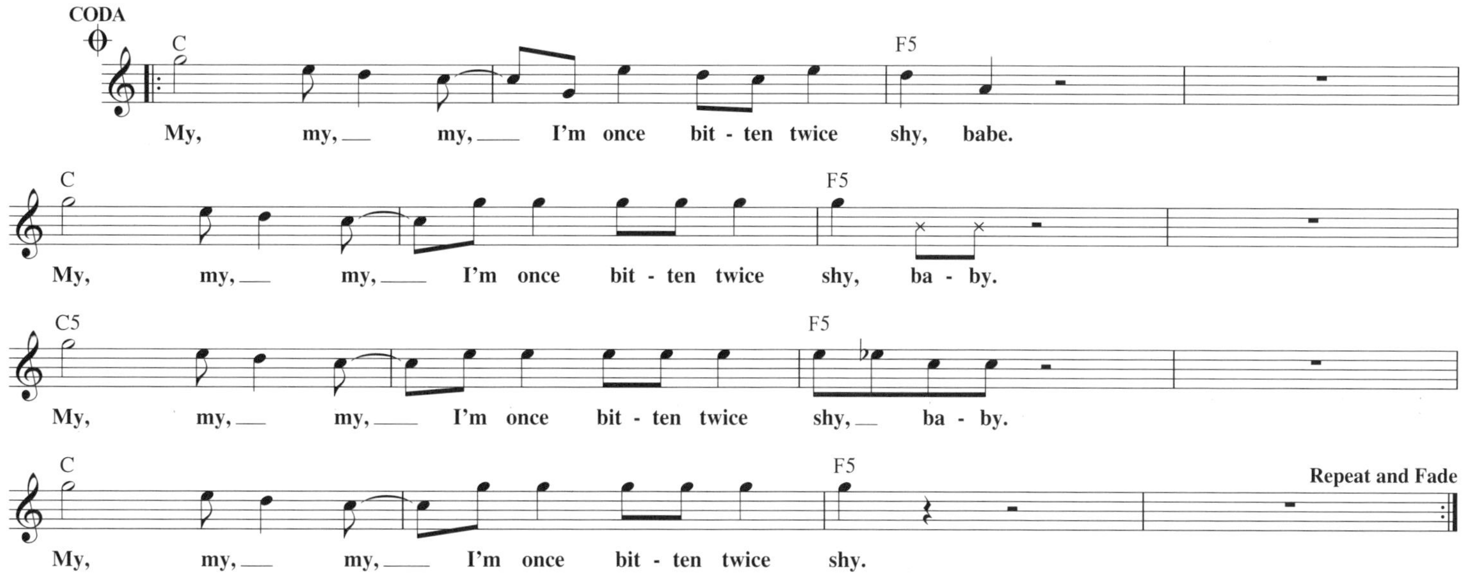

OH, OH I'M FALLING IN LOVE AGAIN

Words and Music by DICK MANNING, AL HOFFMAN and MARK MARKWELL

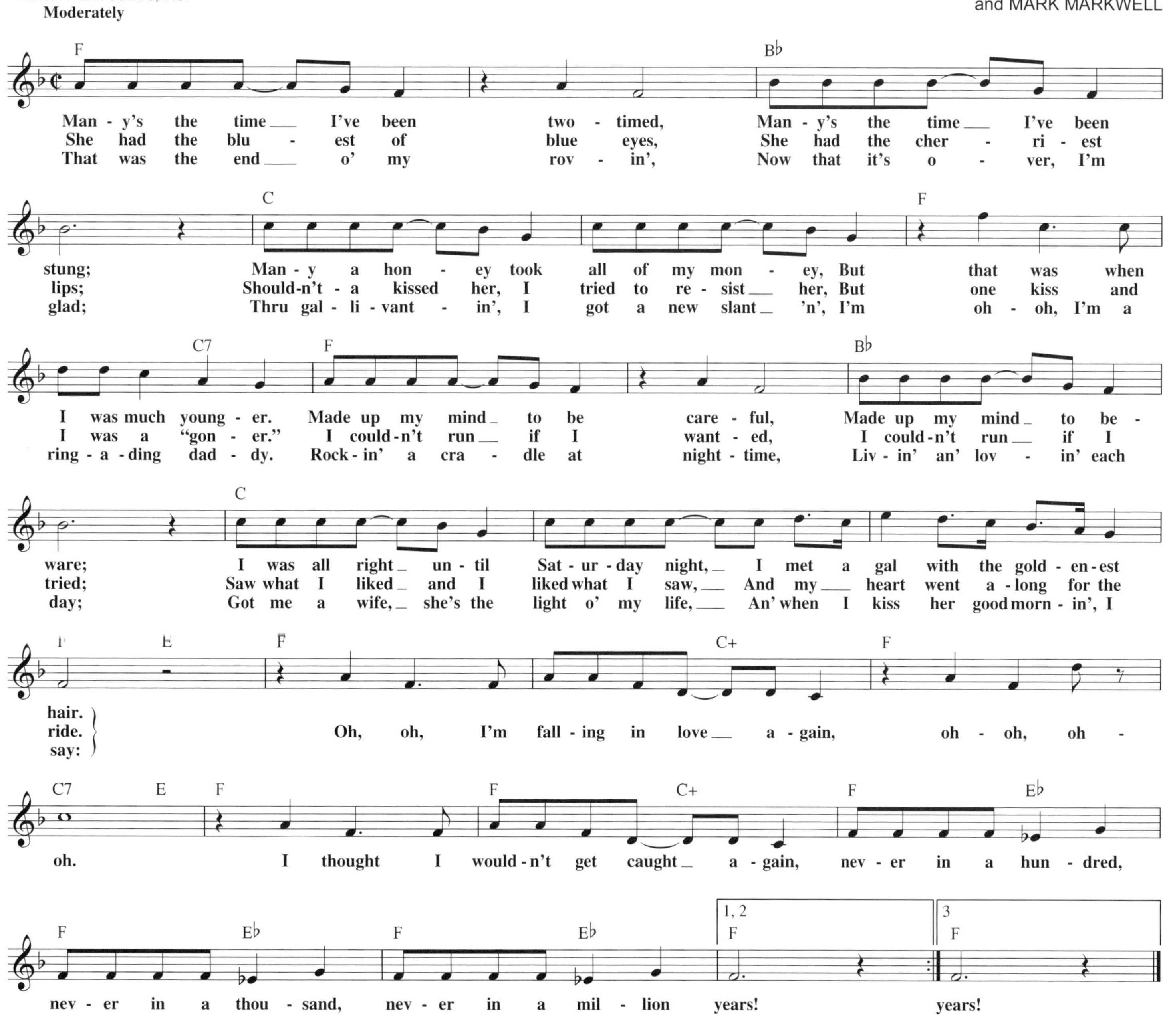
Moderately
F Bb
Man - y's the time I've been two - timed, Man - y's the time I've been
She had the blu - est of blue eyes, She had the cher - ri - est
That was the end o' my rov - in', Now that it's o - ver, I'm
C F
stung; Man - y a hon - ey took all of my mon - ey, But that was when
lips; Should-n't - a kissed her, I tried to re - sist her, But one kiss and
glad; Thru gal - li - vant - in', I got a new slant 'n', I'm oh - oh, I'm a
C7 F Bb
I was much young - er. Made up my mind to be care - ful, Made up my mind to be -
I was a "gon - er." I could-n't run if I want - ed, I could-n't run if I
ring - a - ding dad - dy. Rock - in' a cra - dle at night - time, Liv - in' an' lov - in' each
C
ware; I was all right un - til Sat - ur - day night, I met a gal with the gold - en - est
tried; Saw what I liked and I liked what I saw, And my heart went a - long for the
day; Got me a wife, she's the light o' my life, An' when I kiss her good morn - in', I
F E F C+ F
hair.
ride.
say:
Oh, oh, I'm fall - ing in love a - gain, oh - oh, oh -
C7 E F F C+ F Eb
oh. I thought I would - n't get caught a - gain, nev - er in a hun - dred,
F Eb F Eb 1, 2 F 3 F
nev - er in a thou - sand, nev - er in a mil - lion years! years!

100 YEARS

Words and Music by
JOHN ONDRASIK

Moderately fast
G C Am7 D7sus G/B
I'm fif - teen for a mo-ment, caught in be - tween ten and twen-ty and I'm just dream - ing,
Em Am7 Dsus D G C
count-ing the ways to where you are. I'm twen - ty - two for a mo-ment
Am7 D7sus G/B Em Am7
and she feels bet - ter than ev-er and we're on fire, mak-ing our way back from Mars.
D G D C(add9) G D C(add9)
Fif - teen, there's still time for you. Time to buy and time to lose.
G D C(add9) Em7 D C(add9)
Fif - teen, there's nev-er a wish bet-ter than this when you on-ly got a hun-
G/B G5/C Em7 D G/B C(add9) Em7 Dsus G
-dred years to live. (Instrumental) I'm thir - ty - three
C Am7 D7sus G/B Em
for a mo-ment, I'm still the man, but you see I'm a they; a kid on the way, a
Am7 Dsus G C Am7 D7sus
fam-'ly on my mind. I'm for - ty - five for a mo-ment, the sea is high and I'm head-ing in-to
G/B Em Am7 Dsus D G
a cri - sis, chas-ing the years of my life. Fif - teen, there's
D C(add9) G D C(add9) Em7 Dsus
still time for you. Time to buy and time to lose your-self with-in a morn - ing star.

C(add9) G D C(add9) G D C(add9)
Fif - teen, I'm all right with you. Fif - teen, there's nev-er a wish
Em7 D C(add9) C
bet-ter than this when you on - ly got a hun - dred years to live. Half time goes by,
Dsus Em Fmaj7 C(add9)
sud-den-ly you're wise. An-oth - er blink of an eye, six - ty - sev - en is gone. The sun is get-ting high,
Dsus G C Am7 D7sus G
we're mov - ing on... I'm nine - ty - nine
C(add9) Am7 D7sus G/B Em
for a mo-ment, I'm dying for just an-oth-er mo-ment and I'm just dream - ing, count-ing the ways
Am7 Dsus D G D C(add9) G
to where you are. Fif - teen, there's still time for you. Twen - ty - two,
D C(add9) G D C(add9) G D C(add9)
I feel her too. Thir - ty - three, you're on your way. Ev - 'ry day's a new day...
G D Em7 C(add9) G D Em7
Ooh, ooh, ooh.
C(add9) G D Em7 C(add9)
Fif - teen, there's still time for you. Time to buy and time to choose.
G D Em7 D C(add9)
Hey, fif - teen, there's nev-er a wish bet-ter than this when you on - ly got a hun -
G C Am7 Dsus
- dred years to live. (Instrumental)

ONE NIGHT

Words and Music by DAVE BARTHOLOMEW
and PEARL KING

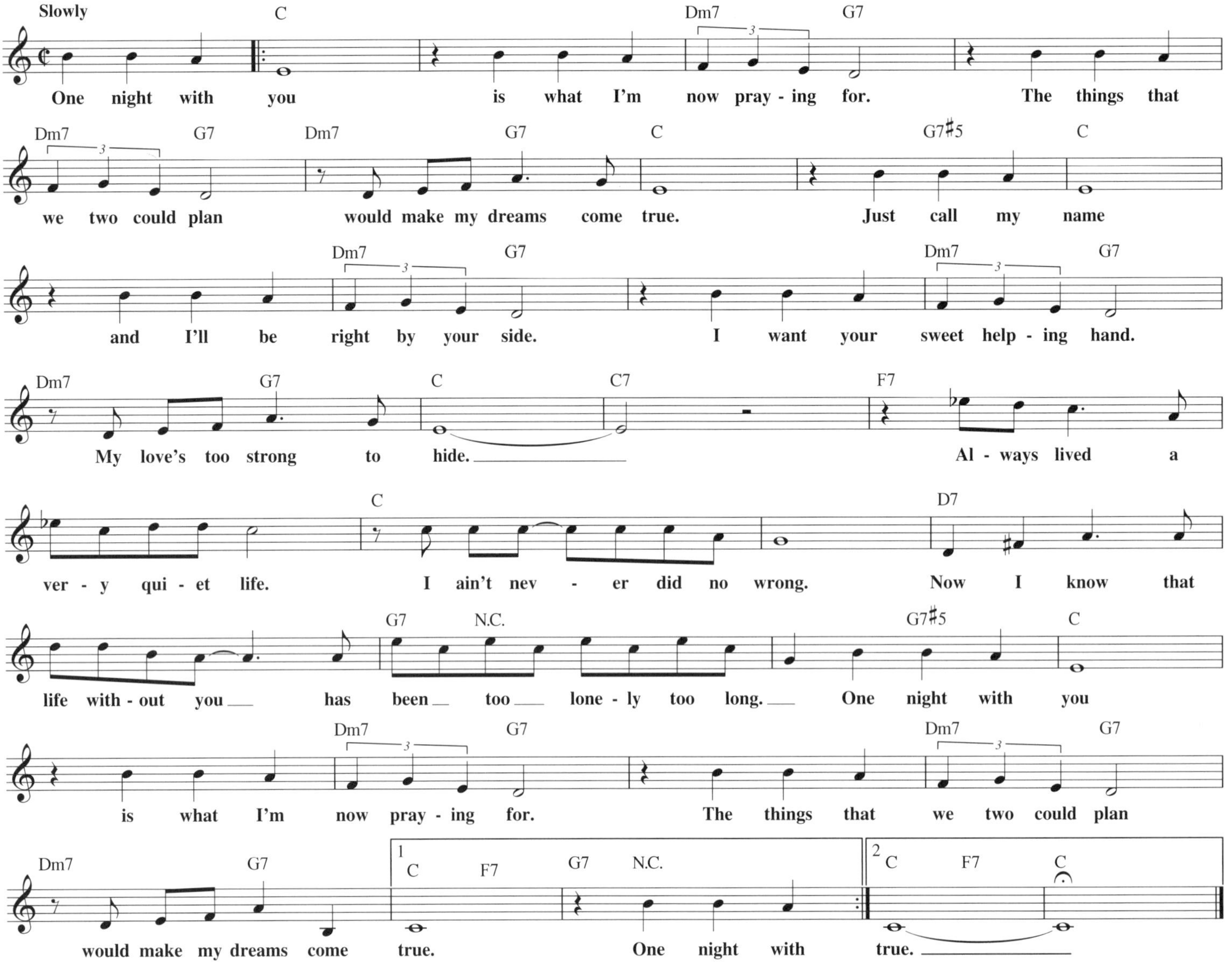

Slowly

C Dm7 G7
One night with you is what I'm now pray - ing for. The things that

Dm7 G7 Dm7 G7 C G7♯5 C
we two could plan would make my dreams come true. Just call my name

Dm7 G7 Dm7 G7
and I'll be right by your side. I want your sweet help - ing hand.

Dm7 G7 C C7 F7
My love's too strong to hide. Al - ways lived a

C D7
ver - y qui - et life. I ain't nev - er did no wrong. Now I know that

G7 N.C. G7♯5 C
life with - out you has been too lone - ly too long. One night with you

Dm7 G7 Dm7 G7
is what I'm now pray - ing for. The things that we two could plan

Dm7 G7 1 C F7 G7 N.C. 2 C F7 C
would make my dreams come true. One night with true.

OOBY-DOOBY

Words and Music by WADE L. MOORE
and RICHARD A. PENNER

Bright Rock
N.C.
Hey, ba - by, jump o - ver here. When you do the oo - by doo - by, I wan - na be near. Oo - by
G7 D7
doo - by. Oo - by doo - by. Oo - by
A7 G7 D
doo - by. Oo - by doo - by oo - by doo - by doo wah doo wah doo wah. Well, you
D
wig - gle to the left. You wig - gle to the right. Do the oo - by doo - by with all
wig - gle and you shake like a big rat - tle snake. You do the oo - by doo - by till you
you've been a strut - ting 'cause now you know how to do the oo - by doo - by. Now,

G7
D7
your might. Oo - by doo - by.
think your heart will break. Oo - by doo - by. Oo - by doo - by.
ba - by, let's go. Oo - by doo - by.
To Coda
A7
G7
D
Oo - by doo - by oo - by doo - by oo - by doo - by doo wah doo wah doo wah.
G7
D7
1
2
D.S. al Coda
Well, you Well,
CODA
G7
D7
doo - by doo - by doo wah doo wah doo wah.

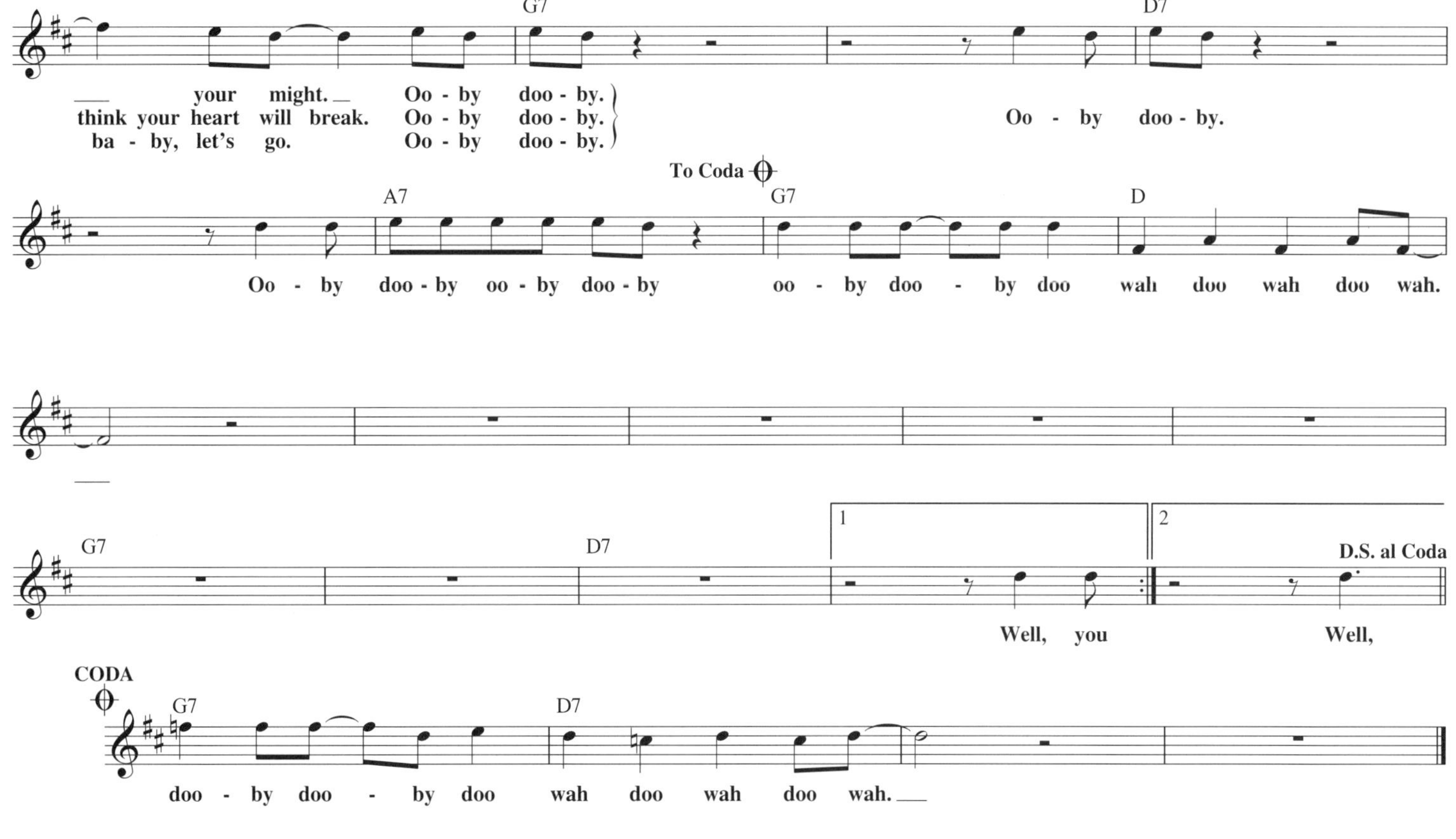

OUR DAY WILL COME

Words by BOB HILLIARD
Music by MORT GARSON

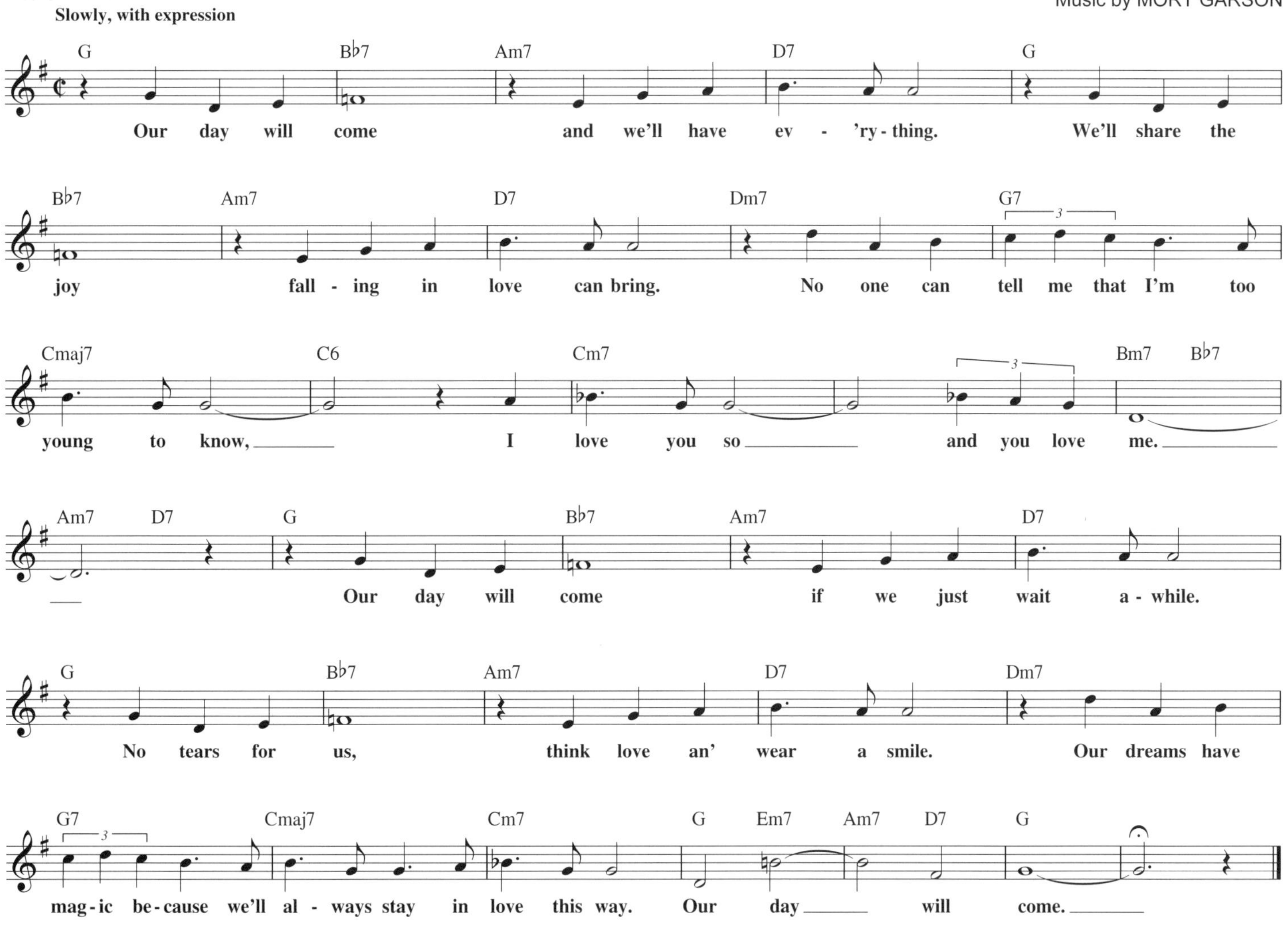
Slowly, with expression
G
B♭7
Am7
D7
G
Our day will come and we'll have ev - 'ry - thing. We'll share the
B♭7
Am7
D7
Dm7
G7
joy fall - ing in love can bring. No one can tell me that I'm too
Cmaj7
C6
Cm7
Bm7
B♭7
young to know, I love you so and you love me.
Am7
D7
G
B♭7
Am7
D7
Our day will come if we just wait a - while.
G
B♭7
Am7
D7
Dm7
No tears for us, think love an' wear a smile. Our dreams have
G7
Cmaj7
Cm7
G
Em7
Am7
D7
G
mag - ic be - cause we'll al - ways stay in love this way. Our day will come.

ONLY YESTERDAY

Words and Music by RICHARD CARPENTER
and JOHN BETTIS

Moderately fast
E♭ Fm/E♭ B♭7/E♭
Af - ter long e - nough of be - ing a - lone, ev - 'ry - one must face
E♭ B♭/D Cm F7/A
their share of lone - li - ness. In my own time, no - bod - y knew
B♭ Gm7 A♭ Fm7 E♭/B♭ B♭
the pain I was go - in' through, and wait - in' was all my heart could do.
E♭ F/E♭
Hope was all I had un - til you came.
Ddim7/E♭ B♭/E♭ E♭ B♭/D Cm
May - be you can't see how much you mean to me. You were the dawn
F7/A B♭ Gm7 A♭ F/A
break - ing the night, the prom - ise of morn - ing light, fill - ing the world sur - round -
B♭ D♭ Fm
- ing me. And when I hold you, ba - by, ba - by, feels like may - be things will be al - right.
D♭ D♭/C♭ Fm7/B♭ B♭7
Ba - by, ba - by, your love's made me free as a song, sing - in' for - ev - er.
E♭ Fm7 B♭ E♭
On - ly yes - ter - day when I was sad and I was lone - ly, you showed me the way
Fm7 B♭ G7
to leave the past and all its tears be - hind me. To - mor - row may be e - ven bright -

Cm Csus(add2) C Fm B♭ Fm7/E♭
- er than to - day since I threw my sad - ness a - way,
To Coda
E♭ Fm/E♭
on - ly yes - ter - day.
(Instrumental)
B♭7/E♭ E♭ B♭ E♭
F/E♭ Fdim7/E♭
B♭/E♭ E♭ B♭ E♭ Fm/E♭
I have found my home here in your arms;
B♭7/E♭ E♭ B♭/D
no - where else on earth I'd real - ly rath - er be.
Cm F7/A B♭ E♭maj7/G A♭
Life waits for us; share it with me. The best is a - bout to be, and
F/A B♭
so much is left for us to see. And when I hold you,
D.S. al Coda
CODA
E♭
day.
B E F♯m7 B
On - ly yes - ter - day when I was sad and I was lone - ly,
E F♯m7 B G♯7
you showed me the way to leave the past and all its tears be - hind me. To - mor - row may
C♯m C♯sus(add2) C♯ F♯m
be e - ven bright - er than to - day since I threw my
B F♯m/E E B
Repeat ad lib. and Fade
sad - ness a - way, on - ly yes - ter - day.

ON AND ON

Words and Music by
STEPHEN BISHOP

Moderately
C Am7(addD) C Am7(addD) C Am7(addD)
Down in Ja - mai - ca they got lots of pret - ty wom - en. Steal your mon - ey, then they
Poor ol' Jim - my sits a - lone in the moon - light. Saw his wom - an kiss an -
sun on my shoul - ders and my toes in the sand. Wom - an's left me for some
Dm7 F/G C Am7(addD) C Am7(addD)
break your heart. Lone - some Sue, she's in love with ol' Sam. Take
oth - er man. So he takes a lad - der; steals the stars from the sky.
oth - er man. Ah, but I don't care. I'll just dream and stay tan.
Dm7 F/G C A7sus A7 Dm7
him from the fire in - to the fry - ing pan. On and on, she just keeps
Puts on Si - na - tra and starts to cry. On and on, he just keeps
Toss up my heart to see where it lands. On and on, I just keep
F/G Cmaj7 A7sus A7 Dm7
on try - ing. And she smiles when she feels like cry - ing. On and on, on and
on try - ing. And he smiles when he feels like cry - ing. On and on, on and
on try - ing. And I smile when I feel like dy - ing. On and on, on and
To Coda
F/G C Am7(addD) 1 C Am7(addD) 2 C Am7(addD)
on, on and on. When the
on, on and on.
on, on and on.
Fmaj7 Em7 Dm7 F/G Cmaj7
first time is the last time, it can make you feel so bad. But if you
Fmaj7 Em7 Am7 D9 Fmaj7/G
know it, show it. Hold on tight. Don't let her say good - night.
C Am7(addD) C Am7(addD) C Am7(addD) C Am7(addD) D.C. al Coda
Got the
CODA
C Am7(addD) Dm7 F/G C Am7(addD) C A7
On and on, on and on, on and on. On and on,
Dm7 F/G C Am7(addD) C Am7(addD) C Am7(addD) C(addD)
on and on, on and on.

THE OTHER WOMAN

Words and Music by
JESSIE MAE ROBINSON

Slowly and freely

Bbmaj7 Gm7 Cm7 F7
The oth - er wom - an finds time to man - i - cure her nails. The oth - er wom - an is

F#dim Gm7 Cm7 F7
per - fect where her ri - val fails, and she's nev - er seen with pin curls in her hair. The

Bbmaj7 Gm7 Cm7 F7
oth - er wom - an en - chains her clothes with French per - fume. The oth - er wom - an

F#dim Gm7 D7 G7
keeps fresh cut flow - ers in each room. There are nev - er hair - pins scat - tered ev - 'ry - where and when her

Cm7 Ab7 Bbmaj7 G7
man comes to call, he'll find her wait - ing like a lone - some queen. 'Cause when she's

C7 F7
by his side it's such a change from old rou - tine. But, the oth - er

Bbmaj7 Gm7 Cm7
wom - an will al - ways cry her - self to sleep. The oth - er wom - an

F7 F#dim Gm7 Cm7
will nev - er have his love to keep. And as the years go by the oth - er wo - man will

1. F7 Bbmaj7 Gm7
spend her life a - lone.

Cm7 F7
But the oth - er

2. Cm7 F7 Bbmaj7
spend her life a - lone.

OUR HOUSE

Words and Music by
GRAHAM NASH

Moderately slow
A A/G♯ F♯m7 A/E D
I'll light the fire; you place the flow - ers in the vase that you bought
A/C♯ Bm7 D/F♯ D/E A A/G♯
to - day. Star - ing at the fire for hours
F♯m7 A/E D A/C♯ Bm7 D/C♯
and hours while I lis - ten to you play your
D/E D/C♯ Bm7 D/C♯ D/E D/C♯ A A/G♯ F♯m7
love songs all night long for me, on - ly for me.
A/E D F/C A A/G♯
Come to me now and rest
(Come to me now.)
F♯m7 A/E D A/C♯ Bm7
your head for just five min - utes; ev - 'ry - thing is done.
D/F♯ D/E A F♯m7
Such a co - zy room. The win - dows are il - lu -
(Such a co - zy room.)
A/E D A/C♯ Bm7 D/C♯ D/E D/C♯
- mi - nat - ed by the eve - ning sun - shine through them:
Bm7 D/C♯ D/E D/C♯ A A/G♯
Fi - ery gems for you,
F♯m7 A/E D F/C A
on - ly for you. Our

A/G♯ F♯m7 A/E D
house is a ver - y, ver - y, ver - y fine house, with two cats in the yard.
A/C♯ D A/C♯ D6
Life used to be so hard; now ev - 'ry - thing is eas -
A/C♯ D Bm7 D
- y 'cause of you. And, ah.
A A/G♯ F♯m7 A/E
La la la la la la la la la la la la la la la la
1
D A/C♯ Bm7 D/F♯ D/E
la la la la la la la la la la la la la la la la
2
D F/C A A/G♯
la la la la la la la la. Our house is a
F♯m7 A/E D A/C♯
ver - y, ver - y, ver - y fine house, with two cats in the yard. Life
(ver - y, ver - y, ver - y fine house)
D A/C♯ D A/C♯
used to be so hard; now ev - 'ry - thing is eas - y 'cause of
D Bm7 D
you. And, ah,
Slowly
A A/G♯ F♯m7 A/E
I'll light the fire, while you place the flow - ers in the vase
D F/C A
that you bought to - day.

OUT OF THE BLUE

Words and Music by
DEBORAH GIBSON

Bright Rock

With - out __ you, with - out __ you, I al - ways thought _ that ev - 'ry - thing was
I need _ you, I need _ you, and ev - 'ry day ____ I love you more and

fine with - out __ you, nev - er know - ing you'd be mine. Sun - den - ly ___ my world _
more with - out __ you. I know __ what it's __ all for. Sud - den - ly ___ I see ___

___ has changed _ and I just won - der why. __ All it took __ was just one
___ you there ____ and ev - 'ry - thing's __ O. K. ____ Don't know why __ I feel this

smile. ________
way. ________
Now with you out of the blue __ love ap - peared __ be - fore my eyes with

you, dream come true. __ I nev - er thought __ I'd re - al - ize what love __ was, __ what

love __ was, _ what love ______ was. ______ __ Here with you. ________

We are to - geth - er now. ___ Nev - er take __ my heart a - way. ____

All the love ____ I found ______ is here to stay.

Out of the blue __ wo, ______ wo, ________ wo, ________ it's like a

dream come true. __ I nev - er thought __ I'd fall in love with you. __________

Out of the blue ___ love ap - peared ___ be - fore my eyes with you.

Repeat ad lib. and Fade

PATCHES

Words and Music by GENERAL JOHNSON
and RONALD DUNBAR

Moderately
C Em E
I was born and raised in Alabama on a farm way back in the woods. I was so ragged folks called me Patches.
One day a strong rain came, washed all the crops away. And at the age of thirteen I felt like I was carrying
F A7 Dm
Papa used to tease me 'bout it, but inside he was hurt because he'd done the best he could.
the weight of the whole world on my shoulders. Mama knew what I was going through.
G6 F6
My pa - pa was a great old man. I can see him with his shov - el in his hand, see
Two days later Pa - pa passed a - way and I be - came a man that day. So
Ev - 'ry day I've had to work the fields 'cause that's the on - ly way we got our meals. See
G6 F6
ed - u - ca - tion Dad - dy nev - er had. But he did won - ders when the times got bad but
I told Ma I want - ed to quit school. She said that was Dad - dy's strict - est rule so
I was the old - est of the fam - i - ly and ev - 'ry - bod - y else de - pend - ed on me.
G6 F6
lit - tle mon - ey from the crops he raised. Bare - ly paid for bills he made.
ev - 'ry morn - ing 'fore I went to school I fed the chick - ens and I chopped wood,
Ev - 'ry night I heard my ma - ma pray "Lord, give him strength to face an - oth - er
C E♭ F C
Life whipped him down to the ground and when he tried to get up life would kick him back down. Then that day
too. Some - times I felt like I could - n't go on. I want - ed to leave, just run a - way from home. Then I'd
day." Years passed and ev - 'ry - bod - y is grown, my ma - ma is liv - in' in a brand new home. Lord
E♭ F C To Coda
Pa - pa called me to his dy - ing bed, placed his hands on my shoul - ders and in tears he said, he said,
re - mem - ber what my dad - dy said with tears in his eyes on his dy - ing bed. He said,
knows it took a lot of sweat and tears and my dad - dy's voice to help us through the years, say - ing,
Em
"Patch - es, I'm de - pend - ing on you son, to pull the fam - 'ly through.
I tried to do my best.
C7 C F A Dm 1 A Dm G 2 A Dm G D.S. al Coda
My son it's all left up to you."
It's up to you to do the rest."
CODA
C Em
"Patch - es, I'm de - pend - ing on you son, to pull the fam - 'ly through.
C7 C F A Dm G Repeat and Fade
My son it's all left up to you."

PANAMA

Words and Music by DAVID LEE ROTH, EDWARD VAN HALEN, ALEX VAN HALEN and MICHAEL ANTHONY

Bright Rock beat
Jump back. What's that sound? Here she comes, foot tap-pin', top down. Hot shoe burn-in' down the av-e-nue. Mod-el cit-i-zen, ze-ro dis-ci-pline.
Ain't noth-in' like it, her shin-y ma-chine. Got the feel for the wheel. Keep the mov-in' parts clean. Hot shoe burn-in' down the av-e-nue. Got an on ramp cut-ting through my bed-room.
Don't you know she's com-ing home to me?
You'll lose her in the turn. I'll get her.
Pan-a-ma, Pan-a-ma.
Pan-a-ma, Pan-a-ma.
(Instrumental)
(Spoken:) Yeah, we're running a little bit hot tonight.
I can barely see the road from the heat coming off it.
I reach between my legs and ease the seat back.
She's blind-in'. I'm fly-in'.
Right be-hind in the rear-view mir-ror now. Got the fear-in', pow-er steer-in',
pis-tons pop-pin'. Ain't no stop-ping now. Pan-a-ma,

D/E A/E G/E E A/E D/E A/E D/E A/E G/E E A/E D/E A/E
Pan - a - ma. Pan - a - ma,
D/E A/E G/E E A/E D/E A/E D/E A/E G/E E A/E D/E A/E
Pan - a - ma. Pan - a - ma,
D/E A/E G/E E A/E D/E A/E D/E A/E G/E N.C.
Pan - a - ma. Pan - a - ma.

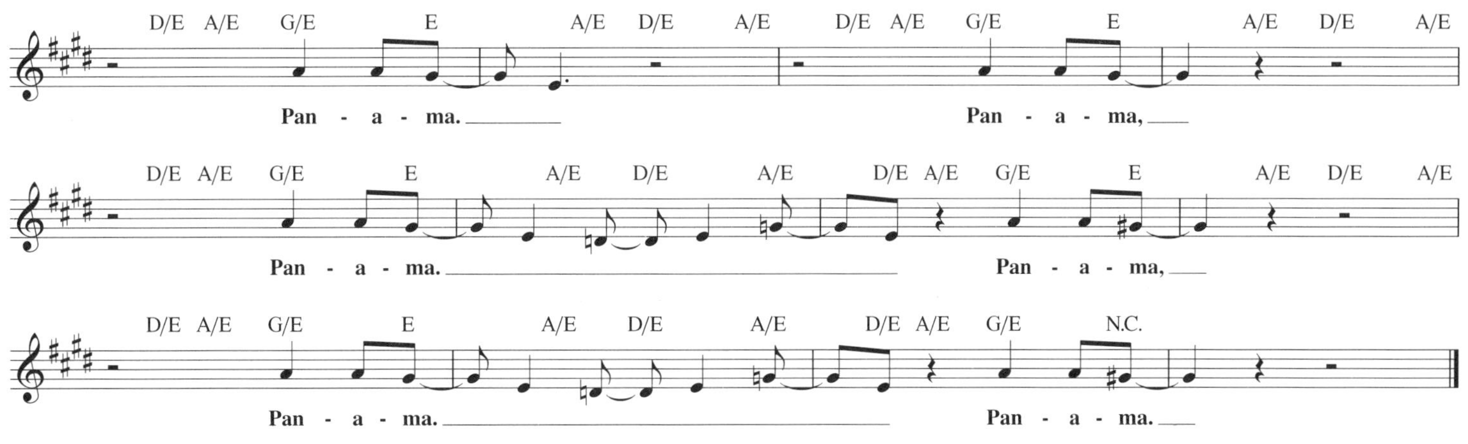

PAPERBACK WRITER

Words and Music by JOHN LENNON
and PAUL McCARTNEY

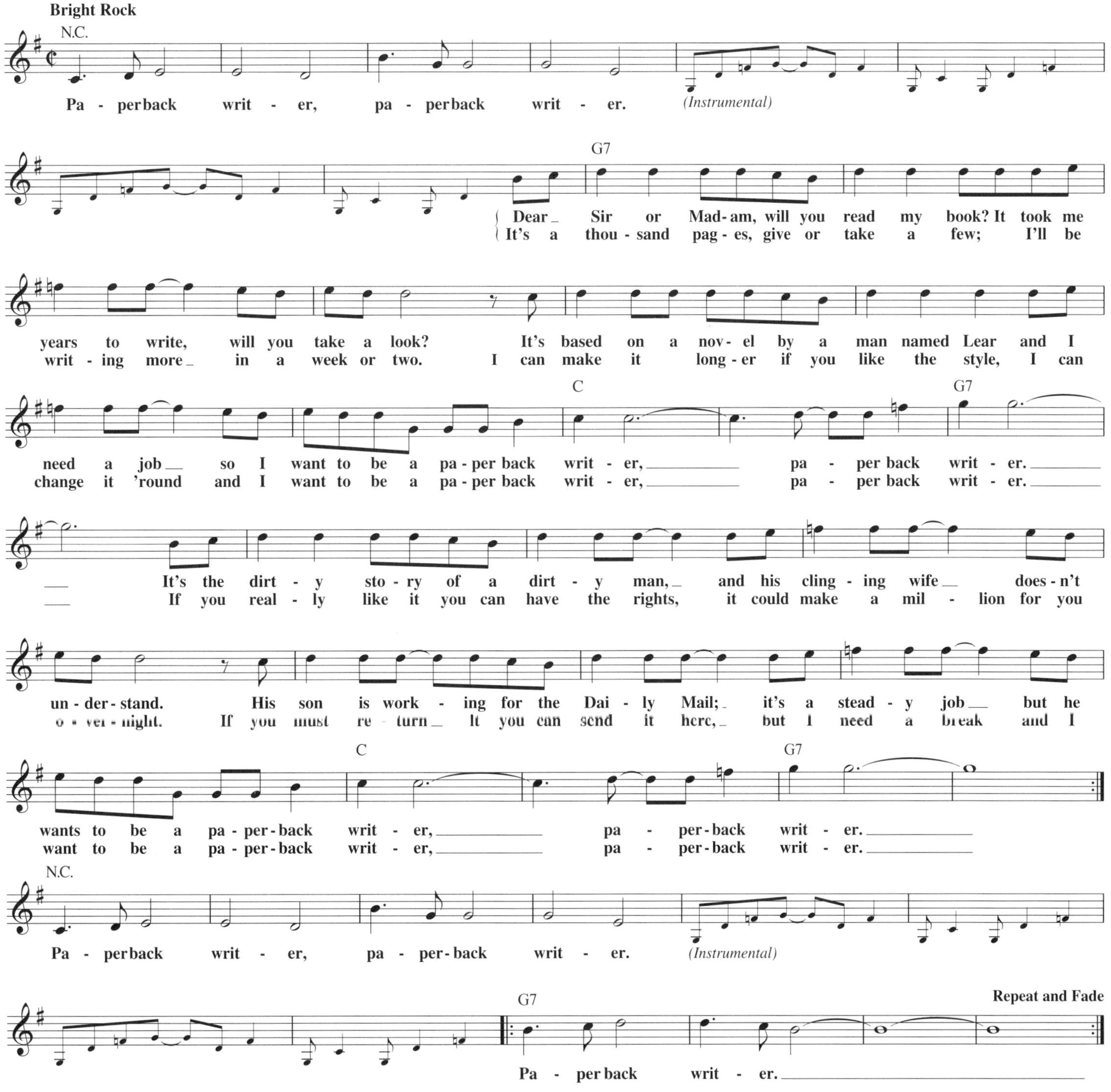
Bright Rock
N.C.
Pa - perback writ - er, pa - perback writ - er. (Instrumental)
G7
Dear Sir or Mad - am, will you read my book? It took me
It's a thou - sand pag - es, give or take a few; I'll be
years to write, will you take a look? It's based on a nov - el by a man named Lear and I
writ - ing more in a week or two. I can make it long - er if you like the style, I can
C G7
need a job so I want to be a pa - per back writ - er, pa - per back writ - er.
change it 'round and I want to be a pa - per back writ - er, pa - per back writ - er.
It's the dirt - y sto - ry of a dirt - y man, and his cling - ing wife does - n't
If you real - ly like it you can have the rights, it could make a mil - lion for you
un - der - stand. His son is work - ing for the Dai - ly Mail; it's a stead - y job but he
o - ver - night. If you must re - turn it you can send it here, but I need a break and I
C G7
wants to be a pa - per - back writ - er, pa - per - back writ - er.
want to be a pa - per - back writ - er, pa - per - back writ - er.
N.C.
Pa - perback writ - er, pa - per - back writ - er. (Instrumental)
G7 Repeat and Fade
Pa - per back writ - er.

PARADISE CITY

Words and Music by
W. AXL ROSE, SLASH, IZZY STRADLIN',
DUFF McKAGAN and STEVEN ADLER

Moderately

G C
Take me down_ to the par - a - dise ci - ty, where the grass is green and the girls are pret - ty.

Fadd9 C G C5 F5 C5 G5
Oh, won't you please take me home._____

G5 C5 1 F5 C5 G5

2 F5 C5 G5 Bb5 G5 C5 Bb5 G5 Bb5 G5 F5 C5 Bb5

G5 Bb5 G5 C5 Bb5
1. Just a ur - chin liv - in' un - der the street._ I'm a_____ hard case that's tough to beat._ I'm your
2.– 4. *(See additional lyrics)*

G5 Bb5 G5 C5
char - i - ty case,_ so buy me some - thing to eat._ I'll pay you at an - oth - er time.

1 N.C.
Take it to the end of the line._

2 N.C.
Ev - 'ry - bod - y's do - in' their time._

G5 C5
Take me down_ to the par - a - dise cit - y, where the grass is green and the girls are pret - ty.

F5 C5 G5
Oh, won't you please take me home,_____ yeah,_ yeah._ Take me down_ to the par - a - dise cit - y, where the

C5 F5 C5 G5
grass is green and the girls are pret - ty. Take me home._____

N.C.
Tell me who ya gon - na be - lieve?
G5
Take me down to the par - a - dise cit - y, where the
C5
grass is green and the girls are pret - ty.
F5 C5 G5
Take me home, yeah, yeah.
F5 C5
Oh, won't you please take me home.
To Coda
G5 F5 G5 B♭5 G5 C5 B♭5 G5 B♭5
Yeah.
G5 F5 C5 B♭5 A5 C5 A5 D5 C5 G5 B♭5 G5 C5
So
D C D C
far a - way. So far a - way. So
D.S. (take 3rd ending) al Coda
C B♭
way.
CODA
G5
home.
Take me home to the par - a - dise cit - y, where the
C5
grass is green and the girls are pret - ty.
F5 C5 G5
Take me home, yeah, yeah.
F5 C5 G5
Oh, won't you please take me home, home.
Double time
(Lead gtr. & vocal ad lib after 2nd time)
G5 C5 F5 C5 G5
Repeat and Fade

Additional Lyrics

2. Ragz to richez, or so they say.
Ya gotta keep pushin' for the fortune and fame.
It's all a gamble when it's just a game.
Ya treat it like a capital crime.
Everybody's doin' their time.
To Chorus

3. Strapped in the chair of the city's gas chamber,
Why I'm here I can't quite remember.
The surgeon general says it's hazarous to breathe.
I'd have another cigarette but I can't see.
Tell me who ya gonna believe?
To Chorus

4. Captain America's been torn apart.
Now he's a court jester with a broken heart.
He said, "Turn me around and take me back to the start."
I must be losin" my mind. "Are you blind?"
I've seen it all a million times.
To Chorus

PICK UP THE PIECES

Words and Music by JAMES HAMISH STUART, ALAN GORRIE, ROGER BALL, ROBBIE McINTOSH, OWEN McINTYRE and MALCOLM DUNCAN

Funk

Fm7 B♭7 Fm7 1 2 B♭7sus C7♯5(♯9) Fm7 B♭7 Fm7

To Coda B♭7 C7♯5(♯9)

D.S. al Coda

Pick up the piec - es, uh huh, pick up the piec - es, oh, yeah. Pick up the piec - es, yeah, pick up the piec - es.

CODA
B♭7sus
C7♯5(♯9)
(Sung:) Pick up the piec - es.
Pick up the piec - es.
1
2
Pick up the

PEG

Words and Music by WALTER BECKER
and DONALD FAGEN

Moderately

D♭maj7 A♭(add2) D♭maj7 A♭(add2) D♭maj7 A♭(add2)

1., 4. I've seen your pic - ture, your name in lights a - bove it.
2. pin shot, I keep it with your let - ter.
3. (Instrumental)

D♭maj7 A♭(add2) G♭maj7 D♭(add2) G♭maj7 D♭(add2) D♭maj7 A♭(add2)

This is your big de - but, it's like a dream come true.
Done up in blue - print blue, It sure looks good on you.

D♭maj7 A♭(add2) A♭maj7 E♭(add2) G♭maj7 D♭(add2) 1 D♭maj7 A♭(add2)

So won't you smile for the cam - 'ra? I know they're gon - na love it, Peg.
So won't you smile for the cam - 'ra? I know I'll love you
(Continue instrumental)

D♭maj7 A♭(add2) 2, 4 D♭maj7 A♭(add2) D♭maj7 A♭(add2) D♭maj7 A♭/C

I got your bet - ter.
love it.
(Instrumental) Peg, it will come

B♭7sus Fsus D♭ A♭/C B♭7sus Fsus B♭/D D♭

back to you. Peg, it will come back to you. Then the shut - ter

To Coda

A♭6 G7 Cm7 F7♯9 B♭m7 E♭9 D♭maj7 A♭(add2)

falls you see it all in "Three D." It's your fa - v'rite for - eign mov - ie.

D.S. 3 D.S. al Coda

D♭maj7 A♭(add2) Gm7 Cm7 Fm7 Cm7 D♭maj7 D♭maj7 A♭(add2) D♭maj7 A♭(add2)

(Instrumental) (End instrumental) I've seen your

CODA

D♭maj7 A♭/C B♭7sus Fsus D♭maj7 A♭/C B♭7sus Fsus

(mov - ie)
Peg, it will come back to you. Peg, it will come back to you.

Repeat and Fade

B♭/D D♭ A♭6 G7 Cm7 F7♯9 B♭m7 E♭9 D♭maj7 A♭(add2)

Then the shut - ter falls you see it all in "Three D." It's your fav-'rite for - eign mov - ie.

PLEASANT VALLEY SUNDAY

Words and Music by GERRY GOFFIN
and CAROLE KING

Moderately fast
A
The local rock group down the street is trying hard to learn their
G/A A
song. They serenade the weekend squire who just came
G/A C F
out to mow his lawn. Another Pleasant Valley
Another Pleasant Valley
C F C F C
Sunday, (Sunday) charcoal burning ev'rywhere.
Sunday, (Sunday) here in status symbol land.
D E A D A E
Rows of houses that are all the same, and
Mothers complain about how hard life is and the
Bm7 F♯m7 D6 A E To Coda E7 A
no one seems to care. See Missus Gray;
kids just don't understand.
G/A D/A
she's proud today because her roses are in bloom.
A G/A
And Mister Green, he's so serene; he's got a T-V in ev'ry room.
D/A D.S. al Coda CODA E7 A/E
Creature comfort goals,
E7 A/E E7 A/E
they only numb my soul and make it hard for me to see.

E7 A/E E7 A/E E7
My thoughts all seem to stray to plac - es
A/E E7 A/E E7 Bm/E
far a - way. I need a change of sce - ner - y.
A Em/A A Em/A A
Ta ta ta ta
G/A
ta ta ta ta ta ta ta ta ta ta ta ta ta.
A
Ta ta ta ta ta ta ta ta ta ta ta ta ta ta ta ta.
G/A C F C
An - oth - er Pleas-ant Val - ley Sun - day,
F C F C Dm7 C/E
(Sun - day) char - coal burn - ing ev - 'ry - where.
F B♭ F B♭ F
An - oth - er Pleas-ant Val - ley Sun - day, here in
B♭ F A Em/A
sta - tus sym - bol land.
A Em/A A Asus D/E A
An - oth - er Pleas-ant Val - ley Sun - day.
Repeat and Fade
Asus A Asus D/E
Pleas - ant Val - ley Sun - day.
An - oth - er Pleas - ant Val - ley

PIECES OF APRIL

Words and Music by
DAVE LOGGINS

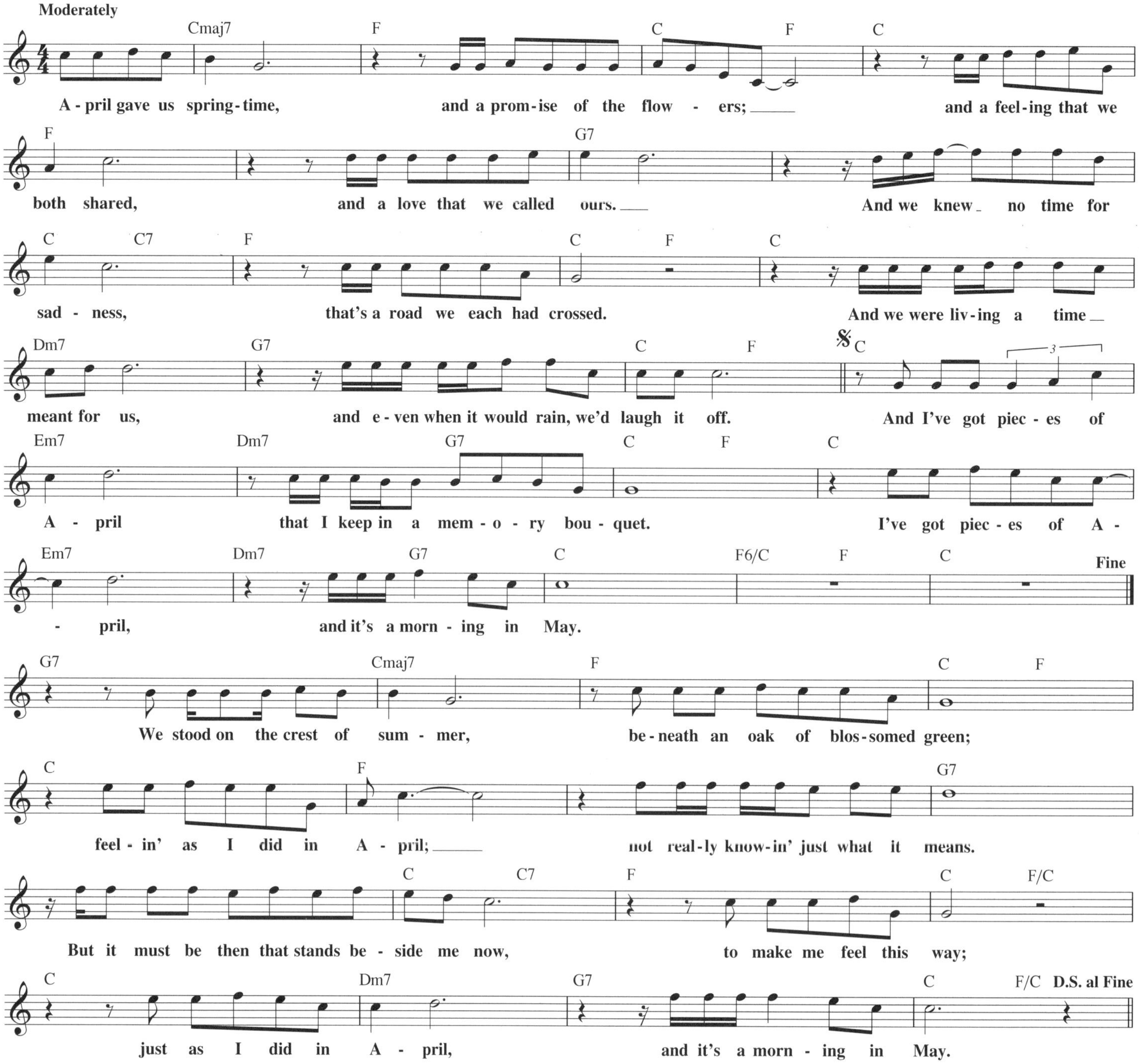

Moderately

Cmaj7 F C F C
A - pril gave us spring - time, and a prom - ise of the flow - ers; and a feel - ing that we

F G7
both shared, and a love that we called ours. And we knew no time for

C C7 F C F C
sad - ness, that's a road we each had crossed. And we were liv - ing a time

Dm7 G7 C F 𝄋 C
meant for us, and e - ven when it would rain, we'd laugh it off. And I've got piec - es of

Em7 Dm7 G7 C F C
A - pril that I keep in a mem - o - ry bou - quet. I've got piec - es of A -

Em7 Dm7 G7 C F6/C F C Fine
- pril, and it's a morn - ing in May.

G7 Cmaj7 F C F
We stood on the crest of sum - mer, be - neath an oak of blos - somed green;

C F G7
feel - in' as I did in A - pril; not real - ly know - in' just what it means.

C C7 F C F/C
But it must be then that stands be - side me now, to make me feel this way;

C Dm7 G7 C F/C D.S. al Fine
just as I did in A - pril, and it's a morn - ing in May.

PLEASE LOVE ME FOREVER

Words and Music by OLLIE BLANCHARD
and JOHNNY MALONE

Very slow
E♭ Gm A♭ E♭ Gm7 F♯m7
Please love me for - ev - er, don't for - get me ev - er. Lis - ten to my
Fm7 C9♯5 F7 A♭m6 B♭7 E♭ Gm
plea, please don't stop lov - ing me. You're in my dreams night - ly,

A♭ E♭ Gm7 F♯m7 Fm7 C9♯5 F7 B♭7♭9
don't take my love light - ly. Beg - ging on my knees, please don't stop lov - ing
E♭ Dm7 G7 Dm7 G7 C7
me. Oh, when I lay me down to sleep, I pray the Lord your love I'll keep.
Cm7/F F9 Cm7/F F9 B♭7 B♭dim B♭7 B♭+ E♭
If I should die be - fore I wake, I'll come back for you, that's no mis - take. Oh, I'll love you for -
Gm A♭ E♭ Gm7 F♯m7
ev - er, can't for - get you ev - er. Our love was meant to
Fm7 C9♯5 F7 B♭7♭9 E♭ F9 B♭7 E♭
be. Please don't stop lov - ing me. me.

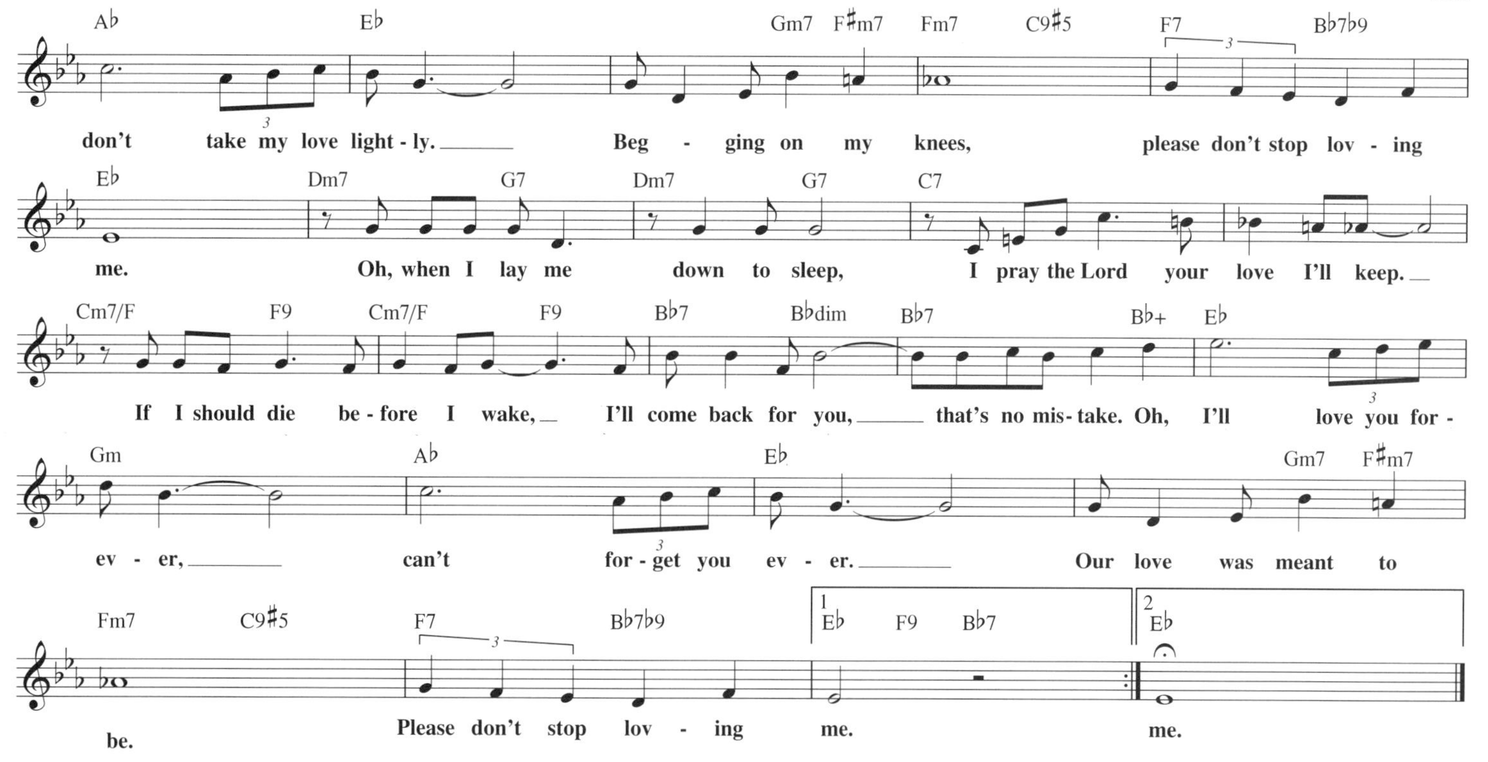

PLEASE PLEASE ME

Words and Music by JOHN LENNON
and PAUL McCARTNEY

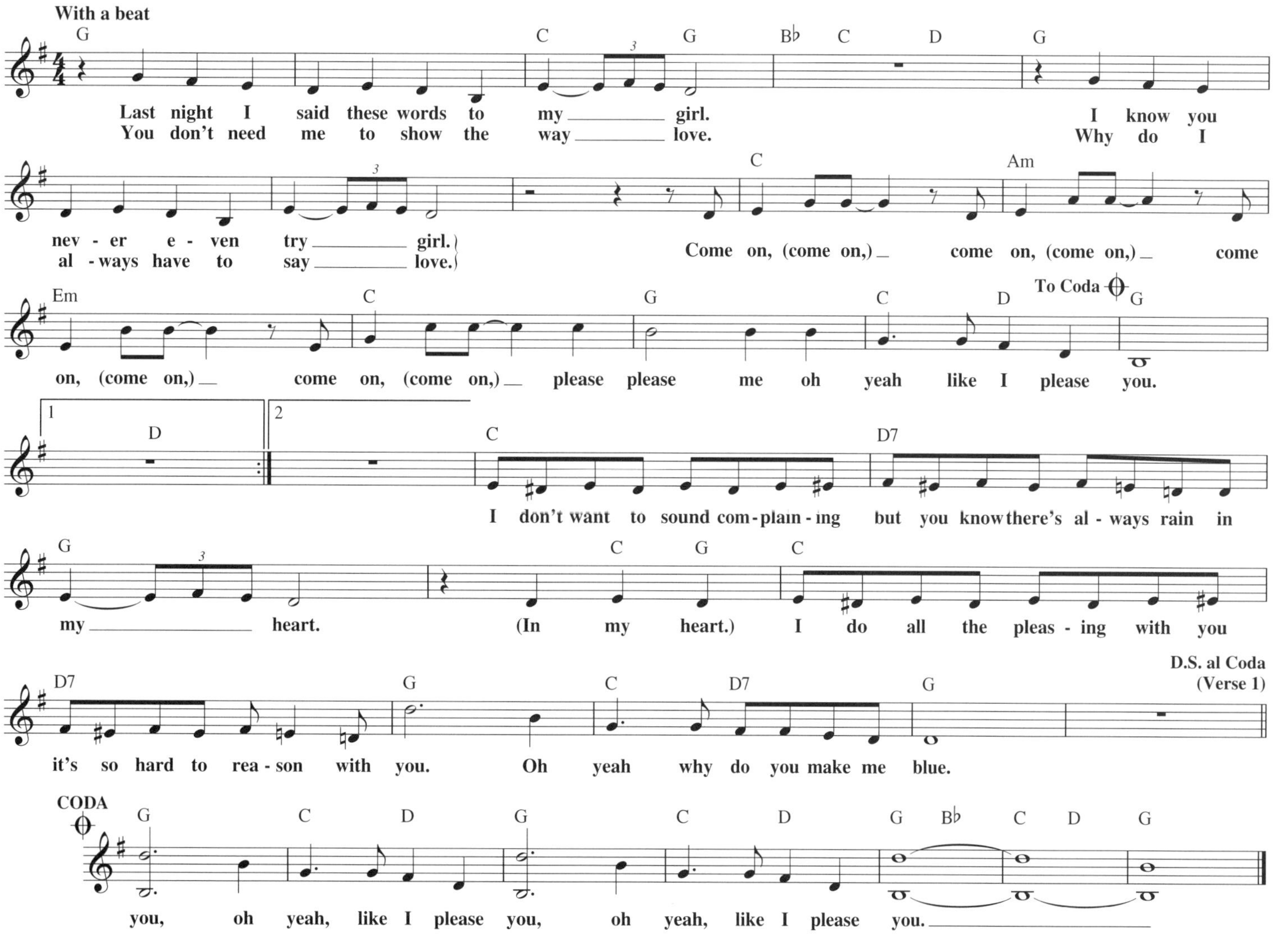
With a beat
G C G B♭ C D G
Last night I said these words to my girl. I know you
You don't need me to show the way love. Why do I
C Am
nev - er e - ven try girl.
al - ways have to say love.
Come on, (come on,) come on, (come on,) come
Em C G C D To Coda G
on, (come on,) come on, (come on,) please please me oh yeah like I please you.
D C D7
I don't want to sound com - plain - ing but you know there's al - ways rain in
G C G C
my heart. (In my heart.) I do all the pleas - ing with you
D7 G C D7 G D.S. al Coda (Verse 1)
it's so hard to rea - son with you. Oh yeah why do you make me blue.
CODA
G C D G C D G B♭ C D G
you, oh yeah, like I please you, oh yeah, like I please you.

PERFECT WORLD

Words and Music by
ALEX CALL

Moderate Rock
1. Ev-'ry-bod-y's look-in' for a per-fect world, where you could have ev-'ry-thing your heart de-sires.
2. (See additional lyrics)
The per-fect boy will meet the per-fect girl, and their per-fect love will set the world on fire.
What you gon-na do when one and one makes three and a vi-sion of the fu-ture is im-pos-si-ble to see?
No-bod-y's per-fect, not e-ven the per-fect fool. If you have faith in me I'll keep faith with you.
Ain't no liv-in' in a per-fect world. There ain't no per-fect world an-y-way.
Ain't no liv-in' in a per-fect world, but we'll keep on dream-in' of liv-in' in a per-fect world.
Keep on dream-in' of liv-in' in a per-fect world.
To Coda
D.S. al Coda
CODA
Repeat and Fade
Keep on dream-in' of liv-in' in a per-fect world.

Additional Lyrics

2. Everybody's got secrets; you know that it's true.
They talk about me and they'll talk about you.
Something happens to the pledges of trust.
Down through the years they begin to rust.
Now here we are amid the tears and the laughter,
Still waitin' for our happily ever after.
We'll keep on dreamin' as long as we can.
Try to remember and you'll understand.
To Chorus

POETRY MAN

Words and Music by
PHOEBE SNOW

Moderately

Am7 A7sus A7 Dmaj7

You make me laugh 'cause your eyes, they light the night, they look right through me.
ge - nie. All I ask for is your smile each time I rub the lamp.
gain it's time to say so long and so re - call the lull of life.

Am7

La la la la. You bash - ful boy. You're
La la la la. When I am with you, I have
La la la la. You're go - ing home now. Home's

A7sus A7 D

hid - ing some - thing sweet; please give it to me, yeah, to me.
a gig - gling teen - age crush though I'm a sul - try vamp, yeah, a sul - try vamp.
that place some - where you go each day to see your wife, yeah.

G Dmaj7

Oh talk to me some more. You don't have to go. You're the po - e - try man.

A7sus 1, 2 D 3 D

You make things all rhyme. Yeah, yeah. You are a right.
So once a -

POOR LITTLE FOOL

Words and Music by
SHARON SHEELEY

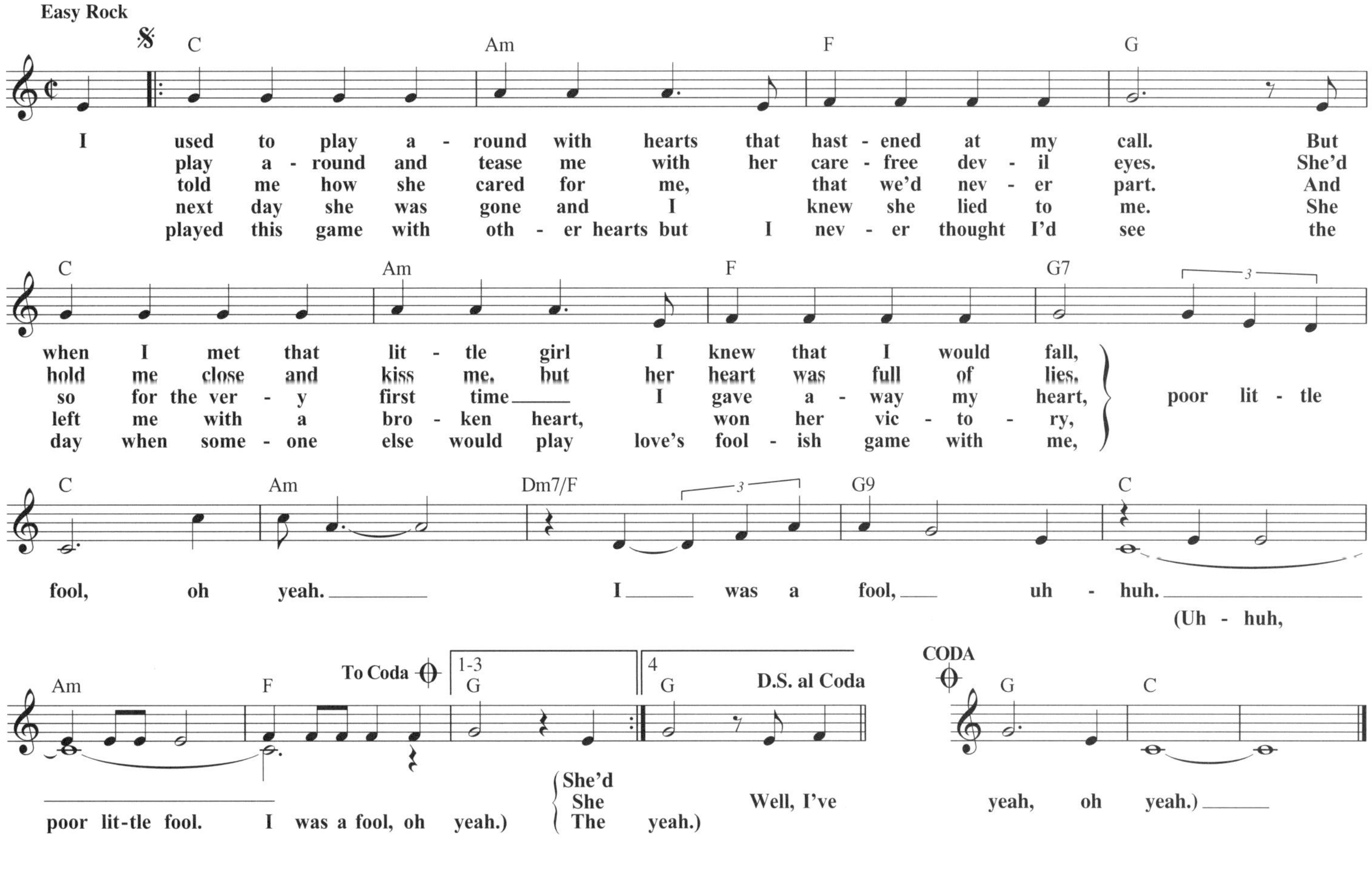

Easy Rock

C Am F G

I used to play a - round with hearts that hast - ened at my call. But
play a - round and tease me with her care - free dev - il eyes. She'd
told me how she cared for me, that we'd nev - er part. And
next day she was gone and I knew she lied to me. She
played this game with oth - er hearts but I nev - er thought I'd see the

C Am F G7

when I met that lit - tle girl I knew that I would fall,
hold me close and kiss me, but her heart was full of lies,
so for the ver - y first time I gave a - way my heart,
left me with a bro - ken heart, won her vic - to - ry,
day when some - one else would play love's fool - ish game with me,
poor lit - tle

C Am Dm7/F G9 C

fool, oh yeah. I was a fool, uh - huh.
(Uh - huh,

Am F To Coda 1-3 G 4 G D.S. al Coda CODA G C

poor lit - tle fool. I was a fool, oh yeah.)
She'd
She Well, I've
The yeah.)
yeah, oh yeah.)

PROUD MARY

Words and Music by
JOHN FOGERTY

Moderately
D
Left a good job in the cit - y, work - in' for the man ev - 'ry night and day. And, I nev - er lost one min - ute of sleep - in', wor - ry'n' 'bout the way things might have been.
Cleaned a lot of plates in Mem - phis, pumped a lot of 'pane down in New Or - leans. But, I nev - er saw the good side of the cit - y till I hitched a ride on a riv - er - boat queen.
If you come down to the riv - er, bet you gon - na find some peo - ple who live. You don't have to wor - ry 'cause you have no mon - ey. Peo - ple on the riv - er are hap - py to give.
A
Big wheel, keep on turn - in', proud Mar - y keep on burn - in'.
Bm
D
Roll - in', roll - in', roll - in' on the riv - er.
To Coda
1
2
- in' on the riv - er.
C A C A G F D F D
(Instrumental)
A Bm D
Roll - in', roll - in', roll - in' on the riv - er.
C A
(Instrumental)
C A G F D F D
D.C. al Coda

CODA
- in' on the riv - er. Roll - in', roll -
Repeat and Fade
- in', roll - in' on the riv - er. Roll -

PUPPY LOVE

Words and Music by
PAUL ANKA

Moderately slow
Gm7 C7 F
And they called it pup-py love, oh, I guess they'll nev-er know,
Am7 Dm7 Gm7 C7 F G♭maj7
how a young heart real-ly feels, and why I love her so.
F N.C. Gm7 C7 F
And they called it pup-py love just be-cause we're in our teens,
Am7 Dm7 Gm7 C7 F G♭maj7
tell them all it is-n't fair to take a-way my on-ly dream.
F F7 B♭ B♭m F C7
I cry each night my tears for you, my tears are all in
F F7 B♭ Am7 D7 G7
vain. I'll hope and I'll pray that may - be some day you'll be back in my arms once a -
C7 Gm7 C7 N.C. Gm7 C7
gain. Some-one help me, help me please, is the an-swer up a -
F Am7 Dm7 Gm7 C7
bove? How can I, how can I tell them this is not a pup-py
1. F G♭maj7 F N.C.
love? And they called it pup-py
2. F D♭7 G♭maj7 Fmaj9
love?

PURPLE RAIN

Words and Music by
PRINCE

Slowly

Gm7(add4) F

I never meant 2 cause U any sorrow. I never meant 2 cause U any

E♭(add2) B♭sus2 Gm7(add4)

pain. I only wanted 2 one time see u laughing. I

F B♭ N.C.

only want to see U laughing in the purple rain. Purple rain, purple rain.

E♭(add2) B♭sus2 Gm7(add4)

Purple rain, purple rain. Purple rain, purple rain.

F

I only wanted 2 see U bathing in the purple

B♭ B♭sus2 Gm7(add4)

rain. I never wanted to be your weekend lover.

F E♭(add2)

I only wanted 2 be some kind of friend.

B♭sus2 Gm7(add4)

Baby, I could never steal U from another.

F B♭ N.C. E♭(add2)

It's such a shame our friendship had 2 end. Purple rain, purple rain.

B♭sus2 Gm7(add4)
Pur - ple rain, pur - ple rain. Pur - ple rain, pur - ple rain.
F
I on - ly want 2 see U un - der - neath the pur - ple
B♭ N.C. B♭sus2
rain. Hon - ey, I know, I know, I know times r chang - ing.
3
Gm7(add4) F E♭(add2)
It's time we all reach out 4 some - thing new.
B♭sus2 Gm7(add4)
U say U want a lead - er, but U can't seem 2 make up your mind. I think U bet - ter close
F B♭ N.C.
it, and let me guide U 2 the pur - ple rain. Pur - ple rain, pur - ple rain.
E♭(add2) B♭sus2 Gm7(add4)
Pur - ple rain, pur - ple rain. Pur - ple rain, pur - ple rain.
F
I on - ly want 2 see U, on - ly want 2 see U
B♭ B♭sus2 Gm7(add4)
in the pur - ple rain.
(Instrumental)
F E♭(add2) B♭sus2

PRETTY LITTLE ANGEL EYES

Words and Music by TOMMY BOYCE
and CURTIS LEE

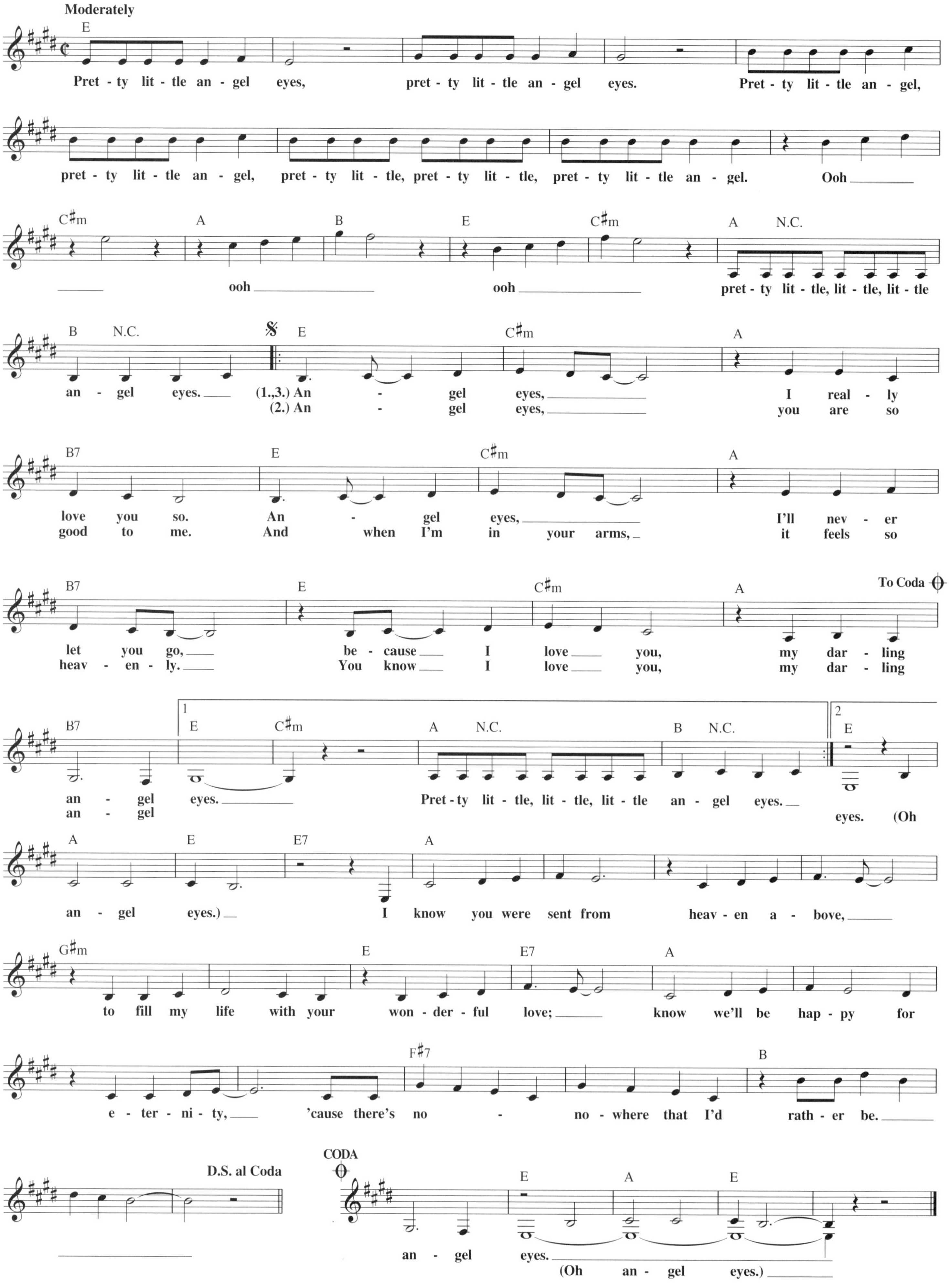

Moderately

E
Pret - ty lit - tle an - gel eyes, pret - ty lit - tle an - gel eyes. Pret - ty lit - tle an - gel,
pret - ty lit - tle an - gel, pret - ty lit - tle, pret - ty lit - tle, pret - ty lit - tle an - gel. Ooh

C♯m A B E C♯m A N.C.
ooh ooh pret - ty lit - tle, lit - tle, lit - tle

B N.C. 𝄋 E C♯m A
an - gel eyes. (1.,3.) An - gel eyes, I real - ly
(2.) An - gel eyes, you are so

B7 E C♯m A
love you so. An - gel eyes, I'll nev - er
good to me. And when I'm in your arms, it feels so

B7 E C♯m A To Coda
let you go, be - cause I love you, my dar - ling
heav - en - ly. You know I love you, my dar - ling

B7 1. E C♯m A N.C. B N.C. 2. E
an - gel eyes. Pret - ty lit - tle, lit - tle, lit - tle an - gel eyes.
an - gel eyes. (Oh

A E E7 A
an - gel eyes.) I know you were sent from heav - en a - bove,

G♯m E E7 A
to fill my life with your won - der - ful love; know we'll be hap - py for

F♯7 B
e - ter - ni - ty, 'cause there's no - no - where that I'd rath - er be.

D.S. al Coda

CODA
E A E
an - gel eyes.
(Oh an - gel eyes.)

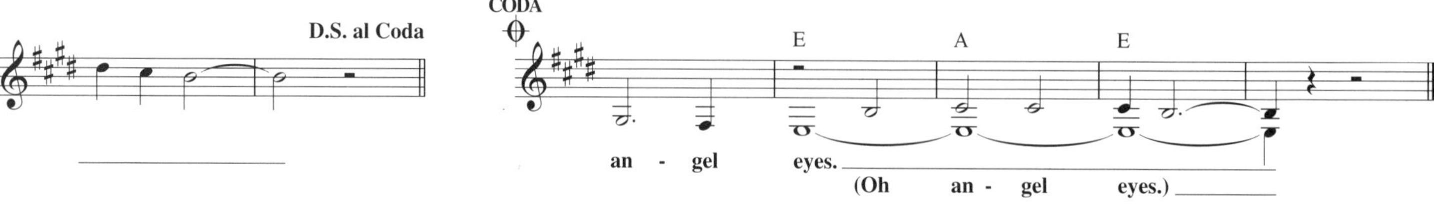

QUE SERA, SERA
(Whatever Will Be, Will Be)
from THE MAN WHO KNEW TOO MUCH

Words and Music by JAY LIVINGSTON and RAY EVANS

Moderately bright

C Dm7
When I was just a lit - tle girl, I asked my moth - er, "What will I be?
G7 Dm7 G7 Dm7 G7 C
Will I be pret - ty? Will I be rich?" Here's what she said to me:
N.C. F F6 F F6 C C6 C
"Que se - ra, se - ra, what - ev - er will be, will be. The
C6 G7 Dm7 G7 Dm7 G7 C F C
fu - ture's not ours to see. What will be, will be."

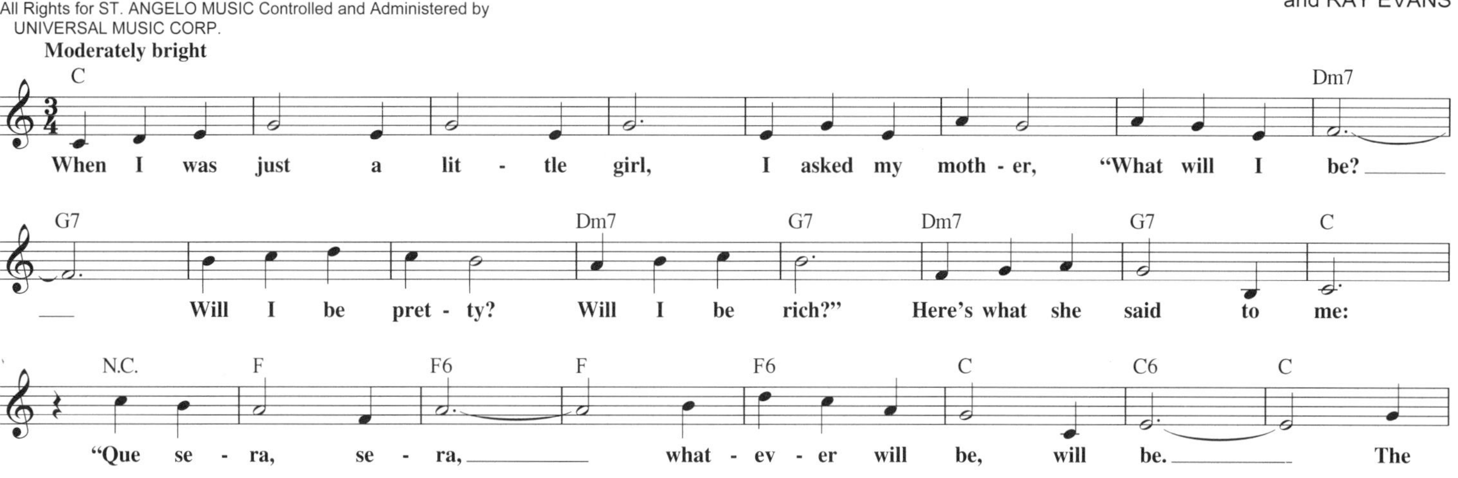

QUIET VILLAGE

Music by LES BAXTER

Lazy tropical tempo

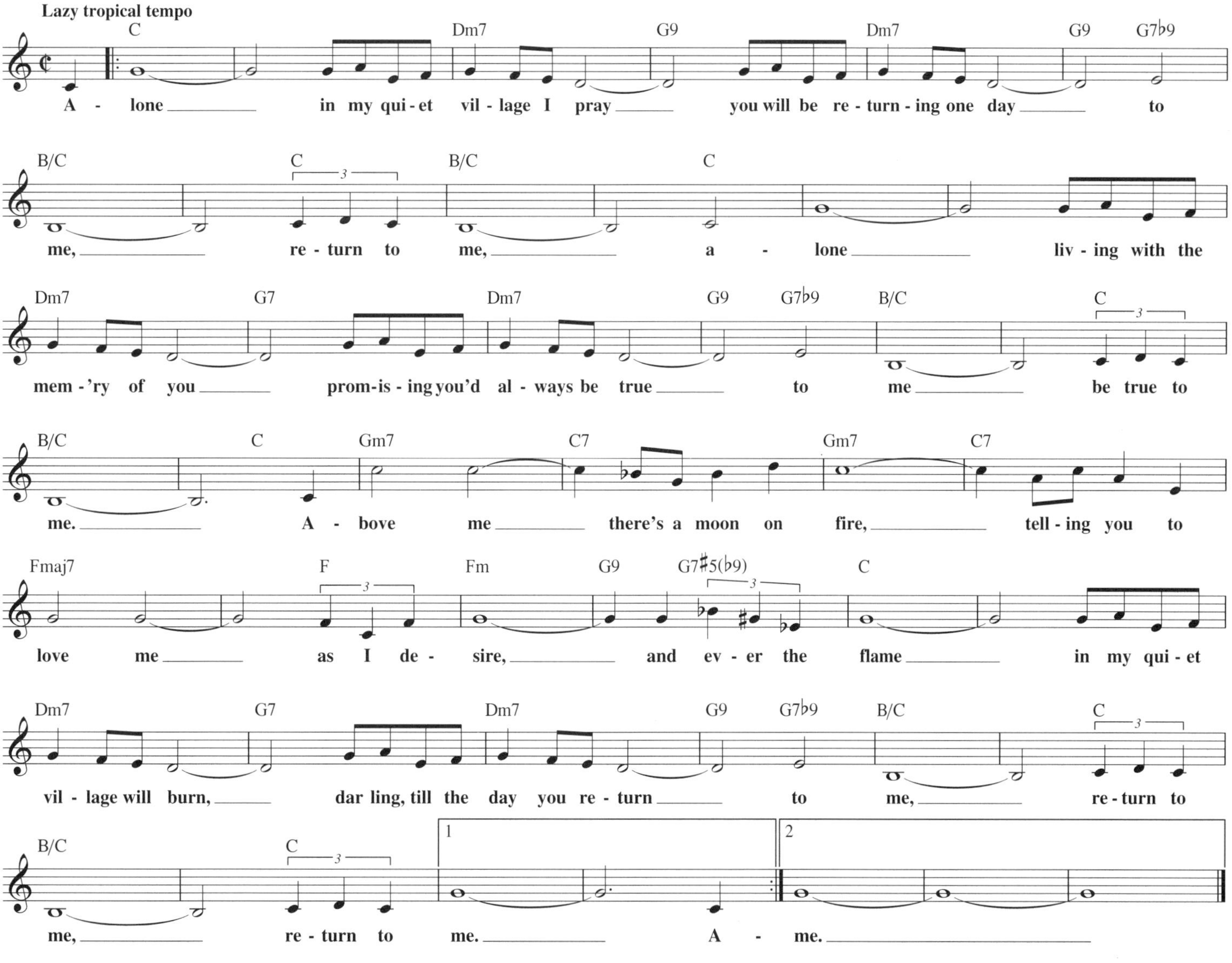

C Dm7 G9 Dm7 G9 G7♭9
A - lone in my qui - et vil - lage I pray you will be re - turn - ing one day to
B/C C B/C C
me, re - turn to me, a - lone liv - ing with the
Dm7 G7 Dm7 G9 G7♭9 B/C C
mem - 'ry of you prom - is - ing you'd al - ways be true to me be true to
B/C C Gm7 C7 Gm7 C7
me. A - bove me there's a moon on fire, tell - ing you to
Fmaj7 F Fm G9 G7♯5(♭9) C
love me as I de - sire, and ev - er the flame in my qui - et
Dm7 G7 Dm7 G9 G7♭9 B/C C
vil - lage will burn, dar ling, till the day you re - turn to me, re - turn to
B/C C 1 2
me, re - turn to me. A - me.

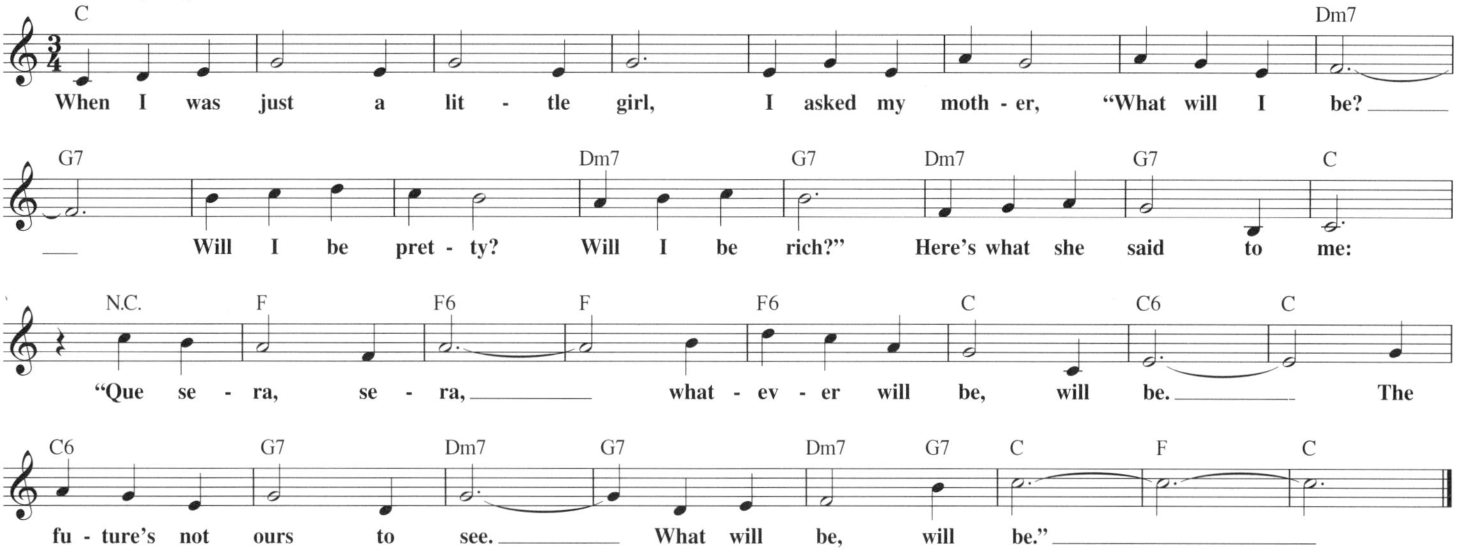

READY TO TAKE A CHANCE AGAIN

(Love Theme)
from the Paramount Picture FOUL PLAY

Words by NORMAN GIMBEL
Music by CHARLES FOX

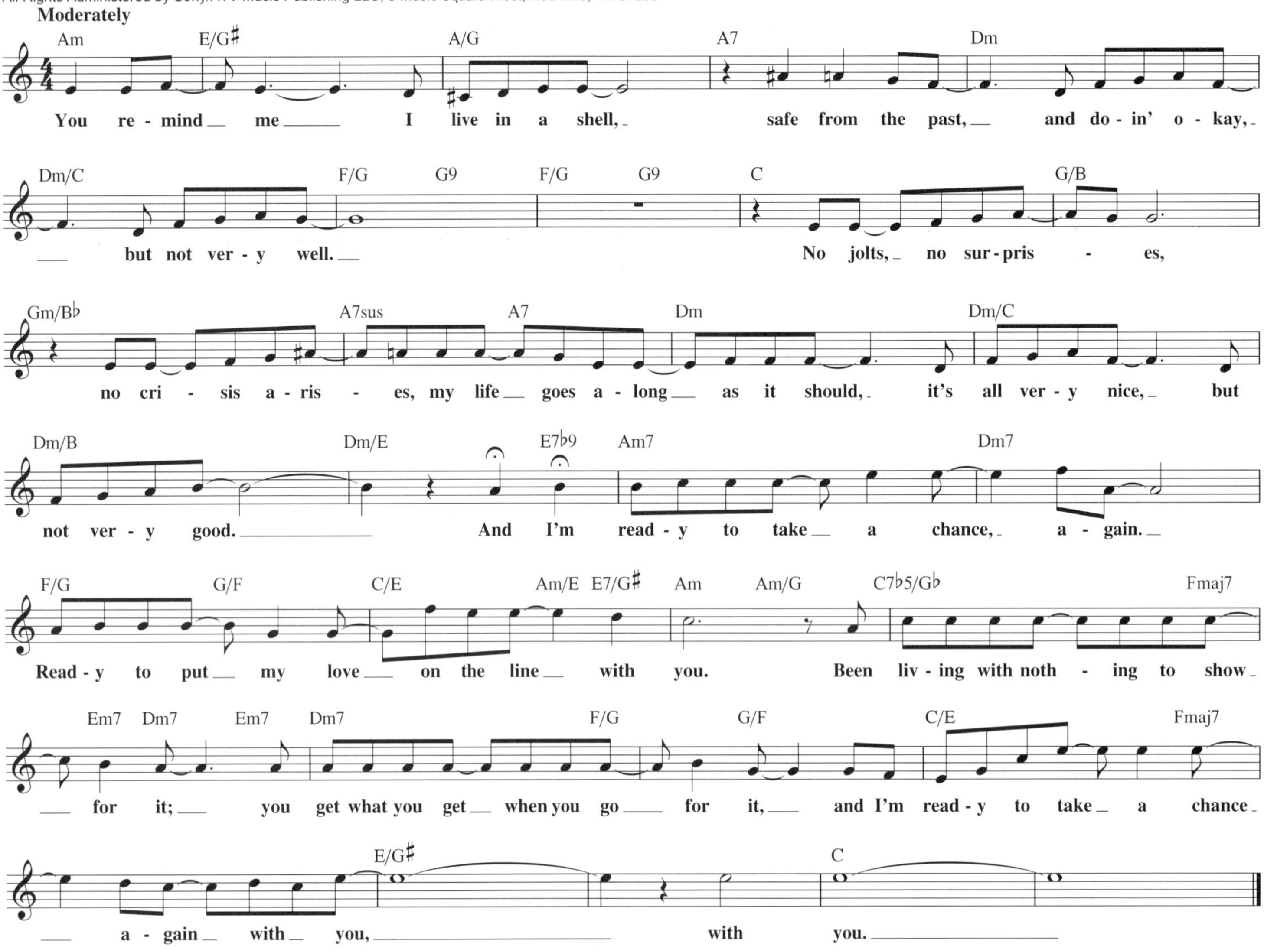
Moderately
Am E/G♯ A/G A7 Dm
You re - mind me I live in a shell, safe from the past, and do - in' o - kay,
Dm/C F/G G9 F/G G9 C G/B
but not ver - y well. No jolts, no sur - pris - es,
Gm/B♭ A7sus A7 Dm Dm/C
no cri - sis a - ris - es, my life goes a - long as it should, it's all ver - y nice, but
Dm/B Dm/E E7♭9 Am7 Dm7
not ver - y good. And I'm read - y to take a chance, a - gain.
F/G G/F C/E Am/E E7/G♯ Am Am/G C7♭5/G♭ Fmaj7
Read - y to put my love on the line with you. Been liv - ing with noth - ing to show
Em7 Dm7 Em7 Dm7 F/G G/F C/E Fmaj7
for it; you get what you get when you go for it, and I'm read - y to take a chance
E/G♯ C
a - gain with you, with you.

REACH OUT AND TOUCH (SOMEBODY'S HAND)

Words and Music by NICKOLAS ASHFORD
and VALERIE SIMPSON

Moderate Waltz (easy flowing)
G7 Cmaj7 Am7 Dm7 G7
Reach out and touch some - bod - y's hand, make this world a bet - ter place if you
C Am7 G7 Cmaj7 Am7 Dm7 G7
can. Reach out and touch some - bod - y's hand, make this world a bet - ter place if you
Em7 Am7 Cmaj7 F F+
can. (Just try.) Take a lit - tle time out of your bus - y day, to give en -
If you see an old friend on the street and he's down, re -
F6 Dm7/G Em Em7 Am7 Cmaj7
cour - age - ment to some - one who's lost the way. (Just try.) Or would I be talk - ing
mem - ber, his shoes could fit your feet. Just try a lit - tle kind - ness and

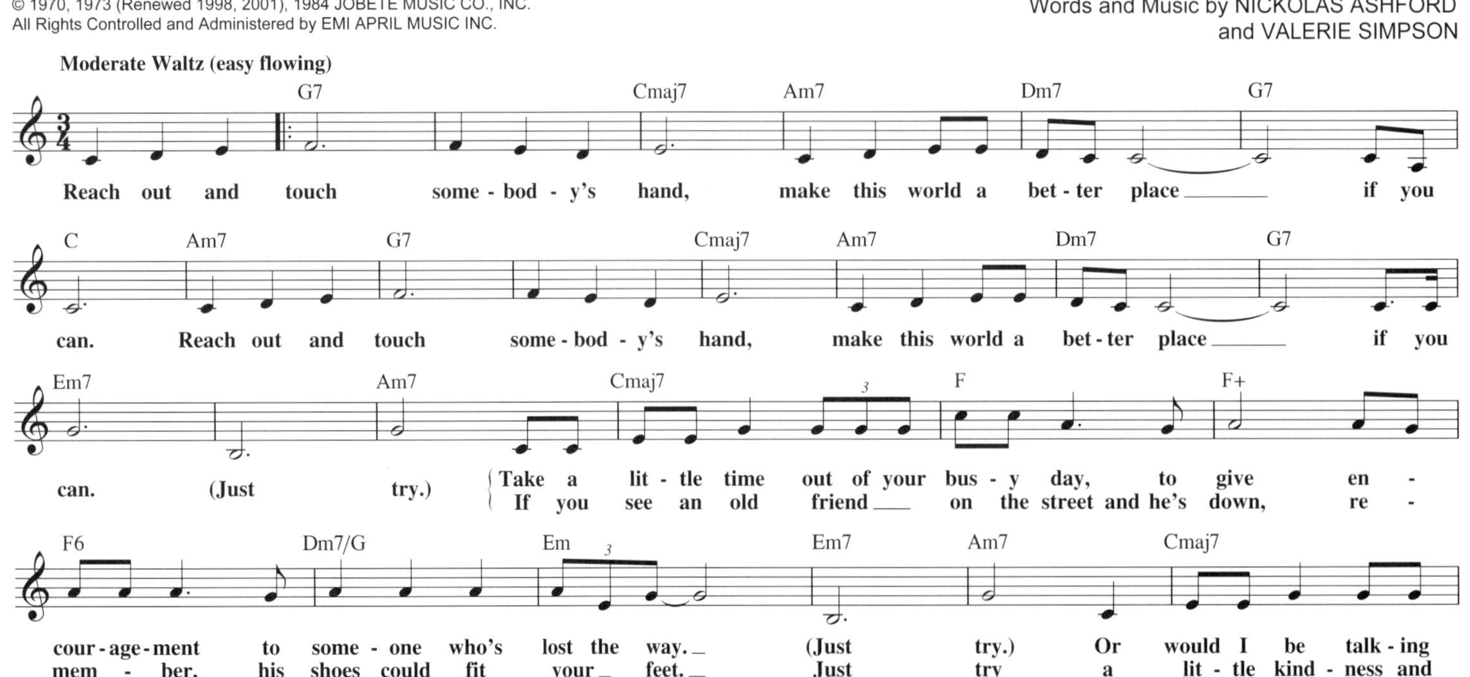

F F+ F6 Dm7/G Gm7 A7
to a stone if I asked you to share a prob - lem that's not your own?
you'll see some - thing that comes ver - y nat - ur - al - ly.
C7 F Am Dm7
We can change things if we start giv - ing.
We can change things if we start giv - ing.
1 G9 Am7
Why don't you reach out and
2 G9 Am7 Dm7/G Cmaj7
Why don't you (Why don't you) reach out and touch some - bod - y's hand.

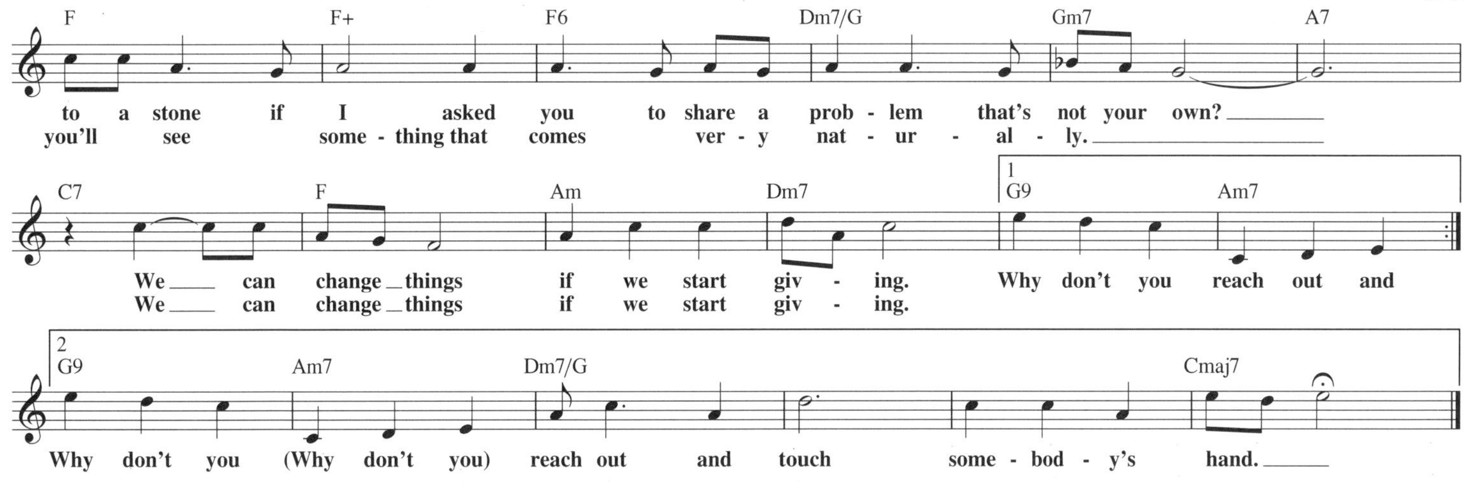

REACH OUT, I'LL BE THERE

Words and Music by BRIAN HOLLAND, LAMONT DOZIER
and EDWARD HOLLAND

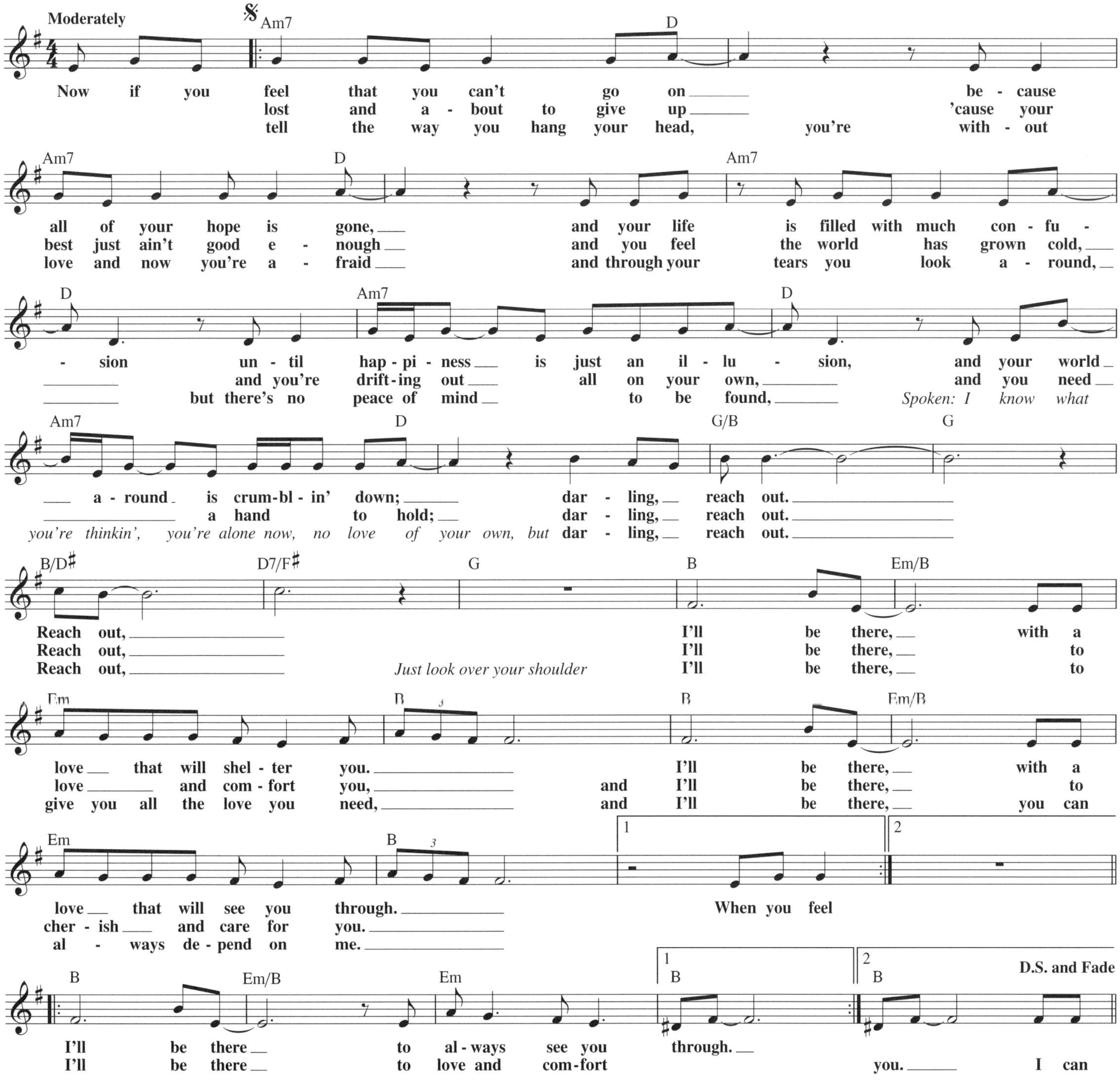

Moderately
Am7 D
Now if you feel that you can't go on because
lost and a - bout to give up 'cause your
tell the way you hang your head, you're with - out
Am7 D Am7
all of your hope is gone, and your life is filled with much con - fu -
best just ain't good e - nough and you feel the world has grown cold,
love and now you're a - fraid and through your tears you look a - round,
D Am7 D
- sion un - til hap - pi - ness is just an il - lu - sion, and your world
and you're drift - ing out all on your own, and you need
but there's no peace of mind to be found, Spoken: I know what
Am7 D G/B G
a - round is crum - bl - in' down; dar - ling, reach out.
a hand to hold; dar - ling, reach out.
you're thinkin', you're alone now, no love of your own, but dar - ling, reach out.
B/D♯ D7/F♯ G B Em/B
Reach out, I'll be there, with a
Reach out, I'll be there, to
Reach out, Just look over your shoulder I'll be there, to
Em B B Em/B
love that will shel - ter you. I'll be there, with a
love and com - fort you, and I'll be there, to
give you all the love you need, and I'll be there, you can
Em B 1 2
love that will see you through. When you feel
cher - ish and care for you.
al - ways de - pend on me.
B Em/B Em 1 B 2 B D.S. and Fade
I'll be there to al - ways see you through.
I'll be there to love and com - fort you. I can

REAL LOVE

Words and Music by MICHAEL McDONALD
and PATRICK HENDERSON

Moderately bright
Dm7 C/D Bbmaj9 Bb6 Bm7b5 A7
Dar - lin', I know I'm just an - oth - er head on your pil - low. If on - ly just to -
Dm7 C/D Bbmaj9 Bm7b5 A7
night, girl, let me hear you lie just a lit - tle. Tell me I'm the
Dm7 C/D Bbmaj9 Bb/C
on - ly man that you ev - er real - ly loved. Hon - ey, take me
back in my mem - o - ry, place when it was all ver - ry right, so ver - y
F6/9 Bb/C C7
nice, so ver - y nice.
F6/9 Bbmaj7/F F6/9 F#dim7 Gm7
Here, dar - lin', stands an - oth - er ban - dit want - ing you. In and out your
Dm7/G Bbmaj7/G Bb/C C7
life, they come and they go. Your days and nights like a
F6/9 F#dim7 Gm7
wheel that turns, grind - in' down a se - cret part of you, deep in - side your
Dm7/G Bb/C C7 F#dim7 Gm7
heart, that no - bod - y knows. When you say com -
F/G C#dim7 Dm7 C/D Dm7 F#dim7 Gm7
- fort me to an - y - one who ap - proach - es, chalk -

F/G
Gm7
C♯dim7
Dm7
C/D
Dm7
Cm7/F
- in' up the hurt,
you live and you learn.
Well, we've both
lived long e-nough to know,
that we'd trade it all right now for just one min-ute of real
To Coda
B♭maj9
Bm7♭5
A7
Dm7
C/D
love,
B♭maj9
B♭6
real love.
Bm7♭5
A7
Real love, I need to be-lieve in real love,
real love, ba-by,
real love, real love, dar-lin', real love.
F6/9
B♭/C
(Instrumental)
Gm7
Gm7/C
D.S. al Coda
F♯dim7
When you say com-
CODA
A♭13
F/A
just one min-ute of real love, real
Repeat and Fade

REMEMBER
(Walking in the Sand)

Words and Music by
GEORGE MORTON

Moderately

Cm Bb Ab Gm7
Seems like the oth - er day my ba - by went a - way.
It's been two years or so since I saw my ba - by go

Fm7 G Cm Bb
She went a - way 'cross the sea. It said that we was through.
and then this let - ter came for me.

Ab Gm7 Fm
She found some - bod - y new. Oh, let me think, let me think. What shall I

G C5 Ab
do? Oh no, oh no. Oh no no no no no. Re-

Faster

Cm Gm Cm Bb Cm Gm
mem - ber walking in the sand. Re - mem - ber walk - ing hand in

Cm Bb Cm Gm Cm Bb
hand. Re - mem - ber the night was so ex - cit - ing. Re -

Cm Gm Cm Bb Cm Gm
mem - ber her smile was so in - vit - ing. Re - mem - ber then she touched my

Cm Bb Cm Gm Cm Bb
cheek. Re - mem - ber with her fin - ger - tips. Re -

Tempo I

Cm Gm Cm G
mem - ber soft - ly, soft - ly we met with a kiss.

Cm Bb Ab Gm7
What - ev - er hap - pened to that girl that I once knew,

Fm7 G Cm Bb
the girl that said she'd be true? Oh, what - ev - er hap-pened to

Ab Gm7 Fm7 G
that night I gave it to you? What will I do with it now?
What would you do with it now?

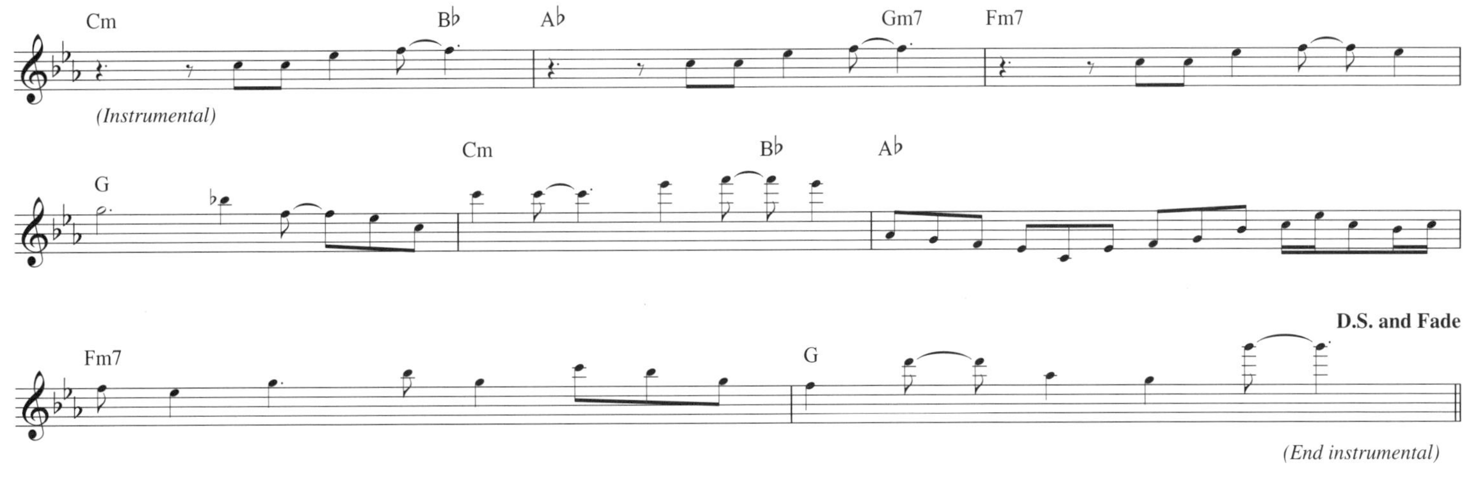

REELING IN THE YEARS

Words and Music by WALTER BECKER
and DONALD FAGEN

Moderately

D A/C♯ Bm7 A D A/C♯ Bm7 A A7/E Adim/E♭ Dm7 A/C♯ D A/C♯ Bm A

Your everlasting summer, you can see it fading fast, so you grab a piece of something that you think is gonna last. You wouldn't know a diamond if you held it in your hand, the things you think are precious I can't understand.

telling' me you're a genius since you were seventeen; in all the time I've known you I still don't know what you mean. The weekend at the college didn't turn out like you planned, the things that pass for knowledge I can't understand.

spent a lot of money and I spent a lot of time, the trip we made to Hollywood is etched upon my mind. After all the things we've done and seen, you find another man, the things you think are useless I can't understand.

Are you reelin' in the

𝄋 Gmaj9 A

years, stowin' away the time, are you gatherin' up the tears, have you had enough of mine? Are you reelin' in the years, stowin' away the time, are you gatherin' up the tears, have you had enough of mine?

F♯m7

1, 2 {You been / I}

3 A — D.S. and Fade

Are you reelin' in the

RAMBLIN' GAMBLIN' MAN

Words and Music by
BOB SEGER

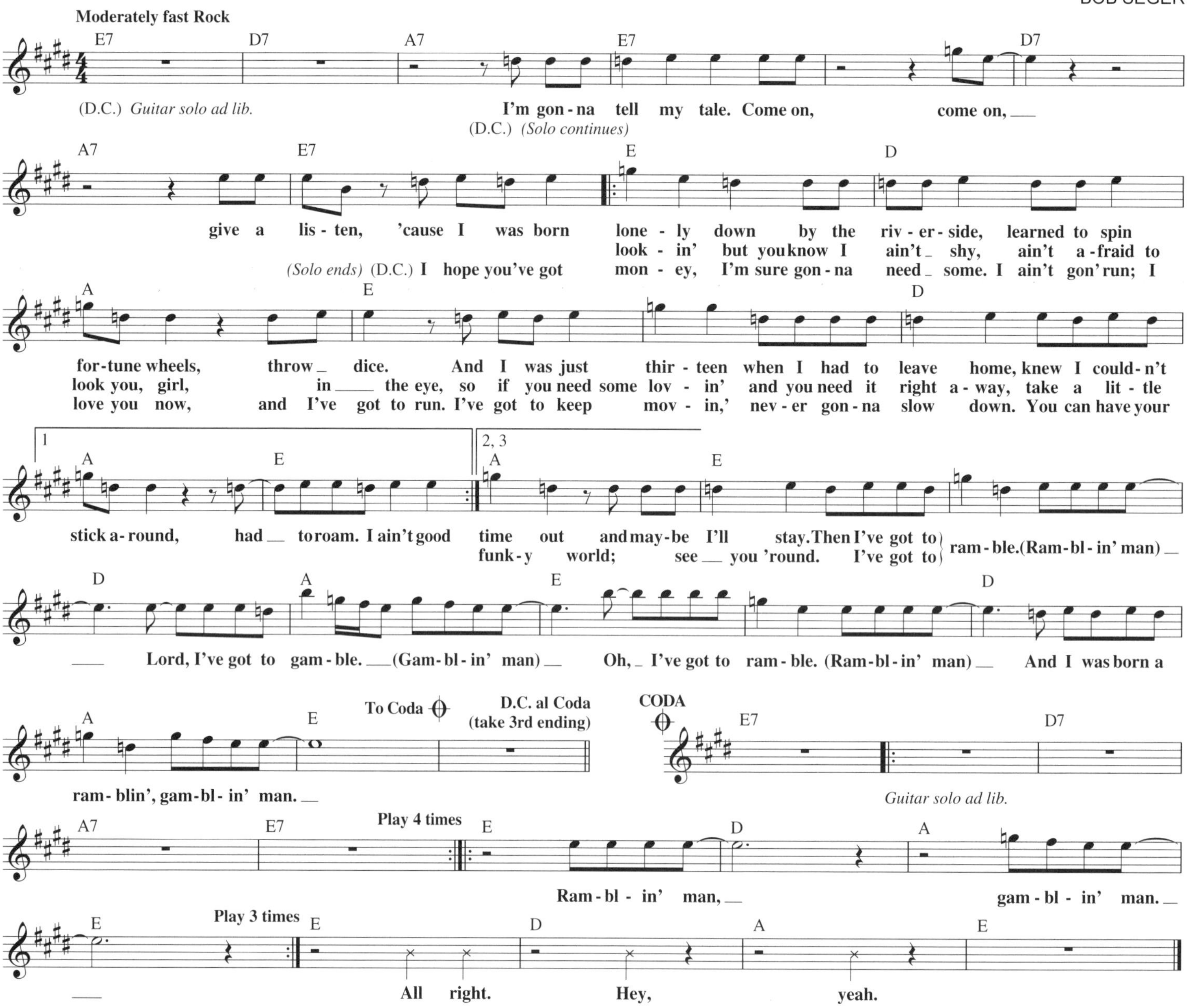

Moderately fast Rock
E7 D7 A7 E7 D7
(D.C.) Guitar solo ad lib.
I'm gon-na tell my tale. Come on, come on,
(D.C.) (Solo continues)
A7 E7 E D
give a lis-ten, 'cause I was born lone-ly down by the riv-er-side, learned to spin
look-in' but you know I ain't shy, ain't a-fraid to
(Solo ends) (D.C.) I hope you've got mon-ey, I'm sure gon-na need some. I ain't gon' run; I
A E D
for-tune wheels, throw dice. And I was just thir-teen when I had to leave home, knew I could-n't
look you, girl, in the eye, so if you need some lov-in' and you need it right a-way, take a lit-tle
love you now, and I've got to run. I've got to keep mov-in,' nev-er gon-na slow down. You can have your
1 A E
stick a-round, had to roam. I ain't good
2, 3 A E
time out and may-be I'll stay. Then I've got to
funk-y world; see you 'round. I've got to
ram-ble. (Ram-bl-in' man)
D A E D
Lord, I've got to gam-ble. (Gam-bl-in' man) Oh, I've got to ram-ble. (Ram-bl-in' man) And I was born a
A E
To Coda
D.C. al Coda (take 3rd ending)
ram-blin', gam-bl-in' man.
CODA
E7 D7
Guitar solo ad lib.
A7 E7
Play 4 times
E D A
Ram-bl-in' man, gam-bl-in' man.
E
Play 3 times
E D A E
All right. Hey, yeah.

RAMBLIN' ROSE

Words and Music by NOEL SHERMAN
and JOE SHERMAN

Moderately
G7 C D7
Ram-blin' Rose, ram-blin' Rose, why you ram-ble no one
on, ram-ble on. When your ram-blin' days are
Rose, ram-blin' Rose, why I want you, heav-en
G7 C7 F C
knows. Wild and wind-blown, that's how you've grown, who can
gone. Who will love you with a love true, when your
knows. Though I love you with a love true, who can
G7
1, 2 C F C
3 C
cling to a ram-blin' Rose? Ram-ble
ram-blin' days are gone? Ram-blin'
cling to a ram-blin' Rose?

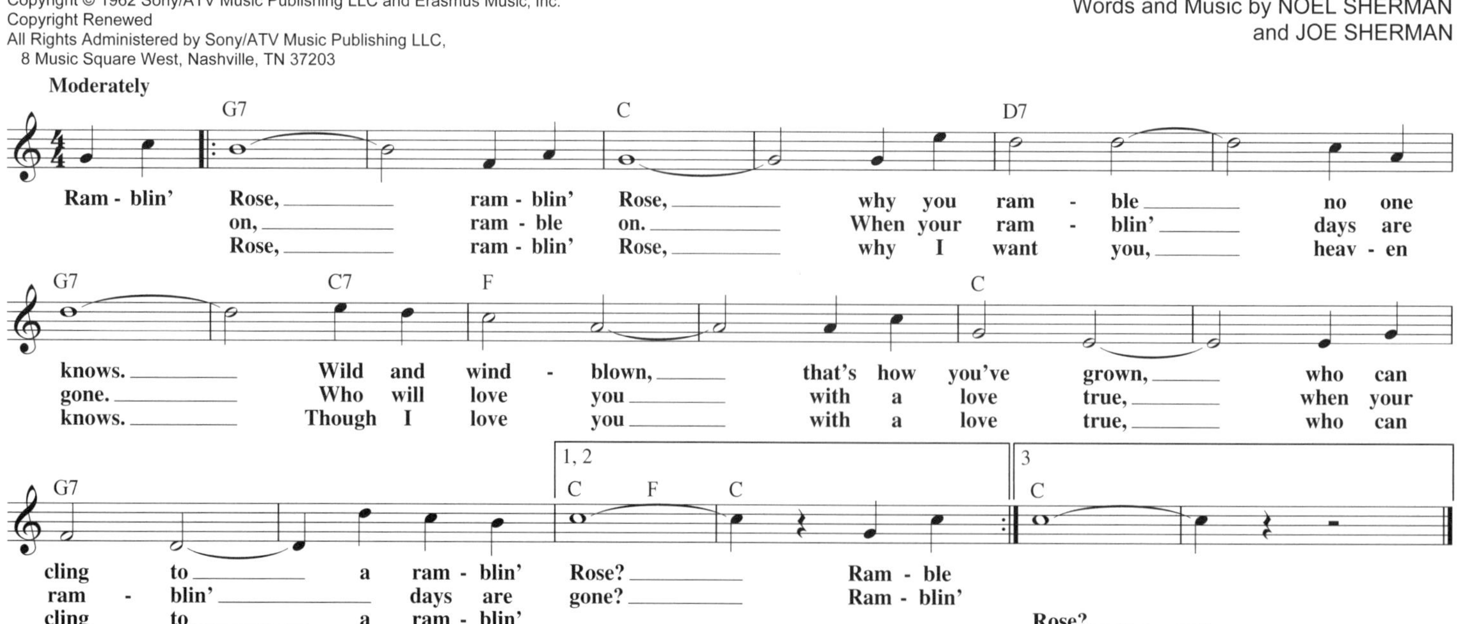

RAPPER'S DELIGHT

By NILE RODGERS
and BERNARD EDWARDS

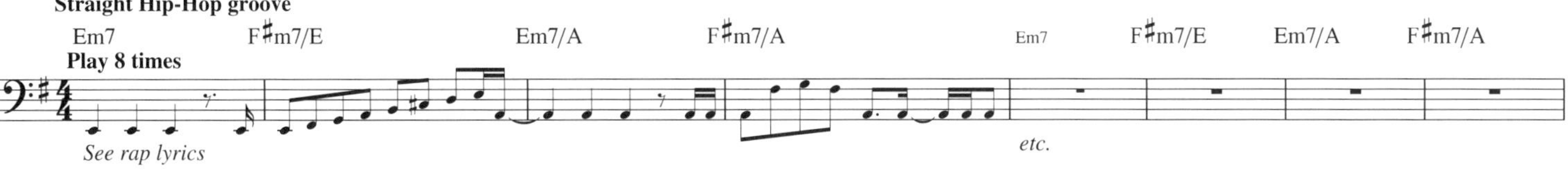

Em7 N.C.

Fade on last time through

Rap lyrics:
Now what you hear is not a test
I'm rapping to the beat
And me, the groove and my friends
Are gonna try to move your feet
See I am Wonder Mike
And I like to say hello
To the black, to the white, the red, and the brown
The purple and yellow
But first I got to bang bang the boogie to the boogie
Say up jump the boogie to the bang bang boogie
Let's rock, you don't stop
Rock the riddle that will make your body rock
Well so far you've heard my voice
But I brought two friends along
And next on the mike is my man Hank
Come on, Hank, sing that song

Check it out, I'm the C-A-S-an-the-O-V-A
And the rest is F-L-Y
You see I go by the code of the doctor of the mix
And these reasons, I'll tell you why
You see I'm six foot one and I'm tons of fun
And I dress to a T
You see I've got more clothes than Muhammad Ali
And I dress so viciously
I've got bodyguards, I've got two big cars
That definitely ain't the wack
I've got a Lincoln Continental and a sunroof Cadillac
So after school, I take a dip in the pool
Which really is on the wall
I got a color TV so I can see
The Knicks play basketball
Hear me talking bout checkbooks, credit cards
More money than a sucker could ever spend
But I wouldn't give a sucker or a bum from the rucker
Not a dime 'til I made it again
Everybody go hotel, motel
What you gonna do today (say what?)
You say I'm gonna get a fly girl, gonna get some spanking
Drive off in a def OJ
Everybody go, hotel motel, holiday inn
Say if your girl starts actin up, then you take her friend
Master Gee, am I mellow?
It's on you so what you gonna do?

Well, it's on and on and on, on and on
The beat don't stop until the break of dawn
I said M-A-S-T-E-R, a G with a double E
I said I go by the unforgettable name
Of the man they call the Master Gee
Well, my name is known all over the world
By all the foxy ladies and the pretty girls
I'm going down in history
As the baddest rapper there could ever be
Now I'm feeling the highs and you're feeling the lows
The beat starts getting into your toes
You start popping your fingers and stomping your feet
And moving your body while you're sitting in your seat
And damn, you start doing the freak
I said damn, right out of your seat
Then you throw your hands high in the air
You're rocking to the rhythm, shake your derriere
You're rocking to the beat without a care
With the sure shot MCs for the affair
Now, I'm not as tall as the rest of the gang
But I rap to the beat just the same
I got a little face and a pair of brown eyes
All I'm here to do, ladies, is hypnotize
Singing on and on and on and on
The beat don't stop until the break of dawn
Singing on and on and on, on and on
Like a hot buttered pop da pop da pop dibbie dibbie
Pop da pop pop you don't dare stop
Come alive y'all give me what you've got

I guess by now you can take a hunch
And find that I am the baby of the bunch
But that's okay, I still keep in stride
Cause all I'm here to do is just wiggle your behind
Singing on and on and on and on
The beat don't stop until the break of dawn
Singing on and on and on, on and on
Rock, rock y'all, throw it on the floor
I'm gonna freak you, here I'm gonna freak you there
I'm gonna move you out of this atmosphere
'Cause I'm one of a kind and I'll shock your mind
I'll put t-t-tickets on your behind
I said 1-2-3-4, come on girls get on the floor
A come alive, y'all a give me what you've got
'Cause I'm guaranteed to make you rock
I said 1-2-3-4, tell me Wonder Mike, what are you waiting for?

I said a hip hop the hippy to the hippy
The hip hip hop, a you don't stop the rock it to the
Bang bang boogie, say up jumped the boogie
To the rhythm of the boogie, the beat
Skiddlee beebop a we rock a scoobie doo
And guess what, America, we love you
Because you rock and you roll with so much soul
You could rock 'til you're a hundred and one years old
I don't mean to brag, I don't mean to boast
But we like hot butter on our breakfast toast
Rock it up baby bubbah
Raby bubbah to the boogie da bang bang da boogie
To the beat beat, it's so unique
Come on everybody and dance to the beat

Ever went over a friend's house to eat
And the food just ain't no good?
I mean the macaroni's soggy, the peas are mushed
And the chicken tastes like wood
So you try to play it off like you think you can
By saying that you're full
And then your friend says, "Momma, he's just being polite,
He ain't finished, uh uh, that's bull."
So your heart starts pumping and you think of a lie
And you say that you already ate
And your friend says, "Man, there's plenty of food."
So you pile some more on your plate
While the stinky food's steaming, your mind starts to dreaming
Of the moment that it's time to leave
And then you look at your plate and your chicken's slowly rotting
Into something that looks like cheese
Oh so you say, that's it, I've got to leave this place
I don't care what these people think
I'm just sitting here making myself nauseous
With this ugly food that stinks
So you bust out the door while it's still closed
Still sick from the food you ate
And then you run to the store for quick relief
From a bottle of Kaopectate
And then you call your friend two weeks later
To see how he has been
And he says I understand about the food
Baby Bubbah, but we're still friends
With a hip hop the hippie to the hippie
The hip hip a hop a you don't stop the rocking
To the bang bang boogie
Say up jump the bookie to the rhythm of the boogie the beat...

RHYTHM OF THE NIGHT

Words and Music by
DIANE WARREN

Lively dance beat

D C/D G/A D C/D Gsus G

(Instrumental)
When it feels like the world_ is on your shoul-ders,
Look out on the street now; the par - ty's just be - gin - ning,

D C/D G D

and all of the mad - ness has_ got you go - in' cra - zy, it's_ time to get out.
the mu-sic's play - ing; a_ cel - e - bra - tion's start - ing. Un - der the street lights

C/D Gsus G D C/D G

Step out in - to the street where all_ of the ac - tion is right there at your feet. Well,
the scene is be - ing set. A night_ for ro - mance, a night you won't for - get. So

A/C♯ G/B Bm G Asus A

(1.) I know a place where we can dance the whole night a - way un - der-neath e - lec - tric stars.
(2., 3.) come join the fun, this ain't no time to be stay - ing home, ooh, there's too much go - ing on.

A/C♯ G/B Bm G **To Coda**

Just come with me and we can shake your blues right a - way. You'll be do - ing fine once the mu - sic
To - night is gon - na be a night like you've nev - er known. We're gon-na have a good time the whole night

Asus A D Em7 D/F♯ A

starts, oh.
long, oh.
Feel the beat of the rhy - thm of_ the night, dance un - til the morn - ing

Bm Em7 D/F♯ A

light. For - get a - bout the wor - ries on_ your mind, you can leave them all_ be -

D Em7 D/F♯ A G

hind. Feel the beat of the rhy - thm of_ the night, oh, the rhy - thm of_ the night,_

1 A D C/D G/A D

oh,_ yeah._ *(Instrumental)*

C/D G/A 2 A Bm A/B A 1 G/A F♯m 2 G/A A Bm **D.S. al Coda**

oh, yeah. *(Instrumental)*

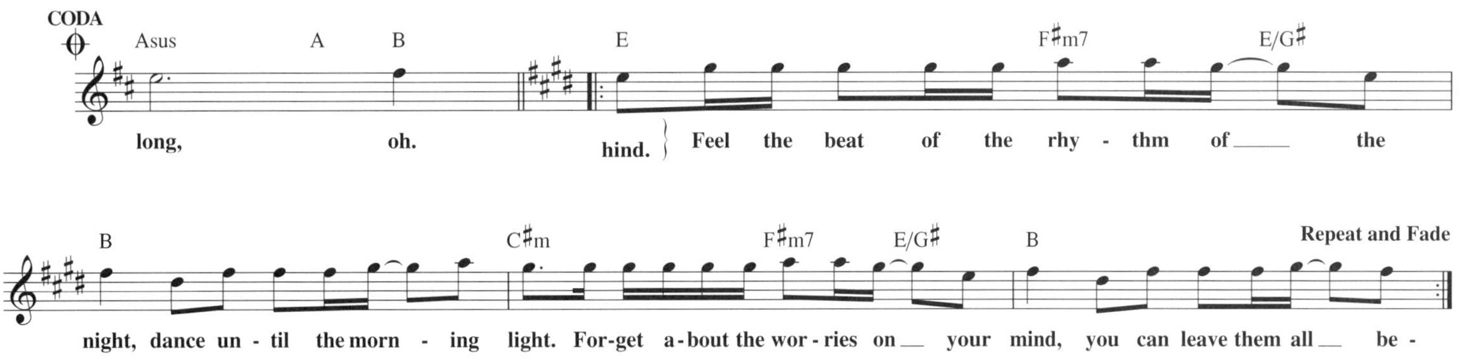

CODA

Asus A B | E F♯m7 E/G♯

long, oh. hind. Feel the beat of the rhy - thm of ___ the

B C♯m F♯m7 E/G♯ B — Repeat and Fade

night, dance un - til the morn - ing light. For-get a-bout the wor - ries on ___ your mind, you can leave them all ___ be -

REFUGEE

Words and Music by TOM PETTY
and MIKE CAMPBELL

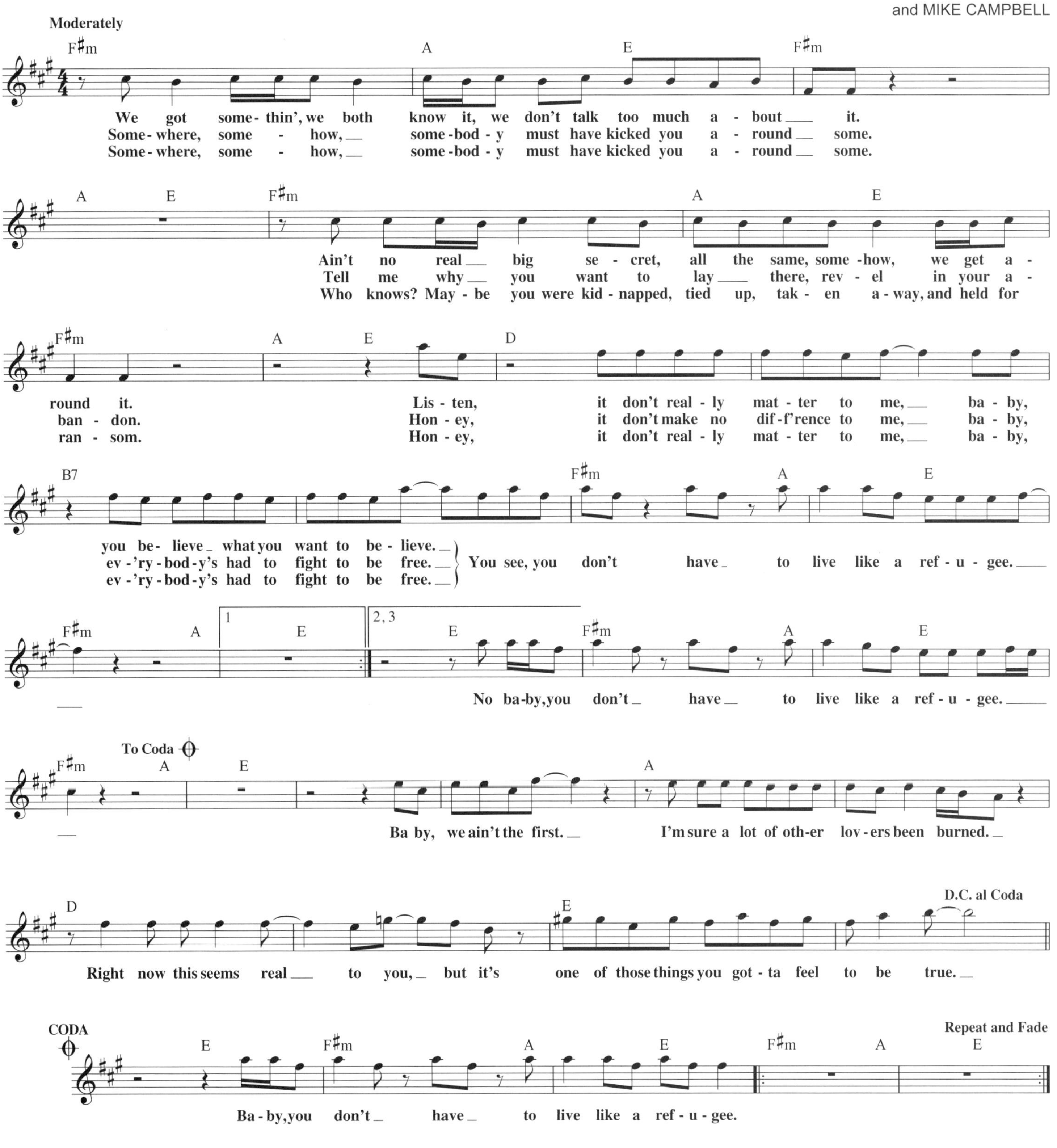

Moderately

F♯m A E F♯m

We got some - thin', we both know it, we don't talk too much a - bout ___ it.
Some - where, some - how, ___ some - bod - y must have kicked you a - round ___ some.
Some - where, some - how, ___ some - bod - y must have kicked you a - round ___ some.

A E F♯m A E

Ain't no real ___ big se - cret, all the same, some - how, we get a -
Tell me why ___ you want to lay ___ there, rev - el in your a -
Who knows? May - be you were kid - napped, tied up, tak - en a - way, and held for

F♯m A E D

round it. Lis - ten, it don't real - ly mat - ter to me, ___ ba - by,
ban - don. Hon - ey, it don't make no dif - f'rence to me, ___ ba - by,
ran - som. Hon - ey, it don't real - ly mat - ter to me, ___ ba - by,

B7 F♯m A E

you be - lieve what you want to be - lieve. ___
ev - 'ry - bod - y's had to fight to be free. ___
ev - 'ry - bod - y's had to fight to be free. ___
You see, you don't have to live like a ref - u - gee. ___

F♯m A | 1 E | 2, 3 E F♯m A E

No ba - by, you don't ___ have ___ to live like a ref - u - gee. ___

To Coda

F♯m A E A

Ba by, we ain't the first. ___ I'm sure a lot of oth - er lov - ers been burned. ___

D E — D.C. al Coda

Right now this seems real ___ to you, ___ but it's one of those things you got - ta feel to be true. ___

REUNITED

Words and Music by DINO FEKARIS
and FREDDIE PERREN

Additional Lyrics

3. Lover, lover this is solid love, and you're exactly what I'm dreaming of.
All through the day and all through the night,
I'll give you all the love I have with all my might, hey, hey!

LYRICS FOR FADE ENDING:

Ooo, listen baby, I won't ever make you cry, I won't let one day go by
without holding you, without kissing you, without loving you.
Ooo, you're my everything, only you know how to free
all the love there is in me.
I wanna let you know, I won't let you go.
I wanna let you know, I won't let you go.
Ooo, feels so good!

RIDE LIKE THE WIND

Words and Music by
CHRISTOPHER CROSS

ROCK AND ROLL IS HERE TO STAY

Words and Music by
DAVID WHITE

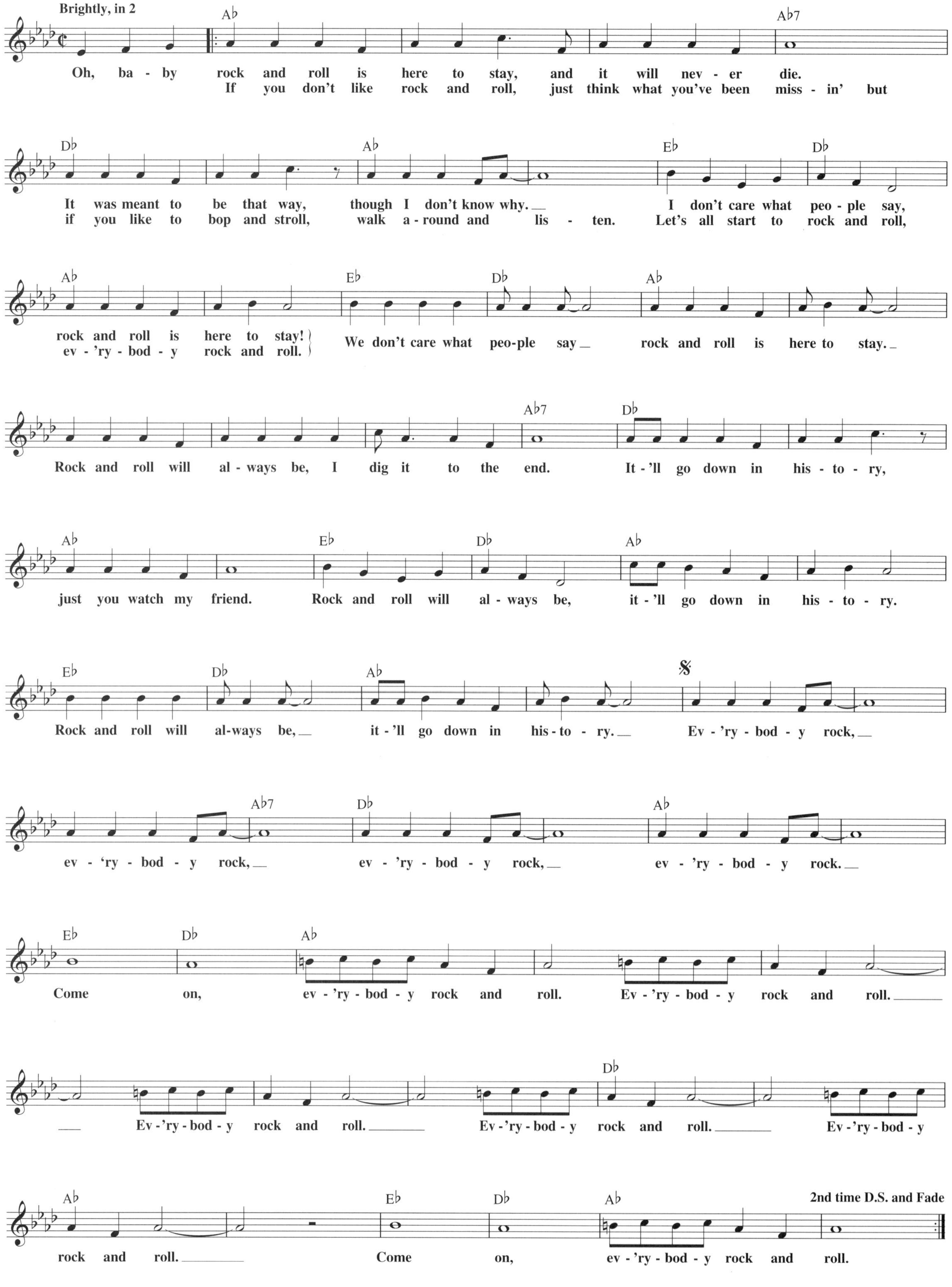

Brightly, in 2

Oh, ba - by rock and roll is here to stay, and it will nev - er die.
If you don't like rock and roll, just think what you've been miss - in' but

It was meant to be that way, though I don't know why. I don't care what peo - ple say,
if you like to bop and stroll, walk a - round and lis - ten. Let's all start to rock and roll,

rock and roll is here to stay! We don't care what peo-ple say rock and roll is here to stay.
ev - 'ry - bod - y rock and roll.

Rock and roll will al - ways be, I dig it to the end. It - 'll go down in his - to - ry,

just you watch my friend. Rock and roll will al - ways be, it - 'll go down in his - to - ry.

Rock and roll will al-ways be, it - 'll go down in his-to - ry. Ev - 'ry - bod - y rock,

ev - 'ry - bod - y rock, ev - 'ry - bod - y rock, ev - 'ry - bod - y rock.

Come on, ev - 'ry - bod - y rock and roll. Ev - 'ry - bod - y rock and roll.

Ev - 'ry - bod - y rock and roll. Ev - 'ry - bod - y rock and roll. Ev - 'ry - bod - y

rock and roll. Come on, ev - 'ry - bod - y rock and roll.

2nd time D.S. and Fade

ROSANNA

Words and Music by
DAVID PAICH

Moderate shuffle

G
All I wan - na do when I wake up in the morn - ing is see your eyes,
I can see your face still shin - ing through the win - dow on the oth - er side,

F(add9)
Ro - san - na, Ro - san - na. Nev - er thought that a
Ro - san - na, Ro - san - na. I did - n't know that a

Em9 G
girl like you could ev - er care for me, Ro - san - na.
girl like you could make me feel so sad, Ro - san - na.

C F
All I wan - na do in the mid - dle of the eve - ning is
All I wan - na tell you is now you'll nev - er, ev - er have to

hold you tight, Ro - san - na, Ro - san - na.
com - pro - mise, Ro - san - na, Ro - san - na.

E♭(add2) Dm9
I did - n't know you were look - in' for more than I could ev - er be.
I ne - ver thought that los - in' you could ev - er hurt so bad.

Gm F/A B♭ E♭/B♭
Not quite a year since you went a - way. Ro - san -

B♭ F Gm F/A B♭
- na, yeah. Now she's gone, and I have to say:

E♭ B♭ F B♭/F B♭/C Cm7 B♭/C
(Instrumental) Meet you all the way,

Cm7 E♭ B♭ F Gm7 B♭/C Cm7 B♭/C Cm7 E♭ B♭ F
meet you all the way, Ro-san - na, yeah.

Gm7 B♭/C Cm7 B♭/C Cm7 E♭ B♭ F Gm7 B♭/C Cm7 B♭/C
Meet you all the way, meet you all the way,

Cm7 E♭6 B♭ F 1 2
Ro - san - na, yeah.

Repeat and Fade

Gm7 C/G Dm/G C/G Gm7 C/G Gm7 C/G Dm/G C/G Gm7 C/G
(Instrumental ad lib)

RIGHT BACK WHERE WE STARTED FROM

Words and Music by
VINCE EDWARDS and PIERRE TUBBS

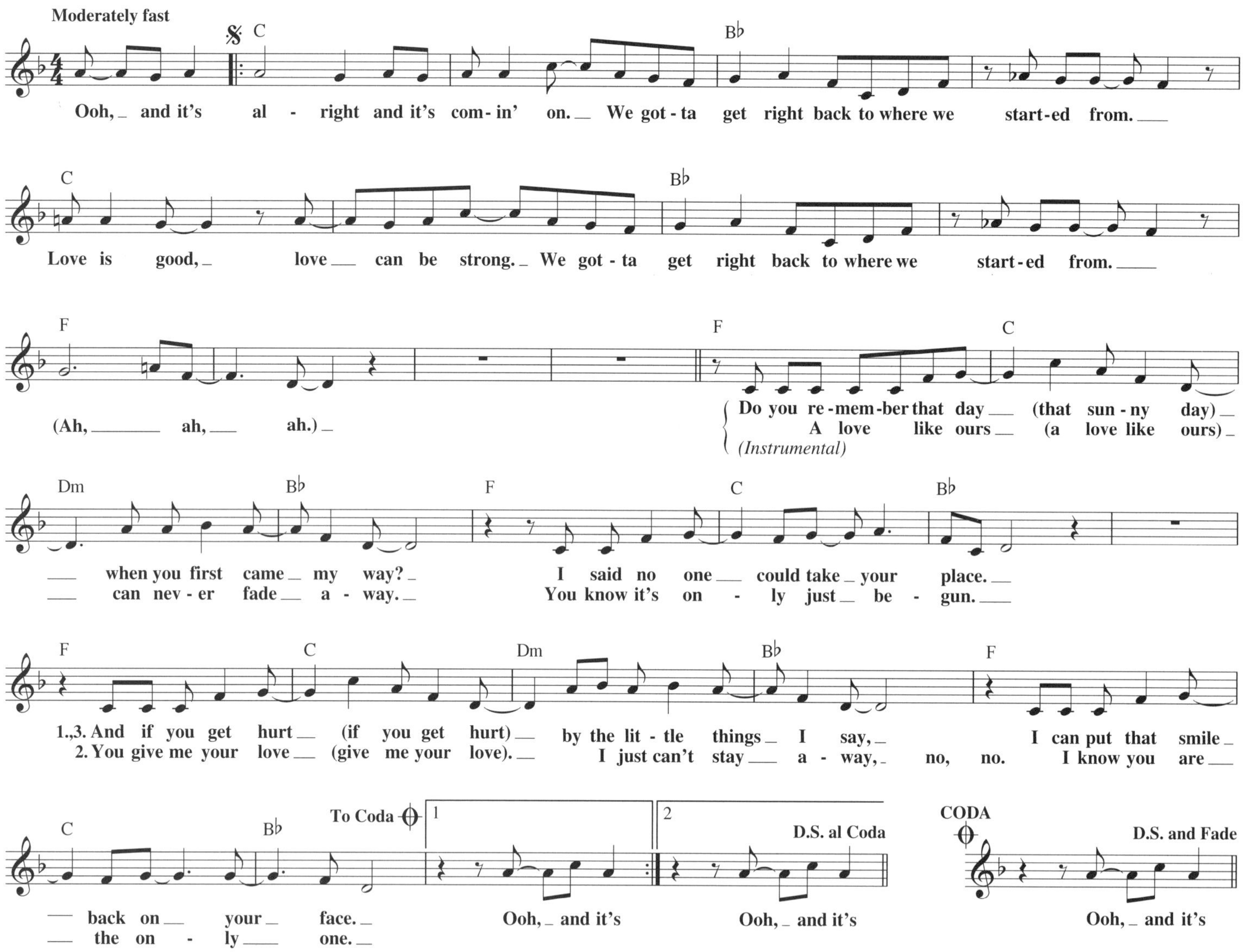

Moderately fast

C Bb
Ooh, _ and it's al - right and it's com - in' on. _ We got - ta get right back to where we start - ed from. _

C Bb
Love is good, _ love _ can be strong. _ We got - ta get right back to where we start - ed from. _

F F C
(Ah, _ ah, _ ah.) _ Do you re - mem - ber that day _ (that sun - ny day) _
A love like ours _ (a love like ours) _
(Instrumental)

Dm Bb F C Bb
_ when you first came _ my way? _ I said no one _ could take _ your place. _
_ can nev - er fade _ a - way. _ You know it's on - ly just _ be - gun. _

F C Dm Bb F
1.,3. And if you get hurt _ (if you get hurt) _ by the lit - tle things _ I say, _ I can put that smile _
2. You give me your love _ (give me your love). _ I just can't stay _ a - way, _ no, no. I know you are _

C Bb
_ back on _ your _ face. _
_ the on - ly _ one. _

To Coda 1
Ooh, _ and it's

2 D.S. al Coda
Ooh, _ and it's

CODA D.S. and Fade
Ooh, _ and it's

ROCK ISLAND LINE

Words and Music by
LONNIE DONEGAN

Moderately
Bb
Oh, the Rock Is - land Line _ it is a might - y good road. _ Oh, the Rock Is - land Line _ it is the
F7 Bb Eb9
road to ride _ the Rock Is - land Line _ it is a might - y good road. _ Well, if you want to ride you got to
Bb Eb9 Cm7 Bb
Fine
ride it like you find it, get your tick - et at the sta - tion for the Rock Is - land Line. _

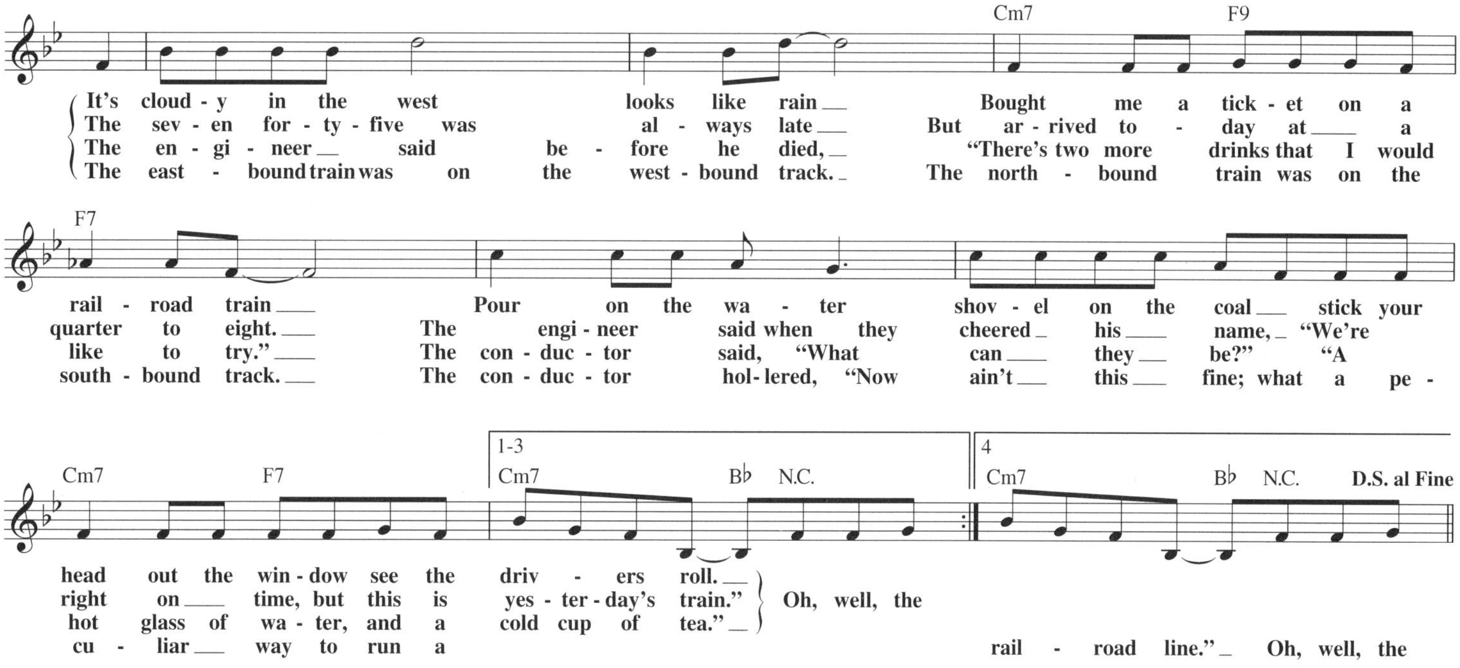

Cm7 F9

It's cloud - y in the west looks like rain __ Bought me a tick - et on a
The sev - en for - ty - five was al - ways late __ But ar - rived to - day at __ a
The en - gi - neer __ said be - fore he died, __ "There's two more drinks that I would
The east - bound train was on the west - bound track. _ The north - bound train was on the

F7

rail - road train __ Pour on the wa - ter shov - el on the coal __ stick your
quarter to eight. __ The engi - neer said when they cheered _ his __ name, _ "We're
like to try." __ The con - duc - tor said, "What can __ they __ be?" "A
south - bound track. __ The con - duc - tor hol - lered, "Now ain't __ this __ fine; what a pe -

Cm7 F7 | 1-3 Cm7 B♭ N.C. | 4 Cm7 B♭ N.C. D.S. al Fine

head out the win - dow see the driv - ers roll. __
right on __ time, but this is yes - ter - day's train." Oh, well, the
hot glass of wa - ter, and a cold cup of tea." __
cu - liar __ way to run a rail - road line." _ Oh, well, the

ROCK ON

Words and Music by
DAVID ESSEX

Slowly, but with a funky double-time feeling

N.C.

Hey, did, y' rock 'n' roll? ____ Rock on! Oh, my soul! Hey, did y' boog - ie, too? _

Did ya? Hey, shout sum - mer - time blues, jump up an' down in the blue suede shoes.

Hey, did y' rock 'n' roll? ____ Rock on! And where do we go __ from here? __

Which is the way that's clear? Still look - in' for __ that blue jean' mov - ie queen, ____ pret - ti - est girl I ev - er seen. _

To Coda

See her shake _ on the mov - ie screen ____ Jim - my Dean! __ James Dean. *(Instrumental)*

D.S. al Coda

And

CODA

Repeat and Fade

Jim - my Dean! Rock on! Rock

ROCKET MAN
(I Think It's Gonna Be a Long Long Time)

Words and Music by ELTON JOHN
and BERNIE TAUPIN

Moderately slow, with a beat

She packed my bags last night pre-flight, zero hour nine A. M.
And I'm gonna be high as a kite by then.
I miss the earth so much, I miss my wife, it's lonely out in space
on such a timeless flight.

And I think it's gonna be a long, long time till touch-down brings me 'round again to find
I'm not the man they think I am at home, oh no no no, I'm a
rocket man.
Rocket man burning out his fuse up here alone.

To Coda

Mars ain't the kind of place to raise your kids,
in fact it's cold as hell.
And there's no one there to raise them if you did.
And all this science I don't understand.
It's just my job five days a week.
A rocket man, A rocket man.

D.S. al Coda

CODA

And I think it's gonna be a long, long time.

Repeat and Fade

ROCK'N ME

Words and Music by
STEVE MILLER

ROLL WITH IT

Words and Music by WILL JENNINGS,
STEVE WINWOOD, EDDIE HOLLAND,
LAMONT DOZIER and BRIAN HOLLAND

Medium Funk
G7
When life is too much, roll with it, ba - by. Don't stop and lose your touch, oh no, ba - by. Hard time knock - ing at your door, I'll tell them you ain't there no more.
that you love is good as mon - ey. I swear by stars a - bove, sweet as hon - ey. Peo - ple think you're down and out, You show them what it's all a - bout.
- 'll be a day, you'll get there, ba - by. You'll hear the mu - sic play, you'll dance, ba - by. You'll leave bad times be - hind, noth - ing but good times on your mind.
C7
G7
Get on through it, roll with it, ba - by.
You can make it, roll with it, ba - by.
You can do it, roll with it, ba - by.
D
Em7
F
C/G
Luck - 'll come and then slip a - way, You've got a move, bring it back to stay.
When this world turns its back on you, hang in and do that sweet thing you do.
Then you'll see life will be so nice, it's just a step up to par - a - dise.
You just
roll with it, ba - by; come on and just roll with it, ba - by, you and me.
To Coda
N.C.
Roll with it, ba - by; hang on and just roll with it, ba - by. Hey. The way
(Instrumental)
Bb
Dm7
Ab
D.S. al Coda
Now there -
CODA
Repeat and Fade

ROXANNE

Words and Music by
STING

RUBY BABY

Words and Music by JERRY LEIBER
and MIKE STOLLER

Moderately
C7
I love a girl and a Ru - by is her name.
Each time I see you, ba - by, my heart cries.
This
Tell yuh,
girl don't love me but I love her just the same.
I'm gon - na steal you a - way from all those guys.
F7
C
Ru - by, Ru - by, how I want yuh, like a ghost I'm a gon - na haunt yuh.
From the hap - py day I met yuh I made a bet that I was gon - na get yuh.
G7
F7
C
Ru - by, Ru - by, Ru - by, will you be mine?
Ru - by, Ru - by, Ru - by, will you be mine?
Ru - by, Ru - by, Ru - by, Ba - by. Ru - by, Ru - by, Ru - by, Ba - by.
F7
C
Ru - by, Ru - by, Ru - by, Ba - by. Ru - by, Ru - by, Ru - by, Ba - by.
G7
F7
C
Ah, ah, ah - ah. I love this girl; I said - a,
Ru - by is her name. When this girl looks at me she just
F7
sets my heart a - flame. Got some hug - gin' and kiss - es too, yeah, and
C
C
F7
I'm gon - na give them - a all to you. Now lis - ten, Ru - by, Ru - by, when will you be
G7
F7
C
G7
F7
C
mine? Ru - by, Ru - by, when will you be mine?

RUN TO YOU

Words and Music by BRYAN ADAMS
and JIM VALLANCE

Driving Rock
She says her love for me could nev-er die. But that-'d change if she ev-er found out a-bout you and I.
She's got a heart of gold, she'd nev-er let me down. But you're the one that al-ways turns me on and keeps me com-in' 'round.
Oh, but her love is cold. It would-n't hurt her if she did-n't know. 'Cause when it gets too much I need to feel your touch.
I know her love is true, but it's so damn eas-y mak-in' love to you. I got my mind made up, I need to feel your touch.
I'm gon-na run to you, I'm gon-na run to you. 'Cause when the feel-in's right I'm gon-na run all night. I'm gon-na run to you.
stay
(Instrumental)
To Coda
Yeah, gon-na run to you.
Oh, when the feel-in's right I'm gon-na run all night, I'm gon-na run to you.
(Instrumental)
D.S. al Coda (lyric 2)
Oh, gon-na
CODA
run to you. Oh, when the feel-in's right I'm gon-na run all night I'm gon-na run to you.
stay
Repeat and Fade
Yeah, gon-na

RUN AROUND

Words and Music by
JOHN POPPER

Brightly
G C Am D G C
Once up - on a mid - night, dear - ie, I woke with some - thing in my head.
shake me and my con - fi - dence 'bout a great man - y things,
- ba, dear, this is the pi - lot speak - ing and I've got some news for you.

Am D G C Am D
I could - n't es - cape the mem - o - ry of a phone
but I've been there; I can see it cow - er like a ner -
It seems my ship still stands no mat - ter what you drop, and there ain't a

G C Am D G C
call and of what you said. Like a game show con - test - ant with a
vous ma - gi - cian wait - ing in the wings. Or a bad play where the he -
whole lot that you can do. Oh sure, the ban - ner may be torn and the wind's

Am D G C Am D
part - ing gift I could not be - lieve my eyes when I saw
roes are right and no - bod - y thinks or ex - pects too much, and
got - ten cold - er. Per - haps I've grown a lit - tle cyn - i - cal. But, I know

G C Am D G C
through the voice of a trust - ed friend who needs to hu - mor me and tell me
Hol - ly - wood's call - ing for the mov - ie rights, sing - ing, "Hey babe, let's keep in
no mat - ter what the wait - ress brings, I shall drink it and al - ways be

Am D G C Am D
lies. Yeah, hu - mor me and tell me lies. And
touch. Hey ba - by, let's keep in touch." But I want
full. Yeah, I will drink it and al - ways be full. Oh,

G C Am D G C
I'll lie too and say I don't mind. And as we seek, so shall
more than a touch. I want you to reach me and show me all the things no one else
I like cof - fee and I like tea. But to be a - ble to en - ter a fi -

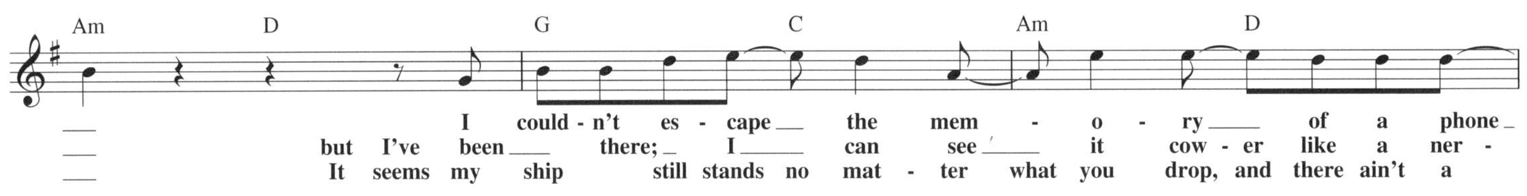

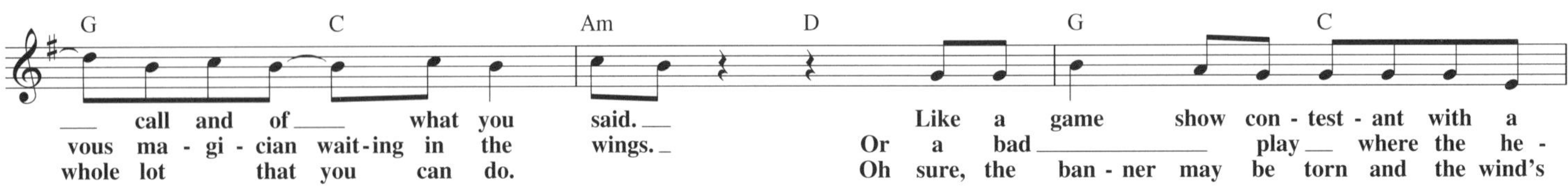

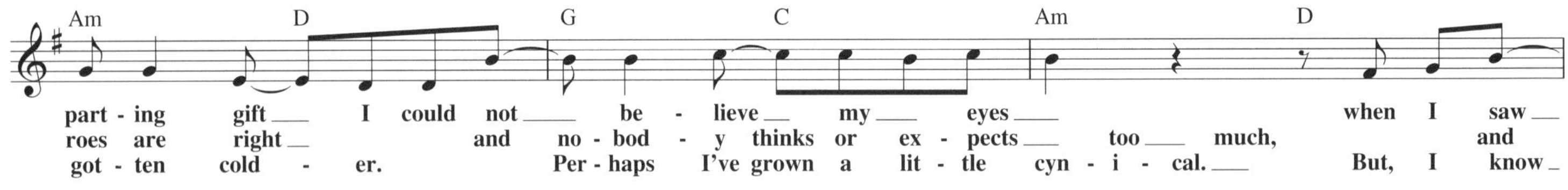

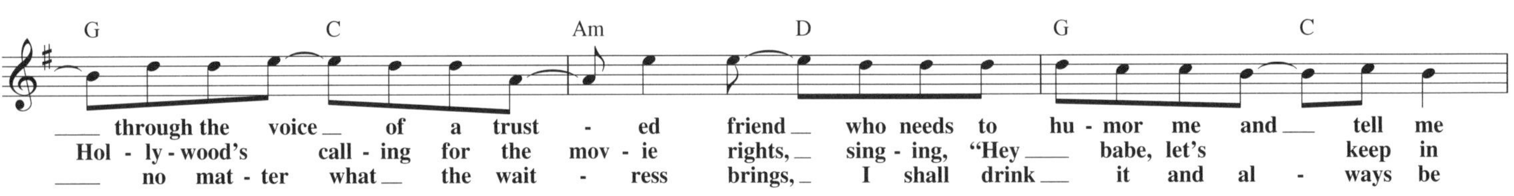

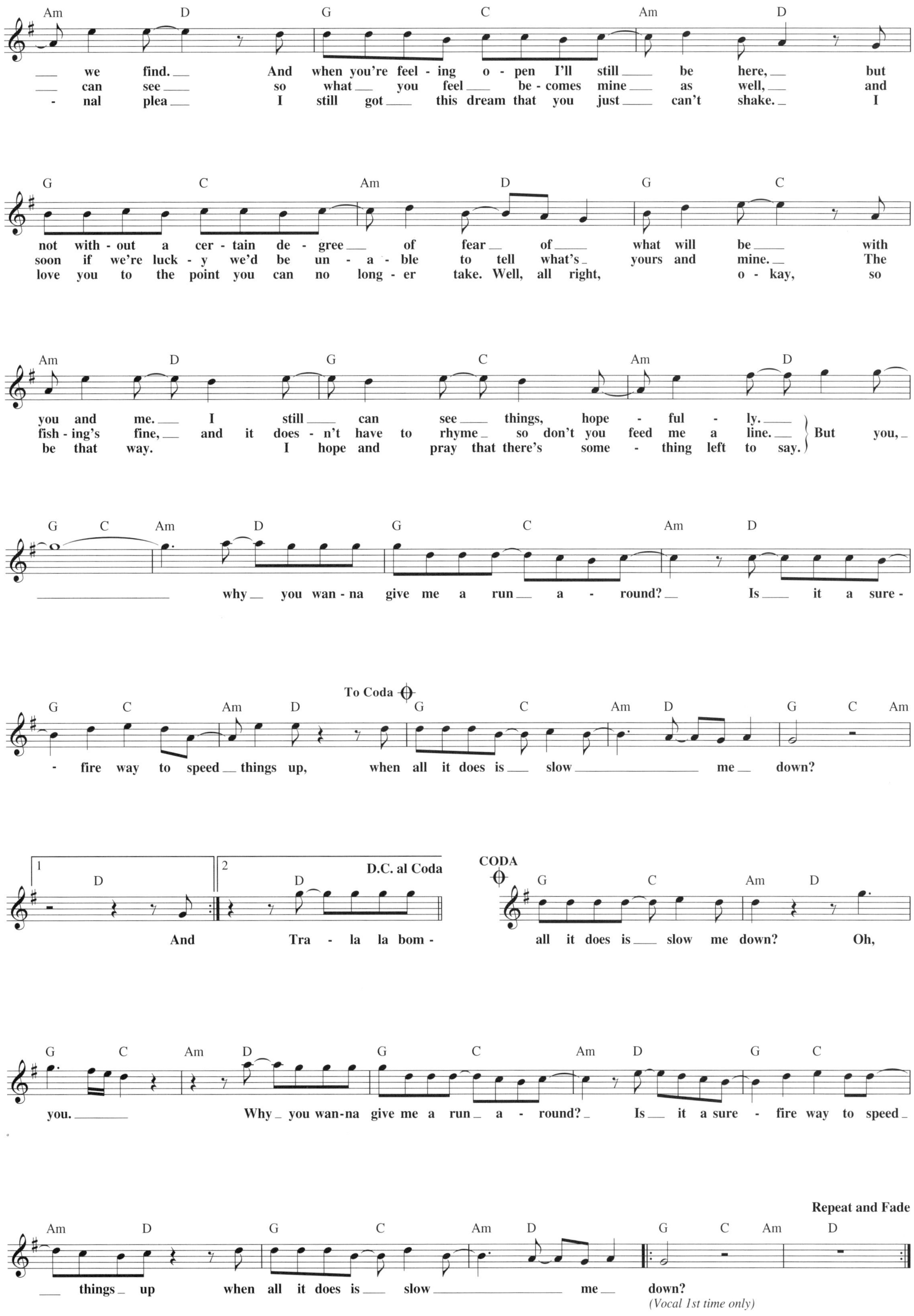

we find. And when you're feel - ing o - pen I'll still be here, but
can see so what you feel be - comes mine as well, and
- nal plea I still got this dream that you just can't shake. I

not with - out a cer - tain de - gree of fear of what will be with
soon if we're luck - y we'd be un - a - ble to tell what's yours and mine. The
love you to the point you can no long - er take. Well, all right, o - kay, so

you and me. I still can see things, hope - ful - ly.
fish - ing's fine, and it does - n't have to rhyme so don't you feed me a line. But you,
be that way. I hope and pray that there's some - thing left to say.

why you wan - na give me a run a - round? Is it a sure -

To Coda

- fire way to speed things up, when all it does is slow me down?

1 And

2 Tra - la la bom -

D.C. al Coda

CODA

all it does is slow me down? Oh,

you. Why you wan-na give me a run a - round? Is it a sure - fire way to speed

Repeat and Fade
things up when all it does is slow me down?
(Vocal 1st time only)

RUNNING SCARED

Words and Music by ROY ORBISON
and JOE MELSON

Moderately
G Am
Just run - ning scared each place we go, so a -
Bm D7 Am7 D7 N.C. G
fraid that he might show. Yeah, run - ning scared;
Am Bm D7
what would I do if he came back and want - ed
G N.C. G Am
you? Just run - ning scared, feel - ing low.
Bm D7
Run - ning scared, you loved him so. Just run - ning
G Am Bm
scared, a - fraid to lose. If he came back,
D7 G G7 C
which one would you choose? Then all at once,
he was stand - ing there, so sure of him - self; his head in the air.
My heart was break - ing, which one would it be? You turned a - round and
D7 1 G N.C. 2 G
walked a - way with me. Just run - ning me.

SAD MOVIES (MAKE ME CRY)

Words and Music by
JOHN D. LOUDERMILK

Moderately
A E7
He said he had to work so I went to the show a - lone. They
A A7
turned down the lights and turned the pro - jec - tor on. And just as the news of the
D A E7 A
world start - ed to be - gin, I saw my dar - ling and my best friend walk in.
E7
Though I was sit - ting there, they did - n't see. And so they sat right
A A7 D
down in front of me. And when he kissed her lips, I al - most died.
A E7 A A7
And in the mid - dle of the col - or car - toon, I start - ed to cry. Oh,
D A A7
sad mov - ies al - ways make me cry. Oh,
D E7
sad mov - ies al - ways make me cry.
A E7
So, I got up and slow - ly walked on home. And ma - ma saw the tears and said, "What's
A A7 D
wrong?" And so to keep from tell - ing her a lie,
A E7
I just said sad mov - ies make me
1 A 2 A D E7 A
cry. He cry.

SATURDAY NIGHT'S ALRIGHT (FOR FIGHTING)

Words and Music by ELTON JOHN
and BERNIE TAUPIN

With a beat

G F

It's get - ting late. _ Have you seen my mates? _ Ma tell me when the boys get here. _ It's
packed pret - ty tight in here to - night; _ I'm look - ing for a dol - ly to _ see me right. I may

C G

sev - en o' - clock and I wan - na rock, wan - na get _ a bel - ly full of beer. _ My _
use a lit - tle mus - cle to get what I need, I may sink _ a lit - tle drink and shout out she's with me. A coup -

F

_ old man's _ drunk - er than a bar - rel full of mon - keys and my old la - dy she don't care. My
- le of _ sounds that I real - ly _ like _ are the sound of a switch - blade and a mo - tor bike. I'm a

C G

sis - ter looks cute in her bra - ces and boots, _ a hand - ful of grease _ in her hair. _
ju - ve - nile prod - uct of the work - ing class _ whose best _ friend floats _ in the bot - tom of a glass, ooh. _

𝄋 D7#9 D7sus C

_ So don't give us none of your ag - gra - va - tion. We've

B♭ F

had it with your dis - ci - pline. _ Oh Sat - ur - day night's al - right _ for fight - in', get _

C

_ a lit - tle act - ion _ in. _ Get _ a - bout as oiled _ as a dies - el train, _ gon -

B♭ F

- na set this dance a - light. _ 'Cause Sat - ur - day night's the night _ I like, _ Sat -

C G E♭6 B♭/D F/C

- ur - day night's al - right _ al - right _ al - right, _ ooh. _

C To Coda 𝄌 1. G Dm F G Dm F G

_ *(Instrumental)* Well they're

2. F/C C F/C C F/C C E♭/B♭ B♭ E♭/B♭ B♭ E♭/B♭ B♭

_ *(Instrumental)*

B♭/F F B♭/F F B♭/F F F/C C F/C C F/C C

D.S. al Coda

CODA
F/C C F/C C F/C C E♭/B♭ B♭ E♭/B♭
Sat - ur - day Sat - ur - day Sat - ur - day Sat - ur - day Sat - ur -
Repeat and Fade
B♭ E♭/B♭ B♭ F B♭/F F B♭/F F C F/C C F/C C
day Sat - ur - day Sat - ur - day Sat - ur - day Sat - ur - day night's al - right.

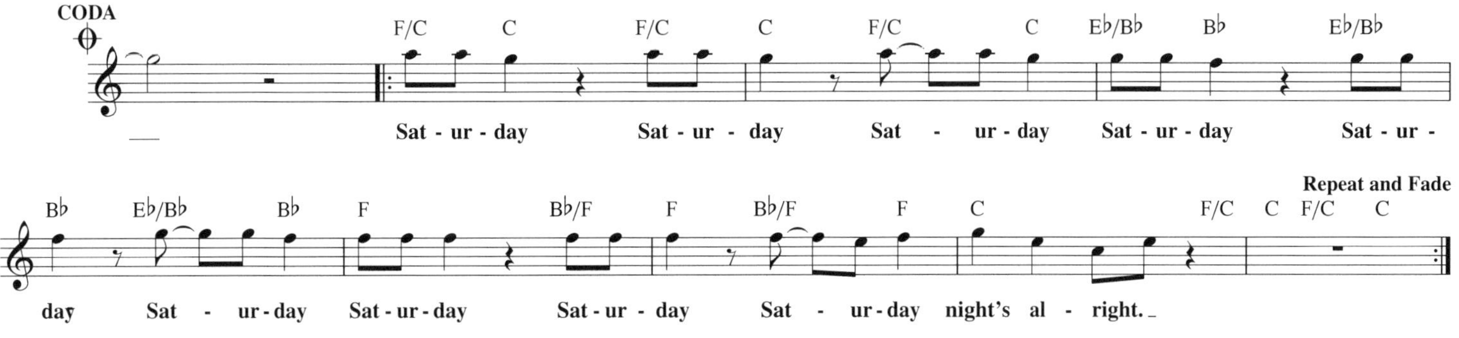

SEE YOU IN SEPTEMBER

Words by SID WAYNE
Music by SHERMAN EDWARDS

Beguine tempo

Fm7 B♭9 Fm7 B♭9
I'll be a - lone each and ev - 'ry night, while you're a - way, don't for - get to write.

Fm7 B♭7 E♭maj7 C7 Fm7
See you in Sep - tem - ber, see you

B♭7 E♭maj7 E♭6 C7 Fm Fm(maj7) Fm7 B♭7
when the sum - mer's thru. Here we are, say - ing good - bye at the

Gm Gm7 C7 Fm Fm7 F7 Fm7
sta - tion, sum - mer va - ca - tion is tak - ing you a - way.

B♭7 N.C. 𝄋 Fm7 B♭7 E♭maj7 C7
Have a good time, but re - mem - ber there is

Fm7 B♭7 Gm7 C7
dan - ger in the sum - mer moon a - bove; will I

Fm7 F♯dim Gm7 To Coda C7 Fm7
see you in Sep - tem - ber, or lose you

B♭7 E♭ Fm7
to a sum - mer love? Count - ing the days till I'll

B♭9 Fm7 B♭7 D.S. al Coda
be with you, count - ing the hours and the min - utes too. Have a

CODA
Cm Fm7
or lose you

B♭7sus E♭ B E♭
to a sum - mer love?

THE SEARCH IS OVER

Words and Music by JAMES M. PETERIK
and FRANK SULLIVAN

Moderately
E♭ A♭maj7
How can I con - vince you what you see is real?
Can we last for - ev - er? Do we fall a - part?
Now at last I hold you. Now all is said and done.
E♭ A♭ Gsus G7/B
Who am I to blame you for doubt - ing what you feel?
At times it's so con - fus - ing, the ques - tions of the heart.
The search is come full cir - cle; our des - ti - nies are one.
Cm B♭/C A♭maj7 E♭ B♭/D
I was al - ways reach - ing. You were just a girl I
You fol - lowed me through chang - es and pa - tient - ly you'd wait till
So if you ev - er loved me, show me that you give a
Cm Gm7 A♭ Gsus
knew. I took for grant - ed the friend I have in you.
I came to my sens - es through some mir - a - cle of fate.
damn. You'll know for cer - tain the man I real - ly am.
G7 F/G G7 C G/B F/A Gsus G7 F/G G7
3
I was liv - ing for a dream, lov - ing for a mo - ment. Tak - ing on
C G/B F/A Gsus G7 F/G
the world, that was just my style.
Now I look in - to your
Now I look in - to your
Then I touched your
E♭ A♭maj7 Fm7 Bdim7
eyes; I can see for - ev - er. The search is
eyes; I can see for - ev - er. The search is
hand; I could hear you whis - per. The search is
Cm To Coda A♭ B♭7 1 E♭ A♭/E♭ B♭/E♭
o - ver. You were with me all the while.
o - ver. You were
o - ver. Love was
2 E♭ B♭/D Cm Gm7
while. Now the miles stretch out be - hind me,
A♭ B♭7 E♭ B♭/D Cm Gm7
loves that I have lost. Bro - ken hearts lie vic - tims of the

A♭ B♭/A♭ A♭ Fm7 Cm
game. Then good luck it fi - n'lly struck like
B♭ Fm7 E♭
light - nin' from the blue; ev - er - y high - way is lead - in' me back to
B♭
D.C. al Coda
you.
CODA
A♭ B♭7 E♭ A♭/E♭ B♭/E♭
right be - fore my eyes.
E♭ A♭/E♭ B♭/E♭ E♭ A♭ B♭ E♭
(Instrumental)

SHARE YOUR LOVE WITH ME

Words and Music by DEADRIC MALONE
and AL BRAGGS

Moderately slow

F Bb F Bb F Am
It's an ill wind that blows no good, and it's a good heart that won't
heart - ache when love is gone, and it's bad and you know it's e-ven

Dm F G7 C7 F Bb
love like I know it should. And oh how lone - some I know you must
sad in the la - ter on; There's no one blind - er than he who just won't

F Am Dm Bbm F C7 | 1 F Bb F C7
be, / see, and it's a shame if you don't share your love with me. It's a

2 F Bb F Am Bb F
me. I can't help it if he's gone you must

Am Dm F G7 C7 F Bb
try to for - get you must live on. Oh how lone - some I know you must

F Am Dm Bbm F C7 F
be, and it's a shame if you don't share your love with me.

Bb Bdim7 F Dm Gm7 C7 C11 F Bb F
Oh yeah it's a shame if you don't share your love with me, yeah.

SEND ONE YOUR LOVE

Words and Music by
STEVIE WONDER

Moderately
A6 G♯7/D♯ Gmaj7 F♯7 Dm Gmaj7
Send her your love with a doz-en ros-es; make sure that she knows it with a flow - er from your
Amaj7 Amaj7♭5 A6 G♯7/D♯ Gmaj7 F♯9
heart. Show him your love, don't hold back your feel-ings. You don't need a
Dm Gmaj9 Amaj7 E♭9 D6 C♯7/G♯
rea-son when it's straight from the heart. I've heard so man-y say that the days of ro-
I know that peo-ple say two hearts beat-ing as
C♯m7♭5 F♯7♯5 Dm7 G9 Amaj7 A6 E♭9♭5
mance are no more and peo-ple fall-ing in love is so old-fash-ioned. But
one is un-real and can on-ly hap-pen in make-be-lieve sto-ries. But
D6 C♯7/G♯ C♯m7♭5 F♯7♯5 Dm7 G9
wait ing are they the day they once let slip a-way, hid-ing need to ful-fill their heart's de-si-re for love's pas-
so blind they all must be that they can-not be-lieve what they see, for a-round us are mir-a-cles of love's glo-
1 C6/9 B6/9 2 C6/9 B6/9 B♭6 A7/E
-sion. Send her your love -ry. (Instrumental)
A♭maj7 G7 E♭m9 A♭maj7 B♭maj7 B♭maj7♯11
Show him your
B♭6 A7/E A♭maj7 G7 E♭m A♭maj7
love, don't hold back your feel-ings. You don't need a rea-son when it's com-ing from your heart.
B♭maj7 E6 E♭6 A♭6/9 A♭maj7 B♭maj7 E6 E♭6 A♭6/9 A♭maj7 B♭maj7 E6 E♭6 A♭6/9 A♭maj7
Huh, huh, huh,
Gmaj9 Dmaj7/E D/E Amaj9 Emaj7/F♯ Bmaj9 G♭maj7/A♭ G♭/A♭ D♭maj9 Cmaj9
huh. Oh, oh, oh.

SENTIMENTAL LADY

Words and Music by
ROBERT WELCH

Moderately slow
You are here and warm_ but I could look a-way_ and you'd_ be gone._ 'Cause
we live in a time_ when mean-ing falls in splin-ters from our lives. That's
why I've trav-eled far, 'cause I come so to-geth-er where you are._ Yes, and
all of the things that I said that I want-ed come rush-ing by in my head when I'm with you.
Four-teen joys and a will to be mer-ry. All of the things that they say are ver-y
sen-ti-men-tal gen-tle wind_ blow-ing through_ my life a-gain._ Sen-ti-men-tal la-dy, gen-tle one._
Sen-ti-men-tal gen-tle wind_ blow-ing through_ my life a-gain._
Sen-ti-men-tal la-dy, gen-tle one._
To Coda
Ooh,_ sen-ti-men-tal
la-dy.
D.S. al Coda
Yes, and
CODA
All of the things that I said that I want-ed come rush-ing by in my head when I'm with you.
Four-teen joys and the will to be mer-ry. All of the things say it a-gain._
Repeat and Fade

SEXUAL HEALING

Words and Music by MARVIN GAYE,
ODELL BROWN and DAVID RITZ

Moderate half time feel
(Whisper) Wake up. wake up. wake up. wake up!
Sing: Oh ba - by now, let's get down to - night.
Ooo
Ba - by, I'm hot just like an ov - en; I need some lov - in'.
Ba - by, I got sick this morn - in', a sea was storm - in' in - side of me.
Ba - by, I can't hold it much long - er; it's get - tin' strong - er and strong - er.
Ba - by, I think I'm cap - siz - in', the waves are ris - in' and ris - in'.
When I get that feel - in' I want Sex - u - al Heal - ing, Sex - u - al Heal - ing.
And when I get that feel - in' I want Sex - u - al Heal - ing, Sex - u - al Heal - ing.
Oh ba - by, makes me feel so fine, helps to re - lieve my mind.
(It's good for me) makes me feel so fine, (It's sumpcherous) helps to re - lieve my mind. (And it's good for us)
Sex - u - al Heal - ing, ba - by, is good for me. Sex - u - al Heal - ing is some - thing that's good for me.
To Coda
When - ev - er blue tear - drops are fall - ing and my e - mo - tion - al sta - bil - i - ty is leav - ing me there is some - thing I can do: I can get on the tel - e - phone and call

Fm7 Gm7 A♭maj7 A♭/B♭ E♭ G7
you up, ba - by. Say, hon - ey, I know you'll be there to re - lieve
A♭maj7 Fm7 Gm7 A♭maj7 A♭/B♭ E♭
me 'cause the love you give to me will be. If you don't know
G7 A♭maj7
the thing you're deal - ing, I can tell you, dar - lin', that it's
Fm7 Gm7 A♭maj7 A♭/B♭ B♭ Cm Gm7 A♭ E♭
Sex - u - al Heal - ing. Get up, get up, get up, get up, let's make love to - night!
B♭ Cm Gm7 A♭ E♭
D.S. al Coda
Wake up, wake up, wake up, wake up, 'cause you do it right!
CODA
E♭ G7 A♭maj7
And it's good for me, and it's so good to me, my ba -
Fm7 Gm7 A♭maj7 A♭/B♭ E♭ G7
by. Oh Oh, come take con - trol. Just grab a hold
A♭maj7 Fm7 Gm7 A♭maj7 A♭/B♭
of my bod - y and mind; soon we'll be mak - in' it, hon - ey, oh we'll be do - in', fine.
E♭ G7 A♭maj7
You're my med - i - cine, O - pen up and let me in. Dar - lin', you're
Fm7 Gm7 A♭maj7 A♭/B♭ B♭ Cm Gm7
so pret - ty, I can't wait for you to op - er - ate. (heavy breathing...................)
A♭ E♭ B♭ Cm Gm7 A♭ E♭
Let's make love to - night! Wake up wake up, wake up, wake up, 'cause you do it right!
Repeat and Fade
B♭ Cm Gm7 A♭ E♭ B♭ Cm Gm7 A♭ E♭
(vocal improvisation)

SHAKE YOU DOWN

Words and Music by
GREGORY ABBOTT

Moderate Rock Ballad
Girl, I been watch-ing you from so far a-cross the floor. Now, ba-
-by, that's noth-ing new. I've watched you so man-y times be-fore. Now, ba-
-by, I see that look in your eyes and what it's tell-in' me. And you know,
ooh, girl, that I'm not shy, I'm glad you picked up on my te-lep-a-thy now.
You read my mind. Girl, I wan-na shake you down. I can give you all the lov-in' you need.
(I'm gon-na love you.) Ma-ma, let me take you down. We'll go all the way to heav-en.
To Coda
Ooh, I been miss-in' you and the way you make me feel in-side. What
can I do? I can tell you got your pride. Now, ba-by, come to me, well, oh, well.
Let me ease your mind. Oh, babe, I got the rem-e-dy, yes, I do.
Now give me just a lit-tle time.
D.S. al Coda
CODA
Spoken: Girl, I been missin' you. And you know, it's funny.
Every time I get to feelin' this way. I wish I had you near me. I wanna reach out and touch you.
I

C/D
G/D
can't stop think-in' of the things we do, the way you call me "ba - by" when I'm hold - in' you. I
D
G/D
D/F♯
C
G
shake and I shiv-er when I know you're near. Then you whis-per in my ear. Oh, babe, well, well.
Em7
G/A
A/D
D
F♯m7
Bm7
Em7
You read my mind. Girl, I wan-na shake you down. I can give
G
G/A
D
F♯m7
Bm7
Em7
G
G/A
you all the lov-in' you need. Come on, let me take you down. We'll go all the way to heav - en.

SHE'S NOT YOU

Words and Music by DOC POMUS,
JERRY LEIBER and MIKE STOLLER

Moderately

F C7 Cdim C7
Her hair is soft and her eyes are, oh, so blue. She's all the

B♭ C7 F F♯dim C7/G N.C.
things a girl should be, but she's not you. She knows just

F C7 Cdim C7 B♭
how to make me laugh when I feel blue. She's ev - 'ry - thing a man could

C7 F B♭ F A7
want, but she's not you. And when we're danc - ing,

F7 B♭
it al - most feels the same. I've got to stop my - self from

A7 N.C. C7 N.C. F C7
whis - p'ring your name. She e - ven kiss - es me like you used to do.

Cdim C7 B♭ C7 F B♭7 F
And it's just break - ing my heart 'cause she's not you.

SHAKE YOUR GROOVE THING

Words and Music by DINO FEKARIS
and FREDDIE PARREN

Bright, with a steady beat

A C/A Bm7/A Bm7/E
Shake it! Shake it!

A C/A Bm7/A
Shake your groove thing, shake your groove thing, yeah, yeah! Show

Bm7/E A C/A Bm7/A
'em how you do it now. Shake your groove thing, shake your groove thing, yeah, yeah!

N.C.
Show 'em how you do it now, show 'em how you do it now.

𝄋 A C/A Bm7/A Bm7/E
Let's show the world we can dance, bad e - nough ta strut our stuff.
We've got the rhy-thm to - night, all the rest know we're the best.

A C/A Bm7/A
The mu - sic gives us a chance, we do more out on the floor.
Our shad-ows flash in the light, twist - in' turn - in', we keep burn - in'.

F♯m G Bm7/E
Groov - in' loose or heart to heart, we put in mo-tion ev - 'ry sin - gle part.
Shake it high or shake it low, we take our bod - ies where they want to go.

F♯m G Bm7/E
Funk - y sounds wall to wall, we're bump - in' boot - ies hav -
Feel the beat, nev - er stop, oh, hold me tight, spin

A C/A Bm7/A
in' us a ball, y'all. Shake your groove thing, shake your groove thing, yeah, yeah!
me like a top!

Bm7/E A
Show 'em how you do it now. Shake your groove thing,

C/A Bm7/A To Coda ⊕ N.C.
shake your groove thing, yeah, yeah! Show 'em how you do it now.

D.S. al Coda
(Instrumental)

CODA

N.C. D C♯

'em how you do it now. There's noth - ing more that I'd like to do

C B Bm7/E

than take the floor and dance with you. Keep danc - in', let's keep

A C/A

danc - in'.

Bm7/A Bm7/E F♯m G

Shake it! Shake it! Groov - in' loose or heart to heart,

Bm7/E F♯m G

we put in mo - tion ev - 'ry sin - gle part. Funk - y sounds wall to wall,

Bm7/E A

we're bump - in' boot - ies hav - in' us a ball, y'all. Shake your groove thing,

C/A Bm7/A Bm7/E

shake your groove thing, yeah, yeah! Show 'em how you do it now.

Repeat and Fade

SING
from SESAME STREET

Words and Music by
JOE RAPOSO

Moderately

C Dm7/C Cmaj9 Gm7/C C7 Fmaj7

Sing! Sing a song, sing out loud, sing out strong. Sing of

G9sus Cmaj9 E7♯5(♯9) Am Am(maj7) D9sus D9 A♭13(♯11) G7sus C

good things, not bad; sing of hap - py, not sad. Sing!

Dm7/C Cmaj9 Gm7/C C7

Sing a song, make it sim - ple to last your whole life long. Don't

Fmaj9 Bm11 E7♯5(♯9) Am7 D9sus D9 G11 G7

wor - ry that it's not good e - nough for an - y - one else to hear. Sing! Sing a

C C F/G

song. La la do la da, la da la do la da, la da da la do la da.

Repeat and Fade

SHE BLINDED ME WITH SCIENCE

Words and Music by THOMAS DOLBY ROBERTSON
and JONATHAN KERR

Funk Rock

E7
It's po - et - ry in mo - tion. She turned her ten - der eyes ___ to me,

as deep as an - y o - cean, as sweet as an - y har - mo - ny.

A7/E A7 A9 G♯9 G9
Mmm, but she blind - ed me with sci - ence *(Spoken:) She blinded me with science!*

E D Em D Em E E9
and failed me in bi - ol - o - gy. ___ Hey, hey.

𝄋
Uh. Ha ah. When I'm danc - ing close to her, ___ (Blind -
When she's danc - ing next to me, ___ (Blind -

- ing me with sci - ence.) Sci - ence!
- ing me with sci - ence.) Sci - ence!

I can smell the chem - i - cals. ___ (Blind - ing me with sci - ence.)
I can hear ma - chin - er - y. ___ (Blind - ing me with sci - ence.)

To Coda ⊕
Sci - ence!
Sci - ence!

E7
Sci - ence! It's po - et - ry in mo - tion.

And when she turned her eyes ___ to me, as deep as an - y o - cean,

A7/E
as sweet as an - y har - mo - ny, she blind - ed me with sci - ence

D.S. al Coda
A7 A9 G♯9 G9 E D Em D Em E
(Spoken:) She blinded me with science!
and failed me in ge - om - e - try.
CODA
E7
It's po - et - ry in mo - tion, And when she turned her
eyes to me, The spheres are in com - mo - tion, the el - e - ments in
A7/E
har - mo - ny. She blind - ed me with sci - ence
(Spoken:) She blinded me with science!
A7 A9G♯9G9 E D Em D Em E N.C.
and hit me with tech - nol - o - gy.
(Instrumental)
E7
(Spoken:) Good heavens Miss Sakamoto - you're beautiful!
G A G A G A G
I... I don't believe it! There she goes again! She's tidied up, and I
F♯m Em G A G A G A G
can't find anything! All my tubes and wires and careful notes and antiquated notions, but..."
Bm7 E7
It's po - et - ry in mo - tion. And when she turned her eyes to me,
as deep as an - y o - cean, as sweet as an - y har - mo - ny,
A7/E A7 A9 G♯9 G9
she blind - ed me with sci - ence. (Spoken:) She blinded me with science!
E D Em D Em E N.C. E
She blind - ed me with... (Instrumental)

(She's)
SEXY & 17

Words and Music by
BRIAN SETZER

Fast Rock
F Bb F
I ain't go - ing to school it starts too earl - y for me.
walk up to the cor - ner and meet my lit - tle Ma - rie.
Spoken: Well, listen man, I ain't
I'm gon - na
Bb7 F
going to school no more, it starts much, much too early for me.
walk up to the cor - ner and meet my lit - tle Ma - rie.
I don't
Well, she's the
C Bb7 F7 1
care a - bout read - in', writ - in', 'rith - ma - tic or his - to - ry.
on - ly one in this whole world who un - der - stands me.
I'm gon - na
2 C7sus F7
Well, she's sex - y and sev - en - teen, my lit - tle
Bb7 F7
rock 'n' roll queen, acts a lit - tle bit ob - scene, got - ta let off a
C Bb7 F
lit - tle steam. Dig that sound and shake it a - round you're mine, mine,
F
mine. John - ny and Ed - die and me and Jim - my and Jack
Fri - day night there's a band that you got - ta hear.
Instrumental
Bb F
are gon - na do a lit - tle num - ber on the teach - er when she turns her back.
Just a dol - lar to get in and twen - ty - five cents a beer.
C Bb7 F7 To Coda
We gon - na cut out - a class and meet the girls by the ra - il - road tracks.
They play rock 'n' roll mu - sic like it has - n't been rocked for years.
1 2 C7sus D.S. al Coda CODA Bb7
Well, ev - 'ry Well, she's When I hear that
Bb9
rock - in' beat I can't sit still up out - a my seat. Come on ba - by shut - tle
G7b9 C9#5 F
'round your feet. Can't learn noth - in' in school they won't teach you on the street. Whoa, whoa,
Bb7 F Bb7
ba - by I like your style. Whoa, whoa,

F C
ba - by I like your style. You don't care what the oth - er kids
B♭7 F7 C7sus F7
say, you go re - al wild. Well, you're sex - y and
B♭7
sev - en - teen, my lit - tle rock 'n' roll queen, acts a lit - tle
F7 C
bit ob - scene, got - ta let off a lit - tle steam. Dig that sound and
B♭7 F 1, 2 3
shake it a - round you're mine, mine, mine, mine. mine.

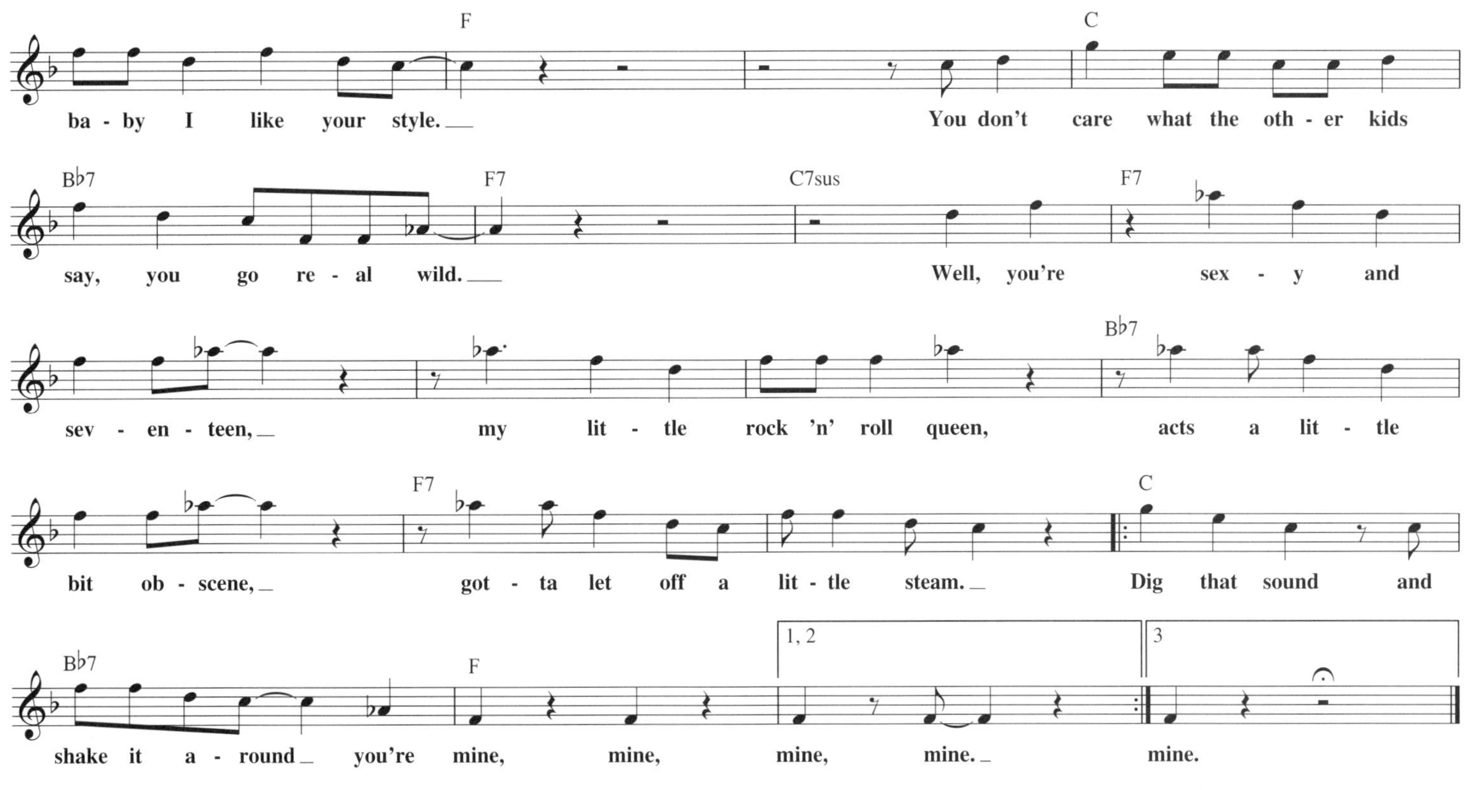

(SEVEN LITTLE GIRLS) SITTING IN THE BACK SEAT

Words by BOB HILLIARD
Music by LEE POCKRISS

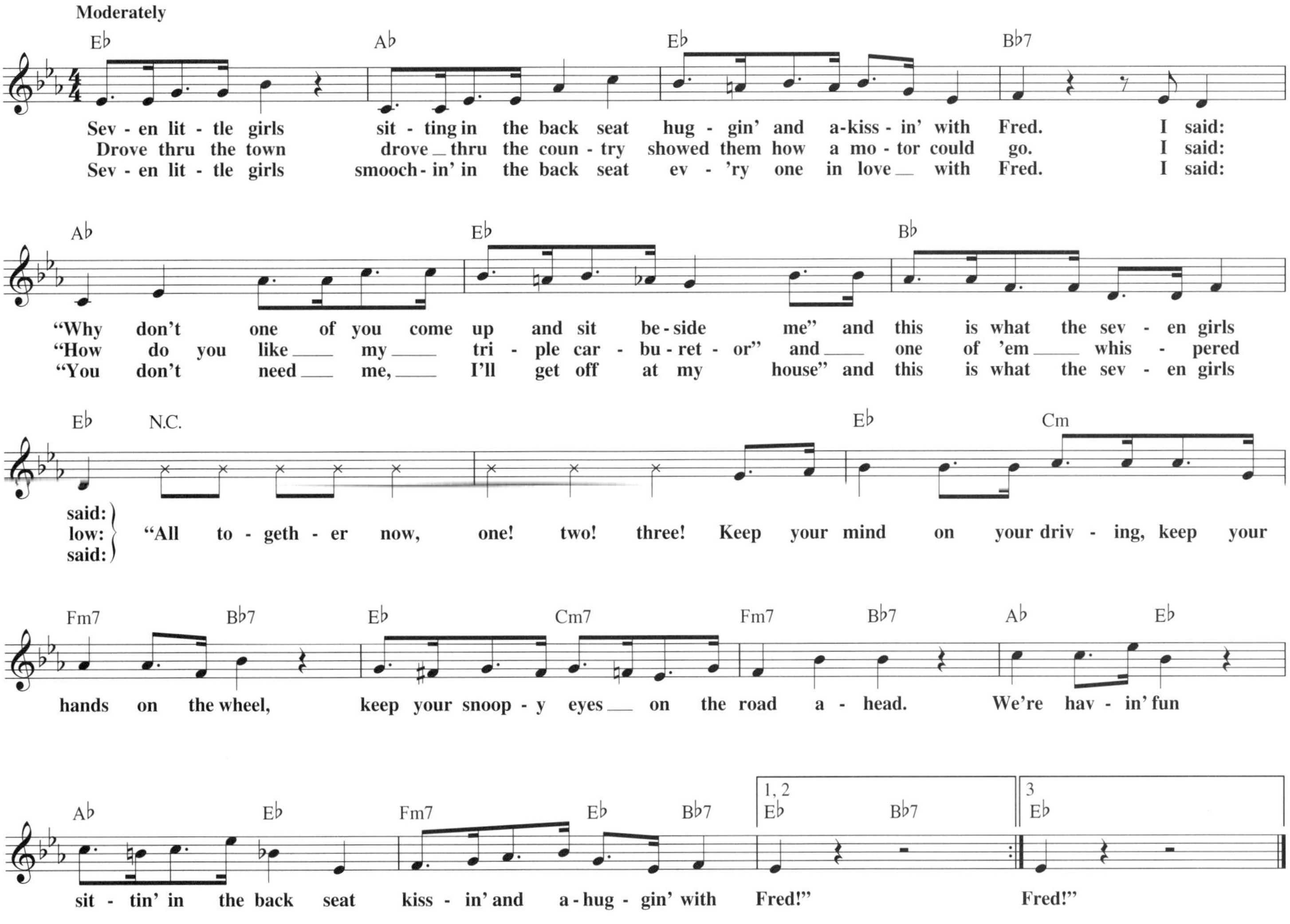
Moderately
E♭ A♭ E♭ B♭7
Sev - en lit - tle girls sit - ting in the back seat hug - gin' and a - kiss - in' with Fred. I said:
Drove thru the town drove thru the coun - try showed them how a mo - tor could go. I said:
Sev - en lit - tle girls smooch - in' in the back seat ev - 'ry one in love with Fred. I said:
A♭ E♭ B♭
"Why don't one of you come up and sit be - side me" and this is what the sev - en girls
"How do you like my tri - ple car - bu - ret - or" and one of 'em whis - pered
"You don't need me, I'll get off at my house" and this is what the sev - en girls
E♭ N.C. E♭ Cm
said: low: said: "All to - geth - er now, one! two! three! Keep your mind on your driv - ing, keep your
Fm7 B♭7 E♭ Cm7 Fm7 B♭7 A♭ E♭
hands on the wheel, keep your snoop - y eyes on the road a - head. We're hav - in' fun
A♭ E♭ Fm7 E♭ B♭7 1, 2 E♭ B♭7 3 E♭
sit - tin' in the back seat kiss - in' and a - hug - gin' with Fred!" Fred!"

SHAMBALA

Words and Music by
DANIEL MOORE

Moderately
Wash a - way my trou - bles, wash a - way my pain, with the rain of Sham - ba - la.
is help - ful ev - ery - one is kind, on the road to Sham - ba - la,
my sis - ter by the flow - ers in her eyes, on the road to Sham - ba - la.
Wash a - way my sor - row, wash a - way my shame, with the rain
Ev - ery - one is luck - y, ev - ery - one is so kind, on the road
I can tell my broth - er by the flow - ers in his eyes, on the road
of Sham - ba - la.
to Sham - ba - la.
to Sham - ba - la.
Ah oo ooh. Yeah, yeah, yeah, yeah, yeah, yeah.
To Coda
Ah oo ooh. Yeah, yeah, yeah, yeah, yeah, yeah. Ev - ery - one
How does your light shine, in the halls of Sham - ba - la?
How does your light shine, in the halls of Sham - ba - la?
D.S. al Coda
I can tell
CODA
How does your light shine, in the halls of Sham - ba - la?
How does your light shine, in the halls of Sham - ba - la? Tell me how
does your light shine, in the halls of Sham - ba - la? Ah
oo, ooh. Yeah, yeah, yeah, yeah, yeah, yeah. Ah
Repeat and Fade
oo, ooh. Yeah, yeah, yeah, yeah, yeah, yeah. Ah

SHOULD I STAY OR SHOULD I GO

Words and Music by MICK JONES
and JOE STRUMMER

Moderately bright

Dar-ling, you've got to let me know: should I stay or should I go?
tease. You're hap-py when I'm on my knees.

If you say that you are mine, I'll be here till the end of time.
One day is fine and next is black. So if you want me off your back,

So you've got to let me know: should I stay or should I go?
well, come on and let me know: should I stay or should I go?

1. It's al-ways tease, tease,
2. Should I stay or should I go now?

Double-time feel

(D.S. only) *¿Me de-bo ir o que-dar-me?*

Should I stay or should I go now?

¿Me de-bo ir o que-dar-me?

If I go, there will be trou-ble. *Si me voy - va pe-li - gro.*

And if I stay, it will be dou-ble. *Me que - do - es do - ble.*

So, come on and let me know. *Me tie-nes que de -*

To Coda

End double-time feel

This in-de-ci-sion's bug-gin' me. *Un - de-ci-sion me mo - les-ta.*

If you don't want me, set me free. *Si no me quie-res lib-ra - me.*

Ex-act-ly who'm I s'posed to be? *Di-ga me que ten-go ser.*

Don't you know which clothes e-ven fit me? *¿Sa-ves que ro-bas me quer - da?*

Come on and let me know: *Me tie-nes que de - sir.*

should I cool it or should I blow? *¿Mi de-bo ir o que-dar - me?*

Should I stay or should I

D.S. al Coda

CODA

sir.

Should I stay or should I go?

SHOW MUST GO ON

Words and Music by LEO SAYER
and DAVID COURTNEY

"Circusy" tempo, in 2

F

Ba - by, al - though I chose this lone - ly life, it seems it's
Ba - by, there's an e - nor - mous crowd of peo - ple; they're all
Ba - by, I wish you'd help me es - cape, help me

C/E F

stran - gling me now. All the wild men,
af - ter my blood. I wish, ba - by, they'd
get a - way. Leave me out - side

C

big ci - gar, gi - gan - tic car. They're all laugh - ing at the lie.
tear down the walls of this thea - tre. Let me out! Let me out!
my ad - dress, far a - way from this mas - que - rade.

C♯dim Dm Am

Oh, I've been used. Ooh, used.
Oh, I'm so blind. Oh, I'm blind.
'Cause I've been blind. Oh, so blind.

Dm Am7

I've been a fool. Oh, what a fool. I broke all the
I wast - ed time, wast - ed, wast - ed, wast - ed time walk - ing on the
I wast - ed time, wast - ed, wast - ed, all too much time walk - ing on the

Dm Am To Coda B♭

rules, oh, yeah. But I must let the show
wire, high wi - re. But I must let the show
wire, high wi - re. But I

F F

go on.
go on.

(Instrumental)

C

1 2 Dm

Oh, I'm so blind. Oh, I'm

Am7 Dm Am7

blind. I wast - ed time, wast - ed, wast - ed, all too much time

Dm Am

walk - ing on the wi - re, high wi - re.

B♭ F D.C. al Coda

But I must let the show go on.

CODA
B♭
must let the show go, I must let the show go, I must let the show go on.
F
F
(Instrumental)
C
Repeat and Fade

SHOT GUN

Words and Music by
AUTRY DeWALT

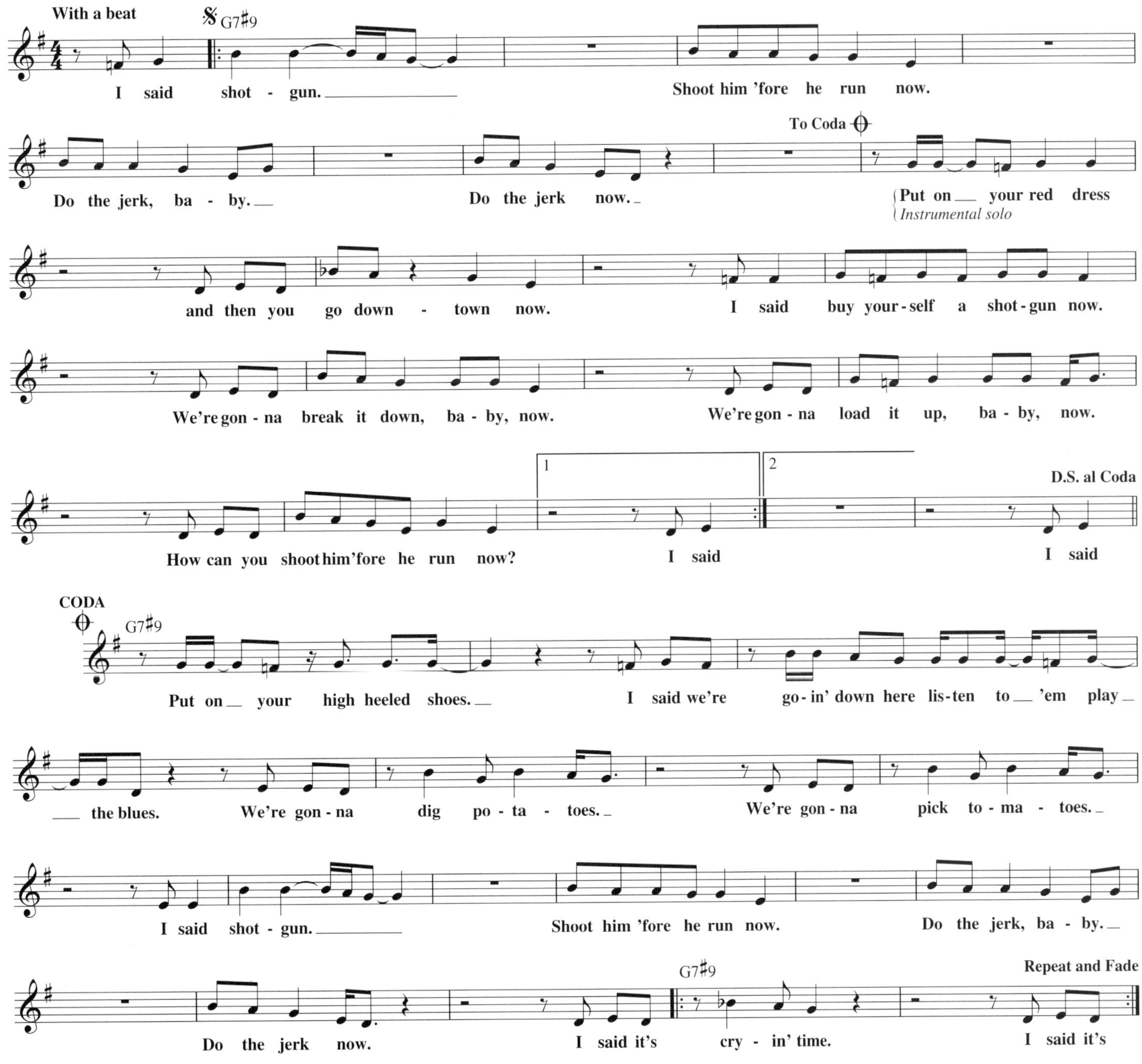

With a beat

G7♯9

I said shot - gun. Shoot him 'fore he run now.

Do the jerk, ba - by. Do the jerk now.

To Coda

Put on your red dress
Instrumental solo

and then you go down - town now. I said buy your-self a shot-gun now.

We're gon - na break it down, ba - by, now. We're gon - na load it up, ba - by, now.

1 2 D.S. al Coda

How can you shoot him 'fore he run now? I said I said

CODA

G7♯9

Put on your high heeled shoes. I said we're go - in' down here lis - ten to 'em play

the blues. We're gon - na dig po - ta - toes. We're gon - na pick to - ma - toes.

I said shot - gun. Shoot him 'fore he run now. Do the jerk, ba - by.

G7♯9 Repeat and Fade

Do the jerk now. I said it's cry - in' time. I said it's

A SIGN OF THE TIMES

Words and Music by
TONY HATCH

Moderately, with a beat

C Em Am Dm7 G7 Dm7 G7

It's a sign of the times __ that your love for me __ is get - ting so much strong - er.
It's a sign of the times __ that you call me up __ when - ev - er you feel lone - ly.

C Em Am Dm7 G7 Dm7 G7

It's a sign of the times __ and I know that I ____ won't have to wait much long - er.
It's a sign of the times __ that you tell your friends _ that I'm your one and on - ly.

Em Dm

You've changed a lot ____ some - how __ from the one I used to know, ____
I'll nev - er un - der - stand ____ the way you treat - ed me. ____

Em Dm 1 Dm7 G7

for when you hold __ me now _ it feels like you nev - er want to let me go. ____
But when I hold __ your hand _ I know you could - n't be the way you

2 Dm7 G7 C

used to be. __ May - be my luck - y star __ at last de - cid - ed to shine.

B♭ Dm7 G7 Dm7 G7

May - be some - bod - y knows __ how long I've wait - ed to make you mine. __

C Em Am Dm7 G7 Dm7 G7

It's a sign of the times __ that you kiss me now __ as if you real - ly mean it.

C Em Am Dm7 G7 Dm7 G7

It's a sign of the times __ and a year a - go __ I nev - er could have seen it.

Em Dm

Don't ev - er change __ your mind _ and take your love a - way ____

Em Dm Dm7 G7

Just leave the fires __ be - hind __ and, ba - by, on - ly think of how it is to - day. __

Repeat and Fade

C Dm7 G7

It's a sign of the times. ____ It's a sign of the times. ____

SIGN YOUR NAME

Words and Music by
TERENCE TRENT D'ARBY

Moderately

C♯ Bm/F C♯/F F♯m

For - tu - nate - ly you have got some - one who re - lies on you. We
Time I'm sure will bring dis - ap - point - ments in so man - y things. It
All a - lone with you makes the but - ter - flies in me a - rise.

C♯ Bm/F C♯/F F♯m

start - ed out as friends but the thought of you just caves me in. The
seems to be the way when your gam - bling cards on love you play. I'd
Slow - ly we make love and the earth ro - tates to our dic - tates.

C♯ Bm/F C♯/F F♯m

symp - toms are so deep it is much too late to turn a - way. We
rath - er be in hell with you ba - by than in cool heav - en. It
Slow - ly we make love.

C♯ Bm/F C♯/F F♯m

start - ed out as friends.
seems to be the way.
Sign your name a - cross my heart. I

B F♯m

want you to be my ba - by. Sign your name a - cross my heart. I

B C♯m7/E 1 C♯7/F 2 C♯7/F D

want you to be my la - dy. Birds nev - er look

A C♯ F♯m D

in - to the sun be - fore the day is done. But oh the light shines bright

A C♯ B C♯ D

on a peace - ful day. Strang - er blue

A C♯ F♯m D

leave us a - lone we don't want to deal with you. We'll shed our stains

A C♯ C♯7 D.C. and Fade

show - er - ing in the room that makes the rain.

SILHOUETTE

By KENNY G

CODA
A7sus
F(add9)
F
Fmaj7
Gm7
Repeat and Fade
B♭/C
F(add9)
F
Gm7
B♭/C

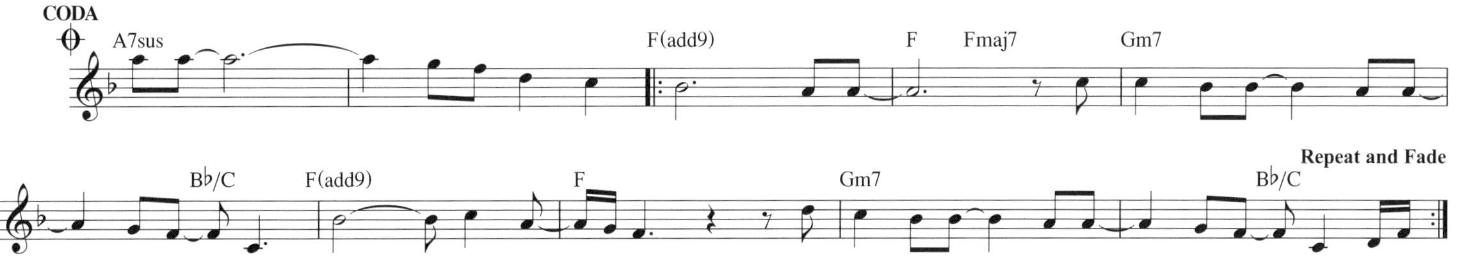

SHE LOVES YOU

Words and Music by JOHN LENNON and PAUL McCARTNEY

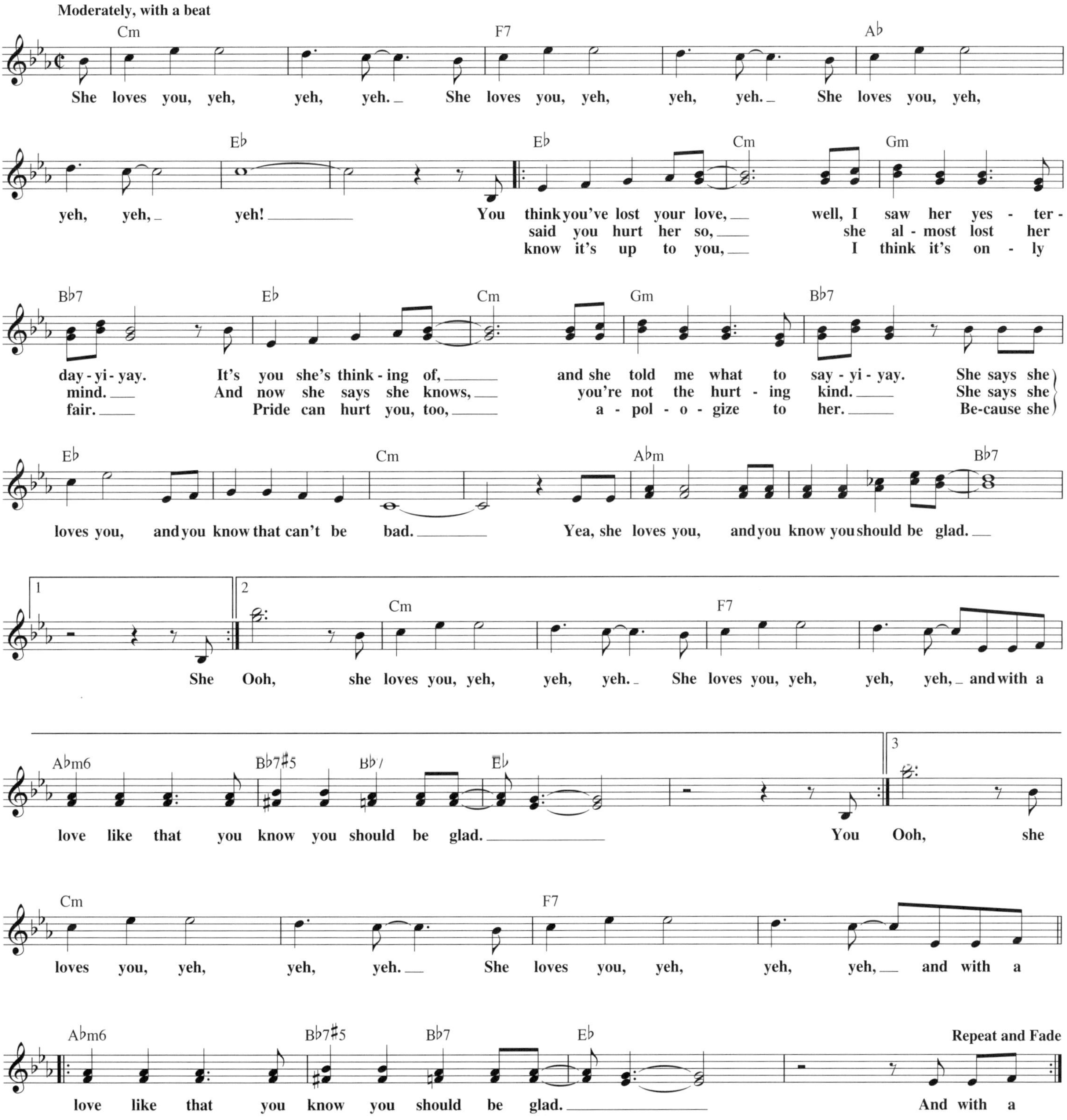

Moderately, with a beat
Cm F7 A♭
She loves you, yeh, yeh, yeh. She loves you, yeh, yeh, yeh. She loves you, yeh,
E♭
yeh, yeh, yeh!
E♭ Cm Gm
You think you've lost your love, well, I saw her yes - ter -
said you hurt her so, she al - most lost her
know it's up to you, I think it's on - ly
B♭7 E♭ Cm Gm B♭7
day - yi - yay. It's you she's think - ing of, and she told me what to say - yi - yay. She says she
mind. And now she says she knows, you're not the hurt - ing kind. She says she
fair. Pride can hurt you, too, a - pol - o - gize to her. Be-cause she
E♭ Cm A♭m B♭7
loves you, and you know that can't be bad. Yea, she loves you, and you know you should be glad.
1
She
2
Cm F7
Ooh, she loves you, yeh, yeh, yeh. She loves you, yeh, yeh, and with a
A♭m6 B♭7♯5 B♭7 E♭
love like that you know you should be glad.
You
3
Ooh, she
Cm F7
loves you, yeh, yeh, yeh. She loves you, yeh, yeh, and with a
A♭m6 B♭7♯5 B♭7 E♭
love like that you know you should be glad.
Repeat and Fade
And with a

SKY HIGH

By CLIVE SCOTT
and DESMOND DYER

Moderately

Am G F Fmaj7 G6
Blown round by the wind,
Up round I've flown then

Am G F Fmaj7 G6
thrown down in a spin.
down down like a stone.

C Fmaj7 Em7
I gave you love, I thought that we had made it to the

C Fmaj7 Em7
top. I gave you all I had to give; why did it have to

A C♯m D Dm
stop? You've blown it all sky high by tell - ing me a

A C♯m D Dm
lie. With - out a rea - son why, you've blown it all sky

F A C♯m
high. You, you've blown it all sky

D Dm A C♯m
high. Our love had wings to fly; we could have touched the

D Dm F
sky. You've blown it all sky high.

D.C. and gradually Fade

SLOOP JOHN B

Words and Music by
BRIAN WILSON

Moderately
G Am7(add4) G Am7(add4) G Am7(add4) G Am7(add4)
We come out in the Sloop John B, my grand - fa - ther and me. A -
first mate, he got drunk. He broke in the Cap-tain's trunk. The
poor cook, he got the fits. He threw a - way all my grits.
G Am7(add4) G D
round Nas - sau town we do roam, drink - ing all
con - sta - ble had to come and take him a - way. Sher - riff John
Then he took and he ate up all of my corn. Let me go

G C Am7
night, got in - to a fight. Well, I
Stone, why don't you leave me a - lone? Well, I
home. Why don't they let me go home? This

G D G Am7(add4) G Am7(add4)
feel so broke_ up I wan - na go home.
feel so broke_ up I wan - na go home. So
is the worst_ trip I've ev - er been on.

G Am7(add4) G Am7(add4) G Am7(add4) G Am7(add4)
hoist up the John B sail, see how the main sail set.

G Am7(add4) G D
Call for the Cap - tain a - shore. Let me go home, let ___ me go

G Am7(add4) G C Am7 G
home. I wan - na go home, oh yeah. Well, I feel so broke up

D | 1, 2 G Am7(add4) G Am7(add4) | 3 G Am7(add4) G
I wan - na go home. The home. ___

SMOKE GETS IN YOUR EYES

Words by OTTO HARBACH
Music by JEROME KERN

E♭ B♭7sus B♭7 E♭ E♭+ A♭ E♭dim E♭
They asked me how I knew my true love was true? ___ I of course re - plied, "Some thing here in -

Fm7 B♭7 E♭ B♭7 E♭ B♭7sus B♭7 E♭ E♭+
side, can - not be de - nied." ___ They said some - day you'll find, all who love are blind. ___

A♭ E♭dim E♭ Fm7 B♭7 E♭
___ When your heart's on fire, you must re - al - ize smoke gets in your eyes. ___

B F♯7 F♯dim F♯7 B
So I chaffed_ them and I gay - ly laughed,_ to think they could doubt my love. Yet to - day,_ my love has

A♭m7 B♭7 E♭ B♭7 E♭ B♭7sus B♭7
flown a - way,_ I am with - out my love. Now laugh - ing friends de - ride, tears I can - not

E♭ E♭+ A♭ E♭dim E♭ Fm7 B♭7 E♭
hide, ___ so I smile and say, "When a love - ly flame dies, smoke gets in your eyes." ___

SMILING FACES SOMETIMES

Words and Music by NORMAN WHITFIELD
and BARRETT STRONG

Moderately
Em F♯m7 Em F♯m7♭9 Em F♯m7♭9 Em F♯m7
Smil - ing fac - es some - times pre - tend to be your friend.
Smil - ing fac - es show no trac - es of the e - vil that lurks with - in.
Smil - ing fac - es, smil - ing fac - es some - times they don't tell the truth.
Smil - ing fac - es, smil - ing fac - es tell lies and I got proof.
To Coda
The
Be -
Your
1
truth is in the eyes 'cause the eyes don't lie, a - men. Re - mem - ber, a
smile is just a frown turned up - side down my friend. So, hear me when I'm say - ing
2
ware. Be - ware of the hand - shake that hides the snake. I'm tell - in' you
be - ware of the pat on the back it just might hold you back.
D.S. al Coda
Jeal - ous - y, (jeal - ous - y) mis - er - y, (mis - er - y) en - vy. I tell you you can't see be - hind
CODA
en - e - my won't do you no harm, 'cause you'll know where he's com - in' from;
D.S. and Fade
don't let the hand shake and the smile fool ya. Take my ad - vice I'm on - ly try - in' to school ya.

SMOKIN' IN THE BOYS ROOM

Words and Music by MICHAEL KODA
and MICHAEL LUTZ

Moderate Rock
D5
Sit - tin' in the class - room think - in' it's a drag.
Check - in' out the hall, mak - in' sure the coast is clear.
Put me to work in the school book - store.
B♭5
Lis - t'nin' to the teach - er rap
Look - in' in the stalls. Nah, there
Check - out count - er and
just ain't my bag. When
ain't no - bod - y here. My
I got bored.
D5
two bells ring you know it's my cue. I'm
bud - dies Sixx, Mick and Tom; to
Teach - er was look - in' for me all a - round.
B♭5
gon - na meet the boys on floor num - ber two.
get caught would sure - ly be the death of us all.
Two hours lat - er you know where I was found.
G5
Smok - in' in the boy's room.
D5
Smok - in' in the boy's room. Now, teach -
A5
- er, don't you fill me
G5
up with your rule 'cause
A5
ev - 'ry - bod - y knows that
G5
smok - in' ain't al - lowed in
1, 2
D5
school.
3
D5
school.
E5 F5 F♯5
G5
Smok - in' in the boy's room.
D5
Smok - in' in the boy's room. Now, teach - er,
A5
I ain't fool - in' a -
G5
round with your rule 'cause
A5
ev - 'ry - bod - y knows that
G5
smok - in' ain't al - lowed in school.
D5 B5 A5 F5 Dsus2

SOME DAY (YOU'LL WANT ME TO WANT YOU)

Words and Music by
JIMMIE HODGES

Moderately

B♭ Cm7 F7 B♭
I know that some day you'll want me to want you, ___ when I'm in love with

B♭7 E♭ G7 Cm Cm7 F7
some - bod - y else. ___ You ex - pect me to be true and

B♭ D7 Gm C7 F7
keep on lov - ing you. Though I am feel - ing blue, you think I can't for -

B♭ Cm7 F7
get you un - til some day you'll want me to want you, when I am strong

B♭ B♭7 E♭ G7 Cm
for some - bod - y new. ___ And though you don't want me

E♭m6 B♭ D7 G7 C7 F7 B♭
now, I'll get a - long some - how, and then I won't want you. ___

SNOWBIRD

Words and Music by
GENE MacLELLAN

Brightly

C Em Dm G7
Be - neath this snow - y man - tle cold ___ and clean ___ the un - born grass lies
I was young my heart was young ___ then, too, ___ and an - y - thing that it would
Spread your ti - ny wings and fly ___ a - way ___ and take the snow back
breeze a - long the riv - er seems ___ to say ___ that he'll on - ly break my

C Em
wait - ing for its coat to turn to green. ___ The snow - bird sings the song he al - ways
tell me that's the thing that I would do. ___ But now I feel such emp - ti - ness with -
with you where it came from on that day. ___ The one I love for - ev - er is un -
heart a - gain should I de - cide to stay. ___ So lit - tle snow - bird take me with you when you

Dm G7
sings ___ and speaks to me of flow - ers that will bloom a - gain in
in ___ for the thing I want the most in life is the thing that I can't
true, ___ and if I could, you know that I would fly a - way with
go ___ to that land of gen - tle breez - es where the peace - ful wa - ters

1-3 C | 4 C G7
spring. ___ When flow. ___ Yeah, ___ if I could ___ you know ___ that I would
win. ___
you. ___ The

F Dm7 C
fly ___ a - way with you. ___

SO INTO YOU

Words and Music by BUDDY BUIE,
DEAN DAUGHTRY and ROBERT NIX

Moderately
Fm
When you walked in - to the room there was voo - doo in the vibes.
so in - to you. I can't think of / get to noth - ing else.
B♭m7
I was cap - tured by your style,
I am so in - to you.
Fm7
To Coda
but I could not catch your eyes. Now I
I can't think of / get to noth - ing else. Think-ing
F7sus
Fm7
Fm7/D♭
Cm
stand here help - less - ly, hop - ing you'll get in - to me. I am
how it's going to be when - ev - er I
Cm
B♭m7
get you next to me. It's gon - na be good. Don't you know,
(Instrumental)
(I'm so in - to you.)
Fm7
B♭m7
from your head to your toe, gon - na love you all o - ver.
Cm
O - ver and o - ver. Me in - to you, you in - to me, me in - to
(I'm so in - to you.)
Fm7
you. Ooh,
D.S. al Coda
(Take 1st ending)
CODA
B♭m7
When you
Come on ba - by.
ba - by, driv - ing me cra - zy.
Fm7
Repeat and Fade
I'm so in - to you. Love the things you do.
Lis - ten
Come on

SOMEWHERE OUT THERE

from AN AMERICAN TAIL

Music by BARRY MANN and JAMES HORNER
Lyric by CYNTHIA WEIL

Moderately, with expression
C(add9) Cmaj7/E C/F F/G C(add9) C/E F Dm7 G/F Em Am
Some-where out there be-neath the pale moon - light some - one's think- in' of me and

Dm7 C/E F Gsus G C(add9) Cmaj7/E C/F F/G C(add9) C/E F
lov - ing me to-night. Some-where out there some-one's say-ing a prayer that

Dm7 G/F Em7 Am Dm7 C/E F/G C F G/F
we'll find one an - oth - er in that big some - where out there. And e - ven though I know how ver - y

F G/F Fmaj7 G/F F G/F
far a - part we are it helps to think we might be wish - in' on the same bright star. And

A♭ B♭/A♭ A♭ B♭/A♭ A♭ B♭/A♭
when the night wind starts to sing that lone-some lull - a - by it helps to think we're sleep-ing un - der - neath the same big

G C Cmaj7/E Fmaj9 F/G To Coda C C/E F Dm7 G/F Em7 Am7
sky. Some-where out there if love can see us through, then we'll be to - geth - er some-where

F G C D/C C D/C C/B♭ B♭maj7 Am/B♭ D/E
out there, out where dreams come true. (Instrumenal)

A C♯m7 A/D D/E A A/C♯ D D+ D6 A/C♯ Bm7 Dmaj7 C♯m F♯m7

Bm7 C♯m D/E A
D.S. al Coda
And
CODA C G/E F Dm G/F
love can see us through, then we'll be to
(love can see us through)

Em7 Am F G C Cmaj7/E C/F G7sus C(add9)
geth - er some-where out there, out where dreams come true.

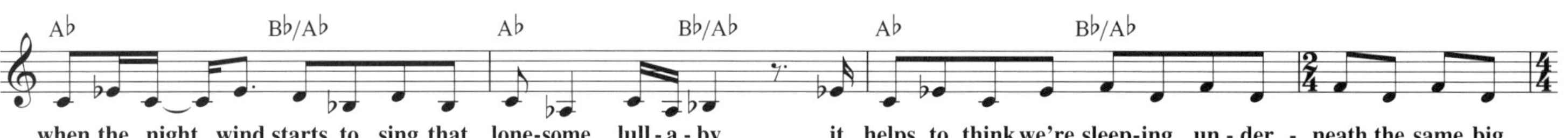

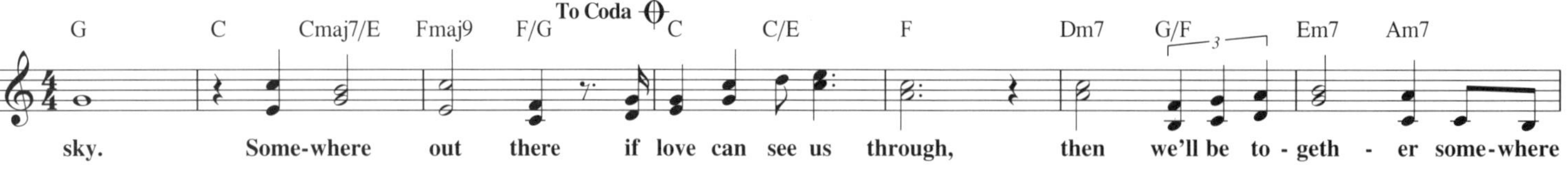

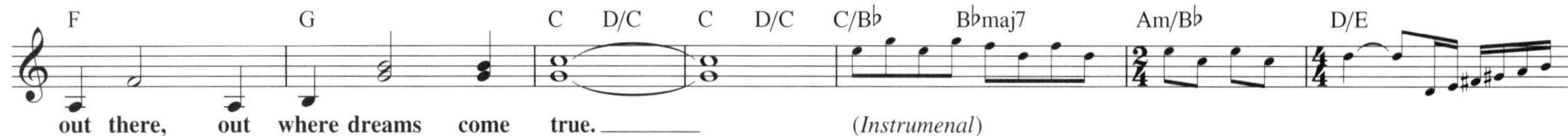

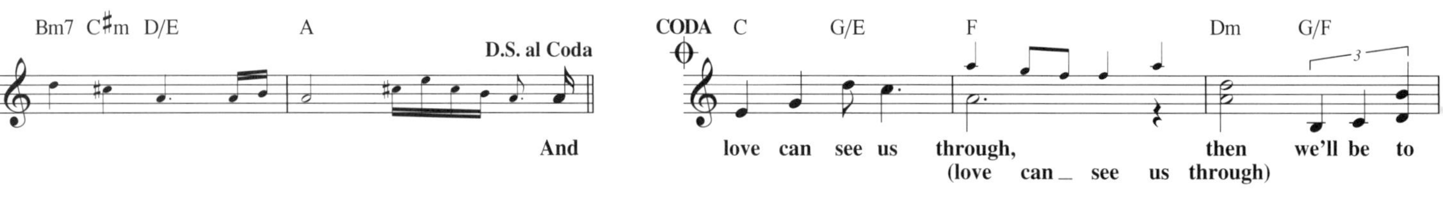

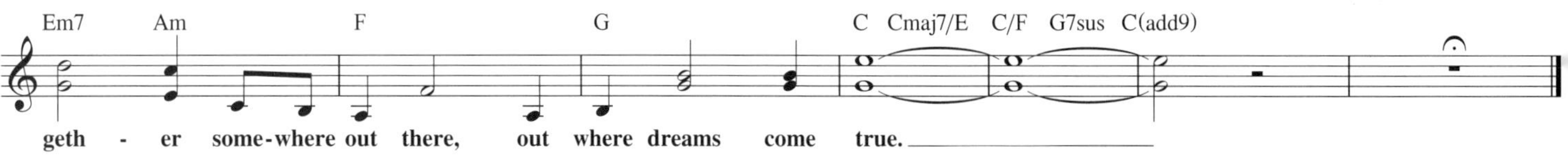

SON-OF-A-PREACHER MAN

Words and Music by JOHN
and RONNIE WIL

Brisk Rock tempo
Bil - ly Ray was a preach - er's son, and when his Dad - dy would vis - it he'd come a - long.
Be - in' good is - n't al - ways eas - y, no mat - ter how hard I try.
When they gath - ered 'round and start - ed talk - in' that's when Bil - ly would take me walk - in'.
When he start - ed sweet talk - in' to me, he'd come and tell me ev - 'ry - thing is all right.
Out thru the back - yard we'd go walk - in'
He'd kiss 'n' tell me ev - 'ry - thing is all right
and then he'd look in - to my eyes,
and Lord knows to my sur - prise, the on - ly one who could
and "Can we get a - way a - gain to - night?" The on - ly one who could
ev - er reach me was the son - of - a - preach - er man.
The on - ly boy who could ev - er teach me was the son - of - a - preach - er man, yes, he was, he was, ooh, yes, he was.
was.
How well I re - mem - ber the look that was in his eyes.
Steal - in' kiss - es from me on the sly, tak - in' time to make time.
Tell - in' me that he's all mine, learn - in' from each oth - er's know - in', look - in' to see how much we've grown and the on - ly one who could ev - er reach me
was the son - of - a - preach - er man.
The on - ly boy who could ev - er teach me was the son - of - a - preach - er man, yes, he was, he was oh, yes, he was.
The
Repeat and Fade

SOUTHERN CROSS

Words and Music by STEPHEN STILLS, RICHARD CURTIS and MICHAEL CURTIS

Moderately Slow
Got out of town on a boat gon' to south-ern is - lands. Sail - ing a
reach be-fore a fol-low-ing sea. She was mak-ing for the trades on the
out-side, and the down-hill run to Pa-pe-e - te. Off the
wind on this head-ing, lie the Mar - que - sas. We got eight - y feet of
sail - ing for to-mor-row. My dreams are a - dy - ing. And my love is an an-chor
wa-ter-line, nice-ly mak - in' way. In a nois-y bar in A-va-lon, I tried to call you.
tied to you, tied with a sil-ver chain. I have my ship, and all her flags are a - fly - ing.
But on the mid-night watch I re-al-ized why twice you ran a - way.
She is all that I have left, and mu - sic is her name.
Think a-bout how man - y times I have fall - en.
Spir-its are us - in' me; larg - er voic - es call - in'. What heav-en brought
you and me can-not be for-got - ten. I have been a -
round the world, look - in' for that wom - an - girl
who knows love can en - dure. And you know it will.
When you see the South-ern Cross for the first time,
So we cheat - ed and we lied and we test - ed.
you un - der - stand now why you came this way.
And we nev - er failed to fail. It was the eas - i - est thing to do.

A
G
D
'Cause the truth you might be run-nin' from is so small. But it's as
You will sur - vive be - ing best - ed. Some-bod - y
A G D Bm A
big as the prom-ise, the prom-ise of a com-in' day. So I'm
fine will come a - long, make me for - get a - bout lov - ing you
1
2
G D A G D
in the South-ern Cross.
(Instrumental)

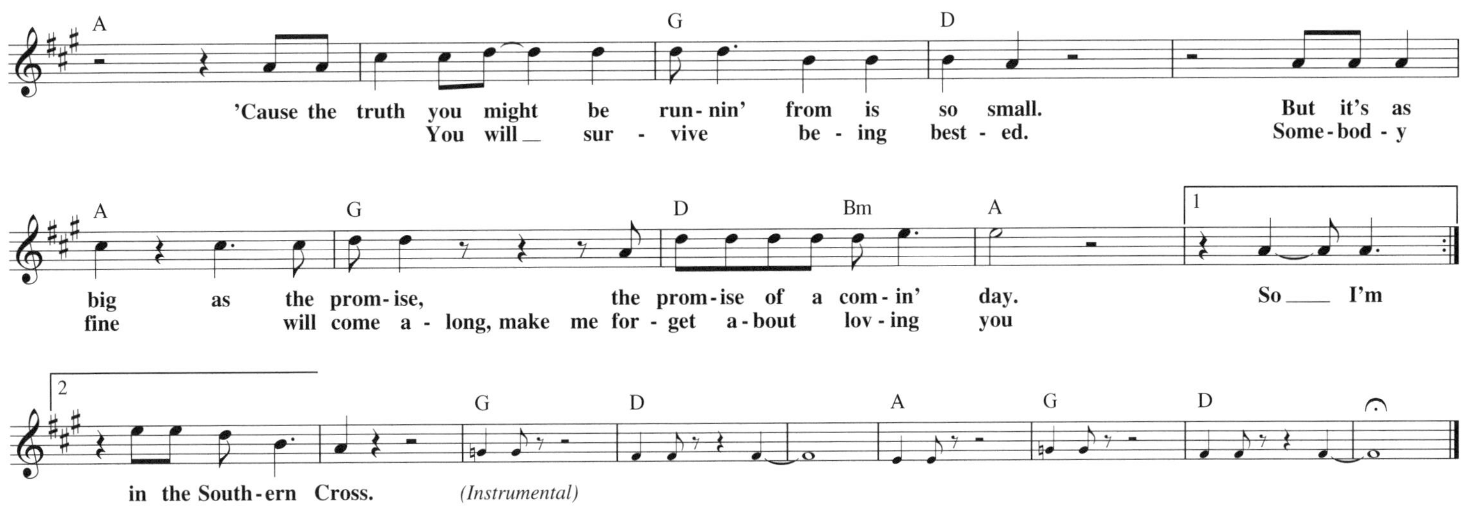

SONG SUNG BLUE

Words and Music by
NEIL DIAMOND

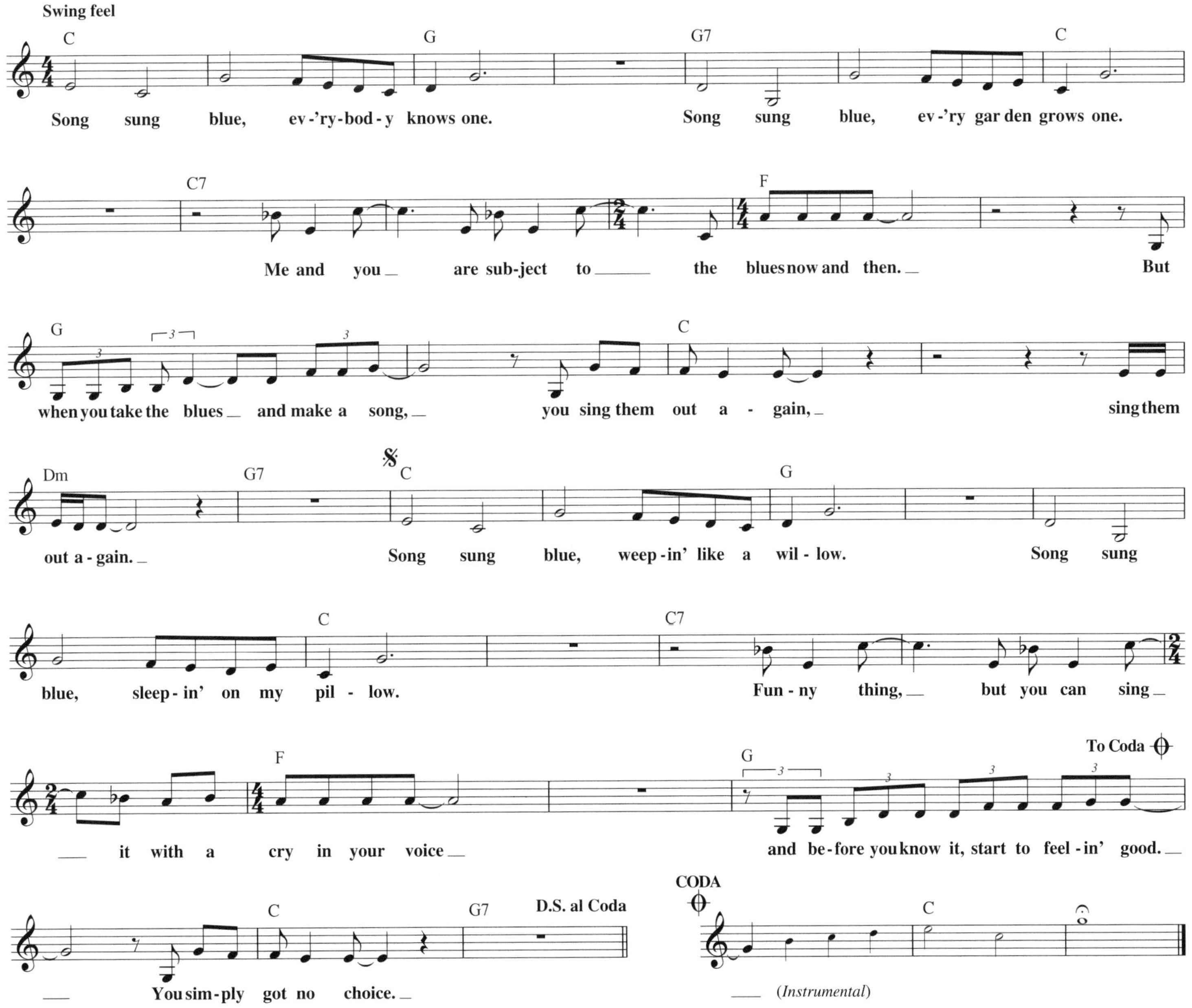

Swing feel
C G G7 C
Song sung blue, ev-'ry-bod-y knows one. Song sung blue, ev-'ry gar den grows one.
C7 F
Me and you are sub-ject to the blues now and then. But
G C
when you take the blues and make a song, you sing them out a - gain, sing them
Dm G7 C G
out a-gain. Song sung blue, weep-in' like a wil - low. Song sung
C C7
blue, sleep-in' on my pil - low. Fun - ny thing, but you can sing
F G
To Coda
it with a cry in your voice and be-fore you know it, start to feel-in' good.
C G7
D.S. al Coda
You sim-ply got no choice.
CODA
C
(Instrumental)

SOUTHERN NIGHTS

Words and Music by
ALLEN TOUSSAINT

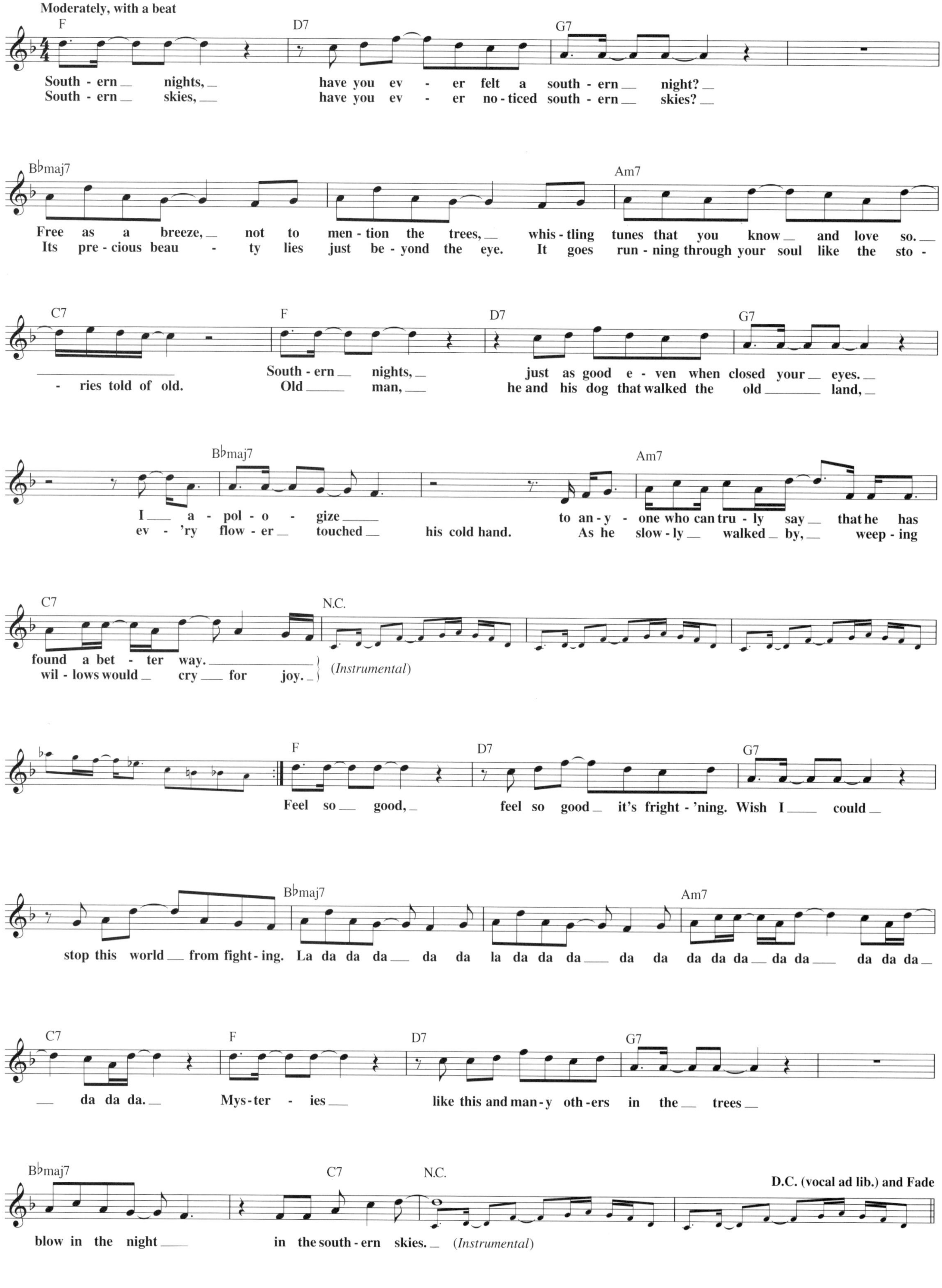

Moderately, with a beat

F D7 G7

South - ern __ nights, __ have you ev - er felt a south - ern __ night? __
South - ern __ skies, __ have you ev - er no - ticed south - ern __ skies? __

B♭maj7 Am7

Free as a breeze, __ not to men - tion the trees, __ whis - tling tunes that you know __ and love so. __
Its pre - cious beau - ty lies just be - yond the eye. It goes run - ning through your soul like the sto -

C7 F D7 G7

South - ern __ nights, __ just as good e - ven when closed your __ eyes. __
- ries told of old. Old ____ man, __ he and his dog that walked the old ____ land, __

B♭maj7 Am7

I __ a - pol - o - gize ____ to an - y - one who can tru - ly say __ that he has
ev - 'ry flow - er __ touched __ his cold hand. As he slow - ly __ walked __ by, __ weep - ing

C7 N.C.

found a bet - ter way. ____
wil - lows would __ cry __ for joy. __
(Instrumental)

F D7 G7

Feel so __ good, __ feel so good __ it's fright - 'ning. Wish I __ could __

B♭maj7 Am7

stop this world __ from fight - ing. La da da da __ da da la da da da __ da da da da da __ da da __ da da da __

C7 F D7 G7

__ da da da. __ Mys - ter - ies __ like this and man - y oth - ers in the __ trees __

SORRY SEEMS TO BE THE HARDEST WORD

Words and Music by ELTON JOHN
and BERNIE TAUPIN

Slowly

Gm D/G Gm7/F Cm7
What have I got to do to make you love me?

F B♭ Am7♭5 D7 Gm D/G B♭/F
What have I got to do to make you care? What do I do when light-ning strikes

Cm7 F B♭ Am7♭5 D7
me and I wake to find that you're not there?

Gm D/G B♭/F Cm7 F B♭ Am7♭5 D7
What do I do to make you want me? What have I got-ta do to be heard?

Gm9 Gm Cm F
What do I say when it's all o - ver? Sor-ry seems to be the hard-est word.

B♭ F/A 𝄋 E♭/G D/F♯ B♭/F Em7♭5
It's sad, it's so sad. (It's so sad.) It's a sad, sad sit - u - a - tion,

Cm/E♭ D7 Gm Am7♭5 D7 E♭/G D/F♯
and it's get-ting more and more ab - surd. It's sad, it's so sad. (It's so sad.)

B♭/F C7/E E♭ Cm7 D D7 To Coda
Why can't we talk it o - ver? Al-ways seems to me that sor-ry seems to be the hard-est

Gm Cm F7 E♭/B♭ F7/A B♭ Am7♭5/G D7/F♯
word. *(Instrumental)*

Gm Cm Cm7 F7 B♭ F D.S. al Coda

CODA

Gm D/G B♭/F Cm F7
word. What do I do to make you love me? What have I got to do to be

B♭ Am7♭5 D Gm Cm Am7♭5 D7♭9
heard? What do I do when light-ning strikes me? What have I got to do,

Gm Cm Am7♭5 D7 B♭ Em7♭5 Cm Gm/D Am7♭5 Dsus D7 Gm9
what have I got to do? Sor - ry seems to be the hard - est word.

SPANISH EYES

Words by CHARLES SINGLETON and EDDIE SNYDER
Music by BERT KAEMPFERT

Moderately

G D7 C G7 Cm Cm6 Ab

Blue Span - ish eyes, tear - drops are fall - ing from your Span - ish eyes. Please, please don't cry. This is just a - dios and not good - bye.
Blue Span - ish eyes, pret - ti - est eyes in all of Mex - i - co. True Span - ish eyes, please smile for me once more be - fore I go.

Soon I'll re - turn, bring - ing you all the love your heart can hold. Please say Si Si. Say you and your Span - ish eyes will wait for me.

Span - ish eyes wait for me, say Si Si!

SPANISH FLEA

Words and Music by
JULIUS WECHTER

Moderately
Bb Am7 D7 G7 C7 C9 F7
There was a lit - tle Span ish flea. A rec - ord star he thought he'd be. He'd heard of
flea? And so he hid in - side a dog - gie from Ma - drid, ar - riv - ing
Bb Eb Ab Db Gb B F N.C.
sing - ers like Bea - tles, The Chip - munks he'd seen on T - V. Why not a lit - tle Span - ish
here in the cit - y still sing - ing his sweet har - mo - ny, as broke as an - y flea could
Bb N.C. Eb Eb7 Ab Eb7
be. He walked a - round as if he owned the town, hum - ming his pint - size mel - o - dy.
rage. I'll put you on the stage in cos - tumes like you've nev - er worn."

A♭ E♭7 A♭7 D♭ D♭7 G♭
With his gui - tar, he knew he'd be a star and in his old home town how
Well, at a glance he knew this was his chance. Yes, all at once a Span-ish
F N.C. B♭ Am7 D7 G7 C7 C9
proud they'd be! Then all at once he met a man who said, "I'll help you if I can."
star was born. For when the peo - ple heard him play they all be - gan to shout, "O - lé!"
F7 B♭ E♭ A♭ D♭ G♭ B F
He list - ened first to the song, then he sang right a - long for you see,
He was the pride of the na - tion, a sing - ing sen - sa - tion was he,
1 N.C. B♭ N.C. 2 N.C. G♭7 F7 B♭
he loved the lit - tle Spanish flea. "You'll be the
though he was just a Span - ish flea.

SPEAK SOFTLY, LOVE

(Love Theme)
from the Paramount Picture THE GODFATHER

Words by LARRY KUSIK
Music by NINO ROTA

Slowly
Cm Fm/C Cm Cm/E♭
Speak soft - ly, love, and hold me warm a - gainst your heart. I feel your words, the ten - der, trem - bling mo - ments

Fm Cm Cm/G G7sus G7
start. We're in a world our ver - y own, shar - ing a love that on - ly few have ev - er

Cm B♭7/D B♭7 E♭ D♭/F Fm6/A♭ G N.C.
known. Wine col - ored days warmed by the sun, deep vel - vet nights when we are one. Speak soft - ly,

Cm Fm/C Cm Fm/C Cm Fm6/C Cm Fm/C Fm
love, so no one hears us but the sky. The vows of love we make will live un - til we die. My life is yours and all be -

Cm Cm/G G7sus G7 1 Cm 2 Cm
cause you came in - to my world with love so soft - ly, love. Speak soft - ly, love.

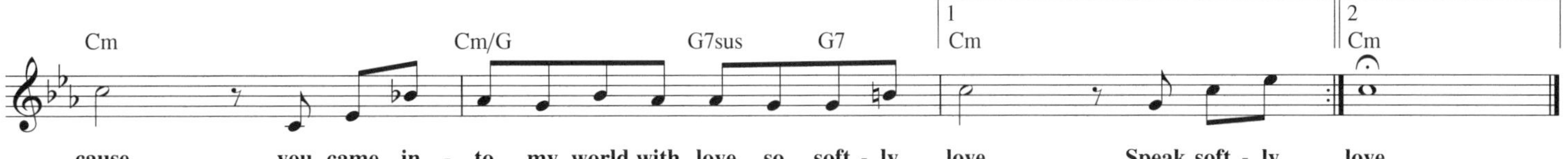

STUCK IN THE MIDDLE WITH YOU

Words and Music by GERRY RAFFERTY
and JOE EGAN

Moderately
D
Well, I don't know why I came here to - night. I got the feel - in' that some - thing ain't right.
stuck in the mid - dle with you and I'm won - d'ring what it is I should do.
Tryin' to make some sense of it all but I can see it makes no sense at all.
(Instrumental)
G7
I'm so scared in case I fall off my chair and I'm won - d'ring how I'll get down the stairs.
It's so hard to keep this smile from my face. Los - ing con - trol I'm all o - ver the place.
Is it cool to go to sleep on the floor? You don't think that I can take an - y - more.
D
(1.-3.) Clowns
(Instrumental)
A C G D
to the left of me, jok - ers to the right. Here I am, stuck in the mid - dle with you.
1,3
Yes, I'm
2,4
(Instrumental ends)
G7
Well, you start - ed out with lov - in' and you found that you're a self - made man.
D G7
And you fan - cy I'll come crawl - in' slap you on the back and say
D Am/D
To Coda
D.S. al Coda (with repeat)
please, please.
CODA
D
(Instrumental)
And I don't know why I came here to - night. I got the feel - in' that some - thing ain't right. I'm so scared
G7 D
in case I fall off my chair and I'm won - d'ring how I'll get down the stairs.
A C G D
Clowns to the left of me, jok - ers to the right. Here I am, stuck in the mid - dle with you.

Yes, I'm stuck in the mid-dle with you.
Stuck in the mid-dle with you.
Here I am, stuck in the mid-dle with you.

SPIDERS AND SNAKES

Words and Music by JIM STAFFORD
and DAVID BELLAMY

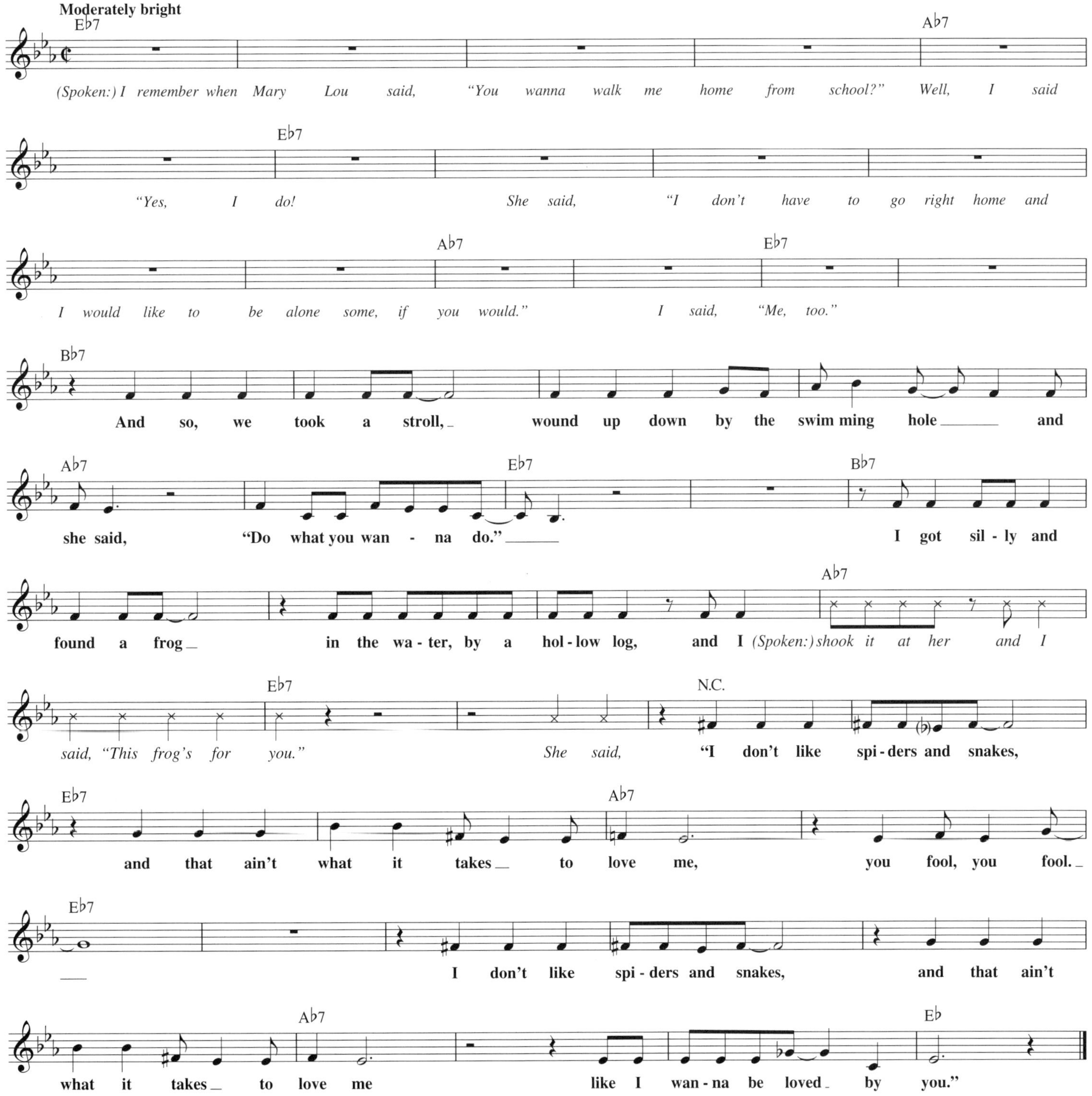

Moderately bright

Eb7 — Ab7

(Spoken:) I remember when Mary Lou said, "You wanna walk me home from school?" Well, I said

Eb7

"Yes, I do! She said, "I don't have to go right home and

Ab7 — Eb7

I would like to be alone some, if you would." I said, "Me, too."

Bb7

And so, we took a stroll, wound up down by the swim ming hole and

Ab7 — Eb7 — Bb7

she said, "Do what you wan - na do." I got sil - ly and

Ab7

found a frog in the wa - ter, by a hol - low log, and I *(Spoken:) shook it at her and I*

Eb7 — N.C.

said, "This frog's for you." She said, **"I don't like spi - ders and snakes,**

Eb7 — Ab7

and that ain't what it takes to love me, you fool, you fool.

Eb7

I don't like spi - ders and snakes, and that ain't

Ab7 — Eb

what it takes to love me like I wan - na be loved by you."

SOUL LIMBO

Words and Music by BOOKER T. JONES, DUCK DUNN,
STEVE CROPPER and AL JACKSON, JR.

STILL

Words and Music by
LIONEL RICHIE

Slowly
Csus(add2) C Fmaj7 Gsus G Gsus G
La - dy, morn - ing's just a mo - ment a - way, and I'm with - out you
Csus(add2) C Csus(add2) C
once a - gain. You laughed at me, you said you've nev - er
Fmaj7 Gsus G Gsus G Csus(add2) C B♭/A C/G
need - ed me. I won - der if you need me now. So man - y
Fmaj7 Dm7 G Cmaj7
dreams that flew a - way, so man - y words we did - n't say.
games that peo - ple play. We made mis - takes a - long the way.
C9 C7 B♭/A C7/G Fmaj7 Dm7/G G Cmaj7
Two peo - ple lost in a storm, where did we go, where'd we
Some - how I know, deep in my heart, you need - ed me. 'Cause I
C9 C7 B♭/A C7/G Fmaj7 Dm7 G
go? Lost what we both had found, you know we
need - ed you so des - p'rate - ly. We were too
Cmaj7 C9 C7 B♭/A C7/G Fmaj7 Am7/E Dm7
let each oth - er down,
blind to see,
but then, most of all, I do love you
To Coda
G Csus(add2) C Csus(add2) C Fmaj7
Whispered: Still.
(Instrumental)
D.S. al Coda
Gsus G Gsus Csus(add2) C C7 B♭/A C7/G
We played the
CODA
Csus(add2) C

STUPID CUPID

Words and Music by HOWARD GREENFIELD and NEIL SEDAKA

With a beat
E♭ E♭7
Stu - pid Cu - pid, you're a real mean guy. I'd like to clip your wings so you can't fly.
A♭ E♭
I'm in love and it's a cry - in' shame, and I know that you're the one to blame.
B♭7 A♭7 E♭ N.C.
Hey, hey, set me free. Stu - pid Cu - pid, stop pick - in' on me. I
E♭ E♭7
can't do my home-work and I can't think straight. I meet him ev - 'ry morn-in' 'bout a half past eight,
A♭ E♭
I'm act - in' like a love - sick fool. You e - ven got me car - ry - in' his books to school.
B♭7 A♭7 E♭ N.C.
Hey, hey, set me free. Stu - pid Cu - pid, stop pick - in' on me.
A♭ E♭
You mixed me up but good right from the ver - y start.
A♭ F7 B♭7
Hey, go play Rob - in Hood with some - bod - y el - se's heart.
E♭ E♭7
You got me jump - in' like a cra - zy clown, and I don't fea - ture what you're put - tin' down.
A♭ E♭
Since I kissed his lov - in' lips of wine, the thing that both - ers me is that I like it fine.
B♭7 A♭7 E♭ N.C. 1 B♭7♯5 2 E♭
Hey, hey, set me free. Stu - pid Cu - pid, stop pick - in' on me. pick - in' on me.

SUFFRAGETTE CITY

Words and Music by
DAVID BOWIE

Medium beat
A F G A F G
Hey man oh leave me a - lone, you know. Hey man oh Hen - ry get off the phone. I got - ta
A B D F G
hey man I got - ta straight - en my face. This mel - low - thighed chick just put my spine out of place.
A F G A F G
Hey man my school day's in - sane. Hey man my work's down the drain.
A B D F G
Hey man well she's a to - tal blam blam she said she had to squeeze it but she and then she. Oh don't
A D C G
lean on me man, 'cause you can't af - ford the tic - ket. I'm back on Suf - fra - gette Cit - y. No don't
A D F G
lean on me man 'cause you ain't got time to check. You know my Suf - fra - gette Cit - y is ou - ta
A
To Coda
sight. She's al - right.
F G
Hey man, ah Hen - ry don't be un - kind, go a - way.
A F G A B
Hey man I can't take you this time, no way. Hey man droo - gie don't crash here. There's
D F G
D.S. al Coda
on - ly room for one and here she comes, here she comes. Ah don't
CODA
A F A
right A Suf - fra - gette Ci -
Repeat ad lib.
E11 A
- ty Suf - fra - gette

SUKIYAKI

Words and Music by HACHIDAI NAKAMURA
and ROKUSUKE EI
English Lyrics by TOM LESLIE and BUZZ CASON

Moderately, with a beat

G Em G Em

(English:) I'll hold my head up high ___ look - ing to the sky ___
I know the night will hide ___ sad - ness I feel in - side. ___
(Japanese:) *U - E - O MU - I - TE A - RU - KO ___*
U - E - O MU - I - TE A - RU - KO ___

G Bm Em Am7 D7

so they won't see all the tears that are in my eyes. ___
No one will know for the smile on my lips won't tell them
NA - MI - DA - GA KO - DO - RE MA - I YO - NI
NI - JI - N - DA HA - SHI - O KA - SO E - TA

G Am C6 B7♯5 B7 Em C

No one will know I'm go - ing through my first lone -
I'm ing you and go - ing through my first lone -
O - NO - I - DA - SU HA - RU - NO - HI HI - TO - RI
O - NO - I - DA - SU NA - TAU - NO - HI HI - TO - TI

Bm Am7 [1. G6 C6 Bm7 Am7] [2. G Em G7]

ly night with - out ___ you. ___
ly night with - out ___ — you. ___
PO - CHI - NO YO - RU. ___
PO - CHI - NO YO - RU. ___

𝄋 C G G7

As I walk a - lone ___ the lone - ly winds seem to say:
SHI - A - WA - SE - WA - KU - MO - NO U - E - NI
KA - NA - SHI - MI - WA - MO - SHI - NO KA - GE - NI

Cm G A9 D7

From this dark - ness on ___ all your nights will be this way.
SHI - A - WA - SE - WA - SO - RA - NO U - E - NI
KA - NA - SHI - MI - WA - TAU - KI - NO KA - GE - NI

G Em G Em

So I'll go on a - lone, ___ pre - tend - ing you're not gone, ___
U - E - O MU - I - TE ___ A - RU - KO ___
U - E - O MU - I - TE ___ A - RU - KO ___

G Bm Em Am7 D7

but I can't hide all the mo - ments of love we knew: ___
NA - MI - DA - GA KO - DO RE MA - I YO - NI
NA - MI - DA - GA KO - DO RE MA - I YO - NI

G Am C6 B7♯5 B7 Em C
Mem - 'ries of you as I go through my first lone -
NA - KI - NA - GA - RA A - RU - KU HI - TO - RI
NA - KI - NA - GA - RA A - RU - KU HI - TO - RI
To Coda
D.S. al Coda
CODA
Bm Am7 G Em G7 G6 C6
ly night with - out you.
PO - CHI - NO YO RU. YO RU.
PO - CHI - NO
Bm7 Am7 G C Bm Am7 G C Bm Am7 G
My first lone - ly night with - out you.
HI - TO - RI PO - CHI - NO YO - RU.

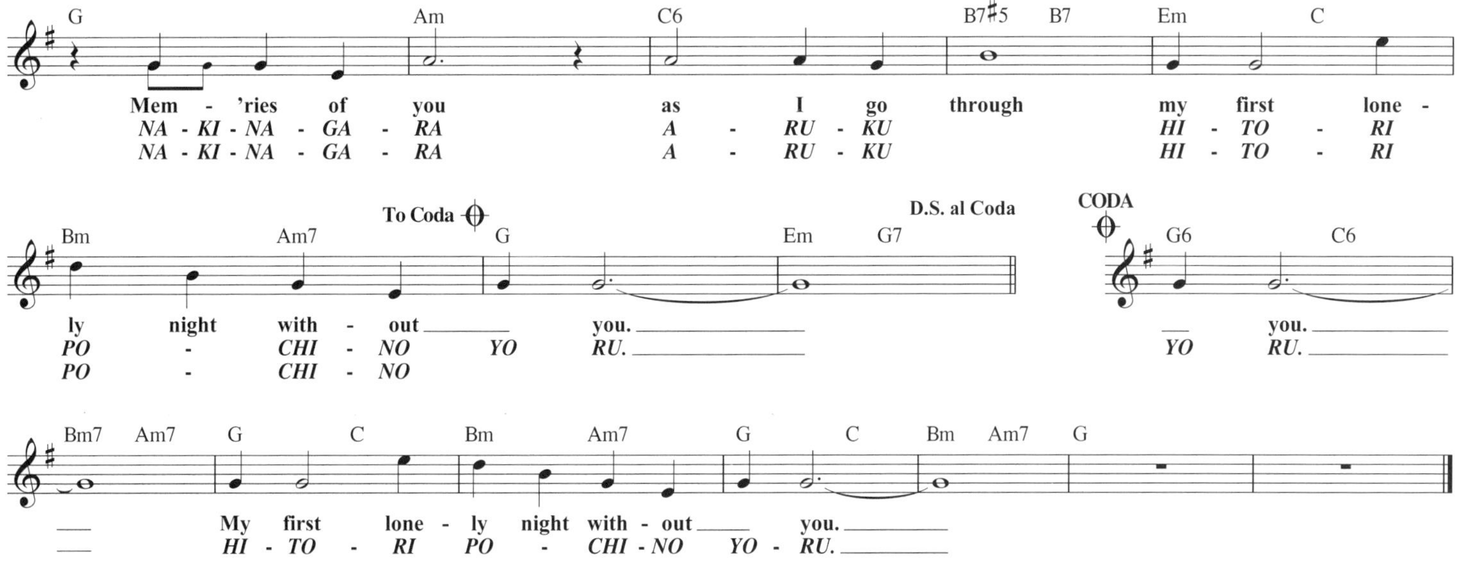

SUMMERTIME, SUMMERTIME

Words and Music by TOM JAMESON and SHERM FELLER

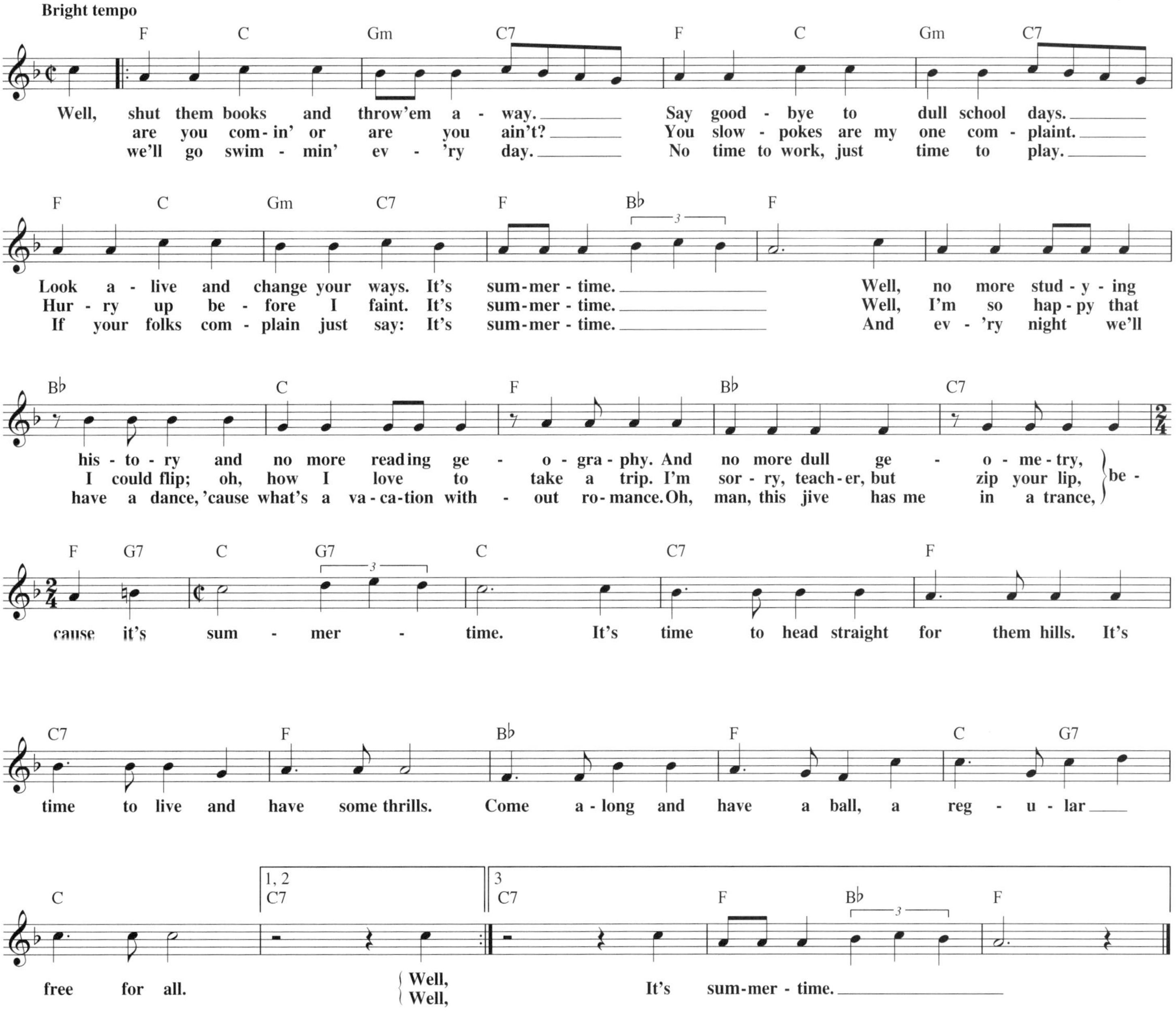

Bright tempo
F C Gm C7 F C Gm C7
Well, shut them books and throw'em a - way. Say good - bye to dull school days.
are you com - in' or are you ain't? You slow - pokes are my one com - plaint.
we'll go swim - min' ev - 'ry day. No time to work, just time to play.
F C Gm C7 F B♭ F
Look a - live and change your ways. It's sum - mer - time. Well, no more stud - y - ing
Hur - ry up be - fore I faint. It's sum - mer - time. Well, I'm so hap - py that
If your folks com - plain just say: It's sum - mer - time. And ev - 'ry night we'll
B♭ C F B♭ C7
his - to - ry and no more read ing ge - o - gra - phy. And no more dull ge - o - me - try,
I could flip; oh, how I love to take a trip. I'm sor - ry, teach - er, but zip your lip,
have a dance, 'cause what's a va - ca - tion with - out ro - mance. Oh, man, this jive has me in a trance,
be -
F G7 C G7 C C7 F
cause it's sum - mer - time. It's time to head straight for them hills. It's
C7 F B♭ F C G7
time to live and have some thrills. Come a - long and have a ball, a reg - u - lar
C 1, 2 C7 3 C7 F B♭ F
free for all. Well, Well, It's sum - mer - time.

STEPPIN' OUT

Words and Music by
JOE JACKSON

Fast Disco
F(add9) Eb Db Eb
Now, the mist a - cross the win - dow hides the lines;
We are young, but get - ting old be - fore our time.
F Eb Db Eb
but noth - ing hides the col - our of the lights
We'll leave the T. - V. and the ra - di - o
Cm7 Db Eb Cm7
that shine. E - lec - tric - i - ty so
be - hind. Don't you won - der what we'll
Db Db/Eb Fmaj9
fine; look and dry your eyes.
find, step - pin' out to - night?
Ebmaj7/F Dm7/F Ab/F Bb/F Eb/F Bb/F Db/F Eb/F Ab/F Eb/F
F(add9) Eb Db Eb
We, so tired of all the dark - ness in our lives,
You can dress in pink and blue just like a child,
F Eb Db Eb
with no more an - gry words to say, can come
and in a yel - low tax - i, turn to me
Cm7 Db Eb Cm7
a - live; get in - to a car and
and smile. We'll be there in just a
Db Db/Eb Fmaj9
drive to the oth - er side.
while, if you fol - low me.
Me, babe, step - pin'
Ebmaj7/F Dm7/F Ab/F Bb/F Eb/F Bb/F Db/F Eb/F Ab/F
out, in - to the night, in - to the
Eb/F Fmaj9 Ebmaj7/F Dm7/F
light. You, babe, step - pin' out,

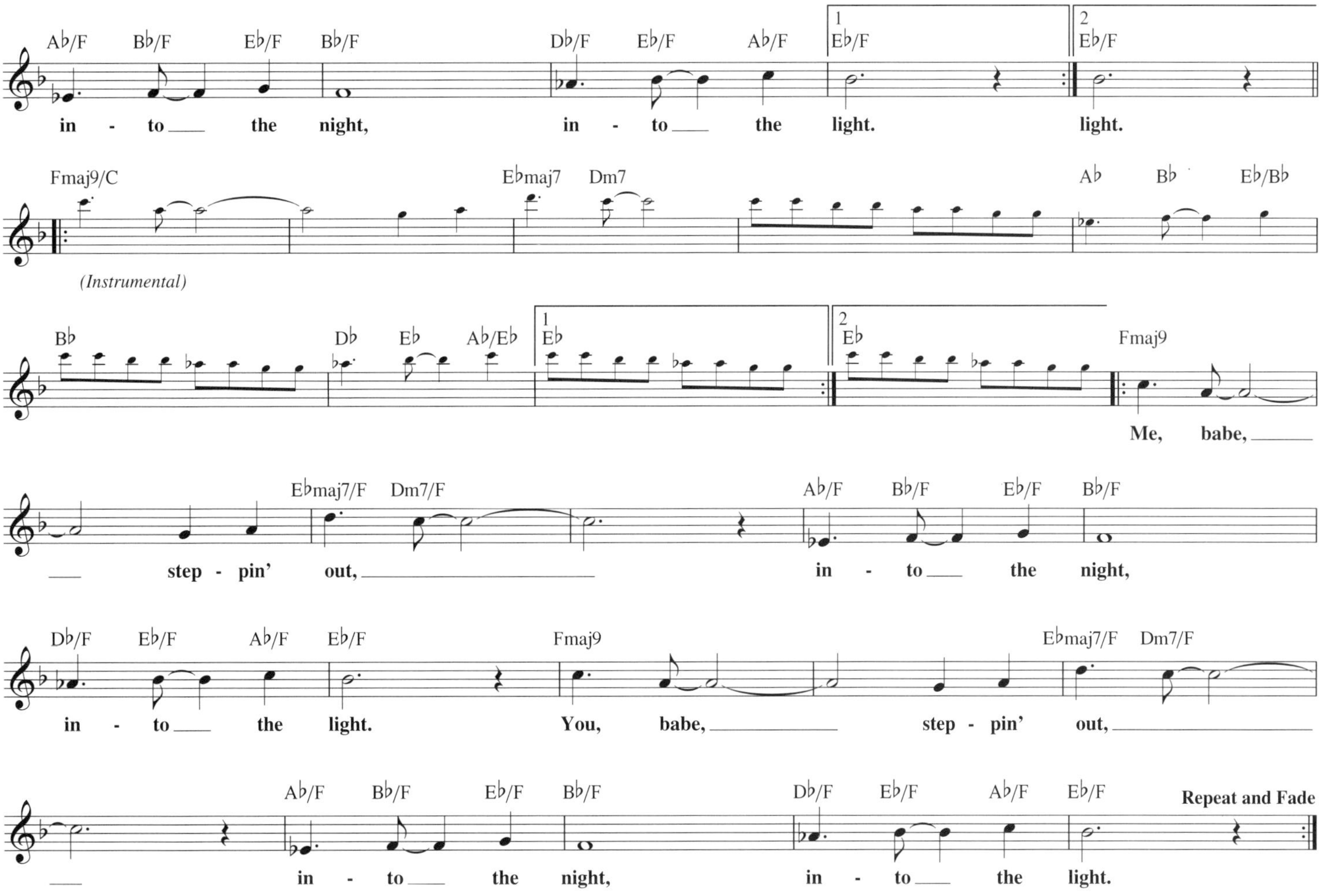

Ab/F Bb/F Eb/F Bb/F Db/F Eb/F Ab/F 1 Eb/F 2 Eb/F
in - to the night, in - to the light. light.
Fmaj9/C Ebmaj7 Dm7 Ab Bb Eb/Bb
(Instrumental)
Bb Db Eb Ab/Eb 1 Eb 2 Eb Fmaj9
Me, babe,
Ebmaj7/F Dm7/F Ab/F Bb/F Eb/F Bb/F
step - pin' out, in - to the night,
Db/F Eb/F Ab/F Eb/F Fmaj9 Ebmaj7/F Dm7/F
in - to the light. You, babe, step - pin' out,
Ab/F Bb/F Eb/F Bb/F Db/F Eb/F Ab/F Eb/F
Repeat and Fade
in - to the night, in - to the light.

SUNNY

Words and Music by
BOBBY HEBB

Moderately
Am C7 F7 E7
Sun - ny, yes - ter - day my life was filled with rain.
Sun - ny, thank you for the sun - shine bou - quet.
Am C7 F7 E7
Sun - ny, you smiled at me and real - ly eased the pain. Oh, the
Sun - ny, thank you for the love you've brought my way. You
Am Am7 Am6 Fmaj7 Fm
dark days are done, and the bright days are here, my sun - ny one shines so sin - cere.
gave to me your all and all. Now I feel ten feet tall.
Oh,
B7b5 E7 Am E7
Sun - ny, one so true, I love you.

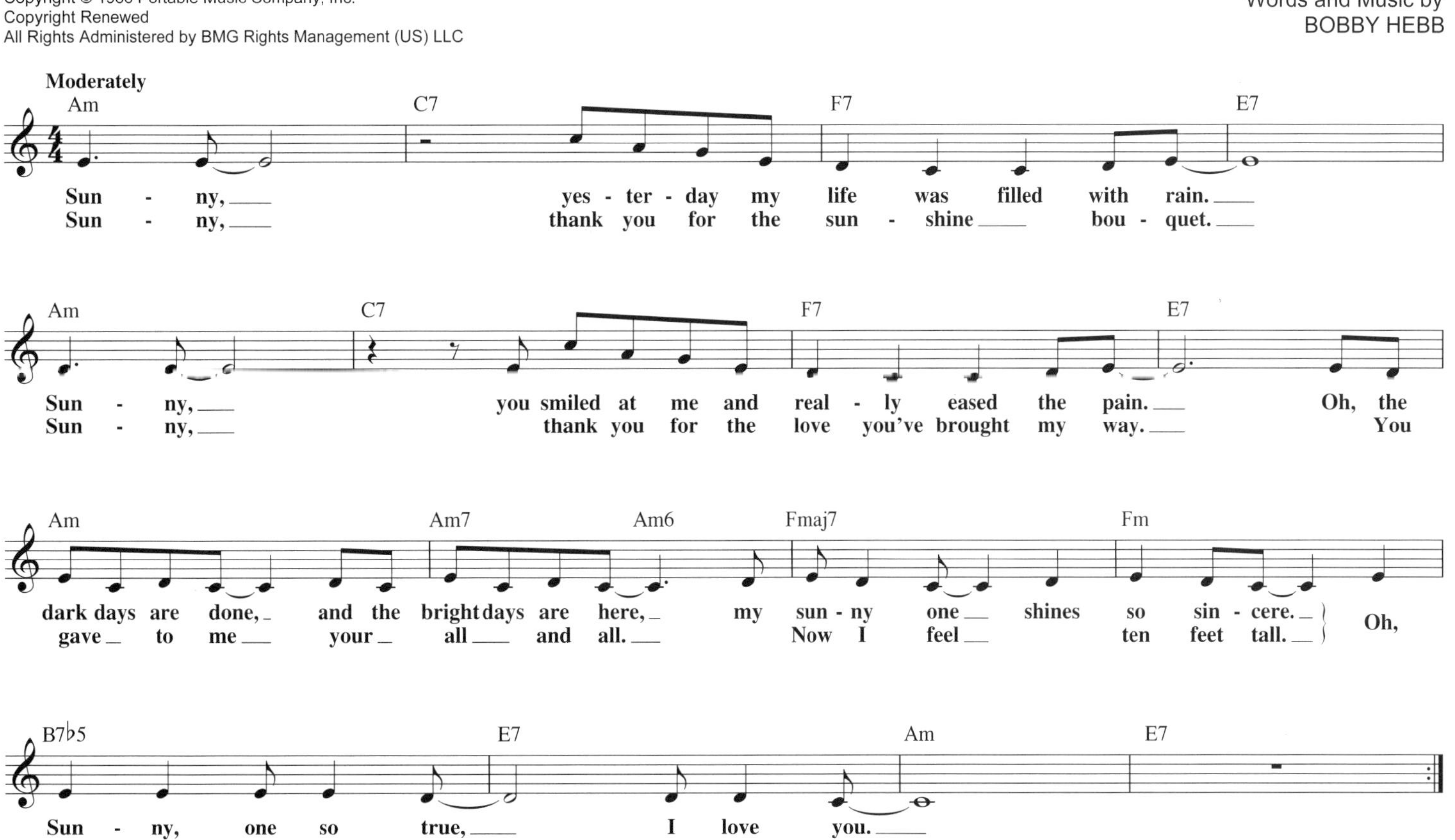

SURRENDER

Words and Music by
RICK NIELSEN

Moderate Rock
C5 G5 F
Moth - er told me, yes, she told me I'd meet girls like you.
Fa - ther says, "Your moth - er's right, she's real - ly up on things."
C5 G5
She al - so told me, "Stay a - way, you'll
Be - fore we mar - ried, Mom - my served in the WACS
F5 C5 F5
nev - er know what you'll catch."
in the Phil - ip - pines."
Just the oth - er day
Now, I had heard the WACS
G5 C5
I heard a sol - diers fall - ing off
re - cruit - ed old maids for the war.
some In -
But Mom -
F5 G5 C5
- do - ne - sian junk that's go - ing 'round.
- my is - n't one of those, I've known her all these years.
C Am7 G5 F5
Mom - my's al - right, Dad - dy's al - right, they just seem a lit - tle weird.
C Am7
Sur - ren - der, sur - ren - der, but don't
G5 F5
give your - self a - way, ay, ay, ay.
B♭ C
(Instrumental)
B♭ C
(End instrumental)

D♭5 A♭5 G♭5
What - ev - er hap - pened to all this sea - son's los - ers of the year?
D♭5 A♭5
Ev - 'ry time I got to think - ing,
G♭5 D♭5 G♭5
where'd they dis - ap - pear? When I woke up,
A♭5 D♭5
Mom and Dad are roll - ing on the couch.
G♭5 A♭5 D♭5
Roll - ing num - bers, rock and roll - ing, got my Kiss rec - ords out.
D♭ B♭m7
Mom - my's al - right, Dad - dy's al - right, they
A♭5 G♭5 D♭
just seem a lit - tle weird. Sur - ren - der, sur - en -
B♭m7 A♭5 G♭5
- der, but don't give your - self a - way,
D♭
ay, ay, ay. A - way.
G♭ D♭ A♭5 D♭
A - way.
Sur - ren - der, sur - ren -
B♭m7 A♭5 G♭5
- der, but don't give your - self a - way. Sur - ren -
Repeat and Fade

SWAY
(Quien sera)

English Words by NORMAN GIMBEL
Spanish Words and Music by PABLO BELTRAN RUIZ

Moderately

F♯dim B7 F♯dim B7 Em
When ma - rim - ba rhy - thms start to play, dance with me, make me Sway.

C9♯11 C9 B9 C9♯11 C9 B7♭9 Em6 B7♭9 Em6
Like the la - zy o - cean hugs the shore, hold me close, Sway me more.

N.C. F♯dim B7 F♯dim B7 Em
Like a flow - er bend - ing in the breeze, bend with me, Sway with ease.

C9♯11 C9 B9 C9♯11 C9 B7♭9 Em6 B7♭9 Em6
When we dance you have a way with me, stay with me, Sway with me.

G6 B♭dim D7 G
Oth - er danc - ers may be on the floor, dear, but my eyes will see on - ly you.

B7 D♯dim B7 Em C9 B7♭9
On - ly you have that mag - ic tech - nique, when we Sway I grow weak. *(Instrumental)*

Em N.C. F♯dim B7 F♯dim B7 Em
I can hear the sound of vi - o - lins, long be - fore it be - gins.

C9♯11 C9 B9 C9♯11 C9 B7♭9 1 Em6 B7♭9 Em6
Make me thrill as on - ly you know how, Sway me smooth, Sway me now.

N.C. 2 Em6 B7♭9 Em6 C B7 Em6
When ma - rim - ba rhy thms Sway me now. Sway me smooth, Sway me now.

SWEET THING (SWEET THANG)

Words and Music by CHAKA KHAN
and TONY MAIDEN

Easy, relaxed groove
Amaj7 Dmaj7 Amaj7 Dmaj7 Amaj7 Dmaj7
I will love you an - y - way, e - ven if you can not stay. I think you are the one for me.
wish you were my lov - er, but you act so un - der - cov - er. Love you child my whole life long.
Amaj7 Dmaj7 Amaj7 Dmaj7
Here is where you want to be. I just want to sat - is - fy you, 'cause
be it right or be it wrong. I'm on - ly what you make me, ba - by. Don't

Amaj7 Dmaj7 Amaj7 Dmaj7
you're not mine and I can't de - ny it. Don't you hear me talk - ing, ba - by?
walk a - way. Don't be so shad - y. Don't want your mind. Don't want your mon - ey. These
Amaj7 Dmaj7 C♯m A G/A A G/A A
Love me now or I'll go cra - zy. Whoa, sweet thing.
words I say, they mighty sound fun - ny, but, whoa, sweet thing.
C♯m F♯m A C♯m A G/A A G/A A
Don't you know you're my ev - 'ry thing. Whoa, sweet thing.
C♯m F♯m A Amaj7 Dmaj7 Amaj7 Dmaj7 Amaj7 Dmaj7
Don't you know you're my ev - 'ry - thing, yes you are.
1 Amaj7 Dmaj7 2 Amaj7 Dmaj7 B♭maj7 E♭maj7 B♭maj7 E♭maj7 B♭maj7 E♭maj7
I Ha, ah, ah, ah, oo.
B♭maj7 E♭maj7 B♭maj7 E♭maj7 B♭maj7 E♭maj7
You are my heat, you are my fire. You make me weak with strong de - sire.
B♭maj7 E♭maj7 B♭maj7 E♭maj7 B♭maj7 E♭maj7
Love you child my whole life long. Be it right or be wrong. I just want to sat - is - fy you 'cause
B♭maj7 E♭maj7 B♭maj7 E♭maj7 Dm7 D♭m7 Cm7 Bmaj7♯11
you're not mine. I can't de - ny it. Don't you hear me talk - ing, ba - by? Love me now or I'll go
B♭maj7 E♭maj7 B♭maj7 E♭maj7
cra - zy.
You're my heat, you are my fire. You're not mine. I can't de - ny it.
Repeat ad lib. and Fade
B♭maj7 E♭maj7 Dm7 D♭m7 Cm7 Bmaj7♯11
Don't you hear me talk - ing, ba - by? Love me now or I'll go cra - zy.

SWEET CITY WOMAN

Words and Music by
RICHARD DODSON

Moderate Shuffle feel
G Am Am/D Am Am/D
Well, I'm on my way to the cit - y lights, to a pret -
coun - try morn - ing, all smoth-ered in dew, ah, she's got
Am Am/D Am Am/D G
ty face that shines her light on the cit - y nights. And I
a way to make a man feel shin - y and new. And she
Am Am/D Am Am/D
got - ta catch a noon train. I got - ta be there on time. Oh, it feels
sing in the eve - ning old fam - i - li - ar tunes, and she feeds
Am Am/D Am Am/D G
so good to know she waits at the end of the line.
me love and ten - der - ness and mac - a - roons.
Am Am/D Am Am/D
Sweet, sweet cit - y wom - an, I can see
Am Am/D Am Am/D G
your face, I can hear your voice, I can al - most touch you.
Am Am/D Am Am/D
Sweet, sweet cit - y wom - an, oh my ban -
Am Am/D Am Am/D G To Coda
- jo and me, we got a feel for sing - ing. Yeah, yeah.
C G
Bon, c'est bon, bon, bon, c'est bon, bon, bon, c'est bon, bon, bon, bon, bon.
C G
Bon, c'est bon, bon, bon, c'est bon, bon, bon, c'est bon, bon, bon, bon, bon.

C
G
D5
G
So long, Ma. So long, Pa.
D5
G
D.S. al Coda
So long, neigh-bors and friends. Like a
CODA
(Instrumental)
Am
Am/D
Am
Am/D
Am
Am/D
Am
Am/D
G
Am
Am/D
Am
Am/D
Da da da da da da da da da do do do do do do. Da da
Am
Am/D
Am
Am/D
G
da da da da da da da da da da da da da da do do do do do do do.
Am
Am/D
Am
Am/D
Sweet, sweet cit-y wom-an. Oh, she's my
Am
Am/D
Am
Am/D
G
sweet, sweet, sweet, sweet cit-y wom-an.
Am
Am/D
Am
Am/D
Sweet, sweet, sweet, sweet cit-y wom-an.
Am
Am/D
Am
Am/D
G
Repeat and Fade
Sweet, sweet, sweet, sweet cit-y wom-an.

SWEET HOME ALABAMA

Words and Music by RONNIE VAN ZANT,
ED KING and GARY ROSSINGTON

Moderately slow
Big wheels keep on turn - ing, car - ry me home to see my kin.
Sing - ing songs a - bout the south - land, I miss ole 'bam - y once a - gain (And I think it's a sin.)
(Instrumental)
Well, I heard Mis - ter Young sing a - bout her.
Well, I heard ole Neil put her down. Well, I hope Neil Young will re - mem - ber
a south - ern man don't need him a - round an - y - how. Sweet home Al - a - bam - a,
where the skies are so blue. Sweet home Al - a - bam - a,
Lord, I'm com - ing home to you. In Bir - ming - ham they love the Gov' - nor. Boo! Boo!
Now Mus - cle Shoals has got the Swamp - ers,
Boo! Now we all did what we could do. Now Wa - ter - gate does not both - er me.
and they've been known to pick a song or two. Lord, they get me off so much;
Does your con - science both - er you? (Tell the truth.)
they pick me up when I'm feel - ing blue. Now how a - bout you?
Sweet home Al - a - bam - a,
where the skies are so blue. Sweet home Al - a - bam - a, Lord I'm com - ing home to you.
D.S. and Fade

SWEET NOTHIN'S

Words and Music by
RONNIE SELF

Moderately
My ba - by whis - pers in my ear, mm, sweet noth - in's.
He knows the things I like to hear, mm, sweet noth - in's.
Things he would - n't tell no - bod - y else. Spoken: Se - cret, ba - by, I keep 'em to my - self. Sweet noth -
- in's, mm, sweet noth - in's. We walk a - long hand in hand,
mm, sweet noth - in's. Yeah, we both un - der - stand, mm, sweet noth -
- in's. Sit - tin' here pass the time read - ing my book.
Spoken: My ba - by gives me that spe - cial look. Sweet noth - in's, mm, sweet noth -
- in's. I'm sit - tin' on my front porch, mm, sweet noth - in's.
Well, do I love you? Of course mm, sweet noth - in's.
Ma - ma turned off the front porch light Spoken: she said: "Come in, dar - lin', that's e -
nough for to - night." Sweet noth - in's, mm, sweet noth - in's.
Sweet noth - in's, mm, sweet noth - in's. Spoken: Sweet noth - in's.

TAKE A CHANCE ON ME

Words and Music by BENNY ANDERSSON
and BJÔRN ULVAEUS

Moderate dance beat
B
If you change your mind, I'm the first in line. Hon - ey, I'm still free,
F♯
take a chance on me. If you need me, let me know, gon - na be a - round.
B
If you got no place to go when you're feel - ing down.
If you're all a - lone when the pret - ty birds have flown, hon - ey, I'm still free,
F♯
take a chance on me. Gon - na do my ver - y best and it ain't no lie.
B C♯m
If you put me to the test, if you let me try. Take a chance on me,
F♯ C♯m F♯ C♯m
take a chance on me.
We can go danc - ing,
Oh, you can take your time, ba - by,
B
we can go walk - ing as long as we're to - geth - er.
I'm in no hur - ry, I know I'm gon - na get you.
C♯m B
Lis - ten to some mu - sic may - be just talk - ing, you'd get to know me bet - ter
You don't wan - na hurt me, ba - by, don't wor - ry I ain't gon - na let you.
G♯m E
'cause you know I got so much that I wan - na do. When I dream I'm a - lone with you, it's
Let me tell you now my love is strong e - nough to last when things are rough, it's
G♯m E F♯ G♯m E
mag - ic. You want me to leave it there, a - fraid of a love af - fair, but I
mag - ic. You say that I waste my time, but I can't get it off my mind. No I
C♯m F♯ C♯m F♯
think you know that I can't let go. If you change your mind,
can't let go 'cause I love you so. If you change your mind,
B
I'm the first in line. Hon - ey, I'm still free, take a chance on me.

F#
If you need me, let me know. Gon-na be a-round, if you got no place to go when you're
B
feel-ing down. If you're all a-lone when the pret-ty birds have flown, hon-ey, I'm still free,
F#
take a chance on me. Gon-na do my ver-y best, ba-by, can't you see,
B
got-ta put me to the test, take a chance on me.
Repeat and Fade
If you change your mind

TAKE A LETTER, MARIA

Words and Music by
R. B. GREAVES

Moderately

G C G
1. Last night as I got home a-bout a half-past ten. There
2.,3. *(See additional lyrics)*
C G
was the wom-an I thought I knew in the arms of an-oth-er man. I kept
C G
my cool, I ain't no fool, let me tell you what hap-pened then. I packed
C G
some clothes and I walked out, and I ain't goin' back a-gain. So take a
G F
let-ter, Ma-ri-a, ad-dress it to my wife.
C G
Say I won't be com-ing home, got-ta start a new life. So take a
F
let-ter, Ma-ri-a, ad-dress it to my wife. Send a
C G 1, 2 3 D.S. and Fade
cop-y to my law-yer, got-ta start a new life. You've been So take a

Additional Lyrics

2. You've been many things, but most of all a good secretary to me,
And it's times like this I feel you've always been close to me.
Was I wrong to work nights to try to build a good life?
All work and no play has just cost me a wife.
Chorus

3. When a man loves a woman, it's hard to understand
That she would find more pleasure in the arms of another man.
I never really noticed how sweet you are to me,
It just so happens I'm free tonight, would you like to have dinner with me?
Chorus

TALK DIRTY TO ME

Words and Music by BOBBY DALL,
BRETT MICHAELS, BRUCE JOHANNESSON
and RIKKI ROCKETT

Up-tempo Rock
G
You know I nev - er, I nev - er seen you look so good. You
nev - er, I nev - er ev - er stay out late. You
call you, I call you on the tel - e - phone. I'm
D
nev - er act the way you should, but I like it.
know that I can hard - ly wait just to see you.
on - ly hop - ing that you're home so I can hear you.
C
And I know you like it too, the
And I know you can not wait, a -
When you say those words to me and
G D
way that I want you. I got to have you. Oh,
wait to see me too. I got to touch you. 'Cause
whis - per so soft - ly. I got to hear you. 'Cause
1
yes I do. I
2, 3
C D
ba - by we'll be at the drive - in,
G C D
in the old man's Ford. Be - hind the bush - es,
G C D
a - 'til I'm scream ing for more. Down the base - ment,
Em C Am7 D N.C. To Coda
lock the cel - lar door, and ba - by, talk dir - ty to me.
G5 D.S. al Coda
You know I
CODA
G5
C. C.,
D5 C
pick up that gui - tar and talk to me!
(Guitar solo)

G C
D C/E D/F♯ G
C G
A7 D N.C.
G
'Cause ba - by we'll be
C D G
at the drive - ins, in the old man's Ford.
C D G F5
Be - hind them bush - es 'til I'm scream ing for more, more, more!
C D Em C
Down the base - ment and lock the cel - lar door, and
Am7 D G Em
ba - by, talk dir - ty to me, yeah. And
C D G D/F♯ Em
ba - by, talk dir - ty to me. Yeah, yeah, yeah, yeah. And
C D N.C. G5
ba - by, talk dir - ty to me.
(Instrumental)

TAKE ME HOME, COUNTRY ROADS

Words and Music by JOHN DENVER,
BILL DANOFF and TAFFY NIVERT

Bright Country tempo
A F♯m E
Al - most heav - en, West Vir-gin - ia, Blue Ridge Moun - tains,
mem - 'ries gath - er 'round her, min - er's la - dy,
D A F♯m
Shen - an - do - ah Riv - er. Life is old there, old - er than the
stran - ger to blue wa - ter. Dark and dust - y, paint - ed on the
E D A
trees, young - er than the moun - tains grow - in' like a breeze. Coun - try
sky, mist - y taste of moon - shine, tear - drop in my eye.
A E F♯m
roads, take me home to the place I be -
D A E
long: West Vir - gin - ia, moun - tain mom - ma, take me
D To Coda A 1 2 F♯m
home, coun - try roads. All my I hear her
E A D A
voice, in the morn - in' hour she calls me, the ra - di - o re - minds me of my
E F♯m G D
home far a - way, and driv - in' down the road I get a feel - in' that I
A E E7 N.C. D.S. al Coda
should have been home yes - ter - day, yes - ter - day. Coun - try
CODA
A E A
roads, take me home, coun - try roads,
E A
take me home, coun - try roads.

THAT'S AMORÉ
(That's Love)
from the Paramount Picture THE CADDY

Words by JACK BROOKS
Music by HARRY WARREN

Moderately
B♭ B♭/D D♭dim7 F7 Bdim7
When the moon hits your eye like a big piz - za pie, That's A - mor - é.
Cm7 F7 B♭
When the world seems to shine like you've had too much wine, That's A - mor - é.
Bells will ring, ting - a - ling - a - ling, ting - a - ling - a - ling, and you'll
D♭dim7 F7 Bdim7 F7
sing, "Vee - ta bel - la."
Hearts will play, tip - py - tip - py - tay, tip - py - tip - py -
B♭
tay like a gay tar - an - tel - la.
When the stars make you
B♭/D D♭dim F7 Bdim7 Cm7
drool just like pas - ta fa - zool, That's A - mor - é.
F7 D7 D7/A♭ G7
When you dance down the street with a cloud at your feet, you're in love.
Cm E♭m B♭
When you walk in a dream but you know you're not dream - ing, Sig - nor - é,
D♭dim7 F7 D♭dim7 F7 D♭dim7 F7
Scuz - za me, but you see, back in old Na - po - li, That's A -
1 B♭ E♭ B♭ F7
mor - é.
When the
2 B♭ E♭m6 B♭
mor - é.

TAKE ON ME

Music by PAL WAAKTAAR and MAGNE FURUHOLMNE
Words by PAL WAAKTAAR, MAGNE FURUHOLMNE and MORTON HARKET

Fast
Bm E A Dmaj7 C♯m7
(Instrumental)
Bm E Bm7 E5
(D.C.) Oh, the
Bm7 E A D C♯m7
Talk - ing a - way, I don't know what I'm to say. I'll
need - less to say, at odds and ends but I'll be
things that you say, is it life or just to play my
Bm7 E A Dmaj7 C♯m7
say it an - y - way. To - day is an - oth - er day to find you.
stum - bling a - way, slow - ly learn - ing that life is o - kay.
wor - ries a - way? You're all the things I've got to re - mem - ber.
Bm7 E7 F♯m D
Shy - ing a - way, I'll be com - ing for your love, o - kay.
Say af - ter me, "It's no bet - ter to be safe than sor - ry."
You're shy - ing a - way; I'll be com - ing for you an - y - way.
A C♯m7/G♯ F♯m D A C♯m7/G♯
Take on me. (Take on me.) Take me
F♯m7 D A C♯m7/G♯ F♯m7
on. (Take on me.) I'll be gone
To Coda
D Esus A E(add4) D6 E E
in a day or two. So,
C♯m G C♯m C♯m7
G Gmaj7 Bm E
N.C.
(Instrumental)
D.C. al Coda
(take repeat)

CODA
D A C♯m7/G♯ F♯m7 D
in a day.
Take on me. (Take on me.)
A C♯m7/G♯ F♯m D A C♯m7/G♯
Take me on. (Take on me.) I'll be
F♯m7 D A C♯m7/G♯ F♯m
gone in a day.
(Take on me.) Take me on.
D A C♯m7/G♯ F♯m7 D
Repeat and Fade
Take on me. (Take on me.)
(Take on me.)

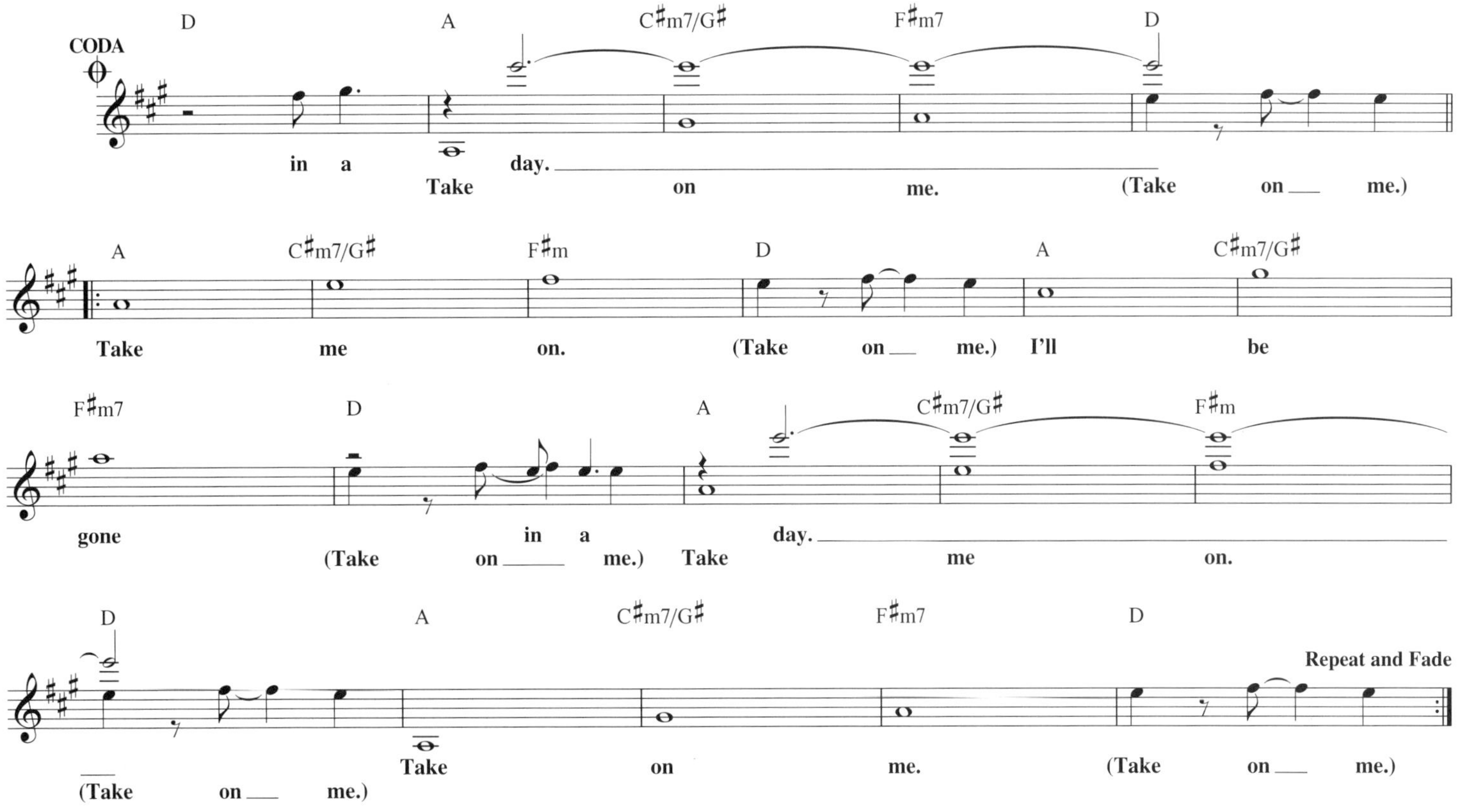

TENNESSEE WALTZ

Words and Music by REDD STEWART
and PEE WEE KING

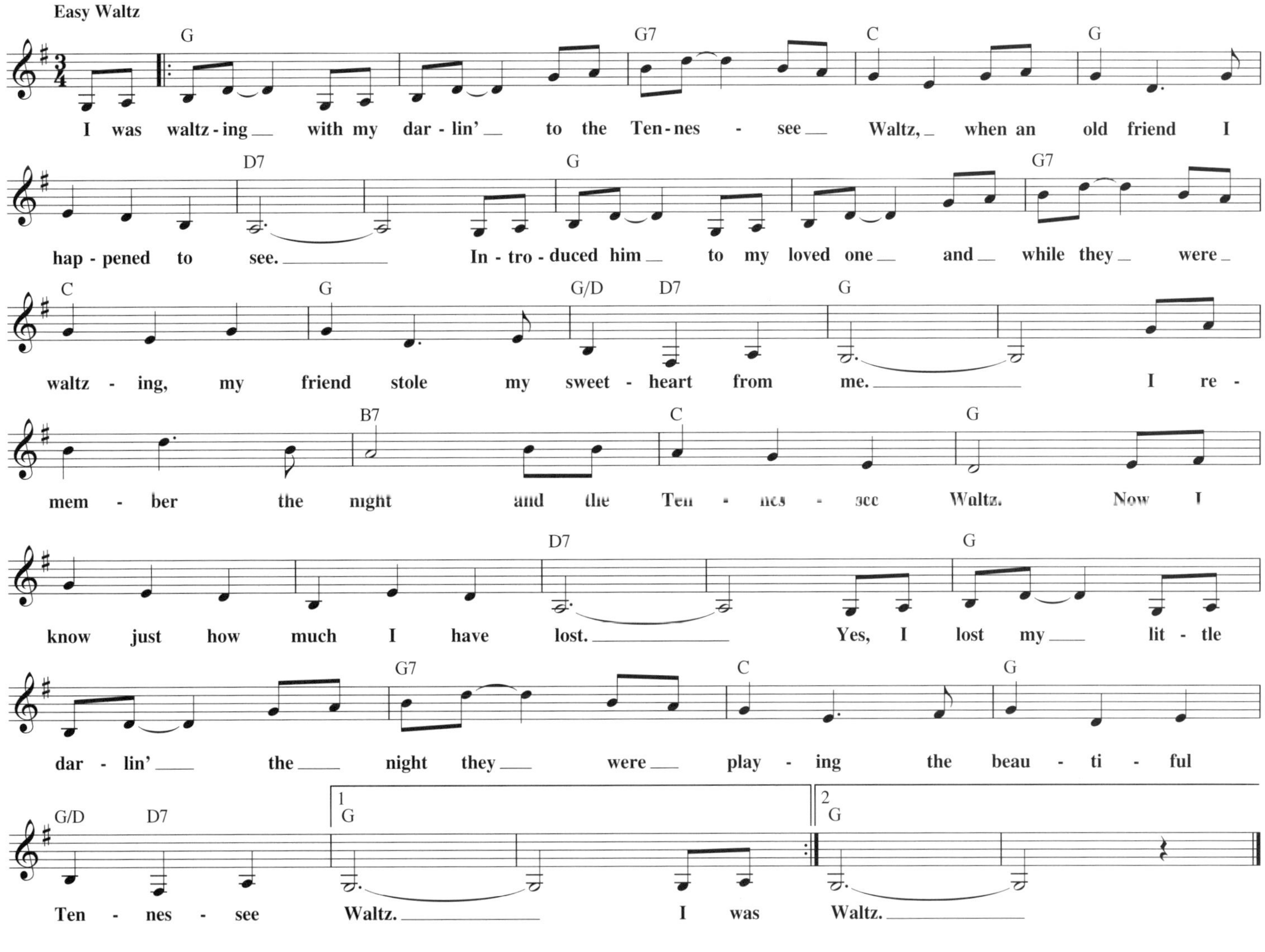

Easy Waltz
G G7 C G
I was waltz-ing with my dar-lin' to the Ten-nes-see Waltz, when an old friend I
D7 G G7
hap-pened to see. In-tro-duced him to my loved one and while they were
C G G/D D7 G
waltz-ing, my friend stole my sweet-heart from me. I re-
B7 C G
mem-ber the night and the Ten-nes-see Waltz. Now I
D7 G
know just how much I have lost. Yes, I lost my lit-tle
G7 C G
dar-lin' the night they were play-ing the beau-ti-ful
G/D D7 1 G 2 G
Ten-nes-see Waltz. I was Waltz.

TALKIN' IN YOUR SLEEP

Words and Music by ROGER COOK
and BOBBY WOODS

Slowly

Three o' - clock in the morn - in' and it looks like it's gon - na be___ an - oth - er
sleep - less night. I've been list'n - in' to your dreams and get - tin' ver - y low, won - d'rin' what
I can do. May - be I'm be - in' fool - ish 'cause I have - n't heard you men - tion an - y - bod - y's
name at all.___ How I wish I could be sure it's me that turns you on, each time you
close your eyes. I've heard it said that dream - ers nev - er lie. You've been talk - in' in___ your___
sleep, sleep - in' in your dreams with some sweet lov - er. Hold - in' on___ so tight, lov - in' her the way___
___ you used to love me. Talk - in' in___ your sleep with lov - in' on your
mind. May be I'm be - in' fool - ish 'cause I have - n't heard you men - tion an - y - bod - y's
name at all.___ How I wish I could be sure it's me that turns you on, each time you close your eyes. I've
heard it said that dream - ers nev - er lie. You've been talk - in' in___ your___ sleep, sleep - in' in your
dreams with some sweet lov - er. Hold - in' on___ so tight, lov - in' her the way___
___ you used to love me. Talk - in' in___ your sleep___ with lov - in' on your
mind. You've been talk - in' in___ your___ sleep.

TALKING IN YOUR SLEEP

Words and Music by JIMMY MARINOS,
WALLY PALMAR, MIKE SKILL,
COZ CANLER and PETER SOLLEY

Fast
Dm Gm C Dm
When you close your eyes and you go to sleep and it's
hold you in my arms at night
Gm C Dm
down to the sound of a heart - beat I can
don't you know you're sleep - ing in a spot - light? And
Gm C Dm
hear the things that you're dream - ing a - bout; when you
all your dreams that you keep in - side; you're
close your eyes and you fall a - sleep
Gm C Dm
o - pen up your heart and the truth comes out.
tell - ing me the se - crets that you just can't hide. You tell
ev - 'ry - thing a - bout you is a mys - ter - y.
C Gm
me that you want me, you tell me that you need me, you tell me that you love me.
B♭ C5 Dm7
And I know that I'm right, 'cause I hear it in the night. I hear the
Gm7 C7 Dm7 To Coda
se - crets that you keep when you're talk - ing in your sleep. I hear the
Gm7 C7 1 Dm7 2 Dm7
se - crets that you keep when you're talk - ing in your sleep. When I talk - ing in your sleep.
Gm7 C7 Dm7
I hear the se - crets that you keep when you're talk - ing in your sleep.
Gm7 C7 Dm7 D.S. al Coda
I hear the se - crets that you keep when you're talk - ing in your sleep. When you
CODA
Gm7 C7 Dm7
I hear the se - crets that you keep when you're talk - ing in your sleep.
Gm7 C7 Dm7 Repeat and Fade
I hear the se - crets that you keep when you're talk - ing in your sleep.

THE TEARS OF A CLOWN

Words and Music by STEVIE WONDER,
WILLIAM "SMOKEY" ROBINSON and HENRY COSBY

Moderately bright
(Instrumental)
Now, if there's a smile upon my face it's only there trying to fool the public; but when it comes down to fooling you, now honey that's quite a diff'rent subject. Don't let my glad expression give you the wrong impression; really I'm sad,
to be carefree, it's only to camouflage my sadness in order to shield my pride I try to cover this hurt with a show of gladness. But don't let my show convince you that I've been happy since you decided to go,
Oh, sadder than sad, you're gone and I'm hurting so bad, like a clown, I pretend to be glad.
I need you so, I'm hurt and I want you to know, but for others I put on a show.
Now there's some sad things known to man but ain't too much sadder than the tears of a clown, when there's no one around.
Oh yeah,
Now, if I appear
Just like Pagliacci did, I try to keep my sadness hid, smiling in the public eye but in my lonely room I cry the tears of a clown, when there's no one around.
Oh yeah, baby!
D.S. and Fade

THAT'S THE WAY OF THE WORLD

Words and Music by MAURICE WHITE, CHARLES STEPNEY and VERDINE WHITE

Moderately
Dmaj7 Am6/D G6/D
Hearts of fire create love desire take you high and higher to the
Gm/D Bdim Dmaj7 Am7/D
world you belong. Hearts of fire create love desire
G6/D Gm/D Dmaj7
high and higher to your place on the throne. We come together on this special
Am/D G6/D Gm/D Bdim Dmaj7
day, sing our message loud and clear. Looking back, we've touched on sor-
Am/D G6/D Gm/D Dmaj7
-rowful days, future pass, they disappear. You will find peace of mind,
D7♭5/A♭ Gmaj7 F♯m7 Gmaj7
if you look way down in your heart and soul. Don't hesitate 'cause the world
F♯m7 Gmaj7 F♯m7 Bm7 Em7
seems cold. Stay young at heart, 'cause you're never, never old.
A7sus Em7/A Dmaj7 D7♭5/A♭ Gmaj7
That's the way of the world, plant your flower and you grow
C9 D/A D9 D7♭5/A♭
a pearl. Child is born with a heart of gold; way
Gmaj7 C9 D/A
of the world, makes his heart so cold. Hearts of fire create
D9 D7♭5/A♭ Gmaj7 C9
love desire take you high and higher to the world you belong.
Repeat and Fade

THOSE WERE THE DAYS

Words and Music by
GENE RASKIN

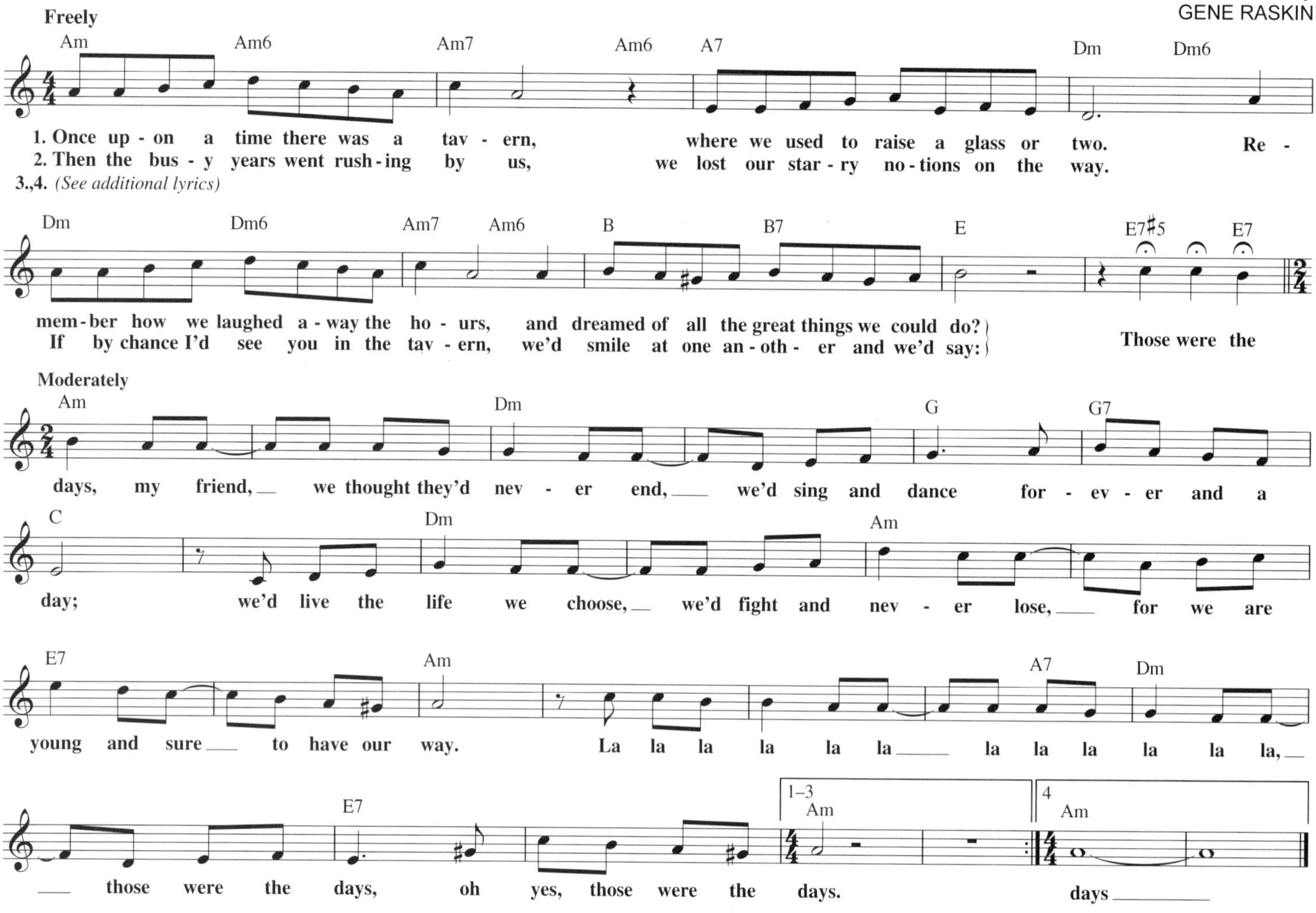
Freely
Am Am6 Am7 Am6 A7 Dm Dm6
1. Once up - on a time there was a tav - ern, where we used to raise a glass or two. Re -
2. Then the bus - y years went rush - ing by us, we lost our star - ry no - tions on the way.
3.,4. (See additional lyrics)
Dm Dm6 Am7 Am6 B B7 E E7♯5 E7
mem - ber how we laughed a - way the ho - urs, and dreamed of all the great things we could do?
If by chance I'd see you in the tav - ern, we'd smile at one an - oth - er and we'd say:
Those were the
Moderately
Am Dm G G7
days, my friend, we thought they'd nev - er end, we'd sing and dance for - ev - er and a
C Dm Am
day; we'd live the life we choose, we'd fight and nev - er lose, for we are
E7 Am A7 Dm
young and sure to have our way. La la la la la la la la la la la la,
E7 1–3 Am 4 Am
those were the days, oh yes, those were the days. days

Additional Lyrics

3. Just tonight I stood before the tavern,
   Nothing seemed the way it used to be.
   In the glass I saw a strange reflection.
   Was that lonely fellow really me?
   Chorus

4. Through the door there came familiar laughter,
   I saw your face and heard you call my name.
   Oh, my friend, we're older but no wiser,
   For in our hearts the dreams are still the same.
   Chorus

THIS LAND IS YOUR LAND

Words and Music by
WOODY GUTHRIE

Moderately bright
C G D7
This land is your land, this land is my land from Cal - i - for - nia
G G7 C G
to the New York is - land. From the red - wood for - est to the Gulf Stream wa - ters;
D7 1–3 G TO VERSE 4 G Am7 G
this land was made for you and me. me.

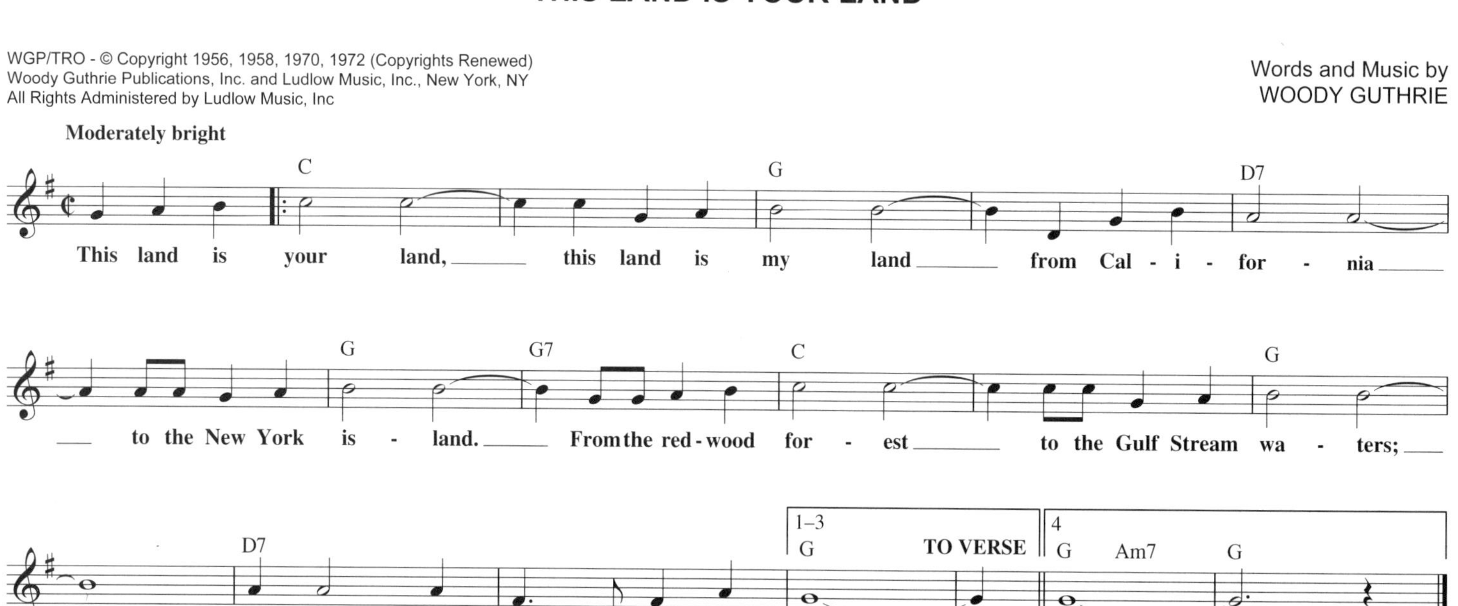

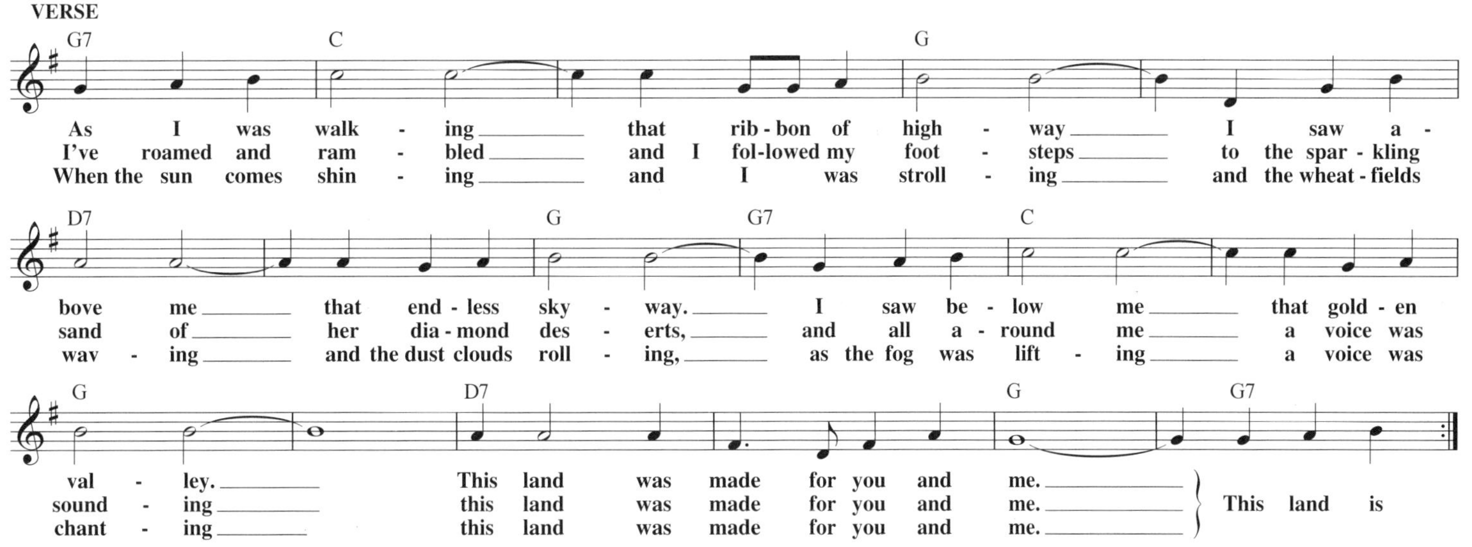

VERSE
G7 C G
As I was walk - ing that rib - bon of high - way I saw a -
I've roamed and ram - bled and I fol - lowed my foot - steps to the spar - kling
When the sun comes shin - ing and I was stroll - ing and the wheat - fields
D7 G G7 C
bove me that end - less sky - way. I saw be - low me that gold - en
sand of her dia - mond des - erts, and all a - round me a voice was
wav - ing and the dust clouds roll - ing, as the fog was lift - ing a voice was
G D7 G G7
val - ley. This land was made for you and me.
sound - ing this land was made for you and me. This land is
chant - ing this land was made for you and me.

THOU SHALT NOT STEAL

Words and Music by
JOHN D. LOUDERMILK

Moderately

Thou shalt not steal. Thou shalt not steal. That's what the Good Book say, ya, ya, ya, ya,

To Coda

thou shalt not steal. Thou shalt not steal. But some - bod - y is a steal - ing you a - way from me. I won - der if he real - ly don't know that he'll reap ex - act - ly what he sows.

If he don't he'll find out some - day when some - bod - y steals you from him. He'll be cry - ing that

D.C. al Coda

CODA

ya, ya.

THROUGH THE YEARS

Words and Music by STEVE DORFF and MARTY PANZER

Moderately

G F♯m7 B7 Em7 Dm7 G7

I can't re - mem - ber when you were - n't there, when I did - n't care
can't re - mem - ber what I used to do, who I trust - ed, who

Cmaj7 D/C Bm7 D11 G

for an - y - one but you. I swear we've been through
I lis-tened to be - fore. I swear you've taught me

F♯m7 B7 Em7 Dm7 G7

ev - 'ry - thing there is, can't im - ag - ine an - y - thing we've
ev - 'ry - thing I know, can't im - ag - ine need - ing some - one so.

Cmaj7 G/B Am7 D11

missed, can't im - ag - ine an - y - thing the two of us can't do. Through the
But through the years it seems to me I need you more and more. Through the

G Em7 Am7 D11 D7 Bm7

years you've nev - er let me down, you've turned my life a - round. the
years through all the good and bad I knew how much we had. I've

Em7 Am7 D11 D7 Bm7 E7♭9

sweet - est days I've found I've found with you. Through the years I've nev - er been a -
al - ways been so glad to be with you. Through the years it's bet - ter ev - 'ry

Am7 D7 D/C Bm7 E7♭9 Cmaj7

fraid, I've loved the life we've made and I'm so glad I've stayed
day, you've kissed my tears a - way, as long as it's o - kay

Bm7 Am7 D11 1 G D11 2 G

right here with you through the years. I
I'll stay with you through the years.

E♭11 A♭ Fm7 B♭m7

Through the years when ev - 'ry - thing went wrong to -
years you've nev - er let me down, you

E♭11 E♭7 Cm7 F7 B♭m7

geth - er we were strong, I know that I be - longed right here with you.
turned my life a - round, the sweet - est days I've found I've found with you.

Eb11 Eb7 Cm7 F7b9 Bbm7 Eb7 Eb/Db
Through the years I never had a doubt we'd always work things out.
Through the years it's better ev'ry day, you've kissed my tears away,
Cm7 F7b9 Db Cm7
I've learned what love's about by loving
as long as it's okay I'll stay with
Bbm7 Eb11 1 Ab 2 Ab
you through the years. Through the
you through the years.

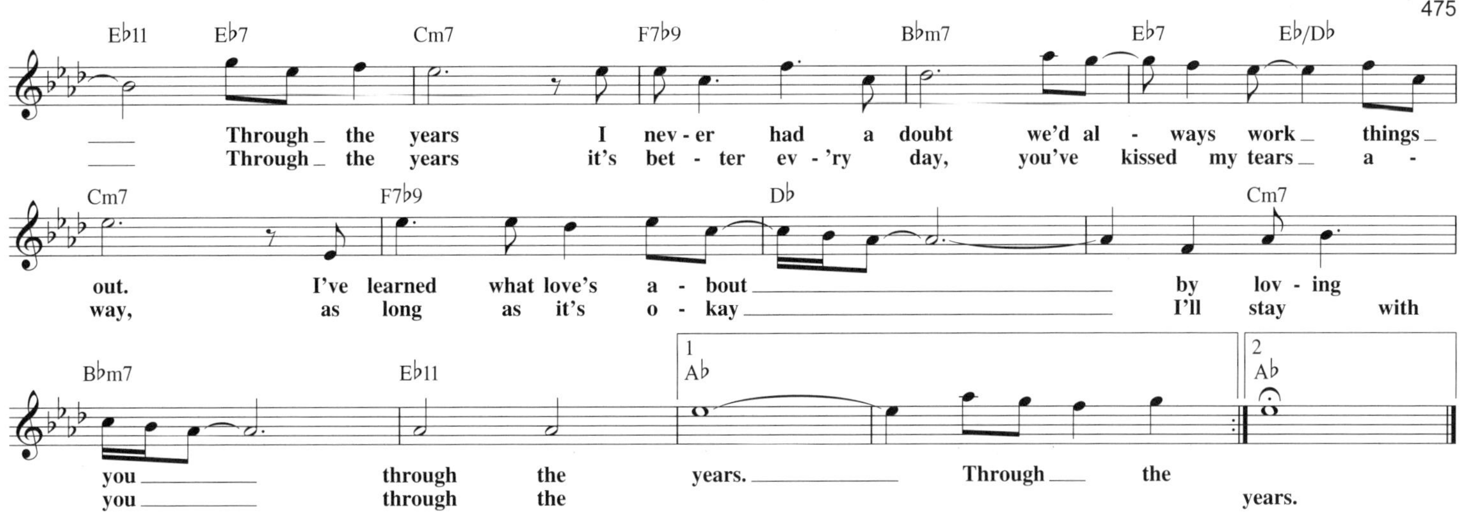

TIJUANA TAXI

Words by JOHNNY FLAMINGO
Music by ERVAN "BUD" COLEMAN

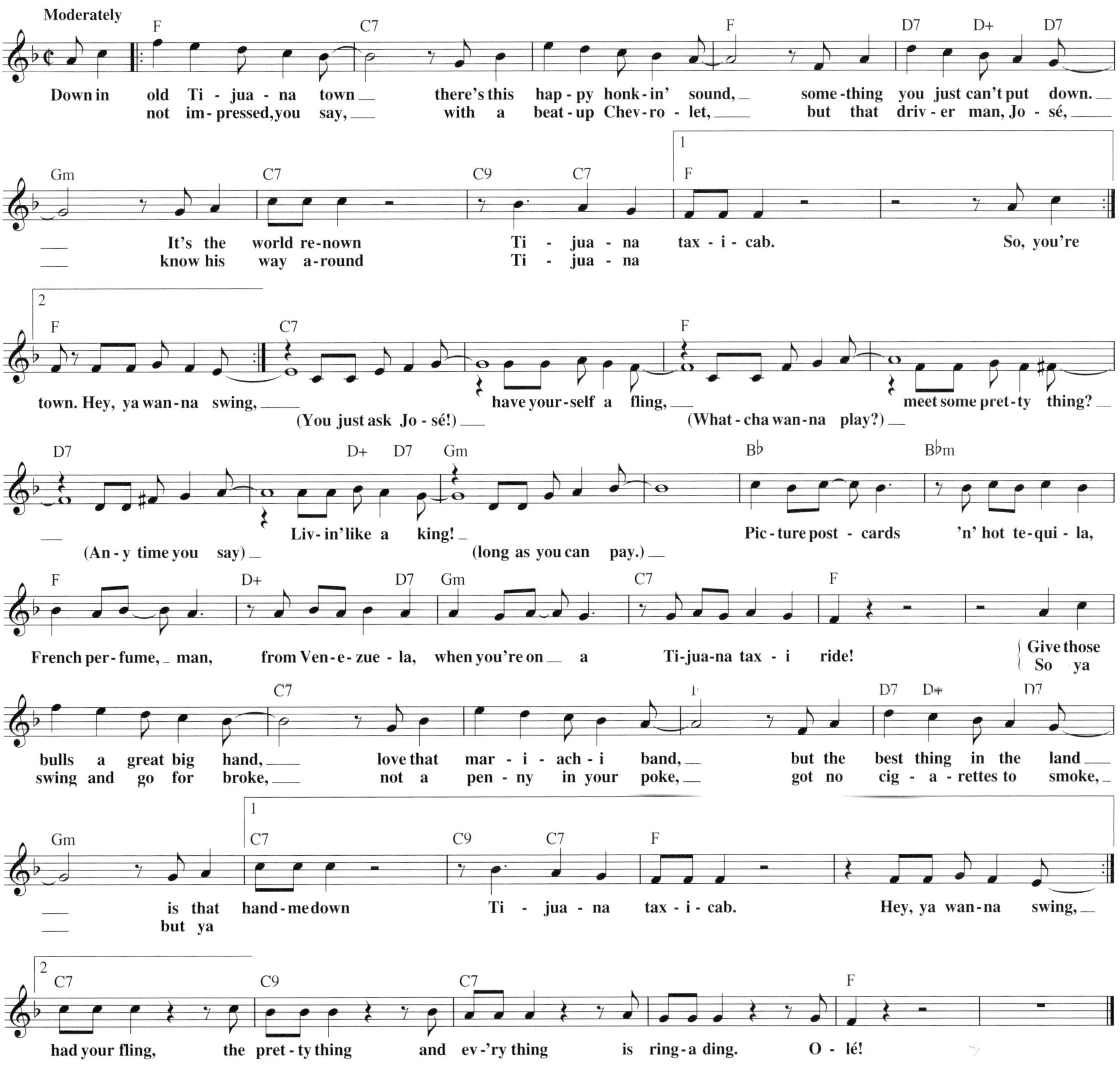
Moderately
F C7 F D7 D+ D7
Down in old Tijuana town there's this happy honkin' sound, something you just can't put down.
not impressed, you say, with a beat-up Chevrolet, but that driver man, José,
Gm C7 C9 C7 1 F
It's the world renown Tijuana taxicab. So, you're
know his way around Tijuana
2 F C7 F
town. Hey, ya wanna swing, have yourself a fling, meet some pretty thing?
(You just ask José!) (Whatcha wanna play?)
D7 D+ D7 Gm Bb Bbm
Livin' like a king! Picture postcards 'n' hot tequila,
(Any time you say) (long as you can pay.)
F D+ D7 Gm C7 F
French perfume, man, from Venezuela, when you're on a Tijuana taxi ride!
Give those
So ya
C7 F D7 D+ D7
bulls a great big hand, love that mariachi band, but the best thing in the land
swing and go for broke, not a penny in your poke, got no cigarettes to smoke,
Gm 1 C7 C9 C7 F
is that hand-me-down Tijuana taxicab. Hey, ya wanna swing,
but ya
2 C7 C9 C7 F
had your fling, the pretty thing and ev'rything is ring-a ding. Olé!

THERE'S A MOON OUT TONIGHT

Words and Music by VINNY NACCARATO, MIKE MINCELLI, NICK SANTAMORIA, FRANK REINA and JOHN CASSESE

Slowly
G Em Am7 D7 G Em
There's a moon out to - night, let's go stroll - in'. There's a girl in my heart,
Am7 D7 G Em Am7 D7
whose heart I've stol - en. There's a moon out to - night, let's go stroll - in' thru the
G Em Am7 D7 G Em Am7 D7
park. There's a glow in my heart I nev - er felt be - fore. There's a
G Em Am7 D7 G Em
girl at my side, that I a - dore. There's a glow in my heart,
Am7 D7 G Em Am D7 G G7 C
I nev - er felt be - fore. Oh dar - lin' where have you
D7 G
been? I've been long - in' for you all my life. Oh ba - by,
C D7
I nev - er felt this way be - fore. I guess it's be - cause there's a moon out to - night. There's a
G Em Am7 D7 G Em
glow in my heart, I nev - er felt be - fore. There's a girl at my side
Am7 D7 G Em Am7 D7
that I a - dore. There's a glow in my heart. I guess it's be - cause there's a
Freely
N.C.
moon out to - night, moon out to - night, moon out to - night, moon out to - night, there's a moon out to -
G C G
night.

TICKET TO RIDE

Words and Music by JOHN LENNON
and PAUL McCARTNEY

Moderate Rock tempo

A

(Instrumental)

A

I think I'm gon-na be sad, _ I think it's to-day ___ yeah! _ The girl that's driv-ing me mad ___ is go-ing a-way. ___
said that liv-ing with me _ is bring-in' her down ___ yeah! _ For she would nev-er be free ___ when I was a-round. ___

Bm7 E7 F♯m D7 F♯m G

She's got a tick-et to ride. ___ She's got a tick-et to ri - hi - hide. _

F♯m E7 1 A 2 A

She's got a tick-et to ride, _ but she don't care! _ She _ I

D7 E

don't know why she's rid-in' so high, ___ she ought-ta think twice; she ought-ta do right by me. Be-

D7 E

fore she gets to say-in' good-bye ___ she ought-ta think twice, she ought-ta do right by me.

A

I think I'm gon-na be sad, ___ I think it's to-day ___ yeah! _ The
She said that liv-ing with me ___ is bring-in' her down ___ yeah! _ For

Bm7 E7 F♯m

girl that's driv-ing me mad ___ is go-ing a-way. ___
she would nev-er be free ___ when I was a-round. ___ Yeah! _ Oh, she's got a tick-et to ride. _

D7 F♯m G F♯m

She's got a tick-et to ri - hi - hide. _ She's got a tick-et to ride, _

E7 1 A 2 A

Repeat and Fade

_ but she don't care! _ I _ My ba-by don't care!

TIME IS TIGHT

Words and Music by BOOKER T. JONES, DUCK DUNN,
STEVE CROPPER and AL JACKSON, JR.

Repeat and Fade

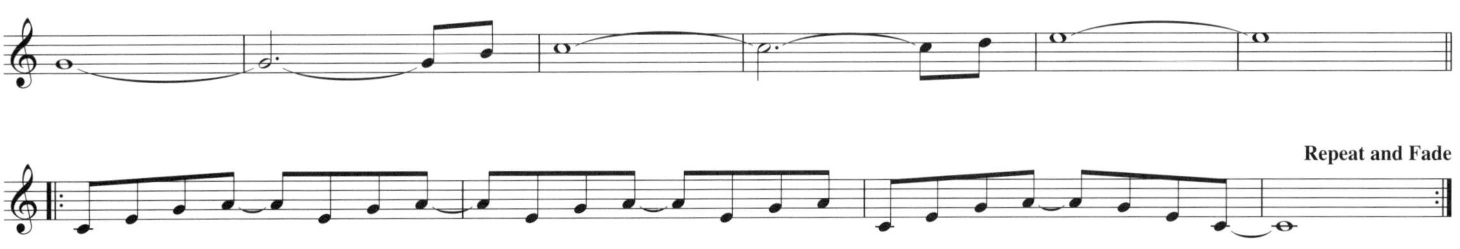

TIMOTHY

Words and Music by
RUPERT HOLMES

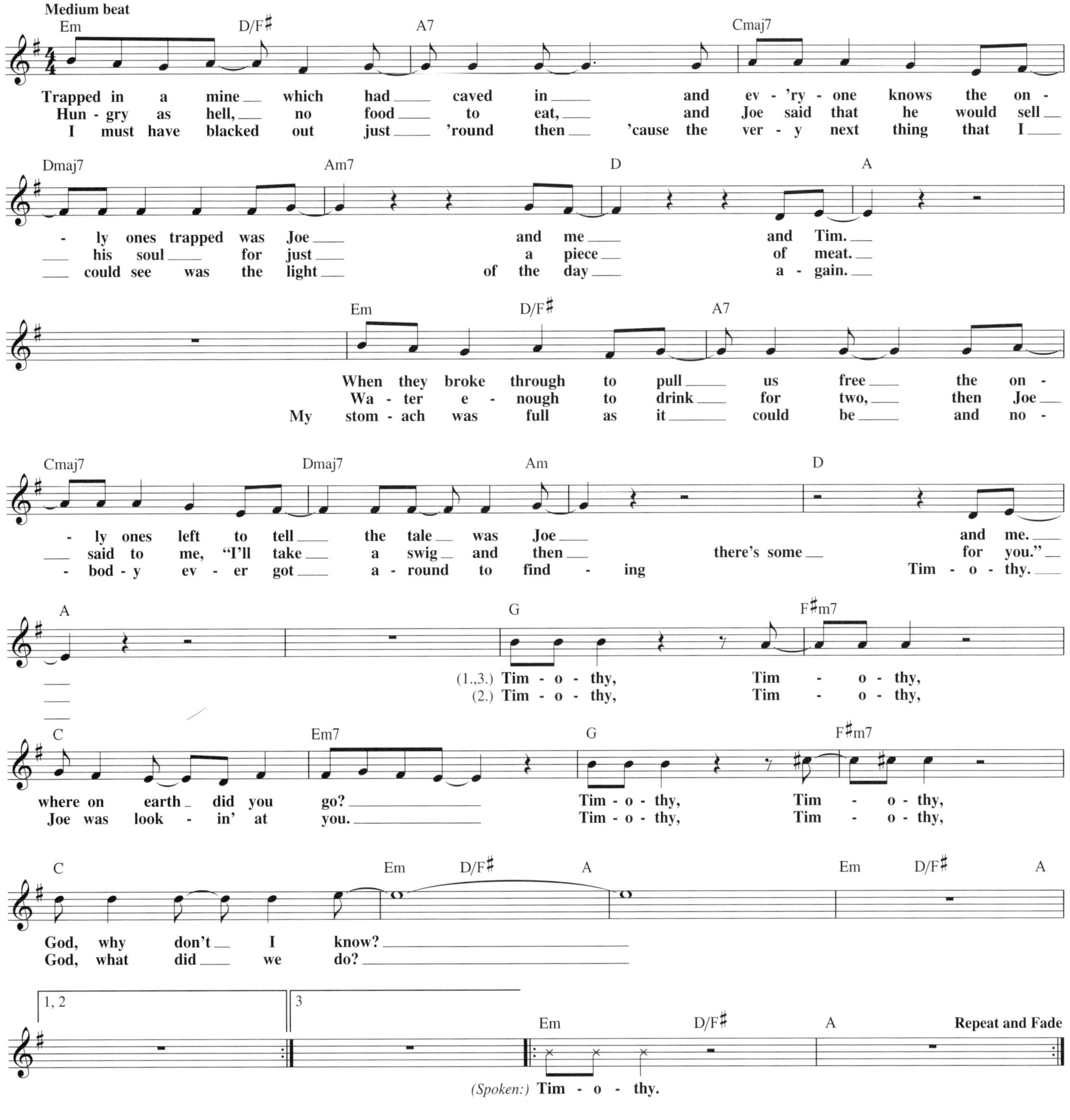
Medium beat
Em D/F♯ A7 Cmaj7
Trapped in a mine which had caved in and ev - 'ry - one knows the on -
Hun - gry as hell, no food to eat, and Joe said that he would sell
I must have blacked out just 'round then 'cause the ver - y next thing that I
Dmaj7 Am7 D A
- ly ones trapped was Joe and me and Tim.
his soul for just a piece of meat.
could see was the light of the day a - gain.
Em D/F♯ A7
When they broke through to pull us free the on -
Wa - ter e - nough to drink for two, then Joe
My stom - ach was full as it could be and no -
Cmaj7 Dmaj7 Am D
- ly ones left to tell the tale was Joe and me.
said to me, "I'll take a swig and then there's some for you."
- bod - y ev - er got a - round to find - ing Tim - o - thy.
A G F♯m7
(1.,3.) Tim - o - thy, Tim - o - thy,
(2.) Tim - o - thy, Tim - o - thy,
C Em7 G F♯m7
where on earth did you go? Tim - o - thy, Tim - o - thy,
Joe was look - in' at you. Tim - o - thy, Tim - o - thy,
C Em D/F♯ A Em D/F♯ A
God, why don't I know?
God, what did we do?
1, 2 3
Em D/F♯ A Repeat and Fade
(Spoken:) Tim - o - thy.

THROWING IT ALL AWAY

© 1986 ANTHONY BANKS LTD., PHILIP COLLINS LTD., MICHAEL RUTHERFORD LTD.
and HIT & RUN MUSIC (PUBLISHING) LTD.
All Rights Controlled and Administered by EMI APRIL MUSIC INC.
Words and Music by TONY BANKS,
PHIL COLLINS and MIKE RUTHERFORD
Moderately
D♭ G♭/D♭ D♭
Need I say I love you need I say I care?
can - not live to - geth - er, we can - not live a - part.
Some - day you'll be sor - ry. Some - day when you're free
G♭/D♭ Fm
Need I say that e - mo - tion's some - thing we don't share?
That's the sit - u - a - tion; I've known it from the start.
mem - ories will re - mind you that our love was meant to be
B♭m G♭ D♭/F E♭m7
I don't want to be sit - ting here try - ing to de - ceive you, 'cause
Ev - 'ry time that I look at you, I can't see the fu - ture, 'cause
late at night when you call my name the on - ly sound you'll hear is the
D♭ E♭m/D♭ 1 G♭ D♭
you know I know, ba - by, that I don't wan - na go. We
you know I know, ba - by,
sound of your voice call - ing,
2, 3 G♭ D♭ D♭maj7 C♭(add9)
I don't wan - na go. Just throw - ing it all
call - ing af - ter me. Just throw - ing it all
G♭(add9) A♭sus D♭maj7
a - way, throw - ing it all a - way.
a - way, throw - ing it all a - way.
To Coda
C♭(add9) G♭(add9)
Is there noth - ing that I can say to
And there's noth - ing that
A♭sus C♭(add9)
make you change your mind? I watch the world go
G♭maj7 C♭(add9)
round and round, and you see mine turn - ing up -
G♭maj7 D♭
- side down. (ooh ooh ooh ooh ooh

G♭/D♭
A♭/D♭
ooh ooh ooh ooh ooh ooh ooh)
C♭/D♭
Throw - ing it all a - way.
D♭
(ooh ooh ooh ooh ooh
G♭/D♭
A♭/D♭
ooh ooh ooh ooh ooh ooh ooh.)
C♭/D♭
D♭
G♭/D♭
Now who will light up the dark - ness and
who will hold your hand?
Who will find you the an - swers
when you don't un - der - stand?
Fm
B♭m7
G♭
Why should I have to be the one
D.C. al Coda
D♭/F
E♭m
E♭m/A♭
who has to con - vince you? 'Cause you know I know, ba - by, that I don't wan - na go.
CODA
G♭(add9)
A♭sus
I can say, ay, ay. (ooh ooh
ooh ooh ooh ooh ooh ooh
Repeat and Fade
We're throw - ing it all a - way.
C♭/D♭
ooh ooh ooh ooh) (ooh ooh

TIME AFTER TIME

Words and Music by CYNDI LAUPER
and ROB HYMAN

Moderately fast Rock
Ly - in' in my bed I hear the clock tick and think of you,
caught up in cir - cles con - fu - sion is noth - ing new.
Flash back warm nights, al - most left be - hind.
Suit - case of mem - o - ries time af - ter. Some - times you
Af - ter my
pic - ture me. I'm walk - ing too far a - head. You're call - ing
pic - ture fades and dark - ness has turned to gray, watch - ing through
to me, I can't hear what you've said. Then you say
win - dows, you're won - der-ing if I'm O. K. Se - crets
go slow. I fall be - hind. The sec - ond hand
stol - en from deep in - side. The drum beats out
un - winds.
of time.
If you're lost, you can look and you will find me, time af - ter time.
If you fall, I will catch you; I'll be wait - ing, time af - ter time.
If you're lost, you can look and you will find me, time af - ter time.
(Instrumental)

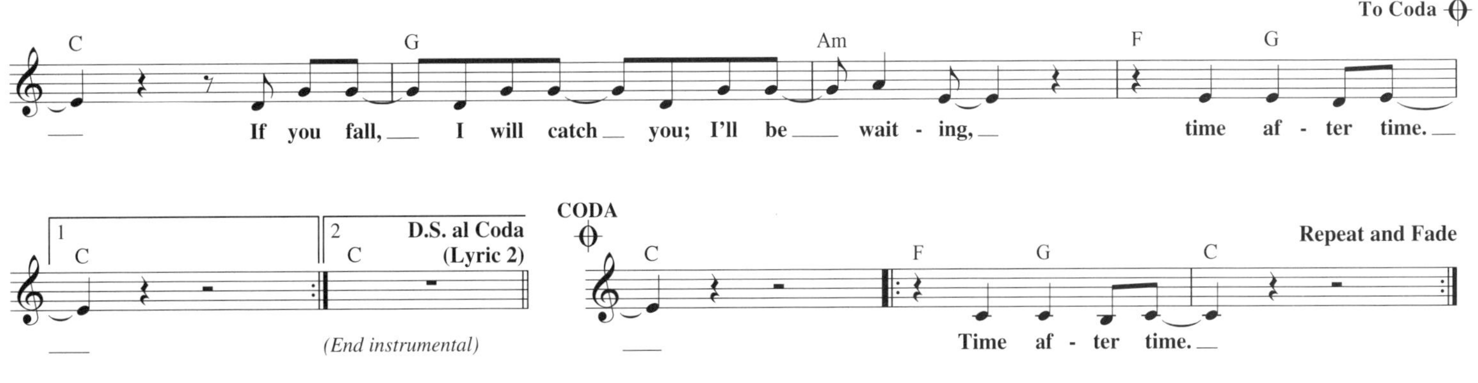

TOO MUCH

Words and Music by LEE ROSENBERG
and BERNIE WEINMAN

Medium Rock

B♭

Hon - ey, I love you too much. Need your lov - in' too much.
You spend all my mon - ey too much. Have to share you, hon - ey, too much.
Ev - 'ry time I kiss your sweet lips, I can feel my heart go flip flip.

E♭7 B♭

Want the thrill of your touch. Gee, I can't hold you too much.
When I want some lov - in', you're gone. Don't you know you're treat - in' me wrong.
I'm such a fool for your charms. Take me back, my ba - by, your arms.

F7 E♭7 B♭ 1

You do all the liv - in' while I do all the giv - in' 'cause I love you too much
Now you got me start - ed, don't you leave me bro - ken heart - ed 'cause I love you too
Like to hear you sigh - in' e - ven though I know you're ly - in' 'cause I love you too

2 B♭

much. }
much. }
Need your lov - in' all the time. Need your hug - gin', please, be mine.

E♭7 B♭

Need you near me; stay real close. Please, please, hear me, you're the most.

F7 E♭7 B♭ 1 (D.C.) 2

Now you got me start - ed, don't you leave me bro - ken - heart - ed 'cause I love you too much. much.

TOTAL ECLIPSE OF THE HEART

Words and Music by
JIM STEINMAN

Rock Ballad
B♭m
A♭
(Turn a - round) Ev - 'ry now and then I get a lit - tle bit lone - ly and you're nev - er com - ing 'round.
part.
(Turn a - round) Ev - 'ry now and then I get a lit - tle bit rest - less and I dream of some-thing wild.
Instrumental solo
B♭m
A♭
(Turn a - round) Ev - 'ry now and then I get a lit - tle bit tired of lis - t'ning to the sound of my tears.
(Turn a - round) Ev - 'ry now and then I get a lit - tle bit help - less and I'm ly - ing like a child in your arms.
D♭
B
(Turn a - round) Ev - 'ry now and then I get a lit - tle bit ner - vous that the best of all the years have gone by.
(Turn a - round) Ev - 'ry now and then I get a lit - tle bit an - gry and I know I've got to get out and cry.
D♭
B
(Turn a - round) Ev - 'ry now and then I get a lit - tle bit ter - ri - fied and then I see the look in your eyes.
(Turn a - round) Ev - 'ry now and then I get a lit - tle bit ter - ri - fied but then I see the look in your eyes.
Solo ends
E
E/A
A
1
(Turn a - round bright eyes) Ev - 'ry now and then I fall a - part.
(Turn a - round bright eyes)
Ev - 'ry now and then I fall a -
2, 3
E
E/A
A
part.
(Turn a - round bright eyes)
Ev - 'ry now and then I fall a - part,
A♭
Fm
and I need you now to - night,
D♭
E♭7
A♭
Fm
and I need you more than ev - er. And if you on - ly hold me tight,
D♭
E♭7
A♭
Fm
we'll be hold - ing on for - ev - er. And we'll on - ly be mak - ing it
D♭
E♭7
D♭/F
E♭/G
right 'cause we'll nev - er be wrong to - geth - er we can take it to the end of the line. Your

Fm
Bb
love is like a shad - ow on me all of the time.
I
Ab
Eb/G
don't know what to do, and I'm al - ways in the dark.
Fm
Bb
We're liv - ing in a pow - der keg and giv - ing off sparks.
I real - ly need you to - night.
Ab/C
Eb/Bb
Ab/C
For - ev - er's gon - na start to - night,
Db
Eb7
for - ev - er's gon - na start to - night.
Ab
Fm
Once up - on a time I was fall - ing in love, but
C
now I'm on - ly fall - ing a - part.
Db
Ab/C
There's
Bbm7
Eb7b9
noth - ing I can do; a to - tal e - clipse of the heart.
Ab
Fm
(Instrumental)
Db
Eb7
Eb/G
Ab
Fm
Once up - on a time there was light in my life, but
To Coda
C
Db
Ab/C
now there's on - ly love in the dark.
Bbm
Eb7b9
Noth - ing I can say; a to - tal e - clipse of the heart.
Ab
Fm
(Instrumental)
Db
Eb7
Eb/G
D.C. al Coda
CODA
Bbm
Eb7b9
Noth - ing I can say; a to - tal e - clipse of the heart.
Ab
Fm
Db
Eb7
Eb/G
Repeat ad lib. and Fade
A to - tal e - clipse of the heart.

TIME
(Clock of the Heart)

Words and Music by
GEORGE O'DOWD, JON MOSS,
MICKEY CRAIG and ROY HAY

Medium Rock
Don't put your head on my shoul - der sink me in a riv - er of tears
make me feel an - y cold - er time is like a clock in my heart
this could be the best place yet but you must o - ver - come your fears
touch me touch was the key too much I felt I lost you from the start
Ooh in time it could have been so much more the time is pre-cious I know
in time it could have been so much more the time has noth - ing to show
be - cause time won't give me time and time makes lov - ers feel like they've got some - thing real
But you and me we know they've got noth - ing but time
To Coda
and time won't give me time won't give me time.
and you know
Don't
D. S. al Coda
Ooh in time
CODA
time won't give me time and time makes lov - ers feel like they've got some - thing real.
Repeat and Fade
But you know

TOWN WITHOUT PITY

from TOWN WITHOUT PITY

Words and Music by DIMITRI TIOMKIN
and NED WASHINGTON

Slowly, with expression
Am Am(maj7) Am7 Am6 Dm Dm(maj7) Dm7 Dm6
When you're young and so in love as we, and be - wil-dered by the world we see, why do
B♭dim A7 Dm C C♭ G7 B7♭5 E7 E7♯5
peo - ple hurt us so, on - ly those in love would know. What a town with-out pit - y can do! If we
Am Am(maj7) Am7 Am6 Dm Dm(maj7) Dm7 Dm6
stop to gaze up - on a star, peo - ple talk a - bout how bad we are, ours is
B♭dim A7 Dm C C♭ G7 G7♯5 C C7
not an eas - y age, we're like ti - gers in a cage. What a town with-out pit - y can do! The young have
F E♭7 D7
prob - lems, man - y prob - lems, we need an un - der - stand - ing heart. Why don't they
G Dm Dm7 F♯dim G7 E7 E7♯5
help us, try to help us, be - fore this clay and gran - ite plan - et falls a - part! Take these
Am Am(maj7) Am7 Am6 Dm Dm(maj7) Dm7 Dm6
ea - ger lips and hold me fast, I'm a - fraid this kind of joy can't last, how can
Gm A7 Dm C C♭ G7 G7♯5 E7
we keep love a - live, how can an - y - thing sur - vive, when these lit - tle minds tear you in two. What a
F G7 G7♯5 E Am E7 Am A♭7 G7 G♭7 F7 E7 E7♯5(♭9)
town with - out pit - y can do! No, it is - n't ver - y pret - ty what a town with - out pit - y can
1 Am Am(maj7) Am7 B7 E7♯5
do. When you're
2 Dm Dm6 Dm7 Dm Am
do.

TRUE BLUE

Words and Music by STEPHEN BRAY
and MADONNA CICCONE

Moderate '50s rock
C
Am
I've had oth - er guys. I've looked in - to their eyes.
I've heard all the lines. I've cried oh so man - y times.
F
G7
But I nev - er knew love be - fore 'till you walked through my door.
Those tear - drops, they won't fall a - gain. I'm so ex - cit - ed 'cause you're my best friend.
C
Am
I've had oth - er lips. I've sailed a thou - sand ships.
So if you should ev - er doubt, won - der what love is all a - bout,
F
G7
But no mat - ter where I go you're the one for me, ba - by. This I know 'cause it's
just think back and re - mem - ber, dear, those words whis - pered in your ear, I said
C
Am
true love. You're the one I'm dream - ing of. Your heart fits me
F
1
G7
like a glove and I'm gon - na be true blue, ba - by. I love you.
2
G7
C
true love. You're the one I'm
true blue, ba - by. I love you 'cause it's This time I know it's true love.
Am
F
dream - ing of. Your heart fits me like a glove. And I'm gon - na be
You're the one I'm dream - ing of. Heart fits me like a glove.

G7
Fmaj7
G
true blue, ba - by. I love you. No, no more sad - ness, I kiss it good -
Fmaj7
G
Am
G
F
bye. The sun is burst - ing right out of the sky. I searched the whole world for some - one like
G
C
you. Don't you know, don't you know, that it's true love. Oh, ba - by, true love, Oh, ba - by.
Am
F
C
Oh love, oh ba - by. True love, it's true. So if you should ev - er doubt,
Am
F
won - der what love is all a - bout, just think back and re - mem - ber, dear,
G7
C
True love. You're the one I'm
those words whis - pered in your ear. I said This love I know it's true love.
Am
dream - ing of. You heart fits me
F
like a glove. And I'm gon - na be
you're the one I'm dream - ing of. Heart fits just like a glove.
G7
C
True blue, ba - by. I love you. True love, oh ba - by.
Repeat and Fade
Am
F
True love, oh ba - by. Oh love, oh ba - by. True love. It's

THE TRACKS OF MY TEARS

Words and Music by WILLIAM "SMOKEY" ROBINSON, WARREN MOORE and MARVIN TARPLIN

Moderately
Do, do, do, doot. Do, do, do, doot. Do, do, do, doot. Do, do, do, do, do, do.
People say I'm the life of the par - ty 'cause I tell a joke or two.
Since you left me, if you see me with an - oth - er girl, seem - in' like I'm hav - in' fun.
Al - though I might be laugh - in' loud and heart - y,
Al - though she may be cute, she's just a sub - sti - tute be - cause
deep in - side I'm blue.
you're the per - ma - nent one.
So take a good look at my face. You'll see my
smile looks out of place.
If you look clos - er
Look a lit - tle bit clos - er,
it's eas - y to trace the tracks of my tears.
I need you, need you. you.
Hey, hey, yeah. (Out - side.) I'm mas - quer - ad - ing. (In -
side.) My hope is fad - ing. (Just a clown.) Ooh yeah, since you put me down. My
smile is my make - up I wear since my break - up with you. Ba - by, take a
good look at my face. You'll see my smile looks out of place. Yeah, just look clos -
- er, it's eas - y to trace the tracks of my tears, ba - by, ba - by, ba - by, ba - by. Take a
Repeat and Fade

TO KNOW HIM IS TO LOVE HIM

Words and Music by
PHIL SPECTOR

Slowly, with feeling

F C7 Dm
To know, know, know, {him / you} is to love, love, love {him. / you.} Just to see {him / you} smile

B♭ F C7
makes my life worth while. To know, know, know {him / you} is to love, love, love {him / you} and I

F C7
do. {I'd / I'll} be good to {him / you} and {I'd / I'll} bring love to {him. / you.}

Dm B♭
Ev - 'ry - one says there'll come a day when I'll walk a - long side of {him. / you.}

F C7 F B♭ F
Yes, yes to know {him / you} is to love, love, love {him / you} and I do.

A♭7 E♭7 D♭7
Why can't {he / you} see how blind {he can / can you}

C7 A♭ F7 B♭m Fm
be? Some day {he'll / you'll} see that

G7 C7 F
{he was / you were} meant for me. To know, know, know {him / you} is to

C7 Dm B♭
love, love, love {him. / you.} Just to see {him / you} smile makes my life worth while. To

F C7 F B♭ F
know, know, know {him / you} is to love, love, love {him / you} and I do.

TUFF ENUFF

Words and Music by
KIM WILSON

Moderate Rock
C
1. I would walk ten miles on my hands and knees. Ain't no doubt a - bout it ba - by, it's
2. For you ba - by, I would swim the sea. Noth - in' I'd do for you that's too
3.,4. (See additional lyrics)
you I aim to please. I'd wres - tle with a li - on and a griz - zly bear. It's
tuff for me. I'd put out a burn - ing build - ing with a shov - el and dirt, and
my life ba - by, but I don't care.
not even wor - ry a - bout get - ting hurt.
Ain't that tuff e - nuff,
E♭ F C
ain't that tuff e - nuff? Ain't that
tuff e - nuff, ain't that tuff e - nuff?
1.,3.
D.S.
2
(Instrumental solo ad lib.)
(Solo ends)
3. I'd
4
Ain't that
tuff e - nuff, ain't that tuff e - nuff? Ain't that
Repeat and Fade
tuff e - nuff, ain't that tuff e - nuff? Ain't that

Additional lyrics

3. I'd work twenty-four hours, seven days a week
Just so I could come home and kiss your cheek.
I love you in the morning and I love you at noon,
I love you in the night and take you to the moon.
Chorus

4. I'd lay in a pile of burning money that I've earned
And not even worry about getting burned.
I'd climb the Empire State Building, fight Muhammad Ali
Just to have you, baby, close to me.
Chorus

TWO DIVIDED BY LOVE

Words and Music by DENNIS LAMBERT,
BRIAN POTTER and MARTY KUPPS

Moderately
E♭ F/E♭ Fm/E♭
Ev - 'ry night your tears come down and I know how you're feel - in' in - side.
I'd be ly - in' to my - self if I said I was get - tin' a - long.
E♭ F/E♭
Lone - li - ness is no one's friend. I've been tak -
All I do is think of you and I know
Fm/E♭ E♭ B♭/D Cm F7 A♭/B♭
- in' the same kind of ride and that just shouldn't be if you're still lov - in' me.
that it's here you be - long. Come on, girl, make your way; we can start from to - day,
N.C. E♭
Come on ba - by Two di - vid - ed by love
put - tin' it back to - geth - er. Two di - vid - ed by love
Gm Cm7 Fm7 B♭7
can on - ly be one and "one" is a lone - ly num - ber.
can on - ly be sad, can on - ly be bro - ken - heart - ed.
E♭ Gm Cm7
Two di - vid - ed by love can on - ly be sad, can on - ly hurt one
Two di - vid - ed and blue should take what they had and go back to where
1
Fm7 B♭7 N.C.
an - oth - er.
2
Fm7 B♭7 Cm Gm
they start - ed. Take a - way the rain from a flow - er and the
Cm Gm A♭maj7
flow - er just can't grow. Take a - way you from me,
A♭/B♭
girl, and out of my mind I slow - ly go.
D.S. and Fade
(Verse 1)

TUBTHUMPING

Words and Music by NIGEL HUNTER, BRUCE DUNCAN, ALICE NUTTER, LOUISE WATTS, PAUL GRECO, DARREN HAMER, ALLEN WHALLEY and JUDITH ABBOTT

Moderately fast
N.C.
I get knocked down, but I get up again. You're never gonna keep me down. I get knocked down, but I get up again. You're never gonna keep me down. I get knocked down, but I get up again. You're never gonna keep me down. I get knocked down, but I get up again. You're never gonna keep me down.
To Coda
Pissing the night away. Pissing the night away. He drinks a whiskey drink, he drinks a vodka drink, he drinks a lager drink, he drinks a cider drink. He sings the songs that remind him of the good times, he sings the songs that remind him of the better times.
Oh, Danny Boy, Danny Boy, Danny Boy.
Don't cry for me, next-door neighbour.
1
I get knocked
2
I get knocked
D.S. al Coda
CODA
(Instrumental)
I get knocked down, but I get up again. You're never gonna keep me down. I get knocked

D G A
down, but I get up a - gain. You're nev - er gon - na keep me down. I get knocked
D G D G
down, but I get up a - gain. You're nev - er gon - na keep me down. I get knocked
D G A
Repeat and Fade
down, but I get up a - gain. You're nev - er gon - na keep me down. I get knocked

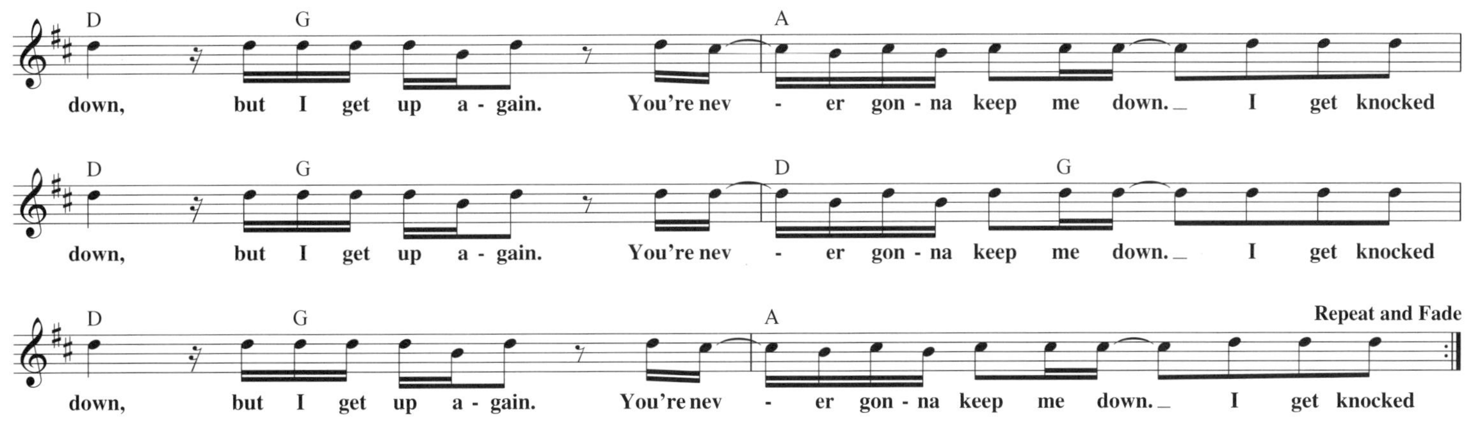

TRULY

Words and Music by
LIONEL RICHIE

Slowly

D♭ Fm/C A♭m6/C♭ A♭m6/B♭ B♭7

Girl, tell me on - ly this; that I have your heart for al - ways and
Now, I need to tell you this; there's no oth - er love like your love and

E♭m D+ E♭m/D♭ D♭/A♭ A♭

you want me by your side whis - per - ing the words "I'll al - ways love you."
I, as long as I live I'll give you all the joy my heart and soul can give.

G♭maj7 Fm7 G♭maj7

And for - ev - er I will be your lov - er.
Let me hold you I need to have you near me.

Fm7 G♭maj7 Fm7 | 1 E♭m7 A♭7sus A♭ A♭sus A♭

And I know if you real ly care I will al - ways be there.
And I feel with you in my arms this

2 E♭m7 A♭7sus A♭ A♭sus A♭ D♭(add2) D♭7

love will last for - ev - er be - cause I'm tru - ly, tru - ly in

G♭maj7 G♭/A♭ D♭(add2) D♭7 G♭maj7

love with you, girl. I'm tru - ly, head o - ver heels with your love.

G♭/A♭ D♭(add2) D♭7 G♭maj7 G♭/A♭

I need you. And with your love I'm free. And

D♭(add2) D♭7 G♭ D♭/F E♭m7 E♭m7♭5 D♭(add2)

tru - ly, you know you're all right with me.

TURN YOUR LOVE AROUND

Words and Music by JAY GRAYDON, STEVE LUKATHER and BILL CHAMPLIN

Moderately, with a beat
Dm9 G Dm9
You got the love, you got the pow - er, but you just don't un - der - stand;
I'm try - ing to show how much I love you, still be - liev - ing in ro - mance;
G Dm9 Dm7/G
girl, you've been charg - ing by the hour for your
you're tak - ing way too man - y chanc - es with our
1 Cmaj7 A7♭9
love.
2 Cmaj7 A7♭9
love. I re - mem - ber when
Fmaj7 Fmaj7/G Fmaj7 E7
you used to be the talk of the town; all you'd get is lone - ly.
of yes - ter - day, and he stays at home, all they get is lone - ly.
Am7 Fmaj9 E7♭9 E7♯9 Am7
Turn your love a - round; don't you turn me down.
Fmaj9 E7♭9 E7♯9 Am7 Fmaj9 E+ E7♭9 Fmaj7
To Coda
I can show you how; turn your love a - round.
E+ E7♭9 Dm9 G Dm9 A7♭9
Dm9 G Dm9
With - out the wom - an I can make it, but I need the girl to stay.
G Dm9 Dm7/G
Ah, don't you let the la - dy take it all a -
Cmaj7 A7♭9
D.S. al Coda
way. When the wom - an needs a taste
CODA
Fmaj7
round.
Bm7 E+ E7♭9 Am9 C/D Bm/D Am/D Bm/D
Oh, girl, you know me, I'm a - lone un - til you show

Fmaj9 E+ E7♭9 E+ E7 Am9
me that you're still in love with me. We're gon - na make
Am7/G Fmaj9 E7♯9 Am7
it; we're gon - na take it back where we be - long. Turn your love a - round;
Fmaj9 E7♭9 E7♯9 Am7 Fmaj9 E7♭9 E7♯9
don't you turn me down. I can show you how;
Repeat and Fade
Am7 Fmaj9 E+ E7♭9 Fmaj7 Dm7/G E+ Am7
turn your love a - round. Turn your love a - round;

UNCHAINED MELODY

from the Motion Picture UNCHAINED

Lyric by HY ZARET
Music by ALEX NORTH

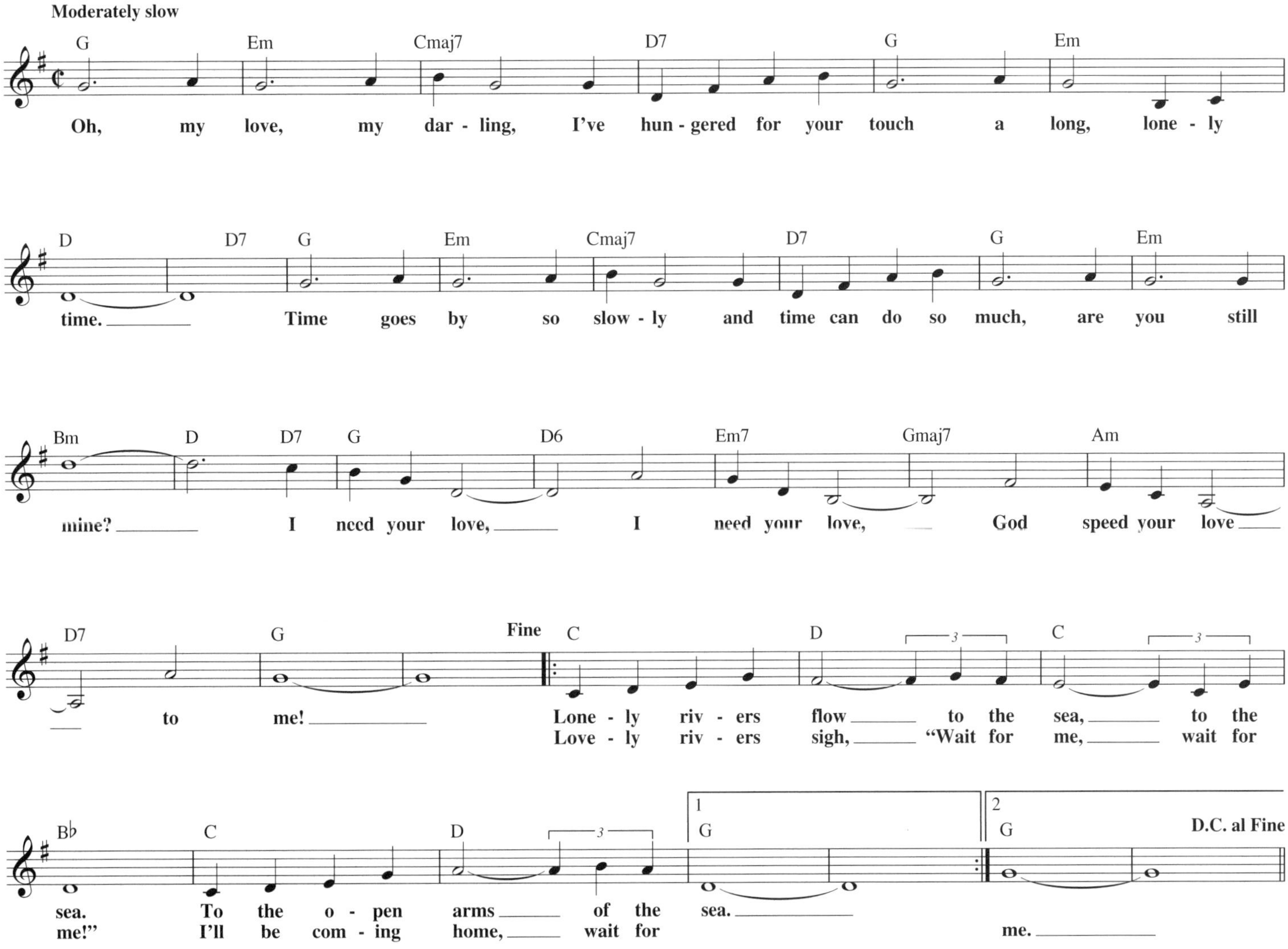

Moderately slow

G Em Cmaj7 D7 G Em
Oh, my love, my dar - ling, I've hun - gered for your touch a long, lone - ly

D D7 G Em Cmaj7 D7 G Em
time. Time goes by so slow - ly and time can do so much, are you still

Bm D D7 G D6 Em7 Gmaj7 Am
mine? I need your love, I need your love, God speed your love

D7 G **Fine** C D C
to me! Lone - ly riv - ers flow to the sea, to the
Love - ly riv - ers sigh, "Wait for me, wait for

B♭ C D 1. G 2. G **D.C. al Fine**
sea. To the o - pen arms of the sea.
me!" I'll be com - ing home, wait for me.

UNCLE ALBERT/ADMIRAL HALSEY

Words and Music by PAUL McCARTNEY
and LINDA McCARTNEY

Slowly
Am7/D D Am7/D
We're so sor - ry, Un - cle Al - bert, we're so sor - ry if we caused you an - y pain.
D Am7/D D Gm7 C C♯
We're so sor - ry, Un - cle Al - bert, but there's no one left at home and I be -
D Gm7 C Gm7 C Gm7 C
lieve I'm gon - na rain. (Instrumental solo)
Gm7 C C♯7 D Am7/D D Am7/D
We're so sor - ry, but we have - n't heard a thing
D Am7/D D Gm7 C C♯
all day. We're so sor - ry, Un - cle Al - bert, but if an - y - thing should hap - pen we'll be
D Gm7 C9 Gm7 C9 Gm7 C9
sure to give a ring. (Instrumental solo)
Gm7 C C♯7 D C D Am7/D
(Spoken): We're so sor - ry, Un - cle
D Am7/D D Am7/D
Al - bert, but we have - n't done a blood - y thing all day. We're so sor - ry, Un - cle
D Gm7 C C♯ D
Al - bert, but the ket - tle's on the boil and we're so eas - 'ly called a - way.
Gm7 C Gm7 C Gm7 C Gm7 C C♯ D C
(Instrumental solo)
B♭ Gm Am C Am C Am C Em
C Am Dm G7 F A B♭ C
Hands a - cross the wa - ter, (wa-ter) heads a - cross the sky.
Am Dm G7 To next strain C Fine C
Hands a - cross the wa - ter, (wa-ter) heads a - cross the sky. sky.
Am C Am C
Ad - mi - ral Hal - sey no - ti - fied me, he had to have a berth or he could - n't get to sea, I

Am C Em C Am Dm
had an-oth-er look and I had a cup of tea and a but-ter pie.
Hands across the wa-ter, (wa-ter)
G7 F A♭ B♭ C Am Dm G7
heads across the sky.
Hands across the wa-ter, (wa-ter) heads across the sky.
Faster
C
Live a lit-tle, be a gyp-sy, get a-round, (get a-round) get your feet up off the
1 G7 C
ground, live a lit-tle, get a-round.
2 G7 C
ground, live a lit-tle, get a-round.
Slowly-Tempo I
D.S. al Fine
(Instrumental solo)

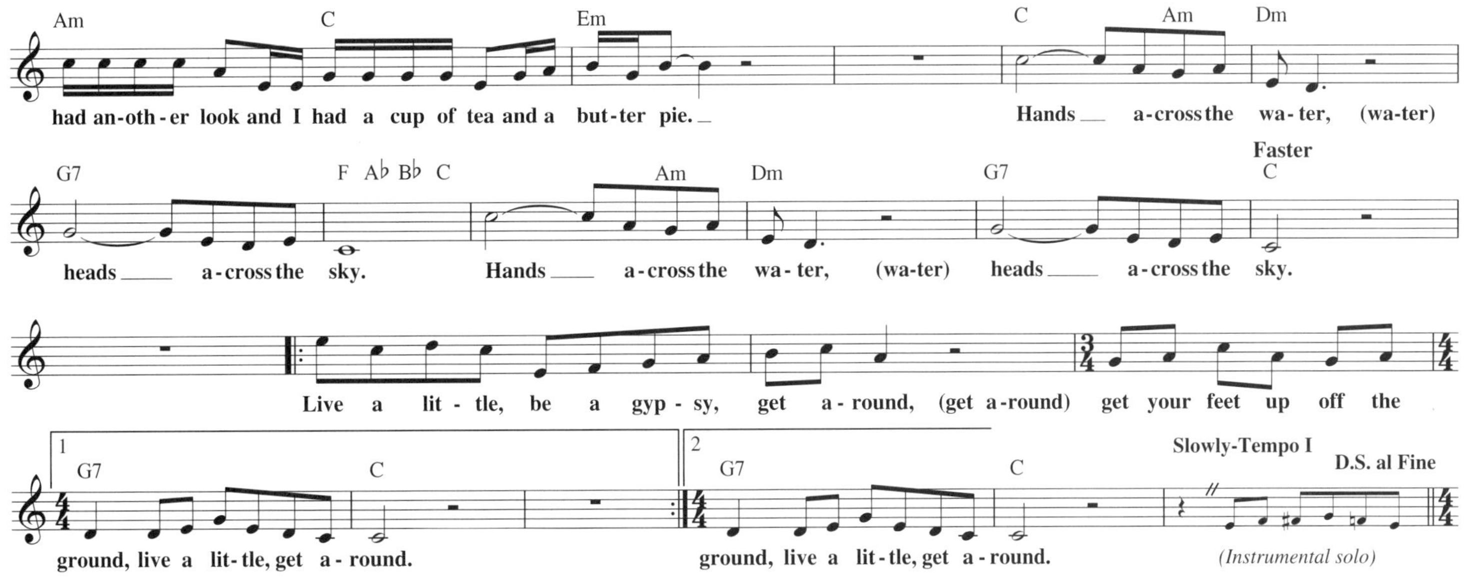

UNITED WE STAND

Words and Music by ANTHONY TOBY HILLER
and JOHN GOODISON

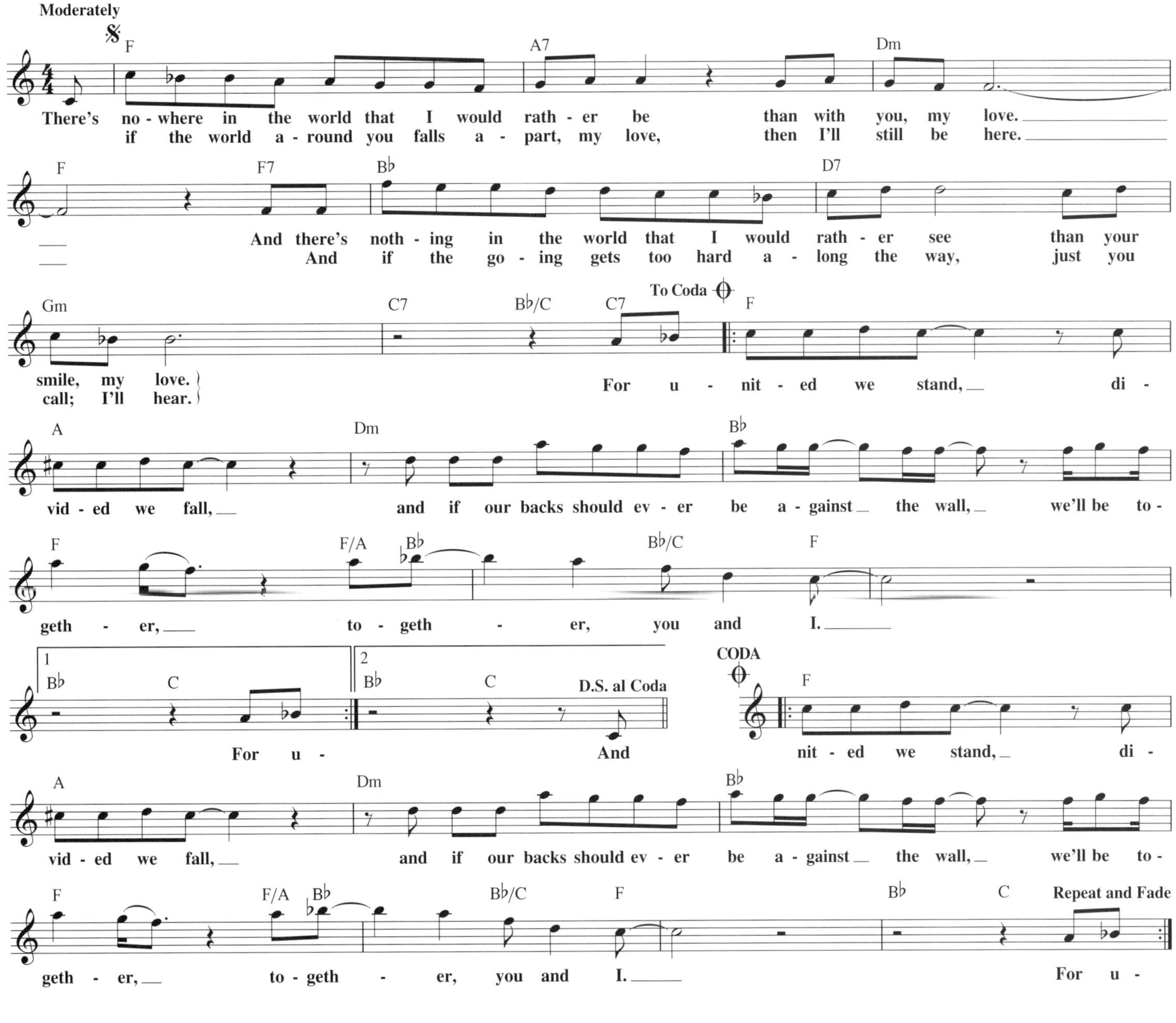

Moderately

F A7 Dm
There's no-where in the world that I would rath-er be than with you, my love.
if the world a-round you falls a-part, my love, then I'll still be here.

F F7 B♭ D7
And there's noth-ing in the world that I would rath-er see than your
And if the go-ing gets too hard a-long the way, just you

Gm C7 B♭/C C7 To Coda F
smile, my love.
call; I'll hear.
For u-nit-ed we stand, di-

A Dm B♭
vid-ed we fall, and if our backs should ev-er be a-gainst the wall, we'll be to-

F F/A B♭ B♭/C F
geth-er, to-geth-er, you and I.

1 B♭ C
For u-
2 B♭ C D.S. al Coda
And

CODA
F
nit-ed we stand, di-

A Dm B♭
vid-ed we fall, and if our backs should ev-er be a-gainst the wall, we'll be to-

F F/A B♭ B♭/C F B♭ C Repeat and Fade
geth-er, to-geth-er, you and I.
For u-

VIDEO KILLED THE RADIO STAR

Words and Music by BRUCE WOOLLEY,
TREVOR HORN and GEOFF DOWNES

Bright tempo
I heard you on the wire - less back in fif - ty - two, ly - ing a - wake in - tent - ly
tun - ing in on you. If I was young it did - n't stop you com - in' through.
Oh, oh. They took the cred - it for your sec - ond sym - pho - ny,
And now we meet in an a - ban-doned stu - di - o.
re - writ - ten by ma - chine on new tech - nol - o - gy. And now I un - der - stand the
We hear the play - back and it seems so long a - go. And you re - mem - ber the
prob - lems you can see. Oh, oh. I met your chil - dren. Oh, oh.
jin - gles used to go: Oh, oh. You were the first one. Oh, oh.
What did you tell them?
You were the last one.
Vid - e - o killed the ra - di - o star. Vid - e - o killed the ra - di - o star.
Pic - tures came and broke your heart. Oh, uh uh uh oh.
In my mind and in my car, we can't re - wind; we've
gone too far. Oh, uh uh uh oh. Oh, uh uh uh oh.
Vid - e - o killed the ra - di - o star. Vid - e - o killed the ra - di - o star.

D A/C♯ G/B D A/C♯ G/B
In my mind and in my car, we can't re - wind; we've gone too far.
D A/C♯ G/B D/A A G(add2)
Pic - tures came and broke your heart. Put the blame on V. C. R.
D/F♯ G6 Asus A D/F♯ G6 Asus
You are a ra - di - o star.
1 A 2 A D G
Repeat and Fade
You Vid - e - o killed the ra - di - o star.

WALKIN' AFTER MIDNIGHT

Lyrics by DON HECHT
Music by ALAN W. BLOCK

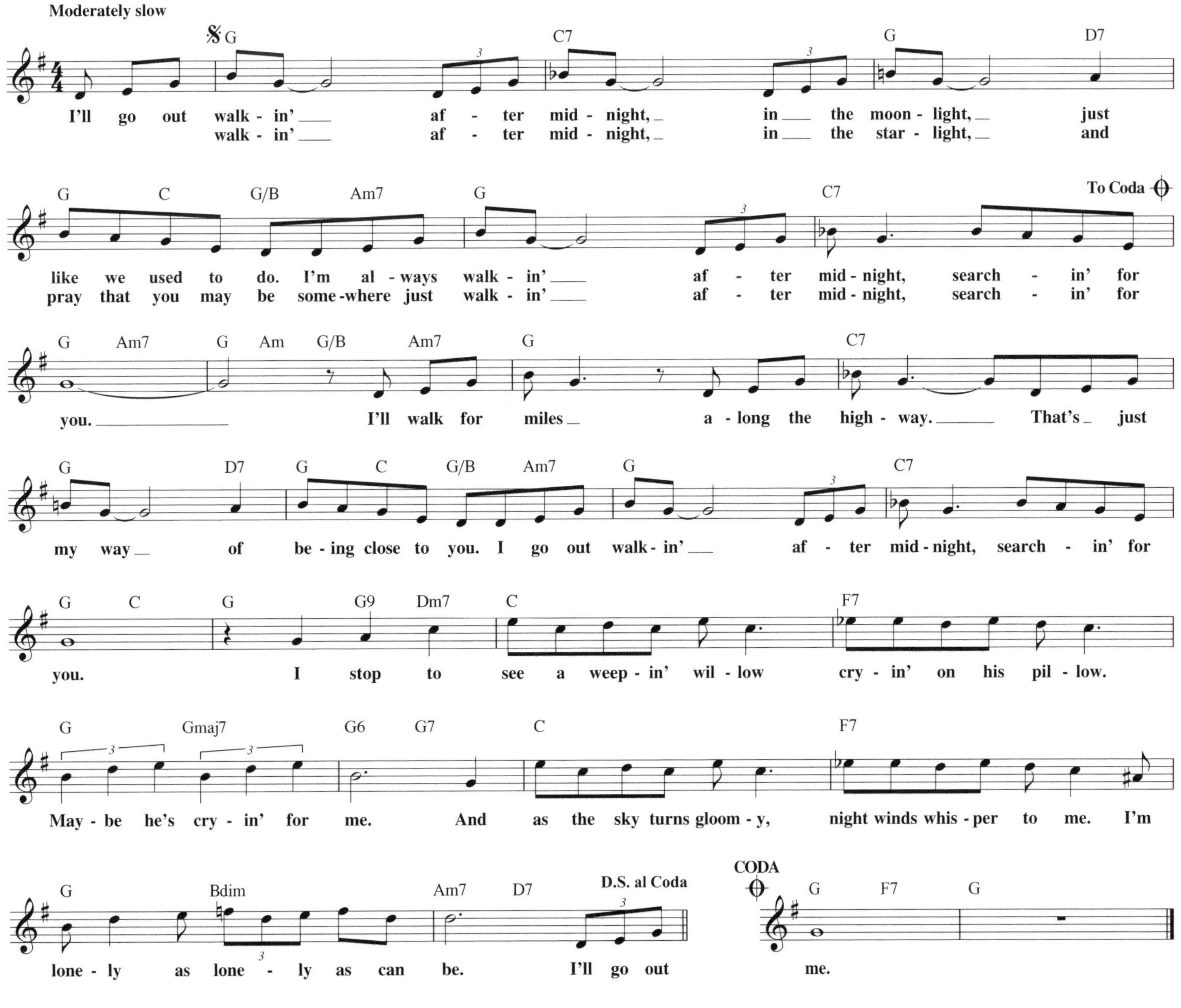

Moderately slow

G C7 G D7
I'll go out walk - in' af - ter mid - night, in the moon - light, just
walk - in' af - ter mid - night, in the star - light, and

G C G/B Am7 G C7 To Coda
like we used to do. I'm al - ways walk - in' af - ter mid - night, search - in' for
pray that you may be some - where just walk - in' af - ter mid - night, search - in' for

G Am7 G Am G/B Am7 G C7
you. I'll walk for miles a - long the high - way. That's just

G D7 G C G/B Am7 G C7
my way of be - ing close to you. I go out walk - in' af - ter mid - night, search - in' for

G C G G9 Dm7 C F7
you. I stop to see a weep - in' wil - low cry - in' on his pil - low.

G Gmaj7 G6 G7 C F7
May - be he's cry - in' for me. And as the sky turns gloom - y, night winds whis - per to me. I'm

G Bdim Am7 D7 D.S. al Coda CODA G F7 G
lone - ly as lone - ly as can be. I'll go out me.

WALKING IN MEMPHIS

Words and Music by
MARC COHN

Moderately fast

F5 G5 C5 A5 F5 G5 C5 A5 F5 G5 C5
Put on _ my blue _ suede shoes _ and I board - ed the plane. Touched down _ in the land of the

A5 F5 G5 C5 A5 F5 G5 C5
Del - ta Blues _ in the mid - dle of the pour - ing rain. _ W. _ C. Han-
(dou - ble - u) _

A5 F5 G5 C5 A5 F5 G5 C5 A5 F5
- dy, won't you look down o - ver me? _ Yeah, _ I've got a first - class _ tick - et but I'm as

G5 C5 Am F G C Am
blue as a boy _ can be. Then I'm walk - ing in Mem - phis. Was walk - ing with my

F G C Am F G C Am
feet ten feet off of Beale. _ Walk - ing in Mem - phis, but do I real - ly

F G F5 Gsus F5 C/E Dm F5 Gsus F5 C/E Dm F5
feel the way _ I feel? _ Saw the ghost of El - vis

Gsus F5 C/E Dm F5 Gsus F5 C/E Dm F5
on Un - ion Av - e - nue, fol - lowed him up to the gates of Grace - land, then I

Gsus F5 C/E Dm C/E F5 Gsus C Am F5
watched him walk _ right through. _ Now se - cur - i - ty, they did not _ see him; they just

Gsus C Am F5 Gsus C Am
hov - ered 'round his _ tomb, but there's a pret - ty lit - tle thing _ wait - ing for the King _

F5 C F G C Am
down in the Jun - gle Room. When I was walk - ing in Mem - phis I was walk - ing with my

F G Am7 F G C Am7 F G
feet ten feet off of Beale. _ Walk - ing in Mem - phis, but do I real - ly feel the way _ I feel? _

C7sus C7 C7sus C7 C7sus
They've got cat - fish on the ta -
C7 C7sus C7 C7sus C7
- ble; they've got gos - pel in the air,
Suddenly slowly, freely
C7sus C E7 F7 F♯dim
and Rev-er-end Green be glad to see you when you have-n't got a
a tempo
G7 F5 G5 C5 A5 F5
prayer, but, boy, you've got a prayer in Mem - phis.
G5 C5 A5 F5 G5 C5 A5 F5 G5 C5
Now Mu-ri-el plays pi-an-o ev-'ry Fri - day at the Hol-ly-wood,
A5 F5 G5 C5 A5 F5 G5 C5 A5
and they brought me down to see her and they asked me if I would,
F G7sus C Am F G7sus C Am F G
well, do a lit-tle num - ber, and I sang with all my might. She said, "Tell me, are you a Chris -
C Am7 F5 C F G C
- tian, child?" and I said, "Ma'am, I am to-night." Walk-ing in Mem - phis.
Am7 F G Am F G C
I was walk-ing with my feet ten feet off of Beale. Walk-ing in Mem - phis,
Am7 1 F C/E Dm C Am7 2 F G F5
but do I real-ly feel the way I feel? Walk - ing in Mem- feel the way I feel?
G5 C5 A5 F5 G5 C5 A5 F5 G5 C5
Put on my blue
A5 F5 G5 C5 A5 F5 G5 C5
suede shoes and I board-ed the plane. Touched down in the land of the
A5 F5 G5 C5 A5 F5 G5 C
Del - ta Blues in the mid-dle of the pour - ing rain. Touched down in the land of the
Am F G F5 G5 C5 A5 F5 Gsus G C
Del - ta Blues in the mid-dle of the pour - ing rain.

THE WARRIOR

Words and Music by NICK GILDER
and HOLLY KNIGHT

Moderate Rock
1. You run, run, run a - way; it's your heart that you be - tray. Feed - ing on your
2. (See additional lyrics)
hun - gry eyes, I bet you're not so civ - i - lized. Well, is - n't love
prim - i - tive, a wild gift that you wan - na give? Break out of cap - tiv - i - ty and
fol - low me, ster - e - o jun - gle child. Love is the kill, your heart's still wild.
Shoot - ing at the walls of heart - ache, bang, bang. I am the war - ri - or.
Well, I am the war - ri - or, and heart to heart you'll win, if you sur - vive
the war - ri - or, the war - ri - or. war - ri - or. I am the
war - ri - or.
(Instrumental solo ad lib.)
4 times
Shoot - ing at the walls of heart - ache, the war - ri - or,
(Shoot - ing at the walls of heart - ache.)
I am the war - ri - or, and heart to heart you'll win, heart to heart you win,
if you sur - vive the war - ri - or the war - ri - or.
D.S. and Fade

Additional Lyrics

2. You talk, talk, you talk to me,
Your eyes touch me physically.
Stay with me, we'll take the night
As passion takes another bite.
Who's the hunter, who's the game?
I feel the beat, call your name.
I hold you close in victory.
I don't wanna tame your animal style;
You won't be caged in the call of the wild.
Chorus

WASTED ON THE WAY

Words and Music by
GRAHAM NASH

Moderately, in 2
Look a - round me. I can see my life be - fore me, run - ning
you were young, did you ques - tion all the an - swers? Did you
rings a - round the way it used to be. I am
en - vy all the danc - ers who had all the nerve? Look a -
old - er now. I have more than what I want - ed, but I
round you now. You must go for what you want - ed. Look at
wish that I had start - ed long be - fore I did.
all my friends who did and got what they de - served.
And there's so much time to make up ev - 'ry - where you turn,
So much time to make up ev - 'ry - where you turn,
(D.S.) So much love to make up ev - 'ry - where you turn,
time we have wast - ed on the way.
time we have wast - ed on the way.
love we have wast - ed on the way.
So much wa - ter mov - ing un - der - neath the bridge.
Let the wa - ter come and car - ry us a - way.
To Coda
Oh, when
D.S. al Coda
CODA
Let the wa - ter come and car - ry us a - way.

WATERLOO

Words and Music by BENNY ANDERSSON,
BJÖRN ULVAEUS and STIG ANDERSON

Moderate beat
D E/D A/C♯ G/B A D
My, my, at Wa - ter - loo Na - po - le - on did sur - ren - der. Oh yeah, and I
I tried to hold you back but you were strong - er. Oh yeah, and now
E/D A/C♯ G/B A Bm
have met my des - ti - ny in quite a sim - 'lar way. The his - to - ry book on the shelf
it seems my on - ly chance is giv - in' up the fight. And how could I ev - er re - fuse,
Bm7 E7/G♯ A D
is al - ways re - peat - ing it - self.
I feel like I win when I lose.
Wa - ter - loo, I
G A
was de - feat - ed you won the war, Wa - ter - loo, prom - ise to love you for - ev -
D A D G
er - more. Wa - ter - loo, could - n't es - cape if I want - ed to,
A D
Wa - ter - loo, know - ing my fate is to be with you, Wa, Wa, Wa, Wa, Wa -
A To Coda 1 D
ter - loo, fi - nal - ly fac - ing my Wa - ter - loo. My, my
2 D Bm E
ter - loo. And how could I e - ven re - fuse I feel like I win when I lose.
A7 D.S. al Coda CODA D A
Wa - ter - loo. Wa, Wa, Wa, Wa, Wa - ter - loo, know - ing my fate is to be
D A Repeat and Fade
with you, Wa, Wa, Wa, Wa, Wa - ter - loo, fi - nal - ly fac - ing my Wa -

'WAY DOWN YONDER IN NEW ORLEANS

Words and Music by HENRY CREAMER
and J. TURNER LAYTON

Moderate bounce

'Way down yon - der in New Or - leans __ in the land __ of dream - y scenes __ there's a gar - den of
E - den that's what I mean. __ Cre - ole ba - bies with flash - ing eyes __
soft - ly whis - per with ten - der sighs, __ "Stop! Oh! won't you give your la - dy fair __
__ a lit - tle smile?" Stop! you bet your life you'll lin - ger there __ a lit - tle
while { There is hea - ven right here on earth __ with those beau - ti - ful queens }
{ They've got an - gels right here on earth __ wear - ing lit - tle blue jeans }
'way down yon - der in New Or - leans. leans. __

THE WAY YOU DO THE THINGS YOU DO

Words and Music by WILLIAM "SMOKEY" ROBINSON
and ROBERT ROGERS

Moderately, with a beat

You got a smile so bright, you know you could - 've been a can - dle.
are, you know you could - 've been a flow - er.
I'm hold - ing you so tight, you know you could - 've been a han - dle.
If good looks caused a min - ute, you know that you could be an hour. __
The way you swept me off my feet, you know you could - 've been a broom. __
The way you stole my __ heart, you know you could - 've been a cool crook.
The way you smell so sweet, you know you could - 've been some per - fume. __ }
And Ba - by you're so smart, you know you could - 've been a school book. __ }
Well, __ you could - 've been an - y thing that you want - ed to and I can tell. __ The way you do the things you
do. __ Ah, Ba - by. As pret - ty as you - by. Yes! __

WE BELONG

Words and Music by DAVID ERIC LOWDEN
and DANIEL NAVARRO

Moderately
F5 Bbsus2
Man - y times I tried to tell you; man - y times I've cried a - lone.
May - be it's a sign of weak - ness when I don't know what to say.
F5 Bbsus2
Al - ways I'm sur - prised how well you cut my feel - ings to the bone.
May - be I just would - n't know what to do with my strength an - y - way.
G5 F/A Bb5
Don't wan - na leave you, real - ly; I've in - vest - ed too much time
Have we be - come a hab - it? Do we dis - tort the facts?
G5 C5
to give you up that eas - y to the doubts that com - pli - cate your mind.
Now there's no look - ing for - ward, now there's no turn - ing back when you
F Bb C5
say: We be - long to the light, we be - long to the thun - der. We be -
F Bb C5
long to the sound of the words we've both fall - en un - der. What -
F Bb C5
ev - er we de - ny or em - brace, for worse or for bet - ter, we be - long,
F Bb C5
we be - long, we be - long to - geth - er.
1 2
N.C. F5
(drums)
Close your eyes and try
Bbsus2 F5
to sleep now. Close your eyes and try to dream. Clear your mind and do
Bbsus2 G5
your best to try and wash the pal - ette clean. We can't be - gin
F F/A Bb5 G5
to know it, how much we real - ly care. I hear your voice
C5 F
in - side me; I see your face ev - 'ry - where. Still you say: We be - long to the

B♭ C5 F
light, we be - long to the thun - der. We be - long to the sound of the
B♭ C5 F
words we've both fall - en un - der. What - ev - er we de - ny or em -
B♭ C5 F
brace, for worse or for bet - ter, we be - long, we be -
B♭ C5
long, we be - long to - geth - er.
Repeat and Fade

WHATEVER GETS YOU THROUGH THE NIGHT

Words and Music by
JOHN LENNON

Moderate Rock

N.C. 𝄋 A C G

What-ev-er gets you thru' the night 'sal - right, 'sal - right.
life 'sal - right, 'sal - right.
light 'sal - right, 'sal - right.

A C G

It's your mon - ey or your life 'sal - right, 'sal - right.
Do it wrong or do it right 'sal - right, 'sal - right.
Out the blue or out of sight 'sal - right, 'sal - right.

Em D C G 1

Don't need a sword to cut thru' flow - ers, oh no, oh no. Whatev - er gets you thru' your
Don't need a watch to waste your time,
Don't need a gun to blow your mind,

2, 3 Em A7

(Instrumental)

D7 A7 D7 A7 D

(Instrumental ends) Hold me dar - lin', come on lis - ten to me.

A7 D A7 D

I won't do you no harm. Trust me dar - lin', come on lis - ten to me, come on

C G Em A7

lis - ten to me, come on lis - ten, lis - ten. *(Instrumental)*

C G N.C. D.S. and Fade

(Instrumental ends) What ev - er gets you to the

WE'RE READY

Words and Music by
TOM SCHOLZ

Medium Rock beat
E5 B/E A/E E A/E E G(add2) Asus2
I'm read-y for more, the feel-in' now that I'm be-side you. We'll o-pen the door, do
an-y-thing that we de-cide to. And I
G D A
know that there's some-thin' that's just out of sight.
feel like it's time we were off on our way.
C D G Em7
And I feel like I'm fi-nal-ly see-in' the light. Hold-in' on, girl, I
We can go so much far-ther than we've come to-day. Hold-in' on, girl, and
Am D Dsus N.C. A5/E B5/F♯
know it's right. I know it's right. We're read-y!
come what may, come what may, we're read-y!
1
You and I (ooh) will find a rea-son to
sim-pli-fy a change of sea-son. And I
2
We're read-y, we're read-y, we're read-y.
C♯m
Come on! Come on! Come
on!
A B G♯m F♯m7
Come on!
(Instrumental)
A(add2)
We can find a way.

To Coda
E5 B/E A/E E A/E E A5 B7sus4 E5 B/E A/E
We're read-y now, catch-in' a wave to
E A/E E G(add2) Asus2 E5 B/E A/E E A/E E
ride on. Stead-y now, head-in' where we de-cide on. And I
G D A C D
know that there's some-thin' that's just out of sight. And I feel like we're try-in' to
G Em7 Am D
do some-thing right. Come on make it if we hold on tight, hold on tight. We're
N.C. A5/E N.C. B5/F♯ A5/E N.C. A5/E N.C. B5/F♯ N.C. A5/E
read-y! Yeah, yeah. We're read-y! Yeah, yeah.
N.C. B5/F♯ A5/E N.C. A5/E N.C. B5/F♯ A5/E N.C. A5/E N.C. B5/F♯ A5/E
We're read-y! Ooh. We're read-y. We're
N.C. A5/E N.C. B5/F♯ N.C. A5/E N.C. B5/F♯ A5/E N.C. A5/E
read-y. Yeah, yeah. We're read-y. Yeah. We're read-y.
One! Two!
D.S. al Coda
N.C. B5/F♯
Three! Four! Come
CODA
A5 B7sus E5 B/E A/E E A/E E
We're read-y now. (Ooh.) We're read-y now.
G(add2) Asus2 E5 B/E A/E
Freely
A(add2) A(add2)
Repeat and Fade
We're read-y now. (Ooh.)

WE ARE THE WORLD

Words and Music by LIONEL RICHIE and MICHAEL JACKSON

Moderately slow
E A/E B/E E
There comes a time when we heed a cer - tain call, when the
A B7 E B/E E A/E E C♯m
world must come to-geth-er as one. There are peo-ple dy - ing and it's
G♯m F♯m7 F♯m7/A Bsus B
time to lend a hand to life, the great - est gift of all.
E A/E B/E E A B7
We can't go on pre - tend-ing day by day that some-one, some-where will soon make a
Send them your heart so they'll know that some - one cares and their lives will be strong-er and
E A/E E C♯m G♯m
change. We are all a part of God's great big fam - i - ly and the
free. As God has shown us by turn-ing stone to bread, so we
F♯m7 F♯m7/A Bsus B E/G♯ A B
truth, you know, love is all we need.
all must lend a help-ing hand.
We are the world, we are the chil -
E A B E
- dren, we are the ones to make a bright - er day, so let's start giv - ing. There's a
C♯m G♯m F♯m7 A/B
choice we're mak - ing, we're sav-ing our own lives, it's true; we make bet - ter days, just you and me.
1 E A/E B/E A/E E A/E B/E A/E 2 E C D E A/E E
When you're down and out, there seems no hope at all, but if you
C D E C♯m
just be - lieve, there's no way we can fall. Let us re - al - ize that a
G♯m F♯m7 F♯m7/A Bsus B
change will on - ly come when we stand to-geth-er as one. We are the world,
A B E A B
we are the chil - dren, we are the ones to make a bright - er day, so let's start giv -
E C♯m G♯m
- ing. There's a choice we're mak - ing, we're sav-ing our own lives, it's true;
F♯m7 A/B E E/G♯ Repeat and Fade
we make bet - ter days, just you and me. We are the world,

WE'RE IN THIS LOVE TOGETHER

Words and Music by KEITH STEGALL
and ROGER MURRAH

Moderately bright 4
B♭maj7 Gm7/D Cm7 Cm7/F B♭maj7
It's like a dia - mond ring, it's a pre - cious thing, and we
It's like a rain - y night and can - dle light, and,
Gm7/D Cm7 Cm7/F B♭maj7 Gm7/D
nev - er want to lose it. It's like a fa - vor - ite song that we love
ooh, it's so ro - man - tic. We got the whole thing work - ing out
Cm7 Cm7/F B♭maj7 Gm7/D Cm7 Cm7/F
to sing, ev - 'ry time we hear the mu - sic.
so right, And it's just the way we planned it.
B♭maj7 Gm7 Cm7 Cm7/F
And we're in this love to - geth - er; we got the kind that - 'll last for -
B♭maj7 Gm7 Cm7 Cm7/F B♭maj7 Gm7
ev - er. (Instrumental) We're in
Cm7 Cm7/F G♭/A♭
this love to - geth - er; and like ber - ries on the vine it gets
Cm7/F Cm7 B♭maj7 E♭ F/G
sweet - er all the time. (Instrumental)
Cmaj7 Am7 Dm7 Dm7/G
We're in this love to - geth - er; we got the kind that - 'll last for -
Cmaj7 Am7 Dm7 Dm7/G
ev - er. (Instrumental)
Cmaj7 Am7 Dm7 Dm7/G
We're in this love to - geth - er; we got the kind that - 'll last for -
Repeat and Fade
Cmaj7 Am7 Dm7 Em7 A♭/B♭ F/G
ev - er and ev - er - more. (Instrumental)

THE WAY YOU MOVE

Words and Music by ANTWAN PATTON, PATRICK BROWN and CARLTON MAHONE

Moderate groove
N.C.
Boom, boom, boom, hah, hah.
Rap 1: (See rap lyrics)
Rap 2: (See rap lyrics)
etc.
Cm7
I like the way you move.
I like the way you move. Woo,
A♭/C
I love the way you move.
I love the way.
G7
I love the way.
Cm7
I love the way you move.
I love the way you move. Woo,
A♭/C
I love the way you move.
I love the way.
1
G7
I love the way.
2
G7
I love the way. Hey,
Cm7
baby girl, don't you stop it. Come on, lady, dance all around me. You
A♭/C
look so fine, look so fine. Look so fine, driv-in' me out of my mind,
G7
out of my mind.
Cm7
If I could, I would just leave with you, ba - by. Ooh, 'cause you light
A♭/C
me, and ex-cite me. And you know you got
G7
me, ba - by.

Cm7
I like the way you move. I like the way you move. Woo,
Ab/C
G7
Repeat and Fade
I love the way you move. I love the way. I love the way.

Rap Lyrics

Rap 1: Ready for action, nip it in the bud.
We never relaxin'. OutKast is everlastin'.
Not clashin', not at all.
But see, my nigga went up to do a little actin'.
Now that's for anyone askin'.
Give me one, pass 'em.
Drip, drip, drop, there goes an eargasm.
Now you comin' out the side of your face.
We tappin' right into your memory banks, thanks.
So click it or ticket, let's see your seatbelt fastened.
Trunk rattlin' like two midgets in the back seat wrestlin'
Speakerboxxx vibrate the tag.
Make it sound like aluminum cans in the bag.
But I know y'all wanted that eight-o-eight.
Can you feel that B-A-S-S, bass?
But I know y'all wanted that eight-o-eight.
Can you feel that B-A-S-S, bass?

Rap 2: The whole room fell silent. The girls all paused with glee.
Turnin' left, turnin' right, are they lookin' at me?
Well I was lookin' at them, there, there on the dance floor.
Now they got me in the middle feelin' like a man whore.
Especially the big girl. Big girls need love too.
No discrimination here, squirrel. So keep your hands off my cheeks.
Let me study how you ride the beat, you big freak.
Skinny slim women got the the camel-toe within 'em.
You can hump them, lift them, bend them,
Give them something to remember.
Yell out "timber" when you fall through the chop shop.
Take a deep breath and exhale.
Your ex-male friend, boyfriend was boring as hell.
Well let me listen to the story you tell.
And we can make moves like a person in jail....
On the low, hoe!

WHERE HAVE ALL THE FLOWERS GONE?

Words and Music by
PETE SEEGER

Moderately slow, with simplicity

C D7 G7 C
1. Where have all the flow-ers gone? Long time pass-ing. Where have all the flow-ers gone?
3.,5. *(See additional lyrics)*
F G C G7
Long time a-go. Where have all the flow-ers gone? The girls have picked them ev-'ry one.
F G7 C F G7 C
Oh, when will they ev-er learn? Oh, when will they ev-er learn?

D7 G7 C
2. Where have all the young girls gone? Long time pass-ing. Where have all the young girls gone?
4.,6. *(See additional lyrics)*
F G C G7
Long time a-go. Where have all the young girls gone? They've tak-en hus-bands ev-'ry one.
F G7 C F G7 C
Oh, when will they ev-er learn? Oh, when will they ev-er learn?

Additional Lyrics

3. Where have all the young men gone? Long time passing.
Where have all the young men gone? Long time ago.
Where have all the young men gone?
They're all in uniform.
Oh, when will they ever learn?
Oh, when will they ever learn?

4. Where have all the soldiers gone? Long time passing.
Where have all the soldiers gone? Long time ago.
Where have all the soldiers gone?
They've gone to graveyards, every one.
Oh, when will they ever learn?
Oh, when will they ever learn?

5. Where have all the graveyards gone? Long time passing.
Where have all the graveyards gone? Long time ago.
Where have all the graveyards gone?
They're covered with flowers, every one.
Oh, when will they ever learn?
Oh, when will they ever learn?

6. Where have all the flowers gone? Long time passing.
Where have all the flowers gone? Long time ago.
Where have all the flowers gone?
Young girls picked them, every one.
Oh, when will they ever learn?
Oh, when will they ever learn?

WEAR MY RING AROUND YOUR NECK

Words and Music by BERT CARROLL
and RUSSELL MOODY

Bright tempo
C G7 C
Won't you wear my ring up a - round your neck to tell the
ring up a - round your neck to tell the
C7 G7 C
world I'm yours, by heck. Let them see
world I'm yours, by heck. Let them know
C7 F C G7 N.C.
your love for me, and let them see by the ring a - round your
I love you so, and let them know by the ring a - round your
1, 3 C F C N.C. 2, 4 C F7 C7 F7
neck. Won't you wear my neck. They say that go - ing
C C7 F7
stead - y is not the prop - er thing. They say that we're too young to know the
C C7 F7 C
mean - ing of a ring. I on - ly know I love you and that you love me
D7 G7 D7♭5 G7 N.C.
too. So, dar - ling, please do what I ask of you. Won't you wear my
C
ring a - round your neck to tell the world
C7 G7 C C7
I'm yours, by heck, let them see your love for
let them know I love you
F C G7 N.C. To Coda
me, and let them see by the ring a - round your
so, and let them know by the ring a - round your
C F7 G7 N.C. D.S. al Coda
neck. Won't you wear my
CODA
C F7 C
neck.

WHAT ABOUT LOVE?

Words and Music by BRIAN ALLEN, SHERON ALTON and JIM VALLANCE

Moderately
Dm Bb F C Dm Bb F C
I've been lone - ly. I've been wait - ing for you. I'm pre - tend - ing, and that's all I can do.
Dm Bb F C Bb Bbsus2
The love I'm send - ing ain't mak - ing it through to your heart. You've been
Dm Bb F C Dm Bb F C
hid - ing, nev - er let - ting it show, al - ways try - ing to keep it un - der con - trol.
tell you what you're feel - ing in - side. And I can't sell you what you don't want to buy.
Dm Bb F C Bb
You got it down, and you're well on your way to the top. But there's
But some - thing's miss - ing and you got - ta look back on your life. You know
C F/A Bb C
some - thing that you for - got.
some - thing, it just ain't right.
What a - bout love? Don't you want some - one to care a - bout you? What a - bout
F/A Bb C F/C C F/A Bb To Coda 1 C
love? Don't let it slip a - way. What a - bout love? I on - ly want to share it with you. You might
Bb Dm C/D Bb/D C/D
need to some - day. Yeah. I can't
2 C Bb C Bb C
share it with you. (Instrumental)
Bb C Dm C D.S. al Coda
What a - bout
CODA
C G/D C/D D G/D C/D D Repeat and Fade
share it with you.
Vocal ad lib: (What about love? What about love?)

WE'VE GOT TONIGHT

Words and Music by
BOB SEGER

Moderately slow
B F# E/G# F#
I know it's late. I know you're wea - ry. I know your plans
I've been so lone - ly. All of my hopes
B/D# Emaj7 E6 B F# B
don't in - clude me. Still, here we are,
fad - ing a - way. I've longed for love
Emaj7 E6 B Emaj7 E6
both of us lone - ly, long - ing for shel - ter from all that we
like ev - 'ry - one else does. I know I'll keep search - ing e - ven af - ter to -
B F# B/D# Emaj7 E6 B/F# F#
see. Why should we wor - ry? No one will care, girl. Look at the stars
day. So there it is, girl. I've said it all now. And here we are,
B/D# Emaj7 E6 B/F# F# B Emaj7 E6
so far a - way.
babe. What do you say?
We've got to - night. Who needs to - mor -
B B/D# Emaj7 E6 1 B
- row? We've got to - night, babe. Why don't you stay?
2 B D
Deep in my soul stay? I know it's late. I know you're
B D B
wea - ry. I know your plans don't in - clude me. Still, here we
E G B Emaj7 E6 B Emaj7 E6
are, both of us lone - ly, both of us lone - ly.
B Emaj7 E6 B
We've got to - night. Who needs to - mor - row? Let's make it last.
Emaj7 E6 B F# B Emaj7 E6
Let's find a way. Turn out the light. Come take my
B B/D# Emaj7 E6 To Coda B
hand now. We've got to - night, babe. Why don't you stay?

Emaj7 E6 B
We've got to-night. Who needs to-mor - row? Let's make it last.
Emaj7 E6 B F♯ B Emaj7 E6
Let's find a way. Turn out the light. Come take my
B B/D♯ Emaj7 E6 B D.S. al Coda
hand now. We've got to-night, babe. Why don't you stay? Oh, we've got to-night.
CODA
B Emaj7 E6 B/F♯ F♯ F♯7 B
stay? Oh. Oh, why don't you stay?

WHERE OR WHEN
from BABES IN ARMS

Words by LORENZ HART
Music by RICHARD RODGERS

Moderately

E♭ E♭6 E♭maj7 Fm7
It seems we stood and talked like this be - fore. We looked at each oth - er in the same way then,

Fm7/B♭ E♭maj7 Cm7 Fm7 B♭7 E♭ E♭6 E♭maj7
but I can't re-mem - ber where or when. The clothes you're wear - ing are the clothes you

Fm7 Fm7/B♭
wore. The smile you are smil - ing you were smil - ing then, but I can't re - mem - ber where or

E♭maj7 Dm7♭5 G7 Cm Fm7 Dm7 G7 Dm7 G7 Cm
when. Some things that hap - pen for the first time, seem to be

Fm7 Cm7 F7 Fm7 B♭7 E♭ E♭6 E♭maj7 E♭7♯5 A♭6
hap - pen - ing a - gain. And so it seems that we have met be - fore, and laughed be -

Gm7 Fm7 Gm7 C7 Fm7 B♭7 E♭6 A♭m E♭
fore, and loved be - fore, but who knows where or when!

WHAT IN THE WORLD'S COME OVER YOU

Words and Music by
JACK SCOTT

Slowly
G B7 C
What in the world's come o - ver you? Seems we nev - er get a -
G G7 C G Em A7
long. Ev - 'ry night I rem - i - nisce, dream - ing of your
D7 G B7
ten - der kiss - es. What in the world's come o - ver you?
G G7 C
Will you ev - er change your mind? If you do, I'll
G Em A9 D7 G D7
still be here, dear, wait - ing, long - ing for you. All my life I've
G A7
loved you so, nev - er dreamed I'd miss you so. Now a - lone in my
D7 N.C. D7
room at night, my heart, it cries, "It's just not right!" Oh,
G B7 C
what in the world's come o - ver you? Could you ev - er change your
You're still mine, you're from a -
G G7 C G Em 1 A9 D7
mind? If you do, I'll still be here, dear, wait - ing, long - ing for
bove; guess you'll al - ways be my one and
G 2 C D7 G C G
you. on - ly, on - ly real love.

WHEN DOVES CRY

Words and Music by
PRINCE

Medium tempo

Am Dm/A G E7♯5/G♯ E7/G♯
Dig, if U will, the pic - ture of U and I en - gaged in a kiss. The

Am Dm/A G E7♯5/G♯ E7/G♯
sweat of your bod - y cov - ers me. Can U, my dar - ling, can U pic - ture this?

Am Dm/A G E7♯5/G♯ E7/G♯
Dream, if U can, a court - yard, an o - cean of vi - 'lets in bloom.
Touch, if U will, my stom - ach. Feel how it trem - bles in - side.

Am Dm/A G E7♯5/G♯ E7/G♯
An - i - mals strike cu - ri - ous pos - es. They feel the heat, the heat be - tween me and
You've got the but - ter - flies all tied up. Don't make me chase U. E - ven doves have

𝄋 Am Dm/A G E7♯5/G♯ E7/G♯
(Both times)
How can U just leave me stand - ing a - lone in a world that's so cold?
U.
pride.

Am Dm/A G E7♯5/G♯ E7/G♯
May - be I'm just 2 de - mand - ing. May - be I'm just like my fa - ther 2 bold.

Am Dm/A G E7♯5/G♯ E7/G♯
May - be U're just like my moth - er. She's nev - er sat - is - fied.

To Coda 𝄌

Am Dm/A G E7♯5/G♯ E7/G♯
Why do we scream at each oth - er? This is what it sounds like when doves cry.

F Am G F Am G F Am G F Am G F Am G

F Am G F Am G

1. F Am G

2. F Am G

D.S. al Coda

CODA 𝄌

E7♯5/G♯ E7/G♯ Am
when doves cry.

WHEN I NEED YOU

Words and Music by CAROLE BAYER SAGER and ALBERT HAMMOND

Moderately
G D7/F♯
When I need you, I just close my eyes and I'm with you, and
D7 D♯dim7 Em
all that I so want to give you, it's on - ly a heart - beat a -
D G
way. When I need love, I hold out my hands and I
D7/F♯ D7 D♯dim7 Em
touch love, I nev - er knew there was so much love
D Em
keep - ing me warm night and day. Miles and miles of emp - ty space in be -
It's not eas - y when the road is your
D Em D
tween us, a tel - e - phone can't take the place of your smile. But you
driv - er, hon - ey, that's a heav - y load that we bear. But you
G Em Am Am7
know I won't be trav - el - ing for - ev - er. It's cold out, but
know I won't be trav - el - ing a life - time. It's cold out, but
Dsus/A To Coda D7 G
hold out and do like I do. When I need you, I
hold out and do like I
D7/F♯ D7
just close my eyes and I'm with you, and all that I
D♯dim7 Em
so want to give you, babe, it's on - ly a
D D.S. al Coda
heart - beat a - way.
CODA D7 G
do, when I need you.

WHEN THE CHILDREN CRY

Words and Music by MIKE TRAMP
and VITO BRATTA

Smoothly, with motion
G D/F♯ Em Bm C G
Lit-tle child, dry your cry - in' eyes. How can I ex-plain the
Lit-tle child, you must show the way to a bet - ter day for
(Guitar solo ad lib.)
Em D G D/F♯ Em Bm
fear you feel in - side? 'Cause you were born in - to this e - vil world
all the young. 'Cause you were born for the world to see
To Coda
C G Em D C Bm
where man is kill - ing man and no one knows just why. What have we be - gun?
that we all can live with love and peace. No more pres - i - dents,
(Solo ends)
Em Bm C G Em D Dsus
Just look what we have done. All that we de - stroyed you must build a - gain.
and all the wars will end; one u - ni - ted world un - der God.
D Em Bm C G Em Bm
When the chil - dren cry, let them know we tried. 'Cause when the chil - dren sing, then the
D.C. al Coda
CODA
C D D Dsus D C Bm
new world be - gins. gins. What have we be - gun?
No more pres - i - dents,
Em Bm C G Em
Just look what we have done. All that we de - stroyed, you must build a -
and all the wars will end; one u - nit - ed world un - der
D D Dsus D Em Bm C
gain. God. When the chil - dren cry, let them know we
G Em Bm C D Em Bm
tried. 'Cause when the chil - dren fight, let them know it ain't right. When the chil - dren pray, let them
C G Em Bm C D
know the way. 'Cause when the chil - dren sing, then the new world be - gins.

WHIP IT

Words and Music by MARK MOTHERSBAUGH
and GERALD CASALE

Quickly
E7sus
Crack that whip, give___ the past the slip.
Step on a crack,_ break___ your mom-ma's back.
E7sus
(1.,D.S.) When a prob-lem comes a-long, you___ must whip it. Be-fore the cream sits out too long, you___ must whip it. When some-thing's go-ing wrong, you___ must whip it.
(2.) When a good time turns a-round, you___ must whip it. You___ will nev-er live it down un-less you whip it. No one gets their way un-til they whip it.
To Coda
1
C G D C
Now whip it in-to shape, shape it up, get straight,
G D C
go for-ward, move a-head. Try to de-tect it. It's not too late to whip it, whip it good.
2
E5 G5 C5 E5 G5 D5
I say whip it, whip it good.
E7sus
D.C. al Coda
Play 8 times
(Instrumental)
CODA
C G D C G
Now whip it / to whip it in-to shape, shape it up, get straight, go for-ward, move a-head,
D C E7sus
try to de-tect it. It's not too late to whip it, whip it good.

WHO CAN IT BE NOW?

Words and Music by
COLIN HAY

Moderate beat
E Dmaj7 C♯m B
1. Who can it be knock-ing at my door? Go a-way, don't come 'round here no more.
2. Who can it be knock-ing at my door? Make no sound, tip-toe a-cross the floor.
3. (Instrumental)
Can't you see that it's late at night? I'm ver-y tired, and I'm not feel-ing right.
If he hears, he'll knock all day. I'll be trapped and here I'll have to stay.
All I wish is to be a-lone, stay a-way, don't you in-vade my home.
I've done no harm, I keep to my-self. There's noth-ing wrong with my state of men-tal health.
Best off if you hang out-side, don't come in, I'll on-ly run and hide.
I like it here with my child-hood friend. Here they come, those feel-ings a-gain.
(Instrumental ends)
C♯m E/B
Who can it be now? Who can it be now? Who can it be now?
To Coda
Who can it be now?
1 2
F♯m B7 E E/B
Is it the man come to take me a-way? Why do they fol-low me?
It's not the fu-ture that I can see, It's just my fan-ta-sy.
C♯m7
D.C. al Coda
CODA
Who can it be now?
B6
Play 3 times
Ah, ah. Who can it be now? Ah, yeah, yeah, yeah.
F♯m7/B

WHAT HAVE I DONE TO DESERVE THIS?

Words and Music by CHRIS LOWE, NEIL TENNANT and ALEE WILLIS

Moderate Pop
Cadd9 B♭add9 Cadd9 B♭add9
1. You al - ways want - ed a lov - er I on - ly want - ed a job.
2. I come here look - ing for mon - ey and end up leav - ing with love.
3. You al - ways want - ed me to be something I wasn't. You al - ways want - ed too much.
Cadd9 B♭add9 B♭/C C
I've al - ways worked for a liv - ing
Now you've left me with noth - ing (can't take it.)
Now I can do what I want to for ever
How am I gon - na get through?
B♭/C C C
How am I gon - na get through? get through? get through?
(to Chorus) (to Chorus)
Chorus
F Em Am
I brought you drinks, I brought you flowers, I read your books and talked for
At night the peo - ple come and go. They talk too fast and walk too
F Em Am
hours. Ev - 'ry day so man - y drinks such pret - ty flowers so tell me
slow. Chas - ing time from hour to hour. I pour the drinks and crush the
F Em Am F
what have I / flow - ers. what have I, what have I done to de - serve this? What have I, what have I,
Em Am N.C.
what have I done to de - serve this? What have I? What have I? What have I? Since you went a -
C Dm7 Dm
way I've been hang - ing a - round. I've been won - der - ing why
G C Dm7
I'm feel - ing down. You went a - way, it should make me feel bet - ter, but
Dm B♭ C
I don't know oh how I'm gon - na get through,
(what have I, what have I, what have I done to deserve this?)
B♭ C B♭ C
how I'm gon - na get through. (to verse 3) how I'm gon - na get through. Repeat 5 times
(what have I......) (what have I......)

F Em Am F F Em Am

How I'm gon-na get through.

F Em Am F Em Am

How I'm gon-na get through. How I'm gon-na

F Em Am F Em Am

get through. We don't have to fall a-part. We don't have to fight. We don't need

F Em Am F Em Am F

to go to hell and back ev-er-y night. We could make a deal.

Em Am F Em Am F

We don't have to fall a-part. We don't have to fight. We don't need to go to hell and back

Em Am F Em Am Repeat and Fade

ev-er-y night. What have I, what have I, what have I done to de-serve this?

WHY

Words and Music by BOB MARCUCCI
and PETER DeANGELIS

Moderately

G6 Gmaj7 G6 Gmaj7 Am7 D7 Am7 D7 Am7 D7

I'll nev-er let you go, why, be-cause I love you. I'll al-ways love you

Am7 D7 G6 Gmaj7 G6 Gmaj7 Dm7

so, why, be-cause you love me. No bro-ken hearts for us, 'cause we love each

Cm7 B♭ Am7 D7

oth er. And with our faith and trust, there could be no oth-er, why, 'cause I love you,

Am7 D7 G Gmaj7 G6 Gmaj7 Am7 D7 Am7 D7

why, 'cause you love me. I think you're aw-f'ly sweet, why, be-cause I love you.

Am7 D7 Am7 D7 G Gmaj7 G6 Gmaj7 Dm7

You say I'm your spe-cial treat, why, be-cause you love me. We found a per-fect love, yes a

C Cm6 G Gmaj7 Am7 D7 1 G Gdim7 Am7 D9 D7♭9 2 G

love that's yours and mine. I love you and you love me all the time. time.

WISHING YOU WERE HERE

Copyright © 1974 by Universal Music - MGB Songs and Big Elk Music
Copyright Renewed
Words and Music by
PETER CETERA
Moderately
Dm7 E/D E♭/D Dm Dm
(Instrumental)
A D A Dm
Sleep - less hours and dream - less nights and far - a - ways.
Same old show in a dif - f'rent town on an - oth - er time.
On the road it's a heav - y load, but I'll get by.
Oo,
Gm7 C7 Dm B♭ C A D A
wish - ing you were here.
(Wish - ing you were here.)
Heav - en knows, and, Lord, it shows when
E - ven though you're far a - way, you're
Pay the price, make a sac - ri - fice and
Dm Gm7 C7 To Coda Dm Dm7
I'm a - way.
on my mind.
still I'll try.
Oo, wish - ing you were here.
(Wish - ing you were here.)
Oo,
E/D E♭/D Dm Dm7
Oo.
E/D E♭/D Dm B♭ C Dm
B♭ C Dm C B♭ F B♭/F
And I'd like to change my life, and you know I would, just to be with you to - night,
F B♭/F F B♭ C Dm C B♭
ba - by, if I could. But I've got my job to do, and I do it well,
F B♭ Dm7 E/D
so I guess that's how it is.
Oo, wish - ing you were here.

E♭/D
Dm
Dm7
E/D
Oo, wish-ing you were here.
Oo.
(Wish-ing you were here.)
D.S. al Coda
CODA
E♭/D
Dm B♭ C
Dm
C B♭ C
(Wish-ing you were here.)
Here.
Oo. Wish-ing you were
(Wish-ing you were here.)
Dm7
E/D
E♭/D
Dm
D
Oo.
here. (Instrumental)

WILL YOU LOVE ME TOMORROW

(Will You Still Love Me Tomorrow)

Words and Music by GERRY GOFFIN
and CAROLE KING

Moderately

G C C/D G

To-night you're mine com-plete-ly, you give your
Is this a last-ing treas-ure, or just a
I'd like to know that your love is love I

C C/D Bsus B

love so sweet-ly. To-night the light of
mo-ment's pleas-ure? Can I be-lieve the
can be sure of. So tell me now and

Em Em/D♯ Em/D Em/C♯ C C/D Am/G To Coda

love is in your eyes.
mag-ic of your sigh?
I won't ask a-gain.
Will you still love me to-mor-

1. G 2. G C Bm

row? row? To-night with words un-spo-ken,

C G C

you say that I'm the on-ly one, but will my heart be

Bm Em7 A Am7 D D.C. al Coda

bro-ken when the night meets the morn-ing sun?

CODA

G C C/D N.C.

row? Will you still love me to-mor-

Em Em/D♯ Em/D Em/C♯ C D G

row? *(Instrumental)*

WHO PUT THE BOMP (IN THE BOMP BA BOMP BA BOMP)

Words and Music by BARRY MANN and GERRY GOFFIN

Slowly
F7 Bb Gm Cm7 F9
I'd like to thank the guy who wrote the song that made my ba - by fall in love with me.
With a beat
Bb Gm Cm7 F7 Bb Gm Eb
(Instrumental)
Who put the bomp in the bomp ba bomp ba bomp? Who put the ram in the
F7 Bb Gm Eb
ram - a - lam - a - ding - dong? Who put the bop in the bop sh - bop sh - bop? Who put the dit in the
F7 Bb D7 Eb Edim7
dit, dit, dit, dit - da? Who was that man? I'd like to shake his hand. He
Bb/F Gm Cm F7 Bb Gm
made my ba - by fall in love with me.
When my ba - by heard
Time that we're a - lone,
Eb F7 Bb Gm Eb
bomp, ba - ba - bomp, ba - bom - ba - bomp - bomp, ev - 'ry word went right in - to her heart.
bomp, ba - ba - bomp, ba - bom - ba - bomp - bomp, sets my ba - by's heart all a - glow.
F Bb Gm Eb F9#5 Eb7
And when she heard them sing - ing ram - a - lam - a - lam - a - lam - a - ding - dong,
And ev - 'ry time we dance to ram - a - lam - a - lam - a - lam - a - ding - dong,
Bb/F Gm Cm F7 1 Bb 2 Bb
she said we'd nev - er have to part.
she al - ways says she loves me so.

WITH A LITTLE HELP FROM MY FRIENDS

Words and Music by JOHN LENNON
and PAUL McCARTNEY

Moderate Swing feel

E B/D♯ F♯m B7

What would you do if I sang out of tune? Would you stand up and walk out on me?
What do I do when my love is a - way? (Does it wor - ry you to be a - lone?)
(Would you be - lieve in a love at first sight?) Yes I'm cer - tain that it hap - pens all the

E B F♯m

Lend me your ears and I'll sing you a song and I'll try
How do I feel by the end of the day? (Are you sad
time. (What do you see when you turn out the light?) I can't tell

B7 E D A

not to sing out of key. Oh, I get by with a lit - tle help from my friends.
be - cause you're on your own?) No, I get by with a lit - tle help from my friends.
you but I know it's mine. Oh, I get by with a lit - tle help from my friends.

E D A E

Mm, I get high with a lit - tle help from my friends. Mm, I'm gon - na try
Mm, I get high with a lit - tle help from my friends. Mm, I'm gon - na try
Mm, I get high with a lit - tle help from my friends. Oh, I'm gon - na try

A | 1 E B7 | 2,3 E

with a lit - tle help from my friends.
with a lit - tle help from my friends. (Do you need
with a lit - tle help from my friends. (Do you need

C♯m F♯m7 E D A

an - y - bod - y?) I need some - bod - y to love. (Could it be
an - y - bod - y?) I just need some - one to love, (Could it be

C♯m F♯7 E D To Coda A D.C. al Coda

an - y - bod - y?) I want some - bod - y to love.
an - y - bod - y?) I want some - bod - y to love.

CODA

A D A

Oh, I get by with a lit - tle help from my friends.

E D A E

Mm, I'm gon - na try with a lit - tle help from my friends. Oh, I get high

A E D

with a lit - tle help from my friends. Yes, I get by with a lit - tle help from my friends.

A C/G Am9 E

with a lit - tle help from my friends.

WITH YOU I'M BORN AGAIN

Words by CAROL CONNORS
Music by DAVID SHIRE

Freely, expressively
Dm Am7 B♭maj7 Am7
Come, bring me your soft - ness. Com - fort me through all this mad - ness.
Gm7 A7♭9sus A7♭9 Dsus D Dm(add2) Am11
Wom-an, don't you know, with you I'm born a - gain. Female: Come give me your sweet-ness.
B♭maj9 Am11 Gm7 A9sus A7 Dsus
Now there's you, there is no weak-ness. Ly - ing safe with - in your arms, I'm born a - gain.
D Gm7 Am7 B♭maj7 Am7 Gm9
Male: I was half, not whole; in step with none. Female: Reach-ing through this
Am7 E♭maj9 Dm7 Cm9 Dm Am7
world in need of one. Both: Come show me your kind-ness.
B♭maj7 Am7 Gm9 A7♭9sus A7 Dm
In your arms I know I'll find this. Male: Wom-an, don't you know, with you I'm born a - gain.
Slower
Dm/C B♭maj7 A7sus A
Female: Ly - ing safe with you, I'm born a - gain.
Moderately, steadily
Dsus D A/D
D Dsus D A/D D Dm7
Female: (Ah,
Male: Come bring me your

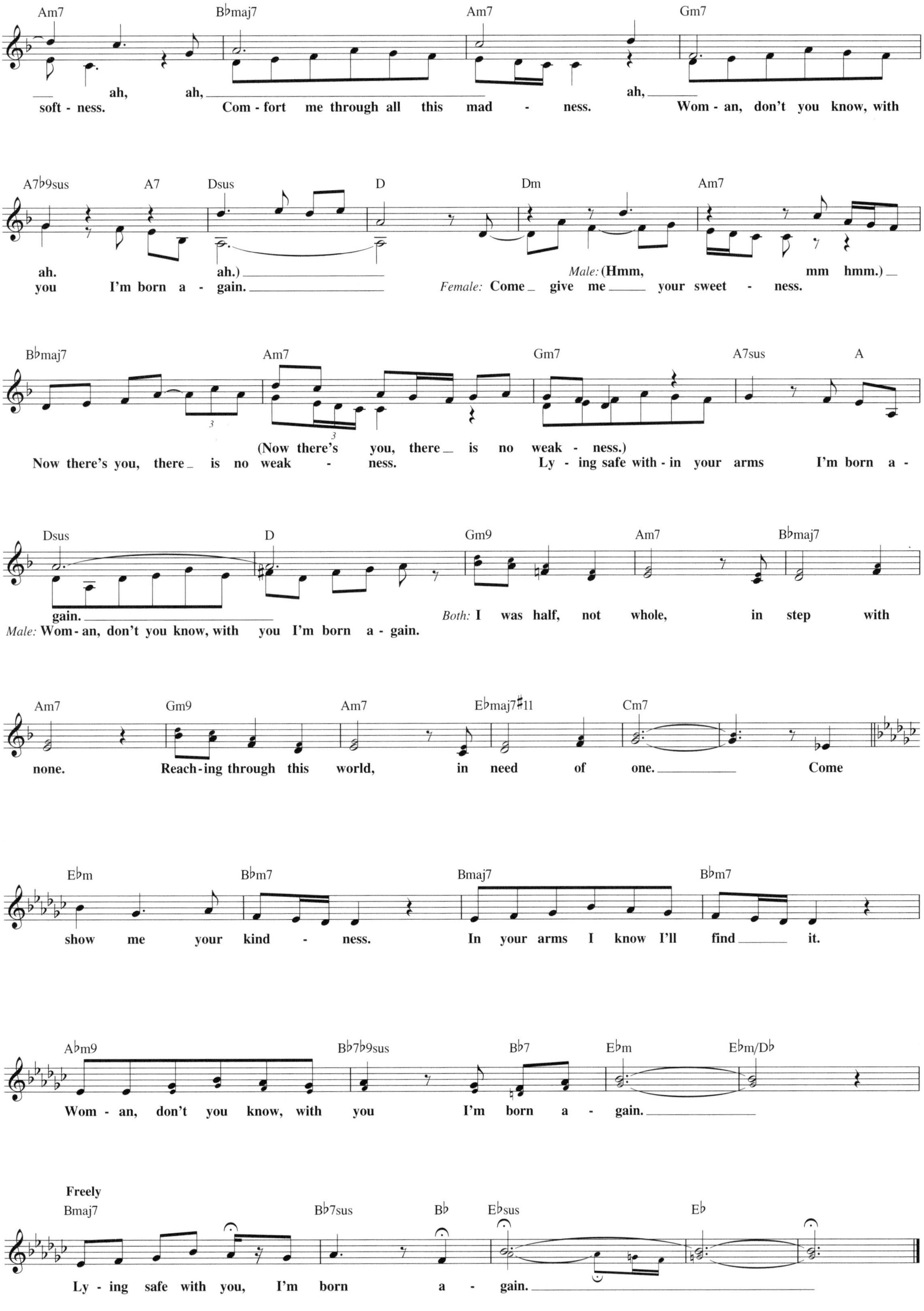

Am7 B♭maj7 Am7 Gm7

ah, ah, ah,

soft - ness. Com - fort me through all this mad - ness. Wom - an, don't you know, with

A7♭9sus A7 Dsus D Dm Am7

ah. ah.) *Male:* (Hmm, mm hmm.)

you I'm born a - gain. *Female:* Come give me your sweet - ness.

B♭maj7 Am7 Gm7 A7sus A

(Now there's you, there is no weak - ness.)

Now there's you, there is no weak - ness. Ly - ing safe with - in your arms I'm born a -

Dsus D Gm9 Am7 B♭maj7

gain.

Male: Wom - an, don't you know, with you I'm born a - gain. *Both:* I was half, not whole, in step with

Am7 Gm9 Am7 E♭maj7♯11 Cm7
none. Reach - ing through this world, in need of one. Come

E♭m B♭m7 Bmaj7 B♭m7
show me your kind - ness. In your arms I know I'll find it.

A♭m9 B♭7♭9sus B♭7 E♭m E♭m/D♭
Wom - an, don't you know, with you I'm born a - gain.

Freely
Bmaj7 B♭7sus B♭ E♭sus E♭
Ly - ing safe with you, I'm born a - gain.

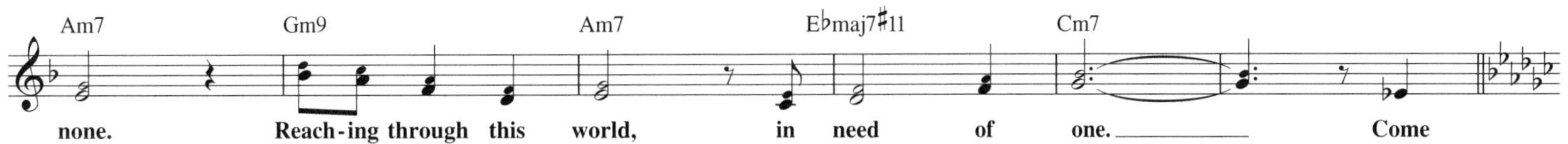

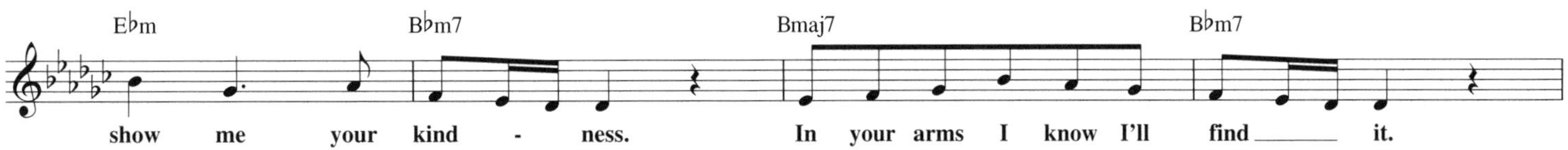

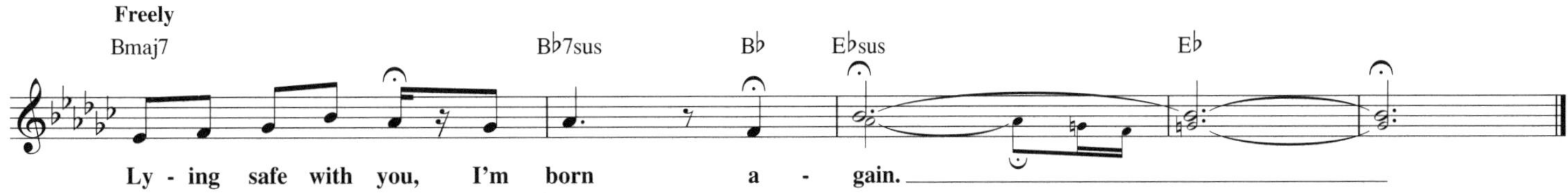

WIVES AND LOVERS

(Hey, Little Girl)

from the Paramount Picture **WIVES AND LOVERS**

Words by HAL DAVID
Music by BURT BACHARACH

Moderately fast

Fm7

Hey, lit - tle girl, comb your hair, fix your make - up, soon he will o - pen the
Day af - ter day there are girls at the of - fice and men will al - ways be

Bb7 Gm7

door. ___ Don't think be - cause there's a ring on your fin - ger
men. ___ Don't send him off with your hair still in curl - ers,

C9 Cm7

you need - n't try an - y - more. ___ For wives should
you may not see him a - gain. ___ For wives should

F7b9 Am7b5 D7 Ebmaj7

al - ways be lov - ers too. Run to his arms ___ the mo - ment
al - ways be lov - ers too. Run to his arms ___ the mo - ment

Am7 D7 Dbmaj7 Gm7 C7

he ___ comes home to you. I'm warn - ing you. ___
he ___ comes home to you. He's al - most here. ___

Fm7

Hey, lit - tle girl, bet - ter wear some - thing pret - ty, some - thing you'd

Bb9 Eb6 Edim Fm7

wear to go to the cit - y. And dim all the lights, pour the

Bb9 Ebmaj7

wine, start the mu - sic, time to get read - y for love. ___

C7b9 Fm7 Bb7 Fm7

___ Oh, time to get read - y, time to get

Bb9 Fm7 Bb9 Eb6

read - y, time to get read - y for love. ___

WOMAN, WOMAN

Words and Music by JIM GLASER
and JIMMY PAYNE

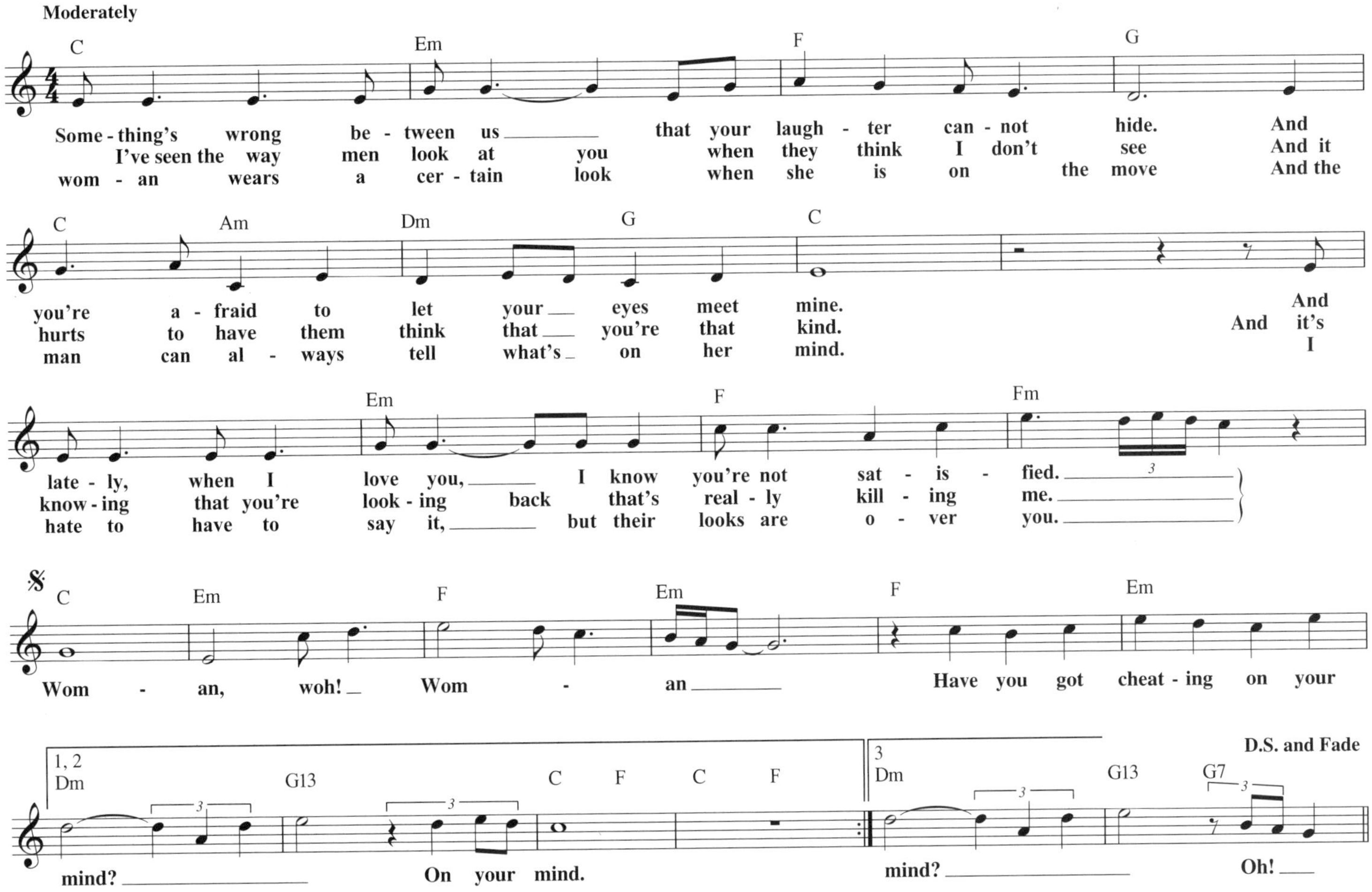

Moderately
C Em F G C Am Dm G C Em F Fm
Some - thing's wrong be - tween us that your laugh - ter can - not hide. And you're a - fraid to let your eyes meet mine. And late - ly, when I love you, I know you're not sat - is - fied.
I've seen the way men look at you when they think I don't see And it hurts to have them think that you're that kind. And it's know - ing that you're look - ing back that's real - ly kill - ing me.
wom - an wears a cer - tain look when she is on the move And the man can al - ways tell what's on her mind. I hate to have to say it, but their looks are o - ver you.
C Em F Em F Em
Wom - an, woh! Wom - an Have you got cheat - ing on your
1, 2 Dm G13 C F C F
mind? On your mind.
3 Dm G13 G7 D.S. and Fade
mind? Oh!

THE WONDER OF YOU

Words and Music by
BAKER KNIGHT

Slowly (with much expression)
F Dm Gm7 C7 F Dm Gm7 C7
When no one else can un - der - stand me, when ev - 'ry - thing I do is wrong, you give me love and con - so - la - tion. You give me hope to car - ry on, and you
And when you smile, the world is bright - er. You touch my hand and I'm a king. Your kiss to me is worth a for - tune. Your love to me is ev - 'ry - thing, and you're
You'll nev - er know how much I love you. My love is yours and yours a - lone, and it's so won - der - ful to have you, to have you for my ver - y own. Guess I'll
F F7 Bb C7 F D7 Gm7
try to show your love for me in ev - 'ry - thing you do. That's the won - der,
al - ways there to lend a hand in all I try to do. That's the won - der,
nev - er know the rea - son why you love me as you do. That's the won - der,
C7 1, 2 F Gm7 C7 3 F
the won - der of you.
the won - der of you.
the won - der of you.

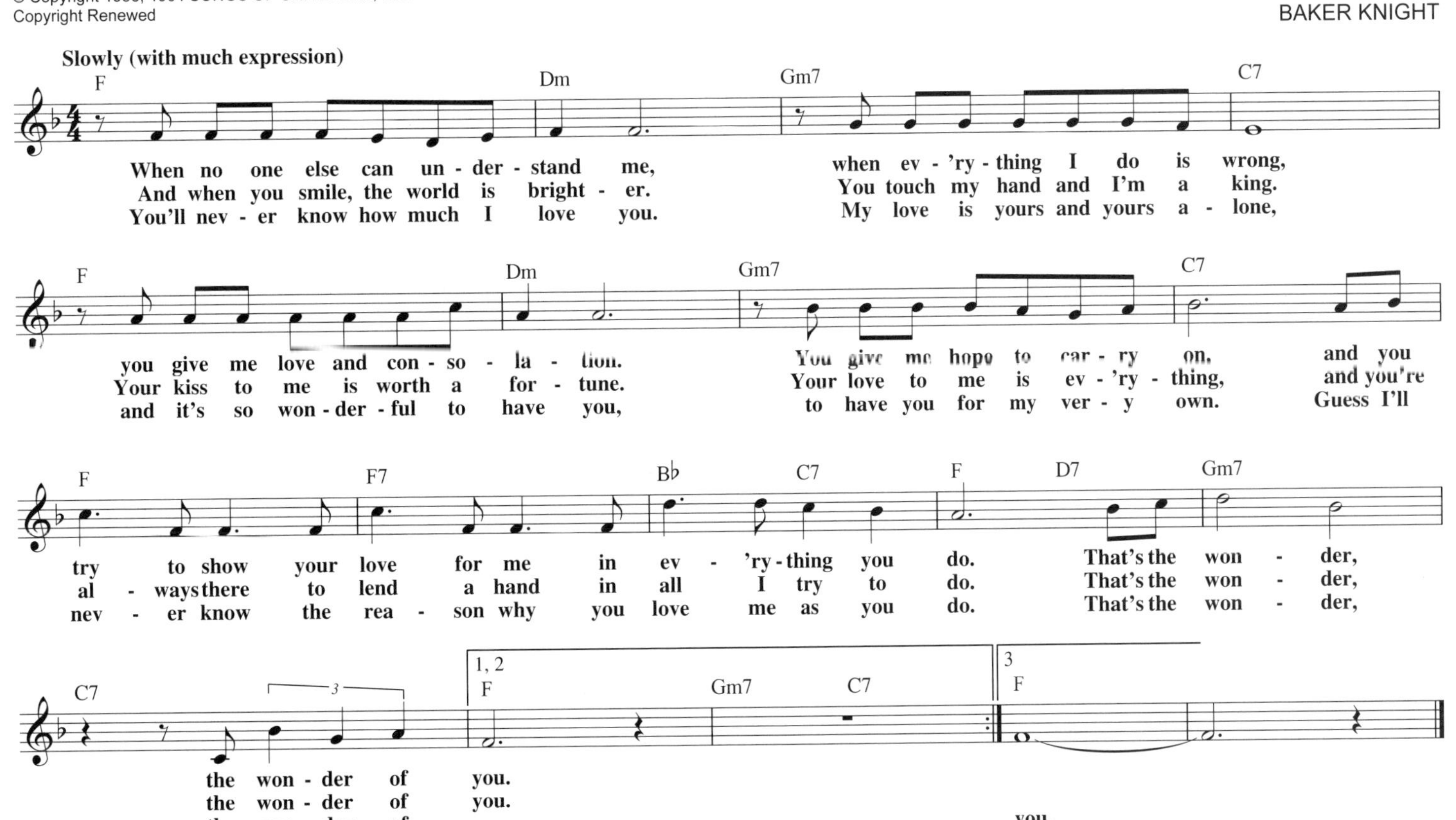

WONDERWALL

Words and Music by
NOEL GALLAGHER

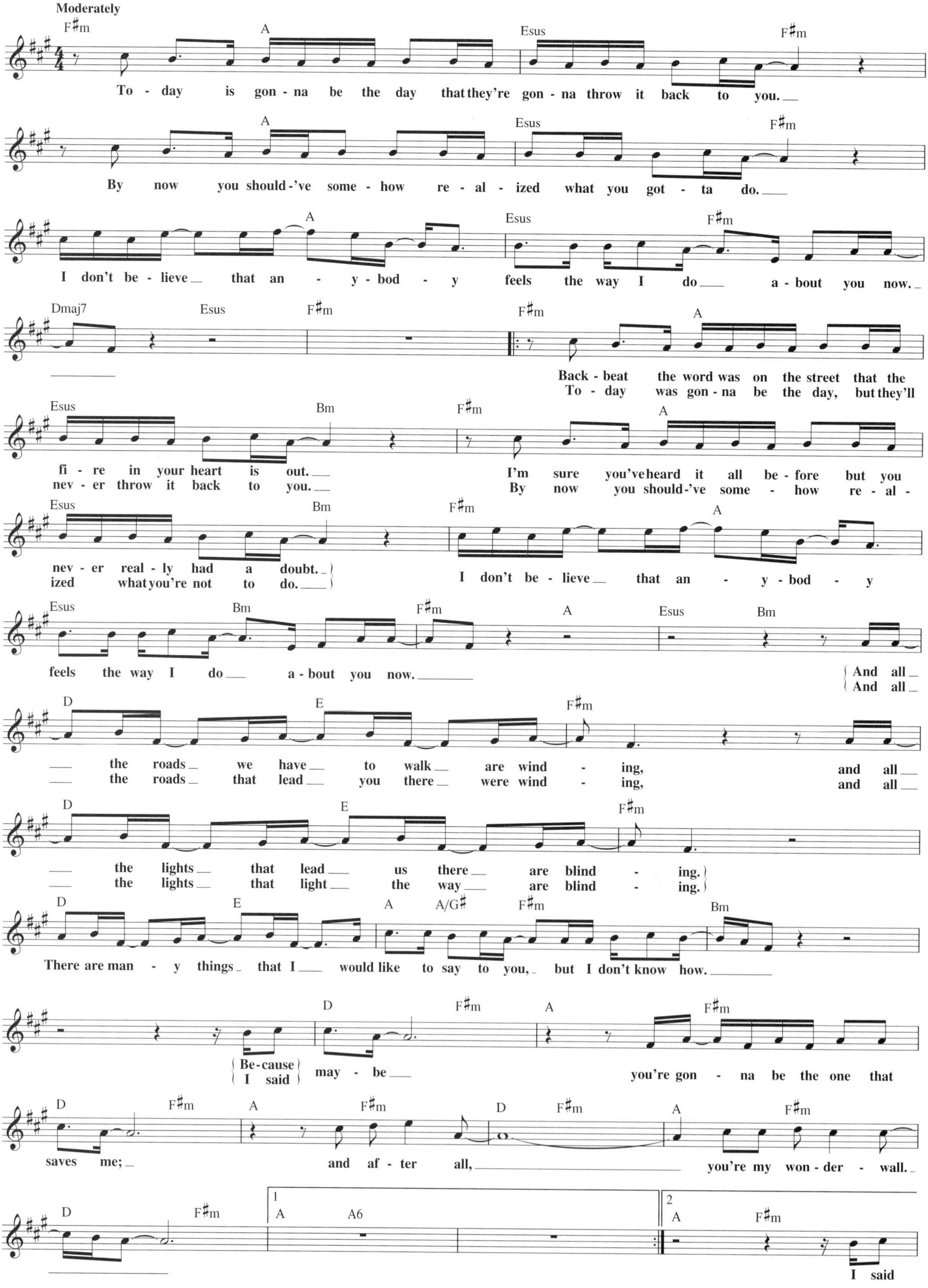
Moderately
F#m A Esus F#m
To - day is gon - na be the day that they're gon - na throw it back to you.
A Esus F#m
By now you should - 've some - how re - al - ized what you got - ta do.
A Esus F#m
I don't be - lieve that an - y - bod - y feels the way I do a - bout you now.
Dmaj7 Esus F#m F#m A
Back - beat the word was on the street that the
To - day was gon - na be the day, but they'll
Esus Bm F#m A
fi - re in your heart is out. I'm sure you've heard it all be - fore but you
nev - er throw it back to you. By now you should - 've some - how re - al -
Esus Bm F#m A
nev - er real - ly had a doubt.
ized what you're not to do.
I don't be - lieve that an - y - bod - y
Esus Bm F#m A Esus Bm
feels the way I do a - bout you now.
And all
And all
D E F#m
the roads we have to walk are wind - ing, and all
the roads that lead you there were wind - ing, and all
D E F#m
the lights that lead us there are blind - ing.
the lights that light the way are blind - ing.
D E A A/G# F#m Bm
There are man - y things that I would like to say to you, but I don't know how.
D F#m A F#m
Be - cause
I said
may - be you're gon - na be the one that
D F#m A F#m D F#m A F#m
saves me; and af - ter all, you're my won - der - wall.
D F#m
1 A A6
2 A F#m
I said

D F♯m A F♯m D F♯m
may - be you're gon - na be the one that saves me;
A F♯m D F♯m A F♯m D F♯m
and af - ter all, you're my won - der - wall.
A F♯m D F♯m A F♯m
I said may - be you're gon - na be the one that
D F♯m A F♯m D F♯m
saves me, you're gon - na be the one that saves me.
A D F♯m A F♯m D F♯m A F♯m
Play 3 times
(Instrumental)

WOODEN HEART

Words and Music by BEN WEISMAN, FRED WISE, KAY TWOMEY, and BERTHOLD KAEMPFERT

Moderately

E♭ Fm7 B♭7 E♭
Can't you see I love you? Please don't break my heart in two, that's not hard to do, 'cause I

Fm7 B♭7 E♭ Fm7 B♭7 E♭ Fm7 B♭7
don't have a wood - en heart. And if you say "Good - bye" then I

E♭ Fm7 B♭7
know that I would cry. May - be I would die 'cause I don't have a wood - en

E♭ A♭ E♭ Fm7 B♭7 E♭ B♭7 E♭
heart. There's no strings up - on this love of mine, it was

A♭ E♭ Edim7 B♭7 E♭ Fm7 B♭7 E♭
al - ways you from the start. Treat me nice, treat me good, treat me like you real - ly

Fm7 B♭7 E♭ A♭ E♭
should, 'cause I'm not made of wood, and I don't have a wood - en heart.

WORDS OF LOVE

Words and Music by
JOHN PHILLIPS

Moderate Ragtime tempo
G F B♭ A7 D
Words of love so soft and ten - der won't win a girl's heart an - y - more.
G F B♭7 A7
If you love her, then you must send her some - where where she's nev - er been be - fore.
Gm F B♭/F F B♭ A A♭ N.C.
Worn - out phras - es and long - ing gaz - es won't get you where you ought to go.
No!
With a Rock feel
G F7 E♭7 D
Words of love soft and ten - der, won't win her.
Em Am F D7
You ought to know by now. You ought to know. You ought to know by now.
Tempo I
Tempo II
G F7 E♭7 D7
Words of love soft and ten - der, won't win her an - y -
G F B♭ A D G F
more.
(Instrumental)
E♭ D N.C.
Tempo I
Em Am
You ought to know by now.
Tempo II
F D7 G F
You ought to know. You ought to know by now. Words of love soft and ten - der won't
B♭ A7 D7 G F
win a girl's heart an - y - more. If you love her, then you must send her
B♭ A Gm F
some - where where she's nev - er been be - fore. Worn - out phras - es and long - ing gaz - es won't
B♭ A A♭ N.C. G F
get you where you ought to go. Words of love soft and ten - der won't
E♭7 D E♭ D G
win her an - y - more. An - y - more.

WRAP IT UP

Words and Music by ISACC HAYES
and DAVID PORTER

Moderately fast
E♭5
I've been watch - in' you for days now, ba - by. I just love your sex - y ways now, ba - by. You know
my love will nev - er stop now, ba - by. Just put your lov - in' in my box, ba - by. Wrap it up,
D♭5 G♭ To Coda A♭
I'll take it. Wrap it up, I'll take it.
E♭5
No more will I shop a - round, ba - by. I know I got the best thing in town, ba - by. I've
seen all I wan - na see, ba - by. Bring your lov - in' straight to me, now ba - by. Wrap it up,
E♭5 D♭5 G♭5 1 A♭5
I'll take it. Wrap it up, I'll take it. Wrap it up,
2 A♭5 E♭5
it. Good God al - might - y, come on.
Cm
Ooh, I'm gon - na treat you like the queen you are; bring you sweet things from my
can - dy jar, 'cause you've got treats you ain't nev - er used. Give it, give it to me. You
B♭ D.C. al Coda
won't get a - bused.
CODA
A♭5 E♭5
it. Wrap it up, I'll take
D♭5 G♭5 A♭5
it. Wrap it up, ooh, wrap it up,
E♭5 D♭5 G♭5 A♭5 Repeat and Fade
I'll take it. Wrap it up, I'll take it. Wrap it up,

A WONDERFUL TIME UP THERE

(Everybody's Gonna Have a Wonderful Time Up There)

Words and Music by
LEE ROY ABERNATHY

With spirit
G
Lis - ten, ev - 'ry - bod - y, 'cause I'm talk - ing to you. Je - sus is the on - ly one to
Lis - ten here, my sis - ter, we're not leav - ing you out. may not be a preach - er but you
When the trib - u - la - tions seem to dark - en the way, that's the time to get down on your
get your Ho - ly Bi - ble in the back of the book, book of Rev - e - la - tion, that's the
D7 G
car - ry you through. Now you bet - ter get you read - y for I'm tell - ing you why,
sing and shout. What's the use to wor - ry if you've been re - deemed, 'cause
knees and pray. Ev - 'ry - bod - y gon - na have their trou - bles, too.
place you must look; If you un - der - stand it and you can if you try,
Edim7 D7 G
Je - sus is a - com - ing from His throne on high; Man - y are the wea - ry and the
Heav - en's e - ven bet - ter than a mis - er dreamed; Think a - bout the trou - ble you could
Got - ta be so care - ful 'bout the things we do; we're go - ing down the val - ley, go - ing
Je - sus is a - com - in' from His throne on high; Read - in' in the Bi - ble all the
D7
lone and sad, They're gon - na wish they had - n't done the things they had.
save some soul, Tell them what to do to reach the shin - ing goal,
one by one, Gon - na be re - ward - ed for the things we've done.
things that He said, Said He was a - com - in' back to raise the dead,
G A9 D13
How're you gon - na feel a - bout the things He'll say on that judg - ment
Sure - ly you can show them how to find the light, make the whole thing
When we get to Heav - en and the prom - ised land, then we'll un - der -
Are you gon - na be a - mong the cho - sen few, will you make it
G C
day? right. stand. through? Ev - 'ry - bod - y's gon - na have re - li - gion in glo - ry, Ev - 'ry - bod - y's gon - na be
G D7
sing - ing that sto - ry, Ev - 'ry - bod - y's gon - na have a won - der - ful time up there, Oh,
G
glo - ry hal - le - lu - jah! Broth - er, there's a reck - on - ing a - com - ing in the morn - ing,
C G
Bet - ter get you read - y 'cause I'm giv - ing you the warn - ing. Ev - 'ry - bod - y's gon - na have a
D7 G C/G 1–3 G 4 G
won - der - ful time up there.
(4.) Now

YELLOW SUBMARINE

Words and Music by JOHN LENNON
and PAUL McCARTNEY

March tempo
D C G Em Am Cmaj7 D G
In the town where I was born lived a man who sailed the sea. And he
D C G Em Am Cmaj7 D G
told us of his life in the land of sub - mar - ines. So we
D C G Em Am Cmaj7 D G
sailed up to the sun till we found the sea of green. And we
D C G Em Am Cmaj7 D
lived be-neath the waves in our yel - low sub - mar - ine.
G D G
We all live in a yel - low sub - mar - ine, yel - low sub - mar - ine, yel - low sub - mar - ine.
D G
We all live in a yel - low sub - mar - ine, yel - low sub - mar - ine, yel - low sub - mar - ine.
And our
As we
D C G Em Am Cmaj7 D G
friends are all on board, man - y more of them live next door. And the
live a life of ease, ev - 'ry one of us has all we need. Sky of
D C G
band be - gins to play:
blue and sea of
(Instrumental)
G Em Am Cmaj7 D
D.S. and Fade
green in our yel - low sub - mar - ine.

Y.M.C.A.

Words and Music by JACQUES MORALI, HENRI BELOLO and VICTOR WILLIS

Disco
G
Em
1. Young man, there's no need to feel down. I said, young man, pick your-self off the ground. I said,
2. Young man, there's a place you can go, I said, young man, when you're short on your dough. You can
3.-6. (See additional lyrics)
C
D/F♯
C/E
D
C
G/B
D/A
young man, 'cause you're in a new town there's no need to be un-hap-py.
stay there and I'm sure you will find man-y ways to have a good time.
D7
G
It's fun to stay at the Y. M. C. A. It's fun to stay at the
Em
Am
Am(maj7)
Am7
Y. M. C. A. They have ev-er-y-thing for young men to en-joy. You can
Am7/D
G
hang out with all the boys. It's fun to stay at the Y. M. C. A. It's fun to stay at the
Em
Am
Am(maj7)
Am7
Y. M. C. A. You can get your-self clean, you can have a good meal. You can
Young man, young man, there's no need to feel down. / are you lis-t'ning to me?
D11
1
D.C.
D
2
D.C.
D7
3
D.S. ad lib. and Fade
D
do what-ev-er you feel.
Young man, young man pick your- / what do self off the ground.
you want to be?

Additional Lyrics

3. Young man, are you listening to me?
I said, young man, what do you want to be?
I said, young man, you can make real your dreams
But you've got to know this one thing.

4. No man does it all by himself.
I said young man put your pride on the shelf.
And just go there to the Y.M.C.A.
I'm sure they can help you today.
Chorus

5. Young man, I was once in your shoes
I said, I was down and out and with the blues.
I felt no man cared if I were alive.
I felt the whole world was so jive.

6. That's when someone come up to me
And said, "Young man, take a walk up the street.
It's a place there called the Y.M.C.A.
They can start you back on your way."
Chorus

YOU BELONG TO ME

Words and Music by CARLY SIMON
and MICHAEL McDONALD

Moderately
Why'd you tell me this while you look for my re - ac - tion?
What do you need to know? Don't you know I'll al -
- ways be the one. You don't have to prove to me you're beau -
- ti - ful to stran - gers. I've got lov - in' eyes
of my own. You be - long to
me in this life. An - y - one could tell. An - y fool can
see who you need. I know you all too well. You don't have to
prove to me you're beau - ti - ful to stran - gers. I've
got lov - in' eyes, and I can tell.
You be - long to me. Tell him you were fool - in'. You be - long to
me. You be - long to me. Tell him he's a stran - ger. You be - long to
me. (Instrumental)
You be - long to
me. You be - long to me. You be - long to
Repeat and Fade

YOU ARE

Words and Music by LIONEL RICHIE
and BRENDA HARVEY-RICHIE

Moderately
C G/C F/C C F/C G/C C Am7 G/A
Ba - by, you'll find there's on - ly one love, yours and mine.
Tell me it's true; I can't be - lieve you do what you do.

Am G C G/C
I've got so much love. And need - ing you so,
I've got so much love. And my love, you'll see,

F/C C F/C G/C C Am7 G/A Am
my love for you I'll nev - er let go. I've got so
we'll stay to - geth - er, just you and me. I've got so

Am/G F G C
much love. All I want is to hold you. Let me show
much love. On - ly you know me. Tell me how

F G C F
how much I love you, ba - by. I don't mind and I don't mind.
to love you, ba - by. I don't mind and I don't mind.

G C F F/G C G/B
(Lov - ing you.) Girl, I love you. There's no one a - bove you.
(Tell me.) Girl, I love you, al - ways think - ing of you.
You are the sun,

Am Gm6 Fmaj7 F/G G C G/B
you are the rain that makes my life this fool - ish game. You need to know

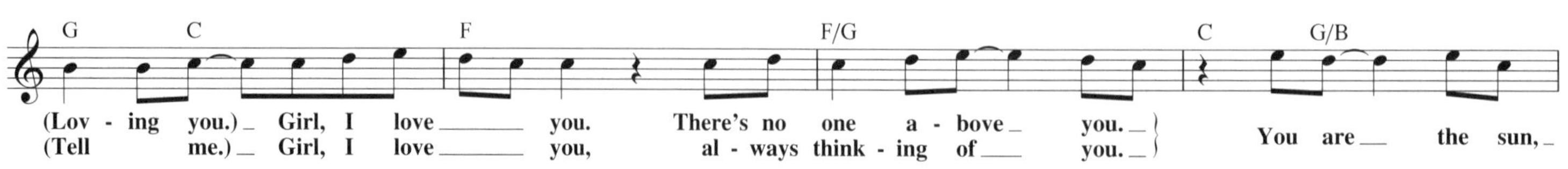

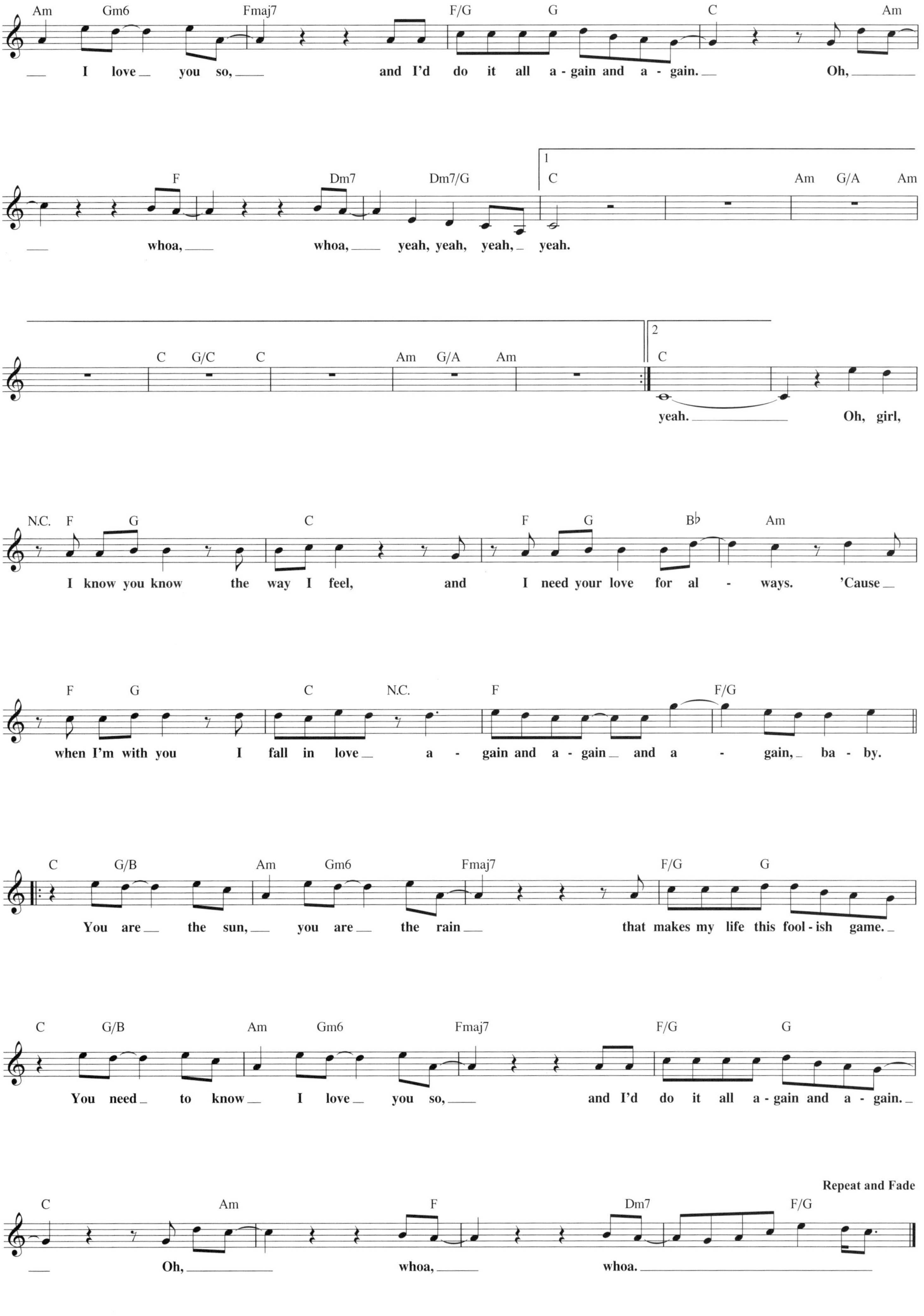

Am Gm6 Fmaj7 F/G G C Am

I love you so, and I'd do it all a-gain and a-gain. Oh,

F Dm7 Dm7/G 1 C Am G/A Am

whoa, whoa, yeah, yeah, yeah, yeah.

C G/C C Am G/A Am 2 C

yeah. Oh, girl,

N.C. F G C F G B♭ Am

I know you know the way I feel, and I need your love for al-ways. 'Cause

F G C N.C. F F/G

when I'm with you I fall in love a-gain and a-gain and a-gain, ba-by.

C G/B Am Gm6 Fmaj7 F/G G

You are the sun, you are the rain that makes my life this fool-ish game.

C G/B Am Gm6 Fmaj7 F/G G

You need to know I love you so, and I'd do it all a-gain and a-gain.

YOU DIDN'T HAVE TO BE SO NICE

Words and Music by JOHN SEBASTIAN
and STEVE BOONE

Moderately
Eb Gm Ab Bb7
You did - n't have to be so nice
I would have liked you an - y - way
And when we've had a few more days
I won - der if I'll get to say
If you had just looked once or twice
and gone up - on your qui - et way.
you did - n't have to be so nice
I would-'ve liked you an - y way.
To-day said the time was right for me to fol - low you
I knew I'd find you in a day or two and it's true
you came up - on a qui - et day
you sim - ply seemed to take your place
I knew that it would be that way
the min - ute that I saw your face.
You did - n't have to be so nice
I would have liked you an - y - way
If you had just looked once or twice
and gone up - on your qui - et way.
(Instrumental)
1
2

YOU'RE IN MY HEART

Words and Music by
ROD STEWART

Moderately
E D#m7 C#m7 B
I did-n't know what day it was when you walked in - to the room. I
I took all those hab-its of yours that in the be - gin-ning were hard to ac - cept. Your
said hel - lo un - no - ticed; you said good - bye too soon.
fash - ion sense for Beards-ley prints I put down to ex - pe - ri - ence. The

E D♯m7 C♯m7 B
Breez - in' through the cli - en - tele, spin-ning yarns that were so lyr - i - cal,
big - bos - omed la - dy with the Dutch ac - cent who tried to change my point of view, her
E D♯m7 C♯m7 1 B E
I real-ly must con - fess right here the at - trac - tion was pure-ly phys-i - cal.
ad lib. lines were well re - hearsed, but my heart cried out for
D♯m7 C♯m7 B 2 E A D
you. You're in my heart; you're in my
A A/C♯ D A A/C♯ D
soul. You'd be my breath should I grow old. You are my lov - er; you're my best
A D C♯m Bm7 A Adim7 E
friend. You're in my soul.
My love for you is im-meas -
You're an es - say in glam - our. Please
D♯m7 C♯m7 B E
- ur - a - ble; my re - spect for you im - mense. You're age - less, time - less,
par - don the gram - mar, but you're ev - 'ry school - boy's dream. You're Cel - tic u - nit - ed,
D♯m7 C♯m7 B E
lace and fine - ness; you're beau - ty and el - e - gance. You're a rhap - so - dy, a
but, ba - by, I've de - cid - ed you're the best team I've ev - er seen. And there have been
D♯m7 C♯m7 B E
com - e - dy; you're a sym - pho - ny and a play. You're ev - 'ry love song
man - y af - fairs and man - y times I've thought to leave. But I bite my lip and
D♯m7 C♯m7 1 E A
ev - er writ - ten, but hon - ey, what do you see in me? You're in my heart;
turn a - round, 'cause you're the warm - est thing I've ev - er found.
2 E A D A A/C♯ D
You're in my heart; you're in my soul. You'd be my breath should I grow
A A/C♯ D A D C♯m Bm7 A
old. You are my lov - er; you're my best friend. You're in my soul.

YOU GOTTA BE

Words and Music by DES'REE
Additional Music by ASHLEY INGRAM

Funk
F(add2)
G
Am7
C
Lis ten as your day un - folds,
chal-lenge what the fu - ture holds.
Try and keep your head up to the sky.
Lov-ers, they may cause you tears,
go a - head re - lease your fears.
Stand up and be count - ed, don't be a-shamed to cry.
You got-ta be, you got-ta be bad, you got-ta be bold, you got-ta be wis - er.
You got-ta be hard, you got-ta be tough, you got-ta be strong-er.
You got-ta be cool, you got-ta be calm, you got-ta stay to-geth - er.
A♭maj9
Gm7(add4)
All I know, all I know,
B♭
love will save the day.
Her-ald what your moth - er said,
read - in' the books your fa - ther read,
try'n' to solve the puz - zles in your own sweet time.
Some may have more cash than you,
oth - ers take a dif - f'rent view,
lis-ten as your day un - folds,
chal-lenge what the fu - ture holds,
try to keep your head up to the sky.
Lov - ers, they may cause you tears,
go a - head re - lease your fears,
To Coda
my, oh my, hey, ay.
You got-ta be bad, you got-ta be bold, you got-ta be wis - er.
You got-ta be hard, you got-ta be tough, you got-ta be strong-er.
You got-ta be cool, you got-ta be calm, you got-ta stay to-geth - er.

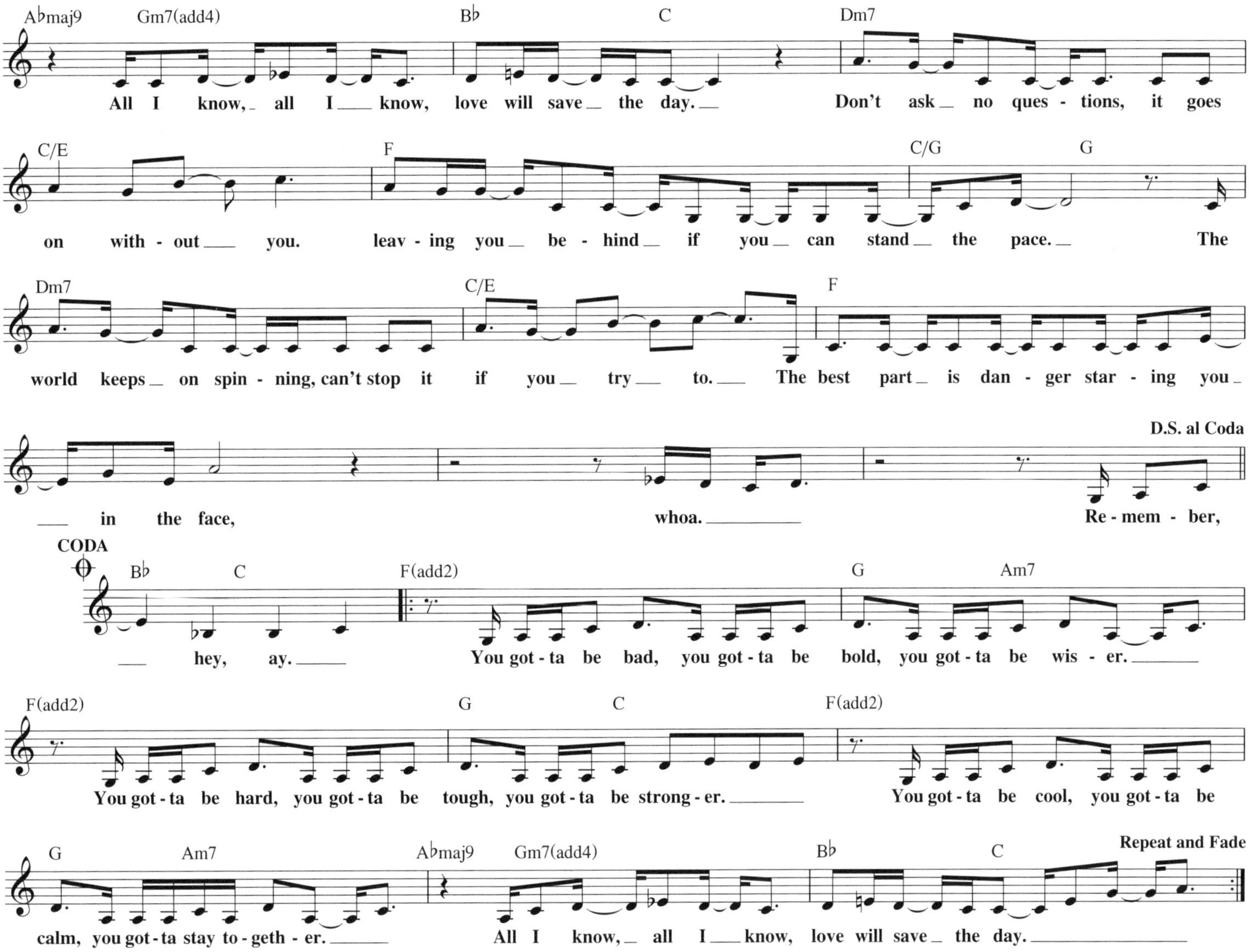
A♭maj9 Gm7(add4) B♭ C Dm7
All I know, all I know, love will save the day. Don't ask no ques - tions, it goes
C/E F C/G G
on with - out you. leav - ing you be - hind if you can stand the pace. The
Dm7 C/E F
world keeps on spin - ning, can't stop it if you try to. The best part is dan - ger star - ing you
D.S. al Coda
in the face, whoa. Re - mem - ber,
CODA
B♭ C F(add2) G Am7
hey, ay. You got - ta be bad, you got - ta be bold, you got - ta be wis - er.
F(add2) G C F(add2)
You got - ta be hard, you got - ta be tough, you got - ta be strong - er. You got - ta be cool, you got - ta be
G Am7 A♭maj9 Gm7(add4) B♭ C
Repeat and Fade
calm, you got - ta stay to - geth - er. All I know, all I know, love will save the day.

YESTER-ME, YESTER-YOU, YESTERDAY

Words by RON MILLER
Music by BRYAN WELLS

Moderately
Dm7 G7 C Dm7
What hap - pened to the world we knew, when we would
Where did it go, that yes - ter - glow when we could
seems those yes - ter - dreams were just a
G7 C E7 Am D7 G7 C F
dream and scheme and while the time a - way,
feel the wheel of life turn our way, yes - ter - me, yes - ter - you, yes - ter - day.
cruel and fool - ish game we used to play,
1, 3 C Fine 2 C Dm G7 C E7 Am
I have a dream, so did you. Life was warm, love was true.
When I re - call what we had, I feel lost, I feel sad
D7 G7 G Dm C/E E♭m Dm7
1st time D.S.
2nd time - D.S. al Fine
Two kids who fol - lowed all the rules, yes - ter - fools, and now, now it
with noth - ing but the mem - 'ry of yes - ter - love,

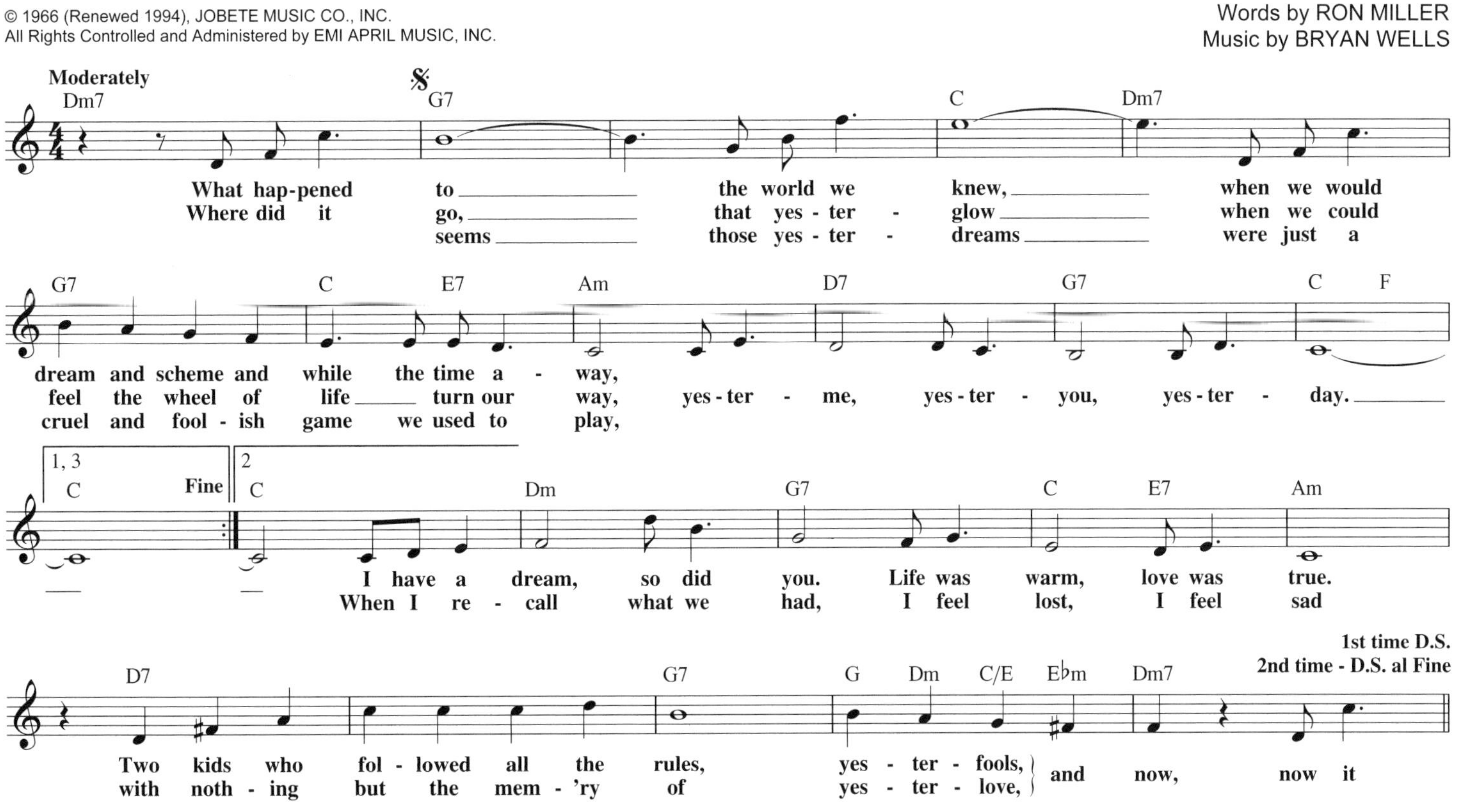

YOU HAVEN'T DONE NOTHIN'

Words and Music by
STEVIE WONDER

Moderately
E♭m7 E♭7sus/B♭ A♭ E♭m7 E♭7sus/B♭ A♭ E♭m7 E♭7sus/B♭ A♭
We are a - mazed but not a - mused by all the things you say that you'll do.
much con - cerned but not in - volved with de - ci - sions that are made by you.
1 E♭m7 E♭7sus/B♭ A♭
You're
2 E♭m7 E♭7sus/B♭ A♭ A♭7 G7 G♭7 F7
But we are (1.,2.) sick and tired of hear - ing your song,
(D.S.) keep on mak - ing us hear your song,
tell - in' how
tell - in' us
F7/A B♭7
you are gon - na change right from wrong.
how you are chang - ing right from wrong.
'Cause if you
E♭m7 D7 D♭7 C7 B7 B♭7
real - ly want to hear our views,
you have - n't done noth -
1 E♭m7 E♭7sus/B♭ A♭ E♭m7 E♭7sus/B♭ A♭ E♭m7 E♭7sus/B♭ A♭
in'. (Instrumental)
It's
E♭m7 E♭7sus/B♭ A♭ E♭m7 E♭7sus/B♭ A♭
not too cool to be ri - di - culed but you brought this up - on your - self.
would not care to wake up to the night - mare that's be - com - in' real life,
E♭m7 E♭7sus/B♭ A♭ E♭m7 E♭7sus/B♭ A♭ E♭m7 E♭7sus/B♭ A♭
The world is tired of pac - i - fiers, we
but when mis - led, who knows a per - son's
E♭m7 E♭7sus/B♭ A♭ E♭m7 E♭7sus/B♭ A♭ E♭m7 E♭7sus/B♭ A♭
want the truth and noth - ing else, yeah.
mind can turn as cold as ice, umm.
And we are
Why do you
2, 3 E♭m7
in'.
Jack - son Five join a - long with me, sing
Jack - son Five sing a - long a - gain, say
doo doo wop hey hey hey doo doo woop wow wow wow
doo doo wop naw naw naw doo doo wop co co co
To Coda
D.S. al Coda
(take repeats)
doo doo wop bum bum bum doo doo wop We
CODA
doo doo wop bum bum bum
Repeat and Fade
doo doo wop bum bum bum Doo doo wop bum bum bum. Sing it loud for the peo - ple, say

YOU RAISE ME UP

Words and Music by BRENDAN GRAHAM
and ROLF LOVLAND

Moderately slow
E♭5 E♭sus E♭5 E♭/G A♭sus2
When I am down and oh, my soul's so wea - ry, when trou - bles come and my heart bur - dened
B♭(add4) A♭(add2) A♭ E♭(add2)/G E♭/G A♭ E♭ B♭7/E♭
be, then I am still and wait here in the si - lence un - til you come and sit a while with
E♭ Cm A♭ E♭/G B♭/D Cm A♭
me. You raise me up so I can stand on moun - tains. You raise me up to walk on storm - y
E♭/G B♭ E♭ A♭(add2)/C E♭/B♭ E♭/G A♭
seas. I am strong when I am on your shoul - ders. You raise me
E♭/B♭ B♭7 E♭ F Fsus
up to more than I can be. There is no life no life with - out its
F F(add2)/A B♭ F/C C
hun - ger each rest - less heart beats so im - per - fect - ly. But when you
B♭/D B♭ F/A B♭ F/C C7sus F C/E
come and I am filled with won - der, some - times I think I glimpse e - ter - ni - ty. You raise me
Dm C/B♭ B♭ F/A C/E Dm C/B♭ B♭
up so I can stand on moun - tains. You raise me up to walk on storm - y
F/C Csus C F F/G F/A B♭sus2
seas. I am strong when I am on your shoul - ders. You raise me
F/C C7sus F B♭/F Gm/F F
up to more than I can be. You raise me
Repeat and Fade

YOU'RE BEAUTIFUL

Words and Music by JAMES BLUNT,
SACHA SCARBECK and AMANDA GHOST

Moderately slow
E♭ B♭11/D Cm7 A♭9
My life is bril - liant, my love is pure. I saw an an - gel, of that I'm sure. She smiled
E♭ B♭11/D Cm7
at me on the sub - way, she was with an-oth-er man. But I won't lose no sleep all night, 'cause I've
A♭9 B♭11/D E♭ A♭9 B♭11/D
got a plan. (1.,2.) You're beau-ti - ful. You're beau-ti - ful. You're beau-ti - ful, it's true.
(3.) You're beau-ti - ful. You're beau-ti - ful. You're beau-ti - ful, it's true.
E♭ A♭9 B♭11/D E♭ B♭11/D Cm7 To Coda II
I saw your face in a crowd-ed place. And I
There must be an an - gel with a smile on her face when she
A♭9 B♭sus Cm7 B♭11/D A♭9 B♭sus To Coda I E♭ B♭11/D
don't know what to do, 'cause I'll nev - er be with you.
Cm7 A♭9 E♭ B♭11/D Cm7
Yes, she caught my eye as I walked on by. She could see from my face that I was
A♭9 B♭11/D E♭ B♭11/D Cm7
fuck-ing high. And I don't think that I'll see her a - gain, but we shared a mo-ment that will last
D.S. al Coda I
till the end.
CODA I
E♭ A♭9 Cm7 A♭9 Cm7
La la la la. La la la la.
A♭9 Cm7 Fm7 B♭ D.S. al Coda II
La la la la la.
CODA II
A♭9 B♭sus E♭ Cm7
thought up that I should be with you.
A♭9 B♭sus Cm7 A♭9 B♭sus E♭
But it's time to face the truth; I will nev - er be with you.

YOU'RE MY EVERYTHING

Words and Music by NORMAN WHITFIELD,
ROGER PENZABENE and CORNELIUS GRANT

Moderately
C Dm/C C
1. You sure - ly just know mag - ic, girl, 'cause you changed my life.
2., 3. (See additional lyrics)
F Em Dm C Dm/C C
It was dull and or - di - nar - y, but you make it sun - ny and bright.
F Em Dm Em7 F Em Dm Em7 F Em Dm
I was blessed the day I found you; gon - na build my whole world a - round you. You're
F Em Dm F Em Dm F Em Dm F Em Dm G7
To Coda
ev - 'ry - thing good, girl, and you're all that mat - ters to me.
2. When my way
C Bm C/A Dm7/G G7 C Bm
You're a part of ev - 'ry thought I think each day. Your name is in ev - 'ry
C/A Dm7/G F G7
phrase my lips say, ev - 'ry dream I dream is a - bout you, hon - ey, I could - n't live with - out you.
Dm7/G G Dm7/G G C
Ba - by, ba - by, ba - by, you're my ev - 'ry - thing, you're my
D.C. al Coda
Dm/C Em F Em Dm
ev - 'ry - thing. Yes, you are, you're my ev - 'ry - thing. 3. Girl, you're the
CODA
Repeat and Fade
C Dm7/C G7
You're my ev - 'ry - thing, you're my ev - 'ry - thing, you're my

Additional Lyrics

2. When my way was dark and troubles were near,
Your love provided the light so I could see.
Girl, just knowing your love was near when times were bad
Kept the world from closing in on me, girl.
I was blessed the day I found you; gonna build my whole world around you.
You're everything good, girl, and you're all that matters to me.

3. Girl, you're the girl I sing about in every love song I sing.
You're my winter, baby, my summer, my fall, my spring.
I was blessed the day I found you; gonna build my whole world around you.
You're everything good, girl, and you're all that matters to me.

YOUNG TURKS

Words and Music by ROD STEWART, KEVIN SAVIGAR, CARMINE APPICE and DUANE HITCHINGS

Moderate Rock
Fm Fm/A♭ Cm7
Bill - y left his home with a dol - lar in his pock - et and a head full of dreams.
Fm Fm/A♭ Cm7
He said some-how, some way it's got - ta get bet - ter than this.
Fm Fm/A♭ Cm7
Pat - ti packed her bags, left a note for her mom-ma, she was just sev - en - teen. There were
Fm Fm/A♭ B♭
tears in her eyes when she kissed her lit - tle sis - ter good - bye. They
Fm Fm/A♭ Cm7
held each oth - er tight as they drove on through the night, they were so ex - cit - ed. We got just
dise was closed so they head - ed for the coast in a bliss - ful man - ner. They took a
(Instrumental solo)
Bill - y wrote a let - ter back home to Pat - ti's par - ents try - in' to ex - plain. He said we're
Fm Fm/A♭ Cm7
one shot of life, let's take it while we're still not a - fraid. Be - cause
two - room a - part - ment that was jump - ing ev - 'ry night of the week.
both real sor - ry that it had to turn out this way. But there
Fm Fm/A♭ Cm7
life is so brief and time is a thief when you're un - de - cid - ed. And like a
Hap - pi - ness was found in each oth - er's arms as ex - pect - ed.
ain't no point in talk - ing when there's no - bod - y list - 'ning so we just ran a - way.
To Coda
Fm Fm/A♭ B♭
fist - ful of sand, it can slip right through your hands. ooh!
Bill - y pierced his ears, drove a pick - up like a lun - a - tic, (Instrumental ends) Young
Pat - ti gave birth to a ten pound ba - by boy, yeah!
E♭ Cm Gm B♭ E♭ Cm Gm
hearts, be free to - night. Time is on your side.
1, 2
A♭ C♭ D♭ E♭
Don't let them put you down, don't let 'em push you a - round,
A♭ C♭ B♭
don't let 'em ev - er change your point of view. (Instrumental)
E♭/B♭ B♭ E♭/B♭

D.S. al Coda
CODA
Par - a -
(Spoken): Come on now!
E♭ Cm Gm
hearts, be free to - night.
E♭ Cm Gm
Time is on your side.
Repeat and Fade
Young

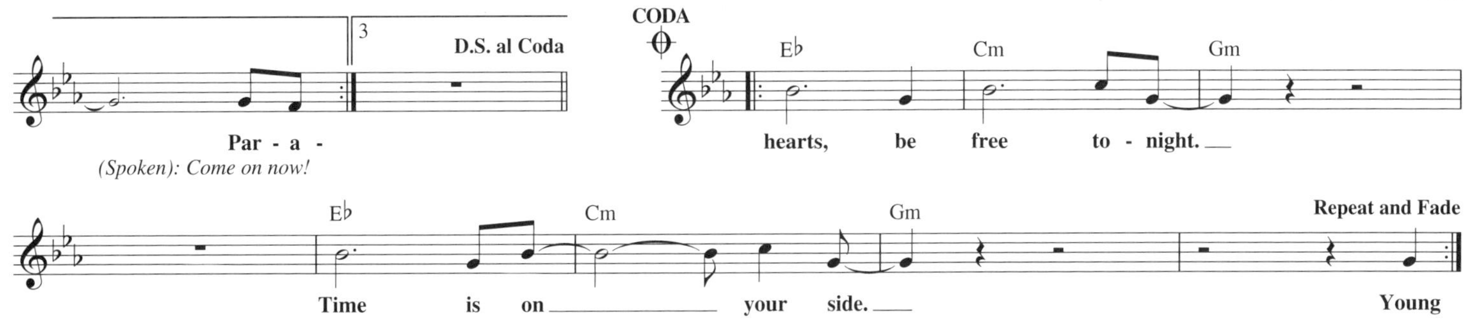

YOU CAN'T SIT DOWN

Words and Music by DELECTA CLARK,
CORNELL MULDROW and KAL MANN

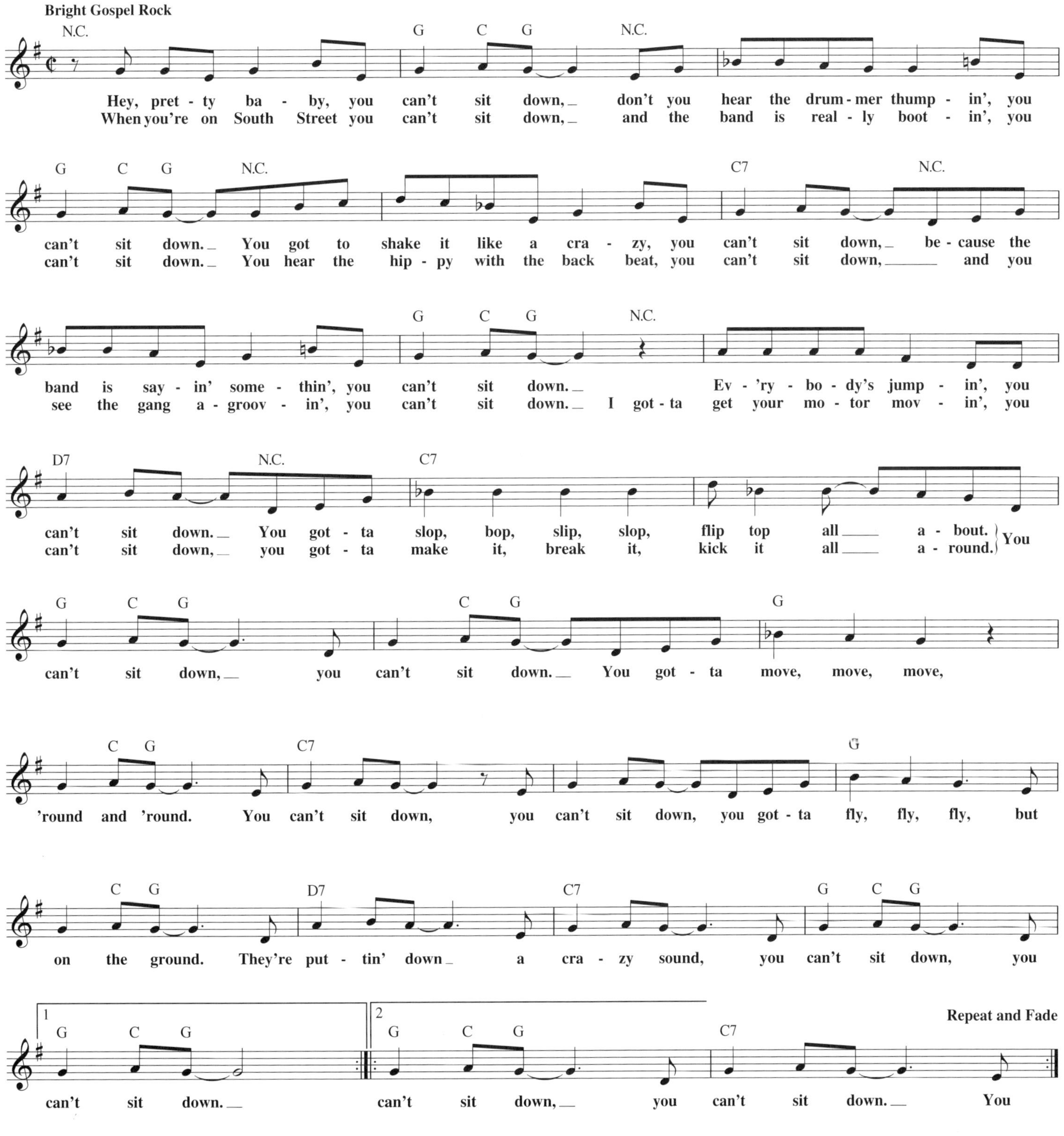

Bright Gospel Rock
N.C. G C G N.C.
Hey, pret - ty ba - by, you can't sit down, don't you hear the drum - mer thump - in', you
When you're on South Street you can't sit down, and the band is real - ly boot - in', you
G C G N.C. C7 N.C.
can't sit down. You got to shake it like a cra - zy, you can't sit down, be - cause the
can't sit down. You hear the hip - py with the back beat, you can't sit down, and you
G C G N.C.
band is say - in' some - thin', you can't sit down. Ev - 'ry - bo - dy's jump - in', you
see the gang a - groov - in', you can't sit down. I got - ta get your mo - tor mov - in', you
D7 N.C. C7
can't sit down. You got - ta slop, bop, slip, slop, flip top all a - bout.
can't sit down, you got - ta make it, break it, kick it all a - round.
You
G C G C G G
can't sit down, you can't sit down. You got - ta move, move, move,
C G C7 G
'round and 'round. You can't sit down, you can't sit down, you got - ta fly, fly, fly, but
C G D7 C7 G C G
on the ground. They're put - tin' down a cra - zy sound, you can't sit down, you
1 G C G
can't sit down.
2 G C G C7
can't sit down, you can't sit down.
Repeat and Fade
You

YOU'RE ONLY LONELY

© 1979 EMI BLACKWOOD MUSIC INC.
Words and Music by
JOHN DAVID SOUTHER
Moderately
A F♯m D E7
When the world is read - y to fall on your lit - tle shoul - ders,
When you need some-bod - y a - round on the nights that try you, re-mem-ber,
and when you're feel - in' lone - ly and small, you need some - bod - y there to hold you.
I was there when you were a queen, and I'll be the last one there be - side you.
You can call out my name
So you can call out my name
when you're on - ly lone - ly.
Now, don't you ev - er be a - shamed. You're on - ly lone - ly.
1
2
- ly. (You're on - ly lone - ly.) (You're on - ly lone - ly.)
(You're on - ly lone - ly.)
When the world is read - y to fall
on your lit - tle shoul - ders,
and when you're feel - in' lone - ly and small, you need
some-bod-y there to hold you.
So don't you ev - er be a - shamed when you're on - ly lone -
- ly. You can call out my name when you're on - ly lone - ly. (You're on - ly lone - ly.)
Vocal ad lib.
(You're on - ly lone - ly.) (You're on - ly lone - ly.)
Repeat and Fade